War and Diplomacy

War and Diplomacy

The Russo-Turkish War of 1877–1878 and the Treaty of Berlin

edited by

M. Hakan Yavuz

with Peter Sluglett

Utah Series in Middle East Studies

THE UNIVERSITY OF UTAH PRESS

Salt Lake City

Utah Series in Middle East Studies
M. Hakan Yavuz, series editor

 The Defiance House Man colophon is a registered trademark
of the University of Utah Press. It is based upon a four-foot-tall,
Ancient Puebloan pictograph (late PIII) near Glen Canyon, Utah.

15 14 13 12 11   1 2 3 4 5

LIBRARY OF CONGRESS CATALOGING-IN-PUBLICATION DATA

War and diplomacy : the Russo-Turkish War of 1877–1878 and the
Treaty of Berlin / edited by M. Hakan Yavuz with Peter Sluglett.
       p. cm.
   Proceedings of a conference held at the University of Utah in 2010.
   Includes bibliographical references and index.
   ISBN 978-1-60781-150-3 (cloth : alk. paper)
   ISBN 978-1-60781-185-5 (ebook)
1. Russo-Turkish War, 1877–1878 — Diplomatic history — Congresses.
2. Treaty of Berlin (1878) — Congresses.   3. Turkey — History — 1829–1878 —
Congresses. 4. Balkan Peninsula — History — 19th century — Congresses.
5. Caucasus — History — 19th century — Congresses.   6. Political violence —
Turkey — History — 19th century — Congresses.   7. Political violence — Balkan
Peninsula — History — 19th century — Congresses.   8. Political violence —
Caucasus — History — 19th century — Congresses.   I. Yavuz, M. Hakan.
II. Sluglett, Peter.
   DR573.3.W37 2011
   949.6'03872 — dc23

                                                           2011017775

Index by Andrew L. Christenson

Printed and bound by Sheridan Books, Inc., Ann Arbor, Michigan.

Contents

PART III. THE BEGINNING OF THE END IN EASTERN
ANATOLIA: THE MASSACRES OF ARMENIANS

PART IV. ETHNO-RELIGIOUS CLEANSING AND POPULATION
TRANSFERS IN THE BALKANS AND THE CAUCASUS

Illustrations

A Note on Transliteration

Modern Turkish spelling is used, adopted from the system of the *International Journal of Middle East Studies* with minor modifications.

Acknowledgments

This book is the outcome of a generous gift from the Turkish Coalition of America. We would like to thank the Turkish Coalition of America for its support for the Turkish Studies Project at the University of Utah. We owe a debt of gratitude to Kemal Sılay of Indiana University and Ali Yaycıoğlu of Fairfield University for reading and commenting on the entire manuscript.

Introduction

Laying the Foundations for Future Instability

M. Hakan Yavuz and Peter Sluglett

As an attempt at a definitive solution to the Ottoman or "Eastern question" in Europe, the Treaty of Berlin (1878) permanently transformed the political landscape in the Balkans and the Caucasus. In addition, it planted the seeds of future conflict, from World War I to the recent civil wars and ethnic cleansing in the former Yugoslavia. Indeed, 1878 was the defining moment for the viability of the Ottoman polity. As the most powerful and most developed Muslim state in the world and the seat of the caliphate, it was the focus of political and religious allegiance and aspirations for Muslims from North Africa to South Asia, Central Asia, the Malay peninsula, and the Indonesian archipelago. The magnitude of the defeat of the Ottoman Empire by Russia and the human, material, and territorial losses that followed proved fatal to the project of liberal reform and modernization known as the Tanzimat launched in the middle of the nineteenth century by Sultans Mahmud II and 'Abd al-Majid.

Under the cover of pan-Slavic solidarity, Russia had declared war on the Ottoman state in the hope of extending its influence in the Balkans and gaining access to the Mediterranean. The Russo-Turkish War of 1877–78 resulted in the loss of nearly all Ottoman territory in the Balkans, the cession of a large part of eastern Anatolia to the Russian army, and the subsequent massacre or expulsion of millions of Balkan and Caucasian Muslims. This in turn would lead to the adoption of pan-Islamic ideology by the Ottoman state under Sultan Abdülhamid II as a vehicle to resist Western imperialism that still has resonance in the wider Muslim world today. The main motive for Russian intervention in the Balkan conflict was its pan-Slavic and pan–Orthodox Christian foreign policy. In practice, Moscow's main goal was to carve out a vast Bulgarian state as the center of pan-Slavic activism, consisting of most of Ottoman Macedonia with access to the Aegean. Russian troops were to stay in Bulgaria in order to assist in the consolidation of the newly established Bulgarian state. The terms of the Treaty of San Stefano led to major concerns in London, because one of Britain's paramount strategic goals was to prevent imperial Russia from gaining control of the Straits and having a base in the Mediterranean. In order to temper the effect of the Russian gains and also to protect Istanbul from further Russian expansion, the British Empire agreed to come to the Ottomans' aid and concluded a secret agreement under which Britain would be allowed to occupy the strategically important island of Cyprus.

Habsburg Austria-Hungary was also deeply concerned by the rise of pan-Slavism and Russian imperial gains in the Balkans. With the support of Great Britain and other European powers, it pressed the participants at the Congress of Berlin to revise the Treaty of San Stefano. The Treaty of Berlin was signed at the end of the Congress of Berlin (June 13–July 13, 1878) by the major Continental powers — Great Britain, Austria-Hungary, France, Germany, Italy, Russia, and the Ottoman Empire.

The treaty marked the end of Ottoman hegemony in the Balkans by formally recognizing the independence or de facto sovereignty of Romania, Serbia, and Montenegro and the autonomy of Bulgaria. The *sancak*s of Novi Pazar and Bosnia were placed under the administration of Austria-Hungary. Macedonia remained under Ottoman rule, while Romania received the Dobruja region, an important agricultural area between the lower Danube and the Black Sea. Montenegro obtained most of the Albanian-inhabited territories of Nikšić, Podgorica, and Bar. The various territorial concessions inflamed the Albanian and Slavic Muslim communities (Pomaks, Torbes, and Bosnians) against the sultan. They started to develop their own separate nationalism outside the Ottoman state to forestall further ethnic cleansing and subjugation. Eastern Rumelia, which included large Muslim and Greek minorities, became an autonomous province under a Christian governor. Russia retained southern Bessarabia in the Balkans, as well as Ardahan, Batum, and Kars in eastern Anatolia. Finally, the treaty did not address the question of the border between the Ottoman Empire and the new Greek state. After the treaty, the Ottoman state was too weak to defend itself in this region and was forced to cede Thessaly to Greece in 1881. The treaty consolidated the principle of nation-states in the diverse societies of the region and planted the future seeds of tragic conflict in the Balkans, Anatolia, the Caucasus, and the Middle East.

Given the wide-ranging significance of the Treaty of Berlin, remarkably few studies have been written, particularly in English, on the treaty and its implications for much of the political, cultural, and territorial structure of a significant part of the globe. Only three volumes have been published on the Russo-Turkish War of 1877–78 and the Treaty of Berlin. The first work, W. N. Medlicott's *The Congress of Berlin and After: A Diplomatic History of the Near Eastern Settlement, 1878–1880*, is a diplomatic history entirely based on British sources which totally ignores the treaty's impact on the people of the region.

The second work, *Der Berliner Kongress von 1878: Die Politik der Grossmächte und die Probleme der Modernisierung in Südosteuropa in der Zweiten Hälfte des 19. Jahrhundert*, edited by Ralph Melville and Hans Jürgen Schroeder, focuses primarily on southeastern Europe and is more a top-down analysis of the Russo-Ottoman War than of the treaty itself.[1] It is also structured within the framework of European balance-of-power politics and focuses on the interaction among the major Western actors to the detriment of the Balkans, Anatolia, and the Middle East. This book provides a rich diplomatic history of the activities of the Continental powers but no clear analysis of the impact of the war and the subsequent peace treaty on the Ottoman state itself or on the broader Muslim world. Moreover, it does not discuss the impact of the war on the Caucasus and especially on the Armenian issue in Anatolia.

The third work, *The Ottoman-Russian War of 1877–78*, edited by Ömer Turan, is very disjointed; it focuses on crisis diplomacy during the war and was published in Turkey with very limited distribution. This study is also more concerned with the short-term causes of the war and the diplomatic negotiations preceding it rather than the treaty and its long-term impact.

Our volume, unlike these three earlier works, seeks to provide a mixture of perspectives, both top-down (diplomatic) and bottom-up (social, cultural, geopolitical), by emphasizing the role of social, cultural, and political actors at both the national and international levels. Its main strength is that it is interdisciplinary and takes a broader perspective by comparing and contrasting the different Ottoman and European policies. It also highlights the seminal role played by this attempt at settling the "Eastern question" in shaping the current international system, for better or worse.

THE ORIGINALITY OF THE COLLECTION

This book is the outcome of careful planning and a two-day intensive conference of leading scholars at the University of Utah. We received the first draft of the papers before the conference and asked a series of questions of each contributor to bring their different perspectives together. Our approach was to compile an interdisciplinary and comparative examination of the treaty and its sociopolitical implications for the Balkans and the Caucasus by utilizing the theoretical tools and approaches of political science, sociology, history, and international relations. The papers also include comparative dimensions of nation-state formation, ethnic cleansing, transnational movements of identity and resistance, and the various imperial policies that tried to contain or counter ethnic nationalisms in Anatolia, the Balkans, and the Caucasus.

Our volume demonstrates that the destruction of much of the remaining Ottoman political presence in the Balkans following the Treaty of Berlin not only brought about the destruction of a multiethnic imperial polity but also initiated widespread ethnic cleansing and the destruction of a number of indigenous Muslim and Christian communities. It shows how this attempt to resolve the Eastern question in Europe had broad effects on issues such as universal standards of human rights, the notion of "humanitarian intervention," and the future of Muslim-Western relations both in the region itself and over a much wider area. In many ways it acted as a template for ethnic cleansing and even for genocide in the first half of the twentieth century and for many continuing geopolitical and identity conflicts in the contemporary world.

A NEW PERSPECTIVE ON VITAL CONTEMPORARY ISSUES: THE ORIGINS OF MODERN ETHNIC CLEANSING IN EUROPE AND WEST ASIA

The papers underscore that the 1878 Treaty of Berlin provided a foundational framework for the establishment of a new regional order in the Balkans, Anatolia, and the Caucasus. It helped to codify and implement the principles of "monoethnic" sovereignty and ethnicity in its attempt to create homogeneous nation-states. The new principles of ethnic sovereignty and the establishment of nation-states resulted in a new comprehensive strategy of ethnic or religious cleansing that would have tragic consequences both at the time and later. The lofty principle of national self-determination collided with the reality that none of the newly independent states were demographically homogeneous; this, in turn, led to campaigns of major demographic reengineering. In short, the Treaty of Berlin was based on the paradoxical foundations of progress (recognizing national self-determination) and destructive regression (ethnically cleansing multicultural communities).

A CENTURY OF PEACE?

These papers illustrate very clearly that much of post-Napoleonic nineteenth-century Europe was not blessed with a long period of peace (1815–1914) as has traditionally been claimed but rather was the fulcrum for a century of ethnic and religious cleansing and of course for two world wars. A number of chapters shed new light on these disturbing phenomena, providing details of ethnic conflict and atrocities that speak directly to present-day controversies and ethno-national conflicts in the Balkans, the Caucasus, Anatolia, and the Middle East.

PAN-SLAVISM AND PAN-ISLAMISM: THE RISE OF TRANSNATIONAL POLITICAL, IDEOLOGICAL, AND IDENTITY MOVEMENTS

Like the "Jewish question," the Eastern or Ottoman-Muslim question in Europe and its attempted settlement at the Congress of Berlin proved to be particularly tragic and vexing. Pan-Slavic and pan-Christian ideologies, including liberal ones grounded in ostensibly universal standards of human rights, presented the Ottoman territorial presence in Europe and its treatment of minority communities as an abomination while simultaneously pursuing destructive imperial expansion into the non-Western world and laying the ground for charges of ethnic and religious double standards and civilizational fault lines. This period also witnessed the rise of pan-Slavism, pan-Europeanism, and pan-Islamism.

The dismembering of the Ottoman state and the ethnic cleansing of the Muslim populations of the Balkans and the Caucasus further politicized, radicalized, and mobilized transnational Islamic networks and leaders to challenge Western imperialism. These events marked the origins of the pan-Islamic policies of the Ottoman sultan Abdülhamid II (r. 1876–1909). Ethnic and religious mobilization had several social and political implications — it enhanced ethno-religious fault lines and politicized them, with tragic consequences in the wider region.

REFORMS

The reform policies that the European powers imposed on the Ottoman state as a result of the Treaty of Berlin generally provoked the Muslim populations against their Christian neighbors, which eventually led to the breakdown of communal coexistence in Anatolia. Reforms that were supposed to calm ethno-nationalist conflict simply served to undermine the framework of the *millet* system, which had facilitated multiethnic and confessional coexistence for centuries. Non-Muslim ethnic groups began to challenge the structure of the *millet* system, hoping to gain exclusive sovereignty in territories that were still multiethnic and multireligious. In order to receive the patronage of one or more of the major European powers, they sought to secede or gain autonomy from the Ottoman state, often by pioneering insurgent tactics and using terrorism to provoke a harsh response from the state, as in the example of the Internal Macedonian Revolutionary Organization (IMRO).

KOMITACILIK: COUNTERINSURGENCY WARFARE

The Ottoman state confronted a new form of warfare in the Balkans. Its army was trained in the German military tradition of offensive and defensive strategies, which generally held that encirclement and envelopment were the best way to defeat the enemy. None of these strategies was useful in coping with insurgent nationalist guerrillas, especially when they were supported by the rival Balkan powers and Russia. Their goal was to rebel against Ottoman authority and establish a communal power structure with the purpose of transforming rural populations into ethno-nationalists pitted against other ethnic groups. The revolutionary committees posed a far greater threat to the Ottoman Empire than less unified and less ideological insurgencies had presented in the past. These new structures were network groupings with bases of support in the local society, consisting of educated and well-to-do strata with links to external support. This new form of insurgency had both political and military wings and activities. In response, the Ottoman state developed two divergent counterinsurgency strategies in the Balkans and the Caucasus. A number of papers examine the origins and purposes of these two divergent counterinsurgency strategies in terms of the significance of territory and the lack of economic resources.

The gradual dismantling of the Ottoman state also had profound consequences for the future development of Middle Eastern and world politics. With the collapse of the Ottoman state, the Muslim world lost its core hegemonic state and market institutions and was unable to emerge successfully from Western imperialism, unlike China or India. Needless to say, this circumstance, along with the creation of Israel, has contributed to systemic regional conflict that has gradually spread outside the confines of the area.

This book will be of great interest for scholars who study these issues as well as broader themes such as nation-state formation, nationalism, population movements, ethnic cleansing, war and counterinsurgency, and Western-Muslim relations in the late nineteenth and twentieth centuries.

CONTENTS

*Part I. European Diplomacy and
the Exclusion of the Ottoman "Other"*
The book consists of four integrated parts, along with an introduction and a conclusion. In the first chapter M. Hakan Yavuz sets out the social and political context of the Ottoman state and society before the Treaty of Berlin by stressing the penetration of European capitalism, ideas, and institutions among the Ottoman elite. The Crimean War helped the Ottoman state to be recognized as part of the European state system, and its territorial integrity and sovereignty were fully guaranteed. Chapters 1 to 4 examine how this short-lived consensus came to an end and how some European powers, especially Great Britain, concluded that the collapse of the empire was inevitable. They also stress how the problematic of "Turkey in Europe" underscored the cultural and religious basis of European trans-national identity and how constructs of the "other," such as Jews and Muslims, proved to be particularly vexing. After examining the Russo-Turkish War, these chapters examine the long-term and short-term implications of the Treaty of Berlin as the foundational document of the regional sub-system in the Balkans, Anatolia, and the Caucasus.

These chapters assess the foreign policies of the major European powers during and after the Treaty of Berlin by examining the nature of late nineteenth century balance-of-power politics and the role of the major powers in the establishment of a system of nation-states in the Balkans. Even though the international peace conference sought to deal with the messy social and political consequences of the last major Russo-Turkish War, it created a new set of problems. Both the debates at the congress and the limits on participation in it reflected the self-confidence of the European powers vis-à-vis the Balkan peoples.

Feroze A. K. Yasamee examines how the Ottoman state, especially Sultan Abdülhamid II himself, tried to cope with the new external and internal challenges stemming from major losses of territory and the expulsion of over a million Muslims from the Balkans.

Sean McMeekin's paper takes up some of the general themes discussed by Yasamee by stressing the new "international order" through an examination of the assertive role of Germany and the policies of Otto von Bismarck during and after the congress. He illustrates the gap between Bismarck's rhetoric and Germany's actual policies toward the Ottoman Empire in general, and the Balkans in particular, through Bismarck's notion of *Realpolitik*.

Mujeeb R. Khan's paper illustrates the new norms of this "international" system that marginalized the minorities and denied rights to certain cultural groups in the Caucasus and the Balkans in the name of a notion of a civilizational progress radiating out from Western Europe. He examines the problematic origins of Western human rights and humanitarian interventionist policies in the various attempts to address the Eastern question. Khan underscores how the tension between universal standards and values on the one hand and particular identities and interests on the other lay at the very foundation of the nascent humanitarian agenda and indeed continues to afflict world politics; compare the widespread non-Western perceptions of double standards on Bosnia, Chechnya, Iraq, and Palestine. He also illustrates how the template for the ethnic cleansing of the Ottoman Muslim "other" would directly shape *Vernichtungspolitik* (ethnic cleansing campaigns) against a whole host of populations in Europe, Anatolia, and the Middle East.

Part II. The Emergence of the Balkan State System
This section includes six chapters that examine how local populations reacted to the Treaty of Berlin and how the newly independent states sought to carry out the dual process of nation and state building. Mehmet Hacısalihoğlu examines how the treaty provoked a series of revolts among Muslims and Christians in the Balkans. First he examines the Orthodox Christian resistance to the treaty in Macedonia, using both Ottoman and Macedonian archives. Then he discusses the second major reaction, by the Pomak Muslim community in Western Thrace. In short, the treaty further radicalized the local populations because the division of the region was based on keeping the "balance of power" in the Balkans without paying any attention to the actual social and political needs of ordinary people. This was the beginning of mass mobilization in the Balkans, which would gradually undermine long-standing communal ties and lead to a series of conflicts.

Miroslav Svirčević focuses on the impact of the Treaty of Berlin on Serbia and provides a detailed analysis of how the Serbian state sought to "nationalize" the population and the territories inhabited by the Muslim population. Utilizing Serbian archives, he demonstrates the pattern of Serbian state nationalization polices and forced population movements.

Edin Radušić examines how British policy ignored the needs of the local people and largely developed within the framework of Continental balance-of-power politics. He analyzes the reaction from the Bosnian Muslim community at the time.

Aydın Babuna further disaggregates the Bosnian Muslim community and discusses the reasons why certain sectors of the population became mobilized against the occupation of Bosnia by Austria-Hungary. His paper, based upon original archival work, focuses on local agrarian and economic conditions before and after the Congress of Berlin to indicate the causes of Bosnian resistance and interethnic conflict.

Isa Blumi's paper examines how ethnic identities translated into maps and borders with collective violence. This mapmaking in the Balkans "entails as much destruction as construction"; in particular, the introduction of new life-worlds led to gradual mobilization and resistance by the local population.

Gül Tokay examines how the European intervention under the guise of reforms further enhanced the secessionist movements of different Christian groups in Macedonia. This paper offers an interesting distinction between the two types of reforms in terms of their origins and implications: the first was undertaken by the Ottoman state for the purpose of enhancing its territorial integrity; the second was imposed by the major European powers to fragment the Ottoman state and enhance their own national interests. Tokay succinctly argues that the issues that the Treaty of Berlin covered "became major causes of regional conflicts." The current map of the Balkan nation-state system was first drawn by the Congress of Berlin without much regard for the local needs of the population. Tokay analyzes how the process of "mapmaking" through border demarcation and the refugee problem further destabilized the region and "destroyed the pluralist order: the newly independent Balkan states adopted the idea of a single ethno-linguistic nation based on European models." By focusing on the European reforms of 1903 in Macedonia, she offers a convincing narrative showing how the reforms provided the necessary legal framework for the creation of a new "Macedonian" nation through the amalgamation of different ethnic and religious groups.

Part III. *The Beginning of the End in Eastern Anatolia: The Massacres of Armenians*

Most of these papers examine the context of the Armenian struggle for self-determination. They provide both diplomatic and social history to analyze the shift of the Armenian communities from being the most "loyal community" of the empire to mounting an assertive national struggle to carve out an independent state. The process of this shift is an outcome of the interaction between domestic and international factors.

Brad Dennis questions the contention in Turkish and Armenian historiography that the Treaty of Berlin was the beginning of the "Armenian question" as well as the idea of a linear connection between the Treaty of Berlin and the massacres of the Armenians in the 1890s. Although article 61 of the treaty was instrumental in polarizing Armenian and Muslim communal relations, many other social and political factors need to be considered in order to provide a satisfactory explanation of the violence. Dennis focuses on economic and social relations between Kurds and Armenians at a local level to explain the causes of violence, utilizing the Ottoman archives to provide a bottom-up reading of conflict and violence in eastern Anatolia.

Garabet K. Moumdjian argues that territorial losses in the Balkans shaped the way in which Abdülhamid II viewed Armenian demands for autonomy and European intervention on the Armenian side. He suggests that the 1878 defeat provided an opportunity to bring the Armenian question to the forefront. He rejects the argument that the Congress of Berlin marked the beginning of Armenian separatism within the Ottoman Empire while contending that the notion that foreign intervention led the Ottoman Armenians to make political demands is inadequate. This paper examines the connection between the politicization of the Armenian communities and the internationalization of the Armenian question after the Treaty of Berlin. Did this internationalization help or hinder Armenian national aspirations? How did Abdülhamid II react to the various Armenian claims and the way in which Armenian communities reacted to Ottoman policy?

The papers of Edward J. Erickson and Bayram Kodaman deal directly with Ottoman polices toward Armenian demands after the Congress of Berlin. Erickson argues that the Treaty of Berlin left indefensible borders and furthered the nationalist aspirations of the non-Muslim minorities in the Balkans and the Caucasus. After examining the new nationalist insurgency in the Balkans, he analyzes the causes of two divergent Ottoman counterinsurgency practices, focusing on defense spending, manpower, geography, and the importance of the region for the Ottoman State. Erickson argues that the Ottomans learned to cope with nationalist insurgencies by studying the contemporary examples of the Boer War and the U.S. campaigns in the Philippines and Cuba. He contextualizes Ottoman counterinsurgency tactics within the larger context of Western imperial pacification of indigenous resistance during the period. Erickson contends that Abdülhamid II's policy of establishing tribal militias, the Hamidiye Regiments, further increased the security concerns of the Armenian communities.

Bayram Kodaman examines the factors that led to the establishment of the tribal militia regiments and their transformation as a result of changing conditions. He argues that the Ottoman state's purpose in establishing these institutions was to ensure Kurdish loyalty, settle seminomadic tribes, and organize more effective tax collection and also to use these "militias" against pro-Russian Armenian insurgents. The Hamidiye Regiments consisted mostly of Kurdish tribes, with some Karapapak and Arab tribes. These irregular cavalry regiments were commanded by their own tribal chieftains.

The leaders of the Armenian Church, like those of many other minority communities, came to the conclusion that the imminent collapse of the Ottoman state was nigh. The leadership sent a delegation headed by the patriarch, welcoming Russian expansion and actually asking the Russian military command to support the creation of an autonomous Armenia in eastern Anatolia. Indeed, article 16 of the Treaty of San Stefano was slightly revised during the Congress of Berlin. In order to keep Russia out of the Middle East, Britain pledged its support for the Armenian cause and agreed to supervise extensive political reforms in those provinces inhabited by Armenians under article 61 of the treaty. In fact, not only was the Armenian question internalized by the Treaty of Berlin but the impact of the counterinsurgency on the identity and organizational structure of the army was so deep that it shaped the operational role of the Ottoman army in World War I. The insurgency in the Balkans further channeled the mindset of the Ottoman army in the direction of Turkish nationalism, which became the dominant ideology among young Ottoman military officers. Moreover, the counterinsurgency not only provided autonomy to field officers but also undermined the hierarchical discipline of the military.

Part IV. Ethno-religious Cleansing and Population Transfers in the Balkans and the Caucasus

The four papers in this section examine the causes and processes of ethno-religious cleansing of part of the Muslim population in the Balkans. The authors address a number of vital questions. Why did the European powers fail to protest against the killing and cleansing of Muslims in the Balkans? Why was the Ottoman Muslim presence in Europe viewed as being so problematic? Why was Muslim identity such a concern for the new Balkan states? What was the Ottoman reaction to this "othering" of Islam and Muslim communities in the Balkans? What were the major lessons and legacies of the Treaty of Berlin in the context of cosmopolitanism, ethnic homogenization, and the interaction between religion and nationalism?

Justin McCarthy provides detailed statistics on the major population movements after the new boundaries were drawn at the Congress of Berlin. His paper examines how the Congress of Berlin ignored the basic human rights of the local people in the Balkans and Caucasus. By analyzing the demographic data, he reveals the widespread ethno-religious cleansing in the Balkans to create new, homogeneous states. Moreover, by failing to establish a mechanism to protect the rights of minorities, the Congress of Berlin planted the seeds of future wars and constant conflict in the Balkans. McCarthy shows that the Treaty of Berlin sought to "solve" the Muslim presence in the Balkans through religious cleansing and massacres. The last part of the paper examines the internationalization of the Armenian question in Anatolia.

Mustafa Tanrıverdi describes forced population movements and ethnic cleansing in the Caucasus under Russian occupation. He examines the local conditions that led to major population movements from Ardahan, Kars, and Batum to different Ottoman cities, arguing that these forced population movements mobilized the Muslims of Anatolia against both Russian and Armenian forces and communities, with fateful consequences.

Tetsuya Sahara's detailed and original examination of the Batak Massacre is very important in assessing the formation and utilization of anti-Muslim agitation in the Balkans. The paper illustrates William Gladstone's political manipulation of the incident to promote a liberal Christian European identity. Sahara compares primary source material from the Batak case with popular contemporary accounts in the British press.

Ömer Turan's paper focuses on the Pomak Muslim rebellion against the dictates of the Treaty of Berlin. The Muslims of the Rhodopes used arms, diplomatic initiatives, and the media to prevent the occupation and partition of the region. Although they did not have the means to resist the Russian occupation, they managed to prevent Russian penetration into the Rhodopes. The lack of external support resulted in the dismemberment of the region from the Ottoman state, however, and the population of the region became a permanent minority with no political rights. This paper also indicates that the Congress of Berlin totally failed to take local concerns and the basic rights of the Muslims into account.

This volume concludes with Frederick F. Anscombe's provocative paper, which challenges many key arguments put forward by other contributors. He argues that the 1875–78 period was less a major turning point in Ottoman history than a way-marker for reversion to patterns seen earlier in the nineteenth century. While conceding that the Russo-Turkish War and the subsequent settlement resulted in a loss of vast territories and a huge influx of Muslim refugees from the Balkans into what was left of the Ottoman Empire, he contends that these cataclysmic events do not seem to have caused a major shift in Abdülhamid II's policies. Anscombe provides an audit of the eighteen chapters in this volume that includes reassessments of some key assumptions and conclusions. He concludes that the Treaty of Berlin did not affect basic Ottoman political principles because it did not alter the fundamental goal of reform: to strengthen the state's ability to defend itself against the European powers. We ask readers to reassess the papers in light of Anscombe's comprehensive essay and draw their own conclusions.

NOTES

1. See also Richard Millman, *Britain and the Eastern Question, 1875–1878*; and Michael R. Milgrim, "An Overlooked Problem in Turkish-Russian Relations: The 1878 War Indemnity."

PART I

European Diplomacy and
the Exclusion of the Ottoman "Other"

1

The Transformation of "Empire" through Wars and Reforms

Integration vs. Oppression

M. Hakan Yavuz

As Carlton J. H. Hayes noted, "If before 1878 the 'Eastern Question' concerned one 'sick man,' after 1878 it involved a half-dozen maniacs. For the Congress of Berlin drove the Balkan peoples mad."[1]

EMPIRE VS. NATION

Empires are different political systems than nation-states. They do not seek homogenization or attempt to govern daily life; rather, they seek to control diverse populations through cooptation, various institutions, and webs of integration. Imperial institutions generally encourage social, political, and economic amalgamation. They reduce the cost of coercion and provide a necessary sense of authority among their diverse populations by creating order and predictability within diverse communities. Through its institutions and practices, the Ottoman Empire was able to generate a diffuse political legitimacy that allowed these communities to live together by living apart. This sense of legitimacy helped unify the elite and the people on the street through various means, including social and political networks of incorporation and a sense of justice that the state provided.

Empires come to an end in unique ways and under varied conditions. Some empires outlast others, and some select coercion over cooptation (inclusion). The Ottoman case is important in understanding how empires persist and how they come to an end. Empires generally collapse either as a result of a major military defeat or when their component parts (such as peripheries) begin gaining independence, as seen in modern times. This was particularly true when nationalism as a political ideology reached its zenith in the nineteenth and twentieth centuries. It became clear for many an empire that maintaining control over diverse communities under an imperial system was simply too costly.[2] The principles of nationalism (homogenization and self-determination) are intrinsically in conflict with the structure of empires; as nationalism became the worldwide vogue, the imperial framework faced delegitimization. In this respect, the military weakness of an empire provides the most opportune moment for peripheral agitation and secessionism. Both the Ottoman Empire and Habsburg Empire, for instance, came to an end as a result of unsuccessful reforms, wars, and nationalist agitations.[3] For the Ottomans, the wars in the Balkans (1878, 1896, 1912–13) not only resulted in the draining of an already bankrupt state treasury and a great loss of manpower but also emboldened the masses to take advantage of Ottoman weakness and European patronage. The state becomes ineffective when it is too enfeebled to resist internal and external challenges, and more powerful groups begin to compromise its autonomy. The balance of power gradually shifts to the detriment of state autonomy. New social groups emerge with a whole spate of demands to restructure the political system and even the political boundaries of the state in question. The principles of self-determination and nationalism are in direct conflict with the logic of empire. In this respect, nationalist movements are very effective in delegitimizing the imperial system.

In this paper I argue that the Ottoman-Russian War of 1878 and the Treaty of Berlin that followed were a "shock," both at the level of the state institutions and across the "collated" Ottoman society.[4] It was the single most devastating event for the late Ottoman state, with several detrimental social and political implications. The map that emerged after the Treaty of Berlin ignored natural boundaries as well as land and trade routes, and most of all it "recast the Ottoman Balkan possessions in such a way that it was no longer militarily feasible to defend them against either foreign aggression or internal insurrection."[5] This vulnerable geographic position triggered long-lasting insurgencies and wars.[6] Prominent Ottoman historians Stanford Shaw and Ezel Kural Shaw sum up the outcome:

> The Ottoman Empire was forced to give up two fifths of its entire territory and one fifth of its population, about 5.5 million people of whom almost half were Muslims. It also lost substantial revenues though it was partially compensated by the tribute paid by the remaining vassals and the agreement of the newly independent states to assume a portion of the Ottoman public debt. In so far as England was concerned, the Russian threat had been weakened but for

the Ottoman empire the Congress of Berlin was a terrible defeat, depriving it of territory, people and finances and making it difficult for what was left to survive.[7]

In order to understand the sociopolitical implications of this devastating war, the first part of this paper discusses the political background of the events and then the "making of the new polity" through the Treaty of Berlin. The second part examines the political context of the war and the treaty through an analysis of their major consequences. The last part analyzes the policies of the Ottoman state in coping with the challenges posed by the homogenization of new states through forced population movements, the search for legitimacy, and the separatist insurgency in Anatolia. After the treaty, the Ottoman sultan was obsessed with the eventual and gradual dismemberment of the Ottoman state because of the reforms that were imposed in part to enhance separatist movements in the Ottoman state by the European powers. In short, the Christian minorities, especially Armenian communities, assumed that the Ottoman state was too weak and that it was their turn to carve out a homeland through revolutionary tactics; the sultan, in turn, overestimated their power and did not hesitate to use all necessary means to suppress them.

By analyzing the Armenian issue, this paper challenges some dominant theses of Turkish historiography about the role of Britain in the Armenian question. After 1878 Britain became the "protector" of the Armenians in order to counter Russian influence among them and also to prevent a possible Russian penetration into Anatolia. Britain used the "Armenian reform" issue to get more concessions from the Ottoman state and also to win over public opinion among Armenians as well as in Britain itself. Britain was only paying lip service to the issue of reform and the welfare of the Armenians, however, because London did not take any concrete steps to improve Armenian living conditions. By not providing any financial support to the bankrupt Ottoman treasury, which could be used toward reforms, and instead insisting on debt repayment, Britain made a mockery of the reform talks. It would be a mistake to conclude from the British initiatives that Britain was in favor of an independent Armenia.

THE SOCIOPOLITICAL BACKGROUND, 1838–1876

According to Engin Akarlı, the Ottoman state confronted two major problems during the period of Sultan Abdülhamid II: pervasive foreign intervention in every aspect of domestic and foreign policies and economic failure due to the dire state of public finances, such as the monstrous public debt and the economic impact of the capitulations granted to major European powers, which undermined Ottoman industrial activities.[8] As a result, the government could not extract sufficient resources from the population to pursue its goals. Abdülhamid II tried to cope with these challenges by developing relations with other states in order to counterbalance British domination over the Ottoman state and by pursuing a series of internal reforms in education, transportation, agriculture, and the administration of tax collection.

The political rivalry between Russia and Britain restricted Abdülhamid II's geopolitical maneuverability.[9] The main goal of British policy in the early nineteenth century was to prevent any power from taking control of the Straits and Asia Minor, which would in turn endanger British preeminence and interests in the Indian subcontinent, Britain's most important colony. London preferred weak and ineffectual Ottoman control to Russian hegemony and therefore pursued a policy of maintaining Ottoman territorial integrity; Britain already had full access to the Ottoman market with the Anglo-Ottoman Convention of 1838.[10] This convention was in fact the main reason why most British statesmen supported Ottoman territorial integrity. Without this British support the dissolution of the empire would have been accelerated. The ensuing collapse of the Ottoman state would have brought Russia to the Straits, Asia Minor, and the eastern Mediterranean, thereby directly threatening Great Britain's access to India via the Suez Canal and also ending its "liberal" trade with the Ottoman economic sphere. Thus, for economic and strategic reasons, British policy was primarily concerned with the "protection" of the Ottoman state as a shield against Russian expansion in the eastern Mediterranean.

One of the fundamental unintended outcomes of the 1838 Convention was the weakening of local industry within the Ottoman Empire and the conversion of the Ottoman state into a British "economic colony." This relationship of dependency between the Ottoman state and Great Britain was in part regulated by Mustafa Reşit Paşa, who managed to attain considerable influence with British support. The 1856 Crimean War against the Russian menace further enhanced Ottoman-British relations. The Ottomans allied with Britain and France against the Russian attempt to change the balance of power in Europe, while Austria maintained a neutrality detrimental to Russia. With the defeat of Russia, the Ottoman state granted further capitulations to Britain in Serbia, Moldavia, and Wallachia. Moreover, the Russian Black Sea fleet was destroyed; the Black Sea was effectively demilitarized, and Britain was allowed access to the Danube. Some Ottoman statesmen as well as British prime minister Lord Palmerston (1784–1865) firmly believed that free trade and European investment in the Ottoman state would help bring more resources, along with tax revenues, to rebuild the Ottoman army.[11] In following this open trade policy, however, the British had the ulterior motive of empowering the Christian population of the empire with the goal of liberating it. In other words, a major contradiction existed between the British policy of preserving the territorial integrity of the empire as a "free-trade space" and the British commitment to the freedom of Christians from Ottoman rule. In fact, the free-trade policy, which aimed to bring legal and political equality between the Muslims and Christians, ultimately empowered the Christian minorities and made them the brokers in economic relations. Palmerston, for example, believed that free trade would help create a new "class" with a European outlook and lifestyle.[12] Indeed, with the 1838 Convention, Christian merchants who benefited from and were protected by these treaties became de facto agents of the European powers and consequently provided the necessary support for the nationalist separatism in the provinces. Thus the British policy of protecting the Ottoman territorial integrity and "strengthening" the Ottoman state through "free trade" in fact further weakened the empire and enhanced separatist nationalism.

As European goods began to invade Ottoman markets, new consulates were also created in order to protect the legal and commercial interests of Europeans in accordance with the capitulation treaties. European consuls were stationed in nearly all major Ottoman cities and were "quick to take up" any complaints against local officials "with the Bab-i Ali (the Sublime Port), or government offices."[13] Many Christian communities did have legitimate complaints about the local officials, but European powers used these communities for their own interests. As Donald Quataert observes, the "West Europeans' assumptions that Ottoman Christians — because they were Christians — were somehow more trustworthy as business partners than Muslims certainly played a role. As *protégés* of European merchants, Ottoman Christians obtained powerful tax exemptions (in the form of *berats*), that allowed them to buy and sell goods more cheaply than Muslim merchants."[14] The consuls acted as another counterweight to the power of the governors in cities and thereby created an alternative source of protection for the Christian population of the empire.[15] These consuls took the local complaints to their embassies in Istanbul, which in turn were addressed to the Ottoman authorities; as a consequence the Ottoman foreign ministry grew in importance. The locus of power eventually shifted from the imperial palace to the ministerial headquarters, known as the Sublime Porte. After the Crimean War, the Ottoman bureaucracy "borrowed heavily from London and even more from Paris, mortgaging its land revenue to get the loans."[16] In order to pay his mounting debts, the sultan had to increase land taxes. This either angered the farmers or in some cases provoked the Orthodox Slav peasants, with the help of some urban leadership, to revolt against the Ottoman authorities, as happened in Bosnia and Hercegovina.

THE CONVERGENCE OF DOMESTIC AND INTERNATIONAL FACTORS: TURMOIL

In April 1875 the Slavic Orthodox tenant-farmers in Hercegovina rebelled against the harsh tax and tenure obligations. The Ottoman state suppressed the rebellion with harsh measures, and many Orthodox took refuge in Montenegro and Serbia.[17] This population movement, in turn, mobilized public opinion in Serbia and Montenegro against the Ottoman state; the public, especially the church leadership, called for Serbia and Montenegro to declare war against the Ottoman state.[18] The Slavic Orthodox revolt against the local Ottoman rulers also gained widespread sympathy among the pan-Slavic circles in Russia. While the rebellion was spreading in the Balkans in October 1875, the Ottoman state suspended the interest payment on its foreign debt, which in turn undermined Ottoman credibility in many capitals, especially London. This anti-Ottoman sentiment was combined with the horror over the reported Ottoman suppression of the Bulgarian insurgency in Batak and surrounding areas (see chapter 17). The European governments reacted negatively to these policies and called for an international conference to discuss the situation of the Christians in the Balkans. A major debate occurred in Britain over British policy toward the Ottoman Empire. Although there was widespread public support (led by former prime minister William Gladstone) for the liberation of Balkan Christians, especially the Bulgarians, from Ottoman rule, current prime minister Benjamin Disraeli was skeptical of Russian intentions and media coverage of the events. It became too costly to "shelter" the Ottoman state against Russia: it was time to rethink the British policy of protecting Ottoman territorial integrity.[19] The future of the Ottoman state in the Balkans became part of British domestic politics, as the two leaders took opposing positions. This led to a major confusion in British foreign policy that was subsequently reflected throughout the crisis.

This sociopolitical milieu resulted in the abdication of Sultan Abdülaziz on May 29, 1876. Six days later he was found dead. Abdülaziz's brother, who was close to him, became Sultan Murad V. After having a mental breakdown over the circumstances of the killing of his brother, he was deposed on August 31, and Abdülhamid II became the new sultan. Both Serbia and Montenegro, with the support of pan-Slav circles in Moscow, decided to take advantage of this deepening political crisis and power vacuum in Istanbul and declared war against the Ottoman state in July 1876. The Serbian forces were headed by the Russian general M. G. Cherniav, a devoted pan-Slavist. Even though Istanbul was in political turmoil, it was still powerful enough to send its army to the gates of Belgrade in October 1876, but a Russian ultimatum stopped the Ottoman advances. The confrontation between the Ottoman state and Russia increased fear over the prospect of a wider war and possible Russian expansion into the Balkans. Under these conditions, Russian diplomatic pressures resulted in the Istanbul Conference on December 23, 1876, in the assembly of the Ministry of the Navy. In order to secure British support and overcome the pressure exerted by the European powers on behalf of the Balkan Christians, Midhat Paşa decided to proclaim a constitution on the day of the Istanbul Conference, much as the previous reform decrees of 1839 and 1856 had been declared for external reasons.[20]

Midhat closely cooperated with the Young Ottomans to counterbalance the power of the sultan and enhance the power of the bureaucracy.[21] Although the supposed purpose of the Istanbul Conference was to address the political situation of the Balkan Christians, its main goal was to decide the future of the Ottoman state in the Balkans. Britain, France, and Italy joined the conference, which excluded Ottoman officials from the preliminary discussions. The Ottoman state rejected the proposed terms at the Istanbul Conference for several reasons. One of the critical factors was ambiguity in the British position. Due to the rivalry between Disraeli and Gladstone, the British policy was in confusion. Furthermore, the Foreign Office played its "double" policy by not angering the Russians while also showing that Great Britain was still on the side of the Ottomans. It was the British delegation under Lord Salisbury which helped the Russians prepare the terms of the conference in Istanbul. Sir Henry Elliot, the ambassador to Istanbul, encouraged the Ottoman state to reject the proposal. The Ottoman statesmen interpreted his position as the true British policy and rejected the proposals of the Istanbul Conference, finding them unacceptable because they violated the basic principles of a sovereign state. Although some scholars present this genuine disagreement between Salisbury and Sir Henry Layard as a strategic plot, the two British officials had a major disagreement due to their divergent understanding of the future of the Ottoman state.[22] Finally, the Ottoman bureaucracy thought that the

major European powers would maintain their commitments under the
Treaty of Paris to guarantee the territorial integrity of the Ottoman state
against any Russian advances.[23]

When the Ottoman state rejected the proposal, the Russian government approached the European powers with a draft protocol calling for
the implementation of reforms on behalf of the Christians of the Ottoman
Balkans. With the help of Britain, the terms of the protocol were watered
down. The revised protocol was signed by the British foreign secretary
and the ambassadors of the Great Powers to London on March 31, 1877.
This second attempt was also rejected by the Ottoman state for several
important reasons. The Ottoman state felt that the protocols were too
harsh and that it would be giving up its sovereignty by accepting them. The
Ottomans thought that Russia was lacking in resources and ill prepared to
launch an attack; even if Russia attacked, the Ottoman army was capable
of defending and containing the Russians. Britain was ready to provide
the necessary financial means, including military support, in the event of
defeat. More importantly, the Ottoman statesmen failed to understand
the gravity of the situation and the military leadership in Istanbul misled the sultan over preparations. According to Mesut Uyar and Edward J.
Erickson, "war became inevitable and bad crisis management and public-
ity isolated the Ottoman Empire further."[24]

THE WAR OF CHOICE?

Russia declared war against the Ottoman state on April 24, 1877, after
reaching an agreement with the Dual Monarchy and Germany.[25] Russian
victory was not swift, but it was devastating for the Ottomans. The expected aid from the British side never materialized: Britain only threatened Russia when Istanbul, the Ottoman capital, was likely to fall into
Russian hands. After the Russian army had advanced to within seven kilometers of Istanbul and almost all of the eastern Balkan provinces had been
invaded by Russian forces, the threat of British intervention finally halted
the Russian advance. Thus the government in Istanbul was a hostage to
British whims.

The Russian advances forced the Ottomans to sign the Treaty of San
Stefano on March 3, 1878. The Ottoman state agreed to cede most of its
territories in the Balkans and eastern Anatolia, which become almost a
"protectorate" of Russia. The most important stipulation established an
independent Bulgaria, which included most of Macedonia and extended
to the Danube and from the Aegean to the Black Sea. In establishing this

new Bulgarian state, which seemed likely to become a Russian satellite, St. Petersburg underestimated the fears of Great Britain, which did not want to see an expansion of Russian power in the eastern Mediterranean. Moreover, the Dual Monarchy feared that Russia might encourage Slavic and Orthodox solidarity at the expense of Austrian influence in the Balkans. In short, the terms of the Treaty of San Stefano created a situation that was untenable for the other powers, thus threatening the balance of power in Europe and causing the major powers to call for an international conference. This conference was scheduled to meet in Berlin in June 1878, and Britain tried to use this as an opportunity to enhance its position with the Ottomans.

The Ottoman defeat was the beginning of the end for the Ottoman state. Great Britain began to adjust its policy toward making the empire's dissolution as orderly as possible. During the Istanbul Conference, Britain contemplated the occupation of Egypt but decided against it for the time being because of potential conflict with France. Instead Britain focused on Cyprus due to its strategic significance for the eastern Mediterranean. It became the "protectorate" in eastern Anatolia from which Britain could watch Russian activities. On May 23, 1878, the British government demanded that the Ottoman state sign on to British demands within forty-eight hours. Thus the Ottoman state was forced to sign the Cyprus Convention in order to acquire British support just before the Congress.[26]

The Cyprus Convention stated:

> If Batum, Ardahan, Kars or any of them shall be retained by Russia, and if any attempt shall be made at any future time by Russia to take possession of any further territories of his imperial majesty the Sultan in Asia, as fixed by the definitive treaty of peace, England engages to join his imperial majesty, the sultan, in defending them by force of arms.
>
> In return, his imperial majesty the sultan, promises to England to introduce necessary reforms, to be agreed upon later by the two powers, into the government, and for the protection of the Christian and other subjects of the Porte in these territories.[27]

The sultan reluctantly accepted the demands with a few minor modifications: Britain would support the Ottoman position at the Berlin Congress, the occupation of Cyprus would be temporary, and Britain would help the Ottoman state to carry out reforms in eastern Anatolia in order to improve the situation of the Armenians.[28]

The Ottoman delegation participated in the congress with expectations that the British would support the Ottoman aim to overturn Russian gains. The Congress of Berlin convened on June 13, 1878, with an opening speech by the Austrian foreign minister, Count Gyula Andrássy. During the Congress, Britain did not fulfill any of its promises and focused on maintaining the balance of power in Europe, especially keeping Russia out of the Straits. Sultan Abdülhamid II lost his faith in Britain after the Treaty of Berlin, which resulted in the loss of most of the Ottoman Empire's Balkan territories; the loss of Cyprus to Britain and Bessarabia, Batumi, and Erzurum to Russia; and the occupation of Bosnia-Hercegovina by Austria-Hungary. Greater Bulgaria, which was created by the Treaty of San Stefano, was divided into three parts: the Bulgarian Principality under Ottoman suzerainty; autonomous Eastern Rumelia under Ottoman sovereignty; and Macedonia, which was returned to the Ottoman state with the condition of a series of reforms under European supervision. The Treaty of Berlin also left Albanian-inhabited territories to Montenegro and Serbia and divided Rumelia into two provinces. The independence of Serbia, Montenegro, and Romania was recognized, and Romania was compelled to cede southern Bessarabia to Russia, in exchange receiving Dobruja from the Ottoman Empire.

The major loser of the war was clearly the Ottoman Empire. The major European powers humiliated Russia, however, by reducing its initial gains in the Treaty of San Stefano. Given the financial burden of the war on the Russian economy and the death of 120,000 Russian soldiers during the war, Moscow became the second loser of this costly congress.[29] Ultimately, the winners were Britain, Austria-Hungary, and some Balkan states.

This Russian move increased the anxiety in Berlin about the possibility of an alliance between Russia and France over the division of the Balkans. Thus Otto von Bismarck worked hard to bring Russia and Austria together so that they could coordinate their actions in the Balkans, thereby allowing Germany to maintain its policy of isolating France. But Austria-Hungary did not want any Russian influence in the Balkans, fearing that Russian influence would increase at its own expense. When it realized that war was inevitable, however, the Dual Monarchy focused on Bosnia-Hercegovina in order to enhance its influence. In fact, the Austro-Hungarian military command convinced Emperor Franz Joseph I that possessing Bosnia was vital for the defense of Dalmatia. Indeed, during his visit to Bosnia in 1875, the emperor received many petitions from diverse Christian communities to expand his authority over them. After the visit, he developed a set of strategies for invading Bosnia and Hercegovina.[30] In return for Bosnia-Hercegovina, the Dual Monarchy signed an agreement with Russia to become the "benevolent protector" of the western Balkan people against the Ottomans.

Russian intentions were aimed at ending the post–Crimean War order established in 1856 and enhancing its influence in the Balkans by using pan-Slavism and rebuilding its fleet in the Black Sea. Russia behaved extremely cautiously to avoid alienating Germany and made an agreement with the Dual Monarchy in its efforts to coordinate the policies of all major European powers against Istanbul.[31] Russia was also able to convince Britain that its ultimatum would not threaten British interests in the Middle East or routes to India. Great Britain was not inclined to trust Russia, however, and thus pursued a policy of threatening Russia with war and, at a few points, with the dismemberment of the Ottoman Empire on its terms. Britain's main concern was the alliance between Russia and the newly emerging German state. Consequently, it used all the means at its disposal to prevent alliances among the three European powers. Furthermore, the British would not commit themselves to Ottoman territorial integrity as long as vital British interests were threatened by Russia. Instead they developed a series of smaller tactics, which they could implement if need be. The Ottoman higher bureaucracy unconditionally surrendered itself to Britain in order to contain the Russian threat. But Abdülhamid II opposed this policy of ceding everything to Britain and wanted to pursue a policy that would balance the European powers against each other.[32]

POLITICAL CONSEQUENCES:
HOMOGENIZATION, REFORM, AND LEGITIMACY

The Treaty of Berlin clearly demonstrates the shift in the constitutive rules of the Eurocentric international system in terms of the acceptance and promotion of the nation-state, the encouragement of population exchange, and the conversion of the Ottoman state into a "protectorate" on the basis of Christian rights. The treaty planted the seed of hope for diverse ethnic groups by insisting on political reforms that eventually transformed the center-periphery relations and encouraged these groups to win independence from the "Sick Man of Europe." The reforms (the process of decentralization and localization of authority by building communal political institutions) engendered fears among the European Muslim communities that their position would deteriorate.

The Treaty of Berlin redefined sovereignty in terms of national homogeneity. The logic of the treaty played an important role in the subsequent evolution of national mapmaking in the Balkans. It partitioned the territories along ethnic, religious, and national lines and thus legitimized

the forced deportation of "different" ethnic and religious groups under
the banner of nation-state formation. Under this new international system, ethnic homogenization and the nation-state became the new founding principles. Essentially this was a shift from the Vienna system of 1815,
which accepted and promoted multiethnic and multireligious empires and
states, to the Berlin system *qua* the Eastern question: a state is presumed to
represent a "nation" and becomes a nation-state through forced expulsion
of populations or violent ethnic cleansing. Thus the Treaty of Berlin marks
the beginning of the modern international system, not only by linking the
population to sovereignty but also by providing a framework in which
cleansing of the "religious Others" (Muslims) from Europe became possible. In this respect, J. A. R. Marriott's definition of the Eastern question
in 1918 reflects the diplomatic logic of the time: "The primary and most
essential factor in the problem is, then, the presence, embedded in the living flesh of Europe, of an alien substance. That substance is the Ottoman
Turk."[33] Thus the target of European diplomacy in the nineteenth century
was to eliminate this "alien substance": Ottoman Muslims. As Mujeeb R.
Khan aptly argues, "the Eastern Question was not simply about diplomacy
or border revisions, but about the cultural, religious, and even quasi racial
demarcation of Europe and the final subjugation of the non-West by the
West. Implicitly it also meant the ethnic cleansing and genocide of the
'alien' Ottoman Muslim presence in Europe."[34] The post-Berlin period was
the beginning of the "ethno-religious cleansing" of Muslim Turks from
the Balkans.

Population homogenization thus came to be regarded as natural and
necessary for stability in the postimperial Balkans. Hence the post-Berlin
regional system celebrated and promoted the homogenization of population through deportations, voluntary population exchanges, and massacres
of the undesirables embedded in the fabric of multiethnic and multireligious societies. The post-Berlin order redefined sovereignty in terms of the
representation of the "collective will" via an ethnically and/or religiously
homogeneous population. In order to realize this nation-state goal, the
Balkan states became engaged in a series of wars with the sole aim of further homogenization. It would not be wrong to treat the wars after the
1878 Treaty of Berlin as a function of the principle of homogenization.[35]

The origins of the Berlin system were rooted in the London Protocols
of 1830, which led to the independence of Greece. This was the first move
to link a specific population with the principle of sovereignty, in that the
Greek state was regarded as the sole representative of the Greek people. It
was not the patriarch but rather the "ethnic Greek" state that was regarded
as the representative of the Greek Orthodox population. After its inde-

pendence, Greece used a series of strategies to achieve a Greek majority in its territories, including the cleansing of the Ottoman Muslim population.[36] Although the London Protocols of 1830 recognized the rights of Muslims in Greece, they provided no mechanism to protect them from forced deportation. This principle, on which the independence of Greece was based, was later utilized by the Congress of Berlin to carry out massive population exchanges.[37] Indeed, following the Balkan Wars (1912–13), the countries in the region had to sign a number of treaties providing a legal basis for this new international nation-state order.[38] The Treaty of Berlin and its implementation would also provide the basis for the Paris peace settlement from 1919 to 1923 that shaped the post–World War I system. The key principles of the establishment of nation-states, the linkage between population and sovereignty, and the practice of population exchange were all institutionalized within the Treaty of Berlin and later fully implemented under the terms of the Paris peace settlement. In short, the genesis of the current nation-state is very much rooted in the articles of the Treaty of Berlin.

In August 1878 Sir Henry Layard, the perceptive British ambassador, already foresaw the oncoming of further problems:

> But we must not shut our eyes to the fact that the arrangements come to at Berlin, so far from having "settled" the Eastern question, may contain the seeds of future disorders and troubles, if not of future wars. The impulse given to aspirations and pretensions of "nationalities," and the sanction afforded to the new political doctrine of "autonomy," are already producing their fruits. Greeks, Albanians, Armenians, Pomaks, Bulgarians, Servians, and the innumerable other races scattered over the Turkish Empire, are encouraged to believe that they have each their special political rights, and a future, which have been sacrificed, for a time, to brute force or to political necessities. Those who think themselves strong enough to support their aspirations by arms will be ready to rebel against the authority under which they believe they have been placed in violation of justice and of the principle of "nationality." Those who cannot recur to force will have recourse to intrigue and conspiracy. Both processes have already begun. It would require a wiser and stronger Government than that of the Porte, unless some great change takes place in it and it is supported by Europe, to arrest them. If foreign Powers interfere, as they will probably do hereafter, it may be with the object of promoting their own special and particular interests.[39]

Nationalists in or outside of the empire came to believe that the imperial system was doomed to collapse. Accordingly, they all sought ways to carve out their own "ethnic" and "homogeneous" territories. The defeat of the Ottoman Empire was so deep and humiliating that it not only lost large chunks of its territories in the Balkans and Caucasus but practically became a "protectorate" of Britain.[40] Perhaps the greatest loss, however, was the legitimacy of the empire in the eyes of its multiethnic and multireligious populations. Having suffered an erosion of its legitimacy, the Ottoman state pursued a number of strategies to restore and enhance its power. But the lack of economic resources (because the Ottoman finances were under the tight control of European powers) and limited manpower very much dictated limits to the policy options at the disposal of the state.

THE DISCOURSE OF REFORM: EROSION OF LEGITIMACY

Faced with the major Ottoman military defeat that shocked both Muslim and Christian subjects of the empire, the Armenian, Albanian, and some Macedonian-Bulgarian revolutionary leaders were seeking to carve their own piece from the collapsing empire. In order to contain these nationalist aspirations, the Ottoman state introduced a number of reforms under the pressure of the major European powers.

The attempts to reform the empire through the distribution of sovereignty to ethnic and religious groups and the introduction of equality to its subjects further intensified the crisis and gradually undermined the legitimacy of the Ottoman state. The reforms exposed the question of legitimacy and the feeble sense of belonging that existed among the diverse populations. In other words, the reforms did not enhance the legitimacy of the empire but rather reinforced the aspirations of Christian minorities to carve out their own territory. When reforms were implemented in Greece, Lebanon, Macedonia, and Anatolia, they followed trajectories of their own, influenced by the preexisting norms, interests, and aspirations of the local communities. Thus they were developing their own orientations that were usually at odds with Istanbul's desire to enhance the power of the state. Reform projects that aimed to contain nationalism bled into conflict and eventually destroyed the empire. Even if the sultan issued the reform project either voluntarily or under duress, local functionaries such as governors and *kaymakam*s decided whether projects of reform would be implemented and, if so, where, when, and for what purpose. The degree to which the reforms were implemented was very much determined by the local configuration of forces, illustrating the very limited power of the central government.

The European economic penetration into Anatolia after the Ottoman-British Trade Agreement in 1838 and the Tanzimat reforms of 1839 contributed to the creation of socially differentiated and politically unified, autonomy-seeking ethno-religious communities, such as the Armenians and Macedonians. Jeremy Salt, a leading authority on Christian missionaries and the Armenian reforms, argues that "pressure on the reform question was serving only to inflame relations between Muslims and Christians."[41] In other words, these reforms led to the evolution and strengthening of a sense of political "difference." That in turn provided the grounds for the emergence of separatist nationalisms (for example, Armenian, Albanian, or Macedonian). This was especially true as the center was seeking to create a new sense of political legitimacy based on Islam and Islamic identity in order to hold the empire together, thus alienating the Christian periphery, which was also searching for its own political destiny. Indeed, a parallel search for legitimacy was occurring both at the center around Islam and at the periphery among Armenians on the basis of "self-determination." The cultural and political distance between the center and periphery gradually increased, and the inequality between the groups provided the necessary source for agitation toward political autonomy. In short, the forced political reforms imposed by Britain strengthened the empire's centrifugal ethno-religious tendencies by weakening the central authority. Indeed, the reforms of the Ottoman Empire promoted the separatist national identities and eventually led to the weakening of the center.

By analyzing the social and political impact of this military defeat and the failure of the reform projects to recognize the political claims of the various ethnic groups, we can understand when and under what conditions the ethnic groups of the periphery came to the conclusion that living within the empire was no longer feasible and that secession was the only possible outcome. Scholars of nationalism and ethnic conflict maintain that peripheral elites who are marginalized by the metropole and not respected by the central authority turn to nationalism as a way of agitating the masses for more political power.[42] These agitations, combined with increasing state repression, encourage peripheral societies to think that they would be better off separated from the imperial system. I would also argue that the impact of war, if it results in a major defeat for the central authority, opens an unexpected opportunity for peripheral actors to assert their power. Thus the debacle of 1878 was not only the turning point for the empire in terms of displaying its military and political weakness

but also provided an opportunity for the peripheral actors to make political claims and call for the redistribution of sovereignty along ethnic and
religious lines.

Shortly after the defeat in 1878, Armenian elites in eastern Anatolia
and Cilicia, just like the Albanians and others in the Balkans, played a
leading role in demanding political autonomy. When their demands were
not granted by Istanbul, they turned to nationalism in order to legitimize
their position and conversely to delegitimize the imperial framework.
The question, then, is: when did the Ottoman Empire lose its legitimacy
among the peripheral communities? The sociopolitical conjuncture of the
Treaty of Berlin was the beginning of the end of the Ottoman Empire.
British ambassador Sir Henry Layard aptly concludes in his memoirs that
"the year 1878 sealed the fate of the Ottoman Empire and proved to me
that all hope of restoring to it even something of its former power and
independence would have been to be abandoned. Its final dismemberment
was only a question of time."[43] Indeed, in order to avoid its dismemberment, Abdülhamid II tried to address the destructive consequences of the
Treaty of Berlin by restructuring his foreign and domestic policies.

Great Britain capitalized on the Ottoman weaknesses and formally
occupied Egypt in 1882. Aware of the possibility of a similar fate, the sultan
pursued the primary foreign policy goal of enhancing the state and playing
one European power against another to protect the territorial integrity
of the empire. In some cases, such as the Dual Monarchy's occupation of
Bosnia and Hercegovina, Abdülhamid II grudgingly recognized the occupation in order to balance Austria-Hungary against Great Britain. The
Ottoman sultan also developed working and peaceful relations with Russia to counter British ambitions. In the economic domain, Abdülhamid II
believed in closer ties with Germany for the development of the empire's
infrastructure. He was sensitive to the exigencies of legitimacy for the state
and used the limited means at his disposal to patch up the weakening state.
In this he was relatively successful. Furthermore, he used Islam as a new
source of solidarity to bring Muslims together and raise Muslim political
consciousness.

THE SEARCH FOR LEGITIMACY: ISLAMISM AS NATIONALISM

The simultaneous search for a new source of legitimacy both at the center
and on the periphery took place after a major military defeat and large territorial losses in the aftermath of the Treaty of Berlin. This defeat not only
undermined the state's legitimacy but also "transformed the Ottoman

state into a largely Muslim one whose main territory lay in Asia Minor and the Middle East."[44] This, in turn, forced the Ottoman state to search for new sources of legitimacy to keep the Muslim majority together.

During the long reign of Sultan Abdülhamid II, the Ottoman state began to restructure Islamic practices and identity in order to construct an Islamic nationalism. Profound social and political changes within and outside the Ottoman state facilitated the promotion of this Islamic political consciousness.[45] The cycle of wars and large population movements, especially European-imposed reforms to alleviate the situation of the Christians, gave life to religious-based identities: the nineteenth-century Ottoman nationalist discourse was framed in terms of Islamic identity. The Ottoman political elite utilized Islamic concepts to promote the idea of territory as the new foundation for statehood and to disseminate the view that the fatherland constituted the space that was necessary for the survival of this Islamic community. By the end of the nineteenth century the Ottoman elite had begun to use fragments of Ottoman-Islamic political thinking to articulate new concepts such as homeland (*vatan*),[46] nation (*millet*), and public opinion (*kamuoyu*).[47]

These bureaucrat-led reforms, such as Tanzimat, sought to shift the center of loyalty from the sultan to a more broadly based understanding of legal citizenship and to promote the concept of "Ottoman" nationhood. Realizing the difficulty of creating a nation through strictly legalistic means, the state bureaucrats stressed the necessity of a common cultural axis for forming a nation. Islam was presented as a vital part of the cultural glue that would hold the population together. The state invoked an Islamic identity to blend various Muslim ethnic groups into a "Muslim nation" after the 1877–78 War. This constituted a major revolution in the Ottoman state tradition. The source of legitimacy began to move away from the Ottoman dynasty and toward the caliphate and the Muslim community; a new center of loyalty began to develop, along with a more concrete concept of homeland. This feeling, in turn, gave impetus to the rise of the notion of citizenship in the Ottoman state. The existence of the state was rationalized by the need to ensure the survival of the *Muslim* nation.

The 1877–78 War resulted in a massive influx of Balkan and Caucasian Muslim refugees into Anatolia.[48] The atrocities that these Muslims described served as a catalyst for a new Islamic political and national consciousness following the 1878 treaty. The treaty reduced Ottoman territory by two-fifths and detached one-fifth of its subjects.[49] The total Ottoman population before the war "is estimated at 35 million–15 million in Europe and 20 million in Asia and Africa. Muslims numbered 21 mil-

lion compared to 14 million Christians."[50] After the Treaty of Berlin, the
population declined to 17.1 million, including approximately 12.5 million
Muslims and 4.5 million Christians.[51] The Treaty of Berlin left Muslims
as the clear majority in the Ottoman state, thus making its promotion as
the spiritual home of Muslims much easier. Over 4 million Muslims had
migrated from the Crimea, the Caucasus, and the Balkans to settle in Anatolia and Eastern Thrace. The migrations from territories ceded to European powers under the Treaty of Berlin transformed the multireligious
empire into a Muslim country. This influx of migrants also required that
the Ottoman state provide some conceptual framework that would help
unite these newcomers, many of whom were non-Turks (Albanians, Bosnians, Circassians, Chechens, and others) speaking several different languages. The migrants, who had been expelled or forced to leave due to
their religion, found in Islam the source of their common bond with the
people of Anatolia. The sultan sought to strengthen this common bond
and to replace the various group loyalties and identities with loyalty to
and identification with an Islamic state apparatus — the institution of the
caliphate.[52]

Only British-Russian rivalry kept the Ottoman Empire from being dismembered totally in 1878. The sultan recognized that he needed to forge
strong political unity among the remnants of the empire in order to have
any chance of preserving it. In the aftermath of the treaty and following the
occupation of Egypt by the British in 1882, Sultan Abdülhamid II sought
to integrate the Anatolian, Arab, and Balkan regions of his state through a
series of new administrative, economic, and cultural programs. In particular, he tried to create among his Muslim subjects a political consciousness
and sense of unity based on the twin pillars of state (*devlet*) and religion
(*din*). In practice, however, religion was subordinate to the state and acted
primarily as a shield for its preservation. Abdülhamid II pursued his efforts to create a form of Islamic nationalism through numerous avenues,
such as the centralization of authority and the building of schools; an
emphasis on the role of Arabic culture in the empire; the creation of new
communication and transportation channels, such as the Hijaz railroad
and telegraph lines; the provision of financial support to select Arabic and
Turkish newspapers; the retention of leaders of Sufi orders as advisors; and
investment in the protection and reconstruction of Mecca and Medina.[53]

Sultan Abdülhamid II also took steps to form connections with the
widespread networks of Sufi orders and to emphasize the pilgrimage to
Mecca and Medina and the caliph's role as organizer of this important
Muslim activity.[54] He invited the sheikhs of the prominent Sufi orders to

Istanbul and established a close relationship with the leaders of the Shazli and Ritai orders, who became his advisors. He resumed use of the title "caliph" to show Muslims around the world that he served as guarantor of the holy places in Mecca, Medina, and Jerusalem.[55] But the sultan's objective of reconstituting imperial society along Islamic lines and integrating the Kurds into the system was in direct competition with the Christian communities' desire for political autonomy.

The Treaty of Berlin had introduced the political principle of the nation-state that would become the new basis of mapping the Balkans and the Caucasus. The treaty also sanctioned the deportation of populations in order to create homogeneous nation-states. The forced migration and deportation of large Muslim communities from the Balkans and the Caucasus and the indifference of the major European powers to the plight of these people shaped the Ottoman perception about other future acts of demographic engineering.

The treaty's lack of concern for the welfare of the people caused a series of reactions against it (see chapter 5). It forged a temporary Muslim-Christian alliance in Bosnia as they rallied a stiff resistance against the Dual Monarchy; the Albanians organized themselves and launched an all-out rebellion against Montenegro's government; the Pomak Muslims resisted the Bulgarian occupation of their territories; and the treaty increased the anxiety among Muslims in eastern Anatolia about the possibility of their territories becoming an Armenian state. In other words, the Treaty of Berlin planted the seeds for a long series of future conflicts and wars in the Balkans and eastern Anatolia. Stavrianos aptly sums the long-term implications of the treaty: "The direct and logical outcome of the Berlin settlement was the Serbian-Bulgarian War of 1885, the Bosnian crisis of 1908, the two Balkan wars of 1912–1913, and the murder of Archduke [Franz] Ferdinand in 1914."[56] Indeed, the Berlin settlement not only poisoned inter-Balkan relations but also provided the necessary conditions for the formation of nationalist committees and serious bloodshed in mixed Balkan communities.

SECURITIZATION OF MINORITIES
VIA INSURGENCIES AND OPPRESSION

After the Treaty of Berlin, the revolutionary Armenian committees organized a series of rebellions and insurgencies and even tried to assassinate Abdülhamid II. All of these Armenian actions were aimed at eliciting foreign intervention against the Ottoman state. These acts resulted in the

construction of a new political language that redefined the legitimate political community as "Muslim" by defining the Armenian Christians as the
"other" or the "fifth-column" of the major European powers. Furthermore,
not only had the definition of community been altered, but the politics
of the empire were redefined in Carl Schmitt's terms of "enmity" and "exclusion": the state began treating the Christian minorities, especially the
Armenians, as an "existential threat."[57] The Ottoman state regarded the
stipulations of the Treaty of Berlin as the blueprint for the partition of the
state and, as such, the possible end of Ottoman sovereignty. Armenian
demands for autonomy threatened both the territorial integrity and the
sovereignty of the state. Ole Waever argues that "state security has *sovereignty* as its ultimate criterion, and societal security has *identity*. Both
usages imply survival. A state that loses its sovereignty does not survive as
a state; a society that loses its identity fears that it will no longer be able to
live *as itself*."[58] In short, the Armenian insurgency, which aimed to bring
about European intervention, resulted in the securitization of the community during the reign of Abdülhamid II. By referring to "securitizing"
Armenian minorities, I mean that the Ottoman bureaucracy began to consider the Armenians "an existential threat, requiring emergency measures
and justifying actions outside the normal bounds of political procedure."[59]
After framing the Armenians as a "security threat," the state developed a
series of strategies to criminalize the political, civil, and religious activities of the group. In addition, through securitization, the state initiated
the mobilization of the Muslim population against the non-Muslims and
subsequently justified their actions.

The Ottoman Empire used a series of strategies (reforms or coercion)
to deal with peripheral mobilization for ethnic autonomy and well-
organized insurgency movements. Nineteenth-century Ottoman history
is the story of the mutually constitutive relationship between reforms and
increased insurgency. The reforms forced on the Ottoman Empire by the
European powers were not effective in controlling dissent and political
opposition. The gap between reforms and demands increased, and eventually the periphery started using all possible means to break away from the
center. The most critical factor for the failure of the reform projects was
the lack of resources. Very limited attempts were made to address the social
conditions that were generating dissent and revolt, and the Ottoman system tried to address the issue in terms of law and order. It had only limited
resources, but it used them to assert control over rebellious peripheries
such as the Balkans and Caucasus. In addition, it used coercion in terms
of counterinsurgency tactics, new formal and informal institutions, and

political reforms with the purpose of control and integration. Indeed, the Ottomans were not the only ones who invoked counterinsurgency tactics to maintain control over the periphery (see chapter 13). Although coercion was very effective, it was ultimately very costly. Thus peripheral resistance movements constantly changed their tactics to increase the costs for the center. Michael Doyle argues that the metropole controls a peripheral society when the periphery is politically divided and socially integrated.[60] Thus empires lose control when the periphery becomes socially differentiated and politically unified. Therefore the reforms of the Tanzimat era, along with the penetration of European capitalism, played an important role in the growing gap between the center and the periphery in the empire.

Ottoman counterinsurgency tactics and coercive politics did not bring lasting peace and further radicalized the increasingly unified Armenian communities across the Anatolian plateau. These tactics not only caused huge costs for the state budget but also engendered long-term resentment that created a unified sense of "us" against the oppressive state. Rather than seeking to diffuse Armenian discontent over a series of policies, the Ottoman tactics of repression created more support among the periphery for separatist movements. This does not mean that coercion was not effective. In fact, coercion can be very effective if it is not arbitrary and excessive. The failed reform policies in the Balkans, the European desire to partition the Ottoman territories, and the activities of the Armenian and Macedonian revolutionary committees radicalized Ottoman policies toward the periphery. The relatively tolerant Ottoman attitude toward non-Muslim communities gradually ceased after the Treaty of Berlin; the Ottoman state started using coercion more than persuasion in regard to the nationalist revolutionary movements.

Any form of revolt or insurgency was perceived by the metropole as a threat to the territorial integrity and sovereignty of the state. Some Ottoman bureaucrats had a sense that the empire had lost the Balkans because of the political reforms made on the heels of the Tanzimat period. Thus the empire opted for coercion rather than concession to deal with the Armenian revolutionary organizations. With the excessive use of force by the Hamidiye Regiments (irregular Kurdish tribal forces), the Armenian communities came to the conclusion that the use of force by the state to control and discipline communities was abusive, so the state lost legitimacy among the Armenians.[61] Although the Hamidiye Regiments were generally successful in integrating the Kurds into the system, they were also key to the erosion of Ottoman legitimacy and the Armenian rejection of imperial rule.[62] Because of the lack of economic resources, the Ottomans were forced to depend on irregular forces (Circassians and Kurdish tribal militias). Indeed, due to financial constraints, the Ottoman state had to relinquish its monopoly on state violence to these irregular forces, which lacked discipline and ignored the traditional customs of warfare, thus becoming involved in a series of atrocities against the civilian population.

THE SHADOW OF THE PAST: THE DIVERGENT STRATEGIES

Kurds

Yet the same empire that used coercion against the Armenian revolutionary organizations was able to develop a series of formal and informal institutions not only to co-opt the Kurds but also to integrate the Kurdish tribes further into the system.[63] Why were these diametrically opposed policies used toward different imperial subjects? In order to prevent the rise of centrifugal forces among the Kurds and gain their full loyalty, the Ottoman bureaucracy engaged the Kurdish periphery by means of social and political incorporation. Through a number of institutions, the Ottomans integrated the Kurdish periphery into the rest of the empire in order to develop pan-Islamic identity.

Abdülhamid II emphasized both secular and religious education to socialize the periphery into the empire; furthermore, he provided new opportunities for secular and religious Kurdish elites to participate in local political processes. The sultan used Islam, as a form of soft power, to "make power seem legitimate in the eyes of [the] other."[64] Through Islamism, the Ottoman state developed a new ideology that encouraged the Muslim communities to follow the empire's lead and remain loyal to its institutions. The Kurdish periphery became integrated into the Ottoman Empire through Islamism (recruiting local religious leaders and recognizing their authority), the Hamidiye Regiments (recruiting Kurdish tribes as soldiers), and the educational system. Abdülhamid II further managed to socialize the Kurdish elite into his dominant Islamic-Ottoman system, which in turn consolidated hegemonic Ottoman power. In short, when it came to the Kurds, the Ottomans were willing to take risks and integrate them into the system through a number of strategies, especially by stressing the socialization of the elite into the imperial system. On the basis of G. John Ikenberry and Charles Kupchan's article examining the competing British policies in India and Egypt, I would argue that the Ottoman state regarded the Kurds as an asset and "socializable" into the imperial system.[65] In contrast, after the Berlin Congress, it treated the Armenians as a "security concern," which became a "threat" after the rebellion in Sasun in 1894. Stephen Duguid argues that "the Armenians came to be seen as a threat and a source of trouble" by 1894.[66] Indeed, the Muslim population and the Ottoman bureaucracy reached the conclusion that "all Europeans were in league with the [Armenian] revolutionaries and were interested only in overseeing the disintegration of the Empire."

Abdülhamid II's socialization policies for the Kurdish elite consolidated the legitimacy of the Ottoman imperial system and served to contain potential Kurdish nationalism. The Ottoman state used education, ideology, and empowerment as effective methods for integrating the Kurds into the Ottoman state. In addition to socialization, the second most important strategy for integrating the periphery into the system was political participation. The elite are the most critical force in the construction and dissemination of nationalism, so it was very important for the empire to co-opt the peripheral elite into governance. The more members of the peripheral elite were included in the decision-making processes and recognized by the state in terms of rank or title, the more they would be integrated into the empire. If the empire isolated certain ethnic or religious groups from the metropole, this would create conditions for the nationalist discourse of secessionism. According to Michael Doyle, some empires, including the Ottoman Empire, survived longer than others because they were more successful in including the peripheral elite in political processes. Moreover, Benedict Anderson locates the origins of nationalism in Latin America because of the exclusion of the native and Creole elite from the system. In short, the failure of the Spanish Empire to include Creole and native elites in the political system gave rise to colonial nationalism there. Although Michael Hecter calls for federalism and decentralization to give recognition to the local elite and keep diverse groups within one state, Doyle argues that too much decentralization is likely to fragment the state and increase the appetite of local leaders for full independence.[67] Doyle contends that the most successful way for the Roman Empire to manage and contain its conflicts was to incorporate peripheral leaders into the central government, not through direct rule, due to the lack of modern technology and communication. Hecter argues that the source of nationalism is "direct rule" resulting from the development of technology and communications.[68]

Armenian Nationalism and the Empire

Turkish historiography explains the Armenian rebellions and insurgency activities in two ways. The "provocation" thesis suggests that the Armenian rebellions aimed to bring about European intervention and provoke the

Ottoman security forces. The other thesis is that the British, and in some cases the Russians, engineered actions to weaken the Ottoman state by advocating an independent Armenia. On the basis of my study, I have found that the provocation thesis is partially useful to understand not so much the sociopolitical causes of the revolts but rather their utilization. The objective of some high-profile public attacks, such as the terrorist attack on the Ottoman Bank and the attempt to kill the sultan, was to win over European public opinion in hopes of triggering European intervention. For instance, after the Hunchak Party demonstrations in Istanbul in 1896, British ambassador Philip Currie wrote to London, "There is good reason to suppose that the object of the 'Hindchag' [Hunchak] was to cause disorder and bloodshed with a view to inducing the Powers of Europe to intervene on behalf of the Armenians."[69] This argument makes sense in explaining some of the major urban terrorist attacks but does not explain the rebellions in provinces and rural areas. In order to understand these rebellions, we need to contextualize them by examining the sociopolitical conditions under which Armenians were living. The problem with the provocation thesis is that it ignores the largely miserable social and political conditions of the Armenian communities in Anatolia. These communities had good reasons to rebel against the corrupt and ineffective authorities. As far as the second thesis is concerned, neither Britain nor Russia wanted an independent Armenia. Britain worried that an independent Armenia might become a Russian instrument and thus threaten its interests in the region. The Russian Empire also was not keen to see an independent Armenia because it did not want to set an example for its own Armenians and other ethnic groups. The second thesis is helpful in explaining the rebellions in terms of British and Russian policies, but it ignores domestic factors and denies the Armenian communities as well as the Ottoman officials any form of independent agency. The sociopolitical causes of these rebellions and their utilization by different groups and states are not the same.

The Armenian communities were much better educated due to the diligent work of the Christian missionaries. Moreover, Armenian merchants were better integrated into the global economic structure than their Muslim counterparts and were in full control of the trade within and across borders. The work of Christian missionaries and the new economic realities facilitated the formation of a new political consciousness among the Armenian elite, who sought equality and recognition.[70] The same processes that facilitated the formation of a new Armenian political consciousness also helped to create a series of social and political cleavages within the Armenian community, such as revolutionary versus religious, nationalist versus conservative, and pro-Ottoman versus pro-Russian. This evolving political consciousness coincided with the tectonic events of wars, population transfers, and the worsening economic situation in eastern Anatolia. When the new Armenian elite, educated in missionary schools and European universities and influenced by Russian revolutionary anarchist ideology, started to make political demands and seek better economic conditions for the peasants in Anatolia, the Ottoman state was ineffective in meeting these expectations of equality and security. Thus the mostly secular and revolutionary Armenian elite sought more radical solutions in realizing their goal of autonomy and then independence.

Although the Armenian question did not start with the Treaty of Berlin, this was a wake-up call for the Ottoman state in regard to the loyalty of the Armenian leadership and communities. The Armenian mood was already restless before the 1877–78 War.[71] They, like many other communities, had long-standing grievances over taxation, equality, land grabs, and insecurity. But these were all common problems of nineteenth-century Ottoman Anatolia. What really transformed the Ottoman perception of the Armenians "as a security concern" was the occasional Armenian cooperation with the occupying Russian troops and the active involvement of Patriarch Nerses Varjabedian in the Congress of Berlin. He was active in sending letters to Bismarck and Salisbury and also sending a delegation to fight for an "autonomous Armenia."[72] The Treaty of Berlin not only internationalized the Armenian claims for autonomy but also destroyed the possibility of coexistence between the Muslim and Christian communities.

Even though the Ottoman troops fared a little better in eastern Anatolia, they still lost the traditional Muslim cities of Doğu Beyazıt, Ardahan, Kars, and Erzurum. Some unruly Kurdish tribes and Armenian nationalists, motivated by the expectation of better economic conditions, supported the Russian troops and even moved eastward with them as they withdrew. Some Armenians, especially the peasants, allied themselves with the Russian troops for a number of reasons: the grab of Armenian agrarian land by the Kurds; the lack of security and the ineffective Ottoman provincial bureaucracy; the heavy taxation of the peasants; and the Russian policy of defending Christian rights and freedoms in the Ottoman state. Also, many Armenians lived in Russian territory in the Caucasus, including some who were commanders of the Russian army. Beybut Shelkovnikov, Mikhail Loris-Melikov, Ivan Lazarev, and Arshak Ter-Ghukasov all served as generals. Again Armenian political organizations based in

Tbilisi openly supported the Russian adventure in Anatolia.[73] The Russian advance into both Anatolia and the Balkans encouraged many Armenian intellectuals, religious leaders, and merchants to believe that the collapse of the Ottoman Empire was imminent and that Russia was there to stay. This belief that the Ottoman state could not maintain its sovereignty in the larger Balkan and Anatolian landscape further motivated the Armenian leadership to speak out against the Ottomans and become fully allied with the Russians at San Stefano in 1878.

The defeat was so great that every group was seeking to save itself and also benefit from the problematic situation in which the state found itself. For instance, the Armenian delegation (headed by the patriarch Nerses Varjabedian) went to San Stefano to welcome the Russians and ask Grand Duke Nicholas for help in creating an independent Armenian state in Anatolia. The grand duke did not bring the Armenian demand of independence to the negotiation table, but he forced the Porte to undertake massive political reforms in the provinces inhabited by the Armenians and to protect them from the Kurds and Circassians. Article 16 of the Treaty of San Stefano states:

> As the evacuation of the Russian troops of the territory which they occupy in Armenia, and which is to be restored to Turkey, might give rise to conflicts and complications detrimental to the maintenance of good relations between the two countries, the Sublime Porte engages to carry into effect, without further delay, the improvements and the reforms demanded by local requirements in the provinces inhabited by Armenians, and to guarantee their security from Kurds and Circassians.[74]

Before the Congress of Berlin, Patriarch Nerses visited British ambassador Sir Henry Layard on March 17, 1878, and expressed the Armenian demands:

> Your Lordship [Lord Salisbury] will remember that last year his Eminence [Nerses] was anxious to persuade me that they greatly preferred remaining under it [Ottoman rule] to being transferred to that of Russia. His Eminence admitted to me when I saw him yesterday that such had been the case. But he said that since the Russian success, and especially since it had become known that Russia had stipulated in one of the Articles of the Preliminaries of Peace for administrative reforms for Armenia, the state of affairs had completely changed.[75]

Nerses lobbied for the autonomy for the Armenian people pointing out that the Christian population of the Balkans had gained their autonomy and independence. The patriarch informed Layard that "if they could not obtain what they asked from the justice and through the intervention of Europe, they would appeal to Russia, and would not cease to agitate until they were annexed to her." Indeed, Nerses asked for an autonomous Armenia. When Layard asked him to define the borders of this autonomous Armenia, the patriarch said that "Armenia should contain the Pashalics of Van, Sivas, the greater part of that of Diarbekir, and the ancient kingdom of Cilicia." Layard informed Nerses that in all those provinces he asked for "the very large majority of the population consisted of Mussulmans."[76] Even if the Armenians were in the majority in the eastern Ottoman provinces, the British government was not in favor of any form of autonomous Armenia because it feared that this entity might become a Russian post in Anatolia, which would give Russia a great military advantage and thus threaten British policies in the Middle East. (The belief that an autonomous Armenia would become an extension of Russia was widespread not only among the Ottoman bureaucracy but also among the British elite.) Thus the primary goal of the British policy was not Armenian autonomy but rather the reversal and prevention of Russian gains within Anatolia.

The Treaty of Berlin reformulated the provisions of the Treaty of San Stefano in relation to the Armenian question. According to article 61 of the Treaty of Berlin, the Russian troops were to withdraw immediately from eastern Anatolia without waiting for the implementation of reforms. The Ottoman state would implement the reforms for the Armenians under the loose supervision of the European powers, especially Britain; the Ottoman state promised Britain that it would "introduce necessary reforms" in Anatolia under the Cyprus Convention.[77] In fact, article 16 of the Treaty of San Stefano was almost identical to article 61 of the Treaty of Berlin, which stated:

> The Sublime Porte undertakes to carry out, without further delay, the improvements and reforms demanded by local requirements in the provinces inhabited by Armenians, and to guarantee their security against the Circassians and the Kurds. It [the Sublime Porte] will periodically make known the steps taken to this effect to the Powers, who will superintend their application.[78]

The only change was the immediate withdrawal of Russian troops from eastern Anatolia and the reassignment of Russian supervision to the European powers to oversee the implementation of the reforms. The

Treaty of Berlin was signed on July 13, 1878. It not only internationalized the Armenian issue but also transformed it into a weapon in the hand of the European powers, especially Britain, against the Ottoman state. The Armenian delegation was not satisfied with the outcome of the Treaty of Berlin, which did not include a "territorialized" Armenia.[79] Article 61 called upon the Ottoman state to carry out reforms in the "provinces inhabited by Armenians" but did not specify the nature or the scope of these reforms. Moreover, the treaty had also asked the Russian troops to withdraw from the eastern provinces.

The Treaty of Berlin raised suspicion among Ottoman bureaucrats and the sultan himself regarding the loyalty of some peripheral communities such as the Armenians, who heretofore had been known as *Millet-i Sadıka* (The Loyal Millet). Armenian author Kevork Pamukciyan stresses that "Patriarch Nerses Varjabedyan made a mistake by sending an Armenian delegation to the Berlin Congress in 1878 since [this act] had damaged, in the eyes of the Palace and the government, the eminence and reliability of the Armenians, who up to that point had been known as a Loyal Nation."[80] Similarly Lord James Bryce, a devoted friend of the Armenians, highlighted the critical role of the Berlin Treaty as a landmark in the deterioration of the relations between the Ottoman state and the Armenians:

> Before the Treaty of Berlin the Sultan had no special enmity to the Armenians nor had the Armenian nation any political aspirations. It was the stipulations then made for their protection that first marked them out for suspicion and hatred, and that first roused in them hope of deliverance whose expression increased the hatred of their rulers. The Anglo-Turkish Convention taught them to look to England, and England's interferences embittered the Turks.[81]

The Treaty of Berlin gave rise to the rumor that the eastern Anatolian provinces might become the basis for a new "independent Armenia," thus arousing the fears of the Muslim population in the region. Apprehension about the future rather than the actual situation mobilized the local Muslim notables into believing that they might lose their land and be forced to live under the control of Russians or Armenians.[82]

The perceived conditions of the Treaty of Berlin and the transmutation of the Kurdish-Islamic movement are closely linked. The war not only caused the collapse of security but also brought famine, migration, and devastation to the region. Under these sociopolitical conditions Kurdish Nakşibendi Sheikh Ubeydullah said: "What is this I hear; that the Armenians are going to have an independent state in Van, and the Nestorians are going to hoist the British flag and declare themselves as British subjects. I will never permit it, even if I have to arm the women."[83] The Kurdish notables were united in preventing the implementation of reforms for the Armenians. In fact, a major Kurdish rebellion against the Ottoman state occurred in 1880 as a result of security concerns after the 1877–78 War, including the fear of an independent Armenia and the gradual destabilization of the region.[84] The war not only interrupted regular agricultural activity due to lack of rain, seeds, and labor but also played an important role in transforming subsistence farming into cash crops such as opium and tobacco.[85] Moreover, during and after the war, the trade links between Trabzon and Tabriz and Diyarbakır and Batum and Van were interrupted, creating a major economic problem.[86]

The war and Russian occupation destroyed the local economy: crops went unharvested, resulting in widespread hunger in eastern Anatolia. These events not only interrupted routine agricultural activities but shattered the normal situation of law and order. The region had devolved into a state of anarchy, thus turning the raiding Kurdish tribes into a deadly force. The Kurds, with the support of local officials, were "plundering the peaceful inhabitants of both Musulman Turks and Armenians, destroying their villages and crops, and committing many instances of cruelty."[87] Although the Ottoman government in Istanbul decided to take measures against the Kurdish tribes and improve the security situation, not much was done; "they had not the means at their disposal to enforce them against tribes which had at all times maintained a kind of independence of the Porte and had defied its authority."[88] Moreover, the provincial bureaucracy in eastern Anatolia was beset by corruption and bribery, and its effectiveness had been eroded by Kurdish tribal loyalties. Due to the lack of resources and the political will of local functionaries, the Ottoman state failed to improve the security situation of the Armenians. Thus a worsening social, economic, and security context provided the necessary grounds for the Armenian revolutionary organizations to challenge more cautious Armenian groups and also to radicalize Armenian peasants. The provocation of the Armenian revolutionary organizations against the Ottoman state and the Muslim population resulted in a massive retaliation.[89] The revolutionaries had two aims: the mobilization and unification of the Armenians against the Ottoman state and the solicitation of intervention by major European powers by turning public opinion against the Ottoman state.[90]

In order to understand the tactics and strategies of the Armenian revolutionaries in the second half of the nineteenth century, we have to examine the processes of cross-fertilization of ideas and strategies between Russian radicalism and the revolutionaries, who were mostly educated in

Russian universities. In short, the Armenian revolutionary movement originated in the Russian Empire, especially among the Tbilisi Armenians. Russian radicalism intensely shaped the Armenian revolutionary movement in terms of ideas, organizational structure, and strategies of raising the political consciousness of the masses. The radical ideas of Russian intellectuals and activists such as Sergei G. Nechaev, Pyotr L. Lavrov, and Pyotr N. Tkachev deeply shaped the Armenian revolutionary movement.[91] Nechaev's ideas of revolutionary organization, leadership, and tactics in particular were internalized by Armenian revolutionaries, who stressed sacrifice, responsibility, absolute devotion, and vanguardism in order to free the Armenian people at any cost. For instance, in 1890 a group of revolutionaries under the leadership of Russian Armenian Sarkis Gugunian tried to enter Ottoman Turkey to prepare the peasants for rebellion.[92] They were all killed by Ottoman forces. The imprints of Russian revolutionary ideas on the evolution of the Armenian revolutionary movement were ubiquitous. The founders and the first members of the revolutionary and nationalist Hunchak (Bell) Party, established in Switzerland in 1887, were Russian Armenians or were educated in Russian universities and influenced by the intellectual debates in Russia.[93] The leader of the party (Avetis Nazarbekian) and his fiancée (Maro Vardanian) had connections with the Russian revolutionary parties. According to Louise Nalbandian, the most prominent authority on the Armenian revolutionary groups, the main policy of the Hunchak Party was to use violence as a political tool to raise nationalist consciousness among the "passive" Armenian peasants. She describes the Hunchak strategies as "Propaganda, Agitation, Terror, Organization, and Peasant and Worker Activities."[94] Hratch Dasnabedian argues that the party's main goal was "inciting popular revolt" and "revolution."[95] Indeed, the Hunchak organized attacks and incited the people to revolt in almost all towns where Armenians lived. When its leadership was challenged from within, the Armenian community and some leaders were exiled from the Ottoman state, the second Armenian revolutionary and nationalist organization, Hai Heghapokhagan Tashnagtsoutioun (Armenian Revolutionary Federation: Dashnaks), was established in Tbilisi in 1890. These Armenian revolutionaries, just like the Russian populists, thought that the peasantry had a potential key role in social change and in the establishment of the "new system."[96]

The initial goal of the Dashnaks was not independence but rather self-rule for the Armenians in the Six Provinces (Vilayet-i Sitte) by arming the Armenians, attacking state officials, and killing Armenian "traitors" who were not followers. According to Benjamin C. Fortna, a leading

Ottoman historian, these organizations' "extremely aggressive terrorist policy intended to catch the attention of the Western powers ultimately proved disastrous. Following the strategy of the Bulgarian nationalists in the 1870s, the Armenian revolutionaries frequently incited violence which was calculated to draw Muslim reprisals and trigger an international intervention."[97] After the establishment of these political parties, Abdülhamid II took a series of measures. In order to prevent the further breakup of territories by Russia and also to contain Armenian nationalism, he established the Hamidiye Regiments of irregular Kurdish troops/militias in the middle of 1892.[98] These regiments were primarily composed of Kurdish tribes and had a high degree of administrative autonomy. Their main purpose was to establish law and order in the eastern provinces. The regiments used violence against the Armenian population of the region, which further alienated the two communities and consolidated Armenian nationalism.

The fear of an independent Armenia gradually undermined communal relations. When communal conflict turned into violence, Abdülhamid II developed a number of strategies; their implementation was dictated by the availability of resources.[99] The lack of resources forced him to rely on the voluntary Kurdish tribal militias in order to protect the territorial integrity of eastern Anatolia and also to integrate the Kurds into the system. Abdülhamid II's counterinsurgency policies toward the Armenians, primarily based on the unruly Kurdish militias, further radicalized the Armenian communities and resulted in a series of massacres. The major turning point was the reaction to some radical Armenian provocation at Sasun and Zeytun in 1894. The Hamidiye Regiments brutally suppressed the provocation, resulting in the massacre of thousands of Armenians. This bloodshed created a major reaction outside the Ottoman state. Foreign media started to call Abdülhamid II the "red Sultan." A series of fact-finding missions attempted to study the tactics of the Hamidiye Regiments. One of the British reports detailed the gruesome tactics of the Hamidiye Regiments and asked the sultan to dissolve them. The main purpose of these rebellions was to trigger European intervention, so the British forced the Ottoman state to establish a commission with some European representation. The government established a commission of inquiry on January 23, 1895, to examine the events.[100] When Armenian groups learned of the establishment of a commission, they reported the atrocities to the European embassies, who informed their respective governments.[101] In response to some of the bloody tactics of the Hamidiye Regiments, the British, French, and Russian ambassadors asked the sultan to implement a reform package for Armenians known as the "Memorandum and Project of Reforms for the Eastern Provinces of Asia Minor" on May 11, 1895.[102] The Ottoman government rejected the memorandum and the "territorialization" of the Armenian question in terms of the Six Provinces. In September 1895 the Hunchak Party organized a mass demonstration of thousands of Armenians at the Sublime Porte demanding the implementation of the May Reform Project. This provocation and challenge to governmental authority required a swift response from the Ottoman government: a number of people were arrested and hanged.

In order to influence European public opinion and also push toward the implementation of the 1895 Reform Project, the Dashnak leaders organized a major attack on Ottoman military headquarters in Van. It degenerated into a civil conflict within the city, and many innocent people were killed.[103] The most important Dashnak revolutionary attack took place on August 16, 1896, in Istanbul. The revolutionary Dashnaks, under the leadership of Papken Siuni, an eighteen-year-old student, engineered the takeover of the Ottoman Bank. Siuni was killed during the takeover, and Karekin Pastermadjian (known as Armen Karo) took over control of the group. They wanted more European intervention against the Ottoman state and also an end to the massacres of Armenians by Kurds and some Ottoman troops in the eastern provinces.[104] The terrorist attacks in Istanbul further radicalized the Ottoman government, which started to use more heavy-handed tactics against the Armenians. The Armenian communities of Istanbul became a target of random attacks by state officials and some local gangs. This radicalized the Armenian community and further isolated it from the government.

The Armenian nationalist movement would gradually become secessionist as the policies of Istanbul failed to meet its demands and would become more dependent on Russia for a number of reasons. The Ottoman policies against the Armenian revolutionary organizations forced the Armenians to become more radical and also "collaborationist" against their own state/sultan. The series of massacres and deportations alienated the Armenian community from the larger Muslim society as well as from the state under which they had lived for centuries.

Alexander Wendt, a leading political theorist of international relations, argues that "authority requires legitimacy, not mere influence or power."[105] Indeed the Ottoman sultan lost his legitimacy among the Armenians particularly because of the Hamidiye Regiments' abusive policies. The Armenian peripheral elite started to believe that the Ottoman state had no right to control their society and thus justified all forms of violence against the state. Many Armenians came to the conclusion that they could not go on living under the constant abuse of the Hamidiye Regiments. The lesson from the interaction between the Hamidiye Regiments and the Armenians was that the more coercive the empire became, the more the Armenians rejected Ottoman legitimacy. (Of course, Ottoman coercion might also be viewed as a response to Armenian radicalism.) We might argue that the more the Kurds became integrated into the imperial system, the more they identified with the empire and became its loyal citizens. What took place in Anatolia after the Treaty of Berlin was the conflict between the logic of empire and the logic of nationalism. The Armenian tragedy was the ultimate outcome of this contradiction.

To conclude, the Treaty of Berlin had four major (un)intended impacts on the social and political situations of the Ottoman society and state. First, it exposed the military and economic weakness of the central government, which in turn undermined the legitimacy of the state. Second, when the Armenian leadership tried to benefit from this "weakness" by grabbing a share of their own from the failing Ottoman state, as Megerditch Khrimian called for, "the most loyal nation" became a security "concern" in the eyes of the Ottoman officials. This securitized nearly the entire Armenian body politic and its activities.[106] Third, in order to protect the eastern Anatolian provinces against Armenian "autonomy" and insurgency, the local Muslim population gradually became mobilized and radicalized against the Armenian communities. Fourth, the Ottoman state, by arming the Kurdish tribes to protect the territories and also to bring law and order, further increased the insecurity of the Armenians, who in turn armed themselves against the Kurds and the central authority. In return for their loyalty, the Kurds asked the state to look aside when they grabbed Armenian land. This security concern and the lack of state loyalty created a fertile ground for Armenian radical groups to convert religious peasants into revolutionaries and ultimately into militias.

CONCLUSION

The Treaty of Berlin triggered a series of processes that led to the demise of the Ottoman Empire by weakening its institutions, undermining its legitimacy, and creating an indefensible territory in the Balkans and Anatolia. Moreover, the treaty exposed Ottoman weaknesses and encouraged peripheral minorities to use them as an opportunity to carve out a state of their own. This created a sense of anxiety among the Muslim population over the future of the state and encouraged the search for a new source of legitimacy, which resulted in the construction of a Muslim-only nation. The forced population movement of Muslims from the Balkans and the Caucasus greatly transformed the Ottoman demographic structure, and the Muslim migrants' memories of war and exile provided a basis for revanchist forces in Istanbul. The guarantee of war and the bankrupt state of Ottoman finances forced the state to rely on the irregular militias and led to acts that would further undercut the legitimacy of the state among its Christian Armenian population. In fact, reforms in terms of centralization and introduction of equality were detrimental to the existence of the Ottoman state as an empire.

NOTES

My profound thanks go to Feroze Yasamee, Gül Tokay, Kemal Sılay, Mujeeb R. Khan, Peter Sluglett, Ramazan Hakkı Öztan, Umut Uzer, Perparim Gutaj, William Holt, Nihat Ali Özcan, and Ali el-Husseini. Without their help I could not have written this paper. I am also indebted to the Turkish Coalition of America, whose financial support made possible an ideal environment in which to research and write it.

1. Carlton J. H. Hayes, *A Generation of Materialism, 1871–1900*, 33.
2. Solomon Wank, "The Disintegration of the Habsburg and Ottoman Empire: A Comparative Analysis," 98.
3. The collapse of empires is the outcome of imperial overreach and the emergence of new great powers, wars, and nationalist movements. Paul Kennedy, *The Rise and Fall of the Great Powers: Economic Change and Military Conflict from 1500*.
4. By "collated" Ottoman society, I mean the amalgamation of diverse groups that shared a sense of legitimacy and, in a limited way, a political language. Michael Doyle argues that an imperial government "is a sovereignty that lacks a community" and "shared commitments." This has to do with the nature of imperial societies that were not "integrated" but consisted of a collection of communities. M. W. Doyle, *Empires*, 35–36.
5. Mesut Uyar and Edward J. Erickson, *A Military History of the Ottomans, from Osman to Atatürk*, 213.
6. F. A. K. Yasamee, *Ottoman Diplomacy: Abdülhamid II and the Great Powers, 1878–1888*, 45. Yasamee argues that "the Treaty of Berlin…left the Empire with almost no defensible frontiers in Europe, and a seriously weakened frontier in Asia."
7. Stanford Shaw and Ezel Kural Shaw, *History of the Ottoman Empire and Modern Turkey*, 2:191.
8. Engin Akarlı, "The Problem of External Pressures, Power Struggles, and Budgetary Deficits in Ottoman Politics under Abdülhamid II (1876–1909): Origins and Solutions."
9. For the best comprehensive analysis of Abdülhamid II's foreign policy, see Yasamee, *Ottoman Diplomacy*, 41–52.
10. Sevket Pamuk, *The Ottoman Empire and European Capitalism, 1820–1913: Trade, Investment and Production*, 29.

11. Although Palmerston defended the independence of Greece in 1830, he was in favor of the territorial integrity and rejuvenation of the Ottoman state as a "barrier" for two reasons: to prevent a Russian military presence on the Bosphorus and to counterbalance France's influence in Egypt.

12. Ronald Robinson, John Gallagher, and Alice Denny, *Africa and the Victorians: The Climax of Imperialism in the Dark Continent*, 78.

13. Jeremy Salt, *Imperialism, Evangelism and the Ottoman Armenians, 1878–1896*, 10–11.

14. Donald Quataert, *The Ottoman Empire, 1700–1922*, 68.

15. Salahi R. Sonyel, *The Ottoman Armenians: Victims of Great Power Diplomacy*.

16. Robinson et al., *Africa and the Victorians*, 79.

17. Ibid.

18. L. S. Stavrianos, *The Balkans since 1453*, 402. Stavrianos also indicated the power struggle between the Serbian and Montenegrin leadership over the unification of the Slavs. Milorad Ekmečić, a leading Serbian nationalist historian, who wrote the first Ph.D. dissertation on the causes of the 1875 Hercegovinian rebellion, argues that the revolt of 1875 was a reaction to declining agricultural prices and the increasing tax payment in cash imposed by the Ottoman authorities. This rebellion was a peasant revolt that evolved into a regional and European crisis with the help of Austrian military agents as well as a power struggle between political actors in Serbia (the rival Karadjeordjevic family vs. the ruling Obrenovich family) and Montenegro. Milorad Ekmečić, *Ustanak u Bosni 1875–1878*. I would like to thank Perparim Gunaj for reading and summarizing the book for this paper.

19. The most important book that vilifies the Turks and Muslims and supports Bulgarian autonomy is William Gladstone's *Bulgarian Horrors and the Question of the East*. Ali Suavi, a leading Young Ottoman, responded to the book: see "Letters by Ali Suavi Efendi," *Diplomatic Review* 24 (October 1876): 270–76. The British establishment still wanted to keep Russia out of the Straits, and "the line of defence against Russia was still the Turkish empire in Asia." Robinson et al., *Africa and the Victorians*, 82.

20. Roderic Davison, *Reform in the Ottoman Empire, 1856–1876*, 358–408. For more on the sociopolitical context that led to the promulgation of the constitution and the reaction, see Robert Devereux, *The First Ottoman Constitutional Period: A Study in the Midhat Constitution and Parliament*, 82–92.

21. Abdülhamid II retained most of his power, however, and the constitution declared that the "caliph is not responsible for his acts" and is a sacred person. In short, sovereignty and even infallibility rested within the person of the sultan. The Assembly first convened on March 19, 1877, and war was declared on April 24 by Russia.

22. For more on Salisbury's views, see Yasamee, *Ottoman Diplomacy*, 57; Stavrianos, *The Balkans since 1453*, 406.

23. The Ottoman diplomacy after 1856 was based on two pillars: reliance on Britain as a superpower and reliance on the Paris Treaty of 1856. According to the treaty, the Ottoman state admitted members of the Concert of Europe and all signatories pledged jointly to maintain "the integrity of the Ottoman Empire" and guaranteed its independence. The Ottoman state was expecting Britain to defend the treaty. During the Berlin Conference, the Ottoman state officials always reminded the

Europeans that the Ottoman state was one of the European powers and a major actor, not an object of the diplomacy of other powers.

24. Uyar and Erickson, *A Military History of the Ottomans, from Osman to Atatürk*, 183. This book provides an excellent analysis of the military situation and the shortcomings of the Ottoman military. Several books have been written on the military side of the war; see *History of the Turko-Russian War*; Valentine Baker, *War in Bulgaria: A Narrative of Personal Experiences*; Ibrahim Ethem Paşa, *Plevne Hatıraları (Sebat ve Gayret, Kıyametten Bir Alamet)*.

25. W. N. Medlicott, *The Congress of Berlin and After: A Diplomatic History of the Near Eastern Settlement, 1878–1880*.

26. Christopher J. Walker, *Armenia: The Survival of a Nation*, 114–15.

27. Ibid., 114.

28. Dwight E. Lee, *Great Britain and the Cyprus Convention Policy of 1878*; İsmail H. Uzuncarsılı, "II. Abdülhamid'in İngiliz Siyasetine dair Muhtıraları."

29. Richard G. Weeks, "Peter Shuvalov and the Congress of Berlin: A Reinterpretation."

30. Stavrianos, *The Balkans since 1453*, 399. Stavrianos offers an essentialist reading of the history of the Balkans. He presents the nineteenth-century conflicts as "the centuries old religious conflict" (399); his perspective on the Ottoman state and Muslims reflects typical European prejudice, as if Muslims are an "alien" presence in the Balkans. Stavrianos freely describes the Ottoman attempts to control rebellions in terms of "barbarous brutality by Turkish irregulars" (401). He hardly criticizes the brutality against the indigenous Muslims by the unruly Orthodox forces. This is still an important book, however, and every historian of the Balkans must read it with the understanding that this is a typical representation of an essentialist reading of the events in the Balkans.

31. Russia did not want to repeat the mistake of the Crimean War by taking unilateral action against the Ottoman state and uniting the major European powers against itself. Before engaging in any military operation in the Balkans, Russia sought to build alliances and negotiate with major European powers, especially with the Austro-Hungarian Empire. Russia promised to support the Dual Monarchy's expansion toward Bosnia and Hercegovina. Alan J. P. Taylor, *The Struggle for Mastery in Europe: 1848–1918*, 242.

32. Yasamee, *Ottoman Diplomacy*, 47.

33. J. A. R. Marriott, *The Eastern Question: An Historical Study in European Diplomacy*, 3.

34. I would like to thank Mujeeb R. Khan for allowing me to cite his unpublished paper.

35. Antony Anghie, *Imperialism, Sovereignty and the Making of International Law*; Gerrit W. Gong, *The Standard of "Civilization" in International Society*.

36. A series of systematic ethnic cleansings against the Muslims and other ethnic groups occurred in Greece; see Michael Mann, *The Dark Side of Democracy*, 113.

37. A. W. Brian Simpson, *Human Rights and the End of Empire: Britain and the Genesis of the European Convention*. For the best debate on the Treaty of Berlin, see Carole Fink, *Defending the Rights of Others: The Great Powers, the Jews, and International Minority Protection, 1878–1938*, 3–40.

38. Fikret Adanır and Hilmar Kaiser, "Migration, Deportation, and Nation-Building: The Case of the Ottoman Empire," 2. For a more polemical, one-sided, and very anti-Turkish debate treating the Turks as the "alien substance" in Europe and dealing with the transfer of populations, see Stephen Ladas, *The Exchange of Minorities: Bulgaria, Greece, and Turkey*.

39. National Archives of the United Kingdom (formerly Public Record Office), Foreign Office Archives, London (FO), FO 424/73 (Layard to Salisbury) 1008/318, August 19, 1878, quoted in Kemal H. Karpat, "The Social and Political Foundations of Nationalism in South East Europe after 1878: A Reinterpretation," 371–72.

40. Yasamee, *Ottoman Diplomacy*, 65.

41. Salt, *Imperialism, Evangelism and the Ottoman Armenians, 1878–1896*, 106.

42. C. B. Lieven, *Empire: The Russian Empire and Its Rivals*.

43. Sinan Kuneralp, ed., *The Queen's Ambassador to the Sultan: Memoirs of Sir Henry A. Layard's Constantinople Embassy, 1877–1880*, 519.

44. Wank, "Disintegration of the Habsburg and Ottoman Empire," 99.

45. M. Hakan Yavuz, "The Patterns of Political Islamic Identity: Dynamics of National and Transnational Loyalties and Identities."

46. Bernard Lewis, "Watan."

47. Şerif Mardin, "Modernization of Social Communication."

48. Nedim İpek, *Rumeli'den Anadolu'ya Türk Göçleri, 1877–1880*.

49. Shaw and Shaw, *History of the Ottoman Empire*, 191.

50. Wank, "Disintegration of the Habsburg and Ottoman Empire," 99.

51. Stanford Shaw, "The Ottoman Census System and Population, 1831–1914," 325–38; Justin McCarthy, *Muslims and Minorities: The Population of Anatolia and the End of the Empire*, 109.

52. Mujeeb R. Khan, "External Threats and the Promotion of a Trans-National Islamic Consciousness: The Case of the Late Ottoman Empire and Contemporary Turkey."

53. See further M. Hakan Yavuz, "Nationalism and Islam: Yusuf Akçura, 'Üç Tarz-ı Siyaset.'"

54. Butrus Abu-Manneh, "Sultan Abdülhamid II and Shaikh Abdulhuda Al-Sayyadi," 139.

55. See further H. A. R. Gibb, "Lutfi Pasa on the Ottoman Caliphate"; idem, "Some Considerations on the Sunni Theory of the Caliphate"; and Halil İnalcık, "Islamic Caliphate, Turkey and Muslims in India."

56. Stavrianos, *The Balkans since 1453*, 412.

57. Carl Schmitt, *The Concept of the Political*, 19–80.

58. Ole Waever, "Securitization and Desecuritization," 67 (emphasis in original).

59. Barry Buzan, Ole Waever, and Jaap de Wilde, *Security: A New Framework for Analysis*, 24.

60. Doyle, *Empires*, 129.

61. Stephen Duguid, "The Politics of Unity: Hamidian Policy in Eastern Anatolia."

62. For one of the best articles on Armenian-Kurdish relations, see Tessa Hofmann and Gerayer Koutcharian, "The History of Armenian-Kurdish Relations in the Ottoman Empire"; see also Garo Sasuni, *Kürt Ulusal Hareketleri ve Ermeni-Kürt İlişkileri (15.yy'dan Günümüze)*.

63. Bayram Kodaman, *Şark Meselesi Işığı Altında Sultan II. Abdulhamid Devri Doğu Anadolu Politikası;* Wadie Jwaideh, *The Kurdish National Movement: Its Origins and Development.*

64. Joseph S. Nye, "The Soft Power," 167.

65. G. John Ikenberry and Charles A. Kupchan, "Socialization and Hegemonic Power," 283–315.

66. Stephen R. Duguid, "Centralization and Localism: Aspects of Ottoman Policy in Eastern Anatolia, 1878–1908," 287.

67. Doyle, *Empires*; Benedict Anderson, *Imagined Communities: Reflections on the Origin and Spread of Nationalism*; Michael Hecter, *Containing Nationalism*, 136–56.

68. Hecter, *Containing Nationalism*, 29.

69. Cited in Justin McCarthy, *Turks in America: The Creation of an Enduring Prejudice*, 108.

70. Salahi R. Sonyel, *The Ottoman Armenians: Victims of Great Power Diplomacy*, 19–26.

71. Cevdet Küçük, *Osmanlı Diplomasisinde Ermeni Meselesinin Ortaya Çıkışı, 1878–1897*, 1–15.

72. Kuneralp, *The Queen's Ambassador to the Sultan*, 445.

73. Vartan Gregorian, "The Impact of Russia on the Armenians and Armenia."

74. Walker, *Armenia*, 111.

75. Bilal N. Şimşir, *British Documents on Ottoman Armenians*, 159.

76. Ibid., 160.

77. Treaty of Berlin, article 61.

78. Walker, *Armenia*, 115. These powers were Great Britain, Germany, France, Russia, the Austro-Hungarian Empire, and Italy.

79. The Armenian autonomy debate added a "territorial" dimension when the European powers defined the scope of Armenian reforms in terms of the "six provinces" (Vilayet-i Sitte) in a May 1895 reform memorandum. These six provinces would later be framed as "Western Armenia."

80. Melek Sarı Güven, "Kevork Pamukciyan'ın Tarih Perspektifinden Olaylara Bakışı," 69–70.

81. Quoted in Guenter Lewy, *The Armenian Massacres in Ottoman Turkey: A Disputed Genocide*, 9.

82. For more on Russian-Armenian connections, see Ronald Grigor Suny, *Looking toward Ararat: Armenia in Modern History*; and Manuel Sarkisyanz, *A Modern History of Transcaucasian Armenia: Social, Cultural, and Political.*

83. Vice-Consul Clayton to Major Trotter, Baskale, July 11, 1880, in National Archives of the United Kingdom (formerly Public Record Office), Parliamentary Papers, London (PP), *Parliamentary Papers* (Turkey, 1881), 5:7.

84. Jwaideh, *The Kurdish National Movement*, 83.

85. The socioeconomic conditions of the region disintegrated into hunger and the sale of children: see the Reverend Samuel G. Wilson (an American missionary), *Persian Life and Customs*; Robert Elliott Speer, *Hakim Sahib, the Foreign Doctor: A Biography of Joseph Plumb Cochran, M.D., of Persia.*

86. Charles Issawi, "The Tabriz-Trabzon Trade, 1830–1900: Rise and Decline of a Route."

87. Kuneralp, *The Queen's Ambassador to the Sultan*, 446.

88. Ibid.

89. Küçük, *Osmanli Diplomasisinde Ermeni Meselesinin Ortaya Çıkışı, 1878–1897*.

90. For more on the provocation thesis, see Lewy, *The Armenian Massacres in Ottoman Turkey*, 17; and Louise Nalbandian, *The Armenian Revolutionary Movement: The Development of Armenian Political Parties through the Nineteenth Century*, 90–178.

91. Richard G. Hovannisian, *Armenia: On the Road to Independence, 1918*, 17.

92. Ronald Grigor Suny, "Eastern Armenians under Tsarist Rule," in *The Armenian People from Ancient to Modern Times*, ed. Richard G. Hovannisian, 132.

93. The founding members of the Hunchak Party were Avetis Nazarbekian, Maro Vardanian, Gabriel Kafian, Gevork Garajian, Ruben Khanazatian, Christopher Ohanian, and Levon Stepanian. Nalbandian, *The Armenian Revolutionary Movement*, 115.

94. Ibid., 110.

95. Hratch Dasnabedian, "The Hunchakian Party," trans. Marine A. Arakelians, *Armenian Review* 4, no. 4 (1988): 22.

96. Gerard J. Libaridian, "Revolution and Liberation in the 1892 and 1907 Programs of the Dashnaktsutiun," 189.

97. Benjamin C. Fortna, "The Reign of Abdülhamid II," 55.

98. Kodaman, *Şark Meselesi Işığı Altında Sultan II. Abdulhamid Devri Doğu Anadolu Politikası*, 7–11.

99. William L. Langer, *The Diplomacy of Imperialism, 1890–1902*; Akdes Nimet Kurat, *Türkiye ve Rusya: XVII. Yüzyıl Sonundan Kurtuluş Savaşına Kadar Türk-Rus İlişkileri 1798–1919*; Arman J. Kirakossian, *British Diplomacy and the Armenian Question: From the 1830s to 1914*; Manoug Joseph Somakian, *Empires in Conflict: Armenia and the Great Powers, 1895–1920*; M. S. Anderson, *The Eastern Question, 1774–1923: A Study in International Relations*.

100. William Miller, *The Ottoman Empire and Its Successors*, 429. According to Miller, the commission was appointed by the Ottoman government at the insistence of Great Britain, which demanded that British, French, and Russian delegates accompany it.

101. Nalbandian, *The Armenian Revolutionary Movement*, 122.

102. This memorandum mentions the Treaty of Berlin and first attempt to territorialize the Armenian question by implying that "Armenia" consists of six provinces (Vilayet-i Sitte).

103. For more on the Armenian rebellion in 1896, see Justin McCarthy et al., *The Armenian Rebellion at Van*, 58–60.

104. "Mobs Killed More Than 3,000," *New York Times*, August 28, 1896.

105. Alexander Wendt, *Social Theory of International Politics*, 208.

106. Megerditch Khrimian (1820–1907) was an Armenian patriarch, a publisher, and the most prominent intellectual of the Ottoman Armenian communities. He also represented the Armenian interest at the Congress of Berlin.

2

European Equilibrium or Asiatic Balance of Power?

The Ottoman Search for Security in the Aftermath of the Congress of Berlin

Feroze A. K. Yasamee

I

The Treaty of Berlin was one of a series of international agreements concluded between 1878 and 1881 by the Ottoman Empire and the six European Great Powers, which collectively formed the Berlin settlement.[1] The settlement was a response to the Russo-Ottoman War of 1877–78 and also to the Eastern Crisis that had preceded and provoked the war. The Eastern Crisis had been driven by a chain of upheavals within the Ottoman Empire, leading to European diplomatic intervention: Christian revolts in Hercegovina, Bosnia, and Bulgaria; local wars with Serbia and Montenegro, both legally Ottoman dependencies; a constitutionalist revolution that deposed two sultans in succession; the Ottoman treasury's default on its foreign debts; and proposals by the Great Powers for radical reforms in the administration of the Ottoman Empire's European provinces. These events, and the subsequent defeat of the sultan's forces in the war with Russia, destroyed European faith in the Ottoman Empire: it was now seen as a failing state, whose demise could not be long postponed. Accordingly, the Berlin settlement was designed with two purposes in mind: first, to deal with the immediate consequences of the Eastern Crisis and the war; and second, tacitly to prepare the way for the Ottoman Empire's final dissolution and enable the European powers to stake out positions in anticipation of that eventuality.

The first of the agreements constituting the Berlin settlement was the preliminary peace of San Stefano, concluded between Russia and the Ottoman Empire on March 3, 1878; though soon revised by the other European powers at the Congress of Berlin, the provisions of this peace set the congress's essential terms of reference, notably by establishing the formal independence of Romania, Serbia, and Montenegro; granting autonomous statehood to the Bulgarians; ceding substantial territories to Russia in Bessarabia and eastern Anatolia; and providing for the implementation of internal reforms in Bosnia and Hercegovina, in other portions of the Balkan peninsula remaining under direct Ottoman rule, and in those provinces of Ottoman Asia inhabited by Armenians. The preliminary peace also obliged the Ottoman Empire to pay Russia a large war indemnity, intended to impede any future Ottoman recovery. To Britain and Austria-Hungary, these terms represented an unacceptable increase in Russia's power and influence in the Near East, and the Russians were quickly persuaded to submit them for revision at a congress of all the Great Powers in Berlin. In anticipation, the British induced the Russians to accept a reduction of their gains of influence and territory in Ottoman Europe and Asia and offered to support Austria-Hungary's acquisition of the Ottoman provinces of Bosnia and Hercegovina, as a counterbalance to Russian influence in the Balkans.

The British attempted to resolve the remaining problem of future Russian preponderance in Asia by inducing the Ottoman government to sign the Cyprus Convention on June 4, 1878. This gave the sultan a unilateral British military guarantee against future Russian aggression in Asia, subject to the conditions that the island of Cyprus be placed under British administration and a British-approved program of internal reforms be introduced in the sultan's Asiatic provinces. The convention represented a British bid to establish, if not a protectorate over the Ottoman Empire, then at least a preponderant influence in the affairs of its Asiatic provinces and, by implication, in their eventual disposal.

The Congress of Berlin duly convened on June 13, 1878, and its deliberations were issued one month later in the Treaty of Berlin, concluded on July 13. This confirmed the independence of Romania, Serbia, and Montenegro and reduced the territorial area in which the Bulgarians would enjoy self-government and also the area to be ceded to Russia in Anatolia. It also stipulated that Austria-Hungary should occupy and administer the provinces of Bosnia and Hercegovina indefinitely, thereby asserting Austria-Hungary's right to a voice at least equal to Russia's in any future revision of the territorial and political settlement in the Balkan peninsula. The treaty confirmed the San Stefano provisions for reforms in the remainder of the Ottoman Balkans and the provinces inhabited by Armenians but made them subject to the approval and supervision of the Great Powers collectively, rather than of Russia alone.

In addition, the Congress of Berlin expressed formal opinions on three vital topics that were not included in the body of the treaty. First, it recommended that the Ottoman Empire make a substantial cession of territory to Greece. Second, it recommended the establishment of a financial commission of experts, to be nominated by the Great Powers, which would examine the problem of the Ottoman government's default on its foreign debts and propose a remedy. Third, the question of the sultan's established right to control the passage of foreign warships through the Straits of the Bosphorus and the Dardanelles was broached in an exchange of declarations by the British and Russian delegations. The British indicated that they would no longer be willing in all circumstances to respect the Ottoman government's right to close the Straits to warships, and the Russians insisted that the closure of the Straits was a European principle that could not be modified by unilateral British action. Finally, mention must be made of certain informal understandings and suggestions. In the course of the congress, German and British representatives privately encouraged France to seize the Ottoman dependency of Tunis—a check that the French duly cashed in May 1881. In similar fashion, Germany's Chancellor Bismarck privately advised the British to help themselves to Egypt—a suggestion that they were not disposed to take up, for the time being.

The Ottoman Empire's liability to pay a substantial war indemnity to Russia was confirmed in a definitive bilateral treaty of peace, concluded on February 8, 1879, while the terms of Austria-Hungary's occupation and administration of Bosnia and Hercegovina and its right to maintain military garrisons in the adjacent Ottoman *sancak* of Novi Pazar were resolved in a bilateral convention dated April 21, 1879. Even so, a range of crucial questions still awaited a definitive resolution: the new frontier between the Ottoman Empire and Greece; a financial settlement between the Ottoman Empire and its European creditors; the nature and extent of the internationally approved reforms to be introduced into the sultan's European provinces and those inhabited by Armenians; and the nature and extent of the reforms to be introduced into the sultan's Asiatic provinces under the terms of the separate Anglo-Ottoman Cyprus Convention. Nor were the full political implications of the settlement immediately clear. It was widely believed that the Ottoman Empire was now so weakened at home and abroad that it would have no choice but to eke out its remaining days as a client or pensioner of one or more of the European Great Powers.

The peace of San Stefano had conjured up the specter of Russian domination, which was conjured away by the Treaty of Berlin; but the Cyprus Convention represented a British counterbid for predominance in Ottoman Asia. The British tried in vain to induce Austria-Hungary to assume a similar role in respect to the sultan's remaining territories in Europe. In reality, no European power would succeed in establishing a virtual protectorate over the Ottoman Empire. None proved capable of achieving this on its own. The evolution of the Great Powers' mutual relations after 1878 precluded any combination that might have achieved this, and the Ottoman Empire proved to be more resilient than had been anticipated. At the time, however, none of this could have been foreseen.

II

For the Ottoman Empire, the terms of the Berlin treaty marked a massive diplomatic defeat, whose implications were every bit as dangerous as those of the preceding military defeat it had suffered at the hands of Russia. The pledges of Ottoman territorial integrity enshrined in the 1856 Treaty of Paris were set at naught, along with the assumption that the Ottoman Empire had been accepted by the European Great Powers as a legitimate and credible member of international society. The sultan was obliged to surrender considerable territories in Europe and in Asia not only to the victorious Russians and their Balkan allies but also to Austria-Hungary, Greece, and Great Britain (through the Cyprus Convention) in a form of compensation arrangement that appeared to presage the Ottoman Empire's partition. Further, the treaty's provisions for internationally supervised administrative reforms in the empire's remaining European possessions and also on behalf of the Armenians of Asia Minor might yet open the door to a system of provincial autonomies, leaving the sultan's government with no more than a nominal sovereignty in the regions affected.

Just as importantly, the withdrawal of European support symbolized by the treaty was a blow to the prestige and authority of the Ottoman government in the eyes of its own subjects, which served to stimulate separatism among its Armenian and other Christian populations and also among some Albanian and Arab Muslims.[2] The treaty's one saving grace, in the opinion of the Ottoman ambassador to Berlin, Sadullah Paşa, was that it had enabled the empire to ward off the threat of unilateral domination by Russia and thus preserve its independence.[3] Even this was not certain, for the congress's provision for an international commission to investigate the empire's foreign debts might open the way to a system of international control of the state budget, similar to the one existing in Egypt, which would effectively extinguish Ottoman political independence.

These were long-term issues. In the shorter term, the signature of the treaty plunged the Ottoman Empire into a fresh period of crisis. Sultan Abdülhamid II and his advisors had every reason to fear that the implementation of the territorial provisions of the treaty, and also its provisions for measures of internal reform in the Balkan and Anatolian provinces, might provoke an internal collapse or, conceivably, a fresh war with Russia or Austria-Hungary. Either outcome would be fatal and open the way to the empire's definitive partition by the European Great Powers. In addition, the Anglo-Ottoman Cyprus Convention had imposed an important change in Ottoman foreign policy, by drawing the empire into an exclusive peacetime alliance with a European Great Power, for the first time since the 1833 treaty of Unkiar-Skelessi. The British alliance was a new departure and also an unwelcome one. For one thing, it restricted Britain's obligations to the defense of the empire's Asiatic territories and offered no guarantee of its European and African possessions. For another, it was conditional upon the implementation of a British-approved program of administrative reforms in those Asiatic territories that, in the eyes of Sultan Abdülhamid and his ministers, appeared to envisage a form of British protectorate over the empire, or, just as bad, a British plan to sponsor the development of an Armenian successor state in eastern Anatolia.

Not until the latter part of 1879 did these various dangers recede, as the last Russian troops left the Balkan peninsula, thereby enabling Sultan Abdülhamid to escape from his unwelcome alliance with Great Britain and reassert his diplomatic independence.[4] Even then, spontaneous local resistance to the cession of Albanian-inhabited territory would delay a settlement of the new Montenegrin frontier for a further year and of the Greek frontier for six months after that. After 1880 the question of reforms in the sultan's European and Armenian-inhabited provinces slipped from the diplomatic agenda, though it would eventually return. A final settlement with the sultan's European creditors was reached in December 1881, on terms that did not place the empire's finances under comprehensive foreign control; and the British made no fresh attempt to challenge Ottoman rights at the Straits.

How did contemporary Ottoman statesmen explain the diplomatic defeat registered by the Berlin settlement and assess their empire's prospects for recovery and survival in its aftermath? At issue were not simply the ambitions and attitudes of the various European powers and also of the empire's much strengthened Balkan successors, who now emerged for the first time as a serious strategic threat in their own right. It was just as important for Ottoman statesmen to assess the nature and dynamics of the overall international system of which their empire formed a part and upon which its fate depended. Certainly they were familiar with the notion of a Concert of Europe (*İttihad-ı Avrupa*), to which the Ottoman Empire had been formally admitted in 1856. They were also familiar with the ambiguous notions of the equilibrium of Europe (*müvazene-yi Avrupa*) and the equilibrium of the Powers (*müvazene-yi düveliye*) and used them in both the senses identified by Paul W. Schroeder. On the one hand, they designated a "balance of power" system of mutual security based on countervailing power and blocking coalitions. On the other hand, they designated a broader equilibrium intended to guarantee the independence and security of all through a mutual consensus on norms and rules of behavior and a balance of rights, status, and satisfactions rather than of raw power.[5] This paper attempts to explore these issues by examining the diverse responses of four prominent Ottoman statesmen to the situation in which their empire had been left by the Berlin settlement.

III

In early 1880, as the most pressing dangers conjured up by the Berlin settlement appeared to recede and with his hands at last free, Sultan Abdülhamid II initiated a series of consultations with serving and former ministers, with a view to the determination of future policy in a range of areas. The topics covered included a variety of internal administrative reforms, a possible revision of the 1876 Constitution and a recall of the parliament, suspended since 1878, and an ambitious program of public works designed to foster the development of the empire's Asiatic provinces.[6] Foreign policy was not overlooked. In February Abdülhamid instructed two of his former grand viziers, Hayreddin Paşa and Safvet Paşa, to furnish him with reports on the Austro-Prussian War of 1866, the Franco-Prussian War of 1870–71, and the Russo-Ottoman War of 1877–78. Specifically, he wished to know the causes and immediate sources of these wars, their consequences for the belligerents, how they had reshaped Europe, and how they had been perceived by popular as well as expert diplomatic opinion.[7] No true politician, it has been said, asks a question without already knowing the answer, and the questions that Abdülhamid put to Hayreddin and Safvet were hardly innocent. At the very least, they suggest that he had already concluded that the three wars in question had transformed the international system in ways to which the Ottoman Empire would have to accommodate itself. Clearly implicit, too, was the question of assessing the implications of the emergence of a united and powerful German Empire in the heart of the European continent. It can scarcely be a coincidence that within less than two months of requesting these reports Abdülhamid had made his first tentative steps toward a closer relationship with Germany, with a request to Berlin for civilian and military advisors.[8]

Hayreddin Paşa (1821?–90), formerly chief minister of the Ottoman dependency of Tunis, had been installed by Sultan Abdülhamid as grand vizier in December 1878 but dismissed within a few months after the two men had quarrelled over their respective prerogatives and the question of reconvening a parliament. Even so, Abdülhamid evidently maintained a high opinion of Hayreddin's abilities and continued to consult him ad hoc, on a range of domestic and foreign issues.[9] Hayreddin appears to have submitted separate reports on each of the three wars specified by the sultan, but only the report concerning the Austro-Prussian War can be traced in the Turkish state archives. It is slight. Reduced to essentials, the report asserted that the states of Germany, if united, would naturally form the strongest power in Europe; that Austria and Prussia had been engaged in a contest for supremacy in Germany since the Congress of Vienna; that Prussia had owed its eventual victory to its superior military organization and Bismarck's diplomatic skill; and that the German Empire created by the Austro-Prussian War and Franco-Prussian War was now the dominant power in Europe, as confirmed by the role that it had played at the Congress of Berlin.[10] The absence of Hayreddin's reports on the Franco-Prussian War and Russo-Ottoman War is regrettable; the latter, in particular, may have contained assessments of the Ottoman Empire's current international situation and recommendations for its future policy.

Some pointers as to Hayreddin's views, however, are contained in a further report, largely devoted to recommendations for domestic political and administrative reform, which he submitted to the sultan less than two months later, on May 3, 1880.[11] This report divided the European powers into three groups: those that "will not cease to seek the Ottoman Empire's failure in its internal and external affairs, and the continuation of disturbance and revolution within its territories"; those whose interests in the Ottoman Empire were essentially commercial, rather than political, and therefore did not regard the empire's interests and losses as a matter of primary concern; and those that saw in the survival of the Ottoman state "a firm barrier and strong divider" between themselves and Russia and consequently sought its preservation.

The danger was that the empire's disorderly internal conditions were undermining the confidence of this third group, who might otherwise be regarded as well-wishers; they were already inclining toward viewing the empire's territorial integrity with indifference. Hence the importance of internal reform: unless the "political and fundamental affairs of the Imperial Sultanate" were placed on a firm and secure footing, it would be impossible to forestall further European interference in the empire's internal affairs and, in case of need, to achieve an alliance with a European power that might protect the Ottoman state against attack by other European powers and thereby place the empire's external relations on a secure basis. Hayreddin did not indicate which European power he saw as a potential ally, but his reference to the Ottoman Empire's role as a barrier against Russia suggests that he had Britain in mind. This was the inference drawn by an anonymous internal critic, who warned that the Ottoman Empire must not tie itself to any single power but must "adopt policy in accordance with time and circumstance, maintaining and strengthening good relations with all the powers."[12]

The second former grand vizier consulted by the sultan, Mehmet Esad Safvet Paşa (1814–1883), unlike Hayreddin Paşa, was a veteran diplomat who had served on no less than six occasions as foreign minister and had participated first hand in many of the events he was now called upon to explain.[13] Safvet's report is very long and detailed.[14] Superficially, it may appear to be no more than a narrative history of events; but on closer inspection it reveals arguments, explicit and implied, of some sophistication and originality. The report begins with the Congress of Vienna, which concluded the Napoleonic wars. Safvet explained that the "diplomatic equilibrium of Europe" had been established there, through a series of territorial and political adjustments, freely agreed upon. Unprecedentedly, all the powers of Europe were represented at the congress; only the Ottoman Empire was not invited, although it was clearly a European power and had participated in the Napoleonic wars. The equilibrium established at Vienna was not a balance among particular powers but a general balance and included both territorial and institutional elements.

One key element was the position granted to the Austrian Empire as the dominant power in the Italian peninsula and, jointly with Prussia, as the leader of the states forming the newly established German Confederation. The resulting equilibrium would last for half a century, until Austria's position in Central Europe was successfully challenged. Austrian predominance in Italy was challenged from 1848 onward by the kingdom of Sardinia, to which France and then Prussia eventually gave decisive support. It was challenged in Germany by Prussia, which (unfettered by Austria's extensive commitments) had been able to build up its commercial, financial, and especially military strength. The outcome was the Austro-Prussian War of 1866, resulting in Austria's ejection from Germany and also from its remaining Italian possessions. This war was the true turning point in recent international relations. As a result, "Europe's established equilibrium was entirely disrupted," and not to the Ottoman Empire's advantage. It transformed Austria, stripped of its European role and renamed Austria-Hungary, into an aggressive regional power that would look southeast, to the sultan's possessions, for compensation for its losses in Central Europe.

Formally, the outcome of the Austro-Prussian War had preserved the independence of the other German states. But in practice, Safvet noted, they were henceforth no more than "privileged provinces" of Prussia, in a de facto German Empire of 40 million people. The subsequent Franco-Prussian War had merely rounded off this process. Launched by Napoleon III in "an act of madness," it resulted in France's defeat and consequent losses of territory and international influence, incidentally allowing the new Italian state formed by Sardinia to establish Rome as its capital and put an end to the temporal authority of the papacy. For the past ten years France had been left "in a most unfortunate condition," subordinate to German influence, while the new German Empire had gained hugely in influence and moral strength and was "the absolute arbiter of Europe," as demonstrated by the role Prince Bismarck had recently played at the Congress of Berlin. In sum, the six years between 1865 and 1871 had seen changes in Europe that had not occurred "in the course of several centuries."

Safvet Paşa's account of the origins of the most recent Russo-Ottoman War is noteworthy for its understanding tone toward Russia. Russia, he conceded, had been an expansionist power since Peter the Great and under Catherine the Great had conceived the ambition of overthrowing the Ottoman Empire, seizing its capital, and freeing its Orthodox Christian subjects. He noted, however, that it was Russia that had come to the sultan's aid against Mehmet Ali Paşa of Egypt in 1833 and had offered the Ottoman Empire the protection of an alliance at Unkiar-Skelessi; over the next fifteen years (up to 1848) Russo-Ottoman relations had been marked by friendship and mutual confidence. What had later undermined this amity and trust was Russia's apprehension that the Ottoman Empire was falling under British and French influence, as manifested by the Porte's attitude in the Wallachian and Hungarian refugee crises of 1848–49 and subsequently by a fear that Austria might challenge Russia's own influence over the Montenegrins and other South Slavs. The result was that Russia was tempted by the dispute between Catholic and Orthodox clergy over the Christian holy places in Jerusalem into making an attempt to force the Ottoman government to acknowledge Russia's protection of its Orthodox subjects, thereby provoking the Crimean War and its own defeat at the hands of an Anglo-Franco-Ottoman-Sardinian coalition.

For the Ottoman Empire, Safvet continued, the Crimean War had proved to be a pyrrhic victory, for the terms of peace imposed by the subsequent Treaty of Paris were such that Russia would never be reconciled to them: "every word of the said treaty was a stain and black spot on Russia's reputation, honor, and grandeur." The treaty had destroyed Russia's influence in the Orient and placed the Ottoman Empire under exclusive Anglo-French influence. Yet it was natural that Russia, bound by ties of religion and ethnicity to millions of the Ottoman Empire's subjects, would wish to exercise a similar influence there and maintain its prestige among the Orthodox, especially the Orthodox Slavs. Russia proved to have little hope of persuading the other European powers to revise the terms of the Paris settlement, at least until the Franco-Prussian War provided an opportunity to denounce the treaty's Black Sea clauses in 1870. In the meantime Russia had set out to undermine the Ottoman Empire, and its reputation in Europe, by promoting sedition and disturbances among the Orthodox Greeks, Montenegrins, Serbs, and Bulgarians. In this respect, Safvet conceded, the Ottoman government was not blameless: by failing to honor the pledges of equality that it had made to non-Muslims in 1856, particularly in respect to state employment, it inadvertently pushed its Christian subjects into the arms of Russia.

The upshot, in 1875–76, was the disastrous series of Orthodox Slav revolts in Hercegovina, Bosnia, and Bulgaria and the consequent armed conflicts with Serbia and Montenegro. These events led to a major international crisis and a confrontation between the Ottoman Empire and Russia, which resulted in the disastrous war of 1877–78. Even in this instance, Safvet refrained from casting the whole responsibility on Russia. He conceded that Russia had instigated or encouraged each of the revolts and the conflicts with Serbia and Montenegro. But matters had gone further than the Russians intended, confronting them with a crisis that they could not control. For one thing, the revolts provoked a general loss of European confidence in the Ottoman Empire and led other powers to come forward with radical proposals for internal reform in the affected regions. For another, some provocative remarks by the British prime minister in the autumn of 1876 prompted the Russians to order a partial mobilization, with an implied threat of war against the Ottoman Empire.

The Ottoman government refused the program of reforms collectively presented by the European Powers in December 1876 — rightly, in Safvet's view, for no independent state could have submitted to them. The other powers then refused a Russian proposal to impose the program through coercion, resulting in the formulation of a much milder program in the London Protocol of March 1877. This too was refused by the Ottoman government. Russia had been backed into a corner, Safvet argued, for to have submitted to this refusal and been left empty-handed would have been a major blow to its prestige as a Great Power. For Russia, therefore, the option of war with the Ottoman Empire had become "a vital issue." If the sultan's ministers had grasped that Russia must be offered a way out and themselves sought to develop a compromise, war might have been avoided; as it was, they accepted war fatalistically, too confident in the Ottoman Empire's own military strength and in intervention by other powers once hostilities commenced.

The Ottoman government had mishandled the Russians, failing to understand that influence in the Near East and the Ottoman Empire was crucial to Russia's prestige and standing as a Great Power. In similar fashion, Safvet Paşa argued, the Ottoman government had failed to take account of broader European opinion, which had been badly alienated by the Hercegovinian and Bulgarian revolts and also by the Ottoman Empire's simultaneous default on its foreign debt. In principle, the Ottoman Empire had been entirely justified in rejecting the Great Powers' various reform proposals as unacceptable violations of its independence and sovereignty. But in practice such European interference, particularly on behalf of the sultan's Christian subjects, was of long standing and had already created an independent Greek state, a special form of administration in Mount Lebanon, and an autonomous principality in Serbia. The true solution was to forestall such interference through better internal government and, where it could not be avoided, to manage it in ways that would minimize the threat to Ottoman interests and authority.

Safvet's report leaves much unsaid. It notably avoids any serious analysis of British policy. This may have represented an act of political tact, for Abdülhamid's deep suspicions of the British were already well established; but it may also have reflected a belief on Safvet's part that the Ottoman Empire's external security essentially depended upon its relations with the Continental European powers, primarily Russia and Austria-Hungary. Nor did Safvet's report make any explicit recommendations as to future Ottoman policy. Some indication of his views, however, may be derived from two further reports that he submitted in April 1880 on the subject of the Ottoman Empire's remaining European territories.[15] These warned that the recent Russo-Ottoman War, by abrogating the principle of the Ottoman Empire's territorial integrity previously secured by the Treaty of Paris, had "rendered the Ottoman Empire's existence and survival a pending problem, dependent upon transitory requirements and the achievement of unity between the Powers." The securing of the empire's European provinces was vital, for "the continuance and survival of the Ottoman Empire is limited to the time the region of Rumeli remains under its administration." Specifically, Safvet proposed various measures of internal reform designed to render Ottoman rule acceptable to the majority Christian population of these provinces and also to strengthen the Muslim population of Albania, who were now the main prop of Ottoman rule in the Balkans.

Like Hayreddin Paşa, Safvet Paşa regarded internal reform as the key to the Ottoman Empire's credibility in the eyes of the European powers and considered that credibility to be crucial to its external security. In a private letter written some months earlier he had stated:

> If the Ottoman Empire henceforth does not seriously and truly embark upon the path of reform, as necessitated by the position of its own territories, and if it does not fully accept Europe's civilization, and, in sum, if it does not cause itself to be considered an ordered and civilized state, it will never be freed from the influence, trusteeship, and interference of Europe, and losing its influence, rights, and independence from day to day, it will descend to the level of the Empire of Iran and facilitate partition, and there is no need to explain what the result of such a state of affairs must be.[16]

Unlike Hayreddin, however, Safvet Paşa does not appear to have favored exclusive alliances with any of the European powers.

IV

Hayreddin and Safvet were representatives of an older generation. Safvet's views, in particular, reflected the preoccupations of the preceding Tanzimat era, with its belief that the Ottoman Empire's survival depended upon gaining acceptance by the European Great Powers collectively, through reforms designed to bring the empire closer to European civilization and more particularly through an amelioration of the conditions of the empire's Christian subjects. Though periodically consulted by Sultan

Abdülhamid, Hayreddin and Safvet would not hold ministerial office again. Not so the third figure considered here: Küçük Mehmet Said Paşa (1838–1914). Küçük Said was a new man and a creation of Abdülhamid.[17] Having served as the head of the sultan's palace secretariat and then as minister of the Privy Purse, he was first appointed prime minister in October 1879 and would serve as Abdülhamid's prime minister or grand vizier on a further six occasions.

Küçük Said had no direct diplomatic experience, but as head of the palace secretariat from September 1876 to January 1878 he would have seen all major papers on foreign affairs immediately preceding and during the war with Russia; his views on the empire's international position in the war's aftermath were forthright. He repeatedly warned that the Treaty of Berlin had laid a basis for the Ottoman Empire's partition and that the Franco-Prussian War of 1870 had transformed the European equilibrium in ways that were highly dangerous to the Ottoman Empire. Since that date European opinion had abandoned the notion of preserving the Ottoman Empire and turned instead to advocacy of its dissolution. The immediate source of danger, in the aftermath of the Treaty of Berlin, was the Ottoman government's weakness at home and the wretched state of its finances and internal administration, which threatened to provoke a scramble for advantage among the European powers. This could well end in an agreement that would ensure the empire's annihilation. Just as worrying was the sharp impetus that the Treaty of Berlin had given to the aspirations to provincial or regional autonomy of some of the empire's peoples, which, if realized, would prove to be no more than a stepping stone toward a final partition of the sultan's territories among the Great Powers.[18]

Küçük Said Paşa concluded that the key to the empire's external security and survival lay in internal reform and the strengthening of the Ottoman state, though not primarily with a view to ingratiating itself with European or local Christian opinion. In a lengthy report submitted to the sultan in August 1880, he asserted that a revival of the Ottoman Empire would require the development of the three forces of "probity, education, and justice." An upright administration and an incorrupt judiciary were the best means of appeasing local Christian discontents, far better than the Tanzimat policy of bribing the Christian elites with government jobs, which had been tried and failed. Education was "the first condition of sovereignty": a source of capable officials, effective institutions, and popular prosperity. It was also essential to enable the empire's Muslims to catch up with the local Christians, who had overtaken them educationally and economically in the decades since the Crimean War. With a properly organized military, civil administration, and judiciary, the Ottoman Empire could secure itself against the Great Powers: "These are the means to prevent the formation of a concert against the Ottoman Empire, and to secure its preservation as one of the powers of Europe."

As long as the empire remained weak, none of the Great Powers was to be trusted. It is striking that in his August 1880 report Küçük Said went out of his way to warn Abdülhamid against Germany, the very power that the sultan was newly cultivating. Germany, in Küçük Said's view, would seek to secure its own European interests, and its hopes of further expansion in Central Europe, by encouraging other European powers to compensate themselves at Ottoman expense. Germany had facilitated Russia's war with the Ottoman Empire, had promoted Austria-Hungary's acquisition of Bosnia and Hercegovina, and in all likelihood had also promoted the Anglo-Ottoman Cyprus Convention. Germany would not oppose Russia's ambitions in respect to the Ottoman Empire and could also be expected to continue to push Austria-Hungary forward in the Balkans, thereby stimulating Anglo-Russian rivalry in Ottoman Asia and the ambitions of France and Italy. These perils were to be avoided not by seeking alliances with powers other than Germany but by a combination of good government at home and cautious and skillful diplomacy abroad: "acting with the greatest prudence, giving no party justifiable pretext for quarrel, refraining from things that cause mutual hostility between the Powers, maintaining peace internally, and administering the country well." International politics, Küçük Said argued, was at least partially regulated by norms; any power that openly violated those norms by seeking unjustifiable causes of quarrels would be bound to provoke the opposition of other powers, if only "for the sake of their own influence and prestige."

This was not Küçük Said's final word, for in subsequent years he appears to have come to the view that a policy of isolation and nonalignment could furnish the empire with no security. Possibly he was driven to this opinion by the French seizure of Tunis in May 1881 and the British occupation of Egypt in September 1882. Weeks after the latter event he warned the sultan that the Ottoman Empire was "squeezed between all the Christian powers and principalities" and that in this circumstance neither diplomatic finesse nor military strength could provide security: the empire must align itself with one or another of the Great Powers. Two months later he warned that it was essential to "reform the Ottoman Empire's foreign policy and adopt a principled and firm course of action. This appears impossible unless we conclude an alliance with one or two Powers on the basis of mutual interest." He did not specify which powers he had in mind;

but given his continuing mistrust of Germany and Austria-Hungary and also of Russia, it is a reasonable surmise that he had come to favor an alignment with Britain.

v

The fourth Ottoman statesman considered here, Kıbrıslı Mehmet Kamil Paşa (1832–1913), like Küçük Said, was a member of a younger generation who owed his career in central government to Sultan Abdülhamid. It has been suggested that Abdülhamid may have invited Kamil Paşa to join Hayreddin and Safvet in assessing the causes and consequences of the three recent wars; but if so, Kamil's report remains untraced.[19] Kamil might seem an odd choice of advisor, for he had no diplomatic experience and had spent his entire career up to 1879 in provincial administration.[20] He took a serious interest in international affairs, however; unusually for an Ottoman statesman of the period, he had learned English as well as French. In the course of a future career that would include three spells as Abdülhamid's grand vizier he would acquire a reputation as a foreign policy specialist and a persistent and consistent advocate of a permanent alliance with Great Britain as the only practical guarantee of the Ottoman Empire's security and survival.

How did Kamil Paşa arrive at this conclusion? Hayreddin and Safvet had stressed the importance of the Ottoman Empire's moral credibility in the eyes of the European powers and the need to gain acceptance as a worthy partner in the European equilibrium. In contrast, Kamil Paşa took a "realist" view of international relations as being unconstrained by moral or legal rules and governed exclusively by self-interest. As he noted in February 1882:

> In the belief of Europe there is no conscience in politics, and so a European power, for the sake of gaining its interest, will not hold back from implementing whatever is politically necessary, even if it violates justice and rights and the rules of civilization in the eyes of others, and even if crimes like the killing of populations and the wasting of countries occur.[21]

The guarantees of territorial integrity extended to the Ottoman Empire by the European powers under the treaties of Paris and Berlin could offer no security against foreign aggression. Such treaties might have some moral force in peacetime, but no judicial mechanism existed to hold an aggressor state to account. In wartime belligerents were guided by the rule that "might is right," and no third party could be obliged to deter or intervene against an aggressor. "So the Ottoman Empire must rely on its own diplomatic measures and material and moral force to preserve itself from external blows."[22]

It followed that security for any state lay in a favorable balance of power, to be achieved through the conclusion of exclusive alliances with other states. In a report to the sultan in March 1887, Kamil explained:

> As the rivalry that is natural between states impedes loyalty and may even provoke hostility, even the friendly relations between states in peacetime are a matter of official transactions, and a state that adjusts its conduct to this natural rivalry may be secure against aggression. It is necessary and inevitable, in order that a state may be able to attack another state, that it rely upon the opinion and alliance of the two states that are its neighbors, and likewise, in order that a state may defend itself against the aggression of another state, that it rely on the union of neighboring states.... As true sincerity and loyalty between states are impossible, a state, for the sake of an alliance, without seeking a friendly state, may even conclude an alliance with a state whose attack it apprehends. The possibility of achieving alliance between two such rival states derives from every state's need for allies to protect it from attack.[23]

It was, Kamil Paşa noted, these self-interested considerations of the balance of power that governed the attitudes of the European Great Powers toward the Ottoman Empire and that, in some circumstances, had persuaded some of them to uphold and protect it:

> For example, for a Russian attack and aggression against the Ottoman territories to be permitted, in alliance, by neighboring Austria and Germany, it must be conditional upon these two states each gaining a benefit in return for the advantage that Russia will gain in the event of victory. For otherwise, i.e., if Russia monopolizes the benefit, its increase of power and aggrandizement will threaten neighboring states, so it is natural that those neighboring states will not permit such a dangerous state of affairs, which will disrupt the balance between them, and in the treaties of Berlin as of Paris, the Great Powers' guarantee to uphold the territorial integrity of the Ottoman Empire is based on this principle. Similarly, if

the Ottoman Empire and Austria, and, from among the guarantor powers, England, for example, ally to prevent Russia's aggression, the interest that these two powers will seek lies in the prevention of conquest by Russia, for if that is not prevented, even if Russia's conquest of a portion of the Ottoman territories allows them and even other states to take a share of the Ottoman territories for the sake of achieving a balance, the greatest share and most important positions in this partition will still fall to Russia, and a general war, in particular, may arise out of a disagreement between powers over this partition, and so every state, besides securing its own position, will evidently deem the defense of the Ottoman Empire's territorial integrity to be a matter of common interest and seek no other material advantage.[24]

For the Ottoman Empire, the balance of power that counted was not, in the first instance, between any of the Great Powers within Europe but between the British and Russian empires in Asia. Russian policy was "the driving force of political problems in East," for Russia was a power that had long been bent upon "world conquest," as foretold in the alleged testament of Peter the Great. To be more precise, Russia's ultimate ambition was to wrest control of India away from the British; in order to approach this goal, it was obliged to annihilate or subordinate all the intervening independent Muslim states, including the Ottoman Empire. Through conquests in Central Asia and the Caucasus, and through successive wars that weakened the Ottoman Empire, Russia had steadily advanced toward the realization of its ambition. It was idle to hope that friendly relations might deter the Russians from their ambitions: the acquisition of Istanbul and the Straits, in particular, was a "national desire" that no Russian government could withstand.[25]

Britain and the Ottoman Empire therefore had a common interest in resisting Russian expansionism in Asia. The British must grasp that their own interests, properly understood, required them to support and sustain the Ottoman Empire. As Kamil noted in 1886, in a message evidently intended to be passed on to the British prime minister, Lord Salisbury: "In my opinion, Turkey and England are naturally bound by their common interests in Asia.... It is evident that if, through misfortune, at some future time, India is conquered by the Russians, the Ottoman Empire will no longer be able to exist; and just so England will not be able to prevent Russia's aggressions without the existence or assistance of Turkey."[26]

The difficulty, as Kamil acknowledged, was that the Ottoman Empire was not a purely Asiatic state but also a European and North African state. This meant that it was exposed in European regions where the British had no means of defending it and, judging by the refusal to guarantee the empire's European territories in the Cyprus Convention, less interest in doing so. It also meant that the Russians had opportunities to buy off other European powers, who might otherwise join the British in opposing the Russians, by offering them compensation at Ottoman expense: Austria in the Balkan peninsula and France and Italy in the Mediterranean. For these reasons, an Anglo-Ottoman alliance would prove ineffective without the participation of at least one other European Great Power, France and Austria-Hungary being the obvious candidates in the 1880s. In other words, Russia must be diplomatically contained in Europe if it was also to be militarily contained in Asia: the balance of power in Asia depended upon the balance of power in Europe. Unsurprisingly, Kamil Paşa was deeply alarmed by the Three Emperors' Alliance of Russia, Germany, and Austria-Hungary, concluded in 1881, for this appeared to point the way to a Austro-Russian partition of the Balkan peninsula and also to offer Russia a free hand in Asia. He would subsequently identify the collapse of this alliance, and its replacement in 1887 by a system of understandings involving Germany, Austria-Hungary, Italy, and Britain, as the greatest achievement of his own first grand vizierate. Thereafter a revival of the Three Emperors' Alliance remained his permanent nightmare.[27]

As already noted, Kamil held that states had no natural sympathies; a further reason for his advocacy of a British alliance was his fear that the British might turn elsewhere. The reform provisions of the Cyprus Convention, he argued, were a warning that the British, however mistakenly, had been seduced by the notion that an Armenian successor-state in eastern Anatolia might offer an effective barrier to Russian expansion. He detected signs of similar British thinking in respect to Syria.[28] More dramatically, he warned that, if the British ever lost confidence in their ability to hold India, they might be tempted to look for compensation at the expense of the Ottoman Empire, just as they had acquired India as a substitute for their lost possessions in America:

> for if the English, with all their wealth and means of trade, are confined to the island of Britain, and unable, as now, to employ their capital in eastern countries to gain entry there for the products

of their factories, within a short time what they have will be destroyed and they will be ruined; so it is obvious that they must take necessary steps against these misfortunes while there is a chance available. In that case, the countries to which England must pay attention as alternatives to India could be the Arabian peninsula and Africa.[29]

The practical lesson was that the Ottoman Empire could not afford to remain passive in the face of the European powers' rivalries: the British, and also other potential partners like the Austrians, must be persuaded of the Ottoman government's readiness to stand up to Russia. Failing that, they would be driven to settle with the Russians at the empire's expense.

Finally, Kamil argued that entry into a Great Power alliance would offer the Ottoman government important side benefits. One would be financial: a stance of nonalignment or balancing among all the Great Powers was already obliging the empire to maintain armed forces greater than its financial resources could reasonably bear. An alliance, by enabling the sultan to transfer a portion of the burdens of defense and deterrence to his allies, would also bring relief to his treasury.[30] Another benefit would be greater internal security: the demonstrative support of Great Powers would serve as a deterrent to foreign-inspired subversion and also provide the empire with the diplomatic cover necessary for the suppression of domestic disturbances and revolts without risking European interference.[31]

On the face of it, Kamil's views on a British-led alliance as the means to security seem consistent and clear; Sultan Abdülhamid, however, pointed to important ambiguities. For one thing, the sultan objected that entry into an anti-Russian alliance might expose the Ottoman Empire to the risk of a major war, whether provoked by Russia or by its own allies. Kamil regularly insisted that the alliances he advocated were means to preserve the peace; but in an exchange of views conducted through the sultan's principal palace secretary in August 1889 he did suggest that a European war might be in the Ottoman Empire's interest, for the alternative of a shift in European alignments that might entail a peaceful resolution of the Great Powers' differences would expose the empire to the risk of an agreed-upon partition.[32] Was it perhaps Kamil's real view that the Ottoman Empire could not safely accommodate itself to the Berlin settlement and that security would be best achieved not through the diplomatic exploitation of the existing balance of power but through its overthrow in a war that would leave Russia significantly weakened? In similar fashion,

Abdülhamid objected that entry into an alliance with a British-led coalition of powers would amount in practice to acceptance of a protectorate:

> Indeed a state cannot live in isolation, and it is obvious that it needs to conclude alliances with powers that have common interests in the questions that arise, but it is essential that its independence be preserved in this, and it is utterly impermissible to choose to submit to another power's protectorate and so His Imperial Majesty seeks to the utmost to avoid entering on a path that may undermine the preservation of the Ottoman Empire's independence and will under no circumstances accept the opposite course.[33]

The sultan's concern was not unfounded, for in urging Ottoman adhesion to the Anglo-Austro-Italian Mediterranean Entente in September 1888 Kamil had admitted that the empire's prospective partners might render their support conditional on the implementation of unspecified internal reforms — leading an alarmed Abdülhamid to foresee an imposed system of provincial autonomies and provincial and imperial parliaments.[34] Did Kamil Paşa regard a de facto British protectorate, or at least a substantial measure of British influence in the empire's internal affairs, as a price worth paying for the sake of external security?

VI

I hope that this discussion has established the existence of a considerable diversity of views among Ottoman statesmen on the subject of their empire's prospects of external security in the aftermath of the Berlin settlement, going beyond the conventional categories of "pro-British," "pro-Russian," "pro-German," and the like. The four statesmen considered here were in agreement in regarding the Ottoman Empire's situation as fragile, but they differed in their assessments of the external challenges and opportunities that it faced. In their different ways, Hayreddin Paşa and Safvet Paşa held that the central problem was one of acceptance and moral credibility. The Ottoman Empire would survive only if the European powers believed that it deserved to, and the key to winning their confidence was internal reform. Küçük Said Paşa preferred to emphasize the importance of material credibility and the need for a strong domestic administration and armed forces: internal weakness invited aggression. Kamil Paşa saw salvation in alignment and the exploitation and fostering of the Great Powers' mutual rivalries: specifically, he proposed placing the Ottoman

Empire at the heart of an anti-Russian coalition that would secure it
against Russia and also against its own coalition partners.

As it happened, Sultan Abdülhamid II did not adopt any of these pre-
scriptions as a whole, though he adopted parts of all of them. His own
fundamental assumptions may be briefly sketched here.[35] First, he held
that the Ottoman Empire had a vital interest in the maintenance of peace
among the European powers. This ruled out any policy of alignments or
alliances (for example, with Britain or Russia) that might actually provoke war. Second, it was vital that the Ottoman government maintain a
real measure of independence from the European powers. At home, this
implied a policy of reliance on the Muslim element and resistance to any
measures of reform or decentralization that might facilitate Christian
separatism and European penetration; abroad, it ruled out any alignment
or alliance that might enable a European power or group of powers to
establish a de facto protectorate over the Ottoman Empire. Both these
considerations explain Abdülhamid's decision, as of 1880, to cultivate the
closest possible relations with Germany, the newest of the European Great
Powers. On the one hand, Germany had no known designs of its own on
the Ottoman Empire's territory and independence and no clients among
the sultan's Christian populations. On the other, Germany in the 1880s
appeared to occupy the pivotal position in European politics and would
consequently be able to restrain those powers whose designs caused the
sultan most concern — Britain, Russia, and Austria-Hungary. A close relationship with Germany would enable the sultan to maintain a measure of
balance in his relations with all the other powers and thereby safeguard his
independence. This in turn would furnish him with a respite from external
problems and enable his government to devote its energies and resources
to the internal strengthening that alone could safeguard the Ottoman
Empire's independence and survival in the longer term. Such, at least, was
Abdülhamid's hope.

NOTES

1. The literature concerning the Eastern Crisis and the Berlin settlement is consider-
able. Among useful studies are W. N. Medlicott, *The Congress of Berlin and After:
A Diplomatic History of the Near Eastern Settlement, 1878–1880*; idem, *Bismarck,
Gladstone and the Concert of Europe*; Richard Millman, *Britain and the Eastern
Question, 1875–1878*; Dwight E. Lee, *Great Britain and the Cyprus Convention
Policy of 1878*; B. H. Sumner, *Russia and the Balkans, 1870–1880*; Michael R.
Milgrim, "An Overlooked Problem in Turkish-Russian Relations: The 1878 War
Indemnity"; Friedrich Scherer, *Adler und Halbmond: Bismarck und der Orient*

1878–1890, 36–65; Konrad Canis, *Bismarck's Aussenpolitik 1870–1890: Aufstieg und Gefährdung*, 109–40; Mahmud Celaleddin Paşa, *Mirat-i Hakikat*; Ali Fuat Türkgeldi, *Mesâil-i Mühimme-i Siyâsiyye*; and Rifat Uçarol, *1878 Kıbrıs Sorunu ve Osmanlı-İngiliz Anlaşması (Ada'nın İngiltere'ye Devri)*.

2. F. A. K. Yasamee, *Ottoman Diplomacy: Abdülhamid II and the Great Powers, 1878–1888*, 53–65.

3. Mehmed Zeki Pakalın, *Son Sadrazamlar ve Başvekiller*, 267.

4. Yasamee, *Ottoman Diplomacy*, 65–72.

5. Paul W. Schroeder, "Did the Vienna Settlement Rest on a Balance of Power?"; idem, "The Nineteenth Century Balance of Power: Balance of Power or Political Equilibrium?"; idem, "The 19th-Century International System: Changes in the Structure."

6. Atilla Çetin, *Tunuslu Hayreddin Paşa*, 255–81; Said Paşa, *Said Paşa'nın Hatıratı*, 418–36; Celal Dincer, "Osmanlı Vezirlerinden Hasan Fehmi Paşa'nın Anadolu Bayındırlık İşlerine dair Hazırladığı Layıha."

7. Başbakanlık Osmanlı Arşivi (BOA), Y.EE, 79/1/2540/1/16, note by the Principal palace secretary Ali Fuad Bey, 7 Rebiülevvel 1297 [February 18, 1880].

8. Friedrich Scherer, *Adler und Halbmond*, 69–70.

9. Hayreddin Paşa's life and career are covered in Çetin, *Tunuslu Hayreddin Paşa*; cf. Pakalın, *Son Sadrazamlar ve Başvekiller*, 313–77; İbnülemin Mahmud Kemal İnal, *Osmanlı Devrinde Son Sadrazamlar*, 895–960; M. S. Mzali and J. Pignon, "Documents sur Khereddine."

10. BOA, Y.EE, 80/24/2696/1/8, memorandum by Hayreddin Paşa, gurre-i Rebiülahır 97 [March 13, 1880].

11. Text of report dated 22 Cemaziyelevvel 97 in Çetin, *Tunuslu Hayreddin Paşa*, 320–34.

12. BOA, Y. EE. 80/32, "Hayrettin Paşa programının havi olduğu mevadd hakkında mütalaat-ı mahsusadır," n.d.

13. For Safvet's career, see Pakalın, *Son Sadrazamlar ve Başvekiller*, 3–312; İnal, *Osmanlı Devrinde Son Sadrazamlar*, 809–94.

14. BOA, Y.EE, 79/1/2540/1/16, report by Safvet Paşa, 13 Rebiülahır 97 [March 25, 1880] (following quotations from Safvet Paşa also from this source).

15. Pakalın, *Son Sadrazamlar ve Başvekiller*, 305–12; BOA, Y.EE, 79/2/2541/3/4, report by Safvet Paşa, 2 Cemaziyelevvel 297 [April 12, 1880]; cf. Atilla Çetin, "Rumeli Vilayetlerinin Durumu Hakkında Safvet Paşa'nın ıı: Abdülhamid'e Sunduğu 1880 Tarihli İki Önemli Arizası."

16. İnal, *Osmanlı Devrinde Son Sadrazamlar*, 873–74.

17. For an overview of Said's career, see Ercümend Kuran, "Küçük Said Paşa (1840–1914) as a Turkish Modernist."

18. Said Paşa, *Said Paşa'nın Hatıratı*, 388–89 (following quotations from Said Paşa also from this source: 418–39, 467–68, 524–32).

19. Çetin, *Tunuslu Hayreddin Paşa*, 255.

20. For details of Kamil Paşa's career, see Hilmi Kamil Bayur, *Sadrazam Kamil Paşa: Siyasi Hayatı*; cf. İnal, *Osmanlı Devrinde Son Sadrazamlar*, 1347–1472.

21. Bayur, *Sadrazam Kamil Paşa*, 18–23 (quotation on 22).

22. Ibid., 81–91 (quotation on 85–86).

23. BOA, Y.EE. 86/10/1304.C.16/3152/1/2, memorandum by Kamil Paşa, 16 Cemazi-yelevvel 304 [March 12, 1887].

24. Ibid.

25. Bayur, *Sadrazam Kamil Paşa*, 18–23, 81–91; BOA, Y.EE, 86/41/1/2, memoran-dum by Kamil Paşa, 7 Muharrem 304 [October 6, 1886] (quotation); Y.EE, KP/1/96/96, memorandum by Kamil Paşa, n.d. [1886].

26. Bayur, *Sadrazam Kamil Paşa*, 26–29.

27. BOA, Y.EE 86/10/3152/1/2, memorandum by Kamil Paşa, 16 Cemaziyelahira 304 [March 12, 1887]; 86/47/3189/1/4, 19 Receb 307 [March 11, 1889]; 86/22/1310.Z. 29/3164/1/2, 29 Zilkade 1310 [June 14, 1893]; 86/25/3167/1/2, 24 Rebiülevvel 310 [October 15, 1892]; Hikmet Bayur, "Yeni Bulunmuş Bazı Belgelerin Işığında Kamil Paşa'nın Siyasal Durumu," 76.

28. Bayur, *Sadrazam Kamil Paşa*, 73–74, 81–91.

29. Ibid., 18–23.

30. Kamil Paşa, *Hatırat-ı Sadr-ı Esbak Kamil Paşa*, 13–14; BOA, Y.EE, 86/47/3189/1/4, memorandum by Kamil Paşa, 19 Receb 307 [March 11, 1889].

31. Kamil Paşa, *Hatırat*, 43–45, 155–56.

32. Bayur, "Yeni Bulunmuş Bazı Belgelerin Işığında Kamil Paşa'nın Siyasal Durumu," 75–77.

33. BOA, Y.EE, 86/47/3189/1/4, memorandum by Kamil Paşa, 19 Receb 307 [March 11, 1889].

34. Kamil Paşa, *Hatırat*, 43–48; BOA, Mısır İrade no. 1343, 13 Muharrem 306/8 Eylül 304 [September 20, 1888].

35. Yasamee, *Ottoman Diplomacy*, 41–52, 73–86.

3

Benevolent Contempt

Bismarck's Ottoman Policy

Sean McMeekin

The views expressed by Germany's iron chancellor on the Eastern question are justly notorious. Few students of diplomatic history have not heard Bismarck's bon mot that "the entire Orient [*den ganzen Orient*] is not worth the bones of a single Pomeranian grenadier" — although many mistakenly believe that he was referring to the Balkans, full stop, rather than the Ottoman Empire in its entirety.[1] Otto von Bismarck's Machiavellian "Reinsurance Treaty" of 1887 even contained a clause promising that the Germans would remain neutral if the Russians again tried to seize Constantinople as they nearly had in 1878. The chancellor's dismissive view of Turkey's strategic importance seems of a piece with his only slightly less famous disregard for Africa, expressed to the explorer Eugen Wolff: "my map of Africa lies in Europe. Here is Russia and here is France, and we [Germany] are in the middle; that is my map of Africa."[2]

And yet, despite his supposed contempt for the Ottoman Empire and Africa, Bismarck presided over two Berlin congresses dealing with one and then the other, in 1878 and 1884. He not only went along with Germany's acquisition of African colonies in the 1880s but also approved the dispatch of a German military mission at Sultan Abdülhamid II's request in 1882, which planted the potent seed of German influence in the Ottoman army. Germany's famous investment in Ottoman strategic rail began in the Bismarckian, not the Wilhelmine, era: the first stretch of the Baghdad Railway, from Istanbul to İzmit, was completed in 1872. The original Anatolian Railway Company was incorporated in 1889, while Bismarck was still in office.

What are we to make of Bismarck's actual policies vis-à-vis the Ottoman Empire, which seem to contradict his public statements so blatantly? This paper argues that, far from dismissing Turkey's strategic importance, Bismarck in fact felt it only too keenly. The key to the apparent puzzle of Bismarck's Ottoman policy is the vast gulf between what he saw as Ottoman Turkey's minimal importance for Germany and its colossal importance for other powers — Austria, Russia, and France, which were themselves deeply entangled with Germany. (Britain, like Turkey itself, factored into German calculations only at second remove, via its rivalries with Russia and France.) Bismarck's genius, and his curse, was to perceive sooner than anyone else the danger that a collapse of Ottoman authority in the Balkans would provoke a general European war. Preventing such a conflict was his overriding priority from the time of Germany's unification in 1871 until his fall from power in 1890. It is thus not surprising that Bismarck's most famous diplomatic triumph came at the Congress of Berlin in 1878, when he mediated a settlement that (for all its ugly horse-trading at Turkish expense) helped preserve the Ottoman Empire — and the peace of Europe — for a quarter-century.

Unlike his encouragement of German imperialism in Africa, which truly *was* cynical, following the Berlin Conference Bismarck quietly but genuinely promoted the expansion of German influence in Turkey. His goal was to shore up its defenses in order to ward off the predatory intentions of other powers. To do this while not alarming Austria and Russia — France could easily exploit another eastern crisis to attack Germany — was a difficult but not impossible task for Bismarck's unsentimental *Realpolitik*. It proved beyond the abilities of Kaiser Wilhelm II, whose sentimental attachment to the Ottoman Empire paradoxically led him to become an unwitting catalyst in its destruction.

To understand Bismarck's Ottoman policy at the Berlin Conference of 1878, it is necessary to examine his actions during the Balkan crisis that led up to it. From what we know of the diplomatic fallout of the Berlin Treaty — Russia's notorious resentment at the overturning of its own victorious Treaty of San Stefano with the Ottomans, a "defeat" that many in St. Petersburg blamed on Bismarck — we might expect that the chancellor had discouraged Russia from intervening.[3] This, however, is quite far from the case. Bismarck in fact initially greeted the news of unrest in the Balkans in 1875 as a welcome distraction from what he saw as an unhealthy obsession in Europe's chancelleries with the Franco-German question (it is noteworthy that Bismarck himself, fearing just this, had not wanted to annex Alsace-Lorraine in 1871: he was overruled by the military). In much the same way in which he would later encourage colonial gamesmanship in the "Scramble for Africa" to keep France embroiled with Britain, Bismarck believed that a Balkan crisis could lead to closer relations with London at France's expense. For this reason, after the first rumblings of an Ottoman crisis in 1875 — the Bosnian uprising in the summer and the Porte's default on debt interest payments in October — Bismarck offered Germany's un-prompted endorsement of Britain's buyout of the Suez Canal company in November 1875 and instructed Lord Odo Russell, Britain's ambassador, to propose a sweeping agreement on Balkan issues to British prime minister Benjamin Disraeli. The territorial details of this would-be settlement, Germany's chancellor informed Disraeli, mattered not at all: the powers could agree on either the maintenance of the status quo on Ottoman Europe or its ruthless partition: the important thing was that the powers reach an agreement on "what was to be done with Turkey."[4]

During the entire Balkan crisis that unfolded, Bismarck's basic position of disinterest toward territorial changes never wavered. With remarkable prescience (and a dose of his famous cynicism) Bismarck's "offer" to Disraeli in January 1876 anticipated the basic Balkan settlement reached two years — and two wars — later, with Russian gains in Bessarabia offset by Austrian control of (though not sovereignty over) Bosnia-Hercegovina. Whether Russia went to war with Ottoman Turkey or not was a matter of equal indifference to Bismarck: in fact at one point in September 1876 he all but encouraged St. Petersburg to attack, so long as this was done with Austrian approval.[5] It was not that Bismarck particularly desired either the preservation of Ottoman territorial integrity or its violent dismemberment through Russian aggression. In his view the principal German interest, rather, lay in controlling the Balkan crisis so as to prevent the *European* powers from going to war with each other. Because the state he served had no natural frontiers offering a defense against invasion by any of the potentially hostile powers encircling its borders (France, Denmark, and Austria had all recently lost territory to Prussia/Germany), Bismarck was willing to pay almost any price to avoid diplomatic perturbations that might plunge Europe into war. As Lord Odo Russell explained Bismarck's Ottoman policy to London in 1877, "suffice it to say that he is quite ready to divide Turkey for the sake of keeping Germany together."[6]

To modern sensibilities, these episodes in Bismarckian *Realpolitik* seem brazen, if not downright offensive. What business was it of Germany's chancellor to broach plans for partitioning Ottoman Turkey between Austria and Russia — to Britain's prime minister? On what logical, let alone moral or ethical grounds, did third-party Bismarck presume the right to sanctify a Russian war of aggression mounted in the name of "Christianity" against Muslim Turkey, adding only the condition that a fourth party, Austria, give its consent? Certainly contempt is not too strong a word to describe this sort of posture toward the fate of a large multiethnic, multifaith empire that straddled Europe, Asian Anatolia, and the modern Middle East. As Bismarck himself summarized his Ottoman policy in October 1876, "the question as to whether we can come to an agreement on the Oriental rough-and-tumble with England, still more with Austria, and most of all with Russia, is for the future of Germany infinitely more important than Turkey's treatment of its subjects and its relations with the European powers."[7] Or as he notoriously told the Reichstag just two months later, "the entire Orient is not worth the bones of a single Pomeranian grenadier."

Unattractive as all this may seem to modern sensibilities, Bismarck's Ottoman policy contained much good sense. It was not that Bismarck wished Turkey, or Turks, ill. Even as he was sounding out Disraeli on ways in which the powers might agree on partitioning the Ottoman Empire, the chancellor told Britain's ambassador to Berlin that "he did not agree with those who said: 'Things are too bad to last so any longer'; in his opinion Turkey might yet be kept together with a little good-will."[8] The coldness with which Bismarck viewed the diplomatic chessboard left him immune to the fashionable anti-Turkish sentiments of the day. To Disraeli's own distaste, English public opinion was falling hard for William Gladstone's famous pamphleteering against the *Bulgarian Horrors*. More ominously, the Russian press was concocting that dangerous blend of Orthodox Christian "Second Rome" messianism and pan-Slavic irredentism that convinced Tsar Alexander II that his throne would be in jeopardy if he did not do battle for "Christendom," just as Nicholas II would later fatefully believe that he could not fail to mobilize his armies for Serbia and Slavdom in 1914. Bismarck, by contrast, remained largely unmoved by the drumbeat of anti-Turkish horror stories coming from Bosnia and Bulgaria. He saw easily through Russia's efforts to invoke "Europe" and "Christendom" to beatify its crude territorial ambitions in the Balkans, telling Kaiser Wilhelm I that any politician who used such abstractions to justify wars was not to be trusted. Significantly, Bismarck cited the Crimean War to illustrate his point, condemning in that case not the Russians but the "Western powers" (Britain and France) for having sold the conflict as a "European" crusade against Russian barbarism.[9] Although hardly a pacifist, Bismarck believed fundamentally that "any war, even a victorious war, was a misfortune [*ein Unglück*]. It is always a dangerous game to deploy Beelzebub to drive out the devil."[10]

It was particularly dangerous when Russia played the role of Beelze-bub. Bismarck's worst strategic nightmare was that Germany would have to fight a war on two fronts against France and Russia. For this reason the generals in Berlin were gravely concerned *any* time Russia mobilized its army. A little-known aspect of the Ottoman crisis of 1877 is that in January and February, while Russia was mobilizing against Turkey, the Prussian General Staff undertook intensive preparations for a two-front war. With strategic insight no less prescient than Bismarck's diplomatic anticipation, Helmuth von Moltke the Elder drew up a mobilization timetable for knocking France out first before wheeling around to face Russia, which was eerily similar to the modified Schlieffen Plan that his son, Moltke the Younger, would actually deploy in 1914. The great Moltke, like the great Bismarck, had the kind of wisdom born of a tragic sense of life, which led them to prepare for the worst-case scenario in order not to have to live through it.[11]

In an ideal world, Bismarck would rather that St. Petersburg had not intervened in the Balkan crisis—or, even better, that the Bosnian and Bulgarian uprisings of 1875 and 1876 and the vigorous Ottoman response following the declaration of war by Serbia and Montenegro on June 30, 1876, and the refusal of the Turks to buckle to European pressure the following winter had never happened, giving Russia cause to do so. Failing this, Bismarck would much have preferred that Disraeli mediate the burgeoning crisis himself—after all, keeping Russian imperial ambitions in check had been a cardinal objective of British foreign policy for decades. But the British response to Bismarck's overtures in this direction in 1876 was "cool and dilatory."[12] Playing his own version of *Realpolitik*, Disraeli was happy to watch from the sidelines. Why should a British prime minister be obliged to solve Bismarck's Balkan dilemmas for him? In the end it would be up to the chancellor himself to navigate a path for Germany between the treacherous shoals of Russian ambition and Austrian jealousy.

Short of Germany itself declaring war on St. Petersburg, Bismarck could have done nothing after Russia declared war on Turkey on April 24, 1877, but wait and see what the clash of arms would bring. And nothing is just what he did. One of the strangest facts of the entire Balkan crisis is that the German chancellor who famously hosted the conference that brought it to a close was on sick leave from April 1877 to February 1878, ailing from his chronic neuralgia, rheumatism, shingles, and sleeplessness. Bismarck was effectively out of action, that is, for the entire duration of the Russo-Ottoman War. Whether he used ill health as an excuse to "hide" and wait out the war or not, it was clear that he wanted no part of Russia's "European" crusade.[13]

If Bismarck had first hoped the Balkan crisis would inject fresh new obsessions into European diplomacy to replace the stale Franco-Prussian antagonism, by the time the crisis came to a head in February 1878, with the Russian army at San Stefano (today's Yeşilköy) and the British fleet poised menacingly in the Sea of Marmara, threatening to intervene if they marched on Constantinople, he was thoroughly weary of the whole thing. As Bismarck had told Lord Odo Russell following the collapse of the short-lived Constantinople summit that had preceded Russia's declaration of war in April 1877, "he never liked conferences, he never expected any useful result from them and as far as he was concerned he would never go to a conference again."[14]

While Bismarck's health had improved slightly by the time the diplomats descended on Berlin that June, it is a telling commentary on his condition that each day of the conference he had to force down "two or three beer mugs full of strong port wine" simply in order to "get his blood flowing." Bismarck in 1878 was almost a caricature of an Old World diplomat, world-weary, arrogant, largely inebriated, and yet still able to lead complex multinational negotiations in his own German and two foreign languages (mostly French but also English, as Disraeli did not speak French) simultaneously, while constantly avoiding the merest hint of sentiment about the matters under discussion. Above all, Bismarck insisted that the negotiations be conducted speedily, with no time wasted on issues of less than general interest: his health would not permit them to drag on indefinitely. It is testament to the will of the iron chancellor that the conference was confined to only twenty sessions, lasting one month (June 13 to July 13, 1878).[15]

The contrast between Bismarck's sublime indifference to detail and the passionate lobbying of the other diplomats was almost breathtaking. Count Gyula Andrássy, representing Austria-Hungary, moved heaven and earth to wrest Bosnia-Hercegovina from the Turks, whose own diplomats, Alexander Karatheodori Paşa and Sadullah Bey, sought desperately to salvage some scrap of Ottoman Europe from the wreckage of San Stefano. It is largely a matter of taste whether Bismarck showed more contempt to Andrássy or Karatheodori. On Andrássy's cozying up to Disraeli in order to win Balkan gains for Vienna hardly merited by Austria's passivity, the chancellor memorably told Lord Salisbury: "I have heard of people refusing to eat their pigeon unless it was shot and roasted for them, but I have never heard of anyone refusing to eat it unless his jaws were forced open and it was pushed down his throat." As Salisbury interpreted Bismarck's latest bon mot, the chancellor's objection was that "Andrássy insists not only that the Turk shall cede [Bosnia], but that the Turk shall beg him as a favour to take it. The poor Turks make a wry face."[16] As for the "poor Turks" themselves, the iron chancellor told an aide at one point that they were wrong to think that it would be advantageous for them if the conference broke off without result: whether it led to war or peace, "the powers will reach agreement at the expense of the Turks." Still crueler was Bismarck's aside following a minor incident in which his own (rather large) dog had growled at an unfortunate diplomat: "The dog has not finished his training. He does not know whom to bite. If he did know what to do, he would have bitten the Turks."[17]

Despite appearances, however, the month-long Berlin conference of 1878 saw the first stirrings in Bismarck of a new posture toward the Ottoman Empire. To begin with, although the chancellor had at times seemed disrespectful of the Turkish delegation, according to Josef Maria von Radowitz, director of Oriental Affairs at the Wilhelmstrasse, Karatheodori Paşa had won Bismarck's grudging respect for the "tact and intelligent posture" with which he had defended an impossible position at the conference.[18] And it would be foolish to ignore Bismarck's role in arranging the final Treaty of Berlin, which, of course, was far from unfavorable to the Porte, breaking up the "Big Bulgaria" of San Stefano into two roughly equal halves, one of which (Eastern Rumelia) was returned to Ottoman suzerainty, along with Macedonia. True, along with Bessarabia the Russians gained Kars, Ardahan, and Batum — the lost provinces of Elviye-i Selâse that so animated nationalist Turks in 1914, much as the French wanted Alsace-Lorraine back. But the Russian prize from the *diktat* peace of San Stefano that Alexander Gorchakov and Peter Shuvalov wanted most to hold onto — control of the Straits or at least unfettered access to the Mediterranean for Russian warships — was firmly denied them. Although this diplomatic defeat for St. Petersburg owed at least as much to British objections as to Bismarck's machinations, in the coming years most Russian nationalists and pan-Slavists directed their venom at Bismarck, who in this case at least had proved as good a friend as the Turks could have hoped for.

Too much should not be made of these hints of a more pro-Ottoman stance on Bismarck's part. Bismarck was not opposed per se to a partition of the Ottoman Empire among the European powers, so long as it could be arranged without provoking a European war — but this seemed unlikely in light of the war scare of early 1878. Retaining Russia's friendship, or at least its lack of hostility, indeed remained a higher diplomatic priority for Bismarck over his last twelve years in office than relations with Ottoman Turkey. Many volumes have been written on the delicate balancing act between Austria and Russia involved in Bismarck's revival of the Three Emperors' League in 1881 and his concoction of the Byzantine Reinsurance Treaty of 1887, and for good reason. It was a virtuoso performance in balance-of-power diplomacy, well worthy of the attention showered upon it by diplomatic historians.

It is not always understood, however, how central the Eastern question remained to Bismarck's European balancing act and how much his posture vis-à-vis the Ottoman Empire shifted after the Congress of Berlin. It was not that his previous indifference turned into any kind of sentimental attachment to Turkey. Rather, the Porte's ability to survive in the face of Russian aggression and European connivance impressed him. Once Russian resentment over the collapse of San Stefano had been temporarily put on ice by the renewal of the Three Emperors' League in 1881 — which reaffirmed the ban on Russian warships entering the Straits and guaranteed Turkey's borders against possible Bulgarian aggression in Macedonia, although leaving the door open for a possible union of Bulgarian and Ottoman Eastern Rumelia — Bismarck worked to build German influence at the Porte. It was an intriguing reversal when Radowitz, the man Bismarck had dispatched 1875 as special emissary to St. Petersburg charged with coordinating German and Russian policy regarding the Balkans, was appointed ambassador to Constantinople in 1882, this time charged with helping firm up Turkish defenses to ward off Russian aggression. Not coincidentally, this was the same year that Bismarck, upon the request of Sultan Abdülhamid II, authorized Gen.-Maj. Otto Kaehler's military mission to Turkey (taken over after Kaehler's death in 1885 by Lt.-Col. Colmar Freiherr von der Goltz, with whose name the venture is usually associated). Bismarck wrote on one of Radowitz's reports that this mission would provide Germany "with influence and informants" in the Ottoman Empire.[19]

Bismarck had good reasons for the shift in Ottoman policy. The balance-of-power maneuvering that he had engaged in during the Balkan crisis of 1875–78, by which he sought to supervise a peaceful multipower partition of the Ottoman Empire, had been needlessly complex and had ultimately failed to prevent a dangerous war. Although Russia had nearly taken Constantinople in 1878, the effort had clearly exhausted its forces. A repeat performance was not soon in the cards, as borne out by Russia's humiliation in the Bulgarian crisis of 1885–87, in which Russia failed to intervene even after its officers and advisors were recalled owing to in-subordination by its ungrateful protégé Prince Alexander of Battenberg, who had been placed on the throne by his own uncle, Tsar Alexander II. Austria, meanwhile, had shown an appetite for Turkish territory far larger than its waning military strength warranted. Rather than encouraging pre-tensions of a sweeping partition of Turkey in Vienna and St. Petersburg, it would be far simpler for the Germans to shore up the Ottoman Empire in order to ward off Russian temptation and thereby prevent a great power conflagration.

As noted above, Bismarck would ideally have preferred that the British play this role, as they had in the past. By the early 1880s, however, it had become painfully evident that this would not happen. Although he had dispatched the fleet in 1878, just in time to prevent the Russian conquest of Constantinople, Disraeli had pointedly refused to take up the Balkan baton that Bismarck had offered him back in 1876, when decisive British intervention could have prevented the Russian invasion that brought Eu-rope to the brink of war. With the advent of the hysterically anti-Turkish Gladstone government in 1880 as well as its invasion and subsequent oc-cupation of Egypt in 1882, Bismarck's last hope was dashed. It was obvious that Britain would not soon return to its previous role as protector of the Porte against Russian encroachment.

While not quite subscribing to the later pan-German embrace of Tur-key ("Not a pfennig for a weak Turkey," Paul Rohrbach vowed in his clas-sic primer on *The Baghdad Railway*, "but for a strong Turkey we can give everything!"),[20] Bismarck made it clear that he would no longer easily ac-quiesce in the destruction of the Ottoman Empire by any power that eyed it covetously. This included not only Austria and Russia but also Britain: at the height of the "Great Game" war scare in April 1885 a special German commission was created to revamp Ottoman shore defenses and if neces-sary mine the Dardanelles, in case the British fleet sought to attack Russia via the Black Sea.[21] Crowning the new fortifications would be state-of-the-art German artillery, purchased from Mäuser & Lowe, Schichau, and especially Krupp, which sent 440 cannons to Turkey in 1886 alone. Most of the guns reinforced shore batteries at the Bosphorus and Dardanelles; several were also installed on land at the Çatalca lines outside the capital.[22]

It is true that Bismarck made gestures in the opposite direction toward St. Petersburg, most notably in the Reinsurance Treaty of June 18, 1887, which included a hidden clause promising German neutrality in case the Russian tsar "judged it necessary" to dispatch a Russian fleet to "protect the entrance to the Black Sea [e.g., through the Bosphorus] and thus to safeguard Russia's interests." It should be emphasized, however, that this was a "very secret" protocol, designed more to appease Russian suspicions than to commit Germany to any course of action.[23] Like the offers to Disraeli that the chancellor had put on the table prior to the Russo-Ottoman War of 1877, the Reinsurance Treaty cost Bismarck nothing: he was offering things (such as a Russian right of intervention in the Straits) that were not really his to give. Only the chancellor himself, of course, knew which was the "real" Bismarck: the one who was quietly helping the Turks strengthen their Straits defenses or the one who was (even more quietly!) promising not to object if the Russians tried to seize the very same Straits.

While no one can possibly pretend to know what such a complicated man truly believed in his heart of hearts, on balance the evidence suggests that Bismarck was probably more sincere in his efforts to strengthen German influence in Turkey than in purchasing Russian loyalty with specious promises of blanket neutrality. As Herbert von Bismarck, the chancellor's son, who was Germany's state secretary from 1886 to 1890, interpreted the Reinsurance Treaty with a dose of his father's arch-cynicism: "it should, if matters become serious, keep the Russians off our necks six to eight weeks longer than would otherwise be the case."[24] From the German perspective, the treaty was mostly about France and Russia, not Turkey: the clause about Russian naval intervention at the Straits was thrown in at the special insistence of Russia's foreign minister, Nikolai Girs.[25] If Russia did try to seize the Straits by force, after all, German opposition (or acquiescence) would hardly matter: the Turks would defend the Bosphorus as best they could (unofficially helped by German military advisors). If they held out long enough, the usual coalition of powers not wishing to see Russia control Constantinople would coalesce, doubtless including both Austria and Britain. And all this presumed that the Russians would actually try to seize the Straits, which its current limited naval and amphibious capability in the Black Sea rendered virtually impossible.[26] Bismarck's promise of neutrality in case of an operation that had such a small chance of ever occurring does not tell us much about his real views on the matter.

Against these largely symbolic promises to the Russians, we must set Bismarck's real, if largely unpublicized, gestures indicating a commitment to the defense of the Ottoman Empire. Under the able hands of von der Goltz "Paşa" (an honorific given to him in 1895, after ten years' service to the sultan), the Ottoman army was thoroughly reorganized along European and especially German/Prussian lines in the 1880s. The empire was divided up into seven military districts, each assigned a separate numbered army that handled conscription in the area. The first section of reserves (*redif*) was also structured along German lines to match the organization of the regular army, to make them ready for absorption into the army during wartime. A kind of national or home territorial guard (the Müstafiz) was added to this, with an extended service term for draftees. All Ottoman army and guard units were better armed now too: not only with Krupp heavy guns but with "hundreds of thousands of modern Mauser rifles," which replaced the outdated inventory with which the Turks had tried to hold off the Russians in 1877–78. Perhaps most importantly, von der Goltz introduced rigorous officer-training protocols in Turkey, assigning German instructors to the Ottoman Harbiye Academy and sending the most promising Turkish officer-students to the German war academy in Berlin.[27]

In its first significant conflict following the reforms of Kaehler and von der Goltz Paşa, the 1897 war with Greece, the Turks performed exceptionally well, defeating the Greeks decisively at Domokos (Dömeke) and advancing as far as Thermopylae by May. From there, Edward Erickson believes, the Ottoman army commanded by İbrahim Ethem Paşa could, "in all likelihood, have pushed on rapidly to Athens."[28] That it did not do so was due entirely to European (particularly Russian) diplomatic intervention. It was an ironic turnabout from 1878: this time it was the victorious Turks who were forced to stand down under pressure from concerned outside powers rather than the seemingly unstoppable (but in fact exhausted) Russians. Still, buttressed by the German-led military reforms inaugurated under Bismarck, the Porte had its first real military-diplomatic victory in four decades (much, much longer if we discount the Turks' Crimean War "victory," which owed so much to Britain and France), gaining a small part of Greek Thessaly and forcing Athens to pay heavy reparations. Few could have foreseen such a rapid recovery of the Ottoman position after the humiliation of 1877–78.

A little-known factor contributing to the Turkish victory over Greece in 1897 was the use of the German-built Anatolian railway to transport troops from eastern Turkey to the western front. It is true that German investment in Ottoman rail had lain dormant for much of the period when Bismarck was in office, following the completion of the Istanbul-İzmit line in 1872 under the supervision of the Swabian railway engineer Wilhelm von Pressel, known to posterity as the "Father of the Baghdad Railway." But this was the natural result of the Ottoman bankruptcy of 1875, which dashed the hopes of Pressel and others that the Porte would be able to finance construction of a line to Baghdad or Basra, on the Persian Gulf, across the sparsely inhabited semidesert plains of Anatolia, two forbidding mountain ranges (the Taurus, north of Adana, and the Amanus range, which guarded the entrance to the Hatay and Syria), and the malarial wetlands of Mesopotamia. In the 1880s German engineers and moneymen had rediscovered the dream of a Baghdad railway, just as von der Goltz was helping revive the Ottoman army. After Georg von Siemens of Deutsche Bank gave Sultan Abdülhamid II an emergency loan of 30 million marks in 1888, the Anatolian Railway Company was formed on March 4, 1889.[29] Within three years the Istanbul-İzmit line had been extended to Ankara, which greatly accelerated the Turkish mobilization in 1897.[30]

The key to Bismarck's Baghdad railway policy, like the von der Goltz military mission, was inconspicuousness. If we trace the early history of the Baghdad railway concessions, it is remarkable how little attention they received — outside St. Petersburg of course, where Russians viewed them with predictable foreboding.[31] The completion of the İzmit-Ankara extension between 1889 and 1892, although entirely the work of the German-dominated Anatolian Railway Company, was in fact largely financed by bond issues in the City of London (although the Germans did later buy out the British shares), which helped camouflage German intentions.[32] This was classic Bismarckian policy: quiet, gradualist, inexpensive, and in no way alarming to the other powers. So unconcerned were the Russians about German investments in the Ottoman Empire that St. Petersburg itself requested renewal of the Reinsurance Treaty in 1890.

Of course, Bismarck's Byzantine pact was not renewed that summer — Kaiser Wilhelm II had finally pushed the chancellor out of office in March 1890, and the new chancellor, Leo Caprivi, found its terms not so much offensive as beyond his capacity to understand. The speed with which German foreign policy was transformed after this watershed event has sometimes been exaggerated: the Franco-Russian alliance targeting Wilhelmine Germany with Bismarck's nightmare of a two-front war was not fully ratified until 1894 — and even then Berlin remained on fairly good terms with London, if not so much with St. Petersburg. When it came to Turkey, nothing of substance changed on the surface: the von der Goltz mission remained in place, and the Anatolian Railway Company continued work on the İzmit-Ankara extension.

In terms of *style*, however, a tremendous revolution had taken place in Germany's posture toward the Ottoman Empire. In November 1889 the new emperor Wilhelm II (who, at thirty, was then Bismarck's junior by fifty-four years) — over the stout objections of the iron chancellor — had made a grand state visit to Constantinople, falling in love with the city and Ottoman Turkey more generally. Taken into confidence by Sultan Abdülhamid II, who cleverly told the impressionable young Kaiser that "his visit would make the other powers nervous," Wilhelm II began imagining himself as the champion of beleaguered Turks against bullying Europeans.[33]

Just nine years later the German emperor made an even more famous grand tour of Asiatic Turkey, where he memorably pledged himself to protect Turks — and Muslims — everywhere. Wilhelm declaimed that summer in Damascus with dramatic flourish: "May the Sultan and his 300 million Muslim subjects scattered across the earth, who venerate him as their Caliph, be assured that the German Kaiser will be their friend for all time."[34] Thus was born Hajji Wilhelm, as the Kaiser was sometimes called due to his pose as global protector of Ottoman (and even Persian and Indian) Muslims against the hostile predations of the Christian colonial powers. Britain, France, and Russia all ruled over millions of Muslim subjects — the Raj alone counted nearly 100 million. Not surprisingly, diplomats of the powers soon to coalesce into the Triple Entente were thus greatly alarmed by the Kaiser's speech in Damascus. The Kaiser seemed to have substituted the gushing enthusiasms of a diplomatic amateur hour for Bismarck's posture of cool and calculated indifference toward the Ottoman Empire.[35]

It was a new age in German diplomacy, and not only in the person of Wilhelm II. Succeeding the subtle Bismarck *fils* as state secretary in March 1890 was Adolf Marschall von Biberstein, who, in a sign of Germany's new foreign policy priorities, would be appointed ambassador to Constantinople in 1897 — a post he would hold for another fifteen years. Marschall, unlike Bismarck's man at the Porte (Radowitz), made no effort to hide his partiality for Turkey — or, more precisely, for Germany's primacy of position in Turkey: not for nothing did he become known as the "Giant of the Bosphorus." Marschall, backed by Kaiser Wilhelm II, made very clear his support for the sultan following the bloody Armenian uprisings of 1894–96, even as diplomats from the other powers were unanimous in condemning Abdülhamid II. In August 1896 the Kaiser even sent a signed photograph of himself in public celebration of the sultan's birthday, just as everyone else in Europe was condemning the Kaiser's friend as "the bloody Sultan" or "Abdul the Damned."[36] Meanwhile, whereas Radowitz and the two Bismarcks had ever so quietly signed off on German military missions and declared that the Anatolian Railway Company would receive no official support from Berlin, Marschall declared quite openly in 1899, on the eve of the fateful signing of the first Baghdad Railway Convention:

To extend the railway from Haydar-Pasha to Baghdad...to build this line with only German materials and for the purpose of bringing goods and people to [Asia] via the most direct path from the heart of Germany…will bring closer the day when [Bismarck's] remark about the entire Orient not being worth the bones of a Pomeranian Grenadier will seem like a curious historical memory.[37]

A more emphatic repudiation of Bismarckian Ottoman policy could scarcely be imagined.

A brief glance at the particulars of the Baghdad Railway Convention signed in December 1899 indicates just how serious the German commitment to the Ottoman Empire — and the Hamidian regime — now was. As early as June 1898 Abdülhamid, through his ambassador to Berlin, had demanded that the Germans share intelligence on revolutionary opponents of his regime and be ready to deport specifically named "agitators" from Germany on request. In the years following the awarding of the Baghdad concession in 1899, the Kaiser's spies duly provided the Ottoman sultan with regular reports on the whereabouts and activities of his "Young Turk" opponents. In return, Abdülhamid had secretly agreed to give German prospectors working for the railway company generous exploration rights inside his domains, including copper and coal mining grants and broad excavation rights within twenty kilometers of the Baghdad line on either side. A secret Ottoman imperial *irade* (decree) dated November 15, 1899, further gave the Berlin Museum rights to keep artifacts that German miners and archaeologists might discover while excavating on Ottoman territory. The results were dramatic, as anyone who has visited the Museum Island in Berlin knows. Finally, the Baghdad Railway Convention of 1899, unlike the Anatolian Railway Company chartered a decade earlier in Bismarck's last year in office, required a substantial and open-ended German financial commitment — beginning with a straight-up bribe of 200,000 Turkish pounds (then worth $1 million, the contemporary equivalent of over $100 million) deposited directly into the Ottoman state treasury by Deutsche Bank. Poor old Bismarck (who had died the previous year) would have rolled over in his grave if he had learned of this.[38]

With the one-two punch of the Kaiser's Damascus speech of 1898 and the sweeping Baghdad Railway Convention of 1899, the die was essentially cast for the (still unofficial) German-Turkish alliance: the Kaiser and the sultan were now bound together against the rival European powers, for better and for worse. So strong was the relationship that not even the Young Turk Revolution of 1908 and the fall of Abdülhamid after the Otuzbir Mart Vakası (the counterrevolution of April 13, 1909, which led to the sultan's deposition following a Committee of Union and Progress [CUP] countercoup) could dent it. In ironic testimony to the undiminished power of the colossal new German Embassy atop the hill of Taksim in the era of Marschall, the Giant of the Bosphorus, Abdülhamid's secret police chief İzzet Paşa would seek refuge there from the mob during the Young Turk Revolution of July 1908, even as the Speaker of the CUP-dominated parliament, Ahmed Rıza, sought refuge in a German Baghdad Railway Company building during the Otuzbir Mart Vakası.[39] Another sign of the enduring strength of the relationship between Berlin and Constantinople was the playing out of the controversial "Armenian reform" campaign of 1913–14: Marschall's successor, Hans von Wangenheim, kept the Ottoman grand vizier, Said Halim Paşa, informed on everything the Russians were up to. Although the Germans ultimately agreed to go along as part of a general compromise to cool tensions over the "Liman von Sanders affair" (which broke in November–December 1913), Wangenheim left the grand vizier in no doubt that Russia was behind the Armenian reform campaign and that Germany was going along only to keep the peace. Viewing the campaign as essentially a Russian plot, Wangenheim pointedly demanded that Russia's ambassador, Mikhail Girs, personally insist that the Turks agree to controversial points, such as the appointment of European inspectors in the six eastern "Armenian" provinces, so that the Germans themselves could escape Turkish opprobrium. As Girs complained to Wangenheim on October 17, 1913, "it would be dangerous if we alone had to make this demand, as then all of Turkey's exasperation would fall exclusively on us [Russians]."[40] Due to German insistence, the final terms of the reform agreement ratified in February 1914 did not even mention "Armenians" or "Armenian provinces," as both the Russians and Armenian activists pointedly complained.[41] On this as on nearly every important issue facing the Ottoman empire, Germany remained much closer to the Porte than the other powers, as borne out by the signing of the Turco-German wartime alliance on August 2, 1914 (after Vienna, London, and Paris had all turned down Turkish alliance offers).[42]

The romance between Wilhelm II and Ottoman Turkey is oddly appealing, even allowing for the hiccup in 1908–9 in which his friend Abdülhamid was replaced by the pseudo-constitutional regime of the Young Turks. The Kaiser's famous social awkwardness, born in part of an inferiority complex due to his withered left arm (a legacy of a difficult birth that his mother barely survived), lends a kind of pathos to his fitful and ultimately doomed efforts at visionary statesmanship. It is hard not to sympathize with the efforts of Hajji Wilhelm to champion Turkey and the Muslim world, even if his understanding of Islam was necessarily deficient. Compared to Bismarck's cynicism and gestures of outright contempt toward Turkey and Turks, the Kaiser's earnest love affair with the Ottomans is far more attractive to modern sensibilities.

Whether the interests of Germany — and Turkey — were better served by the Islamophilia and Turcophilia of the Wilhelmine era than by Bismarck's cold *Realpolitik* is a very different question. Historians have long speculated about the prospects for European war and diplomacy had Bismarck remained in office longer, with the obvious counterfactual being better relations with Russia (thus preventing the two-front war nightmare) and England (no "Krüger telegram," no German naval program, thus no Entente Cordiale in 1904 and no Anglo-Russian Convention in 1907 to crown the Franco-Russian alliance as a Triple Entente). Of course, the iron chancellor was a ripe old seventy-five when finally pushed from office in 1890 and lived only another eight years, with his ever-precarious health declining rapidly all the time. After a reign in power lasting nearly thirty years, it is hard to imagine that Bismarck's successors would have kept *all* of his policies: surely the Kaiser himself was not alone in wanting meaningful change. The von der Goltz mission and the Anatolian Railway Company had already pointed the way to a more pro-Turkish line in Berlin by the time Kaiser Wilhelm II pushed the chancellor out of office, Bismarck's Reinsurance Treaty of 1887 notwithstanding. It is hardly surprising that these policies took on new meaning in a post-Bismarck era, particularly after the Kaiser's own appointees (like Marschall at the Constantinople Embassy) began promoting them.

If it is clear that Bismarck's careful *Realpolitik* could not have endured unaltered, however, this does not mean that things needed to turn out the way they did, with Germany foolishly provoking its own encirclement — and helping push the Ottoman Empire into World War I. The key to any sensible foreign policy in a multipolar world, as Bismarck understood, is balance. Taking the enmity of France for granted, the goal of his diplomacy following German unification in 1871 was to postpone a Franco-Russian rapprochement for as long as possible, to reverse the legacy of the Crimean War. An essential corollary to this policy was to prevent a serious clash between Austria and Russia over dividing up the Ottoman inheritance in the Balkans, which might tip Europe into a general war that could only end badly for Germany, surrounded as it was by jealous neighbors. To stave off an Austrian-Russian clash, it was fine for Germany to help Turkey shore up its defenses against possible encroachment — but only so long as the policy did not tip over into outright partiality for Turkey against Russia, which would push St. Petersburg into the nightmare alliance with France. Had the Reinsurance Treaty been renewed in 1890, had the Kaiser refrained from his ostentatious embrace of Islam (with its implied rebuke of the other European powers as Christian oppressors of Muslims), had Marschall not insisted that the Baghdad Railway Company be so exclusively German, the Franco-Russian alliance might never have come into being. Once it did, Germany had no way of escaping the dreaded pincers of a two-front war when the inevitable Ottoman or Balkan "accident" occurred. Bismarck may or may not have sincerely cared whether or not the Ottoman Empire survived long into the twentieth century, but his policies, by postponing Europe's Armageddon, gave it a much better chance of enduring than did the Kaiser's reckless romanticism. Wilhelm's repudiation of Bismarckian diplomacy led inexorably to the German tragedy of 1914–18 and the collapse of the Ottoman Empire in the wake of Germany's defeat.

NOTES

1. The original bon mot was uttered before the Reichstag on December 5, 1876. It has been misquoted ever since. For a discussion, see Margaret Lavinia Anderson, "'Down in Turkey, Far Away': Human Rights, the Armenian Massacres, and Orientalism in Wilhelmine Germany," 111.
2. Cited in Niall Ferguson, *Empire: The Rise and Demise of the British World Order and the Lessons for World Power*, 196 n.
3. On Russian reactions to the Berlin Treaty, see William C. Fuller, Jr., *Strategy and Power in Russia, 1600–1914*, 321–22.
4. Winifried Taffs, *Ambassador to Bismarck: Lord Odo Russell, First Baron Ampthill*, 130–31.
5. Otto Pflanze, *Bismarck and the Development of Germany*, 2: 422.
6. Cited in Taffs, *Ambassador to Bismarck*, 195.
7. "Diktat des Reichskanzlers Fürsten von Bismarck, z. Z., in Varzin," in *Die grosse Politik der Europäischen Kabinette*, 2:64 (document no. 246).
8. Cited in Taffs, *Ambassador to Bismarck*, 119.
9. "Diktat des Reichskanzlers Fürsten von Bismarck, z. Z., in Varzin," in *Die grosse Politik der Europäischen Kabinette*, 2:88 (document no. 256).
10. As rendered by Bismarck's son Herbert, in Horst Kohl, ed., *Anhang zu den Gedanken und Erinnerungen von Otto Fürst von Bismarck*, 2:497.
11. Pflanze, *Bismarck and the Development of Germany*, 2:428–49.
12. Ibid., 2:419.
13. Ibid., 2:436–37.
14. Cited in Taffs, *Ambassador to Bismarck*, 174.
15. Immanuel Geiss, ed., *Der Berliner Kongress 1878: Protokolle und Materialen*, xix–xx; on Bismarck's drinking, see Pflanze, *Bismarck and the Development of Germany*, 2:438.
16. Lord Salisbury to Mr. Cross, June 15, 1878, reproduced in Lady Gwendolen Cecil (his daughter), *Life of Robert, Marquis of Salisbury*, 2:282.

17. Cited in Geiss, *Der Berliner Kongress 1878*, xxiiin. 68.

18. Ibid., xxiii n. 70.

19. Cited in Jehuda L. Wallach, "Bismarck and the 'Eastern Question': A Re-Assessment," 27.

20. Paul Rohrbach, *Die Bagdadbahn*, 16.

21. Hajo Holborn, ed., *Aufzeichnungen und Erinnerungen aus dem Leben des Botschafters Joseph Maria von Radowitz*, 2:245.

22. Jonathan S. McMurray, *Distant Ties: Germany, the Ottoman Empire, and the Construction of the Baghdad Railway*, 26–27, 35 n. 51. For the gun placements, see Edward J. Erickson, *Defeat in Detail: The Ottoman Army in the Balkans, 1912–13*, 13–14.

23. The final version of the *Rückversicherungsvertrages* of June 1887, in the French original (including the full text of the "Protocole additionnel et très secret" concerning Russia intervention at the Straits) is reproduced in *Die grosse Politik der Europäischen Kabinette*, 5:253–55.

24. Cited in Pflanze, *Bismarck and the Development of Germany*, 2:251.

25. Girs to Shuvalov, May 25, 1887, in *Die grosse Politik der Europäischen Kabinette*, 5:239–40 (document 1082). As originally proposed by Girs, the demand was for Russian freedom of action in Bulgaria, Eastern Rumelia, or Constantinople.

26. Serious Russian operational planning for an amphibious operation to seize Constantinople did not begin until 1895–96, when the "Armenian uprising crisis" seemed to threaten the rule of Abdülhamid II. Even eighteen years later Russia's foreign minister S. D. Sazonov recalled in his memoirs that a February 1914 conference of leading Russian politicians, generals, and naval officers had concluded that the Black Sea fleet still lacked sufficient amphibious carrying capacity to seize Constantinople by force. Sazonov, *Fateful Years, 1909–1916: The Reminiscences of Serge Sazonov, Russia's Minister for Foreign Affairs — 1914*, 126–27.

27. Erickson, *Defeat in Detail*, 11–14.

28. Ibid., 15.

29. Herbert Feis, *Europe: The World's Banker, 1870–1914*, 343–44.

30. McMurray, *Distant Ties*, 29. On the early years of the Baghdad railway, see also Sean McMeekin, *The Berlin-Baghdad Express: The Ottoman Empire and Germany's Bid for World Power, 1898–1918*, chapter 2.

31. Ibid.

32. Maybelle Kennedy Chapman, *Great Britain and the Baghdad Railway, 1888–1914*, 24.

33. McMeekin, *The Berlin-Baghdad Express*, 8–9.

34. Wilhelm II, "Tischrede in Damaskus (8. November 1898)," 81.

35. Rumors also spread widely through Arab street bazaars following the Damascus speech that the Kaiser had converted to Islam. While German consuls in the area never actually claimed this publicly, they also made no effort to refute these rumors. See McMeekin, *The Berlin-Baghdad Express*, chapter 1.

36. Michael Balfour, *The Kaiser and His Times*, 190.

37. Cited in Erich Lindow, *Freiherr Marschall von Bieberstein als Botschafter in Konstantinopel, 1897–1912*, 48.

38. For these details, see McMeekin, *The Berlin-Baghdad Express*, chapter 2 ("Berlin to Baghdad").

39. Ibid., 72.

40. Girs to Alexander Izvolskii, Russian ambassador to Paris, copied to S. D. Sazonov, October 4/17, 1913, in Arkhiv Vneshnei Politiki Rossiiskoi Imperii (AVPRI), fond 172, op. 514-2, del. 633, list 19.

41. Richard G. Hovannisian, "The Armenian Question in the Ottoman Empire, 1876 to 1914," 2:237.

42. M. Şükrü Hanioğlu, *A Brief History of the Late Ottoman Empire*, 173–74.

4

The Ottoman Eastern Question and the Problematic Origins of Modern Ethnic Cleansing, Genocide, and Humanitarian Interventionism in Europe and the Middle East

Mujeeb R. Khan

INTRODUCTION

The Ottoman or Muslim "Eastern question" in Europe has been seminal in shaping the course of modern history, often in a tragic direction. The rise of this issue and attempts to resolve it directly shaped the problematic and troubling emergence of modern ethnic cleansing, genocide, and even liberal humanitarian interventionism in Europe and the Middle East. The Eastern question emerged with Romanov Russian expansion south toward the Balkans, Crimea, and the Caucasus, which accelerated following Ottoman defeat and the Treaty of Küçük Kaynarja of 1774. This treaty was seminal in that tsarist Russia's claim of the right to represent and intervene on the behalf of Orthodox Christian subjects of the Ottoman Empire would set a precedent for a long series of such interventions by competing European powers on behalf of other Christian minorities and subjects as well as (in the case of the Balfour Declaration of 1917) Jewish immigration to Palestine.[1] Napoleon Bonaparte's landing in Egypt in 1798 would further ignite the classical nineteenth-century balance-of-power struggle on the European Continent, ultimately shifting to Ottoman Europe and west Asia following the Congress of Vienna in 1815. Many historians have viewed the Russo-Ottoman War of 1877–78 and the subsequent Congress of Berlin as marking the apogee of the Eastern question and classical nineteenth-century balance-of-power politics. Of course, the Berlin Congress under the leadership of Otto von Bismarck was able to diffuse the immediate international crisis surrounding the Eastern question, but the outbreak of World War I proved that no permanent solution to the disputes it had raised had been reached. It is not surprising that continental war and diplomacy surrounding the Eastern question have also been fertile ground for international-relations theorists; both the *Realpolitik* school emphasizing *raison d'état* and the constructivist school centered on the role of norms and identities in international politics drew evidence from it to buttress their theories.

This chapter seeks to underscore the seminal role played by the Eastern question in generating and shaping many of the structural issues and conflicts of modern Eastern European and Middle Eastern politics. It also illuminates how the emergence of modern ethnic cleansing and genocide in Europe emerged with campaigns, primarily by tsarist Russia, not only to conquer Ottoman territory in the Black Sea basin but also to expel or exterminate Ottoman Muslim populations there as an "alien" presence in Europe. These tragic events occurred with the silent condoning of many nominally Christian European states at the time and are a subject that continues to be elided in most Western commentary and scholarship on the modern origins of genocide and ethnic cleansing in Europe. This is especially painfully ironic given that Europe's first post-Holocaust genocidal onslaughts targeted the very same last surviving pockets of indigenous European Muslims in the former Yugoslavia and the Caucasus. Attendant upon the rise of modern ethnic cleansing and genocide has been the problematic origin of humanitarian interventionism and the discourse surrounding universal human rights that had its origins in the European concerns for the welfare of Christian subjects of the Ottoman Empire. At the time, however, these very same powers were in the midst of brutal imperial expansions into often largely Muslim areas of Africa and Asia, giving rise to charges of racial and religious double standards in the Western claim of possessing higher and universal standards of human rights and civilization. As we shall see, this divide between "the West and the rest" is still with us in terms of the perceptions of Western foreign policies in Asia, Africa, and Latin America and, in particular, controversy surrounding Western policies in former Ottoman territories in Bosnia, Palestine, Iraq, and Chechnya.

The dénouement of the Eastern question is usually marked by the breakup of the Ottoman state at the end of World War I. As the examples cited above indicate, however, the legacies and unresolved conflicts from this period continue to play a major role in shaping regional politics and Muslim-Western relations more generally. As pan-Islamic movements from Morocco to Indonesia feared at the beginning of the twentieth century, the breakup of the Ottoman state effectively extinguished Muslim power and representation on the international stage and left a fragmented and underdeveloped Middle East/West Asia in its wake.

THE MUSLIM AND JEWISH QUESTIONS
IN EUROPE IN HISTORICAL PERSPECTIVE

In accounting for genocide in the Western world, we must note that precisely those religious and ethnic minorities that have been historically presented as "alien" in a nominally Christianized European body-politic have been most persistently vulnerable to this ultimate evil. In this sense, Jews, Roma, and the Muslims of Iberia, the Balkans, Sicily, the Caucasus, and Crimea have been recurrent victims over the *longue durée* of programs of assimilation, expulsion, and/or extermination.

Indeed, the famous thesis of the Belgian historian Henri Pirenne was that the very notion of "Latin Christendom" and the "West" first emerged from the ruins of classical civilization due to the Carolingian Holy Roman Empire's crusades against northern pagans and Muslim infidels in the south.[2] It is an often overlooked fact that the Islamic presence in Europe was actually coterminous with the establishment of the Christian faith in large areas of the European continent. Prior to this period, it should be remembered, Christianity was largely a North African and west Asian religion. While pagan Celts, Saxons, and Wends were forcibly Christianized and incorporated into the Germano-Latin cultural framework, monotheistic Muslims, like Jews, could not easily be converted and in the name of *cuius regio eius religio* (whose realm, his religion) had to be forcibly assimilated or massacred and expelled from Europe proper. This pattern, with some pauses and interruptions, began under the Normans in Sicily in the thirteenth century and continued recently with the Serbs.[3] From the early medieval period to today's incendiary commentary surrounding Muslim immigration, this "Other" has never been genuinely incorporated into Europe because it has been an essential antimony in the European construction of "Self." Edward Said and later Thierry Hentsch have pointed out that the Islamic world is contiguous to the West both in imagination and in geography: "Alternatively mysterious, menacing, enticing, or repulsive; at once deserted and swarming, barbaric and refined; sometimes violent, sometimes indolent; a place of enchantment, escape, or exasperation — but always present and always other."[4]

While this paper emphasizes the problematic structure of the "Jewish" and "Eastern" or Muslim questions in Europe over the *longue durée*, some modern historians challenge both the possibility of making such transhistorical claims and the conflation of medieval and modern forms of identity and contestation. This critique is derived from earlier historicist approaches associated with the nineteenth- and early twentieth-century thought of Wilhelm Dilthey, Benedetto Croce, and R. J. Collingwood. The rather eclectic term "historicism" has various connotations. As used here it refers to the rejection of appeals to human nature, timeless values or standards, fundamental problems, and overarching theories explicating general historical patterns and underlying causalities over the *longue durée*. A revealing example would be the work of the historian/anthropologist David Nirenberg examining the complex relationship of Muslim, Jewish, and Christian communities in fourteenth-century Catalonia and Aragon. He has challenged prevailing accounts of the breakdown of Iberian *convivencia* and its relevance for understanding later pogroms and "ethnic-cleansings" of European minority populations.[5] In rejecting such metanarratives and transhistorical claims, Nirenberg limits his inquiry to a detailed study of the outbreak of intercommunal conflict during the Christian Holy Week celebration in Catalonia and Aragon through the first half of the fourteenth century. His thesis is that violence of a limited and structured sort was integral to sustaining the centuries-long coexistence of the three communities in Iberia. He confesses, however, that he cannot explain why this *convivencia* fifty years later, with the onset of the Spanish Inquisition in 1391 (and especially in the immediate wake of the conquest of the last Spanish Muslim city of Granada in 1492), led to the eventually complete "cleansing" of the vast indigenous Iberian Muslim and Jewish populations.

Nirenberg notes in his introduction, without acknowledging the difficulty that this presents for his overall thesis, that "[f]ew today would argue, for example, that the study of Jews and attitudes toward the Jews in Germany tells us little about the formation of modern German cultural and national identities. Nor in the wake of current attacks on Muslims in the former Yugoslavia, on 'foreigners' (often Muslims) in Germany, France, and Italy, or on Jews in Russia, is it possible to argue that episodes of violence against minorities are part of a primitive European past which modern societies have left behind."[6] It is precisely the resilience of certain constructs of Self and Other over the *longue durée*, such as the Jewish and

Eastern or Muslim question in Europe, which begs for both a descriptive and a theoretical account.

Similarly, recent scholarly work on the emergence of genocide in twentieth-century Europe sees it commencing with the massacres of Armenians in 1915 and continuing through the Nazi death camps and Soviet gulags. It has tended to emphasize discontinuity with previous episodes of mass killings and persecutions of minorities in insisting that, as a malignant mutation of modernity, modern genocide represents a radically new phenomenon.[7] In insisting on the centrality of technological and bureaucratic domination wedded to a modern instrumental rationality, the sociologist Zygmunt Bauman has written that the Nazi Holocaust was not only unparalleled in history but also largely disconnected from the long history of European anti-Semitism.[8] The historian Omer Bartov, in endorsing the Bauman thesis, has located the origins of modern genocide in the vast mechanized destruction and trench warfare of World War I.[9]

This focus on *fin de siècle* Europe and the onset of World War I has elided earlier instances of genocidal campaigns connected to European imperial expansions that a number of important studies correctly view as prefiguring the mass slaughter of European civilians in World War II. Furthermore, the prevailing view that *Vernichtungspolitik* or deliberate extermination policy directed against European civilians in the modern period was a unique feature of "Totalitarian" systems under Adolf Hitler and Joseph Stalin has completely failed to note that imperial Russian efforts to solve the Ottoman Eastern question in southeastern Europe and the Caucasus entailed a deliberate process of "cleansing" European Muslim (and also some Jewish) populations through a wave of genocidal massacres and expulsions. In his fine study of the Circassian genocide Oliver Bullough recently has underscored the point, which I first made, that the origins of genocide in modern Europe predate World War I and the slaughter of the Armenians and must be located in efforts to liquidate the Ottoman Muslim presence in the Balkans, the Crimea, and the Caucasus.[10]

THE "SICK MAN OF EUROPE" AND THE RISE
OF THE OTTOMAN EASTERN QUESTION

The nineteenth century marked the steady decline of the Ottoman Empire under pressure from competing European powers. Much has been made of the ostensible terminal decline of the "sick man of Europe" giving rise to the Eastern question. While the Ottomans had to struggle to catch up with the more advanced institutions and military technology pioneered by Western European states by the end of the eighteenth century, the decrepitude of the state and its inability to reform have been greatly exaggerated. From the defeat of Peter the Great at Pruth in 1711 and the legendary defense of Plevna in 1878 to the defeat of Allied armies in World War I at Gallipoli and Kut al-Amara, the Ottoman state and military showed a resilience greater than that of corresponding rivals such as the Habsburg Austro-Hungarian Empire. Its efforts at administrative and economic reform would also likely have succeeded if the Sublime Porte had not been faced with continuous military attacks from 1821 to the outbreak of World War I and forced to grant capitulations and effective control over its economy to erstwhile predatory allies like Great Britain and France.

As tsarist Russia sought to fulfill its cherished geopolitical and religious/ideological goal of capturing Constantinople and the Straits while expanding south to the warm waters of the Aegean, its trump card was its ostensible right to represent and seek freedom for Orthodox Christian subjects of the Porte. In playing this card various tsarist ministers and adventurers not only had a seminal role in stirring up revolts in Greece, Serbia, Bosnia, and Bulgaria but also effectively sought to present the conflict to the rest of Europe as a case of Christian liberation from the intolerable yoke of Islamic despotism. This religious/ideological dimension was absent from most European nineteenth-century Great Power politics, as realist international relations theorists would attest. It played a crucial and tragic role in the Eastern question, however, by ensuring that the resulting conflicts and wars of liberation also became ethno-sectarian campaigns of ethnic cleansing and mass slaughter of enemy civilian populations. Mass atrocities against Ottoman Muslim civilians by Balkan *chetas* (irregulars) were central to this strategy and would in turn invite savage Ottoman reprisals against Orthodox civilians, often by irregulars like the *başıbozuks*. Such atrocities, in turn, would form the one-sided grist for the newly emerging popular press in European states, generating outrage against "Turkey in Europe" while invariably ignoring atrocities committed against Muslims, no matter how great.

This pattern commenced with the Serbian rebellions of 1804 to 1812 and continued with the Greek War for independence from 1821 to 1832, in which 20,000 Muslims and 5,000 Jews were massacred in the Morea at the onset of the campaign.[11] The Ottomans responded with savage reprisals of their own in the Aegean islands and by hanging the Greek patriarch, Gregory V. The Greek rebellion aroused enormous passions in the rest of Europe, which was increasingly coming to define itself in exceptional religious, civilizational, and ultimately ethno-racial terms in order to rationalize its own imperial expansions abroad. The Philhellenes were led by fabled figures such as Lord Byron and combined both secular liberals and romantics and Christian Evangelical nationalists. The liberals in particular were not motivated by religious chauvinism, but their one-sided and enthusiastic campaign against "Asiatic despotism" exposed at the onset the Western liberal double standards when it came to dealing with the non-Western world, which many feel still afflict international relations today. This was most apparent in their willingness to overlook or excuse large-scale massacres of Ottoman Muslim civilians, which many Philhellene leaders as well as Western reporters had witnessed firsthand.

Responding to both elite and popular pressure, Britain, France, and Russia intervened to destroy the Ottoman fleet at Navarino Bay in 1827. This combined European assault against Ottoman Muslim suzerainty in Europe was especially notable in that it violated the ostensibly "realist" conservative balance-of-power rules set in place by Lord Castlereagh and Prince Metternich at the Concert of Europe in 1815. In his recent book *Freedom's Battle*, on the origins of human rights and humanitarian intervention, Gary Bass also notes that they originated in attempts to address the Ottoman Eastern question. He concedes that they initially emerged as a defense of fellow European Christians ruled by a non-Christian empire but asserts that these concerns became more universal in the course of the nineteenth century. His examples of humanitarian interventions in the Ottoman Empire, however, belie this contention. All his examples of such ostensibly universal concerns for human rights, from the Greeks and Bulgarians to the Maronites and Armenians, were solely directed at protecting Christian minorities even as the same Western empires engaged in brutal colonial expansions against native populations on five continents.[12]

From the Greek rebellion to the Balfour Declaration of 1917, ceding Palestine as a national home and invariably future state for European Jews, the rights of indigenous Ottoman Muslim populations were ignored in lofty European rhetoric concerning human rights and civilization. In the case of Palestine, Syria, Eastern Rumelia, Bosnia-Hercegovina, Albania, and eastern Anatolia, European powers repeatedly indicated their willingness to sponsor the creation of independent states for Christian minorities, even in territory where the significant majority of the inhabitants were Muslim. The rationale of the various rival European powers was mixed. The British, French, and Russians were interested in co-opting and patronizing various non-Muslim minorities for the sake of their own imperial and commercial interests. But the powerful sense of religious and civilizational solidarity that also fueled these policies to the detriment of native Muslim populations should not be discounted. Left unsaid in all of these cases, but vividly apparent in practice, was that such Western-sponsored states for Christian subjects of the Ottoman Empire (even where they were clear minorities) could only come about through systematic ethnic cleansing of native Muslims, which very rarely elicited outrage in the West. As shown by continuing conflicts in the Balkans, the Caucasus, and Palestine, as well as the Western support for despotic regimes from Morocco to Brunei, this tension between universal values and particular identities and interests still haunts international relations today, dividing what Samuel Huntington has termed the "the West" from "the Rest."[13]

OTTOMAN EXCLUSION AND
THE BOUNDARIES OF EUROPE

At this juncture we should anticipate some potential criticism from the standpoint of realism and balance-of-power politics, which many international relations theorists see as transcending claims of identity and appeals to ideology. Balance-of-power politics were certainly also crucial in determining international politics surrounding the Eastern question and the stillborn attempts to resolve it at the Congress of Berlin by Otto von Bismarck, the archrealist German chancellor and successor to Metternich. In their rivalry to assert influence and ultimately possession of various parts of the Ottoman Empire European states often sought favor with the Sublime Porte as they sought to balance each other. As tsarist Russia ascended to prominence following the defeat of Napoleonic France, its potential overland threat to strategic approaches to India specifically challenged British imperial interests.

Thus at various times both the British and French were willing to buttress the Ottoman Empire in response to Russian threats. This was most clearly seen during the Crimean War of 1853–56. The war itself, however, involved the symbolic politics of control over the holy places in Jerusalem and the right to represent Christian minorities as much as it did purely geopolitical objectives. The Treaty of Paris in 1856 that ended the war was also notable in first explicitly recognizing the Ottomans as legitimate members of the European society of states, from which the Dutch legal theorist Hugo Grotius noted they had long been excluded. This recognition was only provisional, however; strong resistance to full acceptance of the Ottomans remained, as in the case of Turkey and the European

Union (EU) today. Even though many Ottoman administrative practices were less draconian than those of their giant Russian rival, European chancelleries repeatedly demanded that the Ottomans conform to European norms and undertake reforms to benefit the Christian subjects of the empire. These reforms and the attendant capitulations allowed Christian subjects and their European patrons to control the bulk of the empire's trade by the end of the nineteenth century. Needless to say, none of these reforms were considered appropriate or necessary for the millions of Muslims languishing under harsh Western imperial rule in Africa and Asia.

From the standpoint of realist theory, it might be expected that the long European presence of the Ottoman Empire, which had been one of the world's paramount powers for five centuries, with its center of gravity in the quarter of the European continent that it controlled, would have entitled it to much earlier recognition as a member of the European society of states. Yet the often overlooked reality is that the term "European" has always had an overriding cultural and religious connotation as opposed to a geographical or even ethnic one. In an important constructivist international relations article, Iver B. Neumann and Jennifer M. Welsh have demonstrated how the dominant realist paradigm in international relations theory often failed to account for linkages and barriers between states that result from cultural differences.[14] Their main example is the position of the Ottoman Empire in the European society of states. Despite great internal societal changes brought about by the Renaissance and the growth of humanism and secular authority, European attitudes toward their Muslim neighbors showed and continue to show a remarkable continuity with those of the medieval period. As Neumann and Welsh note,

> the dominant Other in the history of the European states system is "the Turk." In contrast to the communities of the "New World," the military might and physical proximity of the Ottoman Empire, combined with the strength of its religious tradition, made it a particularly relevant Other in the evolution of European identity. It can be shown that until the mid nineteenth century, contemporaries saw the frontier of Europe as stopping where the Ottoman Empire began, and the Christians living within the Ottoman Empire as Europeans in exile.[15]

The Ottomans, despite their geographical location and being for the most part Caucasian, could not be considered "European" by many because they represented an essential antonym in this European construction of Self. As noted, the continuity of this existential condition over the *long durée* is evident even today. Despite its long service in Western security and political institutions and the avid attempts to assert a European identity upon the part of its Kemalist elite, the Republic of Turkey is no closer to attaining membership in the European Union than it was three decades ago. Meanwhile East European and Balkan states who were members of the Warsaw Pact and continue to lag behind Turkey in political and socioeconomic development have been assured full membership in the near future.

Revealingly, this includes Serbia, which has been promised a path to membership if it turns over Radovan Karadžić and Ratko Mladić to the International Tribunal at the Hague for the crime of genocide. The International Court in a highly dubious verdict ruled that it did not have enough evidence to charge the Serbian state directly with the acts of genocide committed in Bosnia-Hercegovina. The court admitted it had not reviewed the reams of existing evidence proving that the forces led by Karadžić and Mladić were organized, trained, and directed from Belgrade because of a political deal with Serbia. A number of observers have pointed out that a verdict of genocide against the Serbian state would have made it very difficult for Serbia to gain EU membership in the near future and would also have revealed the close links between Slobodan Milošević and the French, British, and Dutch governments, which had shielded him from military action while imposing an arms embargo on the Bosnian victims. Whereas Serbia has been officially absolved for the crime of genocide for which a number of individual Serbian leaders stand accused, the nearly century-old charge that Turkey committed genocide against the Armenians and failed to acknowledge it fully and make amends has become a major vehicle for the French and German governments in denying Turkey full EU membership.

THE RUSSO-OTTOMAN WAR OF 1877–78: THE TENSIONS OF REALISM, IDEALISM, AND IDENTITY POLITICS

What is notable about the Eastern question is the extent to which realist interests combined and clashed with those of idealism and identity politics. Uniquely, at times identity politics and pan-Christian European solidarity even trumped the pressing exigencies of *raison d'état* due to strong domestic pressure, as seen in the case of Greece in 1821 and the Bulgarians in 1876–77. These wars in the Balkans and the Caucasus were also unique in that they did not just result in the simple transfer of territories and the clash of professional militaries, as was the case in the rest of post-Westphalian Europe. They also involved concerted efforts to change the demographic balance via the wholesale targeting of Ottoman Muslims for expulsion from Europe or extermination. Therein lies the origins of modern genocide and ethnic cleansing in the European continent. In fact this template would later extend to the Armenians in eastern Anatolia and then to the Holocaust, in what Timothy Snyder has termed the "bloodlands" of Eastern Europe contested between Hitler and Stalin.[16] Sadly, the assumption that the defeat of Nazi Germany had exorcised this evil from Europe was proven stillborn with the return of genocidal onslaughts against the few remaining indigenous European Muslim populations in the former Yugoslavia and Chechnya at the end of the Cold War.

The Russo-Ottoman War of 1877–78 was triggered by Russia's expedient use of the harsh suppression of Bulgarian uprisings (deliberately provoked by the pan-Slavist Russian ambassador in Constantinople, Count N. P. Ignatiev) to capture Constantinople and the Turkish Straits. The deaths of 2,100 people from all communities in these uprisings, and in particular accounts of the massacre at Batak spread by a British missionary, launched a wave of fury against the "Turkish Horrors" in all of Europe, as had similar events in Greece in 1821. British prime minister Benjamin Disraeli clearly viewed a unilateral Russian solution to the Eastern question as a grave threat but was unable to offer assistance to the Porte because of the moralistic anti-Islamic crusade launched by his rival William Ewart Gladstone. Gladstone also repeatedly used anti-Semitic innuendo to disarm Disraeli, accusing him of insufficient compassion for Christians and sympathy toward Turks. Gladstone uttered the immortal words that were to be a guiding beacon for ethnic cleansing operations during the war: "[The Turks] one and all, bag and baggage, shall I hope, clear out from the province they have desolated and profaned."[17] The process of "clearing out" was begun by the Russian army and its local Orthodox Christian auxiliaries as soon as they entered Ottoman territory.

It should be noted that by 1870 Muslims constituted nearly half of the population in the southeast corner of Europe controlled by the Ottoman state and were descended either from indigenous converts or from migrants who had settled there centuries earlier, thus making them native to the corner of Europe from which they would be cleansed. While the Congress of Berlin, like the Balfour Declaration of 1917, paid lip service to the rights of non-Christian populations in the region, in practice very little was done to oppose or even condemn the ongoing campaign of ethnic cleansing. Nearly 300,000 Muslims were massacred during the 1877–78 war and its immediate aftermath, and 5 million were ultimately forced to flee to Anatolia by the turn of the century.[18] As the historian Kemal Karpat notes, "The war was in effect a religious war which aimed at destroying the Muslim Ottoman society and replacing it with National states.... In practice the national identity of the new states established in the Balkans after 1878 rested on a religious basis and only secondarily upon language and history."[19] Most of the victims of Serbian atrocities around Niş and Bulgarian operations in the Rhodopes were Slavic Muslims whose dismal fate in these "wars of liberation" did not deflate the sense of smug moral satisfaction that prevailed in much of Europe at the time.[20] In stark contrast to the fate of the Balkan Christians, the fate of European Muslim populations and their right to maintain a territorial presence on the continent were only intermittently addressed and recognized at either the public or the governmental level and seldom defended in practice. British, French, and German consular reports were actively and accurately detailing the vast atrocities being committed in the Rhodopes and Eastern Rumelia after the Ottoman garrison at Plevna fell, yet this failed to generate any sustained public or elite outrage. This was the case even when Queen Victoria herself, driven by the fear of Russian expansion toward India that Disraeli had implanted in her mind, issued strident condemnations of Russian and Bulgarian atrocities.

A revealing example of such atrocities is a report filed by the British consul in Edirne, E. Calvert, to the British ambassador at the Porte, A. H. Layard:

> It would be a needless and painful task to collect, from the different reports that have been addressed to this embassy, the numberless cases of outrages, cruelty, rape and massacre committed during the last few months by the Russians and Bulgarians upon the Mussalmans of Roumelia. It would scarcely be too much to affirm that they exceed in horror and amount the accumulated misdeeds of four centuries of Turkish misrule. Never, have the Turks, even in the worst days of their history, been guilty of indiscriminate slaughter, such shocking outrages on women and female children, such universal destruction of property and such general religious persecution. The deeds of the Bashi-Bazouk at Batah and in other Bulgarian villages, immensely exaggerated by the thoughtless, designing, or unscrupulous men and the consequence of a panic which subsequent events have shown to have been justified, were sufficient to arouse public opinion in England to such an extent against Turkey, that a war unparalleled for its horrors and perhaps for its consequences, has been the result.[21]

Such double standards and indifference or willful ignorance of the fate of Ottoman Muslims have continued even to this day in the historiography of the region and more generally in academic writings on the origins of modern European genocide. For example, in his study of genocide Ervin Staub uses the example of Gladstone's interventions on behalf of Balkan Christians as a leading and commendable model for humanitarian interventionism. Nowhere in the book, however, does he give any indication that in the end the vast majority of civilian victims of the Russo-Ottoman War of 1877–78 were actually Ottoman Muslims.[22] If Staub may be excused for not being a specialist on the Balkans, no such excuse exists for Mark Mazower, a prominent historian of the modern Balkans and European genocide. In his book *Dark Continent* and in a recent comparative article on ethnic cleansing and genocide, Mazower distorts and downplays this seminal campaign of ethnic cleansing. Although he cites Justin McCarthy's assiduously researched and documented work on the subject, *Death and Exile: The Ethnic Cleansing of Ottoman Muslims, 1821–1922*, he is clearly uncomfortable with the findings.[23] Mazower alludes to McCarthy's book as polemical and makes the absurd claim that the vast migration of Ottoman Muslims following the 1877–78 War resulted from refusal to live under non-Muslim rule, while in reality they were fleeing massacre and rape on a scale not to be seen again in Europe until World War II.[24] Such ethnic cleansing operations would continue during the Balkan Wars of 1912–13, as documented by the Commission of Experts for the Carnegie Foundation. A novel dimension of the second round of fighting between erstwhile Balkan Christian allies of the "Holy League" during the Balkan Wars was that Serbian and Greek forces readily employed the same tactics of massacre and rape against Bulgarian and Macedonian Christians when their alliance fell apart.

Prior to this catastrophic assault on Ottoman Muslims in the Balkans, tsarist Russia launched an even greater genocidal onslaught, the first in modern European history, against the Muslim highlanders of the Caucasus from 1862 to 1865. Russian expansion south to the Caucasus had begun under Peter the Great, reaching the Terek River and the foothills of the Caucasus by the rule of Catherine the Great. Russian expansion galvanized the Muslim highlanders into resistance led by Sufi Nakşibendi *tariqat* (orders). It would last well over a century and continues even today in Chechnya and Daghestan. Though resistance was initiated by Sheikh Mansur Ushurma at the end of the eighteenth century, it received legendary stature during the nearly thirty-year resistance of Sheikh Shamil. The end of the Crimean War allowed the Russians to throw their full weight into ending the interminable resistance of the highlanders. They did this through a scorched earth policy that systematically destroyed the *aouls* (hamlets) of the highland tribes, enslaving and massacring men, women, and children alike.

Oliver Bullough captures the nadir of this genocidal policy well in his recent book on the tragic fate of the Circassian tribes, the first victims of modern European genocide. The Russians followed the defeat of Shamil by sending their army in three columns to drive the Circassians literally into the Black Sea. Half of the population of about 2 million perished, while the others were blown to the far edges of the Ottoman Empire as refugees.[25] This spectacle of genocide, far greater than any Ottoman atrocities of the time, also aroused little indignation in Europe capitals, even though their diplomats kept them well informed of the horrific events as they transpired. The Circassian survivors, as Ottoman irregulars, would play a prominent role in seeking vengeance against Orthodox Christians in the Balkans as well as against Armenians in Anatolia. Indeed, the many polemics surrounding the horrific deportations and massacres of the Armenians in 1915 involving both Turkish and Armenian writers and their supporters fail to note that these tragic events cannot be understood without placing them in the broader context of the emergence of genocide as a tool and template for resolving the Eastern question some decades earlier.

THE PERSISTENCE OF THE JEWISH AND MUSLIM QUESTIONS IN TWENTIETH-CENTURY EUROPE

The "Jewish question" in Europe has also been central for much of the Continent's early modern history and for the intellectual inception of the Enlightenment and modernity and their eventual disillusionment in the death camps of World War II. For both French *philosophes* and the German thinkers of the early Enlightenment, the inherent tension between the universal and the particular in human affairs was most vividly exemplified by this issue and the need to abolish difference, tradition, and superstition, which divided societies along numerable fault lines. The Enlightenment and the modern state fully emerging alongside it in the course of the nineteenth century saw the gradual attainment of societal harmony in the abolishment of substantial legal and ascriptive differences among citizens through the universalizing and homogenizing progress of capitalism, science, and positive rationality. In his controversial essay "On the Jewish Question" Karl Marx saw the solution to traditional anti-Semitism as being the assimilation of Jews and all other social particularities into a classless and postreligious society of equals.[26] This "solution," first hinted at by Baruch Spinoza, was also central to the French Revolutionary decree of Jewish emancipation.

The universalizing mission of the Enlightenment, its naïve failure to consider the instrumental and potentially ruthless aspects of human reasoning aside, obviously could not solve the contradiction between universal ideals and particular identities and interests for everyone. The deflation of Enlightenment optimism in the Dreyfus Affair led Theodore Herzl, Otto Pinsker, and other Jewish intellectuals to advocate the particular in the form of Jewish nationalism and political Zionism. This "solution" itself spawned a chasm between the secular worship of the "nation" and traditional Jewish faith, on the one hand, and what would eventually become the moral dilemma of the perennial victims' victimization of the native Palestinian inhabitants of the yearned-for "Zion," on the other.

As noted earlier, a number of important connections exist between medieval and early modern anti-Semitism and anti-Muslim sentiments in Europe. Allan and Helen Cutler have emphasized that medieval massacres against Jews were often tied to Crusades against Muslims in Iberia and the Holy Land, the rationale being that it made little sense to tolerate the presence of those who denied Christ at home while combating similar monotheistic rivals and heretics abroad.[27] This linkage continued even in early modern times with the spread of pogroms in the Pale settlements and Black Sea region of tsarist Russia. Jonathan Klier Doyle has convincingly demonstrated how pan-Slavic promotion of anti-Semitism and pogroms in the late nineteenth century was intimately connected to Russia's great struggle against the Ottoman Empire and suspicion that Jews sympathized with it. As in the case of Gladstone, many pan-Slav agitators particularly blamed Disraeli's Jewish heritage for his pro-Ottoman sympathies during the war of 1877–78.[28]

Tragically, this persistence of the Jewish and Eastern or Muslim questions in Europe continued in the twentieth century, manifesting itself in attempts at mass expulsion and extermination.[29] "Ethnic cleansing" (from etničko čišćenje in Serbo-Croatian) was also a metaphor widely employed by the Nazis in their campaign against European Jewry. They spoke of the extermination of the Jews as being Gesundung (the healing of Europe), Selbstreinigung (self-cleansing), and Juden Säuberung (the cleansing of Jews). Fundamentally, the Judenfrage was, in the words of one German foreign office press chief, "a question of political hygiene."[30]

At this juncture it would be useful to consider causal explanations for the persistence of the Jewish and Muslim questions in Europe over the *longue durée* at a deep structural level and separate them from more contingent and proximate causal factors in explicating genocide in the Holocaust and its shocking reemergence in Bosnia-Hercegovina. One useful avenue to reference is the *Historikerstreit* (historians' controversy) on the Holocaust that raged in the 1980s.[31] The controversy centered on the two camps of "intentionalists" versus "structural-functionalists," divided over the respective role of Hitler, structural factors, and the influence of Stalin's earlier Great Terror and mass killing program in the East. The traditional intentionalist view of the Holocaust emphasized it as a premeditated central obsession of Hitler, dating back to his writings of the 1920s.[32] This view, however, has been greatly modified by more recent research based upon archival records. The decision to radicalize traditional anti-Semitism into a full-blown genocidal campaign certainly did follow the clearly articulated logic of Nazi doctrine, but its particular implementation was greatly influenced by Germany's invasion of the Soviet Union and the lack of suitable territories into which to deport Jews. From the September 1939 invasion of Poland to the fall of France in 1940, the Germans planned to solve their "Jewish problem" through mass expulsion. The Reichsführer-SS Heinrich Himmler and his deputy Adolph Eichmann originally intended to "purify" German conquered territories by sending the Jews to the Lublin reservation east of the Bug and Vistula rivers. As German armies and horizons expanded farther east, Himmler issued a memorandum calling for the expulsion of Jews from Europe to Madagascar. It was only when setbacks in the war made such expulsion plans unfeasible that the Nazis decided upon physical extermination in the fall of 1941.[33]

The recent genocide against Bosnian Muslims also followed a "twisted path": traditional anti-Islamism on the part of Serbia and Europe proper accelerated with the rise of immigration and the Iranian revolution and melded with the geographical isolation of Bosnian Muslims and their republic between covetous Serb and Croat neighbors to render an attempt at expulsion feasible and even desirable. But Serb nationalists did not simply stop at achieving their political and territorial gains, which they easily accomplished against the small and defenseless Bosnian Muslim population in the spring of 1992. Rather, with the rest of Europe and the West looking on, they embarked upon a systematic program to erase the Ottoman Muslim historical legacy in Bosnia as well as physical extermination of much of the Bosnian Muslim population through mass murder and rape. Balance-of-power politics and the fear of entanglement in a Balkan morass did play a significant part in shaping Western inaction in response to the Bosnian conflict, but that does not invalidate the contention that the Muslim identity of the victims also played a crucial role in developments at the regional and international levels.

Genocide in all of these instances resulted from the convergence of proximate geographical and political factors with those of a much deeper historical and structural/ideational nature. As in the case of the Holocaust, historical prejudice against an "alien minority" and the indifference of many who felt no direct connection with the victims combined with the practical exigencies of alliances, geography, and demographics to make Europe's second genocide in the twentieth century against a religious/cultural minority possible at the "End of History."

Genocide by one human population against another is an extreme example of the treacherous path that the Hegelian dialectic of recognition between Self and Other may take. The Other in G. W. F. Hegel's dialectic of recognition between master and slave presented in the *Phenomenology of Spirit* (1807) was enslaved and not annihilated because his existence was necessary for recognizing the master. If this Other transgresses definitional boundaries and undermines the master's certainty of Self, however, recognition is muddled: he must either be expelled to a distance where practical or eliminated when not. This has especially been the case where distinct minorities like European Jews and Muslims find themselves stranded across clearly demarcated frontiers such as the Mediterranean separating Self from Other and "Orient" from "Occident" and thereby seem to undermine the cohesiveness and ideological viability of the self-identity held by the dominant group.

In terms of the modern "Jewish question" (which in the West has abated at least for the time being because of the tragic "success" of the Holocaust and Jewish emigration to Israel and the United States), Jews were the "only non-national nation" to be found throughout Europe and thus both in a religious/ideological and ethnic/national sense "contaminated" the "purity of the nation." The paradox here is that as the leveling process of modernity blurred historic cultural and religious distinctions it undermined the certainty of Self held by the dominant group and spurred still greater efforts at redrawing definitional boundaries and containing this insidious infiltration. As Zygmunt Bauman notes: "In short, they undermined the very difference between hosts and guests, the native and the foreign. And as nationhood became the paramount basis of group self-constitution, they came to undermine the most basic of differences: the difference between 'us' and 'them.'"[34]

Muslim Slavs, similarly, always posed a very vexing problem for Serbian nationalists. They were clearly descendants of fellow Slavic tribes in their very midst, but they espoused the faith of the accursed "Turks," seen as the foe that provoked the direct opposition through which modern Serbian national consciousness first emerged. The mere existence of this South Slav Islamic population problematized and undermined the basic truth claims of Serbian nationalism. While the topic is beyond the scope of this chapter, it should be noted that this problematic of the "Muslim question" and the need for its elimination in the lands of the South Slavs was central both to traditional Serbian epics such as the Kosovo Epic Cycle and *The Mountain Wreath* of P. P. Njegos and to the writings of modern Yugoslav authors such as Ivo Andrić, Dobrica Ćosić, and Vuk Drašković.[35] Furthermore, as is evident in statements given by high-ranking European officials at the time, the existence of this "blond and blue-eyed" European Muslim nation and the prospect that it could be the basis for a Muslim majority state in the heart of Europe were also a source of profound discomfort for many others in prominent positions on the continent.

THE POST–COLD WAR RETURN OF WAR AND GENOCIDE ON THE OTTOMAN MARCHES: EASTERN QUESTION REDUX?

The indifference to the tragic fate of Ottoman Muslims in the nineteenth century clearly continues to resonate in the recent horrific tragedies visited upon the Bosnian, Kosovar, and Chechen Muslim populations. The decision of leading Western countries not to deter the Serbian invasion of the Bosnian Republic and their concerted efforts to cover up the clear evidence of the emergence of a Serbian ethnic cleansing campaign indicated to Belgrade that physical extermination of a large segment of the Muslim population and its historic legacy would not face a great deal of international resistance. This became apparent as the initial Serbian assault and large-scale atrocities in the Drina Valley launched by paramilitaries like Arkan's Tigers and the White Eagles met with silence on the part of Western governments, who did not want to be pressured into intervening to stop ethnic cleansing on their doorstep in spite of having inaugurated the "New World Order" to stop aggression in the heart of the Islamic world with Operation Desert Storm a year earlier. It was then that Serb nationalists decided to expand their campaign of territorial conquest to a more final solution against a problematic Muslim Slav population that posed not a physical threat but a symbolic/ideational one in terms of Serbian national identity.

The Serbian leadership in Belgrade and Pale went to great lengths in exploiting deeply ingrained anti-Islamic sentiments among a broad range of Western societies (even though the Bosnians were the most secular and pacific Muslim population in the world and the only one in the three-way conflict to have upheld the highest "Western" values of democracy and pluralism). The existence of such animus and sinister feelings is not usually made public and is of course dismissed in a barrage of pious protestations by official spokespeople. Such sentiments did, however, play a significant part in the calculations of some key policymakers. One high-ranking French diplomat indiscreetly told John Newhouse of the *New Yorker* that the Europeans "want to prevent a wider war or the emergence of a rump Muslim state in southeastern Europe — one that might become rich, militant, and an inspiration for ethnic or communal strife elsewhere. Europeans also want to discourage a Bosnian Diaspora of the kind that was generated by the war in Palestine half a century ago. 'Our interests are much closer to the Serbs than you think,' a French diplomat says. 'We worry more about the Muslims than about the Serbs.'"[36]

At the time I charged in an article in the journal *East European Politics and Societies* that British and French policy was tantamount to complicity in the genocide of the Bosnian Muslims and that their religious and cultural identity played a major role in the lack of Western action to stop the carnage.[37] The White House historian Taylor Branch recently confirmed this at the highest level in his book *The Clinton Tapes*. In taped interviews with Branch that were released after a ten-year hiatus, President Bill Clinton recounted how the British and French insisted on maintaining the embargo on the defenseless Bosnians:

> They justified their opposition on plausible humanitarian grounds, arguing that more arms would only fuel the bloodshed, but privately, said the president, key allies objected that an independent Bosnia would be "unnatural" as the only Muslim nation in Europe. He said that they favored the embargo precisely because it locked in Bosnia's disadvantage.... When I expressed shock at such cynicism, reminiscent of the blind-eye diplomacy regarding Europe's Jews during World War II, President Clinton only shrugged. He said that President François Mitterand of France had been especially blunt in saying that Bosnia did not belong, and that British officials also spoke of a painful but realistic restoration of Christian Europe.[38]

As the Bosnian Muslims struggled to survive the genocidal onslaught launched by Serbia, the Chechen Muslims of the Caucasus also found themselves in a similar struggle for survival. While the West used its enormous leverage with Moscow at the end of the Cold War to help liberate Eastern Europe and the Baltic states from Russian control, the bid for independence by the Chechens, who had never ceased their struggle for independence, was met with cold indifference. In spite of the carpet bombing of Grozny and vast Russian atrocities against Chechen civilians, Western criticism was lukewarm.[39] President Clinton hailed Boris Yeltsin's ruthless actions as comparable to those of Abraham Lincoln. The charismatic Chechen leader Dzhokar Dudayev was a moderate who sought to contain bloodshed while seeking independence. Like most other Chechens of his generation, he was a survivor of Stalin's attempted genocide in 1944. He grew up to become a general in the Soviet Air Force and as commander of the Tartu airbase played a key role in preventing Communist hard-liners from using force against the nascent Estonian freedom movement championed by the West. This called to mind the earlier fabled resistance of Sheikh Shamil, which had also helped to protect the freedom of a number of East European nations from Russian dominance.

Nonetheless, the favor was not returned in the case of the Chechens, who found that most Western nations were quite willing to sacrifice them and overlook massive atrocities in order to curry favor with Moscow. Dudayev's assassination by a Su-25 fighter-bomber firing a guided missile in April 1996 was a particularly devastating tragedy, plunging the Chechen freedom movement into anarchy and allowing warlords and militants to undermine and discredit the cause, often with direct or indirect assistance from Moscow. Compelling evidence indicates that American intelligence agencies, and in particular the National Security Agency/National Reconnaissance Office (NSA/NRO), played a central role in orchestrating Dudayev's assassination, which took place when Clinton arrived in Moscow seeking to prop up Yeltsin from growing Communist opposition and outrage over the bungled war and corruption. The knowledgeable former NSA American electronic intelligence analyst Wayne Madsen has pointed out that the sophisticated signals intelligence electronic intercept and triangulation of Dudayev's satellite phone (which had been provided by well-placed Turkish supporters) was well beyond the technical capabilities of the Russians. The very rapid and accurate signals intelligence intercept and triangulation could only have been done by American Vortex or Orion satellites.[40] Another significant piece of evidence seems to point to American involvement in the assassination of the Chechen leader. A few years later I was at the prominent Central Asia/Caucasus academic conference held annually at the University of Wisconsin–Madison and traditionally well attended by analysts working for the State Department and the Central

Intelligence Agency (CIA). In a conversation with me (I also happen to be an American citizen) one CIA analyst indiscreetly bragged that the NSA had used an electro-optical photo-reconnaissance satellite (probably a KH-11 Keyhole Satellite) to photograph Dudayev's body, head, and jaw in fine detail immediately after the hit — "confirming the kill," so to speak, before he was retrieved by his bodyguards. Such timing would have only been possible if the NRO electro-optical/photo-reconnaissance satellite had been coordinated and tasked beforehand for the operation. As it was, Dudayev was very careful in the use of the satellite phone and was lured out ahead of time by a false promise of high-level peace talks mediated via a prominent Russian politician.

Such skullduggery of course continued with the rise of Yeltsin's successor, Vladimir Putin. It is well known among academics and intelligence officials that the Russian Federal Security Service (Federal'naia Sluzhba Bezopasnosti: FSB) carried out a series of apartment-building terror bombings in 1999 (including in the city of Ryazan, where it was caught red-handed), in order to drum up popular outrage for the reinvasion of Chechnya. FSB involvement in a number of other atrocities blamed on the Chechens (such as the murder of Red Cross workers) has also been recently revealed. Even as Moscow seeks to rule through the terror of its psychopathic Chechnyan strongman Ramzan Kadyrov, resistance in Chechnya and Daghestan by the indomitable highlanders is far from over.

THE TIES THAT BIND: THE CONSOLIDATION OF TURKISH DEMOCRACY AND THE EMERGING RECONCILIATION WITH THE OTTOMAN MUSLIM PAST

Much has recently been made about Turkey's reorientation back toward leadership in the Muslim world with the "Neo-Ottoman" foreign policy of the Justice and Development Party (AKP) and its dynamic foreign minister, Ahmet Davutoğlu. A rising and democratic Turkey is seeking to bring peace and political and economic integration and development to the core region of the former Ottoman Muslim state and civilization. Much of the fragmentation and internecine conflict that the Middle East witnessed in the twentieth century can of course be traced back to the dénouement of the Eastern question and its unresolved conflicts. While China and India emerged from Western imperialism with continent-sized state and market institutions intact, allowing their respective states and civilizations to develop and resume great power status, the Islamic world has suffered over the last fifty years from the reinforcing variables of internal fragmentation, local despotism, squandered resources, and highly destructive foreign interventions designed to maintain the status quo. The emerging leadership role of a democratic and economically and culturally vibrant Turkey reconciled with its historic Ottoman Islamic history and identity has garnered massive popular support throughout the Muslim world. Turkish prime minister Recep Tayyip Erdoğan handily wins public surveys of the most esteemed and electable Muslim leader.

This reorientation and reconciliation in terms of Turkey's national identity and interests was not predicted by most scholars of Turkish foreign policy.[41] This has resulted from the emergence of a prosperous and electorally dominant Anatolian Muslim bourgeoisie and from the legitimation crisis that Turkey's Kemalist elite suffered in its failure to be fully accepted in the EU or effectively respond to the trauma felt by the Turkish public over the terrible death and destruction in its historic Ottoman Muslim periphery after the end of the Cold War. This failure of the secular authoritarian elites to fill the regional vacuum left by the breakup of the Ottoman state in terms of either socioeconomic development or political legitimation has been particularly acute in the Arab world, leading to the current crisis and growing popular mobilization for change. Along with this has come a significant reappraisal of the shared Ottoman Islamic past for many Turks and Arabs. While the post-Ottoman secular national elites in both Turkey and the Arab world sought to deprecate one another and their shared Ottoman past in order to foster a radically new basis of legitimacy and identity, their efforts never garnered deep popular support. As subsequent scholarly work by both Muslim and Western scholars has shown, the Ottoman state actually enjoyed until the very end the deep popular allegiance of Muslim (particularly urban) populations not only among Arab, Kurdish, and Turkish citizens of the empire but as far afield as North Africa, Central Asia, India, and the Malay Archipelago.[42] This resulted in part, of course, from Sultan Abdülhamid II's successful use of his renovated title "sultan-caliph." For most Muslims around the world, however, their avid interest in the survival and regeneration of the Ottoman state stemmed not from dynastic loyalty but from their realization that its extinction would mean the eclipse of Muslim power within the international system and their own subjugation or worse.[43]

Of course, such developments shaped by the ongoing legacy and impact of the Eastern and Jewish questions have not been universally welcomed, particularly among many Israelis and their supporters, who had long counted on Kemalist Turkey's alienation from the Muslim world to endure. Going back to David Ben-Gurion's peripheral strategy, Israel has long sought to keep the region weak and divided, while partnering with Western Great Powers and local ethnic or sectarian minorities. Increasingly, such a strategy and the fallout from Western military interventions in the region are viewed by Turks of all stripes as unacceptable threats to their own interests and region. The creation of Israel and the "Jewish question" were intimately linked for centuries as a *Schicksalsgemeinschaft* (community of fate) with the Ottoman Eastern/Muslim questions, however, which offers hope for reconciliation. A Turkey reconnected with its Ottoman Muslim heritage and leadership role in the region not only has the potential to serve as a successful model for democratic and socioeconomic development for the rest of the Muslim world but can also once again be the nucleus for achieving regional integration and peace, as in Europe after World War II. Most Turks today are proud of their history of having been the main historic haven for Jews fleeing ethnic cleansing from Iberia to Eastern Europe. While there is strong opposition to a far-right Likud agenda that seeks to crush the Palestinians and promote anti-Muslim bigotry in alliance with erstwhile Armageddon Evangelical allies in the United States, Turkish political parties across the spectrum accept the legitimacy of a Jewish state and its presence in the Middle East. They seek to achieve its peaceful integration into the region while also securing the legitimate rights of the Palestinians. While still far from certain, perhaps, such an enlightened rearticulation and reassessment of the structural/ideational variables represented by the Jewish and Eastern/Muslim questions may finally render them amenable to peaceful and just resolution. This would allow the Middle East/West Asia to emerge from the cauldron of systemic regional conflict, as Jean Monnet and Robert Schumann's European Community did in much of Europe.

NOTES

1. The Russian use of Orthodoxy and the Treaty of Küçük Kaynarja to undermine the Ottoman state is discussed in Barbara Jelavich, *Russia's Balkan Entanglements, 1806–1914.*

2. Henri Pirenne, *Muhammad and Charlemagne.*

3. A mixture of local converts and Arab settlers had given Sicily a Muslim majority by the time of the Norman conquests in the thirteenth century. In Muslim Spain or al-Andalus, Berbers, Arabs, and black Africans were actually minority elements in the population. The majority of inhabitants were Iberian converts to Islam, known as Muwalladun. Thus the point to keep in mind here as well as in the Balkans is that those being expelled were indigenous to Europe. After the Jews were expelled in 1492, the Inquisition against apostates who remained behind lasted from 1500 to 1609. Muslims were expelled in 1502 and the remainder forcibly Christianized

in 1526. The Edict of Philip III in 1609 led to the expulsion of over half a million Moriscos, who were still suspected of furtively practicing their religion. See James M. Powell, ed., *Muslims under Latin Rule, 1100–1300*.

4. Thierry Hentsch, *Imagining the Middle East*, back cover.

5. David Nirenberg, *Communities of Violence: Persecution of Minorities in the Middle Ages*, 5.

6. Ibid., 3.

7. Robert Melson, *Revolution and Genocide: On the Origins of the Armenian Genocide and the Holocaust*.

8. Zygmunt Bauman, *Modernity and the Holocaust*.

9. Omer Bartov, *Mirrors of Destruction*, 12, 29.

10. Oliver Bullough, *Let Our Fame Be Great: Journeys among the Defiant Peoples of the Caucasus*; Mujeeb R. Khan, "From Hegel to Genocide in Bosnia: Some Moral and Philosophical Concerns."

11. Mirko Grmek, Marc Gjidaram, and Niven Simac, *Le nettoyage ethnique: Documents historiques sur une idéologie serbe*, 23–26; also Stanford J. Shaw, *The Jews of the Ottoman Empire and the Turkish Republic*, 189.

12. Gary J. Bass, *Freedom's Battle: The Origins of Humanitarian Intervention*.

13. Samuel Huntington, "The Clash of Civilizations."

14. Iver B. Neumann and Jennifer M. Welsh, "The Other in European Self-Definition: An Addendum to the Literature on International Society."

15. Ibid., 330.

16. Timothy Snyder, *Bloodlands: Europe between Hitler and Stalin*.

17. Gladstone here was specifically referring to the Ottoman administration in "Turkey in Europe." On the ground little distinction was made between Turkish officials and Muslim civilians, however, and the lack of such distinction left moralistic crusaders like Gladstone largely unperturbed.

18. Kemal H. Karpat, *Ottoman Population, 1830–1914: Demographics and Social Characteristics*.

19. Ibid.; Kemal H. Karpat, "The Social and Political Foundations of Nationalism in South East Europe after 1878: A Reinterpretation," 385, (quotation).

20. The Slavic Muslims of Niş numbered 8,300 people, versus 10,000 Christians. By 1879 the Muslim population of the town had been reduced to 300 people. Karpat, "The Social and Political Foundations of Nationalism," 399.

21. Ibid., 398.

22. Ervin Staub, *The Roots of Evil: The Origins of Genocide and Other Group Violence*, 185.

23. Pioneering work on the topic of ethnic cleansing of Ottoman Muslims was done by Bilal N. Şimşir, *The Turks of Bulgaria (1878–1985)*; see also the original: *Rumeli'den Türk Göçleri*.

24. Mark Mazower, "Violence and the State in the 20th Century," note 9. Mazower also downplays the role of Israeli leaders such as David Ben-Gurion in directing the ethnic cleansing of Palestinians in 1948, seeking to blame it on the actions of local commanders. This contention is disproven in the book *The Ethnic Cleansing of Palestine* by the Israeli historian Ilan Pappé.

25. Bullough, *Let Our Fame Be Great*.

26. Karl Marx, "On the Jewish Question."

27. Allan Harris Cutler and Helen Elmquist Cutler, *The Jew as Ally of the Muslim: Medieval Roots of Anti-Semitism.*

28. Jonathan Klier Doyle, *Imperial Russia's Jewish Question, 1855–81.*

29. On a general diplomatic history of the Ottoman Eastern question, see M. S. Anderson, *The Eastern Question, 1774–1923: A Study in International Relations.*

30. Bauman, *Modernity and the Holocaust,* 71.

31. On the *Historikerstreit* and the role of Hitler, see Charles Maier, *The Unmasterable Past: History, Holocaust, and German National Identity.*

32. The standard intentionalist thesis is presented in Lucy Dawidowicz, *The War against the Jews.*

33. Christopher R. Browning, *The Path to Genocide: Essays on Launching the Final Solution,* 3–28, 86–125.

34. Bauman, *Modernity and the Holocaust,* 52.

35. I develop this thesis more fully in Mujeeb R. Khan, "The 'Other' in the Balkans: Historical Construction of 'Serbs' and 'Turks.'"

36. Cited in Rabia Ali and Lawrence Lifshultz, eds. *Why Bosnia?: Writings on the Balkan War,* xlvii.

37. See Mujeeb R. Khan, "Bosnia-Herzegovina and the Crisis of the Post–Cold War International System."

38. Taylor Branch, *The Clinton Tapes,* 9–10.

39. Emma Gilligan has recently documented the appalling atrocities committed by Russian forces against Chechen civilians. She is quite clear that Russia has waged the war in a quasi-genocidal fashion, motivated by ethnic and religious hatred against the Chechen Muslim population. She also underscores how this fact and the massive atrocities that prefigured the Chechen resort to terrorism have been downplayed in Western dealings with Moscow on the Chechen conflict. Emma Gilligan, *Terror in Chechnya: Russia and the Tragedy of Civilians in War.*

40. Wayne Madsen, "Did NSA Help Target Dudayev?"

41. For the first academic article predicting this Turkish reorientation resulting from democratization as well as the trauma of war and destruction in the Ottoman periphery, see M. Hakan Yavuz and Mujeeb R. Khan, "Turkish Foreign Policy and the Arab-Israeli Conflict: Dynamics of Duality."

42. C. Ernest Dawn, *From Ottomanism to Arabism: Essays on the Origins of Arab Nationalism.*

43. Cf. Mujeeb R. Khan, "External Threats and the Promotion of a Trans-national Islamic Consciousness: The Case of the Late Ottoman Empire and Contemporary Turkey."

PART II

The Emergence of
the Balkan State System

5

Muslim and Orthodox Resistance against the Berlin Peace Treaty in the Balkans

Mehmet Hacısalihoğlu

INTRODUCTION

The Treaty of Berlin led to different reactions by the population in the central and western Balkans. It radically changed the status quo of south-eastern Europe and affected different population groups in both a positive and negative manner. Several examples of armed reactions in the Balkans can be cited, as in Thrace, Macedonia, Albania, and Bosnia-Hercegovina. We cannot put all these cases in the same category, however; aside from the Treaty of Berlin, many other factors lay at the origins of these reactions. It would be more precise to see these cases as reactions against a series of developments in the 1870s, of which the Treaty of Berlin was one of the most important triggering factors.

Some of the revolts dealt with in this paper have been well researched in the national historiographies of the Balkan states.[1] The Albanian reaction to the Treaty of Berlin has been studied in detail, particularly in the context of the Albanian national movement. The revolts in Macedonia (in Kresna and Razlog) have also been well researched in the context of the Macedonian question in Bulgaria and Macedonia. The Muslim resistance in Thrace has not been explored much in scholarly writing, however, with the exception of some studies made in Turkey. This paper focuses on these three cases of resistance. Because of its limited scope, it does not cover the resistance in Bosnia and Hercegovina.

It is important to note that the Treaty of Berlin was the result of a series of revolts, wars, and even treaties in the Balkans, which have been called the "Eastern Question." The revolts in Hercegovina in 1875, the Serbo-Ottoman War of 1876, the Bulgarian revolt (the April Uprising) in

1876, the Russo-Ottoman War of 1877–78, and the Treaty of San Stefano on March 3, 1878, are the major developments that took place before the Treaty of Berlin. In all these cases the initiators were local powers. The Treaty of Berlin had to bring this "great crisis" to an end by creating a new order to bring stability to the Balkans. Therefore it has been seen as a turning point in the modern history of the Balkans. The initiators of this treaty were not the local powers but the Great Powers, which were controlling most of the world at that time. Therefore we must take into consideration that the Treaty of Berlin was not a local project of the Great Powers. It was a step within the scope of their broader project to establish a world order. Great Britain was the protector of the Ottoman Empire until this treaty. Although France and Great Britain had been in colonial competition with each other in the rest of the world, they were still able to come together in order to stop Russia in the Crimean War (1853–56). Interestingly, they did not manage to do the same twenty-four years later, during the War of 1877–78. They intervened only at the end of the war. This indicated rather conclusively that the British government was no longer interested in the protection of Ottoman territorial integrity.

The power structure in Europe was not the same as it had been during the 1850s. Only a few years before the Russo-Ottoman War, France had been defeated by Prussia in the War of 1870–71. The Prussian king declared himself emperor of Germany in the French imperial palace of Versailles in January 1871. Furthermore, the newly established German state occupied the French territory of Alsace-Lorraine. For France, the new German state became the most important threat and enemy. The emergence of Germany as a Great Power was an enormous challenge for the balance of powers in Europe. The leaders of the German unification under Bismarck tried to keep good relations with Russia in order to prevent any alliance between Russia and France. Hence in 1873 Germany, Russia, and Austria-Hungary formed the League of the Three Emperors. In 1878 Germany was the host of the congress in Berlin as a "neutral" power between Russia and England. Thus Germany delved into Great Power politics. The Treaty of Berlin brought not only a change in the status quo of the Balkans but also a new era of relations among the powers. Only one year later, in 1879, Germany made a treaty of alliance with Austria. In 1882 Italy joined this alliance. Within four years after the Treaty of Berlin, the Triple Alliance was completed. Consequently we can see the Congress of Berlin as a turning point in the relations of the Great Powers. At the same time, the regulations of this treaty had to balance the interests of the Great Powers in southeastern Europe.

The main question discussed here is whether and to what extent the Treaty of Berlin, which regulated the interests of the Great Powers, could respond to the expectations of the population groups in the Balkans. Other important avenues of discussion offer perspective on the reasons behind these reactions and on the role (if any) played by the Great Powers in the revolts through their consuls or agents. In many cases we know that the local insurrections in the Ottoman Balkans involved the neighboring countries or the Great Powers.

THE ALBANIAN REACTION TO THE TREATIES OF SAN STEFANO AND BERLIN

The Russian advance in the Balkans by defeating the Ottoman military forces affected the Muslim population of the peninsula negatively. A large number of Muslims migrated, and many of them were killed by the Russian military and Bulgarian volunteers. When Russian troops moved up to the Çatalca line and the Ottoman capital was threatened, the Ottoman government was forced to accept the peace conditions dictated by Russia. The Treaty of San Stefano, signed on March 3, 1878, made Serbia and Montenegro independent and established a new Bulgarian state. Some Ottoman territories with dominant Albanian populations were ceded to these Orthodox Balkan states. This provoked the reactions of the Albanians of Kosovo and Albania.

The weakness of the Ottoman government regarding Russia and the occupations led to reactions by the Albanian leaders and intellectuals. They established the Central Committee for the Defense of the Rights of the Albanian Nation (Komitet Qendror për Mbrojtjen e të Kombësisë Shqiptare). The committee made the following declaration on May 30, 1878: "We do not want anything except to live in peace with Montenegro, Serbia, Bulgaria, and Greece. We do not want or demand anything from them. But we are determined to hold what belongs to us. Albanian land must be left to the Albanians."[2] As a result of the opposition to the Treaty of San Stefano, the Albanian notables and intellectuals established the Albanian League (Lidhja Shqiptare) in Prizren on June 10, 1878.

Despite the Albanian reactions, the Treaty of Berlin did not bring any big change to the status of the occupied Albanian territories. The Albanians organized meetings and protested against the decisions of this treaty, demanding that the Ottoman government form an autonomous Albanian province (*vilayet*) including the *vilayet*s of Ioannina (Yanya), Skutari (Işkodra), Kosovo (Kosova), and Monastir (Manastır).[3]

For its part, the Ottoman government was not willing to fulfill the Albanian demands regarding the formation of an autonomous Albanian province. When the Ottoman representative in Berlin, Mehmet Ali Paşa, traveled to Prizren and Yakova (Gjakovë) in August–September 1878 in order to meet the representatives of the Albanian League, he was attacked and killed by the Albanian insurgents.[4] The government under Abdülhamid II pursued a policy of pacification toward the Albanian population. The demands of the Albanian League were perceived as separatist, however, and were rejected. The sultan sought to gain the trust of the Albanian notables by giving them privileges. But this was not enough to prevent the Albanian revolts that occurred during the implementation of the decisions of the Treaty of Berlin.

In the following decades the Albanian movement became one of the most important factors of the Macedonian question. In the beginning it was a defense movement against the ambitions of the neighboring states of Greece, Montenegro, Serbia, and Bulgaria in regard to the Albanian lands, but it increasingly transformed into a national movement against Ottoman rule.

The Balkan states, however, particularly Bulgaria and Serbia, perceived this Albanian reaction as a combined aggression by the sultan and the Albanians against the Christians in the Balkans. The newspaper *Pro Armenia*, supporting the Bulgarian aims in Macedonia, wrote in 1900: "The massacres of the Armenians were not sufficient for the Sultan. He is also preparing atrocities in Macedonia…. Indeed, like the Kurds and the Circassians in Armenia, he uses the Albanians in Macedonia."[5] According to the Bulgarian propaganda, the Albanians served the sultan as instruments (as *başıbozuk*s) to massacre the Christian Orthodox population in Macedonia. According to the same propaganda, the Orthodox population of Macedonia was Bulgarian.

Article 23 of the Treaty of Berlin foresaw the implementation of reforms in Macedonia by the Ottoman government. Nonetheless, the sultan was not willing to implement any radical reforms that would weaken his authority in the region.

The armed or revolutionary movements of the Exarchist (Bulgarian Church) groups in Macedonia, beginning at the end of the nineteenth century, called the attention of Austria-Hungary and Russia to the situation of the Orthodox population in the Ottoman lands. At the end of 1902 both governments prepared a reform program, the "Vienna Points" (Wiener Punktationen), and submitted it to the Ottoman government in February 1903. The Ottoman government accepted this reform program under the pressure of the Great Powers.[6] Among the articles of the program, for example, was the formation of the gendarmerie composed of Muslims and Christians according to their population shares.[7] This and other articles inflamed the Albanian resistance. They regarded this program as a step toward the occupation of the Albanian lands by the Balkan states.

Albanian nationalist Ekrem Bey Vlora gives the following comment on the reform programs:

> The central government in Istanbul decided also to implement these reforms in the three *vilayets* (governments) of Salonica, Bitola, and Kosovo under supervision of a General Inspector (Hüseyin Hilmi Paşa) without taking into consideration that two-thirds of these two last-mentioned provinces were inhabited by the Albanians, who had nothing in common with the mixture of people in Macedonia and who could stop the Greco-Bulgarian bands in their region without getting any help from the Turkish authorities. These measures terrified and irritated the Albanians. One million Albanians were put under a different regime, while another million Albanian people were divided by a corridor (Sandchak Elbasan, which belonged to Bitola). They resisted the implementation of these measures in the Albanian lands, because they were convinced that this implied a proposal to divide Albania according to interests of its enemies. The sentiments against the central authorities became really hostile. The Albanians rightly feared that these reforms would again lead to cession of the parts of the Albanian lands to Serbs, Bulgarians, and Greeks and succeeded in preventing any commingling with the Macedonian Question. These intrigues of certain European powers and their Balkan accomplices give evidence again that the Turks did not understand anything of their European possessions at all, and they became simply a cue ball in the hands of their enemies.[8]

The sultan appointed Ferit Paşa, an Albanian statesman, as grand vizier in order to break this resistance against the reform program. This did not pacify the armed Albanians. Only by using military force could Ferit Paşa overcome this resistance and begin the reform program in Albania.

A revolutionary Albanian Committee was established two years later, however, in 1905. It began taking armed action like the Bulgarian-Macedonian, Greek, and Serbian committees in Macedonia, which had

been active since the beginning of the century.[9] As a result we can state
that the Treaty of Berlin led to Albanian reactions that developed into a
national movement, which then aimed to establish an independent Albanian state.

THE KRESNA-RAZLOG REVOLT
OF THE ORTHODOX SLAVS IN MACEDONIA

The next group deeply influenced by the Treaty of Berlin was the Orthodox Slav population in Bulgaria, Thrace, and Macedonia. The first major
Bulgarian national revolt took place in 1876 (April Revolt). This revolt
was suppressed by the Ottoman authorities, but the Russo-Ottoman War
of 1877–78 resulted in the establishment of a Bulgarian state. According
to the Treaty of San Stefano, the new Bulgarian state extended from the
Danube to the Aegean, including the port of Kavala. Thrace and Macedonia were parts of a new Great Bulgaria. The treaty gave Russia an entry into
the Mediterranean Sea via Bulgaria. Indeed the new Bulgarian state was
occupied by Russia and could become a basis for further Russian operations. The Treaty of Berlin, however, changed this advantageous situation
for Russia. The European powers, particularly Great Britain, wanted to
secure the Mediterranean, protecting it from Russian interference. The
decisions in the Congress of Berlin were made on this basis. The most radical territorial change took place in the new Bulgaria. The northern part of
the Balkan mountains to the Danube became the Principality of Bulgaria,
with great autonomy. The southern part to Kırcaali became an autonomous province named Eastern Rumelia (Şarki Rumeli Vilayeti), whereas
Macedonia and Western Thrace were left for the Ottoman Empire. This
prevented the entry of Bulgaria, and indirectly Russia, into the Aegean.
Moreover, Great Britain occupied the island of Cyprus in order to secure
control in the eastern Mediterranean and the route to India.

The defeat of the Ottoman Empire and the Russian occupation were
welcomed by a part of the Orthodox Slav population in Macedonia and
Thrace. Still, the decisions of the Congress of Berlin, according to which
the territories occupied by Russia were given back to the Ottoman Empire,
were very disappointing, at least for a part of the Orthodox Slav population of the region. Many of them had been engaged into the War of 1877–
78 as volunteers against Ottoman rule. The Treaty of Berlin caused revolts
among this part of the population. The most famous were the Kresna and
Razlog (Razlık) Revolts in northern Macedonia in 1878, close to the borders of the Principality of Bulgaria.[10]

These revolts were characterized as national uprisings in both Bulgarian and Macedonian historiographies. Bulgarian historiography regards them as a Bulgarian national uprising against Turkish rule. According to this view, the Bulgarian population of the region wanted to be unified with Bulgaria. The revolts against the Ottoman rule in 1878 usually have been described under the heading "Resistance to the Decisions of the Congress of Berlin."[11] A Bulgarian historian offers the following description of how the Orthodox population perceived the Treaty of San Stefano:

> The liberation of Bulgaria from the five-hundred-year-old Turkish yoke is one of the happiest events in the history of the Bulgarian folk [*narod*].... the signing of the San Stefano Peace Treaty was perceived by the Bulgarian folk with great enthusiasm, with deep and true gratefulness. The expressions of this were numerous demonstrations and letters to the representatives of the Russian military and civil authorities on the day of the signing of the Treaty.... The happiness of the Bulgarian folk was short, however.[12]

His description of the Treaty of Berlin offers a sharp contrast: "So the Congress of Berlin dismembered the Bulgarian state. It left under the yoke of the Sultan's rule a big part of the Bulgarian population." The Treaty of Berlin is also called the "Dictate of Berlin." Under the title "The Kresna-Razlog Uprising" we read: "The decisions of the Congress of Berlin were perceived by the Bulgarian folk with pangs and outrage. In all Bulgarian lands a large resistance movement was posed to fight against the unjust decisions."[13]

Macedonian historiography, however, has characterized this as a national Macedonian uprising not only against the Turkish rule but also against the Bulgarian aspirations. According to this view, the rebels aimed to establish an independent state of Macedonia:

> [The Kresna Uprising] was the largest and the longest uprising against the Turkish rule in Macedonia during the Eastern Crisis.... The Kresna Uprising took place at a time when Macedonia was in a serious political situation after the Congress of Berlin and was subjected to ruthless pressure and direct interventions by the political representatives of the Bulgarian conservative bourgeoisie whose purpose was to use the uprising toward the establishing of a "Greater" or "San Stefano" Bulgaria [in the Balkans]. On the contrary, the rebels fought for an independent development of the

uprising and the creation of Macedonian state within or outside of Turkey. These two opposite streams caused conflicts with heavy consequences on the development of the uprising and brought about its easy crushing by the Osmanli-Turkish arm. The crush of the uprising had far-reaching and heavy consequences on the later national and political development of the Macedonian nation.[14]

Although the Bulgarian and the Macedonian interpretations of these revolts are contradictory in describing the people's identity (Bulgarian or Macedonian) and the enemy (Turks or Turks and Bulgarians), they share the notion that the Treaty of Berlin caused this armed resistance of the Orthodox Slav population.

The leaders of this revolt were the so-called voivods (*voyvoda*) from the districts Petrič and Melnik, who were organized by Adam Kalmikov, a Russian Cossack officer, for armed resistance to the cession of the region to the Ottoman Empire. The insurgents joined by the rural population attacked the Ottoman military base in Kresna in October 1878. By defeating the Ottoman posts in the region, they occupied the right side of the river Struma. The Bulgarian Orthodox population of villages such as Kresna, Oštava, Mečkul, Senokos, Osikov, and Vrabča took an active part in this revolt against the Ottoman authorities. The regular troops of the Ottoman Empire suppressed the revolt in December 1878. Many insurgents took refuge in Bulgaria. At about the same time an armed group of 376 men from Cuma-i Bala (Gorna Džumaya) attacked the town of Bansko on November 8, 1878. The Ottoman forces, consisting of 50 men, were defeated and killed. Neighboring villages such as Dolna Draglitsa, Gorna Draglitsa, Godlevo, and Dobarsko began to revolt. They attacked the Pomak village Banya. They also decided to attack Mehomiya (Razlog), but the Ottoman forces countered the insurgents. The revolt was suppressed within seven days.[15]

In the course of the suppression of the revolts, many Christians in the villages involved in the revolt fled to Bulgaria, mostly to Dubnica, a city close to the Ottoman borders. Although the majority were given amnesty by the Ottoman government and returned to their homes, a group of them remained in Bulgaria. In retrospect, these migrants were an important core that later evolved into a revolutionary movement against the Ottoman Empire in Macedonia. The famous revolutionary leader Yane Sandanski, for example, was the son of an émigré family from the village of Vlahi in the District of Melnik.[16]

The Kresna-Razlog Revolt was the first armed reaction of the Orthodox population of Macedonia against the Treaty of Berlin. Later revolts and revolutionary movements followed this initial revolt. After the establishment of revolutionary organizations, the first big revolt took place in the district of Cuma-i Bala (close to the Bulgarian borders), in September 1902. One year later Macedonia experienced a great revolt, the so-called Ilinden Uprising, which provoked the interference of the Great Powers in favor of the Christian population through the Mürzsteg Reform Program. The Ottoman government was forced to implement these reforms in Macedonia under the inspection of the representatives of the European powers.

These revolts or revolutionary movements indeed cannot be explained as direct resistance movements against the Treaty of Berlin, but we can categorize them as resistance movements against the status quo created by the treaty. Article 23 of the treaty, however, was the basis of their demands for reforms.

As is well known, this process ended with the Balkan Wars in 1912–13, in which the Balkan states defeated the Ottoman Empire and divided Macedonia between themselves.[17]

THE RESISTANCE OF THE
MUSLIM POPULATION IN THRACE

Tevfik Bıyıklıoğlu has done the most detailed research on the resistance of the Muslim inhabitants of Thrace after the Russo-Ottoman War of 1877–78.[18] He dedicates approximately ten pages to the Muslim resistance in Thrace against the Treaty of San Stefano, characterizing it as the "first Turkish national struggle for freedom." He views this revolt as the source of the "Turkish National Struggle" after World War I.[19] According to Bıyıklıoğlu, the Muslims of the region benefited from the fight against injustice and oppression and formed a provisional government. It was the first time in history that ideas such as nationality, freedom, and resistance to oppression were adopted en masse and expanded into a national movement among the Turks of Eastern Rumelia and the Rhodopes.

This Turkish national movement became a tradition and continued during the following decades. During the annexation of Eastern Rumelia by the Principality of Bulgaria in 1885, the Muslim deputies of the parliament of Filibe (Plovdiv) attempted to meet as a separate parliament.[20] After the Balkan Wars the Muslims of the region formed the Provisional

Turkish Government of Western Thrace (September 1913). In November 1918, following World War I, the Muslims established the Association of Thrace and Paşaeli.[21]

Though Bıyıklıoğlu views the resistance to the Russian-Bulgarian occupation as being the source of all Turkish national movements, this topic of Turkish history has yet to be studied in detail. The Turkish War of Independence overshadowed the Balkan Wars among modern Turkish historians, so it is not surprising that the local resistance movements could not arouse interest.[22]

Maria Todorova notes that the role of the Rhodope Muslims in the suppression of the Bulgarian revolt of 1876 and their movement to resist the Bulgarian authorities is a subject "less known and reluctantly dealt with" in Bulgarian historiography.[23]

The military character of Muslim inhabitants in Thrace became popular before the Russo-Turkish War of 1877–78, during the suppression of the Bulgarian Uprising. Rupços, the southern subdistrict of the district Filibe (Plovdiv), was populated by the Pomaks, Slavic-speaking Muslims who identified themselves with the Muslim Ottoman rule. During the Ottoman rule in the region, they sometimes acted as volunteers in the operations of the Ottoman army (usually referred to as *başıbozuk*s or "Bashi-Bazouks" in Western sources). The Pomak volunteers played an important role, especially during the oppression of the April Uprising. They were then accused of committing massacres in the Bulgarian villages. The well-known Batak Massacre (Bataşkoto Klane) was carried out by Pomak volunteers under the leadership of a man called Ahmed Ağa.[24]

The Batak Massacre and the myths surrounding it have an important place in Bulgarian national consciousness.[25] But Bulgarian historiographers usually do not emphasize the Pomaks as the committers of the "massacre," preferring to describe this incident as an act of Turkish cruelty. They regard the Pomaks as "Bulgarians of Muslim faith," and a case of Bulgarians massacring Bulgarians is difficult to explain within the logic of national history writing. Bulgarian historiography has preferred to conceal the Pomaks and point fingers at "Turks" or "fanatical Muslims," as they were also called.[26] Interestingly, within Turkish historiography, Bıyıklıoğlu also does not emphasize the role of the Pomaks in these historical processes, which he calls a "Turkish national movement."[27]

The Pomak villagers and the Turks in Western Thrace resisted the Russian occupation fiercely during the War of 1877–78.[28] When the Ottoman government signed the Treaty of San Stefano on March 3, 1878, the area, including the Rhodope Mountains, was given to the new Bulgarian state.

The Muslim Pomaks showed resistance to the occupation of the region beginning in April 1878, centered in the Pomak villages of the Rupços sub-district, the villages in the southern part of Tatarpazarcık district, Turkish villages in the southern part of the Hasköy district, the villages of the Çirmen and Ortaköy districts, and the mountainous district of Sultanyeri. The Russian army tried to break this resistance by attacking the region with machine guns, regular troops, and Cossacks. Despite great losses, however, the Russian army could not gain control over the Rhodopes. The resistance movement extended south to the neighboring district of Gümülcine (Komotini).[29] The British consul of Adrianople describes the reasons for this Muslim resistance:

> All accounts agree as to the causes of its origin, namely, the intolerable oppression of the Russo-Bulgarian régime, whose characteristics continue to be the same now when a civil government is organized, as they were at first, when the excesses committed might with some plausibility have been attributed to the confusion entailed by the movement of a victorious army. It was the attempt to carry out in the hill districts the same pitiless system of spoliation and outrage as elsewhere — by disarming the Mussulman inhabitants and then leaving them to the mercy of Bulgarians — that brought the movement to a head.[30]

The consul reports the following example for his statement:

> It was only a day or two before it broke out that the two Turkish villages of Tchirmen-Karagatch and Bildir-Kioi, near Tchirmen, were thus treated. The inhabitants were stripped of everything, even to their very shoes, and two married women and one girl were carried off from the latter village. The father of the girl gave proof of growing exasperation by shooting the ravisher [to] death with a pistol which he had concealed. The Bulgarian, with characteristic cupidity, had offered to forego possession of the girl on payment of 4,000 piastres, a sum which the father did not possess.[31]

The consul argues that this kind of treatment provoked the armed resistance of the Muslim population in that region. When the Russians reminded the Muslim guerrillas of Sultanyeri of the Treaty of San Stefano, according to which the Muslims had to give up their arms, they gave the following reply: "We neither recognize your authority nor that of the

Porte."[32] In this way they made it clear that they did not recognize the Treaty of San Stefano.

According to the reports of the consul, the Muslim guerrillas also included Circassians, Albanians, and men wearing Ottoman uniforms as well as 100,000 Muslim fugitives.[33]

The leaders of this movement were of different origins. In the Rhodopes one of the leaders of the insurgents was a local leader by the name of Hacı İsmail. The other one was an Englishman, Saint Clair ("Senclair" in Bıyıklıoğlu/also "Sinclair"), who was named among the volunteers as Hidayet Bey or Hidayet Paşa. The movement also had other local leaders.[34] Because an Englishman played a leading role in this resistance movement, Valeri Stoyanov describes it as a "resistance movement, inspired by England and the Sublime Porte."[35] He writes that it was "a movement led by British officers, headed by former consul of Varna and Burgas — D. B. Sent-Kler (Hidayet Paša)."[36] Turkish historiography does not emphasize the role of England in this resistance movement. Considering Britain's interests in the region, we can assume that the British government was in favor of a Muslim resistance to Russian occupation. But the British role does not seem to be as dominant as Bulgarian historians have suggested.

On May 4 and 16, 1878, the resistance leaders sent a memorandum to the embassies of the states that had signed the Treaty of Paris.[37] The memorandum, signed by the insurgents as *hükümet-i muvakkate* (the provisional government), declares:

> The European states have to examine why the people under our temporary administration took up arms. We did not rebel against any person. The only reason that we took up arms is to defend our property, lives, and honor. We did not rebel against any legal government. In defending our personal rights we used our most natural rights. The Treaty of San Stefano is invalid so long as the states that signed the Treaty of Paris do not ratify it. Instead of San Stefano a new treaty must be made. The Bulgarian atrocities are huge and indescribable. We cannot tolerate any armed forces advancing to our outstations. The population of our region is completely Turkish and Muslim; furthermore there are a hundred thousand Muslim fugitives among us.[38]

The leaders also described the reason for the establishment of a provisional government:

After the Treaty of San Stefano, Russians and Bulgarians invaded our lands. We were left without government. Although the
Ottoman government left us to the Bulgarian principality, we cannot accept the Bulgarian government as a legal government as long
as the European states did not recognize it. Everywhere they went,
the Russians and Bulgarians committed innumerable atrocities
and unbelievable murders. We took up arms in order to defend
ourselves against the aggressors.[39]

The memorandum ended:

We strongly protest against the Treaty of San Stefano.... We request you not to give any piece of land on the southwestern part of
Maritza to the new Bulgaria, because four million Muslims under
our government would prefer to die instead of obeying a government that stained its name with indescribable murders and that has
always been our enemy.[40]

The British consul of Adrianople, however, reported attacks by Muslim
insurgents against the Bulgarian villagers in the Rhodopes, forcing them to
flee. In particular the Pomaks in Rupços destroyed the Bulgarian village of
Dospat and other villages above Batak in the district of Tatarpazarcık. The
centers of the Muslim movement were the villages of Leskova, Mihalkova,
and Devlen, near the Krıçma (Kričma) River in Rupços. They attacked
the Bulgarian villages of Rahovo, Babalsko, and Çiralsko, forcing their
inhabitants to flee to Stanimaka.[41] These clashes in Rupços proved that the
Treaty of San Stefano caused an ethnic-religious war between the Muslim
and Christian populations in Western Thrace.

The number of armed Muslim mountaineers in the area of Tatarpazarcık, Filibe, and Hasköy was estimated to be 30,000.[42] An Ottoman-Russian
commission tried to pacify the Muslim population of the Rhodope districts in May 1878; but in response the Muslim insurgents said that "so
long as the Porte is, as at present, necessarily powerless to afford them
valid protection they must hold themselves free to disobey its injunctions,
and continue to defend their lives and property and the honor of their
families."[43]

According to a decision made on July 11, 1878, during the negotiations
in Berlin, a commission was formed to examine the situation of fugitives.
The commission visited Kırcaali on August 3–4 and Karatarla on August 5.

Its report on August 27, 1878, described the Russian and Bulgarian atrocities against the Muslim population and fugitives in detail.[44]

Bıyıklıoğlu claims that the echoes of this Muslim resistance in Thrace influenced the revision of the Treaty of San Stefano.[45]

According to the Treaty of Berlin, the main parts of the Rhodope districts were left under the Ottoman Empire. But the center of the Pomak resistance — the Rupços subdistrict — became a part of the province of Eastern Rumelia. The Pomak inhabitants of Rupços rejected the idea of joining this province and continued their resistance movement, because they regarded Eastern Rumelia as an extension of the Bulgarian or Russian occupation. The Ottoman government signed the cession of this region to Eastern Rumelia, so they could not expect any Ottoman support. Consequently they declared themselves to be an independent administration: some fifty villages began to act as a separate state, paying no taxes to Eastern Rumelia or to the Ottoman government. The same took place in Kırcaali, where the population resisted the provincial administration.[46]

In 1880 the representatives of the province of Eastern Rumelia and the Muslims of Kırcaali and Rupços agreed that only Muslim officers would be appointed for the administration of both districts. The provincial government tried to disarm the Muslim population of the Rhodopes, however, so the resistance movement continued.

The Ottoman government was asked to convince the Pomak inhabitants to obey the provincial government, but this mediation was unsuccessful. According to a report prepared on August 5, 1881, sixteen villages in Rupços were refusing to obey the provincial government (see table 5.1).

The report mentioned the following names as the notables from the disobeying villages, who were mostly opposing the unification of their district with the province: "Haci Hasan from Trigrad, Eyub Hoca from Musla, Haci Mehmed from Beden, Hacioğlu Ahmed Ağa from Breze, Mahmud oglu Eyub Ağa from Trigrad, İsmail Ağa from Tamraş (originally from Beden) or Kır Ağası İsmail, brother of Ahmed Ağa, 'the well-known hero of the destruction of Perushtitza.'"[47]

When the Bulgarians proclaimed the annexation of the province of Eastern Rumelia in 1885, Serbia declared war. The Ottoman government also protested against this annexation. At this time Bulgaria sent a delegation to Istanbul to negotiate with the Ottoman government. In January 1886 it was agreed that the Ottoman government should relinquish its right to occupy and to defend the borders of Eastern Rumelia (article 15 of the Treaty of Berlin); in return Bulgaria accepted the cession of Kırcaali and Rupços to the Ottoman administration. This agreement was also con-

TABLE 5.1. Villages in Rupçoz District That Refused to Obey the Provincial Government

NUMBER	NAME	NUMBER OF HOUSEHOLDS	NUMBER OF INHABITANTS	RELIGION	ORIGIN
1	Breze	130	1,050	Muslim	Slavic
2	Beden	120	950	Muslim	Slavic
3	Leskovo	80	700	Muslim	Slavic
4	Mihalkovo	100	850	Muslim	Slavic
5	Çurukovo	80	650	Muslim	Slavic
6	Tamraş	200	1,232	Muslim	Slavic
7	Çereçevo	28	113	Muslim	Slavic
8	Petvar	28	153	Muslim	Slavic
9	Osikovo	60	350	Muslim	Slavic
10	Nastan	70	350	Muslim	Slavic
11	Giovren (Gökviran)	32	145	Muslim	Slavic
12	Grahotna	30	140	Muslim	Slavic
13	Balaban	210	1,950	Muslim	Slavic
14	Trigrad	300	2,400	Muslim	Slavic
15	Mugla	320	1,000	Muslim	Slavic
16	Köstencik	50	4,560	Muslim	Slavic
Total		1,838	13,283 [corrected as] 12,483*		

Source: Report of D. H. Mitoff, August 5, 1881, FO 195/1366.
* Totals as in the original table (actual total 16,593).

firmed by the Great Powers in the Conference of Istanbul on April 5, 1886. The borders of these districts were to be drawn by a mixed commission. In May and June of 1886 a commission consisting of Bulgarian and Ottoman officers determined the borders between the Ottoman administration and Eastern Rumelia (which became a part of Bulgaria).[48]

Rupços was formed as a district within the Vilayet Selanik (Salonika), while Kırcaali became a district of the Vilayet Edirne (Adrianople).[49]

During the First Balkan War this region was occupied by the Bulgarian state. The Ottoman government organized a resistance movement in 1913 but left the region to Bulgaria after an agreement was reached by the

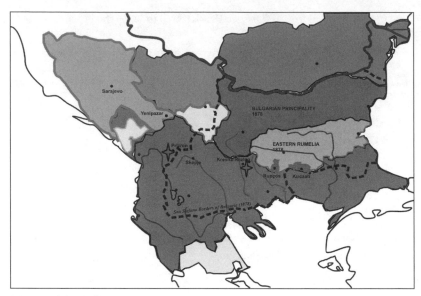

MAP 5.1. The Balkans in 1878

two governments. Despite the agreements, the Muslim inhabitants experienced severe oppression by the Bulgarian administration, and a significant portion of them migrated to the Ottoman state.

The Bulgarian government punished the Pomak population of Rupços in 1913 by forcing them to convert to Christianity and by changing their personal names.[50]

CONCLUSION

When we look at the respective cases in detail we see that two of the resistance movements began before the Treaty of Berlin: the Albanian resistance and the resistance of the Muslims in Thrace. These resistance movements were aimed at the Russian occupation and the Treaty of San Stefano. But they continued after the Treaty of Berlin, which makes it possible also to categorize them as movements established to resist that treaty. We see that the decisions of the Congress of Berlin did not satisfy the Albanians and an important part of the Muslims (Turks and Pomaks) of Thrace, even if its decisions were much more favorable for them than the regulations of San Stefano.

The revolts of Kresna and Razlog in Macedonia were directed against the Treaty of Berlin. Although the Treaty of Berlin adopted the greater part of the decisions of the Treaty of San Stefano, some regions with Orthodox population were left to the Ottoman Empire. This provoked revolts among the Orthodox Christians, who saw Russia as their savior.

Another aspect of these resistance movements is that Britain and Russia were also involved in these revolts to some extent. The organizer of the revolts of the Orthodox Slavs was a Russian Cossack, and one of the leaders of the Muslim resistance in Thrace was an Englishman (Saint Clair).

Although these three cases are far too complicated to be categorized as merely representing resistance to the Treaty of Berlin, they nevertheless make it clear that the treaty could not meet the expectations of the various ethnic and religious communities or organizations in the Ottoman Balkans. Dissatisfaction among the Muslim and Christian populations led to armed movements and revolts. This confirms the view that the Treaty of Berlin was hardly an attempt to solve national problems in the Balkans; rather, it was mostly an attempt to balance the interests of the Great Powers in Europe.

NOTES

1. In the national historiographies in the Balkans the revolts against Ottoman rule have usually been described as "uprisings" or "revolutions" and as liberation struggles of the repressed people against the Turkish oppressors or against the "Turkish yoke."

2. Peter Bartl, *Die albanischen Muslime zur Zeit der nationalen Unabhängigkeitsbewegung* (1878–1912), 117.

3. Peter Bartl, *Albanian: Vom Mittelalter bis zur Gegenwart*, 94–99; idem, *Die Albanischen Muslime*, 115–29; Fikret Adanır, *Die Makedonische Frage: Ihre Entstehung und Entwicklung bis 1908*, 85.

4. Stavro Skendi, *The Albanian National Awakening, 1878–1912*, 57–58.

5. "Les massacres d'Arméniens ne suffisent pas au Sultan: il prépare aussi des tueries en Macédoine.... En attendant, comme les Kurdes et Tcherkesses en Arménie, on lâche les Arnautes en Macédoine." P. Quillard, "Nouvelles d'Orient," *Pro Armenia* 1 (November 25, 1900): 8.

6. Adanır, *Die Makedonische Frage*, 159.

7. Atanas Schopoff, *Les réformes et la protection des Chrétiens en Turquie, 1673–1904*, 571–74; Mihajlo Minoski, *Politikata na Avstro-Ungarija sprema Makedonija i Makedonskoto prošanje (1878–1903)*, 265ff.

8. Ekrem Bey Vlora, *Lebenserinnerungen*, 149–50.

9. Bartl, *Die albanischen Muslime*, 151–52; Mehmet Hacısalihoğlu, *Die Jungtürken und die Mazedonische Frage, 1890–1918*, 144.

10. Dojno Doynov, *Kresnensko-Razloškoto Vȧstanie*, 37ff. In Macedonian historiography this revolt is interpreted as an independence movement of the Macedonian nation against Ottoman rule. See Mihailo Apostolski et al., eds., *Kresnenskoto Vostanie, 1878–1879*.

11. Stojan Germanov, *Makedoniya: Istoriya i Političeskata Sȧdba*, 231.

12. Ibid.

13. Ibid., 232, 234.

14. Manol Pandevski, "Kresnenskoto vostanie vo Makedonija od 1878–1879 godina: Predpostavki, nadvoreshno vlijanie, tek, karakter," 27–57 (English summary on 57).

15. Hristo Silyanov, *Osvoboditelnite Borbi na Makedoniya*, 15–16.

16. For a biography of Sandanski, see Mersiya Makdermot, *Za Svoboda i Săvăršensto: Biografiya na Yane Sandanski*.

17. For more information, see Kathrin Boeckh, *Von den Balkankriegen zum Ersten Weltkrieg: Kleinstaatenpolitik und ethnische Selbstbestimmung auf dem Balkan*; and Hacısalihoğlu, *Die Jungtürken und die Mazedonische Frage*, 367–78.

18. Tevfik Bıyıklıoğlu, *Trakya'da Millî Mücadele*.

19. Ibid., 1:19–31 (quotations on 23, 26).

20. Bıyıklıoğlu gives more information about this attempt: ibid., 1:54.

21. Ibid., 1:23.

22. Only a few studies on the resistance of the Muslims in the Rhodopes have been published by Turkish historians. See particularly Ömer Turan, *The Turkish Minority in Bulgaria (1878–1908)*, 155–63; and idem, "Rodoplarda 1878 Türk-Pomak Direnişi ve Rodop Komisyonu Raporu."

23. Maria Todorova, "Identity (Trans)formation among Bulgarian Muslims," 471–510 (quotation on 475).

24. Mehmet Hacısalihoğlu, *Doğu Rumeli'de Kayıp Köyler: İslimye Sancağı'nda 1878'den Günümüze Göçler, İsim Değişiklikleri ve Harabeler*, 42–43. Ahmed Ağa and his companions, who participated in the suppression of the Bulgarian revolt, were then sentenced to imprisonment for life in a fortress. See British Consular Report, Adrianople, June 25, 1877, National Archives of the United Kingdom (formerly Public Record Office), Foreign Office Archives, London (FO), FO 195/1136.

25. For a recent discussion on Batak, which caused tension in Bulgaria, see Martina Baleva and Ulf Brunnbauer, *Batak kato Mjasto na Pametta: Izložba/Batak, ein bulgarischer Erinnerungsort: Ausstellung*. For an earlier revision of the claims and exaggerations regarding the incident of Batak, see Richard Millman, "The Bulgarian Massacres Reconsidered." For further discussion and revision of the same case, see chapter 17 in this volume. See also Turan, *The Turkish Minority in Bulgaria*, 47–54.

26. For a discussion of this question, see Alexander Vezenkov, "Die neue Debatte über das Massaker von Batak: Historiographische Aspekte," 119–20 (there is also a Bulgarian version of the same article). See also Ulf Brunnbauer, "Ethnische Landschaften: Batak als Ort des Erinnerns und Vergessens" (also in Bulgarian).

27. Bıyıklıoğlu, *Trakya'da*, 19–31.

28. For a description of the Muslim resistance, see Mahir Aydın, *Şarkî Rumeli Vilayeti*, 22–23.

29. British consular report from Adrianople, No. 7, April 20, 1878, FO 195/1184.

30. Ibid.

31. Ibid.

32. Ibid.

33. British Consular Report from Adrianople, No. 8, April 24, 1878, FO 195/1184.

34. Bıyıklıoğlu, *Trakya'da*, 1:26–28.

35. Valeri Stoyanov, *Turskoto Naselenie v Bǎlgariya Meždu Polyusite na Etničeskata Politika*, 63.
36. Ibid. Maria Todorova shares the same view regarding the role of Saint Clair, former consul of Varna and Burgas and volunteer in the Ottoman army, and claims that the British Embassy in Constantinople actively supported the movement. Todorova, "Identity (Trans)formation among Bulgarian Muslims," 475.
37. Aydın, *Şarkî Rumeli*, 23.
38. Bıyıklıoğlu, *Trakya'da*, 1:22.
39. Ibid.
40. Ibid., 1:23.
41. British Consular Report from Adrianople, No. 12, May 2, 1878, FO 195/1184.
42. Ibid.
43. British Consular Report from Adrianople, No. 14, May 11, 1878, FO 195/1184.
44. Bıyıklıoğlu, *Trakya'da*, 1:26–28. For the text of the report in French and its Turkish translation, see Turan, "Rodoplarda 1878 Türk-Pomak Direnişi," 144–56.
45. Bıyıklıoğlu, *Trakya'da*, 1:30–31.
46. Ibid., 1:42–43.
47. Report of D. H. Mitoff, August 5, 1881, FO 195/1366.
48. Bıyıklıoğlu, *Trakya'da*, 1:56–60.
49. For the administrative development of these districts, see Hans-Jürgen Kornrumpf, *Die Territorialverwaltung im östlichen Teil der europäischen Türkei vom Berliner Kongress (1878) bis zu den Balkankriegen (1912/13) nach amtlichen osmanischen Veröffentlichungen*, 67, 84–85.
50. Stoyanov, *Turskoto Naselenie v Bǎlgariya Meždu Polyusite na Etničeskata Politika*; Velichko Georgiev and Stajko Trifonov, *Pokrǎstvaneto na Bǎlgarite Mohamedani 1912–1913: Dokumenti*. For a contemporary report on the forced Christianization of the Pomaks, see Ahmet Akgün, "Bulgaristan'da Asimilasyon ve 'Zavallı Pomaklar' Adlı Bir Risale." See also Turan, "Rodoplarda 1878 Türk-Pomak Direnişi," 140.

6

The Establishment of Serbian Local Government in the Counties of Niš, Vranje, Toplica, and Pirot after the Congress of Berlin

Miroslav Svirčević

INTRODUCTION

Serbia acquired independence as a result of the wars of liberation against the Ottoman Empire in 1876–78 and decisions of the Congress of Berlin in 1878, although its sovereignty was limited. The Treaty of Berlin stipulated six significant obligations for the internationally recognized Principality of Serbia, which had to be fulfilled by the newly established Serbian government. First, it established the effective constitutional equality of all citizens regardless of their religion. Second, Serbia did not have a right to collect any transit fee for goods that were transported through its territory. Third, Serbia did not have a right either to change the legal regime of concessions established for foreign citizens or to alter consular jurisdictions until they were changed by special agreement between Serbia and concerned countries. Fourth, commercial contracts signed between the Ottoman Empire and other countries could not be independently changed by the Serbian government; Serbia was obliged to carry out these contracts until new agreements were made with these countries. Fifth, Serbia was obliged to respect the property rights of *sipahi*s (Ottoman feudal lords) and other Muslim landowners in the former Ottoman territory that was annexed to it. Sixth, Serbia had to take over all Ottoman obligations toward the Austro-Hungarian Society for Exploitation of Railways in European Turkey.

The Treaty of Berlin considerably expanded Serbian territory and increased its population by 299,640.[1] The major towns of the newly liberated areas were Niš, Pirot, Vranje, Leskovac, Prokuplje, and Kuršumlija. The so-called New Areas (*novi krajevi*) were given their final legal shape under a special law.[2] They consisted of the counties of Niš, Vranje, Pirot, and Toplica.[3] The process of establishing the state administration and local government as well as incorporating the newly liberated areas into the legal system of prewar Serbia took five years (1877–82). It was a complex process, fraught with many difficulties. The intention was to bring stability to a backward feudal milieu marked by a volatile political situation, a specific population allocation in these areas, high population density, intense migratory movements, ethnic and religious tensions, and a very low level of economic development. Serbia also had to fulfill the obligations stipulated by the Berlin Treaty noted above. Establishing the state administration and local government in the New Areas was thus a threefold process: (1) legal organization of new local institutions, (2) regulation of agrarian relationships, and (3) colonization of the liberated areas.[4] This paper is devoted to these questions.

THE LEGAL ORGANIZATION OF NEW LOCAL INSTITUTIONS

The Second Serbo-Turkish War broke out on December 1, 1877, and resulted in significant successes within several weeks. Russia started a war against the Ottoman Empire in April 1877 and emerged victorious in January 1878. Excluding other participants in the war, the two sides negotiated a new political situation in the Balkans and signed the Treaty of San Stefano on March 3, 1878. The Ottomans had to accept the creation of an autonomous Principality of Bulgaria controlled by Russia — in fact, a "Greater Bulgaria" as an instrument of Russia's domination in the Balkans.[5]

The Serbian army liberated large areas in the Južna Morava and Nišava river valleys, virtually the entire area of southeastern Serbia. By the time a peace treaty between Russia and the Ottoman Empire was signed at San Stefano, the provisional Serbian authorities controlled the towns and villages of Niš, Prokuplje, Kuršumlija, Leskovac, Vlasotince, Bela Palanka, Pirot, Kula, Gramada, Belogradčik, Caribrod (modern-day Dimitrovgrad), Ginci, Dragoman, Slivnica, Breznik, Trn, Radomir, Klisura, Bosiljgrad, Vranje, Trgovište, Bujanovac, Preševo, Gnjilane, Kamenica, and Novo Brdo as well as the areas of the monasteries of Gračanica (in Kosovo) and Prohor Pčinjski (in Pčinja). The Serbian army had also penetrated close to Priština, Kumanovo, and Kriva Palanka; volunteer units fighting under its command apparently even entered Kustendil (medieval Velbužd).[6]

According to the decisions of the Great Powers at the Congress of Berlin, a portion of the territory that the Serbian army had seized was assigned to the Principality of Bulgaria (Kula, Gramada, Belogradčik, Caribrod, Ginci, Dragoman, Slivnica, Breznik, Trn, Radomir, and Bosiljgrad with its environs) and a portion was restored to the Ottoman Empire (Priština, Kumanovo, Kriva Palanka, Gnjilane, Lab District with Podujevo, and the Bujanovac-Preševo area with Upper Pčinja). At the same time, Serbian rule began to be established in the internationally recognized areas. First, many experienced officials serving in prewar Serbia were sent to the newly liberated areas with the powers of county prefects to exercise their authority in the provisionally constituted territorial units. They were followed by other officials (such as magistrates, notaries, and local treasury officers) to assist in establishing the new local government in accordance with Serbia's state policy.[7]

A project for establishing local government in the areas to be liberated had been created in late 1875, simultaneously with Serbia's war plan (but could not be carried out because Serbia suffered defeat in its first war against the Ottoman Empire in 1876). This may be inferred from a military report on Serbia's armaments dated 1875,[8] which also contained instructions for provisional institutions and officials and fixed the boundaries between the military powers of the Supreme Administration and the civil powers of the Auxiliary Administration.[9]

The main role in establishing civil government was assigned to the very skillful minister of education and religious affairs, Alimpije Vasiljević.[10] As the government's representative in the Supreme Army Command, he was authorized to issue a range of legislation necessary to establish the first domestic local institutions in the liberated areas. Vasiljević was assisted by the highest-ranking military representatives, such as the head of the General Staff and the commander of the division responsible for the ongoing military operations. Serbia started implementing its war plan related to civil-military separation as early as December 1877. With the war still underway, however, the main duty of the civilian authorities was to collect clothes and food for the army.[11]

The process of establishing domestic civil government in the New Areas and incorporating them into the legal system of prewar Serbia passed through two phases: the establishment of provisional local institutions and the establishment of permanent local institutions on the model of those already existing in the Principality of Serbia. The first phase lasted one year: from the arrival of the first officials in December 1877 until December 17, 1878, when the Law on the Division of the Annexed Area into Counties and Districts was passed, finally establishing the structure of local institutions of the new administrative units. The second phase began with the enactment of this law. The process of incorporating the liberated areas into the legal system of prewar Serbia was a painstaking task: it involved removing or at least modifying the effects of Ottoman rule, such as an outdated system, underdeveloped economy, rudimentary state administration, weak public finance, and feudal property relations.

First Period: The Provisional Organization of Local Government
Alimpije Vasiljević signed the first instructions for the provisional organization of local government on December 23, 1877, entitled *Rules for All Officials in the Seized Serbian Areas*.[12] These rules predominantly regulated the conduct of all officials who had begun to work in the new Serbian areas. They reminded the officials of the significance of their role in establishing the principles of law and order. The officials were expected to perform their duties in such a way that the people could feel "all the benefits of a fraternal government," although they were warned not to permit "leniency."[13] One of the interim instructions for the newly established institutions was to settle all "disputes orally and promptly" and to be of assistance to the Serbian army and the population in the New Areas.[14]

The *Rules* also regulated new local, district, and municipal government bodies in the liberated areas. The new districts were administered by a body of three members: "one for the Police, one for the Judiciary, and one for Finance." The chief of police was in charge of maintaining law and order, the chief of the judiciary handled judicial proceedings, and the chief of finance took care of the public revenue for the unit under his jurisdiction.[15]

The officials initially dispatched by the Serbian government to administer the new districts became the heads of local administration.[16] They acted as a liaison with the government member in the Supreme Army Command and answered to him.[17] These officials and their local administrations cannot be identified with real district prefects and prefectures for two reasons. First, the territorial extent of the new districts corresponded more to prewar Serbia's counties than to the new districts. Second, the newly established district administration differed both in structure and in powers from the district prefectures of prewar Serbia (collective bodies, chief of the judiciary, collective governing in the sphere of police, judicial, and financial matters). Therefore the district administration should be viewed as a particular form of civilian government, which was necessary under transitional conditions in the New Areas.[18]

District administrations had several concerns. The first was to make a record of all municipalities, specify the district's inner structure, and establish municipal administrations.[19]

The *Rules* assigned the task of organizing municipal government to the central government officials, who were to consult with distinguished local citizens on the appointment of members to municipal councils; the mayors were to be chosen from persons of "confidence and energy willing and capable to perform their duties to the satisfaction of all." Finally, every municipality was to elect a municipal council of five to fifteen members in accordance with its size and hire several salaried clerks.[20]

Yet the central government's officials often left local institutions as they had been under Ottoman rule. This is obvious from a report by Alimpije Vasiljević, revealing that the Serbian government found it easier to preserve the existing institutions because the people were accustomed to them. Thus the local population was likely to accept the new administration more easily.[21]

In the process of municipal organization, the most significant task of the district administration was to group villages into municipalities and carry out a property enumeration. Several important factors played a part in this process, such as noting the natural boundaries of a municipality, communal orientation points (such as schools, churches, wells, watermills, and craft shops), and the occupations of the population (including farming, cattle-breeding, and crafts). Nevertheless, the procedure could not be uniform for all the liberated areas: different situations in various areas needed to be taken into account. Therefore the newly established authorities had to rely on the advice and opinion of local household heads.[22] It was even more difficult to carry out the enumeration of property, which required military support and assistance. The civil authorities were too weak to prevent the widespread looting of the abandoned Turkish property and frequent raids of armed Muslim Albanians from the Ottoman Empire into the New Areas.

The implementation of the instructions contained in the *Rules* and the experience gained from it led to the first regulation of the legal status of municipalities and municipal authorities, passed by the National Assembly on January 3, 1878: the Provisional Law on the Organization of Liberated Areas.[23] This law defined the legal status of counties, districts, and municipalities in all the liberated territory as well as the responsibilities and procedures for their administrations. Although it made no change to the existing subdivisions, it left room for the district administrations to institute changes "if necessary and in consultation with the distinguished household heads," but only before the process of reorganization was finalized. After that, any change to the structure and name of a municipality required approval from the minister of the interior.[24]

Under the Provisional Law on the Organization of Liberated Areas, territorial subdivisions became typical policing subdivisions with some judicial powers. To judge from its provisions, it was in fact the Law on County Prefecture System and District Prefect Office of 1839 extended to the annexed areas under a *lex specialis*. According to its article 53, every county had its organs of government, such as the county prefect, county treasury officer, and county judge.[25]

As the head of a county, the county prefect exercised police and some judicial powers (in minor civil and criminal cases) in the area under his jurisdiction, assisted by the necessary number of personnel. He was appointed by the prince at the recommendation of the minister of the interior. The prefect managed all county affairs through district and municipal administrations, which he had the power to replace. If a county did not have its military commander, the county prefect fulfilled those duties as well.

The county treasury officer was in charge of economic and financial affairs. He was appointed by the prince at the recommendation of the minister of finance. Judicial power was embodied in the high judge appointed by the prince at the recommendation of the minister of justice. The high judge exercised judicial authority in accordance with his legal powers.[26]

According to article 51 of the Provisional Law on the Organization of Liberated Areas, every county was subdivided into districts.[27] Every district had its government bodies, headed by the district prefect and the district judge. The district prefect, appointed by the prince on the recommendation of the minister of the interior, exercised police and some judicial powers (minor civil and criminal cases) in the area under his jurisdiction. He conducted district affairs through municipal administrations, which he had the power to replace; if the district had no military commander, the district prefect fulfilled his duties as well. Every district had a district judge appointed by the prince on the recommendation of the minister of justice. The judge exercised judicial authority in accordance with his legal powers.[28]

Under the Provisional Law on the Organization of Liberated Areas, districts were subdivided into municipalities, which in turn were classified by size into three groups: small municipalities with up to 200 taxpayers,

medium-sized municipalities with 200 to 500 taxpayers, and large municipalities with more than 500 taxpayers.[29] Every municipality had its organs
of government in the mayor's office. At the second session of the National
Assembly in 1879, a member of the Serbian Parliament (Ćirko Andrejić)
described the procedure for the appointment of municipal mayors in the
New Areas: "At the outbreak of the second war [Second Serbo-Turkish
War], I was authorized by the commander to chose men in my district who
would work properly. And I did: I chose several mayors and they still are
mayors, and no one is unhappy with them."[30]

A municipal mayor was aided by one or two assistants and several
clerks as well as the necessary number of policemen. None of these officials
were elected. The mayor was appointed by the district prefecture "from
among the distinguished household heads in a municipality." Like county
and district prefects in their jurisdiction, he exercised policing and minor
judicial powers in his municipality and fulfilled the duties of a military
commander if the municipality did not have one. As the bearer of administrative powers, the municipal mayor was obliged to "deal with all affairs
of state as required of a municipality." As a judicial authority, he judged
civil cases of no more than fifty dinars and minor criminal cases where the
punishment was limited to five days in prison or a fifty-dinar fine. Even
these minor cases were not under the exclusive jurisdiction of municipal
courts, however; they could be assigned to district courts. Appeals against
the municipal court decisions could be lodged with district courts; the last
level was the so-called grand judge, whose decision was binding.[31]

It is important to note that all judges (municipal mayors, district
judges, and grand judges) tried cases not according to a written law but
based on "conscience, belief, and knowledge of justice and tradition."[32]
They were advised on the local legal customs by councils consisting of local
community members. This procedure was practical, because trials were
quick, although it was more primitive than collegial judging in accordance
with written law.[33]

Every municipality had a council consisting of five, ten, or fifteen members, according to its size. This council was an advisory body, convened and
presided over by the mayor; it discussed a range of issues of importance
for the municipality.[34]

The administrative functioning of municipal (district and county)
government was overseen by the minister of the interior. Various "professional responsibilities" were under the control of the corresponding ministers. During the Serbo-Turkish War, however, all bodies were also subject
to the military authorities.[35]

The relationship between the Provisional Law on the Organization of Liberated Areas and the 1866 Law on Municipalities and Municipal Government (passed under Prince Mihailo and amended by the Alteration and Amendments Law passed in 1875) was regulated under article 87 of the Provisional Law on the Organization of Liberated Areas.[36] If the earlier law contained no provisions for a concrete case and no local custom to abide by could be found, the 1875 Serbian law could be implemented in order to bridge such legal lacunae.[37]

As can be seen, the Provisional Law on the Organization of Liberated Areas envisaged subsidiary use of a Serbian law in effect, thereby paving the way for the incorporation of the New Areas into the legal system of prewar Serbia. The same law also ensured some essential values of civil society, such as the principle of equality before the law and religious freedom. All citizens of the liberated areas were made equal with the citizens of Serbia not only in rights but also in obligations (such as military service and taxation).[38]

Counties and districts were established under the Law on Provisional Administrative Organization of the Liberated Areas of May 14, 1878.[39] All the liberated territory was divided into six counties (Niš, Kuršumlija, Leskovac, Vranje, Pirot, and Kula) with twenty-one districts.[40] Each county and district was allocated the necessary number of policemen as well as financial and judicial officers to alleviate the lack of skilled staff in the newly established local administration.[41] At the same time, the administrative, judicial, and financial professions were completely separated, which was the last step in establishing a provisional domestic government when the borders between the new Balkan states had not been drawn yet. Serbian government extended to all the areas taken by the Serbian army, overcoming (more or less successfully) many ethnic and religious barriers in the process. For example, the borderland between Serbia and Bulgaria (especially in the Šop region) had many difficulties due to the unconsolidated ethnic awareness of the local people, who were influenced by both Serbian and Bulgarian national propaganda.[42]

The *kojabashi* (non-Muslim community leader) of the Ottoman *kaza* of Trn, Arandjel Stanojević, had a very important role in the establishment of Serbian civil government in the liberated Znepolje.[43] He was appointed first president of the local court and then head of the district of Trn. Under the Provisional Law on the Organization of Liberated Areas of January 3 and the Law on Provisional Administrative Organization of the Liberated Areas of May 14, 1878, Trn became the administrative seat of Znepolje, the District of Trn included in the newly formed County of Pirot.[44] Panta

Srećković became the first prefect of the County of Pirot,[45] and Arandjel Stanojević was appointed prefect of the District of Trn. Stanojević persistently campaigned for international recognition of the sovereignty of the Principality of Serbia over all areas taken by the Serbian army on the border with Bulgaria.[46] He also energetically struggled against the propaganda of the Bulgarian Committee from Sofia; against the Exarchate bishops — especially Bishop Eustathius (appointed by the Exarchate on the eve of the war against the Ottoman Empire, as head of the Eparchy of Nišava);[47] and against Pyotr Alabin, the Russian envoy to Sofia, who demanded that the Serbian authorities leave the former *sancak*s of Niš and Sofia so that they could be annexed to Bulgaria in compliance with the Treaty of San Stefano.[48] Bulgarians were aware that Stanojević was prominent in the local community and that the annexation of the *kaza* of Znepolje to Bulgaria would be difficult without Stanojević on their side. Thus Stanojević was offered the role of serving as a deputy of the Bulgarian Constitutional Assembly.[49] The assembly was to establish the first domestic government after the departure of the Russians from Bulgaria.[50] He declined the offer.[51] When the Congress of the Great Powers in Berlin ended on July 13, the borders between the independent Principality of Serbia and the autonomous Principality of Bulgaria were finally defined. The District of Trn and Znepolje became part of Bulgaria, and Stanojević moved to Serbia. He is still remembered in the Pirot region as a man who made personal sacrifices for his homeland.[52]

Second Period: The Permanent Organization of Local Government
As a result of the Berlin Treaty, new states emerged in the Balkans. Serbia had to cede a large portion of the liberated territory to Bulgaria or restore it to the Ottoman Empire. Both the military and civil authorities of the Principality of Serbia withdrew from the ceded and restored territories. A good part of the local population also withdrew, unwilling to acknowledge the new borders. Serbia retained the largest part of the former *sancak* of Niš, while the smaller part and the entire *sancak* of Sofia were annexed to the autonomous Principality of Bulgaria. The *sancak* of Priština was restored to the Ottomans.

From that moment, the process of establishing permanent institutions of local government in the New Areas began. The Serbian government focused all its efforts in the constitutional and overall legal unification of post-Berlin Serbia.

Even before Serbia's legislature made the New Areas administratively and legally equal with prewar Serbia, the government had decreed their political unification by extending voting rights to the new citizens of Serbia, who voted in the parliamentary elections of October 28, 1878. The government's position was that the New Areas had not been conquered but liberated: consequently they should enjoy all constitutional and political rights from day one.[53] The opposition suspected the government of having been guided by party political motives. Indeed, the fear of authorities was greater in the politically uneducated New Areas than in prewar Serbia. The prime minster, Jovan Ristić, could rely on his party's candidates in the New Areas, who firmly supported his government after the elections.[54]

Political unification was followed by administrative and judicial unification. On December 17, 1878, the National Assembly passed the Law on the Division of the Annexed Areas into Counties and Districts.[55] Under this law, the annexed areas were divided into four counties (Niš, Vranje, Pirot, and Toplica) and fifteen districts.[56] In addition, several important provisions of the Provisional Law on the Organization of Liberated Areas of January 3, 1878, were revoked (articles 22, 23, 51, and 52). These mostly regulated the grouping of municipalities into districts, districts into counties, and the seats as administrative centers of districts within counties. This question was settled by a decree issued by Prince Milan Obrenović on February 6, 1879, finally defining the boundaries of districts and counties and the seats of local administration and listing all the villages included in their inner structure (1,001 villages in fifteen districts).[57] Thus the unification, which had been carried out de facto even before the state borders in the Balkans were finally drawn, got its legal framework, resulting in the administrative unification of the whole of the Principality of Serbia.

Judicial unification was carried out under the Law on Legal Proceedings in the Annexed Areas of December 31, 1878.[58] The Serbian laws concerning the judiciary and civil and criminal law (material and procedural) were extended to the New Areas. The only exception was the legislation on immovable property and the Law on Lawyers. The most important exception resulted from Serbia's international obligations as stipulated by the Berlin Treaty. Domestic legislation on the immovable property was not extended to the New Areas because the Great Powers at the Congress of Berlin had met some demands of the Porte and the Ottoman landowners. The limitations imposed on Serbia concerned the obligation to award compensation to the holders of former *spahilik*s in the liberated areas. *Spahilik*s were estates in possession of *sipahi*s. They had two forms: *timar*s and *zeamet*s.

REGULATION OF AGRARIAN RELATIONSHIPS

Article 39 of the Treaty of Berlin stipulated that the Principality of Serbia must strictly respect the property rights of the Muslim-Ottoman land-owners. According to this article, Muslims who were in possession of lands in the territories annexed to Serbia and wanted to settle outside the Principality of Serbia had the right to keep their own immovable property. They could lease their lands or authorize other persons to manage them. A special Serbo-Turkish committee would be formed in order to investigate all the circumstances regarding the civil trading of the immovable property.

The Berlin Treaty stipulated the monetary compensation for the immovable property of the Muslims who did not want to stay and live under the Serbian government but moved or intended to move to the Ottoman Empire. The Serbian government formed two special committees for this purpose. The first committee had the task of investigating the state of property rights in the liberated areas. The second committee was a special agrarian body of the Serbian government, which consisted of two departments (one department for the counties of Niš and Pirot and the second department for the counties of Vranje and Toplica). The main purpose of these committees was to prepare necessary legal sources and make a draft for a Law on Agrarian Relationships in the New Areas and a Law on Settling in New Areas.

It should be noted that the Serbian army found a specific feudal system in the New Areas. The chief of the Supreme Army Command, Gen. Kosta Protić, sent a report on the agrarian relationships found in the New Areas to the Serbian government. According to this report, the main type of *spahilik*s in the area of Leskovac was a *çiftlik* (*čitluk*) (privately owned farm).[59] Available literature shows that this type of Ottoman feudal property was also present in the areas of Pirot, Vranje, and Toplica.[60] *Çiftlik*s were special kind of lands with a determined size, constructed buildings, cattle, and agricultural inventory. According to General Protić's report, two kinds of titleholders existed: landlords (holders of village lands in the area of Leskovac) and *çifchie*s (*čifčije*), that is, *kirayjie*s (*kirajdžije*) (peasants or settlers on other people's lands). Only landlords could be treated as real landholders, while *çifchie*s had only several rights derived from the right of property. Landlords usually divided their lands into small pieces and gave them to *çifchie*s (usually heads of households or nuclear families) to live and work there. *Çifchie*s were obliged to pay a special tax called a ninth (*devetak*) to landlords as a special compensation for a transferred landholding.[61]

*Çifchie*s had holding and some rights coming from the right of property, predominantly *ius utendi* (the right to use something) and *ius frutendi* (the right to enjoy its fruits), rarely *ius abutendi* (the right to put it on the market) over movable and some immovable estates. They had a right to make buildings on a *çiftlik*, to perform daily domestic odd jobs (agricultural works, cattle-breeding, fishing, fruit growing, viniculture), and to leave the *çiftlik* or landlord.[62]

The report shows that peasants in the New Areas resented their obligation to pay compensation for *çiftlik*s because this kind of property was peasant land that had been confiscated during the Ottoman rule. Hence many conflicts broke out between peasants and former Ottoman holders, especially when former landlords wanted to sell their lands or to get paid their agrarian claims.[63]

The Serbian soldiers found that landlords of villages and *çiftlik-sahybia*s (actual, not legal, holders of *çiftlik*s) lived in towns in the New Areas, while *çifchie*s were found only in villages and the suburban part of agricultural areas of Niš, Leskovac, Pirot, and Vranje.[64]

The committee for investigating the Ottoman property and the committee for investigating agrarian relationships did their duty and sent a report to the Serbian government, which examined it in detail. Based on this report, the Serbian government formulated a special agrarian policy for the New Areas in order to carry out its obligations stipulated by the Treaty of Berlin.

The process of regulation of agrarian relationships in the New Areas after the Serbo-Turkish wars had two phases. The first phase lasted approximately ten years (1880–90) and was marked by the efforts of the Serbian government at uniform regulation and resolution of all kinds of agrarian relationships between *çifchie*s and Muslim holders (landlords and *çiftlik-sahybia*s); in this phase the Serbian Assembly passed two very important laws that regulated obligations of peasants in the purchase of lands from *sipahi*s and *çiftlik-sahybia*s: the Law on Agrarian Relationships of 1880 and Law on Agrarian Loan of 1882. The second phase lasted seventeen years (1890–1907). It was marked by the passage of several legal acts and measures for elimination of many negative (predominantly economic) consequences that had appeared after the implementation of the laws in the first phase. The next two laws were passed in this phase: the Law on Protraction of Agrarian Loan in New Areas of 1891 and Law on Amendments on the Law on Protraction of Agrarian Loan in New Areas of 1907.

The most important of these laws was the Law on Agrarian Relationships of 1880, created by minister of justice Vojislav Veljković.[65] According to this law, peasants would became owners of the lands they had cultivated only if they would pay compensation to their former Muslim landlords (articles 5 and 7). The prices of compensation were determined by agreement between interested clients (article 13) or by decisions of the state committees (article 26). The deadline for paying the estimated compensation was five years (article 8). Purchase of land was obligatory for both *sipahi*s and peasants. The legislature obviously wanted to eradicate the feudal-*çiftlik* system in the liberated areas. Therefore it encouraged peasants to pay their purchase price even in situations when they did not want to do that. After political and legal assimilation of the New Areas into prewar Serbia, the social assimilation was also carried out.[66]

The Porte in Istanbul did not accept this model of resolving the agrarian question in the New Areas. It pointed out that Muslim landowners in the counties of Niš, Pirot, Vranje, and Toplica were simply blackmailed and their immovable property was confiscated. The Porte had many objections concerned with the final solution of the agrarian question in the New Areas. One of them was certainly valid. Peasants paid their compensations to former Muslim landlords inaccurately and in an untimely fashion, with fights and tensions. The whole misunderstanding was apparently due to incorrect interpretation of the legal norm from article 8, which prescribed that the compensation had to be paid within five years. This rule was not interpreted as the peasants' obligation to pay the purchase over a period of five years but as an obligation to pay the whole amount of the compensation at the end of fifth year. This situation led the former landowners to a state of hopelessness and despair.

Under the strong pressure of international circumstances, the Progressive Serbian government had to find a solution in order to improve the social status of *sipahi*s. The Serbian Assembly passed the new Law on Agrarian Loan in 1882, which should have guaranteed more regular payment by peasant-*çifchie*s. According to article 1 of this law, the government took over the obligation to pay the compensation to former landowners, and it really did so. The state became a loan holder for redeemed peasants who were obliged to give annual payments within the due date of fifteen–twenty-five years (articles 2 and 3). The Law on Agrarian Loan of 1882 prevented economic disaster for former landowners but at the same time created a very bad position for peasants. All the negative consequences of this law were eliminated in the next two decades. Several laws were passed in the Serbian Assembly in the period from 1890 to 1907, in the second phase of solving the agrarian question in the New Areas.

COLONIZATION OF THE NEW AREAS

The wars in the Balkans in 1877–78 (Serbo-Turkish War and Russian-Turkish War) resulted in fundamental changes in the demographic, ethnic, religious, and social structure in the main part of the Mutasarrıflık (*sancak*) of Niš and Mutasarrıflık of Sofia. After the Congress of Berlin and marking of the new state boundaries of Serbia, Bulgaria, and the Ottoman Empire, this new configuration of the people and nations was officially sanctioned. The number of inhabitants in some areas was crucial for establishment of the domestic local government in the New Areas, but it often changed due to the devastations of war and its consequences (including diseases, hunger, poverty, and bad sanitary conditions). The Serbian government took care to strengthen the Serbian ethnic presence in the liberated areas. It passed various legal acts within the clearly formulated agrarian and population policy. Although this chapter is devoted to the population policy of the Serbian government in the New Areas, it also examines the ethnic-religious structure of the *sancak* of Niš on the eve of the Second Serbo-Turkish War in order to see all consequences of migrations that radically changed the configuration of populations and nations in the central Balkans.

According to the official *Statistical Review*, created on the eve of the liberation (1878), the Mutasarrıflık of Niš had a total of 150,413 male inhabitants.[67] This included 110,386 Christians (73.4 percent) and 40,027 Muslims (26.6 percent) (Turks, Albanians, and smaller numbers of Circassians, Kumans, and Tatars).[68] The whole population was divided into town dwellers and people in rural areas. The male rural Christian population was more numerous than the male Muslim population. The number of male Muslim town dwellers was larger than the Christian urban population. This means that the Christians predominantly lived in villages whereas Muslims lived in towns, although larger mixed ethnic-religious towns also existed, such as Niš, Pirot, Leskovac, and Vranje.[69]

The *Statistical Review* shows that the *kaza* of Niš was 77.7 percent Christian and 22.3 percent Muslim; the *kaza* of Leskovac was 66.6 percent Christian and 33.4 percent Muslim; the *kaza* of Vranje was 70.6 percent Christian and 29.4 percent Muslim; the *kaza* of Pirot was 83.6 percent Christian and 16.4 percent Muslim; the *kaza* of Prokuplje was 42.6 percent Christian and 57.4 percent Muslim; the *kaza* of Kuršumlija was 11.3 percent Christian and 88.7 percent Muslim; and the *kaza* of Trn was 97.9 percent Christian and 2.01 percent Muslim.[70]

It is important to point out that the data on linguistic affiliation of inhabitants are only for the male population. The Albanian-speaking population was dominant in towns, except in Niš and Pirot, where people equally spoke Albanian and Turkish. The Albanian male population spoke exclusively Albanian in Prokuplje and Kuršumlija. These historical data give a notion of the ethnic structure of the Muslim male population in the liberated areas on the eve of the war in 1877–78. It should be noted that the zone of dispersion of the Albanian ethnic element in the Mutasarrıflık of Niš reached Trn, although it was present only in towns. In the town of Trn Albanians represented 2 percent of the whole male population.[71]

This was the overall demographic, social, ethnic, religious, and linguistic structure of the Mutasarrıflık of Niš on the eve of the wars of liberation and independence. It completely changed during the war and especially after the international recognition of Serbia and its territorial enlargement. During the Serbo-Turkish War many massive groups of the Serbian population from the Ottoman Empire escaped to the conterminous areas under temporary Serbian military and civil rule. In the fall of 1878 even a family from the *nahiyes* (districts) of Bitola (Manastir, today in the former Yugoslav Republic of Macedonia) took refuge in this area, away from the Turkish violence. The Serbian government organized a special department to accept and aid the refugees from the Ottoman Empire. Meanwhile 30,000 Muslim inhabitants left their homes and escaped toward Priština, Mitrovica, Vučitrn, Djakovica, Drenica, and Prizren. Most of these people were Albanians from Toplica, Kosanica, Gornja (Upper) Jablanica i Donja (Lower) Jablanica, and Masurica Gornja and the towns of Niš, Prokuplje, Kuršumlija, Leskovac, and Vranje.

These Albanians participated on the Ottoman side as irregular military troops (*başıbozuks*) during the Serbo-Turkish War. The majority of the Muslims, including Albanians, did not want to live in a Christian state. Fearing Serbian revenge due to the violence they had done against the Serbs before and during the war, they withdrew to areas that remained in the Ottoman Empire. But a number of Albanians remained in the New Areas. Albanians who decided to stay in Serbia continued to live in three enclaves: in nine villages of Masurica, in several villages of Gornja Jablanica, and in several villages on the right bank of the River Toplica and on the Kuršumlija-Prokuplje road.[72]

The Ottoman government attempted to locate these escaped Albanians (*muhacirs*) in the new conterminous areas near Serbia, bordered by the Jablanica and Kriva rivers in the south, the Jablanica and Lab rivers in the west, and the Jablanica and Kosanica rivers in the southwest. In planning to locate the *muhacirs* in this way, the Ottoman government wanted to strengthen the new state boundary with Serbia. At the same time, the rest of the Serbian population in this area was subjected to intensive mistreatment by the Muslim population. After the signing of the peace agreement between Serbia and the Ottomans, a number of escaped Albanians went back home to villages in the area of Gornja and Donja Jablanica at the invitation of their tribal heads and the Serbian government. Albanian Sahit-Paša Sailović, originally from the village of Lapaštica (Gornja Jablanica), served as a military commander of the *sancak* of Sofia. He surrendered to the Serbian lieutenant Dragutin Arandjelović and said that he would not fight as a soldier of the Turkish army anymore. He once discussed this with Prince Milan Obrenović in Niš. Sailović expressed his loyalty to the Serbian government and accepted cooperation. He went back home and appealed to Albanians not to leave Gornja Jablanica. Due to this appeal, many Albanian families stayed in villages of Gornja Jablanica (Lapaštica, Tupale, Kapit, Svirce, Djulekare, Dedić, and Grbavce). Sahit-Paša Sailović also had an important political role in the area of Gornja Jablanica and became a close friend of Prince Milan Obrenović.[73] In spite of that, some of the Albanians from Gornja Jablanica definitely moved to Turkey later.

Similar processes can be noted in the *kaza* of Pirot in the *sancak* of Niš. Withdrawal of the Ottoman army from the Pirot area brought about massive flight of the population in the conterminous area toward the town of Pirot. Marking of the new state boundaries between Serbia and Bulgaria and withdrawal of the temporary Serbian military and civil administration led to new migrations. The Serbian population left the areas of Trn, Znepolje, Kustendil, and Vidin and moved to Serbia. Some of these people went to central Serbia: Šumadija, the Resava valley, and the Danube region. Others settled in the area along the Serbo-Bulgarian border. These Serbs had to leave their homeland, fearing Bulgarian revenge. They actively assisted the Serbian temporary administration (like Arandjel Stanojević, *kojabashi* of the *kaza* of Trn) during the war and did not want to deny their Serbian origins. Thus they could be attacked by Bulgarian political leaders. A small number of the Serbs from the villages and towns along the border moved to Bulgaria for different reasons: to save their lands, which were cut by the boundary line, or to improve their trade. But there were political immigrants too: some of them decided to become Bulgarian citizens and identified themselves as "real Bulgarians."[74]

The complete demographic, ethnic, religious, and social structure of the former Mutasarrıflık of Niš changed in this way. The committee investigating the state of property created a report on settled, moved, and displaced populations, immovable property (especially abandoned houses and lands), agrarian relationships, all ethnic changes that came about during the war of liberation and independence, and the possibilities of receiving the new immigrants from Turkey and other countries.[75] This report was a basis for the legal regulation of settling in the New Areas. The Law on Settling was passed by the Serbian Assembly on January 3, 1880. According to this law, each agricultural family had a right to hold four hectares of cultivable land and 2,000 square meters for a homestead, if the head of a family submitted a timely request to the minister of finance (articles 3 and 5). If this kind of request was submitted by a household, it would also have the right to hold two additional hectares for each male older than sixteen (article 5). Craftsmen had a right to hold two hectares of land, including an additional plot for a house and other buildings. The right of property in regard to assigned lands was being acquired after fifteen years of constant holding (article 6).

Due to implementation of this law, the Serbian government successfully controlled the influx of new immigrants from Bulgaria, Montenegro, and the Ottoman Empire. The law had the goal of strengthening the Serbian national presence in the New Areas, enabling the consolidation of the Serbian legal-political order, and ensuring more practical organization of the local administration in those areas. This task was successfully completed by the progressive government of Milan Piroćanac.

CONCLUSION

The incorporation of the newly annexed areas into the legal system of postwar Serbia was successful. According to the norms of the Treaty of Berlin, the Serbian government carried out three reform policies: legal-judicial, agrarian, and social-demographic. These efforts were marked by many difficulties, but they resulted in establishment of the first stable domestic local administration in the New Areas. The newly formed counties of Niš, Pirot, Vranje, and Toplica relatively quickly acquired the same legal form as other local units within the united legal-political order of Serbia. The Treaty of Berlin was of great importance in this regard.

NOTES

1. Before the wars, the Principality of Serbia enjoyed autonomy under the Ottoman suzerainty and consisted of the *paşalik* of Belgrade and the areas that it had acquired by the sultan's decree (Hatt-i Şerif) of 1833: Ključ, Krajina, Crna Reka, Gurgusovac, Banja, Svrljig, Aleksinac, Ražanj, Paraćin, Kruševac, Jadar, Radjevijna, a smaller portion of the region known as Stari Vlah, and the *nahiye* of Novi Pazar. Milan Dj. Milićević, *Kraljevina Srbija — Novi krajevi*, 16.

2. The New Areas were incorporated into Serbia after the wars of liberation against the Ottoman Empire and the Congress of Berlin, and the term came into official usage immediately after liberation in December 1877 and January 1878. Ibid., 15; *Stenografske beleške o sednicama Narodne skupštine za 1879–1880*.

3. In Serbia the county (*okrug*) was the largest unit of local self-government, followed by the district (*srez*) as a medium-sized unit and the municipality (*opština*) as the smallest.

4. For more on the resettlement of Albanians from these areas to Kosovo and influx of Kosovo Serbs into these areas, see Dušan T. Bataković, *The Kosovo Chronicles*, 111–12.

5. The provisions of the treaty, however, were significantly modified by the Treaty of Berlin of July 13, 1878, which did recognize an autonomous but much smaller Bulgaria within the Ottoman Empire.

6. Kustendil is a town in southwestern modern Bulgaria. Vladimir Stojančević, "Jugoistočna Srbija u vreme oslobodjenja 1877–1878."

7. Ružica Guzina, *Opština u Srbiji 1839–1918*, 235.

8. Vidosava Nikolić-Stojančević, *Leskovac i oslobodjeni predeli Srbije 1877–78*, 26.

9. Ibid.

10. Alimpije Vasiljević (1831–1911) was a Serbian politician, member of the Liberal Party, writer, and professor of philosophy at the Great School in Belgrade. His most significant work was *The History of Education in Serbia*. He served several terms as minister of education and religious affairs (including the period of the Serbo-Turkish Wars, 1876–78) and was appointed Serbian diplomatic envoy to Russia twice.

11. A letter from the chief of the General Staff to the minister of the interior on December 11, 1877, shows the most important reasons for civil-military separation. Guzina, *Opština u Srbiji 1839–1918*, 237; Nikolić-Stojančević, *Leskovac i oslobodjeni predeli Srbije 1877–78*, 58–59.

12. "Pravila," 239–41.

13. Ibid., 239.

14. Ibid.

15. Ibid., 240.

16. Slobodanka Stojičić, *Novi krajevi Srbije 1878–1883*, 41; "Pravila," 239.

17. Ibid.

18. Stojičić, *Novi krajevi Srbije 1878–1883*, 41.

19. "Pravila," 241.

20. Ibid., 240–41.

21. Guzina, *Opština u Srbiji 1839–1918*, 239.

22. Ibid., 239.

23. "Privremeni zakon o uredjenju oslobodjenih predela," 251–70.

24. Ibid., articles 1, 2, and 3 on 251.

25. Ibid., article 53 on 261.

26. Ibid., articles 55–57 and 62 on 261–63.

27. Ibid., article 51 on 261.

28. Ibid., articles 25–29, 33, 34, and 36 on 255–57.

29. Ibid., article 18 on 254.

30. *Stenografske beleške o sednicama Narodne skupštine za 1879–1880*, 1063–64.

31. "Privremeni zakon o uredjenju oslobodjenih predela," articles 4–8, 11, 13, 37, and 66 on 251–53, 258, 264.
32. Slobodan Jovanović, *Vlada Milana Obrenovića II*, 13.
33. Ibid., 13.
34. "Privremeni zakon o uredjenju oslobodjenih predela," articles 18 and 19 on 254.
35. Ibid., articles 71 and 73 on 265.
36. Prince Mihailo Obrenović (1823–68), son of Prince Miloš Obrenović, ruled 1840–42 and 1860–68. His rule may be described as enlightened autocracy.
37. "Privremeni zakon o uredjenju oslobodjenih predela," article 87 on 268.
38. Ibid., articles 75–77, 80, and 81 on 266–67.
39. "Zakon o privremenom upravnom podeljenju i snabdenju sa vlastim oslobodjenih predela," 308–15.
40. Under article 2 of the law, the six counties were Niš: Niš, Koprivnica, and Bela Palanka districts; Kuršumlija: Prokuplje, Kuršumlija, Ibar, and Vučitrn districts; Leskovac: Veternik, Vlasina, and Pusta Reka districts; Vranje: Vlasina, Poljana, Morava, and Pčinja districts; Pirot: Viroski, Breznica, Nišava, Trn, and Leskovac districts; and Kula: Kula and Novo Selo districts.
41. "Zakon o privremenom upravnom podeljenju i snabdenju sa vlastim oslobodjenih predela," article 3 on 310–11.
42. The Šop region (Šopluk or Šopsko) is a mountainous area on the modern-day borders of Serbia, Bulgaria, and Macedonia, whose boundaries are quite vague. The term "Šop" has always denoted the common people, highlanders. See Petko Hristov, "Granicite na Šopluka i/ili Šopi bez granica," 67–83.
43. A Serbian popular leader and representative before the Ottoman authorities, Arandjel Stanojević was considered one of the most distinguished figures from Niš to Sofia and from Pirot to Kustendil. Moreover, as a cattle trader he was one of the richest men on the boundary between Znepolje and Vidin (today in Bulgaria). He was respected by the Turks as well. Stanojević spoke Turkish, French, and Greek. After the arrival of the Serbian army he assumed an active role in establishing Serbian rule in the *sancak*s of Niš and Sofia. See Vladimir Stojančević, "Kodžabaša trnske kaze Arandjel Stanojević i srpsko-bugarski spor oko Trna i Znepolja 1878–1879," 195–96.
44. The national feelings of the local population of Znepolje were a highly important matter for the Serbian government and its claims on the liberated areas. Based on field reports, the government was quite confident that the people of Trn, Klisura, and eighty other villages of Znepolje thought of themselves as Serbs. See ibid., 199–200.
45. Panta Srećković (1834–1903) was a professor of history at the Great School in Belgrade and a politician. His historical writing on Serbia's past is somewhat uncritical.
46. Arandjel Stanojević was the representative of the *kaza* of Trn in a deputation to St. Petersburg in April 1878 to petition the Russian emperor for the right of the people of Pirot, Trn, Vranje, and the neighboring areas of Old Serbia to be considered Old Serbs and consequently to remain in Serbia. See Borislava Lilić, *Istorija Pirota i okoline (1878–1918)*, 246.
47. After the abolishment of the Patriarchate of Peć in 1766 and the Archbishopric of Ohrid in 1767, all Bulgarians and Serbian bishoprics came under the jurisdiction

of the Patriarchate of Constantinople, which replaced almost all Slav bishops with ethnic Greeks. This was opposed by all Orthodox Slavs (Serbian and Bulgarian) who strove to emancipate their respective churches from the Greek Patriarchate. Backed by Russia, Bulgarians succeeded in establishing their autonomous church organization. On February 28, 1870, by the sultan's decree, the Bulgarian Exarchate was established; its jurisdiction also extended to many Serb-inhabited areas, including the counties of Niš, Pirot, and Vranje. In the areas under the Exarchate's jurisdiction, Greek bishops and teachers were replaced with Bulgarians.

48. There was a significant gap between Pirot's urban population and its rural surroundings. Many members of the Pirot elite, known as *çorbacı* (*chorbaji*), accepted both the Exarchate and the Bulgarian idea and were unwilling to break their business relations with the markets of northern Bulgaria, Thrace, and Constantinople. The rural people of the Pirot area, by contrast, accepted hardly any change in their life, upheld their customs and traditions, and supported the unification of Pirot and Serbia. The Exarchate sought to exploit this gap, especially under Jordanča-Paşa Bakalov, the *mutasarrıf* (governor of a *mutasarrıflık* [*sancak*]) of Pirot. Lilić, *Istorija Pirota i okoline (1878–1918)*, 247.

49. Stojančević, "Kodžabaša trnske kaze Arandjel Stanojević i srpsko-bugarski spor oko Trna i Znepolja 1878–1879," 209–10.

50. Stationed in Bulgaria during the war, Russian army officers and soldiers behaved as a domestic government.

51. Stanojević was warned that he would be tried by the people's court if he did not declare himself a Bulgarian, which really meant that the Bulgarian Committee would have him executed. Stojančević, "Kodžabaša trnske kaze Arandjel Stanojević i srpsko-bugarski spor oko Trna i Znepolja 1878–1879," 211.

52. Ibid., 209–16.

53. Jovanović, *Vlada Milana Obrenovića II*, 14.

54. Jovan Ristić (1831–99) was one of the most important Serbian politicians of the nineteenth century: a historian, diplomat, and statesman and the unquestionable leader of the Liberal Party. He was a member of the Regency for underage Prince Milan Obrenović (1869–72) and underage King Alexander Obrenović (1889–93). Ristić successfully completed long negotiations on the withdrawal of the Ottoman troops from Serbia under Prince Mihailo Obrenović (1840–42, 1860–68) and worked on the 1869 Regency Constitution. He was minister of foreign affairs at the time of the Berlin Congress and mainly responsible for the international recognition of Serbia. His historical writings include *Foreign Relations of Serbia, 1848–1872* and *Serbian Diplomacy: The Serbian Wars of Liberation and Independence, 1875–1878*.

55. "Zakon o podeli prisajedinjenog zemljišta na okruge i srezove."

56. Article 1 of "Zakon o podeli prisajedinjenog zemljišta na okruge i srezove" established four counties: Niš County with Niš as its county seat included four districts: Niš, Zaplanje, Leskovac, and Vlasotince. Pirot County with Pirot as its county seat also had four districts: Nišava, Visoki, Bela Palanka, and Lužnica. Vranje County with Vranje as its county seat had three districts: Pčinja, Poljanica, and Masurica. Toplica County with Prokuplje as its provisional seat had four districts: Dobrica, Prokuplje, Kosanica, and Jablanica, Ibid., 196–209.

57. Ibid., 196–97.

58. "Zakon o sudjenju i o zakonima, po kojima će se suditi u prisajedinjenim prede-lima," 71–77.

59. Vladimir Stojančević, "Jedan dokument o agrarno-pravnim odnosima posle srpsko-turskog rata 1877–78."

60. Lilić, *Istorija Pirota i okoline (1878–1918)*, 279–86; Milovan Spasić, "Podaci o agrarnim odnosima hrišćana u oslobodjenim krajevima, okruga Topličkog i Vranjskog za vreme turske vladavine."

61. Ibid.

62. Ibid., 280–81.

63. Ibid.

64. Slobodanka Stojičić, *Agrarno pitanje u novooslobodjenim krajevima Srbije posle srpsko-turskih ratova 1878–1907*, 13.

65. "Law on Agrarian Relationships."

66. Jovanović, *Vlada Milana Obrenovića II*, 15.

67. The *Statistical Review* included only male inhabitants.

68. The Turkish *Statistical Review*, which contained data on the demographic-confessional composition of the population in the Mutasarrıflık of Niš in 1873, was taken by the Statistical Department of the Serbian Ministry of Finance. These documents are filled at the Archives of Serbia in Belgrade: Arhiv Srbije (Turski statisticki pregled, Statisticko odeljenje Ministarstva finansija Srbije), Belgrade, PO K-64/421, Register Office of the member of the Supreme Military Command in Niš, No. 2/26, December 1877.

69. Arhiv Srbije, PO K-64/421. The Bulgarian historian Stajko Trifonov pointed out that these towns significantly had possessed the Bulgarian national character that was sanctioned by the Great Powers in Constantinople 1876: Stajko Trifonov, *Istorija na Bulgarija*, 88.

70. Arhiv Srbije, PO K-64/421. Stajko Trifonov claimed that there were 35,000 Orthodox Bulgarians in the *kaza* of Niš, 22,500 Bulgarians in the *kaza* of Leskovac, and 60,500 Bulgarians in the *kaza* of Vranje in 1878. He quoted the statistical data and geographical maps presented by Carl Sax but did not mention where they can be found. This statement is debatable, because Trifonov did not mention any kind of source. It is very difficult to claim that these numbers on the Bulgarian population in the *kaza* of Niš in 1878 are correct, because the population there did not have a clearly consolidated national awareness. This population was subjected to strong Serbian and Bulgarian propaganda, and it often wavered between the two, depending on the concrete situation on the ground. It is much better to classify the population according to religious criteria, which certainly corresponded with the principles of the social system in the Ottoman Empire (Trifonov, *Istorija na Bulgarija*, 88).

71. Ibid.

72. Miloš Jagodić, *Naseljavanje Kneževine Srbije 1860–1861*, 134.

73. Dobrosav Ž. Turović, *Gornja Jablanica: Kroz istoriju*, 89.

74. Lilić, *Istorija Pirota i okoline (1878–1918)*, 270.

75. Spasić, "Podaci o agrarnim odnosima hrišćana u oslobodjenim krajevima, okruga Topličkog i Vranjskog za vreme turske vladavine," 263–69.

7

The Ottoman Wrong Horse?

The Question of Bosnia and Hercegovina in the Last Phase of the Eastern Crisis

Edin Radušić

This paper deals with British policy toward the future status of Bosnia and Hercegovina during the last phase of the Eastern Crisis, focusing on traditional themes and motives of Great Power politics in the Balkans from the perspective of Whitehall. British foreign policy regarding the status of Bosnia and Hercegovina during the Eastern Crisis of 1875–78 went through two distinct periods: the first one starting with the war and ending with the signing of the Treaty of San Stefano and the second one from the time of San Stefano until the Berlin Congress. The main defining characteristic of the first phase was staying the course in guaranteeing the integrity of the Ottoman Empire and keeping Bosnia-Hercegovina within that empire while pushing for internal reforms. The maximum concession that the Ottomans would be forced to make would be administrative autonomy on the local level but not political autonomy for the province. The second phase of Britain's foreign policy was characterized by a totally different approach to Bosnia-Hercegovina and the Eastern question. At that time, the British imperial strategy was focused above all on keeping the Russian Empire away from control of Constantinople and the Straits; it turned to a minimal program in its eastern policy. The newly revised British foreign policy sought to preserve this cardinal goal while allowing "peripheral" territory such as Bosnia-Hercegovina to be sacrificed, in this case by either annexation to the Austro-Hungarian Habsburg Empire or less direct administration by Vienna.

The nineteenth century marked the heyday of multinational empires and Great Power balance-of-power politics. Central to this was the Eastern question, centered on competing European Great Power claims on Ottoman territory. The future status of Bosnia-Hercegovina came to play a central role within this question. Although British policy toward Bosnia-Hercegovina was part of the overall British support of the Ottoman Empire, it deserves special attention because it marked subtle but significant changes in overall British strategy.

Bosnia-Hercegovina enjoyed a number of special attributes. It had a unique geopolitical position on the fault lines of civilization, including a large number of Slavic Muslims (who represented a significant segment of the Ottoman administration of the province), strong interest and claims on Hercegovina by Russia and Austria-Hungary (who frequently used the Bosnian-Hercegovinian Orthodox and Catholic populations to assert their own territorial aims), and the aspirations of the neighboring autonomous principalities, Serbia and Montenegro, to extend their own territory at the expense of Bosnia-Hercegovina. The second half of the nineteenth century in Bosnia-Hercegovina is also the time when the people, characterized until the middle of the century primarily by religious affiliation, started to become receptive to more secular "national" elements in their identity, within the context of changes resulting from reforms in the Ottoman Empire and the Bosnian *eyalet* (province), as well as under the influence and propaganda from neighboring countries. In this period three national identities (Serbian, Croatian, and Bosniak/Muslim) were gelling in Bosnia-Hercegovina, based on the predominant principle of religious and cultural adherence. External factors primarily determined this evolution of national consciousness, although the internal development of Bosnian society in the Ottoman state also influenced this process, which was almost completed during the period of Austro-Hungarian rule.

All these external and internal developments contributed to the complex position of Bosnia-Hercegovina, which required special attention from the British diplomatic and consular service.

The main concern expressed by the British diplomatic and consular representatives was that the consequence of dragging Bosnia-Hercegovina into a series of "unfortunate events" could be an outbreak of a wider European conflict.[1] This explains why Bosnia-Hercegovina came to play such an important role in the overall Eastern question.

A large number of works have been published on the complex issue of the Eastern Crisis, 1875–78 (the uprising in Bosnia-Hercegovina, the Treaty of Berlin, the resistance to the Austrian occupation, and the change of the government) in the historiography of the former Yugoslavia. In the socialist period of Yugoslavia, three important conferences were organized in Sarajevo that should have answered various problems in the historical development of Bosnia-Hercegovina from the uprising of 1875 to the end of the establishment of Austria-Hungarian rule.[2] Considering the large and varied number of publications, it is impossible to come to an academic consensus on this topic; but this paper provides some basic scholarly orientation and characteristics of Bosnian-Hercegovinian historiography and the Eastern Crisis and bibliographic information on this topic.[3] The historiography of the socialist period was under the influence of two political/ideological concepts: Serbian nationalist ideology and the Communist theory of class and dialectical materialism. Both were united in a hostile attitude toward the multinational empires of that time: the Ottoman Empire and the Austro-Hungarian Dual Monarchy. Although they were judged differently in details (the Ottoman Empire was a particular subject of animus for Serbian writers), the general assessment was similar. Both were foreign states that hampered the free development of local populations and their national self-determination as South Slavs, naturally inclined toward the vision of Yugoslavia or a Greater Serbia (indirectly these two terms were taken as synonyms in the official historiography). Because the Serbian autonomous principality was emerging on the free small landholdings protected by the national state (Serbian, Orthodox) it was taken as the rightful pattern for other parts of the South Slavic lands (particularly for Bosnia-Hercegovina).

The identities and aspirations of other non-Orthodox national or religious groups (especially Bosniak Muslims), however, were put aside. So the uprising in Bosnia (1875) was judged to be a popular and righteous revolt against the Ottoman state, which was oppressing the lower classes, who were mostly Orthodox Christians. The Treaty of Berlin was seen as an unjust temporary settlement made by the Great Powers, which prevented the attainment of the "peasant agrarian revolution." The resistance of Bosnians against the Austrian occupation was treated as a popular defensive resistance or even a national liberation war. Although there are some differences between the older and the younger generation of influential historians of nineteenth-century Bosnia, the same overall historiographic attitude continues from the beginning of the first Yugoslavia to the end of the second one (Vaso Čubrilović, Vasilj Popović, Grgur Jakšić, Milorad Ekmečić).[4] Others were under their influence as well, willingly or not.[5] For those who did not agree with this official Yugoslav/Serbian interpretation of history, even a minor effort to venture out of the acceptable narratives was not welcome.[6]

Beginning in the late 1970s a more critical and liberal attitude to the Bosnian-Hercegovinian past could be seen, symbolized by publication of the history of the Socialist Republic of Bosnia and Hercegovina.[7] This kind of Bosnian historiography, which peaked in the 1990s, put Bosnia-Hercegovina and the views of the Bosniak Muslims more in focus. In this narrative, the interpretation of Bosnian society under the Ottoman rule was more favorable than in earlier works, but at the same time the movements for autonomy from the Ottoman Empire were glorified.[8] Although the new approach was a departure from the earlier attitude, Bosnian historiography from that time to the present day has rarely dealt concretely with the Eastern Crisis and the Treaty of Berlin and has not left a strong mark on the study of this topic.[9] Two conferences organized in Sarajevo in 2009, which dealt with the identity of Bosnia-Hercegovina and Austro-Hungarian rule, represent a new beginning in dealing with these issues.[10]

Although the literature written about the Eastern question and the Eastern Crisis of 1875–78 is vast, it treats only some segments of British policy toward Bosnia-Hercegovina in the second part of the nineteenth century, mostly as parts of other topics such as nineteenth-century balance-of-power politics and the general policy of Great Britain toward the Ottoman Empire.[11] Bosnia-Hercegovina rarely has been treated in a framework of such wider topics.[12] Literature on South Slavic languages has focused on events and processes that are only indirectly connected with this topic, except for studies that treat the interests of other European powers in Bosnia and Hercegovina or describe the history of the territory in the nineteenth century on the basis of the diplomatic and consular sources of these countries.[13]

During my work, I have devoted special attention to diplomatic correspondence, dispatches, and reports sent to the British ambassador in Constantinople and to the foreign secretary in London by the consul and vice-consul from Bosnia-Hercegovina. The future policy of Great Britain toward the Ottoman Empire as well as the attitude of the Great Powers toward the future of the provinces of the Ottoman Empire to some extent depended on their reports. The observations of consuls who served for a longer period in the Ottoman Empire were given greater consideration, and their suggestions were for the most part included in the official course of British policy. The viewpoints of William Richard Holmes were especially respected in the embassy in Constantinople and by the Foreign Office at Whitehall. He was a long-serving consul in Bosnia who was commonly believed to know a great deal about Bosnia and the empire as a whole. His opinions and suggestions were valued highly: during the Conference of Constantinople, he was invited to the Ottoman capital together with consul John Elijah Blunt so that he could be of assistance to the British plenipotentiaries in this gathering of representatives of the Great Powers.[14]

The reports and observations of acting consul Edward Freeman, who later became consul and vice-consul in Mostar, were also considered and built into the official policy of London. The opinions of British consular representatives in Bosnia and Hercegovina were especially important in the first phase of the Eastern Crisis (from the beginning of the uprising until the beginning of the Russian-Ottoman war on April 24, 1877), when Bosnia and Hercegovina assumed a central place in the British eastern policy.[15] For example, the instructions to Lord Salisbury on the affairs of Bosnia and Hercegovina, which were his guidelines in representing British interests during the conference, mostly consisted of the reports of Consul Holmes from Bosnia and Vice-Consul Freeman from Hercegovina.[16] In discussing the future of the territory on that occasion Holmes and Freeman advised that existing Bosnia-Hercegovinian institutions should not be abolished but rather should be strengthened and reformed, under obligatory international supervision. This proposal was accepted by the British government.[17] Reports that dealt with the conditions in Bosnia and Hercegovina and particularly in Sarajevo from the signing of the Peace Treaty of San Stefano to the arrival of Austro-Hungarian occupation troops in the country's capital were especially important in helping to shape British polity.[18]

Great Britain was a parliamentary state where the influence of other public institutions and opinion in forging foreign policy was more pronounced than anywhere else in the world. The Cabinet and Foreign Office had to consider domestic political attitudes (of members of Parliament, the Crown, the popular press, the public, church groups, and influential circles with commercial interests in the Levant) in creating foreign policy. Excluding external causes, British foreign policy had to respond to domestic as well as foreign pressures, changing from time to time while consistently attempting to keep its primary goals in focus: peace and the preservation of the balance of power in Europe. Practically speaking, Britain opposed any significant geopolitical change on the Continent, which in this instance meant support for preserving the sovereignty and the territorial integrity of the Ottoman Empire. In keeping with this policy, Britain undertook this obligation on three occasions: in 1856 with the Treaty of Paris and Tripartite Treaty and in 1871 in the Treaty of London. The support extended to the Porte was strengthened by the widespread opinion in London that the alternative to Ottoman rule over southeast Europe and the Near East would mean the expansion of the Russian Empire, threatening trade and the strategic lifeline to India, the jewel in the British imperial crown.

The defense of British interests on a global level required naval mastery and the readiness to use it as a last resort when other methods failed. British policy preferred to protect both the state and the interests of its subjects by using state authority and strong diplomatic and consular pressure. During the second half of the nineteenth century Britain had ten consulates and sixteen vice-consulates in the European part of the Ottoman Empire. The consular service network in the empire was strengthened by the establishment of a consulate in Sarajevo and vice-consulate in Mostar in 1857. The British Bosnian consulate was a political one: its first consul, Henry Adrian Churchill, had to observe how reforms in Bosnia were carried out, along with his usual consular duties. The same obligation was given to the vice-consul in Mostar, James Zohrab, and other British consuls and vice-consuls in Bosnia-Hercegovina until 1878. These included Edward St. John Neale, Churchill, and Holmes; acting consuls and vice-consuls Henry M. Jones, Edward Freeman, Harry Cooper, and Zohrab; and acting vice-consul Aleksandar Đurković.

British consular representatives in Bosnia-Hercegovina and in the surrounding Habsburg territory were specialists on Islam and eastern matters, not on Slavic affairs.[19] This shows that Great Britain's interest was in maintaining Bosnia-Hercegovina within the Ottoman Empire. Before they took duty in the Balkans, the British representatives were in consular service in other parts of the Ottoman Empire or in other Islamic states.

From the establishment of the British Consulate in Bosnia in 1857 until the Treaty of San Stefano in March 1878 British foreign policy was directed toward keeping Bosnia-Hercegovina within the state structure of the Ottoman Empire. After the treaty, due to its isolation, differences in the ruling Conservative Cabinet, and different centers of political power in its political system, Great Britain turned to a minimalist program in its eastern policy. British initiatives and support to enable the conditions in which the reforms in Bosnia-Hercegovina could be implemented were in keeping with Britain's goal of preserving the sovereignty and territorial integrity of the Ottoman Empire. The British believed that only the empire, reformed on modern principles, would be able to survive as an independent state in the face of Russian pressure.

Thus, in the period from the Treaty of Paris to the beginning of the outbreak of war in 1875, British foreign policy in the Ottoman Empire as a whole and especially in Bosnia and Hercegovina and its other European provinces was mostly expressed through the support of internal reforms to be carried out in accordance with the "European pattern."[20] During the Eastern Crisis (1875–78) British support for the Ottoman reforms continued, although Britain's main concern became pacification of Bosnia and Hercegovina.

The British consulate in Bosnia and the vice-consulate in Hercegovina were supposed to help in retaining this province within the frame of the Ottoman Empire. Hence the concrete activity of the consular representatives on the spot had three goals: to preserve peace and stability; to "amortize" the negative influence coming from the Russian and Austrian consulates as well as from the neighboring principalities of Serbia and Montenegro; and to support and induce the provincial Ottoman authority to carry out the reforms. This involved not only observing and reporting on the implementation of reforms but also practical influence on the Ottoman authorities in Bosnia-Hercegovina. The consuls sent suggestions to the British Embassy in Constantinople and the Foreign Office and asked them to use their influence on the Porte.[21]

The protection of the Christians guaranteed by the Treaty of Paris became the collective commitment of the European Powers, and putting it into effect became the task of the British consul in Bosnia and vice-consul in Hercegovina. Until the outbreak of war in 1875, the most important function of the British consulate in Bosnia was a preventive one, as described by Consul Holmes in a dispatch dated March 8, 1872.[22]

When the Eastern Crisis of 1875–78 began, Britons thought that the outbreak of war in Bosnia and Hercegovina in 1875 was primarily caused by interference from abroad. Although they did not deny the difficult socioeconomic conditions of Slavic peasants, they did not consider them the primary cause for the outbreak.[23] The British diplomats did not even use the term "uprising," viewing the outbreak of war in Bosnia and Hercegovina and its bordering territories as a war launched by Serbia and Montenegro against the Ottoman Empire.

At the onset of conflict in Hercegovina in the summer of 1875, Great Britain urged the Ottoman Empire to act promptly and to take the necessary political measures to pacify the rebel districts in order to prevent European intervention, which could, and eventually did, lead to an international crisis. After the Porte's appeal for assistance, however, the British government agreed to join the consular mission in August 1875.[24] After another appeal from the Porte, Britain also took part in the European Concert concerning the Andrássy Note (December 1875), a proposal of reforms made by the Austrian foreign minister.[25] It was strongly supported by Germany and later by other Great Powers, which might be expected to pacify Bosnia and Hercegovina, and called for "equality of religions, abolition of tax-farming, restriction of taxes to the use of the province in which they were raised, land reform and an European commission of revision."[26] That was the turning point for the fate of Bosnia and Hercegovina. After the Andrássy Note became known, the future of Bosnia and Hercegovina depended not on the ability of the Ottoman state to carry out the proclaimed reforms or on the success or failure of insurrection but on relations among the Great Powers.

This minimalist turn in British policy toward the future status of Bosnia and Hercegovina came after the failure of the Berlin Memorandum (May 1876) and especially after the failure of the Constantinople Conference (January 1877). Russia prepared for war and territorial expansion against the Ottoman Empire. The defeat of Serbia had rendered the Reichstadt Convention inoperative and Austria-Hungary had rejected Russian overtures for a parallel occupation of Bosnia and Bulgaria (September 1876), so new diplomatic activities to bring the two countries closer together were undertaken in great secrecy. Although new negotiations had revealed certain divergences of interpretation between the two governments, in the end a secret Austro-Russian Convention was concluded at Budapest, in order to avert a collision of interests in the event of possible Russo-Ottoman conflict.

According to the convention, in return for the promised neutrality and assurance to oppose all collective mediation and not to act upon article 8 of the Treaty of Paris or the triple guarantee treaty of April 1856, Austria-Hungary was assured the right to occupy Bosnia and Hercegovina at the moment that it found most convenient.[27]

An additional convention signed on March 18 reaffirmed the Reichstadt Convention as the basis of a future Austro-Russian joint policy.[28] After obtaining assurance against a possible attack from Austria-Hungary, Russia was able to secure its flank while planning a decisive attack on the Ottoman Empire. With that aim the Russian emperor and his foreign minister, Alexander Mikhailovich Gorchakov, sent Count Nikolai Pavlovich Ignatiev on a mission to London. The count, as a pan-Slavist diplomat and Russian ambassador in Constantinople (after 1864) who played an important role in Russia's foreign policy in Asia in the time of Alexander II, carried a proposal stressing the common attitude of the Great Powers, forcing the Porte to implement reforms and autonomy for the Christian minorities. The choice was not a wise one. Count Ignatiev had long been the chief bugbear of the London Russophobe press, so Lord Salisbury urged postponement, although he entertained the count at Hatfield.

Ignatiev did not succeed in getting London's assent to an understanding on the Eastern question, so the mission was continued by Ambassador Peter Shuvalov, who constantly pressured the British government to sign a protocol as a way to avoid a Russo-Ottoman war. Lord Augustus Loftus professed alarm that "unless difficulty as regards the demobilization can be solved and the Protocol signed, it is my conviction, that the Russian army will cross the Pruth in about three weeks." The Cabinet agreed to sign the protocol without waiting for the conclusion of the Ottoman-Montenegrin peace. Although both Disraeli and Edward Henry Stenly, Earl of Derby, were skeptical about the success of the protocol, they believed that Great Britain was protected from a Russian trap, because the Russian government could not blame London for incorporation and thus find an excuse for war. They trusted that the protocol "can do no harm even if it fails to do any good." In the end the protocol was signed in London on March 31 by Derby and the five ambassadors. It reaffirmed their "common interest in amelioration of the lot of the Christians of Turkey" and advised the Porte to put its armies on a peaceful footing and introduce prompt reforms, in lieu of which they would discuss common action in the interests of the Bosnian Christians. Ambassador Shuvalov, in order to show the conciliatory attitude of the Russian government, suggested that a Turkish envoy should be sent to St. Petersburg, to discuss parallel demobilization.[29]

It is interesting that Derby, not Disraeli, framed the policy of the protocol. The prime minister wrote to Salisbury: "So the Protocol is signed, and everybody writes to me about our triumph and the humiliation of Russia. I can't yet quite make head or tail of it."[30] The Porte considered the protocol derogatory to the sultan's dignity and independence. Musurus Paşa, Ottoman ambassador in London, told the foreign secretary that it would be better for the Ottoman Empire to face the alternative of war, "even if an unsuccessful war," than to accept the terms of the protocol. Everything indicated that the Porte was going to refuse the protocol, as indeed happened. On April 9 the Porte sent a circular dispatch to all the European powers, which contained objections to the protocol.[31]

Apart from this, the Porte refused to send its representatives to Russia to discuss disarmament. Matters became worse after the Ottoman-Montenegrin peace negotiations at Constantinople broke down because of excess territorial demands from the Montenegrin prince. The refusal of the protocol by the Porte gave the Russians an excuse for war, which would only be a matter of time. While Italy, Austria, and France had actively tried to prevent hostilities, Germany had done nothing. Sir Henry Layard made attempts to prevent war, but Derby and Disraeli remained rather passive. Derby thought nothing could be done, and Disraeli was suffering from bad health and had insufficient energy to act decisively. Disraeli viewed the war as a partition of the Ottoman Empire and believed that England would get a share.[32] Because of the isolation imposed on Great Britain during the Eastern Crisis, its relationship with the Ottoman Empire was limited; as was the case in the Crimean War, absolute support for the Porte could not be repeated at that time or in the future.[33]

Russia declared war on the Ottoman Empire on April 24, 1877, a bloody struggle that lasted longer than anybody could have expected. The creators of the British foreign policy quickly recovered from their passiveness caused by the Porte's refusal of the protocol and again became active in the diplomacy of the European Great Powers. From the perspective of this paper it is important to note that the Russian entrance into the war for the moment pushed aside the question of Bosnia and Hercegovina.[34] The same was true for British policy toward Bosnia and Hercegovina, which, amid the complexity of the Eastern Crisis, turned into a sideshow in the Eastern question. This turning point in British policy could be easily explained: Constantinople and control over the Straits became an issue. London had neither an ally on the international political scene nor cohesion in its own government, so it could not lead an effective response to a dramatic shift in the global balance of power. The importance of an international ally for Disraeli and the Queen was perceived by Shuvalov, who reported from London that Great Britain would quickly enter into a war if it found an ally and that it should remain neutral.[35]

The first serious step toward clarifying the relationship between London and St. Petersburg was made by Great Britain. On May 6, 1877, Lord Derby sent a note to Russia, which defined a minimum of British interests in the Near East: keeping open the communication between Europe and the East by the Suez Canal, the safety of the commercial route to the East, Constantinople remaining in the hands of the Porte, and confirmation of the existing arrangements made under European sanction that regulated navigation of the Bosphorus and Dardanelles. The British government also insisted on maintaining the existing status of the Persian Gulf.[36] Even superficial analysis of these British interests in the Eastern question confirms that the issue of Bosnia and Hercegovina became secondary in the policy of the London Cabinet.

Shuvalov had visited St. Petersburg and returned to London with a satisfactory answer. He assured the British government that Russia had "neither the interests, the desire, nor the means" to endanger the British priorities outlined in Derby's note of May 6. Shuvalov also indicated the main terms on which Russia would conclude peace with the Ottoman Empire if the Porte consented to negotiate before Russian troops had crossed the Balkans: a vassal Bulgarian state, administrative guarantees for the Bulgarians south of the Balkans and for the other European provinces, Bosnian autonomy, territorial concessions for Serbia and Montenegro, and Bessarabia and Batum for Russia itself, with Romania receiving compensation in the Dobruja.[37] By promising that British vital interests (Constantinople and the Straits) would not be jeopardized, Russia secured the neutrality of Great Britain during its war against the Ottoman Empire, and the Porte's hope for British military or diplomatic intervention remained unrealized. After an unexpectedly long war, Russia forced the Ottoman Empire to sign the Treaty of San Stefano.[38] The treaty itself showed that Russia did not keep its promises to Vienna (the Reichstadt and Budapest Convention) and London, which naturally led to the possibility of coalition between the deceived parties—Great Britain and Austria-Hungary. The complicated international situation and disagreement in the British Cabinet, where Disraeli could not find enough support for a more active foreign policy, led to a complete reversal in the British attitude toward the future status of Bosnia and Hercegovina.

The Porte, faced with the fall of the fortress of Plevna, accepted an armistice in Edirne on January 31, 1878. The terms of the Edirne armistice proposed the significant territorial enlargement and independence of Romania, Montenegro, and Serbia; a large autonomous Bulgarian principality under an elected Christian prince; and an autonomous organization for Bosnia and Hercegovina. The Treaty of San Stefano sanctioned the terms of the Edirne armistice, proposing establishment of an autonomous "Greater Bulgaria" and territorial enlargement and independence for Romania, Serbia, and Montenegro (significant territorial extension of Montenegro toward Hercegovina, the *sancak* of Novi Pazar, and Albania; territorial enlargement of Serbia through the Bosnian *eyalet* in the region of Mali Zvornik). For Bosnia and Hercegovina it proposed an implementation of the European proposals, which were communicated to the Ottoman plenipotentiaries at the first session of the Constantinople Conference, with certain modifications, on which Austria-Hungary, Russia, and the Ottoman Empire should agree.[39]

The authorities in Bosnia were officially informed by the Porte on May 5 that peace had been signed between Russia and the Ottoman Empire. In the first moment this news was received by the people with extraordinary indifference, although they naturally had some slight anxiety about the exact form of the administrative autonomy of the province. Freeman gave his opinion about the attitude of the domestic population

toward the future of Bosnia and Hercegovina and the possibility of organizing Bosnian autonomy:

> I am inclined to think that among the native Mussulmans, there
> is a growing inclination in favour of Austria. They perceive that
> the power of the Porte in Europe is shattered, they are opposed
> to annexation to either Serbia or Montenegro…and they there-
> fore think that their position would probably be better, and their
> rights and religion be more fully secured to them, were the coun-
> try annexed to Austria…. But I cannot refrain from expressing to
> Your Excellency my conviction of the difficulty, I might almost say
> impossibility of organising an effective administration out of the
> local elements at command. The higher posts in the administration
> have always been held by Osmanlis, and there are but few native
> Mussulmans of sufficient education, or who have had the necessary
> experience to enable them to efficiently perform important official
> functions. Among the Christians there are men of somewhat better
> education, but these are all engaged in trade.[40]

It is well known in historiography that Russia, by secret agreements
arranged in Reichstadt and Budapest, gave its consent for the Austro-
Hungarian acquisition of Bosnia and Hercegovina. Also, from the first
contacts for common accession of the Great Powers, leading to the Constantinople Conference, the Austrian government opposed political autonomy for Bosnia and Hercegovina; so a sharp Austrian reaction against
the terms of the Treaty of San Stefano was expected. Vienna agitated for
the revision of the treaty, with help from Russia's rivals and opponents of
its policy on the Balkans, especially Great Britain.[41] The British government, after perceiving that it should ultimately take action toward Russia to revise the solutions proposed by the Treaty of San Stefano, readily
accepted a collaboration offered by Vienna. This was in accordance with
one of the basic principles of British policy — that Great Britain had to
have a Continental ally if it wanted to act successfully against one of the
other Continental powers — as well as with earlier efforts to maintain the
balance of power.[42]

After the terms of the Preliminary Treaty of San Stefano had become
known, Great Britain and Austria-Hungary started negotiations. This finally resulted in Lord Salisbury's proposal to the Berlin Congress to offer
a mandate to Austria-Hungary to occupy and administer Bosnia and Hercegovina.[43] The possibility that Disraeli mentioned for the first time to the

Queen in the "most confidential Cabinet Memorandum on his Eastern policy," dated May 16, 1876, and written for the occasion of the beginning of an international crisis caused by the emergence of the Berlin Memorandum, now became a reality. On that occasion he contended that it would be better for the Ottoman Empire to give up Bosnia and Hercegovina altogether than to acquiesce in the Berlin Memorandum and that it would also be better for Great Britain that the Ottoman Empire "should do so, than adopt the alternative now offered."[44]

In negotiations with Austria-Hungary, considering the status of Bosnia and Hercegovina and its borders with Serbia and Montenegro, Great Britain took the position that "although the interests of England are not immediately concerned in this matter of boundary, it will be of highest importance that the frontier lines should be traced in such manner that there may not be left perpetual occasions of dispute."[45] When the two governments came into open negotiations it became obvious to the British that the final Austro-Hungarian goal was accession of Bosnia and Hercegovina.

In earlier communication with the British Count Gyula Andrássy had publicly disclaimed any intention of annexing or occupying Bosnia. But on April 6 Count Ferenc Zichy (as instructed by Andrássy) offered Vienna's diplomatic support in attempting to revise the terms of the Treaty of San Stefano if the Ottoman Empire would agree to give up Bosnia and Hercegovina to Austria-Hungary.[46] On April 24 Count Friedrich Ferdinand Beust, the Austro-Hungarian ambassador in London, communicated to Lord Salisbury a long memorandum showing that the autonomy of Bosnia and Hercegovina under Ottoman rule was impossible and that the only satisfactory solution, even from the viewpoint of the Porte, was the annexation of Bosnia and Hercegovina to Austria-Hungary. In his dispatch on the same day Beust informed Salisbury that a partial occupation of Bosnia had been proposed to the Porte.[47] This action had the aim of obtaining the support of Great Britain for Austro-Hungarian acquisition of Bosnia and Hercegovina at the future congress.

The reaction to this memorandum showed that Great Britain had definitely changed the course of its policy toward Bosnia and Hercegovina. Lord Salisbury, the new foreign secretary, stated on May 4, 1878:

> It is not necessary that I should dwell at any length upon the views in respect to Bosnia and Hercegovina, and adjacent territories.... It is impossible to deny the weight of the reasons which he assigned in that despatch for the course which Austria has resolved to take....

But in the absence of any definite knowledge of the views entertained by the Porte, and by the other Powers, it would be difficult
for Her Majesty's Government to enter upon any appreciation of
a measure which in relation to the previous system of Austria is
so entirely novel, and which at the same time has so little bearing
upon the special interests of England.... in the event of such con-
cordant action between the two Powers as they have ventured to
hope for, they will not offer any opposition either in Congress or
elsewhere to this Austrian project.[48]

Salisbury displayed the same attitude toward Bosnia and Hercegovina's
future fate five days later (May 9) in a dispatch to new British ambassador
at Constantinople, Henry Layard, noting that sooner or later the greater
part of European Ottoman Empire, including Bosnia, "must go."[49]

The British diplomatic service in Constantinople was engaged in assurance of Austro-Hungarian interests in Bosnia and Hercegovina. Henry
Layard (the ambassador in Constantinople beginning in April 1878) received instructions from Lord Salisbury on May 11 to give an opinion to
the Porte on the proposed occupation of Bosnia by Austria. He was to
say that "he thinks it would be wiser course not to offer resistance to the
wishes of Austria in this matter" and advise the Porte to use the opportunity to make conditions for the support of Vienna in urging the congress
to accept the line of the Balkans as the boundary of the new Bulgarian
principality.[50] It is clear that the British had a double goal in gaining the
Porte's consent to such a solution of the Bosnian question — supporting
Austrian wishes to consolidate an alliance with Vienna and pushing the
zone under Russia's influence further from Constantinople to protect its
own fundamental goals regarding the Eastern question. In the dispatch
of May 17 Layard reported that he had been informed by the Ottoman
prime minister that the sultan had given him and the other ministers full
authority to examine and report upon the Austrian proposal of provisional occupation and that he was ready to act entirely upon their advice.[51]

Layard understood that the Ottoman prime minister was not personally unfavorably disposed toward the proposal, if he could be assured that
it had no hidden purpose and was not intended as a first step to a permanent occupation. The prime minister expressed his opinion that, "if the
Porte consented to the Austrian proposal, a written agreement should
be come to on the subject between the two Governments, either in the
form of a Convention or of an exchange of notes." This would prevent
Austria-Hungary from departing from or denying its engagements, and

the Ottoman prime minister asked the British government to act accordingly. Layard's dispatch showed that the final proposal made to the Porte was "a very different one from that first put forward by Count Zichy. There was now no question of the cession of Bosnia and Hercegovina, to which there were very grave objections, but of a temporary occupation of these provinces by Austro-Hungarian troops on the invitation of the Porte itself."[52]

The occupation was declared to be in the interests of both the Ottoman Empire and Austria-Hungary and would facilitate the common action of London and Vienna in favor of the Ottoman Empire. The Porte was told that it was at liberty to reserve the sovereign rights of the sultan in Bosnia and Hercegovina. On this occasion Layard, upon instructions from Lord Salisbury, indicated to the Ottoman prime minister the importance of not irritating Vienna by a rapid refusal of the Austrian proposal.[53] The Austrian government, after sounding out the Porte's attitude to the cession of this province, limited its proposal to a temporary occupation, reserving the sovereign rights over Bosnia and Hercegovina to the sultan. The Porte also tried to negotiate an offensive and defensive alliance with Austria for protection of Bosnia, but Count Andrássy expressed his dissatisfaction with such a proposal.[54]

News about a possible Austrian occupation of Bosnia provoked the energetic opposition of its domestic population, particularly of the Bosnian Muslims. Near the end of May 1878 an address to the sultan had been prepared by certain Muslims of Sarajevo and was being circulated for signature. Among other points, it demanded that an Austrian occupation of the country should be resisted to the utmost. This was the beginning of preparations for resistance to the Austrian occupation. The ostensible agents in this matter were Muhamed Efendi Hadžijamaković, a man with good reputation in the town, and Kaukčija Abdulah Efendi, imam of the bey's mosque (chief mosque), with support from even more influential persons. Freeman reported that about five hundred signatures had been affixed to the address by May 27. He believed that the address was signed chiefly by the lower classes and that the more intelligent and respectable Muslims declined to have anything to do with that activity. Also, Freeman wrote that it was rumored that "certain of the authorities themselves are the chief agitators." During the time of the Berlin Congress he suspected that the Ottoman authorities, provincial as well as central, encouraged and supported resistance to the Austrian occupation of Bosnia and Hercegovina.[55]

Like other foreign observers, Freeman also wrongly concluded that the Muslims of this province were so disheartened by their losses and by the result of the war with Russia that they would accept with resignation almost any change of government or administration unless they were aroused to opposition. Convinced that the Porte could no longer afford them efficient protection, they would be quite willing to see the country occupied by Austria. They had no particular liking for that power, "but left to choose between anarchy and annexation to Servia, to Montenegro or to Austria they prefer the latter as the lesser evil." Agitators against the Austrian occupation of the country motivated the Muslims against Austria by telling them that "they will not be permitted the free exercise of their religion, that the seclusion of their women will be intruded on, and that their lands and houses will be taken from them." Also, the Orthodox Bosnians were not favorably disposed toward an Austrian occupation, but their public proclamations that they would prefer to remain Ottoman subjects served a long-term policy that, in the end, should lead to the annexation of Bosnia-Hercegovina to Serbia.[56] On the other side, the occupation of Bosnia by Austria was supported by some Bosnians, mostly the religious Bosnian Catholic elite and many of their flock as well as some influential Bosnian Muslims.[57]

Notables and ordinary people of Sarajevo, Christian as well as Muslim, were summoned a few times and pressed by the authorities to hear the result of communication between the minister of foreign affairs and the governor-general, Mazhar Paşa. The governor-general had asked for instructions on what course he was to pursue with regard to the agitation caused by the rumored approaching occupation of Bosnia by Austria and the alleged departure of a Bosnian deputation to Vienna to advocate annexation to the Austrian Empire. People were told that Safvet Paşa had stated that no deputation from Bosnia had arrived at Vienna, that no Austrian occupation of the country was imminent, and therefore that they had no cause for agitation on this score. According to the Treaty of San Stefano, Bosnia remained under the direct authority of the Porte; but Safvet Paşa announced that a quasi-autonomous administration would be introduced, which gave the population considerable satisfaction.[58] At the beginning of June great agitation among the Muslims of Sarajevo (and, in lesser measure, of other towns) continued in connection with the address to the sultan. Some of the leading Christians had also been invited to associate themselves with the Muslims in this step. The agitation was followed by stormy meetings attended by many people. They decided to forward a petition directly to the Porte, in which the Christians would be invited to take part, asking that measures be taken for the repression of the many abuses of the local government. Finally, eleven individuals were appointed as representatives of the Muslim population to draw up a statement of their grievances and demands; four Orthodox Christians, two Catholics, and two Jews were also invited to take part in those deliberations, which concerned all the people.[59]

Some people also suggested the idea of addressing a petition to the European Congress, but Freeman dissuaded them from that step, saying that "it would only cause further complication and raise hopes which perhaps could not be realised, and assured them at the same time that if Congress met the future of this province would undoubtedly be taken fully into consideration, and the rights of all sects and classes of the population duly respected."[60] Revolt against Austrian occupation slowly became a revolt against Ottoman rule too. People somehow knew that the Ottoman government, willingly or not, was participating in a negotiation deciding their future without their consent. The result of the international crisis and looming occupation resulted in the formation of the National Council on June 5, with members of all creeds. The council named a National Assembly, which should represent the wishes of the whole population of Bosnia and Hercegovina. The movement did not intend to ask for an independent Bosnian state but secured a high degree of administrative autonomy from the Ottoman state.[61]

In return for British support of Austrian administration of Bosnia-Hercegovina, Vienna agreed to ally with Great Britain in opposition to the creation of a Greater Bulgaria while helping to preserve the integrity of the Ottoman Empire. Focusing on the Asiatic part of the empire, where Britain had direct interests, British plenipotentiaries at the Berlin Congress (June 13 to July 13, 1878) would actively pursue this diplomatic course.[62] Shortly before the congress Great Britain came to a definitive agreement with Austria-Hungary and Italy about common goals in the Eastern question and a common attitude toward the current crisis. In a note of June 6, 1878, these three countries precisely defined their common approach on the basis of retaining peace and the status quo in the east as well as preserving the integrity of the Ottoman Empire.[63]

Although Bosnia-Hercegovina was not mentioned directly in this document, acceptance of its cession to Austria-Hungary was probably viewed through the prism of retaining the sultan's sovereign rights in this province. It was not legally in opposition to the postulate of the territorial integrity of the empire. The note also avoided mentioning the principalities of Romania, Serbia, and Montenegro as well as the loss of Bessarabia and lesser parts of the Asiatic Ottoman Empire, although the territorial integrity of the Ottoman state was significantly violated by the terms of the Berlin Congress, which made these countries independent or annexed them to Russia. This change in considerable measure was the result of Salisbury's Foreign Office policy: "the object of Her Majesty's Government is not the independence and integrity of the Ottoman Empire, as has been stated, but the good government and assured peace of those populations of Turkey," as the home secretary Richard Assheton Cross noted, probably after consultation with Lord Salisbury.[64] The congress was organized as a measure against Russia and should neutralize the advances that it gained by arms. Moreover, at the same time this was a warning to the Ottoman government to repudiate its obligations to Russia as the result of military pressure.

In order to assure the support of Russia and the Ottoman Empire for the congress, London activated its diplomacy to persuade them to attend it, because it was going to discuss questions mostly connected with these two countries. Great Britain and its foreign secretary took advantage of Russia's inability to wage another war. Negotiations between London and St. Petersburg began with British objections to the terms of the Treaty of San Stefano, which were communicated to St. Petersburg, through Shuvalov, at the beginning of May.[65]

Thus London insisted on a revision of the entire treaty concluded in San Stefano, not just some parts of it.[66] The final result of negotiations between the two powers was the signing of the Protocol of May 30, which was the basis of an agreement for the future congress. Russia agreed to a division of the "Greater Bulgaria" into two provinces, one autonomous and the other with a large degree of administrative autonomy. Britain agreed to a cession of Bessarabia to Russia and a new cession of Batumi and the greater part of Armenia to Russia.[67] All of this shows that the British government had lost its old pretensions concerning the maintenance of the sovereignty and territorial integrity of the Ottoman Empire and confirms that the British Cabinet's change in policy toward the future status of Bosnia and Hercegovina was part of a general change of course. It was caused by the new international situation and changes in relationship among the Great Powers, as well as by changes on the British political scene. This Russo-British agreement perhaps also shows that the Russian policy and its great appetite expressed in the Treaty of San Stefano may have been part of a game among the Great Powers — ask for maximum gains to attain a more reasonable goal. In that sense we can assume that the tsar and the

Russian government were aware that in the end Bosnia and Hercegovina would go to Austria-Hungary.

As the case of Bosnia and Hercegovina shows, Great Britain negotiated with the Porte about open questions and possible solutions during May 1878. Its policy at that time was concentrated on protection of "the Turkish Asiatic Empire" and an extensive zone around Constantinople and the Straits, which resulted in the cession of Cyprus ("the key to Western Asia") to Britain in return for a defensive alliance for "the protection of Turkey's Asiatic Empire."[68]

The resolution of the Bosnian question at the Berlin Congress was the result of the preparations by Great Britain and Austria-Hungary in the period between the signing of the Treaty of San Stefano and the opening of the Congress, analyzed above. Neither the requests and wishes of the rebels nor the Ottoman government's ability to suppress the uprising and implement the reform measures had any influence on the determination of the future fate of Bosnia and Hercegovina.[69] Great Britain was represented at the Congress by Disraeli, Salisbury, and Odo Russell, the first occasion on which Great Britain sent both its prime minister and foreign secretary to such an event.[70] The selection of the representatives indicated the course of a leading policy, almost halfway between two extremes from earlier times: the views of Disraeli and Gladstone. It was embodied in the personality of the foreign ministry, Lord Salisbury.

The question of the future status of Bosnia and Hercegovina was brought up on June 28. At the beginning of the discussion on the territorial redistribution and revision of article 14 of the Preliminary Treaty of San Stefano in relation to the question of Bosnia and Hercegovina, Count Andrássy stated that the proposed autonomy of these provinces would not produce long-lasting peace. He said that the vital interest of Austria-Hungary was only "a solution of Bosnian-Hercegovinian question which would be likely to bring about the durable pacification of the said provinces, and to prevent the occurrence of events which have put the peace of Europe to such grave danger, and created for Austria-Hungary, while it imposed on her great sacrifices and severe material losses, an intolerable situation, of which she could not admit the continuance." He also declared that his government would be ready to accept any solution that "might give hope of the prompt and definitive pacification of the provinces under discussion." Andrássy presented Vienna's opinion that the task of organizing an autonomous administration in Bosnia, as demanded of the Ottoman state by European powers and article 14, would be difficult or even impossible to fulfill. Among other self-serving reasons, according to Vienna, were the national, religious, and geographical conditions in the provinces at the end of the Eastern Crisis, characterized by the "fanaticism" and "antagonism" that divided the populations. The large number of refugees and the problem of their repatriation, an unsolved agrarian question, disturbances in those countries, and the territorial changes resulting from the war were insuperable obstacles for the Porte in fulfilling its duty.[71]

Lord Salisbury repeated Andrássy's opinions about the problems in the country and inability of the Porte to solve them. He referred to the specifics of Bosnia-Hercegovina: the political importance of its geographical position; the recently concluded insurrection, which had resulted from the religious and social antagonism of the population as well as the unsolved agrarian question; and possible opposition to the Ottoman government stimulated by the recent successes of Serbia and Montenegro and territorial changes. Salisbury declared the necessity of assuring a government that not only would have the means necessary for the establishment of a good administration but would also possess forces sufficient to suppress disturbances. He added that Bosnia and Hercegovina did not contribute to the wealth or strength of the Porte or have strategic value for the Ottoman Empire. Salisbury concluded the proposal with the following words: "For these motives the Government of the Queen proposes to the assembled Powers that the Congress should decide that the provinces of Bosnia and Hercegovina shall be occupied and administered by Austria-Hungary." The proposal was supported by representatives of Germany, France, Russia, and Italy. Ottoman plenipotentiaries expressed opposition to such a proposal and defended the position and ability of their government to fulfil the program of reform, "which may appear at this moment most appropriate to the exigencies of the circumstances." On Bismarck's initiative this protocol remained open for further observations that the Russian plenipotentiaries might wish to offer. At the end of this discussion the Ottoman Empire and its representatives agreed to make an arrangement directly with Austria-Hungary.[72]

Both before and during the congress the sultan and the Ottoman government opposed the occupation of Bosnia and Hercegovina by Austria in every possible way. When this proved impossible, they attempted to share the administration of the country with the Austrians, as a lesser evil.[73] They were obviously aware that the mandate for occupation given to Austria-Hungary without any time limit would probably lead to its final annexation of Bosnia and Hercegovina. The behavior of the sultan and the government was also influenced by some degree by fear of the reaction of the Muslim masses and some influential circles in the Ottoman capital. But all of the Ottoman efforts to stop or limit the occupation were unsuccessful. They only succeeded in persuading Austria-Hungary to conclude a bilateral agreement through direct negotiation. The sultan retained formal sovereignty over Bosnia and Hercegovina as well as some specific rights for Bosnian Muslims and the country itself.

The British government, its representatives at the congress, and its ambassador in Constantinople and consular representatives in Bosnia helped in the realization of the Austrian plan to gain this bordering Ottoman province.[74] The Ottoman government and its representatives at the congress wrongly expected help from the British but in the end learned that Great Britain was the wrong horse to rely upon.[75] Lord Salisbury's proposal that Austria-Hungary should be entrusted with a mandate for the occupation of Bosnia and Hercegovina was the end result of negotiations between the two countries. The British foreign minister himself had given Britain's consent by a secret convention directly concluded with Count Andrássy on June 6. In the Bosnian question Russia was bound by the secret agreements of the Reichstadt and Budapest Convention, which were reactivated after the change in the constellation of powers on the international political scene and by achievement of the alliance of Vienna and London. Germany gave its full backing; France consented in return for a veto of any discussion of Egypt and Syria. Only Italy had some reservations, but it was the weakest country in the concert and completely isolated in this issue. Austria-Hungary could clearly obtain the approval of the European powers for the annexation. But the Porte's opposition and the differing interests of Germans and Magyars in a complicated Dual State system of Austria-Hungary led the Ministry of Foreign Affairs to choose occupation rather than annexation and to exclude the *sancak* of Novi Pazar from the arrangement. The Porte had to accept this decision and agreed to occupation of Bosnia and Hercegovina without any time limit.

At the beginning of July, Austrian consul-general Konrad Wassitsch received news from Andrássy and forwarded it to the governor-general in Bosnia that the European Congress had consented to the occupation of Bosnia by Austria. Representatives of the people of Sarajevo telegraphed the Porte on July 4 to inquire what course it intended to pursue but received no answer. The population reacted very sharply: shops were closed, and the Muslims all took up arms. They proceeded en masse, with some Orthodox Christians, to the *paşa* and declared their intention to oppose Austria. They besieged the barracks, liberated the military prisoners, and insisted on the immediate resignation and departure of the commander of the troops, against whom they had already brought complaints. When the Bosniak troops sided with the people, the situation in the town became critical.

Constantinople sent a message that the question of an Austrian occupation of Bosnia had indeed been brought before Congress and that the Porte was actually engaged in discussing the conditions of such an occupation. This served as a pretext for an outburst of popular feeling and a demonstration against the government, especially against the military authorities. On Friday, July 5, the bazaars and all the shops were closed again; there was great excitement in the town, and all the Muslims were armed. The only troops in the Sarajevo garrison were Bosniaks—the battalion raised in the town and district of Sarajevo. They sided with the people and refused to obey their officers. Governor-general Mazhar Paşa, Mustehsar Constant Paşa, and a few other employees and notables had arrived on the scene and endeavored to calm the people, but they could not be persuaded to disperse.

On July 6 a deputation representing the Muslims, Orthodox Christians, Catholics, and Jews of Sarajevo brought Consul Freeman a request to forward a telegram to the Berlin Congress protesting against any foreign occupation of the country but expressing their readiness to accept the control of a mixed European Commission. This telegram was signed by people of all creeds and classes; but many have acknowledged, as Freeman wrote, that they signed only under the influence of anxiety over the future. Freeman gave his opinion that disturbances proved the absolute necessity of a foreign occupation of the country to carry out reforms: the Ottoman government "has so far lost its influence and prestige with the Mussulmans of the province that they could only be kept in subjection by a large military force." Demonstrations against an Austrian occupation had occurred at Mostar, Travnik, and other towns in the province. In Hercegovina the people were mostly tranquil.[76] Neither the demonstrations expressing the feelings and wishes of Muslims and other Bosnian populations nor the memorandum sent to the Berlin Congress by Orthodox rebels from Bosnia, asking for an annexation of the country to "Serbian principalities," had any influence on British Bosnian policy or the decisions of the Great Powers in Berlin.[77]

Freeman assessed the conduct of the Ottoman authorities in Bosnia as suspicious and wrote that "the Turkish Government was playing a double game and exciting the people to make a show at least of resistance." But

Hafiz Paşa assured Freeman that he had given instructions, as ordered by the Porte, to all the commanders on the frontiers not to oppose the entry of the Austrians by force. Freeman thought that two separate and opposing influences were at work in the country — "both however proceeding from the Government." He concluded his observation on the responsibility of the Ottoman authority if no opposition came "from the people of this province either Mussulman or Christian, to an Austrian occupation, if the Turkish Government acted loyally and abstained from intrigue and instigation."[78] In fact the attitude of the Ottoman authorities toward the armed resistance to Austrian occupation was ambiguous.

As Kemal Karpat correctly concludes, "the upper echelon of the Ottoman administration were sympathetic to the uprising but did not support it openly. To do so would have been a violation of the Berlin Treaty and would have entailed international relations.... The Sultan, despite his formal denials, supported the uprising through secret communication with the Commander-in-chief and religious heads."[79] The people in Bosnia continued their preparations for resistance to the Austrian troops. When Austrian military forces entered Bosnian territory on July 29, intensive fighting started. The Austrians had to use between 82,000 and 300,000 soldiers, wage seventy-six battles, and spend eight days to break the resistance of the Bosnian population.[80] These figures show clearly that it was a broad popular movement. Except for a number of supporters of the Austrian occupation (the majority of the Catholic population and some members of the Muslim upper class), the majority of the Muslims, Orthodox Christians, and, to some extent, Catholics and Jews of all classes took part in the resistance. The population of the territory of present Bosnia and Hercegovina at that time consisted of about 400,000 Orthodox Christians, 330,000 Muslims, 180,000 Catholics, and 10,000 others. The resistance was the Bosnians' response to the Treaty of Berlin.

The Berlin Congress made important decisions on the future of Bosnia and Hercegovina, including independence and territorial concessions to Serbia and Montenegro (Montenegrin territory more than doubled, in great measure at the expense of a former Bosnian *vilayet*). An important article of the agreement for the coming history of Bosnia and Hercegovina and the Balkans was the retention of the *sancak* of Novi Pazar in the framework of the Ottoman Empire, leaving Serbia and Montenegro separated. Austria-Hungary got rights to garrison the *sancak*.[81]

The British representatives were very satisfied with the final epilogue of the congress. As Lord Salisbury reported in the dispatch of July 13,

"The policy which has received the sanction of the Congress of Berlin is generally coincident with that which has been sustained by Her Majesty's Government since the Treaty of San Stefano was published, and which was indicated in the circular of the 1 April."[82] It is noteworthy that this extensive dispatch, which pointed out that all goals of the British policy had been realized after the Congress, did not mention Bosnia and Hercegovina at all.[83]

A long period in the history of Bosnia-Hercegovina under Ottoman rule ended de facto with the Treaty of Berlin. Although the sultan's sovereignty over this part of Europe was maintained until October 1908, this was mainly symbolic. The resistance of the Bosnian population against Austro-Hungarian occupation and the establishment of the new administration was initially fierce (but outside the topic of this paper). Because of unsatisfactory developments on both the international and domestic political scene, Great Britain had one of the most important roles in this process of change from sultan to kaiser and king, as part of the dénouement of this part of the Eastern question. British policy was only a qualified success, however, because it involved a significant departure from Britain's earlier objective of maintaining the territorial integrity of the Ottoman Empire in the face of Russian expansion.

SUMMARY

British foreign policy regarding the status of Bosnia and Hercegovina during the Eastern Crisis of 1875–78 went through two phases. The first one started with the tumultuous uprisings in Bosnia and Bulgaria and ended with the signing of the Peace Treaty of San Stefano; the second one lasted from San Stefano until the Berlin Congress. The first stage was characterized by staying on the course of guaranteeing the integrity of the Ottoman Empire and keeping Bosnia and Hercegovina within that empire, while in the second stage Britain agreed to the cession or appropriation of significant territories located on the margins of the Ottoman Empire while safeguarding the status quo in Constantinople and the Straits. The Congress of Berlin had a decisive impact on the history of Bosnia and Hercegovina and its people, especially the Bosnian Muslims. It was a turning point in the political, economic, and cultural life of Bosnia and Hercegovina, which entered into a new civilizational sphere. But it also sowed the seeds for terrible carnage in the future along geopolitical and civilizational fault lines exacerbated by regional and international powers.

NOTES

1. National Archives of the United Kingdom (formerly Public Record Office), Foreign Office Archives, London (FO), FO 78/2238, Holmes to Granville, London, March 8, 1872.

2. Međunarodni naučni skup povodom: 100-godišnjice ustanka u Bosni i Hercegovini, drugim balkanskim zemljama i istočnoj krizi 1875–1878. godine (Sarajevo, October 1–3, 1975). The papers and discussions were published in *Međunarodni naučni skup povodom: 100-godišnjice ustanka u Bosni i Hercegovini, drugim balkanskim zemljama i istočnoj krizi 1875–1878. godine*. Naučni skup: Otpor austrougarskoj okupaciji 1878. godine u Bosni i Hercegovini (Sarajevo, October 23–24, 1978). The papers and discussions were published in *Naučni skup: Otpor austrougarskoj okupaciji 1878. godine u Bosni i Hercegovini*. Naučni skup: 100 godina ustanka u Hercegovini 1882. godine (Sarajevo, October 21–22, 1982). The papers and discussions were published in Hamdija Ćemerlić, ed., *Naučni skup: 100 godina ustanka u Hercegovini 1882. godine*.

3. See "The Yugoslav Peoples in the XIX Century and the Beginning of the XX Century (to 1914), Bosnia and Hercegovina," 324–39; Nusret Šehić, "Ustanak u Bosni i Hercegovini 1875–78. u jugoslovenskoj istoriografiji u posljednjih deset godina (1965–1975)"; Andrija Nikić, "Bibliografija Hercegovačkog ustanka (1875–1878)"; Dušan Berić, "Pogled na literaturu o otporu austrougarskoj okupaciji 1878. u Bosni i Hercegovini"; Nedim Filipović, ed., *Savjetovanje o istoriografiji Bosne i Hercegovine (1945–1982)*, 37–77; Milorad Ekmečić, "Rezultati jugoslovenske istoriografije o istočnom pitanju 1875–1878," *Jugoslovenski istorijski časopis*, 1–2 (1977); Jelena Maksić, Anica Lolić, *Bibliografija jugoslovenske literature o velikoj istočnoj krizi 1875–1878*, 5–129; Milorad Ekmečić, *Međunarodni naučni skup: Problemi istorije Bosne i Hercegovine 1850–1875*, 15–33; Dušan Berić, "Bosna i Hercegovina od kraja XVIII veka do 1914. u najnovijoj jugoslovenskoj istoriografiji"; "Referati sa Međunarodnog naučnog skupa: Historiografija o Bosni i Hercegovini 1980–1988."

4. Vaso Čubrilović, *Bosanski ustanak 1875–1878*; Vaso Čubrilović, "Istočna kriza 1875–1878. i njen značaj za međunarodne odnose koncem XIX i početkom XX veka"; Vasilj Popović, *Agrarno pitanje i turski neredi za vreme reformnog režima Abdul Medžida (1839–1861)*; Grgur Jakšić, *Bosna i Hercegovina na Berlinskom kongresu*; Milorad Ekmečić, *Ustanak u Bosni 1875–1878*; Milorad Ekmečić, "Istorijski značaj ustanka u Bosni i Hercegovini 1875–1878"; Milorad Ekmečić, "Karakteristike Berlinskog kongresa 1878. godine."

5. For example, Hamdija Kapidžić, "Agrarno pitanje u Bosni i Hercegovini za vrijeme austrougarske uprave (1878–1918)"; Tomislav Kraljačić, *Kalajev režim u Bosni i Hercegovini (1882–1903)*; Iljas Hadžibegović, *Postanak radničke klase u Bosni i Hercegovini i njen razvoj do 1914. godine*; Iljas Hadžibegović, "Radnički socijalistički pokret u Bosni i Hercegovini do kraja prvog svjetskog rata i stvaranje zajedničke države 1918. godine"; Ibrahim Tepić, *Bosna i Hercegovina u ruskim izvorima (1856–1878)*; Đorđe Mikić, "O kolonizaciji stranih seljaka u Bosni i Hercegovini u vrijeme austrougarske uprave."

6. As an example, see discussions in Milorad Ekmečić, ed., *Naučni skup: Otpor austrougarskoj okupaciji 1878. godine u Bosni i Hercegovini*, 404–5, 422–24.

7. Muhamed Filipović, ed., *Socijalistička Republika Bosna i Hercegovina, Separat iz drugog izdanja Enciklopedije Jugoslavije.*

8. Atif Purivatra et al., eds., *ABC Muslimana*; Avdo Sućeska et al., *Istina o Bosni i Hercegovini, Činjenice iz istorije Bosne i Hercegovine*; Ahmed S. Aličić, *Pokret za autonomiju Bosne od 1831. do 1832. godine*; Ibrahim Karabegović, ed., *Bosna i Hercegovina od najstarijih vremena do kraja Drugog svjetskog rata*; Mustafa Imamović, *Historija Bošnjaka*; Robert J. Donia, *Islam pod dvoglavim orlom: Muslimani Bosne i Hercegovine 1878–1914.*

9. Robert J. Donia, *Sarajevo: biografija grada*; Edin Radušić, "Bosna i Hercegovina u britanskoj politici od 1857. do 1878. godine."

10. Međunarodna konferencija: Identitet Bosne i Hercegovine kroz historiju, Institut za istoriju Sarajevo, Sarajevo, September 25–26, 2009; Naučni skup: Bosna i Hercegovina u okviru Austro-Ugarske 1878–1918, Filozofski fakultet u Sarajevu, March 30–31, 2009.

11. Barbara Jelavich, *The Ottoman Empire, the Great Powers, and the Straits Question, 1870–1887*; Kenneth Bourne, *The Foreign Policy of Victorian England, 1830–1902*; R. W. Seton-Watson, *Britain in Europe, 1789–1914: A Survey of Foreign Policy*; R. W. Seton-Watson, *Disraeli, Gladstone and the Eastern Question*; Charles Jelavich and Barbara Jelavich, *The Establishment of the Balkan National States, 1804–1920*; Barbara Jelavich, *History of the Balkans, Eighteenth and Nineteenth Centuries*; M. S. Anderson, *The Eastern Question, 1774–1923*; T. R. Gourvish and Alan O'Day, eds., *Later Victorian Britain, 1867–1900*; Marian Kent, ed., *The Great Powers and the End of the Ottoman Empire*; Michael Scott-Baumann, ed., *Years of Expansion: Britain, 1815–1914*; Llewellyn Woodward, *The Oxford History of England: The Age of Reform, 1815–1870*; R. C. K. Ensor, *England, 1870–1914*; Allan Cunningham, *Eastern Questions in the Nineteenth Century: Collected Essays*; Marvin Swartz, *The Politics of British Foreign Policy in the Era of Disraeli and Gladstone.*

12. Richard Millman, *Britain and the Eastern Question, 1875–1878*; David Harris, *A Diplomatic History of the Balkan Crisis of 1875–1878: The First Year*; Mihailo D. Stojanović, *The Great Powers and the Balkans, 1875–1878*; R. W. Seton-Watson, *The Role of Bosnia in International Politics (1875–1914).*

13. Ekmečić, *Ustanak u Bosni*; Jakšić, *Bosna i Hercegovina na Berlinskom kongresu*; Tepić, *Bosna i Hercegovina u ruskim izvorima*; Čubrilović, *Bosanski ustanak*; Božo Madžar, "Izvještaji austriskog generalnog konzula Vasića…od septembra 1875. do juna 1876. godine"; Midhat Šamić, *Francuski putnici u BiH u XIX stoljeću (1836–78) i njihovi utisci o njoj*; *Međunarodni naučni skup povodom: 100-godišnjice ustanka u Bosni i Hercegovini*; Ekmečić, *Naučni skup: Otpor austrougarskoj okupaciji 1878. godine u Bosni i Hercegovini.*

14. "Derby to Elliot, Foreign Office, 18 November 1876, no. 1014," in Great Britain, Foreign Office, *Turkey, Correspondence respecting Affairs in Turkey, No. 1* (hereafter *Turkey, No. 1*), 635.

15. FO 195/1101, Freeman to Elliot, Bosna Serai, January 7, 1876, no. 2. A copy of the same dispatch was also sent to the Foreign Office, consular no. 5; "Freeman to Derby, Bosna Serai, 7 January 1876, no. 64," in Great Britain, Foreign Office, *Turkey, Correspondence respecting Affairs in Turkey, No. 2* (hereafter *Turkey, No. 2*), 88; FO 195/1101, Freeman to Elliot, Bosna Serai, January 7, 1876, no. 3. A copy of the same dispatch was also sent to the Foreign Office, consular no. 6; "Freeman to Derby,

Bosna Serai, 7 January 1876, no. 64," in ibid., 88; FO 195/1101, Freeman to Elliot, Bosna Serai, February 21, 1876, no. 12. A copy of the same dispatch was also sent to the Foreign Office, consular no. 9; "Freeman to Derby, Bosna Serai, 21 February 1876, no. 27," in Great Britain, Foreign Office, *Turkey, Correspondence respecting Affairs in Turkey, No. 3* (hereafter *Turkey, No. 3*), 12; FO 195/1101, Freeman to Elliot, Bosna Serai, April 21, 1876, no. 20. A copy of the same dispatch was also sent to the Foreign Office, political, no. 12; FO 195/1101, Freeman to Elliot, Bosna Serai, February 3, 1876, no. 7. A copy of the same dispatch was also sent to the Foreign Office, consular no. 7; "Freeman to Derby, Bosna Serai, 3 February 1876, no. 9," in ibid., 5; "Freeman to Derby, Bosna Serai, February 18, 1876, no. 24," in ibid., 10–11. Also see FO 195/1061, Holmes to Elliot, Bosna Serai, July 2, 1875, no. 15; FO 195/1061, Holmes to Elliot, Mostar, September 28, 1875, no. 7; Holmes to Eliot, Mostar, September 28, 1875, inclosure in no. 32 (extract), in *Turkey, No. 2*, 27; "Memorandum by Consul Holmes regarding the Affairs of the Hercegovina, inclosure in no. 67, in Elliot to Derby, Constantinople, 10 March 1876, no. 67," in *Turkey, No. 3*, 39–41; "Derby to Elliot, Foreign Office, March 1876, no. 94," in ibid., 53; "Monson-Buchnanan, Ragusa, 11 March 1876, no. 57," in ibid., 26; "Buchanan to Derby, Wien, 18 March 1876, no. 75," in ibid., 44; "Buchanan to Derby, Wien, 18 March 1876, no. 153," in ibid., 91; FO 195/1101, Freeman to Elliot, Bosna Serai, April 21, 1876, no. 20. A copy of the same dispatch was also sent to the Foreign Office, political, no. 12; "Analysis by Lord Tenterden of the Parliamentary Papers on the Affairs of Turkey and the Conference at Constantinople," in *Turkey, No. 1* and *Turkey, No. 2*, 8.

16. See FO 195/1101, Holmes to Eliot, Bosna Serai, July 15 1876, no. 39; "Holmes to Derby, Bosna Serai, 25 July 1876, no. 6," in *Turkey, No. 1*, 4; FO 195/1101, Holmes to Eliot, Bosna Serai, September 13, 1876, no. 51; "Holmes to Derby, Bosna Serai, 14 September 1876, no. 391," in *Turkey, No. 1*, 309; FO 195/1101, Holmes to Elliot, Bosna Serai, October 26, 1876; "Holmes to Derby, Bosna Serai, 27 October 1876, no. 881," in *Turkey, No. 1*, 601–3; "Holmes to Derby, Bosna Serai, 12 October 1876, no. 763," in *Turkey, No. 1*, 536; "Holmes to Elliot, Mostar, 20 April 1876, no. 189," in *Turkey, No. 3*, 114; "Green to Derby, Scutary, 23 October 1876, no. 862," in *Turkey, No. 1*, 592.

17. FO 195/625, Zohrab to Neale, Mostar, December 24, 1859; FO 195/625, Holmes to Bulwer, Bosna Serai, August 19, 1860, private letter; F.O. 195/950, Holmes to Elliot, Bosna Serai, January 20, 1871, no. 4; FO 195/950, Holmes to Elliot, Bosna Serai, January 20, 1871, no. 4; FO 195/950, Holmes to Baron Eagle, Bosna Serai, May 2, 1870, no. 9; "Holmes to Elliot, Bosna Serai, 26 June 1876, inclosure in Holmes to Derby, Bosna Serai, 14 September 1876, no. 391," in *Turkey, No. 3*, 311.

18. See FO 78/2620, Holmes to Derby, Bosna Serai, April 20, 1877, no. 26, political; FO 195/1212, Freeman to Layard, Bosna Serai, March 8, 1878, no. 12; FO 195/1212, Freeman to Layard, Bosna Serai, March 15, 1878, no. 14; FO 195/1212, Freeman to Layard, Bosna Serai, April 25, 1878, no. 25; FO 195/1212, Freeman to Layard, Bosna Serai, May 27, 1878, no. 33; FO 195/1212, Freeman to Layard, Bosna Serai, May 30, 1878, no. 35; FO 195/1212, Freeman to Layard, Bosna Serai, June 7, 1878, no. 37; FO 195/1212, Freeman to Layard, Bosna Serai, July 5, 1878, no. 44; FO 195/1212, Freeman to Layard, Bosna Serai, July 10, 1878, no. 45.

19. Robin Okey, "British Impressions of the Serbo-Croat Speaking Lands of the Habsburg Monarchy — Reports to the Foreign Office 1867–1908," 61–63.

20. Some scholars believe that such British policy and its strong support of the Ottoman Empire in fact encouraged the Ottoman government in its intransigence. Paul Hayes, "British Foreign Policy, 1867–1900: Continuity and Conflict," 156; Seton-Watson, *Britain in Europe*, 353–54. Lord Palmerston, the leading British political leader of that time, did not share this attitude. He stated in 1853 that the Russian emperor "should be satisfied, as we all are, with the progressively liberal system of Turkey." Seton-Watson, *Britain in Europe*, 358.

21. For more on the British policy in Bosnia-Hercegovina, see Radušić, "Bosna i Hercegovina u britanskoj politici"; Edin Radušić, "Uloga Velike Britanije u promjeni državno-pravnog statusa Bosne i Hercegovine 1878. godine."

22. "With so many different creeds and races, of the most turbulent dispositions, there was constant danger of collision between governors and governed, and among governed themselves. This had to be watched, and if possible controlled, since it might at any moment involve half of Europe in confusion and what affected Europe interested England." FO 78/2238, Holmes to Granville, London, March 8, 1872.

23. "The so-called insurrection in Bosnia might be better termed an invasion by bands openly formed in Austrian Croatia and Servia. It has never extended beyond the range of their operations, and cannot be called a popular movement." "Memorandum by Consul Holmes regarding the Affairs of the Hercegovina, Inclosure in Elliot to Derby, Constantinople, 10 March 1876, no. 67," in *Turkey, No. 3*, 40.

24. "Her Majesty's Government consent to this step with reluctance, as they doubt the expediency of the intervention of foreign Consuls. Such an intervention is scarcely compatible with the independent authority of the Porte over its own territory, offers an inducement to insurrection as a means of appealing to foreign sympathy against Turkish rule, and may not improbably open the way to further diplomatic interference in the internal affairs of the Empire. Since, however, the Porte has begged your Excellency not to stand aloof, Her Majesty's Government feel that they have no alternative. They desire, at the same time, that the Turkish Government is given at their own instance, and that Her Majesty's Government would have thought it better that the Porte should have dealt with the insurgents without foreign intervention of any kind." "Analysis by Lord Tenterden of the Parliamentary Papers on the Affairs of Turkey," 2. Compare with P. J. V. Rolo, "Derby"; on the changed attitude of Lord Derby respecting the Ottoman Empire, see Harris, *A Diplomatic History of the Balkan Crisis*, 86–87.

25. "Elliot to Derby, Constantinople, 13 January 1876, no. 60," in *Turkey, No. 2*, 85; "Derby to Elliot, Foreign Office, 13 January 1876, no. 62," in ibid., 87; "Derby to Buchanan, Foreign Office, 24 January 1876, no. 70," in ibid., 91. Derby personally was not convinced of the possibility of preserving the Ottoman sovereignty and even the Ottomans' existence, because he thought that "Turkish rule and administration were too weak and rotten to be patched." Millman considers that Derby's conviction and his activity contributed to British acceptance of the Andrássy Note. Millman, *Britain and the Eastern Question*, 52.

26. Seton-Watson, *Britain in Europe*, 516.

27. "The Secret Austro-Russian Convention, 15 January 1877," in *Balkanski ugovorni odnosi 1876–1996: Dvostrani i višestrani međunarodni ugovori i drugi diplomatski akti o državnim granicama, političkoj i vojnoj saradnji, verskim i etničkim man-*

jinama, ed. Momir Stojković, 1:60; Seton-Watson, *The Role of Bosnia*, 22; Charles Jelavich and Barbara Jelavich, *The Establishment of the Balkan National States*, 148.

28. Seton-Watson, *Britain in Europe*, 523; Millman, *Britain and the Eastern Question*, 232–33.

29. Millman, *Britain and the Eastern Question*, 254–62 (quotations); "The London Protokol, 31 March 1877," in *Balkanski ugovorni odnosi 1876–1996*, ed. Momir Stojković, 1:69.

30. Seton-Watson, *Britain in Europe*, 524.

31. Ekmečić, *Ustanak u Bosni*, 256.

32. Millman, *Britain and the Eastern Question*, 263–64.

33. J. T. Bury, ed., *The New Cambridge Modern History: The Zenith of European Power, 1830–70*, 492; A. Dž. P. Tejlor, *Borba za prevlast u Evropi 1848–1918*, 234–35.

34. Ekmečić, *Ustanak u Bosni*, 309; Tejlor, *Borba za prevlast u Evropi*, 226.

35. "Analysis by Lord Tenterden of the whole series of the Parliamentary Papers showing diplomatic history of the war in Turkey from 1875 to 1878, Foreign Office, 16 January 1878," in Great Britain, Foreign Office, *Turkey, No. 27, Further Correspondence respecting the Preliminary Treaty of Peace between Russia and Turkey, Signed at San Stefano, 3 March 1878*, 1–23; Seton-Watson, *Britain in Europe*, 524.

36. "P.R.O, F.O. 65/986, Derby to Shuvaloff, Foreign Office, 6 May 1876," in Bourne, *The Foreign Policy of Victorian England*, 407–9. The excerpt from the same document can be found in "Analysis by Lord Tenterden of the whole series of the Parliamentary Papers showing diplomatic history of the war in Turkey from 1875 to 1878," 14–15; Seton-Watson, *Britain in Europe*, 524; Marian Kent, "Great Britain and the End of the Ottoman Empire, 1900–23," in *The Great Powers and the End of the Ottoman Empire*, ed. Marian Kent, 172.

37. "Be good enough to lay these views before Lord Derby, stating to him that the Imperial Cabinet has a right to hope that the Government of Her Britannic Majesty will appreciate them with the same spirit of fairness that induces us to respect the interests of England." "Gortchakow to Schouvaloff, St. Petersburg, 30 May 1877," in "Analysis by Lord Tenterden of the whole series of the Parliamentary Papers showing diplomatic history of the war in Turkey from 1875 to 1878," 15 (quotation); Seton-Watson, *Britain in Europe*, 525.

38. The chronology of the main events before and during the war is as follows. The conference at Constantinople broke up on January 20, 1877. On March 31 the protocol of London was signed. On April 24 Count Shuvalov communicated a circular declaring war against the Ottoman Empire. On May 21 the Romanians declared war and independence. On June 22 the Russians crossed the Danube. On December 10 Plevna was surrendered. On January 9, 1878, the Turkish army in the Şipka Pass surrendered, and the Russians advanced in overwhelming force south of the Balkans. On January 31 the Bases of Peace and Armistice were signed at Kezanlik. On March 3 the Treaty of San Stefano was signed. FO 881/3638, "Notes by Lord Tenterden on the Treaty of San Stefano showing the history and present position of the questions arising under that treaty, Foreign Office, 7 June 1878, printed for the use of the Foreign Office, 13 June, 1878, Confidential (3638)," 21–22; Seton-Watson, *Britain in Europe*, 532–33; Stanford J. Shaw and Ezel Kural Shaw, *History of the Ottoman Empire and Modern Turkey*, 182–89; on Russian

foreign policy in the Eastern Crisis of 1875–78, see N. S. Kiniapina, "Osnovnye Etapi Politiki Rossii v Vostochnom Krizise 1875–1878 gg," 6–22.

39. Stojković, *Balkanski ugovorni odnosi*, 1:76–81; cf. Tepić, *Bosna i Hercegovina u ruskim izvorima*, 473–76; Rade Petrović, "Pokret otpora protiv austrougarske okupacije 1878. godine u Bosni i Hercegovini," 31–32.

40. FO 195/1212, Freeman to Layard, Bosna Serai, March 8, 1878, no. 12. The reaction of the domestic population of Bosnia and Hercegovina to the Austrian occupation and the Eastern Crisis has been very difficult to follow in domestic sources, because only one semiofficial newspaper (*Bosna*) was published in the late phase of the Eastern Crisis and all copies of this newspaper after issue 501 (January 24, 1876) were destroyed or disappeared during the shelling of the libraries and archives of Bosnia and Hercegovina. A reconstruction is possible only by using published books and papers and reports of the foreign consuls.

41. "Derby to Elliot, Foreign Office, 4 February 1878, no. 1," in Great Britain, Foreign Office, *Turkey, Correspondence respecting the Affairs of Turkey, No. 24*, 1; "Russell to Derby, Berlin, 13 March 1878, no. 1," in *Turkey, No. 26*, 1; Petrović, "Pokret otpora," 33; FO 881/3638, "Notes by Lord Tenterden on the Treaty of San Stefano," 62–63.

42. Tejlor, *Borba za prevlast u Evropi*, 240.

43. Radušić, "Uloga Velike Britanije," 271–72. On the British policy from the signing of the Treaty of San Stefano until the end of the Berlin Congress, see Millman, *Britain and the Eastern Question*, 422–32; Ensor, *England, 1870–1914*, 49–52; W. N. Medlicott, *Bismarck, Gladstone and the Concert of Europe*, 3; and Seton-Watson, *The Role of Bosnia*, 23. On searching for the best ally after the Treaty of San Stefano, see Bourne, *The Foreign Policy of Victorian England*, 135; Medlicott, *Bismarck, Gladstone and the Concert of Europe*, 31–32; Hayes, "British Foreign Policy," 157; F. H. Hinsly, ed., *The New Cambridge Modern History*, vol. 11: *Material Progress and World-Wide Problems, 1870–1898*, 547–48; Stojanović, *The Great Powers and the Balkans*, 251–66; Jakšić, *Bosna i Hercegovina na Berlinskom kongresu*, 19–66; and Jelavich, *History of the Balkans*, 1:358–61.

44. "Disraeli's most confidential Cabinet Memorandum on the Eastern policy, enclosed in Disraeli to the Queen, 16 May 1876, Public Record Office, Cab. 41/7, no. 10," in Bourne, *The Foreign Policy of Victorian England*, 406.

45. FO 881/3638, "Notes by Lord Tenterden on the Treaty of San Stefano."

46. Millman, *Britain and the Eastern Question*, 422.

47. FO 881/3638, "Notes by Lord Tenterden on the Treaty of San Stefano," 40; Stojković, *Balkanski ugovorni odnosi*, 1:92; Harris, *A Diplomatic History of the Balkan Crisis*, 31; Seton-Watson, *The Role of Bosnia*, 19; Mustafa Imamović, "Bosna između Osmanske i Habsburške carevine u Istočnoj krizi 1875–1878. godine," 344.

48. "Salisbury to Elliot, Foreign Office, 4 May 1878," in FO 881/3638, "Notes by Lord Tenterden on the Treaty of San Stefano," 40–41; "Elliot to Salisbury, Vienna, 10 May 1878," in ibid., 41.

49. Bourne, *The Foreign Policy of Victorian England*, 413 (quotation); *The Layard Papers: A Memoir of His Embassy to Turkey*, section 13. The *Layard Papers* mainly confirmed explanations and conclusions based on the information obtained from the official diplomatic and consular correspondence as well as from the achievements of historiography. I would like to thank my colleague Gül Tokay, who

kindly gave me some important documents on this topic, including an electronic version of *The Layard Papers*.

50. "Acting upon Lord Salisbury's instructions I urged the Sultan and his Ministers to give Count Zichy's note their favourable consideration and accept the proposal of the Austrian Government." *The Layard Papers*, section 13; FO 881/3638, "Notes by Lord Tenterden on the Treaty of San Stefano," 41; Stojanović, *The Great Powers and the Balkans*, 264–65. Lord Salisbury and Disraeli also pressured the Ottoman plenipotentiaries and through them the sultan and the Porte to accept the Austrian proposal. "Carathédory Pasha to Safvet Pasha, Berlin 16 June 1878, No. 7 (tel.), Top Secret and Confidential," Başbakanlık Arşivi, Istanbul (BBA), HR SYS 1244/2.

51. Bourne, *The Foreign Policy of Victorian England*, 136.

52. FO 881/3628, "Layard to Salisbury, Constantinople, 17 May 1878 (Most Confidential), Printed for the use of the Cabinet"; FO 881/3638, "Notes by Lord Tenterden on the Treaty of San Stefano," 42.

53. "Layard to Salisbury, Constantinople, 17 May 1878," in FO 881/3638, "Notes by Lord Tenterden on the Treaty of San Stefano," 42–43.

54. FO 881/3638, "Notes by Lord Tenterden on the Treaty of San Stefano," 43; on the British-Austrian negotiations, see Millman, *Britain and the Eastern Question*, 422–27.

55. FO 195/1212, Freeman to Layard, Bosna Serai, June 13, 1878, no. 38.

56. FO 195/1212, Freeman to Layard, Bosna Serai, May 27, 1878, no. 33.

57. There was talk about the departure of a deputation consisting of some Catholics and Muslims from Bosnia to Vienna to advocate the annexation of this province to Austria. FO 195/1212, Freeman to Layard, Bosna Serai, March 15, 1878, no. 14.

58. FO 195/1212, Freeman to Layard, Bosna Serai, May 30, 1878, no. 35; cf. "Wassitsch to Wien, Serajevo, 28 Mai 1878, No 8552, 943," in Berislav Gavranović, *Bosna i Hercegovina u doba austrougarske okupacije 1878. godine*, 132; "Andrassy to Zichy, Wien, 3. Juni 1878, pag. 1000, Pr. 5, 4 1878," in ibid., 134.

59. FO 195/1212, Freeman to Layard, Bosna Serai, June 4, 1878, no. 36; FO 195/1212, Freeman to Layard, Bosna Serai, June 7, 1878, no. 37.

60. FO 195/1212, Freeman to Layard, Bosna Serai, June 13, 1878, no. 38; cf. "Wassitsch to Andrassy, Serajevo, 6. Juni 1878, No 32," in Gavranović, *Bosna i Hercegovina u doba austrougarske okupacije*, 134.

61. Kemal H. Karpat, "The Ottoman Attitude towards the Resistance of Bosnia and Hercegovina to the Austrian Occupation in 1878," 170.

62. "Salisbury's private letter to Sir Henry Layard, 9 May 1878, Layard MSS., B.M., Add, MS. 39137," in Bourne, *The Foreign Policy of Victorian England*, 413; Jelavich, *The Ottoman Empire, the Great Powers, and the Straits Question*, 93; Daniela Kodajova, "R. W. Seton-Watson's Views of the Habsburg Monarchy, the Ottoman Empire and Russia," 123; *Hansard's Parliamentary Debates*, vol. 232 (February 8, 1877–March 15, 1877), vol. 1 (1877), 477–572, 712–25.

63. "Nota Austro-Ugarske, Britanije i Italije o stavu prema Istočnoj krizi, 6. juni 1878," in *Balkanski ugovorni odnosi, ed.* Stojković, 1:107–8.

64. Seton-Watson, *Britain in Europe*, 535.

65. "Salisbury's private letter to Disraeli, 21 March 1878, Disraeli MSS., Hughenden

Manor, B/XX/Ce. No. 233," in Bourne, *The Foreign Policy of Victorian England*, 411; "Gortchakow to Schouvaloff, Petrograd, 28 March 1878, no. 2," in *Turkey, No. 27*, 1–10.

66. Stojanović, *The Great Powers and the Balkans*, 235–37.

67. Seton-Watson, *Britain in Europe*, 535–36.

68. "Correspondence respecting the Convention between Britain and Turkey of 4 June, 1878, London 1878," in *Turkey, No. 36*, 3–4; Seton-Watson, *Britain in Europe*, 536–37.

69. Ekmečić, *Ustanak u Bosni*, 316–19; "Protocol No. 8, sitting of 28 June 1878," in Great Britain, Foreign Office, *Turkey, No. 39, Correspondence respecting Affairs in Turkey* (hereafter *Turkey, No. 39*), 112–19.

70. "Correspondence relating to the Congress of Berlin with the Protocols of the Congress (Cross to Beaconsfield and to Salisbury, Foreign Office, 6 June 1878), no. 1," in *Turkey, No. 39*, 1; "Salisbury to Russell, Foreign Office, 8 June 1878, no. 3," in ibid., 2.

71. "Protocol no. 8, sitting of June 28, 1878," in ibid., 112–19.

72. "Carathédory Pasha to Safvet Pasha, Berlin 28 June 1878 No. 57 (tel.)," BBA; "Salisbury to HM' [*sic*] Principal Secretary of State, Berlin, 28 June 1878, no. 16," in *Turkey, No. 39*, 51; "Protocol No. 8, sitting of 28 June 1878," in ibid., 112–19; Anita L. P. Burdett, ed., *Historical Boundaries between Bosnia, Croatia, Serbia, Documents and Maps, 1815–1945*, 281–312.

73. "The Austrian Ambassador pressed for an answer to Count Andrassy's proposal and not being able to obtain one asked for an audience of the sultan in order that he might present the matter personally to H.M. The Porte, I was informed, was altogether opposed to it, principally on the grounds that it would infer a sanction on the part of Turkey of the partition of her territories, which might form a precedent for further demands of a similar nature, and that it would probably lead to European complications." *The Layard Papers*, section 12; Safvet Paşa required that the Ottoman plenipotentiaries try to make an arrangement with the Austrians, ceding of some parts of Hercegovina in order to retain the majority of the province. "Safvet Pasha to the Ottoman plenipotentiaries, Constantinople, 20 June 1878, No 51526/19 (tel.), Very confidential," in Karpat, "The Ottoman Attitude towards the Resistance of Bosnia and Hercegovina," 162–69, 171; Bekir Sitki Baykal, "Pitanje Bosne i Hercegovine i osmanska država 1878. godine," 97–99. A. L. Narochnickij, "Balkanskij krizis 1875–78 gg. i velikie deržavi," 44–46.

74. "The Layard Papers, the inner Ottoman correspondence and already mentioned Freeman reports prove this conclusion." *The Layard Papers*, section 13; "Carathédory Pasha to Safvet Pasha, Berlin 16 June 1878 No. 7 (tel.), Top Secret and Confidential," BBA.

75. The term "wrong horse" was used in regard to the question of the reasonableness of British support for the Ottoman Empire, because of the Ottoman decision to take the opposite side in World War I. Allan Cunningham, "The Wrong Horse? Anglo-Ottoman Relations before the First World War," in *Eastern Questions in the Nineteenth Century*, ed. Allan Cunningham, 227–48. I consider it possible to use the same term in the opposite direction.

76. FO 195/1212, Freeman to Layard, Bosna Serai, July 5, 1878, no. 44; FO 195/1212,

Freeman to Layard, Bosna Serai, July 10, 1878, no. 45 (quotation); Tepić, *Bosna i Hercegovina u ruskim izvorima*, 475.

77. Ekmečić, *Ustanak u Bosni*, 318–19.

78. FO 195/1212, Freeman to Layard, Bosna Serai, July 18, 1878, no. 46.

79. Karpat, "The Ottoman Attitude towards the Resistance of Bosnia and Hercegovina," 171.

80. Petrović, "Pokret otpora," 65.

81. For extensive correspondence relating to the Congress of Berlin, see "Correspondence Relating to the Congress of Berlin with the Protocols of the Congress," in *Turkey, No. 33*, and *Turkey, No. 39*; Seton-Watson, *Britain in Europe*, 539–40; Stojanović, *The Great Powers and the Balkans*, 271; Medlicott, *Bismarck, Gladstone and the Concert of Europe*, 28. According to the terms of the Treaty of Berlin, the Ottoman Empire lost more territory than proposed by the Treaty of San Stefano. Cunningham, "The Wrong Horse?" 229; F. R. Bridge and Roger Bullen, *The Great Powers and the European States System, 1815–1914*, 123–24; Jakšić, *Bosna i Hercegovina na Berlinskom kongresu*, 52–53.

82. "Salisbury to HM' Principal Secretary of State, Berlin, 13 July 1878," in *Turkey, No. 38*. When Disraeli returned to London, he claimed to have won "peace with honour." Mike Byrne, "Foreign Policy 1870–1914," in Michael Scott-Baumann, ed., *Years of Expansion: Britain, 1815–1914*, 393.

83. "Salisbury to HM' Principal Secretary of State, Berlin, 13 July 1878," in *Turkey, No. 38*, 1–3.

8

The Berlin Treaty, Bosnian Muslims, and Nationalism

Aydın Babuna

INTRODUCTION

The Treaty of Berlin was the most important single document in the nineteenth century in tracing the frontiers of the Balkan countries. Romania, Serbia, and Montenegro gained their independence in accordance with the terms of the treaty, while Bulgaria became an autonomous principality. Another important consequence of the treaty was that the Austro-Hungarian Empire was granted the right to occupy Bosnia-Hercegovina even though these provinces would remain under the sovereignty of the Ottoman Empire. This not only changed the political situation in these provinces but also profoundly influenced the national development of the Bosnian Muslims at the turn of the century.[1] The complicated international status of Bosnia-Hercegovina was to exert an important influence on the political developments in the decades to come. The Bosnian Muslims tried to return to the good old days as long as they thought that such a move was possible.

During the Ottoman period the Bosnian Muslims constituted the upper class of Bosnian society and represented the state. After the occupation of Bosnia-Hercegovina by the Catholic Austro-Hungarian Empire, the Muslims were afraid that they might be treated by the new administration on the same level as the kmets (tenants).[2] The Bosnian Muslims, who had lived for centuries under the Muslim Ottoman Empire, also feared assimilation. Though incidents of conversion from Islam to Christianity were limited during the Austro-Hungarian period, they tended to gain ethnic significance and were considered a threat to the very existence of the Muslim community. One of these conversions in 1899 initiated a countrywide

Muslim opposition movement against Austro-Hungarian rule. The wide social impact of the conversion incidents at this time as compared with previous periods shows that during the Austro-Hungarian era the Muslims were undergoing a rapid ethnic development.[3]

After the occupation of Bosnia-Hercegovina the Bosnian Muslims lost first their political status and then, gradually, their economic and social privileges. This led to an inevitable conflict between the Bosnian Muslims and the cultural and religious values of the new administration. Though the nationality policy of the Austro-Hungarian government was based fundamentally on the Muslims, it could not prevent the emergence of a Muslim opposition that would lead to the foundation of the first Muslim political party in Bosnia-Hercegovina, Muslimanska Narodna Organizacija (Muslim National Organization, MNO), in 1906. During Austro-Hungarian rule the Bosnian Muslims came up with political demands in the modern sense for the first time in history. This makes this period particularly important for any analysis of the emergence of Bosnian Muslim nationalism, because "nationalism is a political movement by definition."[4] In contrast to the studies on the Austro-Hungarian period that ignore the emergence of Bosnian Muslim nationalism,[5] this paper explores the place of Bosnian Muslim nationalism in the typology of nationalisms. It shows the crucial importance of Ottoman documents and nationalism theories for the analysis of the national development of the Bosnian Muslims under Austro-Hungarian rule.[6]

THEORETICAL BACKGROUND

Various definitions of "nationalism" have been proposed. According to Paul Brass, nationalism is not a product of relative deprivation or status discrepancy but of the relative distribution of ethnic groups,[7] which compete for important resources and opportunities as well as workplaces in societies undergoing a process of social mobilization, industrialization, and bureaucratization.[8] The process of nationality formation is composed of two stages: transformation from ethnic group to community and from community to nationality.[9] Elite conflicts play a key role in both processes of nationality formation, and the required conditions for both processes are the same.[10] Although nationalism emerges during the transformation from community to nationality it may occur at any time, even in the first stage of the mobilization of the ethnic groups.[11]

The transformation from ethnic group to community takes place in modernizing or postindustrial societies undergoing drastic social changes.

This process does not take place at all in some groups, however, while in some other groups it occurs several times in different periods. According to Ernest Gellner, the nationalities of the Austro-Hungarian Empire underwent this process in the nineteenth and twentieth centuries.[12] In preindustrial and early modernizing societies four different kinds of elite conflicts may take place: (1) between an alien conqueror and the local aristocracy; (2) between the indigenous religious elite and the alien aristocracy; (3) between the religious elites of rival ethnic groups; and (4) between the religious elite and the indigenous aristocracy within an ethnic group.[13]

The elite conflicts that take place during the second stage of nationality formation (from community to nationality) pave the way for the emergence of a nationalist movement. These elite conflicts differ from those of the previous stage (from ethnic group to community) in terms of their magnitude and content and insofar as members of the elite now also demand participation in the decision-making process concerning the distribution of resources and jobs. These demands focus mainly on the schools and the language of the group.[14] One of the main characteristics of the process of nationality formation is that the objective differences between the ethnic groups gradually gain a subjective and symbolic connotation and turn into political demands. These symbols are used by the elite groups to promote group identities and interests. Even though one part of the elite may be profiting from the choice of the symbols to be used, the symbols are basically shaped by the cultural heritage of the ethnic groups.[15]

The ability of effective political organizations to identify themselves with the community as a whole and the treatment of the ethnic groups by the governments were also important factors affecting the future of the nationalist movements. The nationality policies of the governments may shape the nationalist movements and the formation of the elites.[16] These policies may range from genocide to granting autonomy or the formation of a federation. The division of labor and the distribution of the economic resources among the ethnic groups and the linguistic policies constitute two important instruments of the nationality policy of the governments.[17]

Brass's study is mainly based on the movement of the Indian Muslims, which paved the way for the establishment of Pakistan. He focuses on the conflicts between the Muslim and Hindu elites on the one hand and British rulers on the other, as well as on the manipulation of the religious and cultural symbols through different elites. According to Brass, the religious elite used religion as a central symbol for the mobilization of many competing ethnic groups in the colonial territories. Language constituted another important symbol in this process. The local aristocracy, which cooperated with colonial rule, could also mobilize the ethnic group.[18]

THE TREATY OF BERLIN
AND THE OTTOMAN GOVERNMENT

In accordance with the Berlin treaty, Bosnia-Hercegovina was occupied by the Austro-Hungarian Empire in 1878. For the first time in its history the Austro-Hungarian Empire had a compact Muslim community under its rule.[19] According to the census of 1885, 492,710 Muslims lived in Bosnia-Hercegovina, representing 36.88 percent of the total population and forming the second largest community in the province.[20] The occupation of Bosnia-Hercegovina by a Catholic central European state with a powerful bureaucracy led to changes in the Muslim community.[21] These changes would be of great importance in the political and ethnic development of the Bosnian Muslims.

The local population of Bosnia-Hercegovina offered a determined resistance to the occupation of their country by the Austro-Hungarian Empire. Only after a fierce conflict lasting more than two months did the Austro-Hungarian troops succeed in occupying Bosnia-Hercegovina. The Austro-Hungarian Army needed more than 150,000 troops to break the resistance of the local movement.[22] The confirmation of the occupation of Bosnia-Hercegovina by the Ottoman sultan through the Treaty of Berlin had created a reaction in Bosnia-Hercegovina against the Ottoman government. Shortly before the occupation of Bosnia-Hercegovina a commission was established in Sarajevo that would gradually be transformed into an independent organization. This commission was in charge of the preparations of the paramilitary groups against the occupation. Even though the commission was dominated by the Muslims, it also included Serbs as well as some Croats and Jews. The cooperation between the Muslims and the Serbs took place not only in Sarajevo but also in other cities such as Banjaluka and Mostar.[23] It is possible to say that the occupation created a certain sense of unity among Bosnian members of the resistance with different religious backgrounds.

The Ottoman government wanted the resistance to be successful even though it had acquired not only an anti–Austro-Hungarian but also an anti-Ottoman character. Originally the Ottomans planned to delay the occupation of Bosnia-Hercegovina through diplomacy and to change the Treaty of Berlin after the victory of the resistance.[24] Open support for the resistance would create problems for the Ottoman government at the international level, however, so it preferred to offer covert support for the resistance by secretly sending in troops and munitions.[25] Along with some segments of the Serbian community, the Bosnian Muslims constituted the core of the military resistance against the occupation, which shows that by the late Ottoman period they had developed a strong patriotic consciousness. The Muslim fighters were peasants, urban craftsmen, some landowners, and former prisoners who had been released before the occupation.[26] The majority of the landowners preferred to keep their distance from the resistance. The Muslims of the lower class from the cities and the countryside provided the fiercest resistance, while the educated Muslims and notables were more hesitant.[27] During the resistance some Ottoman bureaucrats who stayed in Sarajevo were forced to wear Bosnian clothes,[28] which shows that the resistance was more than a mere self-defense of the local population against the occupation.

After the occupation different waves of migration took place in Bosnian society. The Bosnian Muslim community was most greatly influenced by these migration trends. The majority of the Serbian migrants chose Serbia as their destination, while the overwhelming majority of the Bosnian Muslim migrants preferred different parts of the Ottoman Empire. After 1902 a small number of Bosnian migrants would also leave for America.[29] The Muslims, who in 1885 constituted 36.88 percent of the total population, were reduced to 32.25 percent in 1910, while the Serbs rose from 42.76 percent to 43.49 percent and the Catholics from 19.89 percent to 22.87 percent in the same period.[30] According to the 1906 report of the Landesregierung,[31] the migration was originally confined to former Ottoman officials, bureaucrats, and a few notables.[32] But the introduction of a new military law (Wehrgesetz) in 1881 caused a massive migration among the Bosnian Muslims, which was to continue until 1883. Middle-class Muslims in particular were opposed to the idea of Muslims serving in the army of a non-Muslim state.[33] The new military law extending compulsory military service to non-Muslims constituted the main reason for the uprising against the Landesregierung in 1882.[34] The Serbs from Hercegovina, who had been exempt from military service during the Ottoman period, offered a particularly fierce resistance to this new law.[35] The unsuccessful uprising of 1882, in which some of the Muslims took part, was a contributing factor in the migration of the Muslims.[36]

After a relatively stable period between 1883 and 1898 the number of the migrants increased in 1899 and reached its climax in 1900. Though measures taken by the Landesregierung in 1901 controlled this new wave of migration, the annexation of Bosnia-Hercegovina in 1908 would cause another wave of migration.[37] No exact figure is available for the number of Muslim migrants who left Bosnia-Hercegovina during the Austro-Hungarian period, but according to some estimates it was at most 150,000.[38] Bosnian Muslims were worried by the constant decline in the percentage of Bosnian Muslims in the total population of Bosnia-Hercegovina during the Austro-Hungarian period.[39]

The reasons behind the migration of the Bosnian Muslims were not only political and religious but also economic. In 1891 the Landesregierung started to keep statistics on the migrants based on their ages and professions. The migrants between 1891 and 1897 were composed of members of the following social classes:

Agriculture (including landowners): 3,764 (71.27 percent);
Artisans: 555 (10.50 percent);
Workers and day labourers: 395 (7.48 percent);
Traders: 280 (5.30 percent);
Private jobs: 118 (2.23 percent);
Others: 170 (3.22 percent).[40]

These data show that all the social segments of the Bosnian community, but particularly the peasants, were involved in the emigration. In the following years (1903 to 1906) the free Muslim peasants continued to constitute the overwhelming majority of the migrants.[41] The second largest group after the peasants was the artisans. In addition to the impoverished peasants the small artisans who constituted the majority of the urban population also had difficulties under the new economic conditions, with the local artisans unable to compete with the products coming from the Austro-Hungarian Empire.[42] Prices in Bosnia-Hercegovina had increased dramatically after the occupation, while the prices of the products of the local artisans were in decline. Moreover, their best customers, the Ottoman officials, had left Bosnia. Some of the landowners who had received credits after the occupation faced difficulties in paying them back. These landowners either increased their pressure on their *kmet*s or sold their lands and migrated to Turkey to start a new life there.[43] Finally, the encouraging attitude of some Ottoman officials and some circles in Bosnia also contributed to the migration from Bosnia.[44]

Interestingly enough, both the Ottoman Empire and the Austro-Hungarian Empire accused each other of provoking the migration of the Muslims. Though the Landesregierung had encouraged the migration of the Muslims in the early postoccupation years in order to create room for the new colonists, it tried to stop migration after 1883.[45] The increasing migration of the Muslims upset the demographic balance in Bosnia-Hercegovina in favor of the Serbs, which could pose a threat to the existence of the Austro-Hungarian Empire in the Balkans.[46] According to the Landesregierung, one of the main reasons for the migration was the transition in Bosnia-Hercegovina from a natural economy to a money-oriented economy.[47] The Landesregierung was proud that Bosnia-Hercegovina did not witness a large-scale migration, as was the case in different parts of the Balkans abandoned by the Ottomans.[48] Conversely, the Bosnian Muslims were aware that the Landesregierung had provided them with greater security than any Serbian-Montenegrin or Croatian rule could have done at that time in the Balkans.[49]

The Ottoman government followed an ambivalent policy with regard to Bosnian Muslim migration from Bosnia-Hercegovina. On the one hand, it felt itself obliged to give help to the Bosnian migrants for religious and humanitarian reasons, but, on the other, it was opposed to the Muslim migration for political and strategic reasons.[50] Even though the Ottoman government was strongly opposed to the migration of the Muslims immediately after the occupation,[51] this issue constituted a subject of controversy between the Bosnian and Ottoman *ulema* (high-ranking clerics) and bureaucrats in the years to come. In the end, the strategic interests of the empire gained the upper hand; by the beginning of the twentieth century the Ottoman government was trying to discourage Muslim migration from Bosnia-Hercegovina. The 1901 report of the Ottoman council in Ragusa (Dubrovnik) analyzing the demographic developments in Bosnia-Hercegovina offered some suggestions, including prohibiting the migration of the Bosnian Muslims.[52] This report seems to have shaped Ottoman migration policy.[53] But the Ottoman Empire continued to help the Muslim migrants from Bosnia, who were allowed to settle in different parts of the empire.[54]

THE POLITICAL STRUCTURE

The Austro-Hungarian Empire treated Bosnia-Hercegovina as a colony.[55] After its occupation Bosnia-Hercegovina was placed temporarily under the direct control of the monarch.[56] But the country was ruled for thirty years after its occupation as a sort of no-man's-land. Even after the annexation of 1908 the country belonged neither to Austria nor to Hungary. Bosnia-Hercegovina had no parliament until 1910 and had no representative in either the Reichstag in Vienna or the parliament in Budapest.[57] After

1890 fifty-four agrarian colonies were established in Bosnia-Hercegovina, in which approximately ten thousand foreigners were settled. Though the majority of them had Slavic roots, the settlement of foreigners contributed to the Bosnian Muslims' perception of the Landesregierung as constituting colonial rule. The constantly increasing number of the foreigners during the Austro-Hungarian rule worried the local people.[58] Finally, German and Austrian rhetoric concerning Bosnia-Hercegovina shows that German and Austrian public opinion also considered it a kind of colony.[59]

The complicated international status of Bosnia-Hercegovina after the Treaty of Berlin was of great importance in political developments. According to the treaty, the occupation of Bosnia-Hercegovina by the Austro-Hungarian Empire was only temporary and the country still remained under the sovereignty of the Ottoman Empire. The Yenipazar Convention signed between the two states in 1879 not only confirmed Ottoman sovereignty in Bosnia-Hercegovina but also regulated the rights of the Bosnian Muslims. In accordance with this convention the Muslims were free in the practice of their religion and in their relations with their religious leaders. Properly qualified Ottoman officials would remain in their posts; in the case of replacements, the new officials preferably were to be appointed from among the local people.[60] Ottoman officials encouraged the Bosnian Muslims to be watchdogs of the provisions of the Yenipazar Convention.[61] In the years to come this convention was to provide a suitable basis for the political demands of the Bosnian Muslims.

The political flexibility of the Landesregierung and the dualist structure of the monarchy are other factors that had an important impact on the course of the Muslim opposition. The rivalry between the two parts of the Dual Monarchy over Bosnia-Hercegovina encouraged the Muslim elite to become more active politically. Though the joint minister of finance (Gemeinsame Finanzminister) controlled executive, legislative, and judiciary powers, the variety of the political organizations in the Austro-Hungarian Monarchy allowed the Bosnian Muslims to follow alternative policies. Different Muslim commissions turned not only to the Landesregierung in Sarajevo but also to the Joint Ministry of Finance in Vienna, the Austro-Hungarian delegations, and even the emperor himself to submit their petitions.[62] Even though many of these attempts brought no concrete results, the variety of the political organizations encouraged the Muslims to fight for their rights through legal means and reduced the political tension in the country.[63]

During the Austro-Hungarian period the Ottoman Empire was not only a destination for the Muslim migrants, as noted by many authors,[64] but also one of the players in the political developments in Bosnia-Hercegovina. The occupation had cut the close relations that had been sustained for centuries between the Bosnian Muslims and the Ottoman Empire. But the former official relations were now replaced by unofficial and sometimes secret links, many of which had the character of a "personal network."[65] The Bosnian Muslim migrants and the relatives of the Muslim elite in Istanbul as well as some officials of Bosnian Muslim origin at the Ottoman court were important members of these personal networks. Some Muslims, such as Ali Efendi Džabić, the former mufti (higher clergyman) of Mostar, were directly in touch with the Ottoman government.[66]

During the Austro-Hungarian period the Ottoman sultan still enjoyed considerable prestige among the Bosnian Muslims, who opposed the Landesregierung as long as they nourished hopes of restoring the former order and regaining their previous privileges.[67] In this context the pan-Islamic policy followed by the Ottoman sultan and the relations between the Muslims and Istanbul played a very important role in the national and political development of the Bosnian Muslims.[68] Ottoman documents show that the pan-Islamic policy was a key element as an external factor in the spread of the Muslim opposition movement to different parts of the country.[69] But the annexation of Bosnia-Hercegovina in 1908 and the recognition of the religious autonomy of the Bosnian Muslims by the Landesregierung in 1909 would bring the Muslim movement to a standstill.

MODERNIZATION AND THE BOSNIAN MUSLIMS

Though Ömer Paşa and Osman Paşa carried out some important reforms in the late Ottoman period it was the appointment of Benjamin Kállay as the joint finance minister on June 4, 1882, that marked the beginning of industrialization in Bosnia-Hercegovina.[70] According to Kállay, the improvement of the economic conditions of Bosnia-Hercegovina would be the best way to oppose the idea of the unity of the South Slavs and to keep these provinces under the Austro-Hungarian rule.[71] Almost all the industry of the country and the new financial and transportation networks were established under him.[72] Timber production boomed in Bosnia-Hercegovina and came to challenge Austrian timber exports, while the Bosnian iron industry led to rivalry with Hungary.[73] The Austro-Hungarian period also witnessed the introduction of telephone, postal, and telegraph networks in the Bosnian cities.[74] Despite these achievements Bosnia and Hercegovina still remained one of the least developed parts of the Dual Monarchy. Moreover, the Austro-Hungarian government avoided any radical solution for the agrarian problem and followed a conservative policy.[75]

One of the main features of the Austro-Hungarian period was the introduction of capitalism into Bosnia-Hercegovina. Muslim craftsmen and artisans dominated local trade as the most traditional social class in the city population. After the occupation, however, their products could not compete with better and cheaper products imported from the monarchy. Sectors dominated by the Muslims, such as the production of leather, shoes, knives, swords, and some other weapons, lost their former importance after the occupation.[76] The increasing communication between Bosnia-Hercegovina and Austria-Hungary and the emergence of new economic sectors worsened the situation of the Bosnian Muslims. The outdated guild system was an obstacle to the emergence of Muslim entrepreneurs and also contributed to their economic decline.[77]

The Muslims were the group that suffered most under the changing economic conditions. The majority of the Serbian artisans were also traders and thus were in a relatively advantageous situation, while the lack of capital prevented the Muslim artisans from becoming involved in trade beyond their provincial borders.[78] Despite their difficulties in adjusting themselves to the new economic conditions,[79] the majority of the Bosnian Muslims were unable to change their traditional economic activities.[80] The newly emerging Muslim bourgeoisie was not strong enough to take the lead in the national development of the Bosnian Muslims during this transformation process. Even though there were some Muslim entrepreneurs, they could not exert as much influence on the Muslim opposition as their Serbian counterparts were able to exert on the Serbian opposition.[81]

Centralization was one of the main characteristics of the Landesregierung. The Austro-Hungarian bureaucracy was more extensive and stronger than the previous Ottoman bureaucracy.[82] Kállay had reservations about the compatibility of Islam with the modern world.[83] In his view, a well-organized state was one of the most important differences between Western and Eastern cultures. Kállay wanted to create a state consciousness among the population of Bosnia-Hercegovina and built up a strong centralized state,[84] which remained under the direct control of the Joint Ministry of Finance in Vienna until 1910.[85] The Austro-Hungarian bureaucracy offered new opportunities for the local people.[86] At the same time the Muslim and Serbian opposition movements were trying to increase the number of the local people employed in the Bosnian bureaucracy.[87] Since 1894 the Muslims had been protesting that the dismissal of the Ottoman officials was a breach of the Yenipazar Convention of 1879.[88] The number of Muslim officials gradually increased from 825 in 1908 to 1,644 in 1914.[89]

The first generation of a Muslim intelligentsia was composed of a small group of university students at the turn of the century. In the school year of 1903–4 thirty Muslim students from Bosnia were attending different universities in Vienna and Zagreb,[90] and this number would gradually increase in the following years.[91] Despite the Landesregierung's efforts to raise the educational level of the Bosnian Muslims, 94.65 percent were still illiterate as late as 1910, while among Muslim women the figure was 99.68 percent. Mostar had the highest level of literacy (10.36 percent).[92] This shows that it was no accident that the Muslim opposition movement started in this city.[93] The high percentage of Muslim illiterates points to the difficulties confronting the "intensive communication" among the Bosnian Muslims in the early 1900s, which is important for mass movements. But the Muslims were communicating with each other very successfully through their personal networks.[94] These relations included different kinds of "noncorporate" relations such as marriage alliances, personal friendships, and patron-client and business relations.[95]

THE LANDESREGIERUNG AND THE BOSNIAN MUSLIMS

Rising Serbian nationalism in the 1890s and the rivalry between the Serbian and Croatian nationalists over Bosnia-Hercegovina and the Bosnian Muslims forced the Austro-Hungarian administration to follow a cautious nationality policy. Kállay wanted to direct nationalist tendencies in Bosnia-Hercegovina into harmless paths before it was too late.[96] The policy of Bošnjastvo (Bosniakhood/Bosnianhood) acquired concrete dimensions ten years after the occupation and became the official nationality policy of the Austro-Hungarian government.[97] Kállay, who ruled Bosnia-Hercegovina between 1882 and 1903, was the main promoter of the policy of Bošnjastvo. This nationality policy stressed the common Bosnian roots of the ethnic groups in Bosnia-Hercegovina and tried to create a territorially based Bosnian nation. The Bosnian tradition was considered to be evidence of the distinctiveness of Bosnia-Hercegovina.[98]

The Bosnian tradition was particularly alive among the Bosnian Muslims, but the national consciousness of the Serbs and Croats was strong enough to provide resistance to the policy of Bošnjastvo.[99] Though the policy of Bošnjastvo originally included all the ethnic groups in Bosnia-Hercegovina, Serbian and Croatian resistance gradually forced the Landesregierung to focus on the Bosnian Muslims. The history of Bosnia-

Hercegovina was the most important symbol used by the Landesregierung in its pursuance of the nationality policy. The government tried to revive the pre-Islamic Bosnian traditions and stressed the roots of Bošnjastvo. The medieval Bogomil church as well as the leading role that the Muslim landowners had played in the past constituted some of the most important aspects of this policy. The state schools, the language, official symbols, and the press constituted the most important instruments at the disposal of the government in following the policy of Bošnjastvo.[100]

The question of the official name for the language of Bosnia-Hercegovina constituted the core of the Landesregierung's language policy. Although the Landesregierung still had no clear-cut language policy immediately after the occupation, it was basically pro-Croatian. This policy would meet with resistance from the Serbs, however, who constituted the largest ethnic group in Bosnia-Hercegovina.[101] The Landesregierung seems to have started to change its pro-Croatian policy as early as 1879.[102] In 1880 the Cyrillic alphabet received equal status with the Latin alphabet and was increasingly used in official publications.[103] Language policy became an indispensable part of the nationality policy of the Landesregierung under the Kállay administration, and the language of the country became known as the "Bosnian language."[104] In 1890 the Landesregierung published a grammar of the Bosnian language to be used in secondary schools, but this caused so much discontent in the Serbian and Croatian schools that the Serbs and Croats were allowed to call their own languages Serbian and Croatian.[105] István Burián, Kállay's successor, abandoned his language policy. In 1907 the language of the country was officially recognized as Serbo-Croatian,[106] although the Muslims were allowed to continue to call their language the "Bosnian language" within their own community.

Kállay was accused particularly by nationalist Serbs and Croats of inventing the concept of Bošnjastvo to serve the imperialistic aims of the Austro-Hungarian Empire. As an experienced diplomat and historian, however, Kállay was well aware that the people of Bosnia had relied on different external powers throughout history: the Byzantine emperor, Hungarian king, and Ottoman sultan in the past and now the Austro-Hungarian emperor. In 1893 Kállay told the Austrian delegations that his language policy was capable of meeting the needs of the Bosnian people and was based on a historic tradition.[107] The famous linguist Vatroslav Jagić also supported the use of "Bosnian language" and stressed that this term was not invented by Kállay and had already been in use in the seventeenth and eighteenth centuries.[108] The policy of Bošnjastvo was inherited by Kállay from the Ottomans, having been introduced by the former

Ottoman vizier Ömer Paşa as early as the 1850s. This policy would enjoy the support of some Franciscans in Bosnia, who were sympathetic to the Bosnian tradition for historical reasons. The policy of Bošnjastvo was developed by Topal Şerif Osman Paşa, who ruled Bosnia between 1861 and 1869.[109]

In response to the rising Serbian and Croatian nationalisms, Osman Paşa endeavored to strengthen the ties between the Bosnians and the Ottoman state. During his rule the grammar of the Bosnian language was printed. The main principles of the Bosnian ideology were clarified in an article published in the journal *Bosanski vjesnik* in 1866, which stressed that the Bosnian nation consisted of not only privileged Muslims but the whole of Bosnian society.[110] According to Osman Paşa, the Bosnian nation was historically bound to the Ottoman Empire, regardless of the religious differences, while the administrative structure of the Ottoman Empire provided a suitable basis for the demand for autonomy. The introduction of autonomy to Bosnia already had caused some important economic results, and Bosnia could set an example to the other provinces.[111] During the rule of Osman Paşa the structure of the *vilayet* (province) of Bosnia was reorganized in line with the Provincial Reform Law of 1864. Bosnia-Hercegovina was divided into seven *sancak*s, and new courts were set up with a joint Muslim-Christian Court of Appeal. Each of the new *sancak*s would send two Muslim and one Christian representative to the consultative assembly. In addition, a small executive council (consisting of three Muslims, two Christians, and one Jew) would meet under the governor twice a week.[112]

As part of its nationality policy the Landesregierung tried to avoid making any drastic change in the social status of the Bosnian Muslims. According to the statistics of 1910 the Bosnian Muslims represented 91.15 percent of the landowners with *kmet*s, 70.62 percent of the landowners without *kmet*s, and 56.65 percent of the free peasants. Only 4.58 percent of the *kmet*s were Muslim, while 73.92 percent were Orthodox Serbs and 21.49 percent were Catholic Croats.[113] The Landesregierung avoided any radical solution for the agrarian problem in order to avoid losing the political support of the Bosnian Muslims.[114] But agricultural conditions and relations with the *kmet*s were becoming more and more challenging for the social position of the Muslim landowners.

The *vakf*s (religious foundations), which were of great financial importance for the Muslim community, were put under the control of the Landesregierung after the occupation of Bosnia-Hercegovina. All the revenues of the *vakf*s were collected in a central fund (after 1894 the Zemalska Vakufska Zaklada). Although the Landesregierung had improved the *vakf* system and increased its revenues, government control over the *vakf*s and their expenditure caused discontent among Muslims. The Landesregierung merged the education fund (*mearif fond*) with the *vakf* fund in 1895, thus linking the *vakf* and religious education issues. As a consequence, educational issues became an integral part of the Muslim opposition.[115]

Violent action on the part of the Landesregierung against the Bosnian Muslims was not widespread and was generally confined to particular periods and persons.[116] Interestingly enough, the nationality policy of the government gradually focused on the Bosnian Muslims even though they had constituted the core of the resistance against the occupation. As an important part of the nationality policy the Landesregierung supported the moderate elements in Muslim society; as a result of this well-thought-out policy, a split occurred in the Muslim elite. The relations between the Muslim elites and the state and the rivalry between the radical and the moderates were to shape the ethnic and political development of the Bosnian Muslims throughout the entire Austro-Hungarian period.[117] The Landesregierung showed its political flexibility by negotiating with the Muslim elite in 1901, 1907, and 1908. The recognition of the religious autonomy of the Bosnian Muslims in 1909 is further important evidence of this flexibility.[118]

Though the idea of Bošnjastvo was promoted by some Bosnian Muslim intellectuals such as Mehmet-beg Kapetanović and Safvet-beg Bašagić in the journal *Bošnjak*, it failed to reflect the national identity of the Bosnian Muslims. The nationality policy of the Landesregierung protected and strengthened the distinctiveness of the Muslims in an age of rising nationalism, however, and made an important contribution to their cultural and political development.[119] In this atmosphere Bosnia-Hercegovina witnessed the emergence of a cultural movement referred to in the literature as the cultural or national revival (Preporod) of the Bosnian Muslims.[120] In 1908 there were 124 registered Muslim associations in Bosnia-Hercegovina. All these associations and organizations provided a basis for the further cultural and political development of the Bosnian Muslims as a nation.[121]

THE MUSLIM ELITE AND NATIONALISM

The nationalism of the Bosnian Muslims as an elite phenomenon emerged immediately after the occupation. In the first four years after the occupation the Landesregierung received hundreds of petitions from individuals and a number of different groups. Though these petitions were basically concerned with the mistreatment by government officials, some of them touched upon the common problems of the Muslim community and made some suggestions for the improvement of the political situation.[122] Many of these petitions were submitted by the notables or individual members of the local communities.[123] Though some were isolated initiatives, these petitions constituted a starting point for the later organized Muslim opposition in Bosnia-Hercegovina.[124]

In the early 1900s the Muslim elite was composed basically of three groups: the clerics (*hodzas*), the landowners, and the intellectuals. The national development of the Bosnian Muslims was shaped by the conflict among these groups on the one hand and between these groups and the elites of the other ethnic groups and the state on the other. The Muslim elite groups had no homogeneous structure and were further divided into smaller groups that were also rivals.[125] The Muslim clerics and landowners played a crucial role in the political developments in Bosnia-Hercegovina, while the Muslim intellectuals generally preferred to remain loyal to the Landesregierung.

Conflicts between the Muslim Landowners and the Landesregierung
From the outset the landowners constituted one of the most important components of the Muslim opposition.[126] In different periods the landowners and clerics alternately gained the upper hand and controlled the course of the Muslim opposition. Chronologically the landowners were the first group to initiate opposition activities. Though involved in these activities in Bosnia-Hercegovina, Istanbul, and Vienna as early as the second half of the 1890s (between 1894 and 1899), they failed to turn these actions into a countrywide opposition movement.[127] In order to win over the support of different segments of the Muslim community the landowners not only focused on the agrarian problems but also criticized the deficiencies of the *vakf* system as well as dealing with the religious and educational problems of Muslim society. Religion was an important symbol for the landowners, who exploited religion for political ends by linking their property rights to Sharia law and successfully presented their own economic problems as the problems of the whole Muslim community.[128]

Although Muslim opposition activities were transformed into a countrywide movement under the leadership of the clerics in 1899 and 1900, the Muslim opposition underwent a period of stagnation between 1902 and 1905.[129] The new agrarian reform (Die Zehentpauschalierung), which the landowners perceived as a threat to their existence, was the main reason behind the revival of Muslim opposition in 1905.[130] The second stage of the Muslim movement would pave the way for the foundation of the

Muslim National Organization (MNO) in Slavonski Brod in 1906.[131] The landowners dominated the second stage of the Muslim movement, and the landowner Ali Beg Firdus became the leader of the MNO.[132] In this new period the economic demands of the Muslims would regain importance.[133]

Conflicts between the Muslim Clerics and the Landesregierung

The *hodža*s and the other religious officials constituted another important component of the Muslim opposition and played a key role in transforming the Muslim opposition into a countrywide movement in 1899 and 1900.[134] The *hodža*s from Mostar and Sarajevo constituted the backbone of the Muslim movement, though it also enjoyed the support of the landowners from Travnik and from some other northern provinces.[135] Religion in general and the caliph, the *vakf*s, and the religious language in particular constituted the most important symbols of the Muslim clerics. The relations between the Bosnian Muslims and the Ottoman sultan, who was also the caliph of the Bosnian Sunni Muslims, constituted the most sensitive issue involving the Bosnian Muslims and the Landesregierung. The Muslims were demanding the involvement of Istanbul in the appointment of their religious leader (Reis-ul-Ulema), while the Landesregierung was trying to reduce the relations between the Bosnian Muslims and the Ottoman government. The Landesregierung considered the involvement of Istanbul in the religious affairs of the Bosnian Muslims to be a danger to political stability in Bosnia-Hercegovina.[136] In this sense the institution of the caliphate was the most important symbol for the radical Muslims.[137]

The *vakf*s (which played an important role in the social life of the Muslims) and the language of the religious texts were other important symbols employed by the clerics. Though the Landesregierung improved the *vakf* system that it had inherited from the Ottomans, control over the *vakf* fund caused tension with the Muslims. According to the *hodža*s, the Muslims had the right to control the expenditures of the *vakf* administration. The main aim of the *vakf*s was the foundation of mosques and religious institutions such as *mekteb*s and *medrese*s (religious schools).[138] The *hodža*s tried to strengthen the unity of the Muslim community by demanding the use of the Ottoman-Arabic script in written communications with the Muslim *vakf* and educational institutions.

The Bosnian Muslims experienced a rapid ethnic development during the Austro-Hungarian period. Incidents of conversion from Islam to Christianity were considered ethnic events and caused a wide social impact.[139] The conversion of the Muslim girl Fata Omanović in a village near Mostar in 1899 destabilized relations between the Muslims and the Landesregierung. The immediate consequence of this event was that the rival Muslim groups in Mostar joined forces to set up an action committee under the leadership of Džabić, the former mufti of Mostar, who was to become the most influential leader of the Muslim opposition until 1902. He kept the Ottoman government informed of developments in Bosnia-Hercegovina and received instructions from Istanbul.[140]

The Muslim commission turned to the Landesregierung, the Joint Ministry of Finance, and the Austro-Hungarian emperor in 1899 and referred to the deficient religious education of the Muslims in its petitions.[141] The meetings organized by the Muslims made an important contribution to the spread of the Muslim movement to different parts of the country, while meetings in Kiseljak, Budapest, Mostar, and Sarajevo were particularly influential in the union of the Muslims around a single political program.[142] The submission of a memorandum to the joint minister of finance in 1900 by the Bosnian Muslims initiated a new period in the political life of Bosnia-Hercegovina.[143]

Conflicts between the Muslim and Croatian Clerics

Another important development that shaped the national development of the Muslims under Austro-Hungarian rule was the conflict between the Muslim and Catholic clerics. The proselytizing activities of Josip Stadler, the Catholic bishop of Sarajevo, formed the core of the complaints of the Muslims and increased the tension between the two communities. Though incidents of conversion were limited, Muslims considered them a threat to their community. The Muslim leaders complained about anti-Islamic propaganda on the part of the Croats and accused the government of not putting a stop to it. They stressed that the Muslim community was receiving a poor religious education and that the regulations concerning conversions were being violated.[144] The petitioners described the conversion of Fata Omanović, which sparked a countrywide opposition movement as a result of propaganda against the Muslims.[145]

"The Islamic religion is in danger; we must rescue it" (*Islamski din, islamski vjera u pogibelji, moramo nju osigurat!*) was one of the most important slogans employed by the Muslim leaders.[146] By means of these slogans they were able to get the signatures and mandate (*punomoć*) of the Muslim population, which was important for further opposition activities.[147] Many Muslims gave their support to the leaders of the opposition in order to protect the Islamic religion, which they thought to be in peril, without considering the practical political consequences.[148] The Muslims also complained of the government's neglect of the *vakf* properties, grave-yards, mosques, and other cultural institutions in Bosnia-Hercegovina. According to the Muslim leaders, religious education in the existing *medreses* and *mektebs* was deficient and inadequate in meeting the needs of the Muslim community.[149] Moreover, the *vakf* revenues were not being used for religious purposes as they were supposed to be, while the officials were overpaid and lacked the necessary qualifications.[150]

Conflicts between the Radicals and Moderates

Neither the landowners nor the *hodzas* constituted a homogeneous group, both being composed of radical and moderate wings. The radicals were involved in antigovernment activities, while the moderates were more in-clined to be loyal to the government.[151] The *hodzas* were dominated by the radicals and offered the fiercest resistance against the Landesregier-ung.[152] In contrast, the intellectuals constituted the group in the Muslim elite most loyal to the government and, apart from a few exceptions, did not play any important role in the Muslim opposition. The fear of losing their jobs in the bureaucracy forced the majority of Muslim intellectuals to keep a certain distance from the Muslim opposition. As a group the landowners were in between. They were economically dependent on the decisions of the government and were basically inclined to cooperate with the Austro-Hungarian rule. Generally the landowners changed their posi-tion in accordance with developments in the Muslim movement. Many of the landowners had secret or open contacts with the Landesregierung and were playing a double game.[153] The landowners hesitated between the Landesregierung and the radicals.[154]

The years 1901 and 1902 witnessed a clear polarization between the radicals and the moderates. The rivalry between them for the leadership of the Muslim opposition played a crucial role in the national development of the Bosnian Muslims. In the eyes of the radicals, the Landesregierung and the moderates had failed to protect the interests of the Muslims. One of the most important differences between the political positions of the radicals and the moderates was that the radicals wanted to make an alli-ance with the Serbs while the great Muslim landowners (such as Ali Beg Firdus and Bekir Beg Tuzlić) and traders (such as Mujaga Komadina) were trying to avoid such a move. The Serbs were trying to win over the sup-port of the Bosnian Muslims against the Landesregierung.[155] This alliance was particularly dangerous for the economic interests of the landowners, however, since the majority of their *kmets* were Serbs.[156]

THE BOSNIAN MUSLIMS
AND NATIONALISM

During the Ottoman period the Bosnian Muslims were known as "Bošnaklar," "Bošnak taifesi," "Bosnalı takımı," "Bosnalı kavmi," and other terms and referred to their own language as the "Bosnian language." The uprisings against the Ottoman reforms and attempts at centralization led by the Bosnian *ajan*s (local notables) and the landowners strengthened their Bosniak identity, while their conflicts with the Christians, particularly in the second half of the nineteenth century, stressed their Muslim identity.[157] In the late Ottoman period the Islamic religion played the role of a unifying political ideology and provided a suitable basis for the development of a common culture among the Bosnian Muslims. The Bosnian Muslim community was composed of *sipahis* (landowners), the *ulema*, other social classes in the cities, and *reaya* (peasants) during the Ottoman period.[158]

The occupation of Bosnia-Hercegovina by the Austro-Hungarian Empire initiated a new period in the national development of the Bosnian Muslims. Though the first stage of the political opposition of the Bosnian Muslims continued for only a few years (1899–1902) it marks a turning point for the newly emerging Bosnian Muslim nationalism, with political developments in this short period paving the way for a countrywide Muslim opposition. The Muslim movement, which stagnated after 1902, revived in 1905 and culminated in the foundation of the first Muslim party (MNO) in 1906, which was also the first political party in Bosnia-Hercegovina.[159] Already in 1906 the Muslim press had started to consider the question of national orientation as a nonreligious issue.[160]

The problems of the *vakf* administration and the religious schools were central to the demands of the Bosnian Muslims in the first stage of Muslim opposition. The Muslim movement was often referred to as a struggle for religious and *vakf*-educational autonomy (*borba za vjersku i vakufsko-mearifsku autonomiju*).[161] In the memorandum submitted to the Joint Ministry of Finance in 1900 the Muslims stressed that a non-Muslim state could not run the religious affairs of the Muslims and demanded religious autonomy, stating that the *vakf* fund belonged to the Muslims and ought to be governed by them.[162] According to the detailed proposal (Nacrt Štatuta) for religious autonomy that the Muslim leaders submitted to the joint minister of finance in 1900, the whole school system — not only the religious schools but also the other schools such as the *mekteb-i ibtidaije* (reformed schools) — should be under the control of the autonomous administration.[163] The Muslim leaders demanded the foundation of new *mekteb*s for Muslim boys and girls and *medrese*s for the education of the *hodža*s and that education should be compulsory in the areas that already had *mekteb*s.[164] Not satisfied with the financial aid given by the government for their religious institutions, Muslims tried to gain an increase by calling for financial aid to be proportional to the size of their population.[165]

The Muslims were also interested in the language question, something of great importance for nationalist movements. In the autonomy proposal submitted to the joint minister of finance, Kállay, in 1900 the Bosnian Muslims demanded the use of the Ottoman-Arabic script in written correspondence with the Muslim *vakf* and educational institutions. Only correspondence between these institutions and government offices should be conducted in a Slavic language.[166] They complained that the Ottoman and Arabic languages were not taught in the Dar-ül-Muallimin (school for the education of the *hodza*s).[167] The clerics were trying to strengthen the identity and unity of the Muslim community through the use of the religious language.

The Muslim proposal for religious autonomy went even further and could be considered a well-thought-out political program and a clear indication of the politicization of Muslim ethnicity.[168] According to Kállay, who was also a historian, the Muslims wanted to create a state within a state.[169] Although he was ready to make some important concessions in terms of *vakf* and educational autonomy, anything that might lead to the formation of a political Muslim *narod* (nation) had to be avoided in his view.[170] The formation of a Muslim nation was wholly incompatible with Kállay's conception of a Bosnian nation.[171]

In their daily life the Bosnian Muslims referred to themselves as "Turčin" (Turkish),[172] a term that had no national connotation and simply meant that they belonged to the same religion as the Turks. In Bosnia-Hercegovina "Musliman" (Muslim) and "Turčin" were synonymous.[173] The Muslims often described themselves in their memoranda and petitions as "islamski narod" or "islamski millet" (Muslim nation).[174] The journal *Bošnjak*, which was employed by the government to promote Bosnian ideology, used both "Musliman" and "Bošnjak."[175] Though the majority of the Bosnian Muslims had no clear national orientation, they referred to their language as the Bosnian language or "naški jezik" (our language).[176] The few Muslim intellectuals who had declared themselves Serbs or Croats were not welcomed by the rest of the Muslim community and faced great social pressure.[177]

The religious definitions used by the Bosnian Muslims did not reflect the religious kinship between the Bosnian Muslims and the other Muslim communities and constituted a basis for the later political and cultural development of the Bosnian Muslims as a nation.[178] After the occupation of Bosnia-Hercegovina, the Bosnian Muslims were separated from the Slavic Muslims in Novi Pazar, Montenegro, and Macedonia as well as from the non-Slavic Muslims such as the Albanians and Turks in Kosovo and Macedonia. As another important consequence of the occupation the Sufi orders lost their former influence in Bosnia-Hercegovina. All these various factors would contribute to the development of a distinctive identity of the Bosnian Muslims, with no connection to the Muslim community as a whole.[179]

Different reasons lay behind the use of religious names and definitions by the Bosnian Muslims under Austro-Hungarian rule. First, in contrast to the Bosnian Serbs and Croats, the Bosnian Muslims had identified themselves with the Ottoman state in the past and were deeply influenced by the Ottoman *millet* system, in which religion and nationality were closely intertwined.[180] The concept of Bošnjastvo used by the Bosnian Muslims in the Ottoman period to differentiate themselves from the Ottomans, however, had lost its importance in the Austro-Hungarian period.[181] In this new era religion was the most effective ethnic boundary marker for the Slavic Bosnian Muslims, who wished to distinguish themselves from the Slavic non-Muslim ethnic groups in the country. The concept of Bošnjastvo was promoted by the Landesregierung, which was perceived by the majority of the Muslims as a non-Muslim foreign administration, which was another important reason for its inability to be accepted as the national identity of the Bosnian Muslims. Moreover, the Bosnian Muslims who had lived for centuries under the rule of the Islamic Ottoman Empire were now fearful of becoming assimilated into the Catholic Austro-Hungarian Empire and began to lay stress on their religious roots.[182] Finally, the newly emerging Muslim bourgeoisie and intelligentsia were unable to play a key role in the Muslim opposition and consequently were unable to produce alternative concepts for the national identity of the Bosnian Muslims.[183]

Although the national consciousness of the Serbs and Croats was stronger than that of the Bosnian Muslims during the Austro-Hungarian period, the difference was not as drastic as some historians have claimed. While the Muslim opposition to the Landesregierung had no clear national orientation, it would be wrong to claim that it had no national connotation.[184] During the Austro-Hungarian period the concepts of nationality and religion were still closely intertwined in Bosnia-Hercegovina. According to the report of the Joint Ministry of Finance published in 1906 the differences among the Serbs, Croats, and Muslims still had a dual nature: national and religious.[185]

CONCLUSIONS

Paul Brass's model provides important clues for the analysis of Bosnian Muslim nationalism, which emerged at the beginning of the twentieth century mainly through the elite conflicts in Bosnia-Hercegovina, then a colony of the Austro-Hungarian Empire. Despite the existing similarities, however, Bosnian Muslim nationalism had some distinctive characteristics that differentiated it from the Brass model. Theoretically it is possible to view the period between the beginning of countrywide opposition in 1899 and the recognition of the religious autonomy of the Bosnian Muslims by the Landesregierung in 1909 as the second stage of the nationality formation of the Bosnian Muslims. But my study shows that in the case of the Bosnian Muslims the signs of the two stages of the nationality formation — from ethnic group to community and from community to nationality — occurred simultaneously.

In the case of the Bosnian Muslims the elite conflicts took the following forms: (1) between the Muslim landowners and the Landesregierung; (2) between the Muslim clerics and the Landesregierung; (3) between the Muslim and Croatian clerics; and (4) between the radical and moderate wings of the Muslim elite. Although the elite conflicts played a key role in the national development of the Bosnian Muslims during the Austro-Hungarian period, it would be a simplification to view the Muslim movement as a mere product of the elite conflicts. The Muslim leadership needed the signatures and the mandate (*punomoć*) of the Muslim population to continue with its opposition activities, clearly indicating that not only the Muslim elite but also the rest of the Muslim community was instrumental in shaping the relations between the Bosnian Muslims and the Landesregierung.

Intensive communication is one of the preconditions of mass movements. As late as 1910, 94.65 percent of the Muslims were still illiterate, which means that only a small number of Bosnian Muslims were available for intensive communication. But archival documents indicate very clearly that after 1899 Bosnia-Hercegovina witnessed a countrywide Muslim mass movement. The explanation lies in the relations between the Muslims, who had a form of "personal network." This was not only a local system but extended to Istanbul and constituted an important part of the relations between the Bosnian Muslims and the Ottoman government.

Although Ottoman documents show that the pan-Islamic policy of the Ottoman sultan played an important role in the spread of the Muslim opposition in Bosnia-Hercegovina, the Muslim opposition should not be considered a by-product of Ottoman pan-Islamic policy. The basic reasons behind the Muslim opposition were to be found in Bosnia-Hercegovina.

NOTES

I would like to thank the Boğaziçi University Research Fund for its support (Projekt No. 5087).

1. Aydın Babuna, *Die nationale Entwicklung der bosnischen Muslime, mit besonderer Berücksichtigung der österreichisch-ungarischen Periode*, 42. For the sake of simplicity, the Muslims of Bosnia-Hercegovina are referred to here as Bosnian Muslims.

2. The Muslim landowners with *kmet*s lived on the annual rents they received from them.

3. Aydın Babuna, "Nationalism and the Bosnian Muslims," 214.

4. Paul Brass, "Ethnic Groups and Nationalities: The Formation, Persistence and Transformation of Ethnic Identities," 40.

5. For example, see Robert Donia, *Islam under the Double Eagle: The Muslims of Bosnia-Hercegovina, 1878–1914*; Mark Pinson, "The Muslims of Bosnia-Hercegovina under Austro-Hungarian Rule, 1878–1918"; and Robert Donia and John V. A. Fine, *Bosnia and Hercegovina: A Tradition Betrayed*.

6. This paper draws upon Babuna, *Die nationale Entwicklung der bosnischen Muslime*; and Babuna, "Nationalism and the Bosnian Muslims."

7. According to Brass, ethnic groups differ from the other groups in objective cultural characteristics and contain the elements for a division of labor and for reproduction. Brass, "Ethnic Groups," 2.

8. Paul Brass, *Ethnicity and Nationalism: Theory and Comparison*, 47.

9. Brass, "Ethnic Groups," 8–9.

10. Influential subgroups within ethnic groups and classes: Brass, *Ethnicity and Nationalism*, 14.

11. Ibid., 64–65.

12. Ernest Gellner, *Nationalismus und Moderne*, 24.

13. Brass, "Ethnic Groups," 15.

14. Brass, *Ethnicity and Nationalism*, 45–46.

15. Paul Brass, "Elite Competition and Nation Formation," 89.

16. Gerhard Brunn, Miroslav Hroch, and Andreas Kappeler, introduction to *The Formation of National Elites*, 9.

17. Brass, *Ethnicity and Nationalism*, 9–75.

18. For the role of religion and language in the identity of ethnic groups, see Paul Brass, *Language, Religion and Politics in North India*.

19. Ferdinand Hauptmann, "Die Mohammedaner in Bosnien und Hercegovia," 670.

20. "Landes-Übersicht der einheimischen Bevölkerung von Bosnien und der Hercegovina nach dem Stande vom 1. Mai 1885, die Tabelle über die percentuelle Vertheilung der Bevölkerungsklassen auf Grund der Landesübersicht vom Jahre

1885," in *Ortschafts- und Bevölkerungs-Statistik von Bosnien-Herzegowina nach dem Volkszählungsergebnis vom 1. Mai 1885.*

21. Donia, *Islam under the Double Eagle*, 7.

22. Kemal H. Karpat, "1878 Avusturya İşgaline Karşı Bosna-Hersek Direnişiyle İlgili Osmanlı Politikası," 156. The estimates on the number of the Austro-Hungarian troops range between 150,000 and 270,000. Francine Friedman, *The Bosnian Muslims: Denial of a Nation*, 60.

23. Dimitrije Klicin, "Otpor Muslimana protiv okupacije," 229–30.

24. László Bencze, *The Occupation of Bosnia and Hercegovina in 1878*, 90–91.

25. Karpat, "1878 Avusturya İşgaline Karşı Bosna-Hersek Direnişiyle İlgili Osmanlı Politikası," 195.

26. Mihodil Mandić, *Povijest okupacije Bosne i Hercegovina 1878*, 32; Donia, *Islam under the Double Eagle*, 31.

27. Mandić, *Povijest okupacije*, 32.

28. National Archives of the United Kingdom (formerly Public Record Office), Foreign Office Archives, London (FO), FO 424/74 (from Freeman to Salisbury) 53/2, August 3, 1878, cited in Karpat, "1878 Avusturya İşgaline Karşı Bosna-Hersek Direnişiyle İlgili Osmanlı Politikası," 168.

29. *Bericht über die Verwaltung Bosnien und der Hercegovina*, 14.

30. *Die Ergebnisse der Volkszählung in Bosnien und der Hercegovina vom 10. Oktober 1910*, xlii.

31. The Landesregierung was the Austro-Hungarian government in Bosnia-Hercegovina.

32. *Bericht über die Verwaltung Bosnien und der Hercegovina*, 11.

33. Hamdija Kapidžić, *Der Aufstand in der Hercegovine im jahre 1882: Auszüge*, 76, cited in Babuna, *Die nationale Entwicklung*, 53.

34. Hamdija Kapidžić, "Prilog istoriji hercegovačkog ustanka 1882," 212.

35. Ibid., 214–16.

36. Muhamed Hadzijahić, "Uz prilog Prof. Vojislava Bogičevića," 192.

37. Başbakanlık Devlet Arşivleri Genel Müdürlüğü, *Bosna-Hersek İle İlgili Arşiv Belgeleri*, 307–11.

38. Vojislav Bogičević, "Emigracije Muslimana Bosne i Hercegovine u Tursku u doba austro-ugarske vladavine 1878–1918 god," 182. According to Karpat, the number of the migrants was not over 100,000 and 10–15 percent of them returned to Bosnia. Kemal H. Karpat, "The Migration of the Bosnian Muslims to the Ottoman State, 1878–1914: An Account Based on Turkish Sources," 140.

39. Babuna, *Die nationale Entwicklung*, 169.

40. Bogičević, "Emigracije Muslimana," 183 (percentages slightly revised).

41. *Bericht über die Verwaltung Bosnien und der Hercegovina*, 14.

42. Mustafa Imamović, *Pravni položaj i unutrašnji politički razvitak Bosne i Hercegovine od 1878 do 1914*, 110.

43. Bogičević, "Emigracije Muslimana," 177.

44. Ibid., 178; Imamović, *Pravni položaj*, 110.

45. *Bericht über die Verwaltung Bosnien und der Hercegovina*, 11.

46. Imamović, *Pravni položaj*, 113.

47. Ibid., 109; Bogičević, "Emigracije Muslimana," 184.

48. *Bericht über die Verwaltung Bosnien und der Hercegovina*, 12–13.

49. Spisi Muhamedanske narodne deputacije iz Hercegovine 1899, Arhiv Bosne i HercegovineHercegovina, Sarajevo (ABH), ZMF Pr BH 1397/1899, 13; Haus-, Hof- und Staatsarchiv, Vienna (HHStA), BA. Konst. 444, vom Consul Para an Freiherrn von Braun (K. und K. Geschäftsträger), March 5, 1902.

50. Başbakanlık Osmanlı Arşivi, Istanbul (BOA), Dosya No. 1, Sıra No. 31, Tarih: 1322. 4. 13, Aded: 1. Bab-ali Eyalet-i Mümtaze Kalemi-Osmanlı Arşivi Depo No. 2/3.

51. Ferdinand Hauptmann, *Borba Muslimana Bosne i Hercegovine za vjersku i vakufsko-mearifsku autonomiju: Građa*, 49.

52. Başbakanlık Devlet Arşivleri Genel Müdürlüğü, *Bosna-Hersek İle İlgili Arşiv Belgeleri*, 168–69.

53. Karpat, "The Migration of the Bosnian Muslims to the Ottoman State, 1878–1914: An Account Based on Turkish Sources," 134–35.

54. For the Ottoman government's help to the Bosnian Muslim migrants, see *Osmanlı Belgelerinde Bosna-Hersek: Bosna i Hercegovina u Osmanskim Dokumentima*, 277–317.

55. Clemens Ruthner, "Habsburg's Little Orient: A Post/Colonial Reading of Austrian and German Cultural Narratives on Bosnia-Hercegovina, 1878–1918."

56. Petar Vrankić, *Religion und Politik in Bosnien und der Herzegowina (1878–1918)*, 37.

57. Ruthner, "Habsburg's Little Orient," 6.

58. Noel Malcolm, *Bosnia: A Short History*, 143.

59. For the analysis of this rhetoric, see Ruthner, "Habsburg's Little Orient," 1–16.

60. For the Yenipazar Convention, see Başbakanlık Devlet Arşivleri Genel Müdürlüğü, *Bosna-Hersek İle İlgili Arşiv Belgeleri*, 79–82.

61. Hauptmann, *Borba Muslimana*, 49.

62. The Austro-Hungarian delegation was composed of the members of the Austrian and Hungarian parliaments and met twice a year, like a parliamentary commission.

63. Babuna, "Nationalism," 209.

64. For example, see Pinson, "The Muslims of Bosnia-Hercegovina," 124.

65. Babuna, *Die nationale Entwicklung*, 190.

66. Ibid., 190–91.

67. Todor Kruševać, *Sarajevo pod austro-ugarskom upravom 1878–1918*, 308.

68. Babuna, *Die nationale Entwicklung*, 190–99.

69. BOA-BEO-Mümtaze Kalemi: Bosna, 1/20-(1321.4.22).

70. Peter Sugar, *Industrialization of Bosnia-Hercegovina, 1878–1918*, 39.

71. Ibid., 57, 61.

72. Ibid., 62–63.

73. Ferdinand Hauptmann, *Die österreichisch-ungarische Herrschaft in Bosnien und der Hercegovina 1878–1918: Wirtschaftspolitik und Wirtschaftsentwicklung*, 44, 48.

74. Iljas Hadžibegović, *Bosanskohercegovački gradovi na razmeđu 19. i 20. Stoljeca*.

75. Mustafa Imamović, *Historija države i prava Bosne i Hercegovine*, 227–28.

76. Hauptmann, *Die österreichisch-ungarische Herrschaft*, 229.

77. Ibid., 229–30.

78. Ibid., 232.

79. Babuna, *Die nationale Entwicklung*, 314.

80. Ferdinand Hauptmann, "Privreda i društvo Bosne i Hercegovine u doba austro-ugarske vladavine (1878–1918)," 200.

81. Hauptmann, *Die österreichisch-ungarische Herrschaft*, 245–46.

82. Ibid., 33.

83. Benjamin Kállay, *Die Lage der Mohammedaner in Bosnien, von einem Ungarn* (Vienna, 1900), 81–82, cited in Robin Okey, *Taming Balkan Nationalism: The Habsburg "Civilizing Mission" in Bosnia, 1878–1914*, 98.

84. Benjamin V. Kállay, *Ungarn an den Grenzen des Orients und des Occidents* (Budapest, 1883), 37, 53, cited in Babuna, *Die nationale Entwicklung*, 170.

85. Babuna, "Nationalism," 204.

86. Hauptmann, *Die österreichisch-ungarische Herrschaft*, 238.

87. The Croats were interested in economic activities rather than the bureaucracy.

88. Hauptmann, *Borba Muslimana*, 50.

89. Hauptmann, "Privreda i društvo," 200.

90. İbrahim Kemura, "Proglas muslimanske akademske omladine u Beću od 1907 godine," 334.

91. *Behar* 5 (1904): br. 7, 112; 6 (1905), br. 8, 128, cited in ibid.

92. *Die Ergebnisse der Volkszählung in Bosnien und der Hercegovina vom 10. Oktober 1910*, xlvi.

93. Babuna, *Die nationale Entwicklung*, 177.

94. Donia, *Islam under the Double Eagle*, xii.

95. See Jeremy Boissevain, *Friends of Friends: Networks, Manipulators and Coalitions*, 27, 24.

96. ABH, ZMF, BH, Pr. No. 542/1891, cited in Tomislav Kraljačić, *Kalajev režim u Bosni i Hercegovini (1882–1903)*, 217.

97. Kruševać, *Sarajevo*, 279.

98. Imamović, *Pravni položaj*, 71.

99. Ibid., 77.

100. For the nationality policy of the Landesregierung, see Babuna, *Die nationale Entwicklung*, 203–4.

101. *Sammlung der für Bosnien und die Hercegovina erlassenen Gesetze, Verordnungen, und Normalweisungen 1878–1880*, 319–21.

102. Ibid., 317.

103. Dževad Juzbašić, *Jezičko pitanje u austrougarskoj politici u Bosni i Hercegovini pred prvi svjetski rat*, 12.

104. Ibid., 9.

105. Kraljačić, *Kalajev režim*, 235–37.

106. Juzbašić, *Jezičko pitanje*, 10.

107. "4. Sitzung der 29. Session am 16. Juni 1893," in *Stenographische Sitzungs-Protokolle der Delegation des Reichsrathes* (1893), 199–200.

108. "4. Sitzung der 32. Session am 18. Juni 1896," in *Stenographische Sitzungs-Protokolle der Delegation des Reichsrathes* (1896), 157.

109. Mustafa Imamović, *Historija Bošnjaka*, 376.

110. Vlado Jokanović, "Elementi koji su kroz istoriju djelovali pozitivno i negativno na stvaranja bošnjaštva kao nacionalnog pokreta," 246.

111. Imamović, *Historija Bošnjaka*, 376.

112. Malcolm, *Bosnia*, 128

113. *Die Ergebnisse der Volkszählung in Bosnien und der Hercegovina vom 10. Oktober 1910*, lxviii.

114. Babuna, *Die nationale Entwicklung*, 221; Ivan Božić et al., *Istorija Jugoslavije*, 325.

115. Ferdinand Schmid, *Bosnien und die Hercegovina unter der Verwaltung Österreich-Ungarns* (Leipzig, 1914), 686, cited in Babuna, *Die nationale Entwicklung*, 101.

116. Babuna, *Die nationale Entwicklung*, 47. The suppression of the Muslims took place particularly during and immediately after the occupation. For example, see *Osmanlı Belgelerinde Bosna-Hersek*, 258–66.

117. Babuna, *Die nationale Entwicklung*, 47.

118. Ibid., 317–18.

119. Ibid., 155.

120. For example, see Muhsin Rizvić, *Bosansko-muslimanska knjizevnost u doba preporoda 1887–1918*.

121. Mustafa Imamović, "O historiji bošnjačkog pokušaja," 55.

122. For example, see Hauptmann, *Borba Muslimana*, 50–53.

123. Donia, *Islam under the Double Eagle*, 30.

124. Babuna, *Die nationale Entwicklung*, 316.

125. Ibid., 225.

126. HHStA, BA. Konst. 444. Von Kállay an Goluchowski, February 12, 1902; Hauptmann, *Borba Muslimana*, 39.

127. Babuna, *Die nationale Entwicklung*, 250.

128. Ibid., 254.

129. Ibid., 263.

130. Donia, *Islam under the Double Eagle*, 169.

131. For the establishment of this party, see Aydın Babuna, "The Emergence of the First Muslim Party in Bosnia-Hercegovina."

132. Nusret Šehić, *Autonomni pokret Muslimana za vrijeme austrougarske uprave u Bosni i Hercegovini*, 194.

133. Babuna, *Die nationale Entwicklung*, 251.

134. Ibid., 254–55.

135. ABH, ZMF Pr BH 344/1899.

136. The Landesregierung was also against the idea that the appointed Reis-ul-Ulema should derive his religious mandate from the Ottoman Şeyh-ül Islam.

137. Babuna, *Die nationale Entwicklung*, 259.

138. Spisi Muhamedanske narodne deputacije iz Hercegovine 1899, ABH, ZMF Pr BH 1397/1899, 26.

139. Donia, *Islam under the Double Eagle*, 187.

140. Babuna, *Die nationale Entwicklung*, 198.

141. Spisi muhamedanske narodne deputacije iz Hercegovine 1899, ABH, ZMF PrBH 1397/1899, 5, 6, 14, 15, 21, 22.

142. Donia, *Islam under the Double Eagle*, 129.

143. Babuna, *Die nationale Entwicklung*, 119.

144. ABH, ZMF Pr BH 1670/1900. According to the regulations concerning the conversions, the converts had to be mentally healthy, have reached the legal age, and take the advice of a Muslim cleric before conversion. Ibid., 8.

145. Ibid., 5. Though Fata Omanović had converted to Christianity for private reasons the Muslims thought that she had been duped by a Catholic cleric.

146. ABH, ZMF Pr BH 776/1900; ABH, ZMF Pr BH 1670/1900, 11.

147. ABH, ZMF Pr BH 828/1900.

148. Ibid.; ABH, ZMF Pr BH 865/1900.

149. ABH, ZMF Pr BH 1670/1900, 15–16.

150. Ibid., 25.

151. Babuna, *Die nationale Entwicklung*, 251.

152. Ibid., 315.

153. Ibid., 251–52; HHStA, BA. Konst. 444. Von Kállay an Goluchowski, February 12, 1902.

154. Babuna, *Die nationale Entwicklung*, 315.

155. The Serbs continued the annual celebrations of the accession of the Ottoman sultan to the throne until the annexation of Bosnia-Hercegovina by the Austro-Hungarian Empire in 1908.

156. ABH, ZMF Pr BH 246/1901, 2.

157. Srećko Džaja, *Konfessionalität und Nationalität Bosniens und der Herzegowina: Voremanzipatorische Phase 1463–1804*, 100.

158. Avdo Sućeska, "Neke specifičnosti istorije Bosne pod Turcima," 49.

159. Babuna, *Die nationale Entwicklung*, 166.

160. "Mi," 1.

161. Babuna, *Die nationale Entwicklung*, 101–2.

162. ABH, ZMF Pr BH 1670/1900, 33–34.

163. ABH, ZMF Pr BH 1670/1900 (Nacrt štatuta), 25.

164. Ibid., 28.

165. Ibid., 33.

166. Ibid., 35.

167. Ibid., 14.

168. Babuna, *Die nationale Entwicklung*, 125.

169. Hauptmann, *Borba Muslimana*, 122.

170. "Es sollte jedoch 'alles vermieden werden, was darüber hinausgehend zur Bildung eines politischen mohammedanischen Volk (*narod*) führen konnte.'" Ibid.

171. Babuna, *Die nationale Entwicklung*, 126.

172. ABH, ZMF Pr BH 1068/1900.

173. Kasım Suljević, *Nacionalnost Muslimana: Između teorije i politike*, 15.

174. ABH, ZMF Pr BH 825/1901; ABH, ZMF Pr BH 1670/1900, 2–5 etc. ("islamski narod"); ABH, ZMF Pr BH 825/1901, 4–6 ("islamski millet").

175. Babuna, *Die nationale Entwicklung*, 154.

176. Osman Nuri Hadžić, "Borba Muslimana za vjersku i vakufsko-mearifsku autonomiju," in *Bosna i Hercegovina pod austro-ugarskom upravom*, ed. St. Stanojević (Belgrade: n.p., 1938), 94–95, cited in Babuna, *Die nationale Entwicklung*, 145.

177. Hasan M. Rebac and Osman Đikić, Vardar (Kalendar), 13/1924, 118–20, cited in Rizvić, *Bosansko-muslimanska književnost*, 160.

178. Imamović, "O historiji bošnjačkog pokušaja," 55.

179. Aydın Babuna, "The Bosnian Muslims and Albanians: Islam and Nationalism," 291.

180. Babuna, *Die nationale Entwicklung*, 32.

181. Pedro Ramet, "Die Muslime Bosniens als Nation," 108.

182. The Bosnian Muslims pointed out this fear in different ways in their petitions.

183. Šaćir Filandra, *Bošnjačka politika u XX. Stoljecu*, 18–19.

184. Babuna, *Die nationale Entwicklung*, 154.

185. *Bericht über die Verwaltung Bosnien und der Hercegovina*, 119.

9

Agents of Post-Ottoman States

The Precariousness of the Berlin Congress Boundaries of Montenegro and How to Define/Confine People

Isa Blumi

INTRODUCTION

Among the lingering methodological problems facing scholars working on the nineteenth century is the deference given to categories of distinction found in the documents of emerging state bureaucracies. For many historians since World War I, it is apparently the way in which modernizing states began to manage their human resources that proved crucial to the expansion of government power. This concentration of state capacities, of course, also fits conveniently with a narrative that projects government power in the modern era directly at the expense of historically autonomous social and economic spaces. In particular, the manner in which boundaries began to correspond with an abstract notion of what constituted a "population" and who were citizens of these states became the central concern of scholars. Sadly, as evidenced by the preponderance of studies that in one way or another flaunt the oppressive capacities of modern states, the often contentious and dynamic process of state domination is lost as scholars take the subsequent categories of modern government for granted.

Historians focusing on the Balkans, in particular, tend to treat the "rules" of engagement animating subjects' actions as transcendent of context. Ethno-national and sectarian identities, largely a product of modern methods of governance, are especially taken for granted in the scholarship. In this respect, the Berlin Congress of 1878 has been particularly influential in imposing an epistemology of ethnic and religious difference. In delineating a set of procedures of government in order to impose an "order" to the shifts in imperial power over the Balkans, the congress has served as the foundation to the all-too-readily accepted assertions made by journalists and diplomats about the events in the period covered in this volume. In response, this chapter seeks to challenge a framework of inquiry that perpetuates a codification of ethnic and sectarian truisms still dominating the calculus of analysis among scholars who buy into the essentialism of nationalist historiography.

Much of the scholarship on the period, as evidenced even in this volume, treats the interventions by the Great Powers as an inevitable part of a crucial transforming process. The questions posed throughout this chapter challenge the utility of looking at events "from above" both methodologically and as a practical and accurate reflection of actual events. This chapter suggests that a closer analysis of events on the ground in places like the Hercegovinan/Serbian/Montenegrin/Ottoman frontier during the Berlin Congress and its immediate aftermath may reveal that much of what is taken for granted requires some reconsideration. First, the inhabitants of these regions, initially divided up by imperial cartographers using demographic abstractions that assumed simple religious distinction, thoroughly resisted the implications of the initial drawing of frontiers separating the Ottoman Empire from large parts of its former territories awarded to Montenegro, Serbia, and the Habsburg Empire. Second, the nature of the subsequent resistance ultimately compelled the agents of history so often identified in the history books to modify their strategies dramatically. This was especially the case in the newly recognized states of Montenegro and Serbia, which were confronted with a number of contingencies that few among the chief delegates at Berlin in the summer of 1878 actually bothered to consider. Inspecting the Italian, French, Austrian, British, Turkish, and Albanian state archives makes it clear that the actual presumptions of the modern world order fail to translate on the ground. Local contingencies first forced the powers to redraw the border they had wanted to impose on the region and then, over the long term, forced the reorientation of principal state-building agendas. See map 9.1 for the regions in question and the borders that eventually were drawn to accommodate some (but not all) reactions.

A MODERN WORLD REPEATEDLY REDEFINED

Accessing a revisionist interpretation of the Berlin Congress starts with disaggregating the categories of analysis from the ethno-national, sectarian, and regional to local. Once we challenge the accuracy of the categories

MAP 9.1. Border Areas of the Western Balkans, 1878–1912. Designed by Visar Arifaj.

used by contemporary diplomats and subsequent generations of scholars and state bureaucrats, it is possible to identify numerous tensions that ultimately reveal themselves in the archival material. The imposition of frontiers at the Berlin Congress, for instance, designed in the nineteenth and twentieth centuries to separate what the Ottoman Empire had conjoined over centuries, remains the presumed diplomatic necessity to resolving primordial conflicts between ethnic and sectarian rival peoples. Indeed, breaking up heterogeneous ("mixed") societies that have been the "legacy" of the Ottoman experience has continued to be the preferred diplomatic strategy for the Balkans, the Caucasus, Africa, and the Middle East today.[1] Seen in this light, the complex exchanges among various actors in what became known as Montenegro after the summer of 1878 suggest that the very modern process of delineating identity with territories abstractly defined on a map entails as much destruction as construction, of cities/monuments/states as well as community sensibilities, and toleration for those guilty of mass murder, rape, and ethnic cleansing.

Violent responses to ethnic cleansing are not the only reactions manifested by local populations, however. The violent acts used to protect family and community from the expansion of new states are certainly authentic, but they emanate from a specific set of conditions that did not always exist. This chapter therefore seeks to reconsider the dynamic forces at play along the borderlands separating Montenegro, Serbia, and the Ottoman state when the frontiers were first considered and then imposed during the 1878–85 period. In the process of revealing the intensive give-and-take between an outside diplomatic order and local populations resisting the very idea of delineating a border through their lives, I do not seek to reaffirm the transformative function of the border but to offer a method of observing the process as a series of contingencies reflecting shifting geostrategic, economic, and political contexts.

Among many other questions, we may ask whether we really can be certain that what we observe happening along these frontiers fully addresses the rigid notions of identity and economic propriety imposed by our essentialist analytical categories. Moreover, did the diplomatic and bureaucratic conventions that fixed human relations within the frontiers of nation-states really cover the range of locals' ambitions and anticipated results during these crucial moments of transition? At the heart of such a question lies the need to identify the full range of opportunities offered by these boundaries to hitherto ignored, but strategically vital, local communities. Resistant to simple generalizations, these communities begin to reflect competing interests — the Ottoman, Serbian, and Montenegrin states, factions in each state's bureaucracy, merchants and the political elite, as well as the neighboring powers of Austria-Hungary and Italy — that in turn underwent transformations in the face of events along these contested borders. To make this particularly difficult argument, I focus in detail on the alpine region of Malësi, which became the frontier separating the Montenegrin and Ottoman states. The (re)actions of the Malësorë (inhabitants of the region) in the middle of the 1878–1912 storm offer an especially intriguing set of cases, inasmuch as they demonstrate that power is often not the exclusive resource of the state in moments of institutional and systemic change. Furthermore, events in Malësi highlight that identity politics at that time did not follow our normative modern lines of thinking. Factions that are presumably Albanians and Slavs pitted against each other turn out to have complicated interconnecting interests that often contradict the ethno-national model still shaping the way in which we analyze events in the Balkans today.

The first section of this chapter explores this dynamic from the very process of drawing a frontier by diplomats appointed by the Berlin

Congress. The actual border that they drew was ultimately modified because of the resistance that these officials and subsequent Montenegrin officials faced from local populations living in the highland territories that were to become the frontiers of new states. The process was so contentious that the final settlement of the borders of Montenegro, Serbia, and the Ottoman Empire would take years. This process along the ambiguous frontiers of what were assumed to be cultural, ethnic, and economic fault lines ultimately proves to be a window into the vulnerability of the modern world order and the epistemology of difference that the new powers sought to impose on a previously heterogeneous world.

THE MONTENEGRIN-OTTOMAN BORDER

A close inspection of the proceedings of the Berlin Congress and the events that immediately followed suggests that Russian and Serb ambitions to secure access to the Adriatic were the principal reasons for the expansion of Montenegrin territory into Malësi.[2] To make their case, Belgrade intellectuals and Russian pan-Slavists began a public-relations campaign in the West that asserted Serbian historical claims to "Southern Serbia" (Kosova and northern Albania), of which Montenegro was an extension.[3] Malësi itself became a bone of contention precisely because European powers awarded Montenegro the mountain regions of Gusinje and Plava as a "concession" in response to the Ottoman Empire's continued control over Novi Pazar/Novibazar (separating Serbia from Montenegro) and the redefined *vilayet*s of Kosova and Işkodra. Interestingly, Ottoman negotiators seemed willing to hand over Gusinje and Plava to Montenegro from the very beginning of the Berlin Congress. Judging from Ottoman documents, Istanbul was ready to concede these parts of Malësi largely on the basis of demographic arguments made by Russia at the time. Ottoman officials disowned large tracts of Malësi on the grounds that its population was "Christian," a remarkable demonstration of Hamidian diplomacy at the time, in a policy identified by some as seeking to consolidate the Islamic character of the empire.[4]

While I do not fully subscribe to this reading of Hamidian policy, it is nevertheless intriguing that officials were willing to cede "Christian" territories that had never been captured by Serbian, Russian, or Montenegrin forces and that had been part of Ottoman territory for 500 years. As a result of these narrowly defined diplomatic positions, the region would face a number of outside interventions that affected intercommunity relations. For this reason alone, the subsequent events in Malësi prove worthy of deeper investigation and point to a dramatic shift in the way Istanbul viewed its European provinces after the 1877–78 debacle. Many in Istanbul seemed content to let go of "Christian territories" over which the Ottomans never had any real control in the first place (most of the inhabitants of the area were Albanian-speaking Catholics, with a mixture of Albanian/Slavic-speaking Muslims and Orthodox Christians sharing many of the towns and pasture lands). But important members of the policy-making elite opposed ceding Malësi to Montenegro, including Mehmet Ali Paşa, an Austro-Hungarian convert and veteran of Ottoman rule in the region. This situation helps to illuminate the complexities of the region and the largely ignored dynamics of Ottoman rule in its frontier regions during the Hamidian era.[5]

Ultimately the powers did not approve of Mehmet Ali Paşa's reasoning, which included a compromise proposal that would hand over parts of Hercegovina (populated by Orthodox and Muslim Slavs) in return for keeping Plava and Gusinje within the Ottoman Empire. First, the Habsburgs' interests in Bosnia did not permit the expansion of Montenegro at their expense. Second, none of the European states quite understood why the local opposition predicted by Mehmet Ali Paşa would create problems for implementing the treaty. As a result, the treaty was left to stand as initially planned. To implement the transfer of territory, an Ottoman Montenegrin Delimitation Commission set out to tour the region in early August 1878.[6] The local response was immediate and, as Mehmet Ali Paşa feared, eventually violent.[7]

As news of the formal plans to hand over Gusinje and Plava to Montenegro emerged during the course of the conference, local leaders organized armed units and were quickly joined by groups from neighboring Ipek and Yakova. Resorting to violence, however, was not the first course of action. Instead of using their considerable military power, at this early stage local representatives sent a wave of telegrams to the relevant capitals.[8] Unimpressed by these peaceful methods of allowing local interests to be heard, European delegates pushed ahead with the intended transfer of territory to Montenegro. Apparently, none of the Great Powers understood the depth of the problem. They ultimately assumed that the Ottoman military could compel obedience when it was necessary, an assumption that Ottoman delegates desperately sought to reinforce.

As the powers initiated the process of actual implementation, reports of isolated clashes between Ottoman troops and locals in parts of western Kosova and throughout Malësi emerged. Resistance to the protocols of the Berlin Congress was taking the shape of a general uprising that until that time had been largely deemed local and nonthreatening. Importantly, locals not only targeted Ottoman troops; Montenegro began to report widespread attacks on the advance units that it posted in non-Malësorë territories as well. In addition, as the appointed international boundary delimitation team made its way through the territories in question, it faced organized resistance and was forced to abandon its plans to finalize the boundaries running through Malësi.[9] These initial acts of "insubordination" created a diplomatic stir as the government in Cetinje actively sought assistance from its allies in St. Petersburg and Paris. Events throughout 1879 followed this pattern, representing a stalemate that pitted shepherds and merchants against the diplomatic decrees of Europe's Great Powers.

In an attempt to assuage the rising concerns of the Russians and secure good relations with the rest of the world, the Porte assigned Manastir Vali "Gazi" Ahmed Muhtir Paşa the task of persuading locals that the areas had to be handed over. Ahmed Muhtir Paşa, armed with up to fifteen battalions, began a tour of western Kosova in December 1879. Despite this considerable military might, it is informative that the preferred method of conveying the sultan's displeasure with local "insubordination" was to read a series of declarations. Among other things, Ahmed Muhtir Paşa informed locals in his public statements that "the resistance projected by the inhabitants will result in nothing else but the provocation of the useless spilling of the blood of the unfortunate." The declaration continues: "The spilling of blood for a nonissue is at once condemned by sacred law — Sharia — and reason."[10]

These lines of argumentation fuse notions of imperial sovereignty, religious sanction, and European reason into a misconstrued public-relations campaign that ended up alienating more people than it united. The notion that losing their ancestral homes was "a nonissue" aroused the indignation of locals and signaled to them that Istanbul and local interests were in direct conflict. Later in the same declaration Ahmed Muhtir Paşa called on the region's sense of "patriotism" and stated that any act of resistance to the implementation of the treaty would be considered "an act of moral and material irresponsibility." This most clearly shows the distinct divide between a moral world defined by imperial interests that exclude local concerns and a local reality in which home, livelihood, and family are of primary concern.

Muhtir Paşa's declaration is a consolidation of Ottoman sovereignty claims. The call for loyalty and unity would become the central leitmotif of Hamidian rule in the next thirty years. Local issues often clashed with those universalistic claims, which reveals a great deal about the nature of Ottoman state relations with Ottoman society and its relative success and failure in addressing local concerns. In the course of this initial crisis period, the inhabitants of Gusinje and Plava demonstrated their capacity to go to any length to defend their interests, even risking armed conflict with the Ottoman Empire, to which most still declared partial loyalty. As local and imperial interests diverged on questions of primary loyalty in the future, military repression became the primary option for Ottoman officials.

While the Ottoman state was busy building up its claims to sovereignty (and domination) in areas far removed from Gusinje and Plava, the villagers of these two areas continued their confrontation with Montenegrin forces and the Ottoman state and thereby kept the Berlin Treaty in limbo. This troubled the European powers. As skirmishes took place during the second half of 1879, the Great Powers increasingly pressured Istanbul to impose the kind of "rule of law" evoked in Ahmed Muhtir Paşa's December 1879 declaration. In the end, however, Istanbul's ultimatums were never backed up with the promised force of the fifteen battalions supposedly at his disposal. For Istanbul, the prospects of facing up to 8,000 armed locals in Gusinje was dangerous, because any battle over this issue could ultimately compromise its capacity to rule the region as a whole. The stalemate at the mountain passes leading to Gusinje resulted in a new round of diplomatic measures to settle the potentially dangerous fiasco, which had lasted more than a year. After a particularly bloody round of skirmishes, a compromise drawn up by the Italians (again after failing to consult locals) was proposed and accepted by all powers on April 12, 1880. In return for allowing all of Gusinje and Plava to remain under nominal Ottoman sovereignty, the Italians suggested, the Ottoman Empire should cede areas northeast of Lake Shkodër, including much of the pasture land of Hoti and Gruda. Unfortunately for the European powers, much as happened in the case of Gusinje and Plava, communities in this other part of the Malësore took up defensive positions and threatened armed resistance.[11] As in Gusinje, Montenegro once again had little capacity to capture these areas militarily and had to resort to diplomatic pressure, which also produced few results.

From the perspective of most of the Great Powers, the stalemate was a disaster. All European powers were eager to establish diplomatic order, but resistance in two different areas of Malësi upset the fragile logic of Europe's imperial universe. The most powerful and modern states in the "civilized" world were incapable of imposing their protocols and boundaries, a series of events that could have repercussions throughout the world. A new world order was in danger of falling apart. Ultimately it took the skilled diplomacy of two European veterans of the region — British consul-general

William Kirby Green and his Austro-Hungarian counterpart in Işkodra (Scutari), Franz W. Lippich — to resolve the Montenegrin boundary issue. The two men worked together to draw up new territories that took into consideration the local factors ignored by earlier plans. Instead of Gusinje or Hoti, therefore, Lippich and Kirby Green proposed a plan that would cede the areas west of Lake Shkodër, including the port of Dulcigno (Ulqin) and much of the north bank of the Bojana River. Kirby Green and Lippich correctly calculated that the Malësorë locals had no interest in helping others faced with the prospect of Montenegrin annexation once their own lands had been spared. It is equally significant that Kirby Green and Lippich knew that the new areas in question were located on the coast, so the full might of the Great Powers could be used to enforce the accords, which would be considerably more difficult to accomplish in the Albanian Alps.[12]

It was not a surprise to Kirby Green and Lippich that locals in Ulqin organized to defend their homes and businesses from Montenegrin annexation, just as in the mountains. This specific response, however, is not of immediate concern here. What is important to stress is that the residents of Hoti and Gusinje, people who had fought with great loss of life just weeks earlier, immediately distanced themselves from the events taking place elsewhere. Despite the calls by the inhabitants of Ulqin and even some in the Ottoman state for the population of Hoti and Gusinje to help defend "Albanian," "Muslim/Catholic," or "Ottoman" territory, the issue for the Malësorë was neither Albanian solidarity nor loyalty to the Ottoman project. The issue for them was local interests. The Albanian-speaking inhabitants of Ulqin would have to face the arbitrary boundaries of European powers without the help of the Malësorë. As the next section shows, communities that found themselves on the "wrong" side of a new border did not necessarily face a future of persecution; the policies adopted by the Montenegrin state often reflected a more complicated dynamic than is usually presented in these periods of transition.[13]

THE MONTENEGRIN STATE
AND ITS POST-OTTOMAN REALITIES

At the heart of any successful revision of this period beyond the paradigm of competing nationalisms is recognizing the emergence of newly established zones of government implanted in culturally fused environments in order to enforce a new order based on ethnic difference. How such government actions impacted a large cross-section of the people living in the western Balkans who were suddenly straddling frontiers is perhaps the single most neglected story in the region's modern history. To most citizens, these new borders did not delineate a natural line of demarcation and certainly did not reflect a logic predicated on stable patterns of association or commerce. Thus the complexity of the subsequent decades of government policies attempting to mediate between demands to enforce ethnic differentiation and local resistance is paramount. In the end, instead of clarifying the world with neatly drawn boundaries separating peoples, these borders demonstrated a level of unpredictability and hence proved unmanageable, ultimately transforming the modernizing state.

The imposition of Russian power in the western Balkans by late 1877 shattered the ability of Young Ottoman reformers, including their local allies, to engage state subjects that they had hoped a decade earlier to administer within a single province.[14] A direct consequence of this transition was a process that created new factions in the social and economic elite, which increasingly diverged on how best to govern what was left of the region. The greatest fear of many reformers and local leaders had been realized with the new ethnic and sectarian-based order imposed by the outside world. Therefore local confidence in the Ottoman state and the ability of its new generation of loyalists fragmented into contesting circles, a process that in itself would create new social and political forces that transformed the Balkans forever. For instance, although the new borders imposed a narrowly defined ethno-national area, it was still inhabited by heterodox populations. The subsequent struggle to secure these "rescued" homelands in the face of resistance by those suddenly deemed "minorities" created several mutually exclusive narratives of modern statehood. For many, the new border areas themselves became the domain in which questions of belonging and the collective surfaced in their rawest, most violent form.

Because of this violence, the introduction of new states into the area — Serbia, Montenegro, and Austria-Hungary in Novi Pazar and Hercegovina — led to the creation of bureaucracies geared to reshaping the demographic landscape of the border areas by a combination of colonization, economic marginalization, and more violence. As a result, most Malësorë in the highland territories newly awarded to Montenegro were considered aliens to the state, while Slav Orthodox Christian immigrants from Hercegovina (who were pushed out by Austria-Hungary) were allowed to establish a foothold in the area. This created a new social dynamic of interaction affecting local relations and interactions with the larger world, which in turn led to a new set of questions. The politics of ethnic cleansing, in other words, emerged as a disruptive as well as an animating historical force.

Over time the crisis in Malësi inspired administrative reforms that
sought to mobilize the principal generators of change in the period — the
inhabitants themselves — in new ways. Administrators aimed to incorporate the most aggressive of the local actors into a scheme of differentiation
that would empower them politically while containing their potential for
rebellion. The people living along the newly marked frontiers became a
strategic consideration as well as an object of patronage. In this context,
the application of modern state power basically failed to suppress the concerns of the inhabitants of affected regions. This failure transformed an
imperial ontological fact — a frontier separating different peoples, nations,
and states — into a precarious object of negotiation that made agents of
change out of subjects who had hitherto been ignored.

At the heart of the Great Powers' problem in Malësi was a multiplicity
of largely forgotten, locally determined reactions and counterreactions to
the creation of the Montenegrin/Ottoman frontier. The transfer of large
areas of land not only failed to result in a smooth administrative transition
but opened up a number of avenues for political mobilization and community building across what had previously been substantial economic
divides. Over the course of these highly contentious transitional periods
local communities and, counterintuitively, Prince Nikola of Montenegro's regime itself proved to be far less compliant with the ethno-sectarian
social model than was perhaps assumed when strategies were drawn in
1878.[15] This story therefore must cover a number of angles traditionally
ignored by nationalist historiographies.

Prince Nikola, far from benefiting from a clear-cut and unproblematic transition into independence, would be forced to deal with a number
of dangerous contingencies that emerged because of the 1877–78 events.
Large numbers of people who would have to be incorporated into his new
state did not formally associate historically with his regime. While his
traditional constituents represented a complicated mixture of horizontally
ruled communities that relied on long-established commercial and political alliances with the Malësorë communities, the new Montenegro was
inundated with at least two entirely new clusters of Slav-speaking constituencies who needed immediate political and economic accommodation.
The arrival of large numbers of Slav refugees from Hercegovina and the
incorporation of Dalmatian communities along the Adriatic coast dramatically changed Prince Nikola's political calculations.

Historically Nikola's constituency was less homogeneous than Montenegro's post-Ottoman historiography would imply. In many ways this
cross-section of Gheg, Dalmatian, and Slav coexistence served the region

well, as its inhabitants established economic connections extending far into the Adriatic hinterland. These relations were abruptly severed as a result of the violence in the 1870s and particularly by the Austro-Hungarian occupation of Hercegovina in 1878. Local communities were forced to accommodate large numbers of new arrivals, flooding the region with the political changes taking place in Hercegovina and Dalmatia. For many tense years Nikola and his new, well-armed Hercegovinian subjects interacted in a dynamic and entirely new political economy. At the heart of the problem was economically accommodating the large numbers of refugees, many who settled in Upper Morača. The "invasions" of these areas completely disrupted what some scholars believed were ancient social patterns that included living with non-Orthodox, non-Slavicized communities like the Catholic and Muslim Malësorë in Plava, Guci/Gusi, and Hoti. In place of the traditional pattern of coexistence emerged profiteering from land raids, theft of livestock, and general violence promoted by the Russian officials who were bankrolling the new state.

The international financial elite tied to this new agenda also was directly implicated in the systemic destruction of a well-established regime of communal coexistence. In their quest to command absolute control over the economic resources of the region, the banking interests that influenced the outcome of the Berlin Congress from back rooms had a role for a Nikola-run principality to play. Nikola, much like the Slavic elite in the newly created Serbia farther east, was quickly forced to adopt new policies vis-à-vis his constituencies.

Among the many influences directly affecting Montenegro's early policies was that it had inherited part of the Ottoman debt, on which the Ottomans had defaulted several years earlier. In the face of this debt, Nikola was expected to borrow aggressively to build up an army and navy (with Russian support), fortify borders, and develop an infrastructure. Part of this capital investment included railways that would connect the coast to lucrative mineral resources in the hinterland and other lines (to be built by heavy borrowing) constructed in newly independent Serbia, autonomous Romania, Bulgaria, and a humbled Ottoman state. In the larger context of Ottoman bankruptcy (perhaps the single most important factor behind the diplomatic move to break up Ottoman territories into new states), it becomes clear that Nikola did not have much room for maneuver after gaining independence, although he cannot be completely exonerated from responsibility for the subsequent thirty years. Indeed, by the time the new sultan (in power only since 1876) agreed to sign the Muharram Decree of 1881 that would cede much of the empire's ports and roads to a debt commission charged with collecting revenue on behalf of the banks, all components of the new Balkan order — Nikola, the Ottoman administration, Serbia, and local allies — were expected to participate in the management and regulation of transregional trade.

This is the political economy of the post–Berlin Congress transformation of the region. What is largely lost in this story is the role that locals and the local administrators in Montenegro, Serbia, and the Ottoman Empire played in fulfilling the needs of the day-to-day functioning of the region's economy. Unfortunately, historians eager to identify the origins of the requisite "national rebirth" have overinterpreted these events. If we actually put each event during the entire 1878–80 period into context, it becomes clear that the "resistance" or heroic exploits of militia men and women were not driven by isolated "nationalist" sentiments but represented a series of responses to opportunities that made sense to those who had no direct interest in seeing anything settle down.

A quick review of regional political relations reveals that a social dynamic was at work that parallels the imperial rivalries supposedly shaping the Berlin Congress and the subsequent decades in the Balkans. This dynamic fused confessional, ethno-national, and commercial identities in ways largely contradictory to the crude abstractions based on ethnosectarian divisions that diplomatic historians have focused on, as articulated in the capitulations and so-called *millet* system. For instance, despite their seemingly irreconcilable differences, Christians and Muslims, Slavs and Albanians, maintained integrated social and economic lives that at least initially confounded Ottoman, Austrian, and Russian efforts to assert influence over the populations in the Işkodra and Kosova *vilayet*s in the second half of the nineteenth century. The translation of this factor over time has a great deal of value in arguing against the assertions that present-day historians of the Balkans make about intercommunal relations.

It should be noted that these integrative patterns between assumed "primordial" enemies confounded imperial designs in asserting administrative and even military control of the region after the Berlin Congress of 1878. The first method of state control often was to affirm the confines of its sovereignty by way of territorial frontiers. These frontiers were contested items: regional states searched for ways to circumvent the fact that the communities living within these territories were impossible to categorize along ethno-national lines.[16] The very efforts at centralization practiced by Montenegro, Serbia, Russia, Austria, and the Ottoman state frequently empowered rather than weakened locals, as noted throughout this chapter. By appreciating, in particular, how the Ottoman state's efforts to assert some level of control in its post-Berlin territories created new windows of opportunity for nonstate actors, we may better understand the problems facing the various imperial powers operating in the region.[17] The way in which local opportunities to interact with the world at large translate into a historical narrative can best be demonstrated in this post-Berlin period. During these forty years the so-called forces of modernity were being applied in the region; they were supposed to codify state control over the population along communal lines but instead created new means of engagement for local communities.

In addition to monitoring Ottoman policies in regard to instituting reforms and managing local responses, we can observe how "modernity" and its differentiating ambitions were supposed to have operated through the activities of Russian consuls in the region. These Russians, as the central proponents for the creation of an independent Serbia and Montenegro and the spread of pan-Slavic agendas within Habsburg and Ottoman territories, vigorously asserted their role as the sole protector of Slav Orthodox communities in the Ottoman Balkans, as guaranteed under the capitulations.[18] The responses of Austria and the Sublime Porte to these blatant attempts to change the internal dynamics of the Balkans prove key to appreciating the subsequent efforts to impose control over events on the ground and to maintain local autonomy. Ultimately these dynamic exchanges of regional powers, their bureaucrats, and local populations help us expose the weak foundations of the myths of the ethnic-nation. Local "mixed" communities not only were able to resist Russia's sectarian-based provocations but actively engaged in strategies that empowered their ability to survive the numerous challenges to their autonomy by adopting Ottoman reform measures as much as those introduced by the outside world. In the end the road to demystifying the primordial ethno-national or confessional identity leads through a study of the way in which locals sustained their autonomy in the face of efforts instituted by the various imperial powers.

DISCOVERING THE ALBANIAN:
AUSTRIA COUNTERS PAN-SLAVISM

The primary issue by 1878 was the annexation of Albanian-populated territories by Serbia and Montenegro as a result of the Berlin Congress.[19] Almost immediately the process could only partially be justified by using demographic abstractions of the local population based on their sectarian identities.[20] Modern strategies of statecraft that entailed codifying a universal identity and — as Eugen Weber and others have suggested — the powers granted to the modern state should have spelled the end of multiethnic communities that existed in overwhelmingly rural societies like those in the southwestern Balkans.[21] Indeed, both Montenegro and Serbia actively sought, with Russian money and weapons, to homogenize their newly acquired populations along sectarian lines. Serbia in particular proved adept at instigating large-scale migrations of Albanian-speaking and Turkish-speaking communities from its newly annexed Niş province, much to the dismay of Ottoman officials forced to accommodate those who were expelled.[22]

Despite a number of attempts to populate these border areas exclusively with Orthodox Slav populations, however, neither Serbia nor Montenegro could fully eliminate the indigenous population from the area: the majority were still Albanian-speaking Muslims or Catholics. According to Ottoman and Austrian documents, the central reason for this inability to solidify central control of these areas was the capacity of locals (which included Slav Orthodox neighbors) to resist these homogenizing projects militarily. This material and cultural balance of power had an immediate impact on how diplomacy operated in the Balkans throughout the next ten years and forced Montenegro, in particular, to shift gears dramatically.

After a series of military defeats against local Albanian communities, Montenegro (and to a much lesser extent Serbia) began an attempt to co-opt its frontier populations economically in order to serve their commercial and defensive interests. In the end, this strategy created a security problem for the Ottoman Empire along its frontiers, as locals shifted their loyalties to Cetinje or Belgrade. This shift is intriguing, because it was widely assumed that the Slavic and Orthodox governments of the new independent states and its Albanian, Muslim, and Catholic subjects were "natural" enemies. Quite to the contrary, as evidenced throughout, locals proved perfectly willing to use their key economic and strategic position to play one power off against the other. Consequentially, this capacity to shift loyalties dramatically changed not only Ottoman and Slav policies in the area but Austria's as well. Vienna's subsequent understanding of its role in the region helps us directly question the historical value of long-held assumptions about intercommunity relations and the foundations of ethno-national identities as well as think differently about the rivalry between Austria and pan-Slavism.[23]

The Austrian state's activities among the region's Albanian-speaking populations and especially their leaders demonstrate a clash between assumed imperial interests (and their incumbent capitulatory privileges) and the practical realities on the ground. For Austrian officials operating in the area, this often meant that their state's interests were defined more to reflect how local populations mobilized (or articulated) their communities through a liberal flow of Montenegrin money than by dictates from Vienna or Istanbul, their assumed confessional protectors. The problem posed for both Austria and the Sublime Porte in this period of adjustment therefore was that these populations were categorically "mixed," proving that the diplomatic assumptions asserted in the Berlin Treaty simply did not recognize the inherent complexity of local realities.[24] As Consul Lippich and his successors discovered, loyalties based on faith could not be assumed in the highlands of Ottoman Albania or (as demonstrated below) on the plains of Kosova in regard to the region's Slavic-speaking and Albanian-speaking inhabitants.[25] Austria proved up to the task and modified its initial policies to accommodate the evolving realities on the ground.

In the case of the highland regions of Gruda and Hoti, for instance, an area with a "mixed" Catholic and Muslim Albanian-speaking population, Austrian interests ultimately lay in patronizing these mixed elements of local society to prevent them from being completely dependent on Cetinje's largesse. Such patronage categorically contradicted the Austrian claims of certain privileges in the Ottoman territories based on Vienna's religious affiliation with Albanian Catholics. Catholicism, the assumed wedge whereby Austrian interests were to be framed, had a particular socioeconomic and political role in northern Albania that did not accord with the rigid categorical requirements of the modern diplomatic order. This reality gave locals room in which they could operate in a world order defined by presumed confessional frontiers.

Austria's privileged role in protecting Ottoman Catholics was immediately put into doubt by the growing activities of Albanians based in Işkodra, who were cultivating relations across the frontiers that divided the "Orthodox" world and the Muslim/Catholic Albanians.[26] To add to Vienna's problems, local Albanians also solicited and received extensive assistance from Italy.[27] In sum, it is clear that local Albanian-speaking communities would adopt certain ethnic, sectarian, or political claims to suit the diplomatic capabilities of the various states seeking influence in the region. This ultimately forced Austria (as well as the Russians and the Ottoman state) to adapt to local realities throughout the region.[28]

While Austria quickly learned to adapt its policies to fit local conditions, the fluid sectarian identities of local communities most directly affected Ottoman policy in the area. Although historians of the late Ottoman state focus on Istanbul's imperial pretensions, just as Austrians

discovered in their relations with "Catholics," the Sublime Porte frequently
had to modify its ambitions in regard to its "Muslim" population.[29] One
of the interesting consequences of these sectarian "abnormalities" in local
communities was the dynamic of local power that gave small communities the capacity to balance the Austrians, Russians, and Ottomans against
one another, both by using formal diplomatic structures and by forcing
their modification. This local capacity to mobilize contradictory forces is
clearest in the number of confrontations between local communities and
the Ottoman state as Istanbul sought to consolidate its control of its new
frontiers. Local Albanians often reached out to Austrian consular officials
when seeking protection from Ottoman state persecution.[30] In addition,
as already noted, they welcomed the assistance from Montenegrin Prince
Nikola in arms and money and often served as Cetinje's mercenary army.[31]
Again, the best way to read these events is not in terms of a "failure" or
"success" of the state. Rather, we should observe how local Albanians actively engaged in the state structures present on the ground and actively
challenged the assumed privileges of various agencies in order to secure
local freedom from centralization efforts for at least thirty years.

BUILDING THE MONTENEGRO STATE

In the face of resistance and the eventual ceding of the port of Ulqin to
Montenegro, both the Ottoman and the Montenegrin states adopted administrative strategies that may help us to appreciate the complexity of
the western Balkans when the Berlin Congress cast it into this dramatic
period of transition. The single most dynamic force at play was the tens
of thousands of refugees flowing into both the Ottoman territories and
Montenegro. What scholars such as H. Yıldırım Ağanoğlu and Bilal N.
Şimşir ignore is that this multitude of Ottoman Muslims and Catholics
and Orthodox Christian Slavs who had been expelled from their ancestral
homes immediately transformed the contours of regional politics and the
ability of the Ottoman and Montenegrin states to maintain order in their
Balkan provinces.[32] The influx of homeless Ghegs and Malësorë into the
redrawn provinces of Kosova, Işkodra, and beyond in particular constituted a disruptive force for change that would ultimately transform the
whole Ottoman Empire and its subject population.[33]

The very act of the Montenegrin state in enforcing what appears to
be a policy of ethnic homogenization over the next thirty years also had
a dynamic that is in need of closer study. As already noted, Montenegro's
policy toward the communities straddling the newly established border

became one of selectively expelling non-Slav inhabitants and replacing them with settlers from Hercegovina and Serbia. For the most part, Montenegro's strategy balanced the use of violence with the economic, cultural, and political isolation of the targeted communities. For example, while enforcing widespread ethnic cleansing, at crucial moments Nikola also encouraged targeted groups in key economic sectors to remain. This policy had a long-term economic rationale: extract as much wealth from the indigenous population as possible and then expand the range of trade in the region that would give Montenegro a relative advantage over its Ottoman rival in the medium to long term. Such nuanced policies involved financial inducements for the lowland Albanians who were deemed essential to keeping the state's economy connected to the outside world. This at the very least reveals that Prince Nikola's state-building policies required a flexible approach to his inherited multiethnic population.

In the end Prince Nikola had to treat his Muslim and Catholic subjects cautiously for practical reasons. The Albanians who had long dominated the Adriatic trade from the coast in the areas newly acquired by Montenegro represented a significant portion of the able-bodied male population of the small state in 1878. These men could put up a fight but also sustain the new state's economy. In many ways they held the key to the early Montenegrin state's political stability and economic survival. As noted above, it would have been militarily impossible as well as economically suicidal to force embedded populations in the key port of Ulqin to migrate en masse, all at once. For a start, logistically harnessing the kind of force needed to accomplish such a task was daunting. It was one thing to suppress resistance to transfer sovereignty to Nikola, but it would have been something entirely different to institute a program of depopulating the city. Moreover, there were simply not enough Slav settlers available to replace these economically productive inhabitants. Another political consideration also should be kept in mind, however: maintaining enough politically dependent Albanians in the country gave Nikola leverage over his new Hercegovina constituency.

A closer look at how Nikola carefully managed his expulsion of large numbers of natives is thus crucial to understanding the kinds of pressures on them emerging in the new state. To succeed in putting pressure on the most nonessential Albanians to leave Montenegro without destroying the economic vitality of the country, Nikola's government adopted a subtle long-term strategy that included bureaucratic measures to harass them and slowly apply economic pressure on selected groups. Among the more obnoxious provisions that the Montenegrin state imposed on Muslims in particular was a ban on the burial of deceased members of their community within the first twenty-four hours, as required by Islamic law. In a similar fashion, all Muslim businesses had to cater to local Slav consumption needs, such as selling wine and pork in their shops, while remaining open on Fridays and closed on Sundays. A related demand forced all Muslim children to attend a Slavic-language school, where they presumably would be taught Christianity. In addition, the state made it illegal for the Muslim community to oppose marriage between a Muslim woman and an Orthodox Montenegrin.

Officials using these measures attempted to facilitate the forced assimilation or conversion of the crucial members of the local population who were to remain in the newly formed country. Of course, plenty of measures were adopted that were simply meant to humiliate this group and if possible encourage the departure of many of its members. A particularly egregious provision, for example, required all Muslims to assist in maintaining public toilets.[34] Not surprisingly, these regulations and their heavy-handed enforcement contributed to the "voluntary" emigration of Muslims by the thousands, an exodus condemned by the Ottoman state.[35] It was not enough to humiliate people, however: other measures were also needed.

If all else failed, Montenegrin authorities simply bribed stubborn community leaders to emigrate, using money supplied by Russia. The calculation was that the rest of the community would follow. Austro-Hungarian officials in Bosnia had used this tactic since 1878. This Austrian connection, in fact, goes a long way toward explaining why the Montenegrin government used certain techniques of discrimination. Many of Nikola's henchmen were refugees themselves, so his growing bureaucracy may have made it impossible to sustain a cordial relationship with most of the non-Slav merchants in his country. In a cruel irony, Hercegovinian refugees would use the very same tactics of intimidation against Albanians that the Austro-Hungarian authorities had used against them.

This campaign had nuances, however. In 1880, for instance, officials in Cetinje encouraged the Albanian leaders of the Catholic community to move to Ottoman territories in return for paying considerable amounts of money for the property they left behind.[36] This "peaceful approach" to state building would change by 1883 in the areas bordering Kelmendi, Vukli, and Plava after communities there refused to leave even after offers of money. In these regions the state elected to use violence instead.[37] Nikola was perfecting all forms of the art of ethnic cleansing and was willing to use them all if necessary.[38]

Despite this forced migration, the commercial links between many of these refugees and Montenegro were not cut. Nikola's plans took into consideration their long-term economic impact. Officials allowed refugees newly settled in the border town of Tuz, for example, to maintain their businesses in Montenegro either by negotiating with the state for one member of the extended family to remain behind or by paying new Slav migrants to manage their affairs.[39]

Within a few years these partnerships turned into a new regional dynamic that ultimately brought the Ottoman and Montenegrin states into some form of cooperative understanding. As a result of local pressure, the governments in Cetinje and Shkodër created a commission through which the affairs of those leaving the Montenegrin territories would be handled in a legal and transparent manner. Indeed, emigrants were able to establish formal ownership of the property in the towns they were forced to leave. In addition, an office was apparently established in Podgorica that ensured "fair" compensation for any land that was ultimately issued to others by the Montenegrin state.[40] Both governments wanted to ensure that the careful management and collaboration of locals would reinvigorate a functioning regional economy.

Part of this collaboration is evident in the capital investments that the Montenegrin government made to ensure that the commercial links between the disrupted Albanian communities extended across borders. While expelling most of the Albanian inhabitants from the port town of Antivari and many from Ulqin farther south, the Montenegrin state was at the same time building a road to connect the two port towns and the Ottoman frontier.[41] State authorities envisioned that the road would help facilitate the communication between the core merchant communities that remained in Montenegro and their now displaced partners living in Ottoman territory.[42] Nikola also made direct overtures to Shkodër families, encouraging them to capitalize on the situation by securing much of the trade that had otherwise been disrupted by the creation of the Montenegrin state. This collaboration between Montenegro and merchant families in Shkodër, in fact, seems to have initiated a new era of regional trade and further complicated the way in which the peoples of the region understood the world around them.

Among the more interesting consequences of this transitional process was the emergence of new zones of trade all along the frontiers. The borders themselves, heavily guarded at traditional transit points, created an economic opportunity for people living on both sides. With the regulation of all transactions across the borders, trade that circumvented the Debt Commission customs posts (and hence duty) opened a new range of opportunities for Montenegrin merchants and their allies on the other side of the border. Smuggling became a crucial part of the regional economy and the foundation of a new political order.

By exploring how trade patterns changed in the interior as well as along the coast we begin to appreciate the transformative impact of imposing new territorial unity. To start with, Montenegro invested in the rising flow of smuggled goods by building the road mentioned above. As a result of new economies emerging from the smuggling that was taking place, the process of adjusting to new territorial realities became multilayered. The trade interests of a growing number of agents were pitted against abstract administrative goals that included taxing trade and changing the local perceptions of what constituted a community's interests and how they could be pursued.

The administrator's job in this borderland region was made more difficult over time by Ottoman efforts to impose progress and modernity via the circles of traditional power that had become fragmented because of new, often unrecognized challengers. Ottoman plans to reform and to harness greater revenue from taxes, in other words, directly clashed with new local groups who were developing channels that circumvented all state agencies. A brief history of the trade in commodities in Malësi helps to illustrate the complex nature of economic and imperial relations that were shaped by local collaboration with a new source of patronage: Montenegro.

REGIONAL PARALLEL ECONOMIES

As already noted, the creation of Montenegro established a new set of conditions in the Balkans that completely changed the way in which people conducted their commercial affairs. Because of these frontiers, which were often drawn right across centuries-old trade routes, areas of production and individual and collective properties developed economies of scale that undermined much of what the Ottoman Empire aspired to do with its new frontier economy. Researching the account books of merchants shows that trade between locals did not take place exclusively in the market. Indeed, the heavy duties placed on imported goods proved a disincentive for merchants to buy them in the central bazaar. In response to heavy taxation imposed by the Debt Commission, merchants discovered ways of supplying their long-term customers without paying the duty charged in the markets. Instead of passing through the official customs checkpoints found along the Bojana River and in Shkodër itself, traders began to unload their goods in Ulqin (which had been in Montenegrin hands since 1879) and then transport their goods overland to buyers waiting inside Ottoman territory.[43] It appears that these smuggled goods were prepurchased by regional traders who came to Shkodër and then redistributed them to other markets.[44] The actual goods apparently never reached the city itself. Regional buyers seem to have picked up their purchases at previously arranged areas outside the market (or even beyond the city's limits, to avoid the customs officials guarding the access roads). According to the records available, goods like salt sold at rates considerably below those available in that market.[45]

The Montenegrin government saw an opportunity and ensured that conditions in Ulqin and all along its frontiers would facilitate this smuggling. In addition to the large amounts of state funds that went into investing in road and bridge construction all along these routes it made plans to build a rail line to link the Montenegrin ports of Antivari/Bar to the Ottoman border. This link may have been intended to funnel the goods still passing through Shkodër.[46] In a matter of years Montenegrin officials working with Gheg merchants successfully shifted large amounts of trade revenue away from Ottoman coffers. As shrewd economic policy, Prince Nikola's alliance with Shkodër merchants denied Istanbul much-needed money to develop the empire by strengthening its political and economic leverage over communities living inside Ottoman territory.

The Ottoman state did not sit passively by. Since the creation of an independent Montenegro and the transfer of Ulqin, internationally enforced boundaries cut through long-used trade routes, leaving many traders isolated from their historical zones of activity. To address this and ensure that much of the lucrative trade flowing into the area would continue to go through Ottoman ports, locally based authorities devised a number of strategies of their own. The first was to encourage the legal importation of goods through Ottoman-controlled ports by heavily taxing goods that crossed from what was now a foreign country, Montenegro.[47] Realizing that a great deal of disruption of regional trade had taken place and that many alternative routes, including the one through Ulqin, were attracting traders away from the port of Shkodër, Istanbul initiated projects to modernize its ports all along the Adriatic coast.[48]

As a result of the often conflicting local activities, the states involved all invested resources to monitor events. States that did not monitor the traffic between frontiers inspired administrative innovations, and eventually even cross-boundary cooperation was achieved to address issues of economic sovereignty and the control of commercial flows. Clearly this local power required state officials to spend considerable political and financial capital in co-opting locals to ensure their cooperation. Indeed, much of the post-1878 administration of these areas was shaped by the power that some locals were able to secure. These modifications created new economic spaces and opportunities for those who could make the necessary counteradjustments, transforming the region's political and social dynamic and influencing the very process of nation-building in the twentieth century. At the heart of these border area calculations was the now chaotic circulation of uprooted communities, a political, economic, and social force that compelled the Ottoman state to take drastic steps to settle this potentially dangerous (or useful) mass of humanity.

CONCLUSION

The nature of empire itself was often pushed beyond the artifacts of confrontation (the modern versus traditional, "us" versus "them") because local reactions actually forced the Great Powers to modify their ambitions. In the end the frontiers created in the Balkans to separate "national groups" were as much the legacies of local agency as of imperial power. This aspect of the evolution of the modern imperial state helps us to recalibrate the underlying contradictions that inform our understanding of our world. The natives did have a role in history, and ethno-national interests did not animate it on their own.

The events taking place in the highland distrcits of Kosova and Işkodra provinces during the 1878–1912 period reflected an evolving and increasingly counterproductive relationship between the Ottoman state and its subjects. Over a short period, the initial process of enforcing frontiers created a disastrous set of conditions for communities found on the wrong side of these boundaries. The creation of ethno-national spaces within this would constitute another form of abstraction that further confused the way in which the Ottoman Empire administered its territories. Furthermore, the administrative act of bunching together villages to effect a more "rational" system of taxation and administration created clusters of interests that offered new possibilities for making alliances in an environment that at the same time was experiencing serious confusion because of these changes. This paradoxical chain of transformations ultimately changed the dynamics of power in the communities found within, along, and beyond the various borders established in this period.

NOTES

1. For a crude (and largely unquestioned) attempt to establish national claims to the territories in question, see Jagoš Jovanović, *Stvaranje črnogorske drzave i razvoj črnogorske nacionalnosti: Istorija Črne Goreod pochetka VIII vijeka do 1918 godine* 153–90.

2. Dimitrie Djordjević, *Izlazak Srbije na jadransko more i konferencija ambasadora u Londonu 1912*, 13–15.

3. Noel Malcolm, *Kosovo: A Short History*, 196–201.

4. For comprehensive coverage of these diplomatic events, see Andre Novotny, *Österreich, die Türkei und das Balkanproblem im Jahre des Berliner Kongresses (Quellen und Studien zur Geschichte des Berliner Kongresses 1878)*.

5. For extensive coverage of Mehmet Ali Paşa's objections, see W. N. Medlicott, *The Congress of Berlin and After: A Diplomatic History of the Near Eastern Settlement*, 162, 192, 221. See also Isa Blumi, *Reinstating the Ottomans: Alternative Balkan Modernities, 1800–1912*, chapters 3 and 4.

6. For full details of the commission's work, see Haus-, Hof- und Staatsarchiv, Vienna (HHStA), PA XVII, box 31, Montenegro.

7. See Ottoman reports on early incidents of local resistance to Montenegrin attempts to take over the administration of areas ceded to Cetinje during the Berlin Congress. Başbakanlık Arşivi, Istanbul (BBA), YA.HUS 159/62, 16 Ramazan 1295 [September 14, 1878].

8. For details, see Isa Blumi, *Rethinking the Late Ottoman Empire: A Comparative Social and Political History of Albania and Yemen, 1878–1918*, chapter five.

9. For attacks on Montenegrin forces in Denbosh and their impact on the Delimitation Committee, see a brief report to the palace in BBA, YA.HUS 160/34, 25 Safer 1296 [March 19, 1879].

10. The proclamations were presented in Kalkandelen (Tetova), Prizren, Ipek, and Yakova in December 1879. The quotations are taken from a French translation of the statement provided by the Ottoman Embassy in Vienna, Sawas Paşa to Prime Ministry, December 16, 1879, HHStA, PA XVII, Montenegro Gusinje Frage, box 35, doc. 261.

11. Le Rée to Freycinet, Scutari, April 8, 1880, no. 36, and Annexe à la dépêche du 6 Mai 1880, no. 42, in Archives du Ministère des Affaires Étrangères de France (AMAE), Turquie, Correspondance politique des consuls, Scutari, 1880–83, vol. 22. See also letter sent to Consul Green by leaders of the areas in question in National Archives of the United Kingdom (formerly Public Record Office), Foreign Office Archives, London (FO), FO 195/1303, May 2, 1880.

12. Ultimately the powers sent a flotilla and actually bombed the port of Dulcigno (Ulqin) in an attempt to persuade locals to lay down their arms and allow Montenegro to take over the city: Medlicott, *The Congress of Berlin*, 144–49.

13. I explore these episodes in greater detail in Blumi, *Reinstating the Ottomans*, 207–34.

14. Isa Blumi, "Capitulations in the Late Ottoman Empire: The Shifting Parameters of Russian and Austrian Interests in Ottoman Albania, 1878–1912."

15. See a recent addition to the literature: Elizabeth Roberts, *Realm of the Black Mountain: A History of Montenegro*, 237–57.

16. BBA, YEE 109/17 contains a letter dated Constantinople, September 11/23, 1884, from the Montenegrin representative in Istanbul, G. Vunević, to Marshal Dervis Paşa, aide-de-camp general of the sultan, who was overseeing the delineation of the Montenegrin-Ottoman frontier at the time. The document's value is that it shows how Vunević attempted to negotiate compromises that ultimately highlighted the narrow terms of engagement for local powers. Basically, Vunević offered to stream-line the process by "simply" drawing the border along "racial lines."

17. This is made clear by an extensive report on the emergent political forces inside Kosova as a result of the transformations caused by Ottoman state reforms. See HHStA, PA XII/312 Turkei Liasse XXXIII, dated Prizren, January 26, 1899, Consul Rappaport to Goluchowski, documents 50–53.

18. In a letter from Philadelphia, an American named S. W. King advised the sultan to mistrust the Russians and their overall ambitions, which were being served by the Berlin Congress. The arguments raised against Russian intrigue provide an in-teresting parallel to the views of European diplomats on Russian influences in the region. BBA, YEE 76/25, documents 2a and 2b, dated August 8, 1878.

19. These strategies were already being activated in 1877 as Montenegrin agents, who had commercial ties (and often familial ties) with neighboring Albanian-speaking communities, spent large amounts of Russian money to try to encourage moun-tain communities to rise up against Ottoman forces. See National Archives of the United Kingdom (formerly Public Record Office), Foreign Office Archives, London (FO), FO 78/2628, reports dated Scutari, February 5, 1877, Consul Kirby Green to Foreign Office, document number 8.

20. Perhaps out of this concern about consolidating "control" of the region, Ottoman officials actively played with the demographic composition of the area in early 1877 by importing Circassian colonists who were by-products of the Russo-Ottoman Eastern Front. See FO 78/2628, report dated Scutari, February 10, 1877, Consul Green to Foreign Office, document 9.

21. Eugen Weber, *Peasants into Frenchmen: The Modernization of Rural France, 1870–1914*.

22. See, for instance, BBA, YEE 43/102, 15 Zilhicce 1296 [December 4, 1879], and FO 78/2988, dated Prizren, October 7, 1879, Political Report 24, St. John to Salisbury.

23. See the extensive reports presented to the Porte by Yusuf Ziya Paşa and others during the period in BBA, YEE, 7/23. Compiled by Istanbul on 24 Ramazan 1303 [June 26, 1886], documents 3, 5, and 6.

24. Albanian-speaking communities in northern Albania were often made up of mixed Orthodox, Catholic, and Muslim families. See Isa Blumi, "The Dynamics of Iden-tity: The Albanian in the Ottoman Empire."

25. See Theodore Ippen, "Das religiöse Protectorat Österreich-Ungarns in der Türkei."

26. The Albanian archives contain evidence that economic cooperation between Albanian merchant families in Bar and Ulqin and the new Montenegrin state con-tinued well into the 1890s. See, for instance, Austrian reports attesting to the eco-nomic activity in Montenegro's ports in 1884, Arkivi Qendror Shtetëror (AQSH) F.143.D.1071.f.6–21; D.1073.f.41, 48–50, 53–58, 62–63.

27. Italy became a key rival to Austrian efforts to monopolize Catholic Church affairs in the region. On the rivalry between Italy and Austria over Albania, see Alessan-dro Duce, *L'Albania nei rapporti italo-austriaci, 1897–1913*.

28. This is made clear in the recommendations made by Scutari consul Theodore Ippen to the Foreign Ministry. See HHStA, PA XII/312 Turkei Liasse XXXIV/2, dated Scutari, November 15, 1902, Ippen to Foreign Ministry, documents 53–62.

29. Selim Deringil, "Legitimacy Structures in the Ottoman State: The Reign of Abdülhamid II (1876–1909)."

30. HHStA, PA XII/312 Turkei Liasse XXXIV/2, dated Scutari, January 24, 1902, Kral to Foreign Ministry, documents 12–18.

31. This is made clear in a report by consul Ippen to Vienna; see HHStA, PA XIV/14 LIASSE IX/1, dated Scutari, August 24 1897, Ippen to Goluchowski, documents 9–12.

32. H. Yıldırım Ağanoğlu, *Osmanlı'dan Cumhuriyet'e Balkanlar'ın Makûs Talihi*, 28–45.

33. For a start, it linked previously isolated communities to the outside world as they desperately sought patronage and protection in face of persecution. See letters lobbying the British state in AQSH, F.24.D.5/1.f.1–2, dated July 13, 1878.

34. These measures to harass and offend Montenegro's Muslim population induced them to leave in large numbers throughout the 1880s and 1890s. See Archivio Storico del Ministero degli Affari Esteri, Rome (ASMAE), Serie P Politica 1891–1916, Busta 665, no. 370/165, Consul to Foreign Ministry, dated Scutari, July 5, 1906.

35. Muslim businesses in Podgorica were reportedly targeted by these provisions, a form of harassment that resulted in a decade-long exodus of the once large Muslim Albanian population. BBA, Y.PRK.UM 16/97, 28 Şevval 1307 [June 17, 1890], and BBA, HR.SYS 129/45, report no. 7 from Işkodra *vilayet* to Interior Ministry, dated 27 Zilevvel 1307 [December 17, 1889].

36. See letters and reports from the archbishop's office in Shkodër on the shift of Montenegrin state policies toward Albanian Catholics. AQSH, F.132.D.19.f.1–11, dated between 1880 and 1883.

37. Violence was also used, however, when it expedited the departure of resilient Muslim Malësorë communities. In several reports it is clear that Montenegrin forces targeted Muslims for the specific purpose of expelling them from the country. BBA, Y.PRK.MYD 4/92, 28 Recep 1303 [May 2, 1886], and BBA, Y.PRK.MYD 5/29, 20 Şevval 1303 [June 22, 1886].

38. At the time when Ulqin was being ceded to Slav Montenegrin forces, a long process of forced removal of the port's Albanian inhabitants led to a new practice of arbitrarily confiscating property under the principle of "eminent domain," which resulted in the impoverishment of a historically wealthy community. This plan convinced the Ottoman government in Shkodër to set up a commission in order to monitor the process. This surveillance was undertaken in the hope of ensuring some financial compensation for these Ottoman subjects who were forced to leave their hometowns now under Montenegrin control. BBA, Y.PRK.MYD 1/60, 8 Zilkade 1297 [October 12, 1880].

39. BBA, HR.SYS 129/45, report no. 7 from Işkodra *vilayet* to Interior Ministry, dated 27 Zilevvel 1307 [December 17, 1889].

40. While the details of this agreement remain unclear except for several preliminary guidelines, by 1884 both governments were working in unison to standardize the transfer of land (and to some extent to protect locals), which suggests that enough

pressure was put on these regimes to represent the interests of locals. A copy of the original document in the Montenegrin National Archives used for this study can be found in the Albanian Historical Institute in Tirana: Document number AIH 836/51, Commission Agreement with Seven Articles, dated July 12, 1884.

41. Russian money helped build up the infrastructure of the frontier regions, improving roads and constructing bridges to cut the travel time between the highlands and the coast by days. See an example of such construction at Irjanica near Plava in BBA, Y.MTV 70/174, copy of telegram from Vali Farik Edhem Paşa, 28 Rebiyüla-hir 1310 [June 20, 1892].

42. ASMAE, Serie A Affairi Politici (1881–91) Busta 1, F. 1889, no. 145/82, Consul to Foreign Minister, dated Scutari, April 15, 1889.

43. For evidence of Ulqin's growing significance in regional trade, see a number of protocols written between Montenegrin and Ottoman officials outlining the borderlines. BBA, HR.SYS 861/1, communiqué number 131, Radoviç to Cavid Paşa, February 17, 1886.

44. A detailed report on the upper regions of Malësi reveals how goods passed through the porous borders with considerable economic loss for the Ottoman state. BBA, Y.PRK.MYD 6/14, 4 Cemaziyelahir 1304 [March 1, 1887].

45. Details of this particular kind of transaction may be found in Isa Blumi, "Thwarting the Ottoman Empire: Smuggling through the Empire's New Frontiers in Ottoman Yemen and Albania, 1878–1910."

46. This desire to draw Ottoman trade to Montenegrin-controlled ports was manifested in the proposed plan to construct a railway line connecting Montenegro's other port, Antivari, to Lake Shkodër. Such plans, designed by an Italian firm, clearly worried Ottoman officials. BBA, YA.RES 132/30, Ministry of Trade report no. 99, 15 Cemaziyelahir 1323 [August 18, 1905].

47. For thorough discussions on how the region was to be integrated politically with the empire, see BBA, Y.PRK.MYD 2/1, 5 Rebiyülahir 1298 [March 8, 1881], and BBA, Y.PRK.MYD 2/15, 26 Zilhicce 1298 [November 21, 1881].

48. ASMAE, Serie P Politica (1891–1916), Busta 666, no. 19863/29, Foreign Ministry to Consul Leoni in Scutari, dated Rome, March 3, 1904.

10

A Reassessment of the Macedonian
Question, 1878–1908

Gül Tokay

The Berlin Congress and the treaty that followed were mainly designed to ease the international tension that occurred following the Turco-Russian War of 1877–78 and to safeguard European peace as long as circumstances permitted. The congress left many unresolved local disputes for future arrangements, however, and no doubt brought further complications to the region.[1]

One of the major issues left for future arrangements was the Christian reforms: the Macedonian reforms in Europe and Armenian reforms in the eastern provinces of the Ottoman Empire. In both cases European intervention under the guise of "reforms" no doubt brought complications, not only by further weakening the Ottoman administration but also by encouraging the communities involved to take advantage of the fortuitous circumstances to express their national aspirations. A distinction must be drawn, however, between the European reforms undertaken by the Ottoman statesmen internally, with a view to regenerating the empire, and those imposed on the Ottomans by the European powers. While reforms initiated by the Ottomans were making progress during the late nineteenth century, the same authorities were trying to obstruct the Europeans' projects. The Ottoman authorities always saw in these schemes an element that might challenge the territorial integrity of the empire.[2] Moreover, the border disputes, the refugee question, and the future of those Muslims and Christians who had been separated from their kin by the Treaty of Berlin all became major causes of regional conflicts.

Following the Treaty, however, the Ottomans believed that the survival of the empire depended upon the preservation of their remaining territories in the Balkans. The Bulgarians, who had lost Macedonia at Berlin, also had serious ambitions in these territories, which they viewed as an issue to be exploited when the time was ripe. Therefore the Macedonian question became the core cause of tension not only between these two states but until the end of the Balkan Wars, among the Europeans too. Within this framework, this paper is a reassessment of the Treaty of Berlin and the Macedonian question as it unfolded between 1878 and 1908.[3]

FROM SAN STEFANO TO BERLIN, MARCH–JULY 1878

The European powers implemented a policy of noninvolvement throughout the Turco-Russian War and only started to panic once Ottoman defeat became inevitable.[4] After the preliminary treaty of San Stefano on March 3 in particular, the British and the Austrians began applying pressure on Russia for a general conference with the presence of all signatory powers of the Peace Treaty of Paris. Furthermore, the new British foreign secretary, Lord Salisbury, suggested that the Congress meet in Berlin with Chancellor Bismarck acting as mediator, a recommendation accepted by all the powers.[5]

Salisbury was never going to allow the ratification of the Treaty of San Stefano, which not only established Slav dominance in the Balkans but, more critically, increased Russian influence in the eastern parts of the Ottoman Empire, thus endangering British political and commercial interests in that region.[6] That being said, the British foreign secretary believed that the Crimean system had long become obsolete and that the Ottomans were in need of protection.

Moreover, the Austrians' main concern was the new Balkan map. Their worries focused on the new Bulgarian borders, the existence of Russian troops in the region, the Montenegrin frontiers, and the future of the provinces of Bosnia and Hercegovina. The establishment of Slav dominance and the new geography were a threat to Austrian commercial interests as well as their natural communication lines. The other powers had few major objections to the new settlement. For Bismarck, San Stefano was a final settlement for Near Eastern affairs and only needed to be ratified.[7]

While precongress diplomacy was continuing in the international arena, the British foreign secretary did not want to risk Britain's interests in the region, nor could he wait until the congress was initiated. Through skilled British diplomacy Salisbury succeeded in signing secret agreements with the Russians, Turks, and Austrians prior to the Congress of Berlin. Most importantly, the British, via the Anglo-Ottoman Convention of June 4, succeeded in occupying the island of Cyprus. With Salisbury's diplomatic maneuvering, the congress became not only a formality but also a fait accompli as far as the rest of the plenipotentiaries were concerned.[8]

Most of the sessions of the Congress of Berlin, between June 13 and July 13, dealt with the drawing of a new Balkan map. Issues that were possible sources of conflict between the powers, such as border disputes and Ottoman finances, were momentarily disregarded and left for future arrangements.

One of the major Ottoman concerns was undoubtedly the establishment of the new Bulgarian state, with its many unsettled questions. During the Berlin Congress the San Stefano borders of the Bulgarian Principality were revised and divided into three separate units. First, the Bulgarian Principality was limited to the northern Balkans. Second, an autonomous province of Eastern Rumelia was established under the sultan's suzerainty. Finally, the Macedonian provinces, which had large Slavic populations, were returned to the Ottoman Empire but were promised reforms under the guidance of the European powers.[9] The treaty also guaranteed the protection of the religious and property rights of the Muslims in the Bulgarian Principality and in Eastern Rumelia.

Although the Bulgarian borders were revised, the establishment of a Bulgarian Principality in the middle of the Balkans was viewed as a serious threat. The autonomy of Eastern Rumelia was incomplete and open to Bulgarian influence.[10] Macedonian provinces were returned to the Ottoman Empire; but according to article 23 reforms were to be implemented under European guidance, which was bound to lead to a conflict of authority and encourage the Christians.[11]

On the one hand, the Treaty of Berlin eased international tensions and prevented the likelihood of an Anglo-Russian war; on the other hand, the Eastern Crisis and the treaty destroyed Ottoman prestige both at home and abroad, discredited the Tanzimat policy, and ended the already crumbling Crimean system.[12] Furthermore, the status quo established in Berlin, with a dissatisfied Bulgaria and newly independent Balkan states that had ambitions in "European Turkey" on the one hand and a defeated Ottoman Empire with a young sultan on the other, was almost inevitably going to bring further complications to the region.

THE BERLIN TREATY AND
OTTOMAN-BULGARIAN RELATIONS

After 1878 the main domestic policy goal of the new Bulgarian Principality was to secure stability and economic progress. The main aims of its foreign policy were to gain the support of the European powers for the eventual independence of the principality and to regain the territories that had been lost at Berlin: Eastern Rumelia and Macedonia. Thus the main

Bulgarian ambition was to (re)gain the Macedonian provinces. Immediate issues between Bulgaria and the Ottoman Empire also needed to be resolved, however, such as the border ratifications and the resettlement of refugees. The complications that occurred during the negotiating process certainly led to an ongoing tension between the two states.

Four major issues directly concerned Ottoman-Bulgarian relations after the Treaty of Berlin. In order to understand the escalation of the Macedonian turmoil after 1878, these issues must be explored separately.

The first was the question of the ratification of the borders between Bulgaria and the Ottoman Empire (Macedonia). Under article 2 of the Treaty of Berlin, an international commission was formed by the six signatories of the treaty for the ratification of the new Bulgarian borders with its neighboring states. The commissioners were mostly technical men with military backgrounds. With some exceptions, they worked on the map that was drawn at Berlin without making or suggesting any alterations. In particular, the British commissioner, Col. Edward Bruce Hamley, stated that the frontiers fixed by the treaty were unambiguous and that no revisions of the original document could be carried out. On the other hand, the Russian commissioner complained that it was wrong not to take into consideration the interests of the local population living in the border districts under scrutiny.[13] He was known as a defender of Bulgarian interests, and his proposals were therefore commonly rejected, most emphatically by the British commissioner. For the Ottomans, commissioner Tahir Paşa insisted that the boundary markings had to take into consideration the ability to defend the Ottoman frontiers.[14] Few of the Ottoman suggestions or objections were given any consideration, however; they were in fact seen as Turkish obfuscation of the commissioners' tasks.

As might be expected, problems did occur while the borders between Macedonia and Bulgaria were being drawn. Bulgarians as well as local Ottomans were seen as preventing the commissioners from carrying out their tasks. The Turks complained about the Russian commissioner and were convinced that he was making changes to the treaty proposal in favor of the Bulgarians. Regular complaints were received from the governor-general of Kosovo, claiming that the Bulgarians in the border villages were trying to change the boundary markings after the work had been completed. Furthermore, *başıbozuk*s were a cause for alarm and were preventing work from being carried out at the border villages, especially by the Russian teams. Still, the Bulgarian-Macedonian border commission's work had been completed without major problems by late 1879, to the satisfaction of no one involved. The commissioners were pleased to have completed their task, but it took many years for their work to be ratified by the Otto-mans.[15] Both Bulgarians and Ottomans believed that the borders had been artificially drawn by the European powers without taking the local needs in consideration. Regular border skirmishes occurred during and after the period of markings. These skirmishes became one of the major causes of tension and reasons for mobilization of forces by both states.

The second issue that caused major concern for both states was the problem of resettlement of the refugees, as stated under article 12 of the treaty.[16] The Bulgarian authorities saw two different groups of returning Muslims. The first group consisted of immigrants who were still provision-ally located in different parts of the Ottoman Empire. The second group was made up of those who were being prevented by the Bulgarian authori-ties from crossing the frontier and returning to their homes. The question of the repatriation of the second group of refugees needed to be resolved immediately.[17] Many refugees were stopped at the borders because they did not have visas authorized by the Bulgarian agent in Istanbul, or local Bulgarian authorities would come up with other reasons for not allow-ing them to repatriate.[18] The Jews who were also attempting to return to their homes faced similar treatment.[19] In the meantime many Bulgarian emigrants from Macedonia, who were not subjects of the principality, occupied the Muslims' homes and refused to leave. Bulgarian authorities, even the prince himself, stated that their occupation was a question of humanity and that nothing much could be done on this issue because it was a natural outcome of the war.

Christians in the Macedonian districts had serious worries about what would happen once the Russian troops were withdrawn, because of the ill-treatment meted out to them by the Muslims of the area. Civilian Chris-tians often left or were forced to leave their homes as refugees in areas where the Russian troops were still present. Furthermore, many Christians abandoned their homes and joined the insurgent bands operating in the border districts. The situation for the Bulgarian notables in Macedonia was worse: they were often attacked by the *başıbozuk*s.[20]

No proper preliminary entente existed on the question of refugees or on the work of the mixed Bulgarian-Turkish commissions. This caused misery and suffering for both communities, but the situation for return-ing Muslims was much worse and more difficult to solve.[21] In other words, the Treaty of Berlin destroyed the pluralist order: the newly independent Balkan states adopted the idea of a single ethno-linguistic nation based on European models.[22] This was a natural outcome not only of the war but also of the nation-state building process. Therefore, without upsetting the new settlement, the Bulgarians were going to prevent the repatriation of the Muslims. The Ottomans, for their part, lost some of their multiethnic character as a result of the war and began to generate a Muslim identity, especially in the Balkans, and cling to it more and more. This transformation contributed to the emergence of a political consciousness among the Muslims. It established prejudices among Christians and Muslims as well as a subsequent denial of each other's existence in these lands.[23]

As might be expected, the Macedonian provinces (with their ethno-religious combinations) fueled the existing prejudices between the Muslims and the Christians and intensified the religious sentiments of the communities more than anywhere else in the empire.

The third issue was related to one of the foreign policy aims of the new Bulgarian government, accomplished by Bulgarian unification with Eastern Rumelia in 1885. Soon after the Treaty of Berlin was signed, it was rumored that the Bulgarians, rather than organizing Eastern Rumelia into an autonomous province under the sultan, were waiting for an opportune moment to form a large, semi-independent Slav state to gain independence from the Ottoman Empire in the near future. Russians were already assisting the Bulgarians with ammunition, and noncommissioned Russian officers were involved in the Bulgarian army.[24]

In September 1885 Bulgarian revolutionaries in Eastern Rumelia succeeded in a coup d'état and announced the unification of the province with Bulgaria. This was a clear turning point in Bulgarian-Ottoman relations within the context of the Macedonian developments. First, it affected the balance of power in favor of Bulgaria and threw the Treaty of Berlin into disrepute. Second, it made the Ottomans recognize the existence of a "Bulgarian question" in their Macedonian provinces and further encouraged the activities of the Bulgarian-backed insurgents there. In official Ottoman circles, it was feared that the Macedonian provinces would soon adopt a similar policy and demand unity with Bulgaria.[25]

The final factor was the fundamental ambition of all Bulgarians to regain the lost Macedonian provinces. Soon after the treaty, the Bulgarians increased their activities in the Macedonian provinces through the influence of the Exarchate by establishing cultural ties and sending clergy and teachers from the principality to awaken the national aspirations of the populace. At the same time some revolutionary activists believed that the only way to regain the lost territories was to take up arms.[26] In the meantime, although the prince and the rest of the administration avoided any tension with the suzerain and made sure that they did not upset any of the signatories of the Treaty of Berlin, the political societies and committees that were formed in Eastern Rumelia and Bulgaria were tolerated if not actively encouraged by the Bulgarian authorities. The Ottomans were convinced that the insurgents in Macedonia would not be able to survive if they did not have the support of the Bulgarian government.

For Sultan Abdülhamid II the Bulgarian question emerged in the Macedonian provinces and became the main source of turmoil with the establishment of the Bulgarian Church (the Exarchate) in 1870.[27] The sultan was therefore more tolerant of the activities of other communities on Macedonian soil and endeavored to improve relations with the other Balkan states soon after the treaty was signed to counterbalance the Bulgarian expansionist designs.[28]

ESCALATION OF MACEDONIAN TURMOIL AND EUROPEAN INTERVENTION

The Great Powers, meanwhile, did not want to disturb the 1878 settlement and thus decided to cooperate on the Balkan issues to prevent any further conflict. The most important of these developments was the Austro-Russian Entente of 1897.[29] After the signing of the entente, the two states began cooperating, with the consent of the rest of the powers, on a reform program to improve the living conditions of the Christians in the Macedonian provinces, as stated under article 23.[30] The governments of Austria-Hungary and Russia were aware that the Macedonian problem could not be solved solely by reforms but believed that they would bring temporary relief to the provinces.[31]

Most of the newly established Balkan states, with the exception of Bulgaria, were content with the outcome of the treaty and were more concerned with their internal developments. They kept a constant eye on unfolding events, however, in order to benefit from any future change in the status quo. Soon after the treaty was signed, the turmoil started to escalate in the Macedonian provinces with the increase in the insurgent activities of the different communities. These communities would benefit if the prevailing circumstances were to change. The Bulgarian movement in the provinces was directed not only at the Ottoman administration but at the Greeks as well. The Greek Patriarchate was the oldest institution in the region, and it opposed the expansionistic tendencies of the Bulgarian Church. The principal conflict between the Greeks and the Bulgarians took place in the region of Monastir (Manastir) and its *kazas*, where the Bulgarians were trying to increase their numbers and gain further supporters.[32] Although the Greeks insisted that they were mainly protecting themselves against the designs of other communities, both the Macedonian and mainland Greeks kept the Hellenistic ideal salient via armed struggle as well as through the efforts of the clergy, professionals, and business leaders. Greek activities in Macedonia escalated with the formation of Ethniki Etairia (National Society) in 1894 in Athens. The goal of this secret organization, made up mainly of ex-army officers, was not only to unify the Greeks in Macedonia but also to further their influence over their co-nationals in the rest of the Ottoman Empire. Furthermore, a secret society was formed in Epirus, promoting the idea of pan-Hellenism in the Epirus and Macedonia in cooperation with the Macedonian emigrants in Greece.[33]

Among other Christian communities in Macedonia, the Serbs and the Vlachs also stepped up their activities. In the 1880s many revolutionary bands started to appear in Belgrade and in Bucharest with the aim of fomenting agitation in Macedonia. Two groups existed among the Serbs. One group believed that Serbian activities should be directed from Belgrade. The other group, led by the metropolitan of Üsküp, favored independent action, despite receiving support from the heartland. The Serbs were convinced that the Austrians had ambitions in the region; Bulgarians would never give up their San Stefano borders and would always harbor ambitions in Kosovo, including Novi Pazar, which the Serbs believed should be divided between Montenegro and themselves after the fall of Ottoman Empire. Of course, historical animosities with the Albanians remained.

Serbian activities were essentially directed against the Exarchists on one hand and against the Albanians on the other. The Serbs and the Macedonians in Belgrade simultaneously demanded recognition of their right to religious and educational freedom.[34] The sultan issued *irades* to satisfy Serbian demands but also to prevent the increase of the Exarchists' influence in the area. According to Ottoman sources, Serbs and Bulgarians had been more or less equal in numbers in the Kosovo and Monastir provinces before the war. Despite the Serbs' efforts, the Exarchists succeeded in upending this prewar equilibrium to their advantage soon after the war, especially in Monastir.[35]

For the Vlachs, however, secession from the Ottoman Empire or the establishment of an independent church was not the ultimate aim. Their primary goals were recognition as a distinct community and free use of their language in schools and religious practices. Still, it is necessary to differentiate between the Vlachs who considered themselves Greek and the Vlachs who insisted on a separate identity and were closer to the Romanians. The agitations were carried out mainly by those who wanted to establish a separate identity and use their own language rather than Greek in religious and educational practices.[36] Vlachs cooperated with the Exarchists against the Greeks and also with the Albanians for autonomous rights in the Ottoman Empire.[37]

Among the Muslim communities in Macedonia, the Albanians resented that the Ottomans had to cede certain territories to Montenegro and Greece during the Berlin Settlement that they claimed for themselves. They were also upset that article 23 of the treaty left them out of the European reforms. A committee of Catholic and Muslim Albanians issued a memorandum to the sultan and demanded autonomy, with a reorganization of their provinces under an Albanian governor.[38] These demands were not given much consideration, only attracting some sympathy for the community.[39]

With the onset of the insurgent activities after the Treaty of Berlin, both Christians and Muslims no doubt gained momentum in Macedonia. The Ottomans feared that European intervention, which aimed at reforms in favor of the Christian population, was likely. First, as an immediate response, the Ottomans increased their forces in the region to deter any moves from the neighboring states, mainly Bulgaria. Second, they tried to come up with their own reform packages to prevent European interventions. At the end of 1902 the sultan issued an *irade* entitled *Rumeli Vilayetleri Hakkında Bir Talimat* (Instructions for the Rumelian Provinces) and established the Umumi Rumeli Müfettişliği (Rumelian Inspectorate for Reforms). Hüseyin Hilmi Paşa was appointed the inspector-general of the Macedonian provinces with the approval of the Great Powers in charge of the reorganization.[40] The grand vizier, Said Paşa, came up with a series of reforms in legal, financial, educational, and agricultural areas and reorganized the police and gendarmerie. Furthermore, Said Paşa proposed reforms for the Albanian-populated areas that were left out at Berlin, but the Austrians insisted on the Albanian districts being omitted from the reform program.[41] Ottoman initiatives did not satisfy the local Christian communities, however, who maintained their activities with the expectation of attracting European attention and possible intervention.

The turning point in the Macedonian developments was the Ilinden Uprising, which had always been a part of the Internal Macedonian Revolutionary Organization (IMRO) agenda and started on August 2, the day of St. Elijah ("Ilinden" in Slavonic) in Monastir *vilayet*. The IMRO's objective was to obtain full autonomy within a Balkan federation, and it refused to commit itself to Bulgaria. For the leaders, the only way to obtain autonomy was by means of a popular uprising.[42] Soon after the Ottomans suppressed the uprising, Austria-Hungary and Russia established their reform program, known as the Mürzsteg Reform Program, in October 1903. According to this plan, Hilmi Paşa was appointed governor-general of the *vilayets*, but two European (Austrian and Russian) supervisors were to contribute to his post. The second issue was the gendarmerie reforms. A European general in the service of the Ottoman Empire would be appointed to reorganize the gendarmerie. Military officers of the powers were also to be attached to the general, who would apportion the districts in which they would exercise their duties.[43] Other articles related to the reforms of the financial, judicial, and administrative institutions.[44]

The sultan and the rest of the Ottoman authorities were convinced that the Mürzsteg Reform Program was designed in favor of the Christians of Macedonia and would thus upset the Muslims. They were also concerned that a triple government under an Ottoman governor-general and two foreign assessors would bring confusion. Furthermore, foreign military officers would not be content with the reorganization of the gendarmerie but would interfere with the regular army, which was likely to produce tension between the Ottomans and Europeans. The reformers were not interested in the Ottomans' concerns, however, and the program was implemented by force in early November.[45]

MACEDONIAN REFORMS AND THE ROAD
TO THE YOUNG TURK REVOLUTION, 1904 TO 1908

The major weakness of the Macedonian reforms, which the Europeans failed to see (or chose to ignore), was the fact that there were no "Christian Macedonians" per se; instead there were Bulgarians, Greeks, Serbs, and Vlachs who were Christians but who also harbored nationalist aspirations and were supported by the neighboring Balkan states. Therefore reforms granted to the European provinces of the Ottoman Empire were inevitably going to encourage different Christian communities still living in Ottoman domains.[46]

The Christians in Macedonia, with the exception of the Bulgarians, expressed their satisfaction with the Mürzsteg Reform Program. The Bulgarians were disappointed because they hoped for at least an autonomous Macedonia with a Christian governor-general. Although the Greeks and Serbs stated that they were satisfied with the reforms, this did not prevent them from increasing their activities, in part to extend their sphere of influence in the provinces and in part to prevent Bulgarian expansionism in the region. The authorities in Macedonian lands were more tolerant of the activities of the Greek, Serb, and Vlach bands and their propaganda organs than of their Bulgarian counterparts. For that reason, the Ottomans granted further privileges to the Serbs and Vlachs. The sultan issued an *irade* in 1903, recognizing the Serbs as a separate community. Vlachs were granted representations in assemblies and local councils in 1905, with the right to open their own schools and carry out their own religious practices.[47]

Although the activities of the Greek bands significantly increased, the Greek government insisted that many of these bands did not have any hostility against the Ottomans and were merely defending their co-religionists. They openly stated that hostilities were directed against the Bulgarian bands. The Ottomans thus overlooked many of these Greek activities.[48] Ottoman officials genuinely thought that Europeans were sympathetic to the Bulgarian cause in the provinces and also believed that dividing the Christian communities was one way to fight back.

As the Ottoman authorities had anticipated, the reforms triggered a significant increase in the activities of the Muslims. In particular, the Albanians were unhappy with the European reforms. It was their conviction that the Austrian-led scheme would only benefit the Slavs, especially the Serbs, and diminish the powers of the sultan. Meanwhile the Albanians who lived in the areas in which the reforms were applied believed that the project was pro-Serbian in nature and intent and neglected the needs of the Albanians.[49] In Kosovo, where the Austrians were in charge of reorganizing the gendarmerie, there was constant tension between the Muslim Albanians and the reform officers, including the *eşraf*s (local community leaders) and the ulema, who voiced their concerns in demonstrations. Consequently local Albanian and Turkish Muslim *beys* (notably in Monastir and Kosovo) were displeased with the existence of the European supervision as well as the strict measures introduced by Hilmi Paşa.[50] The control mechanism introduced during the reforms harmed the local Albanian and Turkish *beys*' political and economic interests: before this time they had implemented their own laws and regulations and had distinctive methods of dealing with the local authorities, especially where the officials had a reputation for being weak and corrupt.[51] Under these circumstances a series of local Albanian uprisings took place as a protest and more and more Muslim bands were formed, contributing to the existing turmoil in the provinces.

Despite the difficulties and obstacles, Ottoman and European officials genuinely attempted to improve conditions in the provinces in the early

years of the reforms. Hilmi Paşa's efforts made notable progress in tax collection and in combating corruption. New schools were created for both
Muslims and Christians, and improvements were made in the gendarmerie.
Although Hilmi Paşa was in full control of the Ottoman administrative
machinery, all his actions were controlled by two European supervisors.
Also, a conflict of authority and a clash of personalities emerged between
the European general in charge of reorganizing the gendarmerie and the
governor-general. The major obstacle to the Mürzsteg Reform Program,
however, was the increase in budgetary deficits brought about by the expenditure on the reforms and the increase in military spending. In 1905
the Great Powers decided to form a Financial Commission to regulate
the Macedonian budget and demanded further reforms on the part of the
Ottoman government. The Ottoman administration refused to accept the
formation of the Financial Commission. But when the powers responded
with a naval demonstration supported by the Balkan states, especially the
Greek government, the Ottomans had little choice other than to accept
the commission.[52] It was not the decisions by the Financial Commission
but the extending of the Macedonian reforms that made the Ottomans
believe that Macedonia in effect had become a semiautonomous province
run by international commissions.[53]

The second phase of the reforms, after 1905, certainly witnessed the
decline of the Ottoman administration in the provinces. The central government in Istanbul lost both the respect it once had and the confidence of
the locals in the area. The local Muslims were discontented and frustrated
by the increase in Christian insurgent activities as well as by the presence
of the Europeans and started to organize themselves to prevent further
worsening of their circumstances.[54] More and more Muslim bands (Albanian and Turkish) were formed to counter Christian influence. Moreover,
Muslims of different classes started to organize themselves into various
committees and societies to bring a change to the Macedonian situation.
Interestingly, not only civilian Muslims but also military Muslims in the
provinces were frustrated with developments.[55]

After the Treaty of Berlin, Sultan Abdülhamid started to increase the
forces in the provinces, mainly to prevent any attacks from neighboring
states. Furthermore, he decided to send the best-educated corps to the
region to convince the Europeans that they were capable of dealing with
the insurgency and that no European intervention was needed.[56] The
Ottoman army faced its own difficulties, however, and the possibility of
fighting in Macedonia circumstances merely served to frustrate different
classes of the already discontented soldiery.

The main problem was that the Ottoman army was going through a transformation process, which had a lasting impact on the Third Army in Macedonia. First, differences between the traditional old school soldiery and the liberal educated *mekteblis* (officers with formal training in a military academy) were causing major problems in the corps, making it difficult for the two parties to cooperate.[57] Second, the newly graduated officers had no practical experience in fighting the rebel bands. The continuous clashes between the bands and the difficulties with the Christians were destroying the morale of the soldiery. Third, errors were made in issuing salaries, and *redif*s (reserve soldiers) whose time had expired were not allowed to return to their homes. Moreover, the soldiery did not want to fight against fellow Muslim Albanians. Finally, resentment festered between the military forces and the foreign-led gendarmerie, which was better equipped and better paid. Mutinies began to take place in units of the Third Army.

In the meantime the Europeans were insensitive toward the existing circumstances, ignored the growing tension among the Muslims, and kept increasing their demands under the reform project, genuinely hoping to ease the tension. First, and most importantly, the Foreign Military Commissions decided that in order to cut the military budget (and in response to British pressure) the fights with the bands should be totally transferred from the army to the European-led gendarmerie by the end of 1907.[58] This was viewed as a major insult not only to the military establishment but also to the sovereign rights of the sultan. Second, the 1907 Ambassadors' Conference decided that the Mürzsteg Reform Program and the duties of the foreign officials should be extended another seven years and that salaries and expenses should be covered by an increase in custom duties from 8 percent to 11 percent in 1905.[59] The Ottomans were concerned about these developments for both political and financial reasons. Third, the British foreign secretary, Sir Edward Grey, suggested an autonomous administration as a more viable alternative for the provinces and suggested Montenegrin Prince Mirko as a suitable governor of the provinces. Finally, the Macedonian reforms were also discussed during the Reval Talks between the British and Russians in June 1908, a situation that created major worries in official Ottoman circles.[60]

All these recent developments reminded the Ottomans of the events leading to the Eastern Rumelian unification. More importantly, though, they gave the final impetus to the military and civilian Muslim forces in the provinces to follow the Young Turk Revolution and the restoration of 1876 Constitution soon afterward. It was the Macedonian circumstances that made the revolution inevitable, whatever the later developments might have been. European reforms and foreign intervention encouraged the Christians and frustrated the Muslims. At the same time, the presence and interference of the foreign officials in military and civilian matters provoked anti-Europeanism in the provinces. In addition, the members of the military elite stationed in Macedonia were not satisfied with the Ottoman ruling system, which they believed was the core of the empire's problem, and also observed the deterioration of the conditions in Macedonia. Under these circumstances, it was not difficult for different classes of Macedonian Muslims to come together and demand change.

With the proclamation of the constitution, reform proposals were put aside. Foreign officers were given unlimited leave; only the Financial Commission continued its work as usual. Although the atmosphere immediately after the revolution was joyful, the uncertainties of the new regime brought fundamental changes to the region. In early October Bulgaria declared its independence, Austria annexed Bosnia and Hercegovina, and the crumbling Austro-Russian entente of 1897 came to an end. Evidently the 1878 treaty was being seriously challenged by late 1908. Furthermore, the temporary tranquillity in the provinces was short lived, and both the Christian and Muslim communities stepped up activities again under the new regime. Most importantly, the Balkan states soon overcame their differences, albeit temporarily, and joined forces against the Ottomans on the issue of Macedonia in 1912.

NOTES

1. See W. N. Medlicott, *The Congress of Berlin and After: A Diplomatic History of the Near Eastern Settlement, 1878–1880*; Richard Millman, *Britain and the Eastern Question, 1875–1878*; Ali Fuat Türkgeldi, *Mesâil-i Mühimme-i Siyâsiyye*; and Roderic Davison, "The Ottoman Empire and the Congress of Berlin."
2. Gül Tokay, "The Macedonian Question and the Origins of the Young Turk Revolution, 1903–1908," 2–7.
3. This paper was written during the revision of my original Ph.D. dissertation. Most of the more recent research is based on the Ottoman Foreign Ministerial Archives. For the original study, see Tokay, "The Macedonian Question"; translated into Turkish as Gül Tokay, *Makedonya Sorunu: Jön Türk İhtilalinin Kökenleri, 1903–1908*. For an earlier study on the consequences of the Berlin Treaty in Macedonia, see Gül Tokay, "Macedonian Reforms and Muslim Opposition during the Hamidian Era: 1878–1908." For a full collection of Ottoman diplomatic documents, see Sinan Kuneralp and Gül Tokay, eds., *Ottoman Diplomatic Documents on the Origins of World War One: The Macedonian Issue, 1879–1912*.
4. The Preliminary Peace Treaty of San Stefano was signed by Nikolai P. Ignatiev

(Russian ambassador in Istanbul), Alexander Nelidov (Russian chargé d'affaires), Safvet Paşa (Ottoman foreign minister), and Sadullah Bey (ambassador to Germany) on March 3, 1878.

5. For Lord Salisbury's policy after the Treaty of San Stefano, see Başbakanlık Arşivi, Istanbul (BBA), HRSYS 1218/5 (Ottoman Foreign Ministerial Archives, Political Section), *La Circular de Salisbury*, London, April 1, 1878.

6. BBA, HRSYS 1218/5, *La Circular;* National Archives of the United Kingdom (formerly Public Record Office), Foreign Office Archives, London (FO), FO 65/1004, Salisbury, Foreign Office, London, June 1, 1878.

7. Gül Tokay, "Ayastefanos'tan Berlin Antlaşmasına Doğu Sorunu."

8. Gül Tokay, "Ottoman Diplomacy at the Congress of Berlin, June–July 1878."

9. See Fikret Adanır, *Die Makedonische Frage: Ihre Entstehung und Entwicklung bis 1908*; M. Şükrü Hanioğlu, *Preparation for a Revolution: The Young Turks, 1902–1908*; and Mehmet Hacısalihoğlu, *Die Jungtürken und die Mazedonische Frage, 1890–1918*.

10. Gül Tokay, "Ottoman-Bulgarian Relations, 1878–1908."

11. The reforms were promised in the provinces of Selanik, Monastir, Kosovo, and two independent *sancak*s (Drama and Serres). The Ottoman administration never used the term "Macedonia" and referred to the provinces as *vilayet-i selase* (three provinces).

12. F. A. K. Yasamee, *Ottoman Diplomacy: Abdülhamid II and the Great Powers, 1878–1888*, 13–15.

13. BBA, HRSYS 1247/4, Safved to Chalir, Istanbul, September 23, 1879.

14. For the full collection of the commission reports, see ibid.

15. BBA, HRSYS 1247/3, Edhem to Assim, Vienna, March 9, 1882.

16. It is still very difficult to determine the total number of Muslim emigrants from Bulgaria after the Berlin Treaty. Turkish figures indicate over 1 million emigrants for the years between 1878 and 1912, while the Bulgarian statistics estimate only 350,000. More detailed research no doubt needs to be done, using comparative sources to establish a more convincing number.

17. BBA, HRSYS 318/3, Nihad to Sawas, Sofia, June 4, 1880.

18. BBA, HRSYS 318/3, Sawas to the Representatives of the Powers in Istanbul, September 1880.

19. BBA, HRSYS 318/3, Note Verbale to the Bulgarian agent, November 13, 1879.

20. BBA, HRSYS 319/1, Zancof to Safvet, Istanbul, October 3/10, 1879.

21. For some valuable studies on the refugees and the Turks in Bulgaria, see Bilal N. Şimşir, *Contribution à l'histoire des populations turques en Bulgarie, 1876–1880*; Bilal N. Şimşir, *Rumeli'den Türk Göçleri, 1877–85*; Kemal H. Karpat, *The Turks of Bulgaria: The History, Culture and Political Fate of a Minority*; Ömer Turan, *The Turkish Minority in Bulgaria (1878–1908)*; and Nedim İpek, *Rumeli'den Anadolu'ya Türk Göçleri, 1877–1890*.

22. Kemal H. Karpat, "The Social and Political Foundations of Nationalism in South East Europe after 1878: An Interpretation."

23. Ibid. After 1878 the sultan's inability to deal with the implications of the treaty, such as international reforms, the new status quo in the Balkans, further European intervention in internal affairs, and the escalation in the irredentist activities of the

Christians, no doubt provoked the already existing religious sentiment among the Muslims, especially in the areas with ethno-religious heterogeneity.

24. BBA, HRSYS 314/1, Musurus to Aidine, London, July 15, 1880.

25. Yasamee, *Ottoman Diplomacy*, 153–78; Tokay, "The Macedonian Question," 35–36.

26. In 1893 an organization called the IMRO (Internal Macedonian Revolutionary Organization) was established with the ambition of obtaining full autonomy. Adanır, *Die Makedonische Frage*, 110–15.

27. For the details of the establishment of the Bulgarian Church, see FO 881/3578.

28. For a detailed study on early Hamidian foreign policy, see Yasamee, *Ottoman Diplomacy*.

29. Berthold Sutter, "Machtteilung als Bürgschaft des Friedens: Eine Denkschrift des Botschafter Heinrich von Calice 1896 zur Abgrenzung des Interessensphären zwischen Russland und Österreich am Balkan"; Tokay, "The Macedonian Question," 44–47.

30. The provinces were composed mainly of Bulgarians, Greeks, Serbs, Vlachs, Albanians, and Turks. At the turn of the century, according to the Ottoman sources, there were 1 million Muslim Turks and 750,000 Muslim Albanians (the number might include Albanians outside the reform provinces); 627,000 members of the Greek Patriarchate (including Serbs and Vlachs); 575,000 Bulgarian Exarchists; and 200,000 Jews, Armenians, and Catholics. European sources, however, gave the distribution as 1,500,000 Bulgarians and Serbs; 200,000 Greeks; 300,000 Albanians; 250,000 Turks; and 100,000 Vlachs. Tokay, "The Macedonian Question," 285–86.

31. Steven Sowards, *Austria's Policy of Macedonian Reform*; Tokay, "The Macedonian Question," 55–58.

32. BBA, HRSYS 1082/12, Said to Nabi, Sadaret, April 17, 1894. For one of the best accounts of the Greek question in Macedonia in English, see Douglas Dakin, *The Greek Struggle in Macedonia, 1897–1912*.

33. BBA, HRSYS 1083/16, to Said, Tirhala, June 15, 1894.

34. BBA, HRSYS 1772/19, Ahmed Fevzi to Tevfik, Cetince, February 16, 1896.

35. BBA, HRSYS 1772/26, to Tevfik, Belgrade, April 26, 1897.

36. BBA, HRSYS 1131/1, Süleyman to Sawas, Bucharest, October 4, 1879.

37. Over the years Hellenized Vlachs started to cooperate with the Greeks against the Vlachs who were supported by the Romanians.

38. BBA, HRSYS 130/17, August 2, 1902.

39. Tokay, "Macedonian Reforms and Muslim Opposition," 54–56.

40. Hüseyin Hilmi Paşa was appointed in 1902 and served in the Macedonian provinces until 1908. Previously he had served as the governor of Yemen, where he had established a well-known reputation for the reforms he implemented. The collections on the Inspectorate of the Macedonian Provinces (Rumeli Mufettişliği Tasnifi, BBA, TFR) have many valuable documents on the Macedonian developments after 1903.

41. Said Paşa would have liked to extend the reforms to the *kaza*s of Kosovo (Priştina, Prizren, and Novi Pazar), where there were large Albanian population. Said Paşa, *Said Paşa'nın Hatıratı*, 2:70–173.

42. Adanır, *Die Mazedonische Frage*, 110–12; Tokay, "The Macedonian Question," 38–40.

43. One of the most difficult issues was that the Austrians insisted on being in charge of the Kosovo province in the reorganization of the gendarmerie, despite their hostilities with the Albanians and the Serbs who composed the majority of the population in the province. The Ottomans would have liked to see at least a mixed force in that province, but that was refused by the reformers.

44. Sowards, *Austria's Policy of Macedonian Reform*; Tokay, "The Macedonian Question."

45. Tokay, "Macedonian Reforms and Muslim Opposition," 55–57.

46. Among the Europeans, only the German ambassador, Freiherr Marschall von Bieberstein (1897–1912), was strongly opposed to the European reforms, because he was convinced that the foreign intervention would not only encourage the Christians but also frustrate the Muslims.

47. BBA, HRSYS 1772/39, Tahsin to Ferid; Tahsin to Tevfik, Istanbul, August 30, 1904.

48. BBA, HRSYS 1772/30, Rifat to Tevfik, Athens, November 19, 1904. Only after 1905 did Hilmi Paşa and the rest of the local authorities start to realize that the Greek movement was getting out of control and something had to be done to prevent insurgent activities and the support of the mainland Greeks, including the government.

49. The Austrian authorities viewed the Serbs as economically and intellectually more advanced than the Albanians and thought that including Albanian-populated districts in the reform project would benefit the Albanians and disturb the existing balance with the Serbs. It was in the Austrians' interests not to challenge the existing conditions, so they insisted on leaving the districts where Albanians were in the majority out of the scheme.

50. Gustav Hubka, *Die österreichisch-ungarische Offiziersmission in Makedonien, 1903–1909*, 92–100.

51. BBA, TFR-I KV 204/20353 (Rumelian Collection, Kosovo Section), Kosovo, June 29, 1324 [July 12, 1908]. The Albanians were especially upset with the increase in the local taxes.

52. BBA, HRSYS 1143/3, Sadreddin to Tevfik, Athens, November 30, 1905.

53. For the Règlement of 1905, see FO 881/83876, *Accounts and Papers, CXXXVIII, 1906*, 1171–73.

54. Hubka, *Die österreichisch-ungarische Offiziersmission in Makedonien*, 72–73.

55. See Rıza Paşa, *Hülasa-ı Hatırat*; and Gül Tokay, "Makedonya Reformları ve Güvenlik Güçleri."

56. BBA, Yıldız Resmi, Maruzat Defteri 14340 (9 Zilhicce 1324 [January 23, 1907]).

57. See Tokay, "Makedonya Reformları ve Güvenlik Güçleri," 137–39.

58. See details on the decisions of the Military Commissions' reports in FO 195/2267, Istanbul, December 16, 1907.

59. FO 371/583, "Summary of recent correspondence Macedonian Reforms," June 6, 1908; BBA, HRSYS 1138/1, Tevfik to Hüsnü, Istanbul, March 1908.

60. BBA, HRSYS 593/1, Rıfat to Tevfik, London, June 6, 1908; HRSYS 1094/38, Tevfik to Hüsnü Paşa, Istanbul, June 13, 1908.

PART III

The Beginning of the End in Eastern Anatolia

The Massacres of Armenians

11

Patterns of Conflict and Violence in Eastern Anatolia Leading Up to the Russo-Turkish War and the Treaty of Berlin

Brad Dennis

Most studies on eastern Anatolia have focused on conflict and violence between Muslims and Christians occurring after the Treaty of Berlin. Few studies provide in-depth explanations of the violence occurring before it, and those that do often use the retrospective lens of the events leading up to the massacres of Armenians in the 1890s and in 1915. This paper aims to limit the focus on eastern Anatolian violence to the four decades preceding the war and its immediate aftermath with the hope of overcoming the linear connection often assumed to exist between the war and the treaty and the eventual escalation of violence against the Armenians. It has two main aims. First, it identifies the factors that led to the diversification of actors in eastern Anatolia. Second, it attempts to show how conflicts of interest at local, state, and international levels affected trends of violence and either mitigated or escalated diversity-based tensions. Violence in eastern Anatolia was generally a result of local power struggles rather than state-sponsored violence. But Ottoman centralization efforts, undertaken in response to the threat of Russian incursion, contributed to the erosion of the locally developed conflict mitigation mechanisms in eastern Anatolia. Consequently the Ottoman state was forced to assume responsibility as a mitigating agent in local conflicts of interest. In spite of its economic challenges and its inability to contain eastern Anatolian violence fully, it was actually remarkably effective at minimizing the spread of political violence in eastern Anatolia.

IDENTIFYING ACTORS ON
THE EASTERN ANATOLIAN STAGE

Eastern Anatolia had long been a religiously and ethnolinguistically diverse place. By the mid-nineteenth century the religious demographics
consisted of Sunnis, Sufis of several religious orders (mainly Qadiri and
Nakşibendi), Yezidis, Alevis, Shi'is, Gregorian Orthodox, Catholics,
Protestants, Jacobites, and Nestorians. Linguistic patterns of nineteenth-
century eastern Anatolia reveal that diverse groups had been able to develop rather independently culturally and socially and without significant
influence from the policies of the Ottoman Empire and foreign powers.
Some Kurdish dialects were and still are mutually unintelligible. Sorani
and Kurmanji are significantly distant from each other, to the extent that
the latter's nouns possess gender whereas the former's nouns do not.[1]
Syriac, the language spoken by the Nestorian Christians in the Hakkari
and Urmiye regions, consisted of several vernaculars during the Ottoman
period. According to Arthur Maclean, in his grammar of Syriac published
in the mid-1890s, these were historical developments and not modern
constructions.[2]

Armenian dialects were closer to one another, largely because of the
central role of the Gregorian Orthodox Church in Armenian life. But the
Eastern and Western dialects (spoken in Iran and the Ottoman Empire
respectively) had significant differences in grammar and pronunciation.
Eastern and Western Armenia each had a number of dialects. Herachyah
Adjarian, an Armenian linguist, enumerated seven Eastern dialects and
twenty-one Western dialects in 1909, with eight dialects of the Western
branch being spoken in eastern Anatolia.[3] In some areas, however, linguistic assimilation occurred. One British official in Bitlis observed in 1889
that the inhabitants of the mountainous Sasun region, both Kurdish and
Armenian, spoke a dialect that was a blend of "Kurdish, Zaza, and Armenian languages,"[4] perhaps indicating a degree of cultural fusion there.

Three main factors preserved ethnic and religious diversity in eastern
Anatolia and kept it from becoming homogenized. First, the geographic
ruggedness of the land, both the mountains and the vast desert regions,
provided a natural barrier for locals against long-term outside intervention. Consequently, over the centuries it attracted ethnic and religious
groups seeking land and fleeing persecution from other regions. The land's
difficult physical geography also kept any one indigenous group from assuming any long-term widespread control. Second, the region was distant
from major centers of Russian, Iranian, and Turkish power between the

sixteenth and nineteenth centuries. While Ottoman leaders took control of the land in the early sixteenth century, they maintained only a minimal military presence there to guard against a potential invasion from Iran. The region's barrenness provided little incentive for the Ottomans to invest in fully controlling the land and integrating its population into the state system. The empire generally tolerated linguistic and cultural diversity. Third, because of their physical and political geographic situation, local actors developed indigenous social, political, and economic structures through which to sustain their lifestyles and accommodate long-standing traditional ethnic and religious diversity. Included with such indigenous structures was an internally developed mechanism for resolving conflict and perpetuating the coexistence of multiple ethnicities and religions. The disruption and dissolution of these indigenously developed structures as a result of state intervention during the mid- and late nineteenth century weakened local resilience against social strains between ethnicities and religions.

During the late eighteenth and early nineteenth centuries the number of actors on the eastern Anatolian stage diversified to include Circassians and Western missionaries, travelers, and diplomats. This diversification process had a profound effect on the interchanges between society (as discussed below).

Russian incursions into the Ottoman Empire in the late eighteenth and early nineteenth centuries prompted a gradual movement of the Ottoman state into increasingly threatened peripheral areas. The Russian seizure of Kars in July 1828 and of Erzurum in July 1829 during the Russo-Turkish War of 1828–29 made the Ottoman Empire well aware that its territory was threatened not only in the Balkans but also on its eastern front. The effect of the war on the population in northeastern Anatolia was catastrophic. Ottoman sources estimate that some 100,000 Armenians migrated from the Ottoman Empire to Russia out of fear, force, and persuasion, 21,000 from Erzurum alone.[5] In the wake of the mass exodus, Muslims living in the Ottoman Empire or migrating from Russia seized the lands formerly occupied by Armenians. In spite of these changes in the demographics of northeastern Anatolia, trends of anti-Ottoman rebellion had not occurred among the eastern Armenians on anywhere near the scale of rebellion among the Greeks and the Serbs. This relative calm is attributable in part to the general dispersion of the Armenians throughout the empire and their lack of concentration in any one particular area.

Imam Shamil united a number of Circassian tribes to fight against the Russians in the late 1850s after the Crimean War. When he was eventually defeated, many Circassians left the Caucasus due to a number of unwelcoming economic, political, and social circumstances and also in part because the sultan bade them migrate to the Ottoman Empire. In 1864 Grand Vizier Ali Paşa estimated the number of Circassians (Çerkes) migrating from the Caucasus into the Ottoman Empire between 1858 and 1864 to be approximately 595,000.[6] Many administrators in the Ottoman Empire actually welcomed these new arrivals of immigrants. They hoped to use them as additional manpower for their military forces. They also strategically settled them in areas that had high concentrations of Christians, hoping to blunt the potential force of Christian nationalist movements. This strategy is evident: the Ottomans relocated approximately 400,000 Circassians to Rumelia,[7] a number that far exceeded the Circassians relocated to the much nearer southeastern Anatolia. Of all eastern Anatolian provinces the numbers of Circassians were highest in Trabzon and Erzurum, the *vilayet*s closest to the Caucasus border.[8] The Circassian population was much lower in the *vilayet*s of Diyarbakır and Bitlis, although still substantial. Vital Cuinet gives an estimate of some 10,000 for each province. Van was much lower, with a population of 500.[9]

The consequence of the Circassian migration was that they introduced into the eastern Anatolian socioeconomic and political landscape a new local-level actor that had no domestic or foreign state representation. Despite the Ottoman state's attempts to integrate the Circassians as soldiers, they served only as irregulars (*başıbozuks*). Typically they lived in small communities that they themselves defended and were forced to subsist on agriculture and plunder (allegedly), not receiving sufficient pay for their livelihoods as soldiers.[10] During the 1870s rumors of the Circassians' rapacity abounded among many of the Muslim and Christian inhabitants. Their deteriorating reputation made them particularly unwelcome guests in eastern Anatolia, especially amid the economic and political instability of the era.

The actual effect of the Circassians on eastern Anatolia is much disputed. In 1867 consul J. C. Taylor, on his tour to the southeastern province of Diyarbakır, believed that the "3,000 extra families of 24,000 souls" throughout the province caused significant economic strain, especially since they were crossing the countryside during the grain harvest.[11] Others believed that the influx of immigrant Circassians benefited overall agricultural output by introducing "variations...into its routine by the skills of the newcomers" and created "a desirable fusion of races."[12] Nonetheless, the Circassian migrants' overall lack of political representation at local and state levels made it difficult for them to defend their image and to salvage their reputation. Sufficient evidence to implicate Circassian groups in widespread civil unrest during the 1860s and the 1870s is lacking. Although they may have played a role in plundering and pillaging villages, their tarnished image among the Christians (and Muslims) was sufficient to catch the attention of the Armenian National Assembly, which made a vigorous plea to Russia and Britain to make provisions to contain the Circassians under article 16 of the Treaty of San Stefano and article 61 of the Treaty of Berlin.

Although only a small number of British, American, and Russian diplomats and missionaries served in eastern Anatolia, their influence on international political decisions related to the region and on the local population was so significant that they must be considered actual actors on the eastern Anatolian stage, albeit on an international level. Britain and Russia had kept an eye on the Armenian *millet* since the early nineteenth century. Taking account of the long-standing rivalry between the Armenian Catholic Church and the Gregorian Orthodox Church, the British called for the creation of a separate Armenian Catholic *millet*, which the Ottoman sultan recognized in 1831.[13] British and American Protestant missionaries first went to eastern Anatolia to proselytize the Armenians in the 1810s. They not only had a religious influence on the Armenians through conversion but also had a political influence on them. The missionaries petitioned Western governments for protection of the Protestant Armenians, who in turn petitioned the Ottoman sultan for the creation of a separate Armenian Protestant *millet*, which he recognized in 1848.[14] Missionaries introduced schools to eastern Anatolia, through which they spread Western ideas. For the Kurdish tribes, in contrast, education systems were virtually nonexistent until the 1880s, when the Ottoman state absorbed some of the children of Kurdish tribal elites into the military schools in Istanbul and the major cities of the eastern *vilayets*.[15] Throughout the Tanzimat period the education of Armenians passed from the grasp of the Ottoman state into the hands of Armenian elites and Westerners. Although Armenian education in the east did not spread until the early 1870s, ten years after the establishment of the National Assembly, it grew from 23,000 to 60,000 students between 1872 and 1901.[16]

Missionaries did not directly organize political movements, but they played a crucial role in informing the ethnic identity of the Christian inhabitants of the east and in introducing the poorer classes of Christians to literacy and writing. Toward the end of the nineteenth century, especially after the Russo-Turkish War, missionaries assumed an increasingly political role among the Christian inhabitants as spokespersons for Christian rights and staunch critics of Ottoman governance and in some cases even encouraged violence. For instance consul Albert Charles Wratislaw reported from Erzurum in 1888 that a Protestant school in Harput was teaching students songs "of a rather violent character" that portrayed the Muslims as "religionless" and "pitiless."[17] Foreign diplomats played a more significant role in eastern Anatolia after the Crimean War than they had before it. During the late 1850s and 1860s both Russia and Britain placed consuls in cities throughout the east, including Van, Erzurum, and Diyarbakır.

During the Tanzimat period the traditional horizontal diversity of actors in eastern Anatolia gradually became replaced by vertical diversity. Whereas the earlier type of diversity was based on ethnolinguistic, religious, and lifestyle (nomad, settled, and so forth) differences, the later type was based on differences in class and recognized social status. Ottoman and foreign privileging based on religion and ethnicity was more greatly sensed in eastern Anatolia at the end of the Tanzimat period. An increase of violence between local actors in eastern Anatolia occurred during this period and especially during the Russo-Turkish War (not related to the war itself). The following section seeks to explain the dynamics of and the motivations behind violence during this period by looking at three different levels of conflict: local, state, and international.

LOCAL-LEVEL CONFLICTS OF INTEREST

Local-level conflicts of interest in eastern Anatolia can be defined as disputes between two or more local parties over economic resources and political power that did not directly involve the Ottoman state or its interests. The Ottoman state had been relatively distant from eastern Anatolia until the mid-nineteenth century, so it generally remained a disinterested party in lower-level disputes between local actors and tended to favor groups or individuals who were the most powerful and most in agreement with state interests. In the mid-nineteenth century, however, the Russian threat in the east and sporadic Armenian rebellion prompted it to assume a greater presence in the east.

The main causes of the conflicts of interest at the local level in eastern Anatolia during the early and mid-nineteenth century were related to claims to land, rights of taxation and protection fees, and representative power. Seminomadic pastoral groups, who moved their flocks to different areas depending on the season, often clashed with sedentary agriculturalist groups over the rights to use land as pasture. The seminomadic groups had a military advantage against the sedentary groups, however, because their property was almost entirely mobile and they were more acquainted with the terrain. But the seminomadic groups were not generally united and would often clash with one another over access and rights to political and economic resources.[18] Yet amid tribal politics and power struggles both religious elites (sheikhs) and political elites (*beys* and *mirs*) emerged. They acquired great military prowess and political influence by gaining the support of other tribes, often with the blessing of the Ottoman state. The elites formed tribal confederations throughout eastern Anatolia.

It was not only the tribes who competed for power in eastern Anatolia. A vicious power struggle occurred among the Christians as well. Although Christians are often portrayed by outside observers as a perpetually oppressed group whose plight was only discovered and brought to the attention of outsiders in the mid-nineteenth century, many Christians held high religious and political status. The Catholics of Aghtamar (on an island in Lake Van) held the third highest position in the Gregorian Orthodox Church. Armenians also dominated economic life in Van, Diyarbakır, and Erzurum and were the primary creditors for many prominent state officials in eastern Anatolia. Semiautonomous enclaves of Armenians existed in the Zeytun and Sasun regions. The Nestorian Christians of Hakkari held political power over the region on a par with that of many Kurdish tribes.[19]

Tension had long existed between the Catholic Armenians and the Gregorian Orthodox Armenians. Capt. James Creagh of the British navy observed a great sense of anxiety among Catholic Armenians at Erzurum after the Russians took the city: "they fear[ed] the supremacy of their heretical countrymen, or that of their protecting and sympathetic Russian friends" and "far prefer[red], [according to] their priests[,] the Government of the Sultan to that of the Czar."[20]

The Ottoman state's security and judicial systems did not deeply penetrate eastern Anatolia throughout most of the nineteenth century, so local-level conflicts of interest were generally dealt with by either the tribal confederations or (in cases involving exclusively Christians) the Armenian *millet*.[21] Tribal confederations, which were governed by *mirs* and *beys*, often provided the security for peasants in exchange for a fee and also controlled the resources on the land, being the de facto owners of it. Disputes involving Muslims were handled by Muslim *kadis* (judges), and in eastern Anatolia it was usually the Kurdish elites who occupied these positions.[22] The Kurdish sheikhs of Sufi religious orders and the *beys* played a significant role in conflict resolution between competing Kurdish tribes and between Muslims and Christians.

Major power struggles between elites would often be resolved through brutal and violent means. Yet once a member of a powerful local elite seized power, he could more easily provide security and ensure political stability, albeit in a relatively small region. Bedr Khan (Bedirkhan), for instance, consolidated power in the Bohtan region during the 1830s and 1840s, rising to become one of the most powerful Kurdish *beys* in eastern Anatolia. He gained the support of major tribes and crushed local opposition, including Nestorian tribes in the Hakkari region during the mid-1840s. Bedr Khan's domain during this time was lauded by missionaries and other foreigners for its security.[23] Some historians believe that he "considered Armenians and Kurds on equal terms,"[24] even noting that he arranged marriages between prominent Kurdish and Armenian families, which would take place in the churches.[25]

The paucity of sources makes it difficult to ascertain specifics of local conflict resolution mechanisms in regions other than that of Bedr Khan. Nevertheless it can generally be understood that these mechanisms did not operate by rule of law but in accordance with the preferences of the elites in power. The aforementioned degree of ethnic, linguistic, and religious diversity in the region is an indication that actors were not motivated to commit violence based on ethnic differences alone but that economic and political factors played a role. Economic factors provided an incentive for actors in nineteenth-century eastern Anatolia to maintain order, resorting to violent tactics only in cases where the cost of said violence was less than the potential economic cost that could be incurred without violent action. Violence became a measure of maintaining security amid local disorder. The dissolution of the major *beyliks* (political entity led by a *bey*) by the 1850s (discussed below) left an increasing number of tribes competing with one another for positions of power in the government and for mobile and immobile resources.

Between the 1850s and the 1870s most of the eastern Anatolian countryside witnessed a significant increase in plundering and pillaging by marauding Kurdish nomadic tribes due in part to their poor economic situation and the lack of local and state security. It should be noted that marauding and plundering was not a completely irrational or indiscriminate action on the part of perpetrators. Many of the trends of violence did not appear to be motivated by religious or cultural differences but were a tactic employed to gain economic and political power over the competition. Pastoral tribes regarded Armenian and Muslim peasants as a good source of a protection fee called the *khafir*, and it appears that in most circumstances they were intent on protecting their subjects. For instance, in 1860 Selim Ağa of the Abdurrahmanli clan at Mekkio (in the Van province) killed a rivaling Kurdish *qadi*, Kara Ağaç, for plundering one of his

Armenian subjects' belongings. He subsequently seized the stolen property and returned it to the original Armenian owner.[26]

It is likely that because of the dire economic situation throughout much of eastern Anatolia during the 1860s and 1870s tribes not only attempted to collect the *khafir* at increasingly higher rates but attacked the peasant subjects of rival tribes in order to hurt their economic base. This trend is evident in a report sent by Grigoris Vartabed Aghvanian, the prelate of Muş, to the Armenian patriarch in 1872:

> Whenever [the Kurdish tribes] rise up or engage in hostility against each other, they take their subject Armenians by force, invade each other's territories, and attack particularly Armenian villages, plunder, wound, kill, and then return. The defeated enemy, in order to take revenge, would rise up, invade the villages of the subject Armenians of the enemy, and with...[great] anger, plunder, destroy, ravage, wound, kill, and return.[27]

During and after the Russo-Turkish War this trend appeared to be similar. In July 1877 in the town of Bitlis the Reverend George C. Knapp, an American missionary stationed at Bitlis, reported that a number of local Kurds fended off the attack of an outside Kurdish nomadic group on some local Christians because they regarded them as "their customers."[28] According to a report by Maj. Henry Trotter in 1879, Armenians generally felt the greater threat of violence from Kurdish groups in "neighboring mountains" but were protected by the local *bey*s and *ağa*s, who, in spite of "suffer[ing] terrible oppression at [their] hands," were nonetheless "protected...from external violence."[29]

As noted, in defense of its eastern frontier with Russia the Ottoman state sought throughout the nineteenth century to integrate the eastern Anatolian population into its political and economic system. This led to the rise of a new set of conflicts of interest, as explained in the following section.

STATE-LEVEL CONFLICTS OF INTEREST

Conflicts of interest at the state level include both the Ottoman state's attempts to centralize its power in the east and the local inhabitants' attempts to challenge state authority. Along with the state's centralization efforts came an increase in the drive for taxation and military recruitment, both issues that local eastern Anatolian Muslims and Christians had long tried to avoid. Economic disputes over dues to the state and political struggles over representation and power boundaries caused increasing tension and conflict between locals in eastern Anatolia and the Ottoman state.

Before the Russo-Turkish War two mitigation scenarios for conflicts of interest between the Ottoman state and locals in eastern Anatolia existed. In the first the Ottoman state dissolved local power and enforced its taxation and military policies by force. It provided strong security to prevent opposition movements. In this scenario the state used discriminate violence against specific targets, those ostensibly in opposition to Ottoman policy or deemed to be a threat. In the second scenario the Ottoman state and local actors struck a power-sharing compromise. Typically the Ottoman state would agree to reduce taxes and military obligations on the condition that it would maintain suzerainty over the region. In this scenario the state and local actors engaged in violence against each other when one side believed that the other was overstepping its agreed-upon political boundaries. Violence (when it occurred) was also discriminate, as in the first mitigation scenario, but not as widespread. A third potential mitigation scenario existed in state-level conflict, wherein local actors would entirely secede from state control. Although actors in some subregions of eastern Anatolia did achieve some autonomy, including exemption from taxes and military service, no local political entity ever achieved full independence. The second conflict mitigation scenario between the state and local actors had long played out in eastern Anatolia during most of the Ottoman period. During the late Tanzimat period, however, the first mitigation scenario (wherein the state took increasing control) played out more frequently.

The looming threat of Russia from the east was the major factor that prompted the Ottoman state to integrate eastern Anatolia more into its political and economic system. Once the Ottoman state broke the power of large Kurdish *beylik*s throughout eastern Anatolia with the defeat and exile of Bedr Khan in 1847, it assumed an increasing responsibility for mitigation and resolution of local conflicts in the region (alongside some of the emerging sheikh-dominated tribal confederacies). Its attempts to integrate local actors (both Muslim and Christian) into the administration of the provinces, *sancak*s, and *kaza*s throughout the region during the 1860s and 1870s kept any dominant or popular local leader from gaining a significant degree of power. Yet since the Ottoman state did not have the resources to impose a large number of nonlocal officials on the eastern Anatolian population, it often opted to appoint local elites for the administration of the *kaza*s and *sancak*s.

*Bey*s continued to exist in the Ottoman Empire after the fall of Bedr Khan, but they had less power and were generally more compliant with the Ottoman state than with the sheikhs. As a Russian invasion became more imminent in the mid-1870s, some of the *bey*s in the Van region attempted to play both the Russian and the Ottoman sides to their advantage. For instance, Yusuf Bey, the chief of the *Hayderanlı* tribe (who inhabited the area east of Muş and north of Van), and his son gained increasing power and wealth throughout the early 1870s and threatened to cause civil unrest if the sultan did not give them the rights to the position of *kaymakam* of the Shura-gel region (to the east of Van). The Ottoman officials complied on the condition that the chiefs give them a bribe and conduct raids into Russia (even before the war). To the chagrin of the Ottomans, however, Yusuf Bey also struck a deal with the Russians to supply their armies with grain during the war.[30]

During the 1860s and early 1870s the sheikhs (religious leaders of Kurdish tribes) filled the political vacuum left in the wake of the dissolution of the Kurdish *beylik*s. Like the *bey*s, they commanded the respect of numerous tribes and acted as important figures in local conflict mitigation. Traditionally the sheikhs had been distant from the state, whereas the *bey*s had been relatively close. This is because sheikhs derived their power and wealth not through state-granted administrative status but through their religious devotees, who gave them copious donations of money, material resources, and land. During the Tanzimat period the *bey*s were largely reliant on administrative positions to obtain power and wealth. Bedr Khan Bey, for example, made continual appeals to the *vali*s of Mosul and Diyarbakır during the 1840s to gain privileges in tax collection from the state.[31] Although he did indeed revolt against the Ottomans during the 1840s, he remained a tenuous ally of the state until his death in exile in Syria in 1870. In fact his sons Bedri Bey, Hüseyin Bey, and Ali Shamil Bey gathered more than six thousand volunteers from Istanbul and Syria to fight in the war against Russia in 1877.[32]

In some of the more remote regions the sheikhs became a major impediment to the Ottoman state's centralization efforts, and their allegiance to the Ottoman state was called into question as tensions with Russia increased during the 1870s. The Ottoman state's increased drive to persuade the Kurds in vulnerable regions to pay taxes and to serve in the military prompted many Kurds to side with Iran and Russia in hopes of achieving greater autonomy.[33]

The Dersim region, long a quasi-autonomous enclave between Sivas and Erzincan, illustrates a case in point of the sheikhs' resistance to the

Ottoman state. While the Ottoman state had long enjoyed a strong relationship with the family of Hüseyin Bey during the early Tanzimat period,
Sheikh Süleyman (one of the leading religious figures of the region) remained a perpetual menace for the Ottomans. By the 1860s he is said
to have enjoyed the allegiance of some five thousand followers. Ali Bey,
the grandson of Hüseyin Bey, acting as tax collector over Dersim, faced
significant difficulty in persuading those loyal to Sheikh Süleyman to pay
full taxes to the Ottoman state and to comply with the conventional laws
of conscription.[34] The mounting tension between the sheikhs and the
Ottoman state is further illustrated by the Dersim sheikhs' refusal to negotiate. When the sultan ordered Ahmet Muhtar Paşa to hold talks with
the leading sheikhs and *beys* in the Dersim region to given them an incentive to pledge their allegiance to the Ottoman state, only Hüseyin Bey (the
son of the aforementioned Ali Bey) and Gülâbi Bey (the *kaymakam* of
Mazgirt) participated. Notably absent were Sheikh Süleyman and Mansur
Ağa, another powerful elite leader in the Dersim region. Gülâbi Bey's participation was not taken well by the religious sheikh class, who ambushed
him and killed him upon his return.[35]

During the 1870s the Russians, hoping to sway the inhabitants of
Dersim to their side because of its strategic location near Erzurum, sought
Sheikh Süleyman as an ally.[36] Sultan Abdülaziz commissioned Samih Paşa
to go to Dersim in 1875 to entice Kurdish leaders to side with the Ottomans against Russia. The religious class, having infiltrated tribal politics
more than the Ottoman state expected, remained unmoved in its resistance to the Ottoman state. Sheikh Süleyman managed to accumulate a
large number of weapons from the Russians and to mobilize a formidable
force of 12,000 soldiers, including the militias of numerous tribes, against
the Ottoman forces. Although he led resistance against the Ottoman state,
he was eventually routed and exiled.[37] Despite Ottoman attempts to take
control of Dersim, Russian victories in Kars and Beyazıt during the war
gave Dersimi tribes impetus to engage Ottoman forces once again in the
summer of 1877. The Fourth Ottoman Brigade entered a number of villages in the Toşik mountains to drive out rebels, but local religious elites
called upon Armenian and Kurdish groups to take up arms and fend off
the Turkish invasion.[38]

In the Hakkari region (southeast of Van on the border with Iran) the
Ottoman state made a similar effort in the 1870s to collect taxes and build
its armed forces in order to counteract potential military penetration by
Russia from the north and penetration by Iran from the west and also to
defray the costs of the economic crisis of 1873. By "doubling of the taxes

upon the tobacco production" in 1876, it severely affected the wealth and properties of Sheikh Ubeydullah, who reaped half of the revenue from the tobacco production.[39] Sheikh Ubeydullah was well aware of international politics and the concentration of Armenians to the north of him in Van and feared that they could gain increasing power over his economic and political domains with a Russian occupation. He therefore decided to remain loyal to the Ottoman state. According to Seyit Islam Geylani, Ubeydullah gathered a force of some 40,000 troops from Diyarbakır, Van, Urmiye, and Süleimaniye to fight against the Russians during the Russo-Turkish War of 1877–78.[40]

Fears that the Armenians would completely seize control of Van during the war prompted Ubeydullah and other sheikhs to undertake what seemed to be indiscriminate violence against the Armenians in the region, under orders not from the Ottoman military but from Kurdish elite organizers of volunteer forces. C. B. Norman writes that the Kurdish volunteers acted "in obedience to the summons of...Sheikh Jelaludeen, Obaidulah [*sic*]...[all of whom were] under the command of Kurd Ismail Pasha" and entered Van in fear of an Armenian takeover of the city in the event of Russian penetration in the south. En route to Van they "committed much damage, attacking...[Armenian] caravan[s]..., murder[ing] three chief men..., [and] gut[ting]...villages."[41]

Sheikh Ubeydullah and Sheikh Jelaluddin apparently hoped to use the Ottoman state's war with Russia as leverage to gain increasing independence in the Hakkari and Urmiye (in Iran) regions. Sheikh Jelaluddin of Urmiye had been accused of switching allegiances back and forth between the Ottoman Empire and Iran in order to leverage one against the other.[42] Sheikh Ubeydullah appeared to be operating at the time under Sheikh Jelaluddin in order to promote Kurdish autonomy.[43] Indeed the Ottoman state appeared to perceive Jelaluddin as posing a greater threat than Ubeydullah. Sultan Abdülhamid II ordered the *vali* of Van to poison Jelaluddin as punishment for his treasonous tendencies; however, he punished Ubeydullah only by sending him on a mandatory *hajj* to Mecca.[44]

Generally violence initiated by the Ottoman state against the Kurds was a last resort to impose taxation and military policies. In most cases the state resorted to violence after some attempt at diplomacy and negotiation. Kurdish groups and individuals perpetrating violence against the Ottoman state targeted mainly lower-level state officials, because the Ottoman military was a much stronger force than the Kurdish militias. While Kurdish *beys* (who relied largely on the state for their power) were more open to negotiation and diplomacy, the religious leaders (who derived their political status and legitimacy from local culture) were arguably less open to diplomacy as a means of conflict resolution with the state. As local power in eastern Anatolia became more fragmented and unpredictable, the economy was increasingly strained, the means of law enforcement remained meager, and the pressures of taxation and military enrollment grew, many local Muslim elites saw the cost of violence as lower than the cost of diplomacy. Furthermore, actors increased in their willingness to revolt in these economically trying conditions of the 1860s and 1870s. Their hope was not that they could actually overcome state power but that they might at least be able to increase the burden upon the state to enforce its policy, giving it a disincentive for its drive and either keeping or increasing their autonomy.

The conflict of interests existing between the state and the Armenians was traditionally more indirect than that between the local eastern Anatolian Muslims and the Ottoman state. Historically the Armenian peasants in the east did not serve in the Ottoman military, or at least paid the *bedel* tax to exempt themselves from service after the 1856 Tanzimat edict. Moreover, even after the edict of 1856, Ottoman military leaders were not particularly intent on increasing the number of Christians in their ranks. While the Ottomans did directly tax the Armenians, their grievances about burdensome taxation were mainly against the local Muslim collectors of private protection taxes (*khafir*) rather than the taxes to the state itself. With war looming, however, the Ottoman state's push for taxes and agricultural goods to finance and feed its mobilizing forces grew burdensome for the Armenian peasants. Gen. Ivan Lazarev of the Russian army notes that the Ottoman state demanded from the Armenians in Sasun a monetary sum of two *mecidiye*s (Ottoman coins) as tribute (*imdat*). The onus was so great that many were "forced to sell all of their belongings in order to pay the *imdat*."[45]

Unlike the Kurdish tribes, the Armenian peasants (*rayeh*) had no central local figure such as a *bey* or sheikh around which they could mobilize resistance and force negotiation. The Kurdish tribes could easily hide in the mountains and forestall Ottoman centralization efforts by wreaking havoc, but the Armenian peasants were sedentary and offered an easy target for aggressors. The cost of violence generally outweighed the cost of compliance with heavy demands. Trends of Armenian violence in eastern Anatolia against local Kurdish tribes and the Ottoman state generally involved an external intermediary such as the British, Russians, or expatriate Armenians and can be more fully understood in the light of international conflict.

INTERNATIONAL-LEVEL CONFLICTS
OF INTEREST AND EASTERN ANATOLIA

In short, eastern Anatolia became increasingly subsumed within the general international conflict of interests going on between Russia and Britain throughout most of the nineteenth century. The political objective of Russia since the late eighteenth century had been to expand its hegemony over the Ottoman Empire in order to gain access to the Mediterranean Sea to gain greater commercial dominance. Part of its strategy in accomplishing this objective was to aid and abet nationalist sentiment among the Christian populations in the Balkans and in eastern Anatolia. Claiming to be the protector of the Christians in the Muslim world, Russia systematically sought to attract more Christians to its side and to divide the Ottoman Empire. Initially the Greeks and the Serbs were the target of Russia's instigation efforts; but after Russia captured Erzurum in 1829 (which it later returned to the Ottomans), it gradually sought to pit the Armenians against the Ottoman state.

Britain, fearing Russian encroachment upon its own political domain, sought a number of countermeasures to blunt the force of Russia's invasive foreign policy toward the Ottoman Empire. Too weak to occupy and secure the entire empire by itself, Britain favored Ottoman integrity, although it did seek economic and political control in the empire without formal territorial acquisitions. Britain's policy toward the Christians in the Ottoman Empire can be interpreted as a means to sway them toward the Ottoman side and against the Russians. The various reforms for Christians undertaken throughout the Tanzimat period can generally be understood as the primary product of Ottoman compliance with what were primarily British interests. Yet the political struggle building between Britain and Russia lured the Ottoman state into greater political and economic involvement in eastern Anatolia, which in turn politicized eastern Anatolia's Armenians.

News of significant political decisions and events spread remarkably quickly throughout eastern Anatolia, even apparently in areas distant from modern communication systems (although it should be noted that the information exchanged may not always have been completely accurate). Local inhabitants in eastern Anatolia were well aware of Russia's activities and speculated about the potential political implications of the war not only for the economy and the land but also for their future livelihoods. Hormuzd Rassam, a British diplomat of Assyrian lineage who was sent by Britain in April 1877 to report on the war, notes that during his visit to

Zamboor (a small village in the southeast near Diyarbakır) his hosts were
"all chatting as loud as they could about the war and its consequences."[46] It
is highly likely that the local Muslim inhabitants were acutely aware of the
displacements that the Crimean War had caused because of the increase in
Circassian migrants in eastern Anatolia. They probably feared that, in the
event of a Russian invasion, they could be either killed or forced off their
lands to create an Armenian state. Local Muslim actors were also aware
that they had little potential leverage on the international level (unlike
the situation in their conflicts of interest with the Ottomans). Anxieties
caused by political uncertainties involving powerful external actors induced a relatively large (although small in percentage compared to all
Muslims) group of eastern Anatolian Muslims to employ physical and
economic violence against Christians.

     In the absence of strong central leadership that could ensure economic
sufficiency and political stability for local inhabitants, it was common for
tribes to loot Christians' properties throughout eastern Anatolia at any
time during the 1860s and early 1870s. But major attacks seemed to coincide with significant international events involving the Ottoman Empire.
For instance, the Hercegovina Rebellion of 1875 and the Bulgarian Uprising of 1876 prompted anxiety about the Armenians among many of the
Muslim inhabitants. This is evidenced by an extraordinary attack on the
city of Van (where Armenians constituted a majority) on December 18,
1876, by a group of Kurdish brigands, which resulted in the burning of
"three-fourths of the business quarter of the town, estimated to be from
800 to 1,000 buildings, occupied entirely by Christian traders."[47] Kurdish
raiders also stole most of the Armenians' property before they burned it.
An article in the Armenian newspaper *Mshag* in February 1878 reflects on
the implications of the violence as strictly tied to the palpable fear about
Russian intervention on the part of the Kurds. The Kurds reportedly in-
sulted Armenians, saying: "[Y]ou are of the same belief as these Gavur
Russians!"[48]

     An incident in Bitlis in January 1877 further illustrates conflict out of
anxiety about Russian intervention. The tribes around Bitlis and Muş took
"advantage of the disorganized state of the country and the weakness of
the Government to commence raids on an extensive scale," although the
winter snows had not melted. In this instance, however, it appears that
the Kurdish brigands acted out of a hope of cashing in. It was rumored
that they offered to spare the Christians plunder and robbery, and potential murder, if they were paid a yearly stipend of "200 piastres."[49] Upon

hearing news that the Kurds were advancing on villages, inhabitants barricaded their homes and kept themselves armed. They also closed the bazaars during midday. Significantly, the Ottoman governor-general Samih Paşa, when requested by consul J. Zohrab, said that he could not spare any troops to provide adequate security because if "he gave soldiers to protect every town which was [then] menaced by Koords, he would be left without an army to protect the frontier or garrison the fortresses."[50] Locals should set up their own police forces, he added.

According to Hormuzd Rassam, rumors of Kurdish attacks throughout southeastern Anatolia increased after the war of 1877–78 started. The main reason was that the Ottomans displaced security troops in the southeast interior regions of eastern Anatolia, which were far from the Russian border, to the frontier in order to fortify Ottoman forces against Russian advancements. In addition, Kurdish/Muslim volunteers for the war were not given sufficient supplies and relied on the villages through which they passed to provide food and shelter. Villages were generally lacking in produce themselves (due to the decrease in the number of tillers and the Ottoman demands for supplies), so plundering was often preferred to begging.[51]

Whereas the conflict of interest between the Ottoman state and the Kurds was rooted in the question of autonomy within the state and access to economic resources, the conflict of interest between the Ottoman state and the Armenians by the time of the Russo-Turkish War of 1877–78 was rooted in representation of ethnic/religious interests in the state and the security of peasants in the countryside. The Armenians became the anchor of Russian hegemony in eastern Anatolia and brought international conflicts of interest into the eastern Anatolian playing field as a result of their presence. The Armenian *millet*, while traditionally controlled by the Ottoman state, gradually became the bulwark of international interests. Britain and Russia competed for influence. The British tried to sway the Armenians toward Ottoman loyalty, while the Russians incited them against the Ottoman state.

The *millet* was the structure created by the Ottoman state through which it had long governed its relationship with all of the Armenians throughout the empire. Conflicts of interest between the state and the Armenians had been historically regulated through the *millet*, which served as the intermediary between the state and the non-Muslim populations of the empire. The sultan appointed the head of the Armenian *millet*, who in turn maintained the right to administer the judicial and religious affairs of the empire's subject Armenians. The administrators of the *millet* derived their power and status directly from the state, so they were historically close to the Sublime Porte and the sultan.

Because the center of the Armenian *millet*'s power was western Turkey (mainly Istanbul but also some other cities such as İzmit and Smyrna), the Armenians in eastern Anatolia had little representation. Generally the *millet*'s decision-making reflected the interests of the more educated and commercial *amira* class. The Ottoman state had traditionally relied on its close relations with the Armenian *amira* class, which had a strong influence over the appointment of the Armenian *milletbaşı* (head of the *millet*). In turn the Armenian *milletbaşı* maintained jurisdiction over all political affairs related to Catholic and Gregorian Armenians and Nestorian Christians throughout the empire. Members of the *amira* class supported the integrity of the Ottoman Empire primarily because they partially derived their wealth by funding the Ottoman tax-farming system. The international conflict of economic interests, however, significantly disrupted the traditional relationship between the Ottoman state and the Armenian *millet*. After the Commercial Convention of Balta Liman between Britain and the Ottoman Empire in 1838 (under which the Ottoman sultan agreed to allow Britain to regulate multinational trade) and the Hatt-ı Şerif of Gülhane in 1839 (which abolished the tax-farming system) the *amira* class no longer supplied the bulk of the money to fund the Porte's activities and lost influence in the affairs of the *millet*. Its decline in power opened the doors for non-*amira* Armenian intellectuals and the Armenian merchant class (*esnaf*), who traveled and lived throughout a greater number of the Ottoman lands inhabited by the Armenians, to gain greater representation in the political affairs of the *millet*.

For the Armenians in eastern Anatolia, the *millet* structure was quite burdensome. It was particularly keen on forbidding them from assimilating into the culture of local Muslim neighbors and enforced harsh penalties on critics of the *millet* and violators of its rules. Grievances among Armenian parties were settled through the Gregorian Armenian *millet* and not through the Ottoman state, so Armenians who felt wronged by the *millet* had no recourse in the state. Only Armenians of the Gregorian Orthodox Church were appointed to head the *millet*, creating longstanding tensions between the Gregorian Armenians and the Catholic Armenians. The Catholic population (which had existed in the area since the Crusaders first entered Cilicia in the twelfth century) often accused the Gregorian Armenians of discrimination against them in dispute settlements. The Ottoman state, acting in the interest of maintaining a unified Armenian *millet* under a small and compliant leadership, preferred not to intervene in the affairs of the *millet* on behalf of the Catholic Armenians. It was not until the early nineteenth century that the Catholic Armenians found recourse in the European missionaries, whom they asked to petition the Ottoman Empire on their behalf. After the Ottoman state's granting of a separate Catholic *millet* in 1831, a pattern of external leveraging began to emerge.

External leveraging was a process through which politically conscious but underrepresented Armenian individuals and groups used an external agent such as the Russians, British, or Americans to acquire power within the Ottoman state or to persuade the Ottoman state to act on their behalf. Local eastern Anatolian Armenians would bring their complaints directly to American or British missionaries or travelers, who would lobby their own governments on behalf of a particular Armenian group (mainly the Catholics or the Protestants). The foreign government would then put pressure on the Ottoman government to make legal concessions. Armenians who were not Gregorian Orthodox and did not want to be under the control of the Gregorian *milletbaşı* initially sought recourse through external (generally British or American) missionaries or travelers. By 1850 the Ottomans had created three separate *millet*s for the Armenians at the behest of the British government. This ushered in a period of radical new changes to the *millet*, which drastically affected its role in eastern Anatolian politics.

The implementation of the constitution of the Armenian *millet* in 1860 was a watershed event for the affairs of the Gregorian Armenian *millet*. It provided that the patriarch of Istanbul would be elected, created a national assembly through which *millet* policy was shaped, and offered a way for the previously underrepresented Armenians of eastern Anatolia to have a voice in affairs that no longer concerned only the *millet* but the Armenian nation in the Ottoman Empire. Megerditch Khrimian (1820–1907) is one of the greatest examples of the powerful voice that eastern Anatolian Armenians were acquiring as a result of the changes in the *millet* structure.

An Armenian priest from Van, Khrimian was arguably one of the greatest beneficiaries of the Armenian constitution. Having served in clerical positions in Istanbul, eastern Anatolia, and the Caucasus and published a number of periodicals, newspapers, pamphlets, and booklets during the 1850s and 1860s, he gained popularity among the lower-class Armenians, particularly in eastern Anatolia. His election to the patriarchate of Istanbul in 1869 was in large part due to them. As patriarch he played an active role in lobbying the Ottoman sultanate on behalf of the eastern Anatolian Armenians for increased security, submitting a long line of reports to the sultan about alleged attacks against Armenians. During the chaotic 1860s and 1870s, when the eastern Anatolian Armenians suffered the most at the hands of lawless tribal attacks, Khrimian played a crucial role in leveraging the support of Britain on behalf of the Armenians in the east. It was in Britain's interest to cooperate with Khrimian not necessarily because of the pathos of his plea but because the British favored (even before Khrimian) general Armenian support of the Ottomans and feared Russia's ability to instill the eastern Anatolian Armenians with a pro-Russian political consciousness. Britain hoped to influence Khrimian to sway the eastern Anatolian Armenians against Russia.[52]

It should be noted, however, that members of the wealthy Armenian class in Istanbul were not particularly keen on Khrimian's activism. One wrote that Khrimian spoke so much about the conditions in eastern Anatolia that he "endangered the nation."[53] Frustrated by the western Armenian elite's cold reception and under indirect pressure from the Ottoman state, Khrimian resigned in 1873. Despite his resignation, he remained a popular voice among the Armenians and the de facto representative of the Armenians in eastern Anatolia. He became particularly vocal in 1876 and 1877 when international conflict was looming. In January 1877 Khrimian wrote *Vankoyzh* (The Plight of Van), an elegy for the Armenian victims of the fire at Van in December 1876. Although he did not clearly pronounce support for a Russian invasion, his rhetoric in *Vankoyzh* certainly had an anti-Ottoman and pro-Russian tinge: "[D]o not wait a moment, for our world is winter, snow and frost are on the roofs, but *spring is near*, oh Armenian nation."[54] The Ottoman Empire, concerned that this booklet would incite the Armenians in the east to rebel as the Christians in the Balkans had done, tried to halt its circulation. Khrimian published more copies of the booklet in Tbilisi, and it circulated throughout the major cities and towns of eastern Anatolia.[55]

After the war between Russia and Turkey broke out, Khrimian wrote a second elegy entitled *Haykoyzh* (The Plight of the Armenians), in which he more clearly expressed his lamentation for the whole of the Armenian nation and the call for rebellion: "[O]h how necessary are the sword and blood; indeed are the swordless and bloodless not brought to naught by destitution?"[56] Before the Treaty of Berlin Khrimian had established himself as the primary activist voice on behalf of the Armenians and played a crucial role in Armenian politics, which only added to the already existing tensions within the Armenian *millet*.

Nerses Varjabedian, elected patriarch in 1873 after Khrimian stepped down, took a much different approach to the Armenian question. During the 1860s, while in the National Assembly, he made "acrimonious" speeches against the Russians.[57] In fact during the mid-1870s he showed himself to be more pro-Ottoman than pro-Russian. Particularly notable is an encyclical (*gontag* or *kondak*) that he published on the eve of the Russo-Turkish War in which he lauds the Ottoman Empire, referring to it as a benevolent power and longtime protector of the Armenian peoples for the last five centuries. In this same encyclical he places some blame on the Ottoman Empire for indiscretions and lack of security and even claims that these problems have increased in recent years, but he remarks that "these types of indiscretions injure only the body and are far from the types of indiscretions that injure both soul and body and that threaten the existence of the nation."[58] Even after the Russo-Turkish War started, he continued to refer to the Ottoman state as a "benevolent power" (*parekhnam derutiun*), albeit with some flaws, in an address to the Armenian National Assembly in May 1877. In the conclusion of his address he remarked: "When Midhat Paşa made a visit to the Patriarchate I said that only our Armenian nation is loyal to the Ottoman regime. Be careful lest others benefit from our disunity."[59]

In his novel *The Fool* (*Khente*) Raffi, a pro-Russian Armenian activist who worked with Khrimian, captures the division between Armenians on the eve of the Russo-Turkish War in a fictional dialogue between Tomas Effendi, an Armenian tax collector, and Vartan, an Armenian commoner from the east. Tomas Effendi boasts that Patriarch Nerses Varjabedian referred to him as "my son" but was not too keen on Khrimian, "because he was common and allowed himself to be drawn into talks with the *hamals* [porters] from Moush." In a heated discussion with Vartan, he refers to the Slavic revolutionaries as "fools" for rising up against the Ottoman state. Vartan retorts that it is elitist Armenians like Tomas Effendi who "suck the blood of the Armenians because of the lawless Turkish government" and "will always be supported by the unjust, criminal government."[60]

As Russia's victory over Turkey in the east became clearer during the war, Patriarch Nerses lost significant leverage among the Armenian community to Khrimian. At a meeting with high-ranking Gregorian Armenian bishops at his house in 1877 Khrimian denounced the policy of Patriarch Nerses as "unacceptable" and demanded his replacement.[61] Fearing that his pro-Ottoman tendencies might pit both an increasing number of Armenians and a potential Russian overlord against him, Patriarch Nerses almost immediately began to promote a softer policy toward Russia. In early February 1878 he even met secretly with the Armenian National Assembly and other Armenian elites to compose a memorandum proposing that eastern Anatolia ("the territory as far as the Euphrates") be given to Russia. Despite his ostensible shift in attitude

toward the Russians, Nerses much preferred an independent Armenian
state to Russian control. In private correspondence with Prince Alexander Gorchakov, which he wrote at the time when he was drafting the
memorandum with other Armenian elites, he asked that the Armenians
be able to "live in an Armenia under [their] own rule."[62] Undoubtedly
Khrimian felt vindicated in his decades of activism. On hearing the news
that the British had agreed to lobby for the Ottomans to maintain full
control over eastern Anatolia, Patriarch Nerses, whose legitimacy was
slipping, sent Khrimian to the Congress of Berlin as an advocate on behalf of the Armenians.

Several factors contributed to the Armenian delegation's failure to
gain access or recognition for an independent Armenian state. First,
Khrimian was not a politician but a cleric and was by no means a good
negotiator. When asked how he would communicate his plan to the diplomats and negotiators, he said that he use an international language because he spoke only Armenian and Turkish: "I will cry in front of them,
[for] tears are the shared language of all people. It is not possible that
there will be someone who will not understand."[63] Second, it was not in
the interest of Britain to create an independent or semiautonomous Armenian state, which would be a major advantage to the Russians. Third,
Russia did not actually occupy much of the region inhabited by Armenians. Russian troops only reached as far west as Erzurum and as far south
as Beyazıt. The Van, Diyarbakır, Bitlis, and Sivas regions, which were inhabited by a sizable number of Armenians, were still under full Ottoman
control after the war. Had article 16 of the Treaty of San Stefano (which
stipulated that Russian troops would remain in areas that the Russians
had occupied) remained in force, it would only have applied to a small
portion of the Armenian lands. Even though article 61 of the Treaty of
Berlin stipulated the same provisions for the Armenians as in the Treaty
of San Stefano with the exception of Russian troops, Khrimian promoted
the article as a significant setback for the Armenians in the quest to
achieve independence from the Ottoman state. He vividly expressed his
disillusionment with international politics in regard to the Armenians in
a speech that he gave in Istanbul after returning from the Berlin Conference. Most remarkably, in the speech he called for Armenians to continue
their struggle against tribal indiscretions and the Ottoman state through
armed resistance:

> "Oh Armenian people, understand well what weapons could have
> done and do; therefore beloved and blessed people of Hayasdan

[Armenia], and those in the provinces, when you return to the fatherland give your friends and relatives arms as a bounty one by one, take up arms again and again.... Man must labor by his own strength in order to be saved."[64]

While Khrimian did not physically organize revolutionary groups among the Armenians, his sermons provided legitimacy to those types of groups.

Although international conflicts of interest had no direct effect on most of the inhabitants of eastern Anatolia, they contributed to the motivations behind violence in two ways. First, they created an unpredictable political environment that increased the anxiety of local inhabitants, who consequently became more open to violence as a means of achieving security. Actors did not need to have a complete understanding of the scope and implications of international war and diplomacy to have a local reaction. In many cases actors took swift actions based upon misreadings of international diplomacy. For instance, Sheikh Ubeydullah launched his rebellion against the Ottoman state partly on the notion that the British were colluding with the Armenians and Nestorians to take control of the Van region, which was not the case. He is quoted as saying: "What is this I hear, that the Armenians are going to have an independent state in Van, and that the Nestorians are going to hoist the British flag and declare themselves British subjects? I will never permit it, even if I have to arm the women."[65]

Second, international conflicts of interest disrupted the regular order of state-local and local-local interactions, thus creating opportunities for ambitious actors to seize power. Amid recklessly swift lurches toward power, competing actors would often find themselves in a violent struggle. The attacks of Kurdish tribes upon villages can be interpreted as a product of an intertribal power struggle where the motivating factor was not fear of the Great Powers but fear of the local Muslim rival. This explains the higher incidence of violence in rural regions in southeastern Anatolia during the war, where the victims of violent acts were not only Christian peasants but the *ağas* of Muslim villages and tribal chiefs.[66]

TENUOUS SECURITY AMID LINGERING TENSIONS

The war left the Ottoman Empire economically devastated. In the fiscal year 1877–78 the Ottoman state had a budget deficit of 50 percent below its revenues. In spite of this, its expenses were astronomical. The cost of supporting the armed forces in feeding and housing Muslim refugees from the Balkans reached 2.59 billion kuruş, nearly five times the annual revenue.[67] The Ottoman state emerged from the Russo-Turkish War deeply indebted. The war indemnity imposed upon it by Russia "increased Ottoman indebtedness by one-sixth" and placed the empire's already unstable credit in further jeopardy.[68] Officials kept the repayment of European bondholders as their main priority in order to avoid economic sanctions, so the state was forced to pay its security forces low wages. The Russo-Turkish War also contributed in part to the decline of trade between Trabzon and Tebriz, which had previously been relatively profitable, especially for Christian traders in Erzurum and Van. But Russia's imposition of excises on previously tax-free imports (a frigid political gesture in response to Britain's support of the Ottomans during the war) contributed to the gradual decline of the trade route. The British consul in Tebriz revealed in 1885 that the trade between Trabzon and Erzurum alone, which had grossed 2.4 million pounds in 1875, had since decreased to under 1.1 million pounds.[69]

Famine was widespread throughout the provinces of eastern Anatolia during the summer of 1880. Among the primary causes were the poor harvests due to the lack of young men to "till the ground,"[70] the population influx caused by the settlement of Balkan Muslims in the region (and specifically in the outlying regions of eastern Anatolia), and the increase in raids and depredations of Kurdish tribes against settled peasantry populations due to perceived scarcity of food.[71] The inhabitants of the region bordering Iran and Russia appear to have borne the brunt of the famine. In spite of Britain and France's efforts to alleviate the situation by sending wheat and seeds, the tribes still committed indirect economic violence against the Christian populations by stealing aid and blocking the paths of delivery.[72]

The war and its settlement also indirectly prompted nearly 82,000 Muslims (11,000 from Kars alone) to flee from Russia for various reasons, including fear of reprisal against them for siding with the Ottomans, the decrease in rights, and loss of property.[73] On September 15, 1878, numerous Armenians were reported to have fled Erzurum, seeking asylum in Russia due to fear that Muslims would take revenge upon the Armenians for allegedly aiding in the Russian occupation of the city during the war. Muslims fleeing Russia occupied the lands and properties deserted by the Armenians.[74] Those Muslim refugees from Russia joined hundreds of thousands of other Muslim migrants from the Balkans. The Ottoman government bore the burdensome and costly responsibility of sustaining and settling them. Unlike the Circassian exodus from Russian during the late 1850s and early 1860s, which resulted in a large influx of migrants into the southeastern Anatolian countryside, relatively few of the Balkan Muslims were settled in Diyarbakır and Van. This was not only due to their distance from the Balkans but also at the behest of local Armenian leaders, who feared that new migrants would act as the Circassians had and claimed that the instability of the region made it unsuitable for incoming refugees.[75]

Sultan Abdülhamid II was left with the burden of reintegrating an economically devastated and socially traumatized eastern Anatolia into the political and economic structure of the Ottoman state. The notion that the region could potentially slip into the hands of Russia via the Armenians, and perhaps even via the Kurds to a lesser extent, undoubtedly gave impetus to his defensive policies in regard to eastern Anatolia during the 1880s. Based on an understanding that the continuation of political anarchy in the region would only benefit Russia, the sultan launched a great effort to centralize control by dissolving local power blocs among the tribal leaders and exiling recalcitrant actors. He acted partly out of obligation as a protector of Armenians and partly as a means of clinging onto what little territory the Ottoman Empire had left. Notwithstanding the economic and social woes in eastern Anatolia, it is significant that Abdülhamid II managed to muster up enough force to quell Armenian rebellions in Zeytun in 1878 and 1879,[76] diffuse the revolt of Sheikh Ubeydullah in 1880 (albeit after numerous attempts), and dissolve latent Armenian revolutionary organizations in Van and Erzurum in 1878 and 1882.[77]

A mark of Sultan Abdülhamid II's success in the 1880s was the report on the fact-finding mission in Van, Bitlis, and Muş in the summer of 1889 of Col. Herbert Chermside, the British consul. Despite lingering tensions between Kurds and Armenians, Chermside noted that relations between the Kurds and the Armenians had undergone a marked improvement from the situation during the Russo-Turkish War: "[O]utrages by the Kurds on Christians, inter-tribal feuds, highway robbery, cattle lifting, all exist"; but "none appear to [be] as frequent and as wholesale as they were" ten years ago, when he was last there. Aside from the indiscretions of Musa Bey in the region of Muş, Kurdish attacks on Armenians were "rare."[78] It is beyond the scope of this paper to explain the violence that occurred en masse in eastern Anatolia during the 1890s. But by ending on this note I hope to avoid the all too common assumption that Abdülhamid II's policies in eastern Anatolia were generally a failure. To the contrary, he did manage to achieve a degree of success with regard to centralizing the state's military control over the region. When he inherited the empire from his predecessors, however, the indigenous social and political structures of eastern Anatolia had already been demolished. His exile of Sheikh Ubeydullah put an end to the major local Muslim power-holders in eastern Anatolia. During the reign of Abdülhamid II eastern Anatolia became dependent on the state for security and political stability, but the state at times found itself lacking the resources to fulfill these tasks.

CONCLUSION

Violence in eastern Anatolia before and during the Russo-Turkish War of 1877–78 was generally perpetrated in response to the local-level conflicts of interest. Actors committing the violence were ultimately interested in their own shares of economic and political power, which typically did not extend beyond the immediate eastern Anatolian region. The motivation behind locally perpetrated violence in eastern Anatolia was anxiety over the conditions of livelihood in the event of failing to act violently. The Ottoman state's tenuous central control over eastern Anatolia during the 1860s and 1870s created political anarchy among local actors. It dissolution of the *beyliks* kept strong local actors from emerging and contributed to the perpetuation of local power struggles, in which Christians were often targeted. International conflicts of interest did not directly cause violence in eastern Anatolia. But they created new and more widespread conflicts of interest between local actors. The indigenous population often responded violently.

NOTES

1. Compare Wheeler M. Thackston, *Kurmanji Kurdish: A Reference Grammar*; and Wheeler M. Thackston, *Sorani Kurdish: A Reference Grammar with Selected Readings*.
2. Arthur John Maclean, *Grammar of the Dialects of Vernacular Syriac*, xv–xvi.
3. Herachyah Adjarian, *Classification des dialectes arméniens*, 15, 44.
4. *Bitlis Gazette*, October 17, 1889, cited in Şerif Mardin, *Religion and Social Change in Modern Turkey: The Case of Bediüzzaman Said Nursi*, 254.
5. Kemal Beydilli, "1828–1829 Osmanlı-Rus Savaşında Doğu Anadolu'dan Rusya'ya Göçürülen Ermeniler," 410.
6. Bedri Habiçoğlu, *Kafkasya'dan Anadolu'ya Göçler ve İskanları*, 71.
7. Kemal H. Karpat, "Millets and Nationality: The Roots of the Incongruity of Nation and State in the Post-Ottoman Era," 654.
8. Vital Cuinet estimates the population of Circassians at 60,000 in the 1880s. He does not give a figure for Erzurum, although it can be assumed that the Circassian population was relatively high there because of its proximity to the Russian

border. See Mesrob K. Krikorian, *Armenians in the Service of the Ottoman Empire, 1860–1908*, 48.

9. Ibid., 20, 28, 34. While Cuinet's estimates are extremely loose, it is significant that he estimates the Circassian population of Van to be much lower than in other regions.

10. James J. Reid, *Crisis of the Ottoman Empire: Prelude to Collapse*, 146–47.

11. Cited in A. Üner Turgay, "Circassian Immigration into the Ottoman Empire, 1856–1878," 214.

12. Cited in ibid.

13. John Wooley, "The Armenian Catholic Church: A Study in History and Ecclesiology."

14. Agop Jack Hacikyan, Gabriel Basmajian, and Edward S. Franchuk, *The Heritage of Armenian Literature: From the Eighteenth Century until Modern Times*, 20.

15. Bayram Kodaman, "Hamidiye Hafif Süvari Alayları (II. Abdülhamid ve Doğu Aşiretleri)," 427–80.

16. Pamela Young, "Knowledge, Nation, and the Curriculum: Ottoman Armenian Education (1853–1915)," 96–97.

17. Consul Wratislaw to Sir W. White, National Archives of the United Kingdom (formerly Public Record Office), Foreign Office Archives, London (FO), FO 424/145, no. 58/1, cited in Bilal N. Şimşir, ed., *British Documents on Ottoman Armenians*, 2:557.

18. The defense of honor, as in blood feuds, was another source of conflict and motivation for violence between families and tribes, but this did not take primacy over other preeminent economic and political issues.

19. Michel Chevalier, *Les montagnards chrétiens du Hakkâri et du Kurdistan septentrional*, 195–211.

20. Creagh cited in Maulavi Ali Cheragh, *The Proposed Political, Legal, and Social Reforms in the Ottoman Empire and Other Mohammadan States*, 84.

21. Vartan Artinian, *The Armenian Constitutional System in the Ottoman Empire: A Study of Its Historical Development*, 64–69.

22. We know from research done by Hümeyra Zerdeci in the Müftülük Archives that a sizable number of *ulema* whose biographies are in archives were born in eastern Anatolia (773 out of 5,966), which serves as an indication that they were not supplied from the other parts of the Ottoman Empire. His research shows that the *ulema* born in eastern Anatolia took positions there as well. It is not possible to determine that they were Kurds, but it is likely that many of them were. See Hümeyra Zerdeci, *Osmanlı Ulema Biyografilerinin Arşiv Kaynakları*, 45–46.

23. Sarah Shields, *Mosul before Iraq: Like Bees Making Five-Sided Cells*, 53.

24. Hagop Shahbazian, *Krda-Hay Patmutiune*, 86, cited in Garo Sasuni, *Kürt Ulusal Hareketleri ve Ermeni-Kürt İlişkileri (15.yy'dan Günümüze)*, 71.

25. Celilê Celil, *XIX. Yüzyıl Osmanlı İmparatorluğu'nda Kürtler*, 131–32. I was unable to locate the source from Hagop Shahbazian and Johannes Lepsius that Celil cites. The claim that Kurds and Armenians intermarried is also unsubstantiated, but it is significant that the statement was made by observers in the late nineteenth century.

26. Reid, *Crisis of the Ottoman Empire*, 156–57.

27. Cited in Abraham Giulkhandanian, "Heghapokhakan Sharzhman Skizbe Taroni Mej," 96–97.

28. FO 78-2623, no. 58, Zohrab to Derby, Erzeroum, July 12, 1877, cited in Justin McCarthy, *Death and Exile: The Ethnic Cleansing of Ottoman Muslims, 1821–1922*, 56, n. 73.

29. *Turkey* 10 (1879): 15, cited in Christopher J. Walker, *Armenia: The Survival of a Nation*, 123.

30. Reid, *Crisis of the Ottoman Empire*, 160; Charles Boswell, *Armenia and the Campaign of 1877*, 293.

31. Nazmi Sevgen, *Doğu ve Güneydoğu Anadolu'da Türk Beylikleri: Osmanlı Belgeleri ile Kürt-Türkleri Tarihi*, 63.

32. Ibid., 119.

33. For additional information on Kurdish social structure, see Martin Van Bruinessen, *Agha, Sheikh, and State: The Social and Political Structures of Kurdistan*.

34. İbrahim Yılmazçelik, *XIX. Yüzyılın İkinci Yarısında Dersim Sancağı: İdari, İktisadi ve Sosyal Hayat*, 79–80.

35. Ibid., 80.

36. See General Averyanov's correspondence with the tsar, cited in Celilê Celil, *Intifadat al-Akrad 'Am 1880*, 33.

37. Ibid., 30–31.

38. Celil writes that many songs refer to this battle. Celil, *Intifadat al-Akrad*, 36.

39. Başbakanlık Osmanlı Arşivleri, Istanbul (BOA), A.MKT.MHM 480/66, May 16, 1876.

40. Geylani makes this claim in an interview with Erdost in the 1950s. Muzaffer İlhan Erdost, *Şemdinli Röportajı*, 160.

41. C. B. Norman, *Armenia and the Campaign of 1877*, 296–97.

42. Mr. Layard to the Earl of Derby, Therapia, July 10, 1877, in *British Documents on Ottoman Armenians*, ed. Bilal N. Şimşir, 1:81.

43. Norman, *Armenia and the Campaign of 1877*, 298.

44. Sasuni, *Kürt Ulusal Hareketleri*, 95. The punishment may have been less severe for Ubeydullah because the Ottoman state feared incurring the wrath of his followers, most of whom were within Ottoman borders. Jelaluddin's followers, by contrast, lived in Iran.

45. Ivan Davidovich Lazarev, *Prichiny Bedstvii Armian v Turtsii: Otvetstvennost' za Razorenie Sasuna*, 3–4.

46. Hormuzd Rassam, *Asshur and the Land of Nimrod*, 74.

47. Consul Zohrab to the Earl of Derby, December 24, 1876, Great Britain, Foreign Office, *Turkey, No. 15*, in *Accounts and Papers of the House of Commons* (hereafter *Turkey, No. 15*), 3.

48. *Mshag*, February 24, 1877. Taken from a Russian translation of the originally Armenian article. *Gavur* is a term used to refer to infidels.

49. Consul Zohrab to Sir H. Elliot, January 30, 1877, *Turkey, No. 15*, 146.

50. Ibid.

51. Rassam, *Asshur and the Land of Nimrod*, 87–88.

52. Prelacy of the Armenian Apostolic Church of America, ed., *Hayrig: A Celebration of His Life and Vision on the Eightieth Anniversary of His Death (1907–1987)*, 17.

53. Cited in Gerard J. Libaridian, *Modern Armenia: People, Nation, State*, 62.

54. Megerditch Khrimian, *Vankoyzh: Guzh Me Chur Yur Ayradz Hayrenyats Veray Ge Srsge Khrimian Hayrig* (Tiflis, 1877), 13, cited in Megerditch Gegamovich Nersisian, *Hay Zhogovurti Azatagrakan Paykare Turkakan Brnapetutian Tem 1850–1890*, 205 (emphasis added).

55. Ibid., 204.

56. Megerditch Khrimian, *Haykoyzh*, 5.

57. Mikayel Varandian, *Haykakan Sharzhman Nakhapatmutiune*, 2:127.

58. Ibid., 2:125–26.

59. Arakel Zatiki Sarukhan, *Haykakan Khndire yev Azgayin Sahmanadrutiune Tiurkahayum*, 233–34.

60. Raffi, *The Fool: Events from the Last Russo-Turkish War (1877–78)*, 61–62.

61. Esat Uras, *The Armenians in History and the Armenian Question*, 451.

62. Ibid., 441–43.

63. Cited in Levon P. Dabağyan, *Sultan Abdülhamit II ve Ermeniler*, 111.

64. Megerditch Khrimian, "Kharisayi Gatsan yev Yergatyan Sherepe," cited in Khrimian, *Hayrig*, 57.

65. Enclosure in No. 7, Clayton to Trotter, Bashkale, July 11, 1880, Great Britain, *Turkey No. 5 (1881)*, 7, cited in Wadie Jwaideh, *The Kurdish National Movement: Its Origins and Development*, 83.

66. See Rassam, *Asshur and the Land of Nimrod*, 87.

67. Stanford J. Shaw and Ezel Kural Shaw, *History of the Ottoman Empire and Modern Turkey*, 156.

68. Michael R. Milgrim, "An Overlooked Problem in Turkish-Russian Relations: The 1878 War Indemnity," 522.

69. Charles Issawi, "The Tabriz-Trabzon Trade, 1830–1900: Rise and Decline of a Route," 23–24.

70. Rassam, *Asshur and the Land of Nimrod*, 73.

71. BOA, HR.SYS 78.4, October 14, 1880.

72. BOA, HR.TO 259/13, June 10, 1880.

73. "Kars Oblast."

74. BOA, Y.PRK.BŞK 1/43, September 15, 1878.

75. Nedim İpek, *Rumeli'den Anadolu'ya Türk Göçleri (1877–1890)*, 206.

76. Nejla Günay, *Maraş'ta Ermeniler ve Zeytun İsyanları*, 250–62.

77. Louise Nalbandian, *The Armenian Revolutionary Movement: The Development of Armenian Political Parties through the Nineteenth Century*, 84–89.

78. Consul Chermside to Sir W. White, Inclosure in no. 331, FO 424/162, p. 77, no. 80, in *British Documents on Ottoman Armenians*, ed. Bilal Şimşir, 2:659–64.

12

From Millet-i Sadıka to Millet-i Asiya

Abdülhamid II and Armenians, 1878–1909

Garabet K. Moumdjian

INTRODUCTION

The reign of Abdülhamid II (1876–1909) was one of the longest among Ottoman sultans. A critical study on Abdülhamid II and the Armenian question could easily result in a substantial tome dedicated to the subject.[1] That is not within the scope of this paper.

My purpose here is to present the most important events regarding Abdülhamid II's policies vis-à-vis the Armenian question in a new light. This reevaluation is important because no serious reinterpretation has been attempted since the issue was first tackled in the 1960s. In past decades the majority of historiographic efforts on both sides have focused on producing diverging nationalistic treatises regarding World War I and the ensuing Armenian calamity. Abdülhamid II's period — albeit formative and extremely important in understanding what Armenians experienced during World War I — has been almost neglected. Even the meager historical literature that exists on this era reflects extremely nationalist tendencies on both sides.[2]

Only recently has the subject matter caught the attention of a new generation of historians. It is time to revisit and reevaluate this period with the aim of deconstructing the previous discourses and bringing new facts to light. It is possible to do this by examining the newly produced archival materials from both sides.[3]

This paper uses newly available primary sources to examine events such as the May 1895 Reform Project, the Ottoman Bank incident, the ensuing negotiations with Armenian revolutionary societies, and the revolutionaries' attempt to assassinate Abdülhamid II. Due to lack of space, two important issues related to the subject are dealt with only tangentially: (1) the relations between the Armenian revolutionary societies and the Young Turks; and (2) the relations between Armenian revolutionary societies and their Balkan counterparts, especially the Macedonians.

For a diplomatic historian, the problematic issue in attempting to analyze such discourse is that nationalistic historiographies dealing with the period under discussion have thus far yielded diametrically opposing views. Only a handful of Western historians have tried to produce a somewhat "unbiased" account. The question that asserts itself is whether it is possible for an Armenian and/or Turkish historian to produce a new discussion that can serve as a starting point in the process of reevaluating the blemished historical record. This paper is written with that ambitious objective in mind.

OTTOMAN REFORMS IN PERSPECTIVE

During the Tanzimat period the Armenian *millet* of the Ottoman Empire secured the adoption of a special constitution for "self-governance" in 1863.[4] The constitution provided a sense of pride and victory for Armenians in Constantinople, because it "[r]estricted the patriarch's power within the community, but, for the first time, recognized him as the sole representative of the entire Armenian population of the empire."[5]

The reform project in the Ottoman Empire was an arduous task, as is clear from the writings of Ahmet Cevdet Paşa, one of the most prominent Ottoman civil officials, whose work encompassed over fifty years of the reform project. Reforms within areas inhabited by Armenians were part of the general reform project that had been in the works since the 1830s. One such example was the work of the Fırka'I Islahiyye (Reforming Expedition), commanded by Cevdet Paşa in Cilicia in 1860–61.[6] The mere fact that the reform in Cilicia involved bringing Kurdish and other tribal elements down into the plains and imposing a sedentary way of life on them was in itself a problem for the villagers of the plains, both Armenians and Turks. They now had to compete with the newcomers for scarce arable lands and other natural resources. Thus this also implies that the centralization of power and extraction of taxes from the newly "reformed" populations had started long before Abdülhamid II came to power.

The uprisings in Zeytun since the 1850s had been an important element in publicizing the conditions of Armenians in the Ottoman Empire. Cevdet had another view regarding the local character of the Zeytun incidents:

As for the Istanbul Armenian nationalist groups, they had obtained photographs of the Armenian notables of the four sectors [*mahalle*] of Zeytun and had sent them to France. The Ottoman ambassador to Paris, Cemil Paşa, upon a visit to the French Ministry of Foreign Affairs, was shown those pictures by the foreign minister as if they belonged to Armenian princes. Cemil Paşa stated to the minister: "The photographs are those of herdsmen." Regardless of Cemil Paşa's characterization, French public opinion was more inclined to believe the Armenian side in the matter.[7]

Midhat Paşa's establishment of a constitutional monarchy and the formation of the first Ottoman parliament as well as his subsequent backing of Abdülhamid II in attaining the Ottoman throne, however, created new hopes for Armenians and other Christian communities under Ottoman dominion. All signs demonstrated that Abdülhamid II's reign would be one of reform, thus securing the fledgling constitution and the parliament that it had produced. But the Russo-Turkish War of 1877–78 turned events upside down. After exiling the reformist Midhat Paşa and later executing him, the new sultan not only dissolved the newly formed parliament but also initiated some sort of "police state."[8] This was unique in the Ottoman context: none of his forbears or successors used such a system. It was during the reign of Sultan Abdülhamid II that the Armenian *millet*, which had been called the "Millet-i Sadıka" (Faithful Millet) by the Ottoman authorities, started showing signs of unrest vis-à-vis its social and political conditions in the empire. This in turn transformed this heretofore law-abiding community into a "Millet-i Asiya" (Disobedient [Insurgent] Millet), an appellation usually reserved for the Christian communities of the empire in the Balkans.[9]

THE ARMENIAN QUESTION

Contrary to the common historical view, the issue of Armenian reforms within the eastern Anatolian provinces of the Ottoman Empire (those inhabited by Armenians) was not a result of the Russo-Turkish War of 1877–78 and the subsequent Treaty of San Stefano and Berlin Convention.

The granting of the internal constitution to the Armenian *millet* by Sultan Abdülaziz in 1865 can also be considered a step in this direction.[10] Moreover, the election of Megerditch Khrimian in 1869 as the Armenian patriarch in Constantinople meant that the voice of provincial Armenians would be heard in the capital. The patriarch himself had provincial origins and was well informed about conditions there.

In November 1870 the National Assembly of the Patriarchate commissioned a special investigative committee to examine the effects of the depredations against Armenians in the eastern provinces of the empire. The committee reviewed the reports (*takrir*s in Ottoman) regarding the issue presented to the Porte, which had remained unattended to during the past twenty years (since the institution of the internal Armenian constitution).[11] It recommended that the patriarch request the immediate intercession of the Ottoman central authorities in the resolution of specific issues involving provincial Armenians. The committee also suggested compiling a population census for Armenians living in the Ottoman Empire. This was followed by a new *takrir* in 1876, but to no avail.

As noted above, the ensuing Russo-Ottoman War of 1877–78 expanded the issue out of its internal Ottoman context and made it into an international affair, which the powers of Europe used for their own diplomatic maneuvers in the decades to come.

THE BERLIN CONFERENCE

An Armenian delegation headed by former patriarch Megerditch Khrimian attended the congress and tried to convince the European powers of the perils that Armenians would face if article 16 of the Treaty of San Stefano was not implemented.[12]

An important issue during the Congress of Berlin was the publication of the text of a secret treaty that later became known as the Cyprus Convention. It had been signed by the Ottoman and the British governments just before the Congress.[13]

The difference between article 16 of the Treaty of San Stefano and article 61 of the Berlin Convention is striking: "in comparison with the undertaking of Russia...that of Britain was feeble, since in the former case there was an army in occupation, whereas there was no such British force to compel the sultan."[14]

It follows that Russia, which had "championed" the cause of Armenian reforms and incorporated it in the initial agreement of San Stefano, seemed more than content when the Ottomans (through British intrigue at Berlin) ceded the areas of Kars, Ardahan, Artvin, and Batum to it. It is extremely interesting, however, that no major Armenian relocation into Kars, Ardahan, Artvin, and Batum occurred. The only exception was that thousands of Armenians from Erzurum were allowed to migrate to Akhalkalak and Akhaltsikhe (the region of Javakheti in modern Georgia), while a commensurate number of Turks were brought from those areas to Erzurum. This shows that Russia was keen not to let the number of Armenians in its newly enlarged Armenian Guberniia increase.[15]

This also meant that Russia would no longer press for Armenian reforms in the Ottoman Empire; that task would hereafter be allocated to the British. This situation contains an element of hypocrisy, however: while Britain advocated Armenian reforms within the empire, it did not promise any substantial monetary allocation for this purpose, at a time when Ottoman finances were in shambles (war indemnities and payments on foreign debts) and Istanbul lacked the will to implement such reforms. The obvious question is how reforms in Armenian-inhabited areas could be accomplished when their advocate Great Britain made only verbal commitments and showed no real interest in supporting the process. Such a project could not have been successfully implemented through diplomatic efforts alone. The diplomatic effort, which amounted to pressuring the Sublime Porte for reforms, was in itself a problematic factor that worsened the situation in the very areas that were to be reformed.

The Treaty of Berlin included "[a] right for the Armenians, an Obligation for the Ottoman Empire, and a responsibility for Europe."[16] Events were to show that the European powers would at best deal with this responsibility inefficiently and hence instigate further bloodshed due to their internal rivalries.

THE ARMENIAN REVOLUTIONARY MOVEMENT

During the period after 1878 Armenians in Constantinople were filled with a sense of reformist action. The Armenians of the eastern *vilayets* of the empire were the principal focus. Patriarch Varjabedian was instrumental in the creation of this atmosphere. The task of opening schools and enriching the cultural lives of Armenians in the eastern *vilayets* was delegated to a newly formed United Society. Young teachers and intellectuals soon relocated to the interior. This wave of relocation was indeed a turning point in the formulation of an Armenian renaissance in the provinces.[17]

It is interesting to note that the period from 1878 to 1891 saw no serious action on behalf of Armenians vis-à-vis the implementation of reforms promulgated by the treaties of San Stefano and Berlin. The historical record also shows no malicious policy by Abdülhamid II regarding the Armenians during this same period. Despite the uprisings in Zeytun during the 1870s and the emergence of secret Armenian organizations such as Unity for Salvation (*Miyutyun Ee Pergutyun*) in Van in 1872, Black Cross (*Sev Khach*) in Van in 1878, Defenders of the Fatherland (*Bashdban Hayrenyats*) in Erzurum in early 1881, and Young Armenia (*Yeridasart Hayasdan*) in Tbilisi in 1889, the general Armenian population in the empire was more or less content with its day-to-day life.[18] Some explanations regarding these organizations are in order.

The rebellions of the 1870s in the mountainous area of Zeytun (near Maraş) were local in nature, to avoid paying "excessive" taxes to the central government. Hence it is incorrect to consider these uprisings part of the Armenian revolutionary movement in the Ottoman Empire. Moreover, as noted above, the taxation had been instituted as a result of the reforms initiated in Cilicia by the Fırka'I Islahiyye, led by Mehmet Cevdet Paşa in the beginning of the 1860s. It must be noted that Kurdish tribes in the area of Gavur Dağı and Kurd Dağı had similar problems. The Zeytun Armenians insisted that they had been privileged since the days of Sultan Murad IV to pay only a "nominal" tax, which was to be used to keep the lanterns running at the Hagia Sophia Mosque in Constantinople. Their insistence that such a privilege was granted to them through a decree (*irade*) of Murad IV is yet to be substantiated.

Very little information is available on *Miyutyun Ee Pergutyun* (Unity for Salvation), which was formed in Van in 1872. Garabet Isajanian was the moving force behind the society, which wrote a letter to the Russian viceroy in the Caucasus advocating the opening of a Russian consulate in Van. No information indicates whether the society was still active during the 1877–78 War with Russia.

The *Sev Khach* (Black Cross) was a secret organization with the aim of protecting the Armenian population through armed force if necessary. The society's name signified that those who betrayed it or any of its members would bear a black cross opposite their names in the roster of members and would be assassinated. It is not known whether the society ever carried out such assassination attempts. Despite its secretive nature, this cannot be considered a full-fledged revolutionary organization.

The Sanasarian College opened its doors in Erzurum in 1880 as an institution of higher education. It was in this milieu that a group of students organized the *Bashdban Hayrenyats* (Defenders of the Fatherland) in early 1881. The local Ottoman government uncovered the organization in 1882 and made a series of arrests. Seventy of seventy-six of the arrestees were sentenced to imprisonment, but the appeals court — through the intercession of Patriarch Varjabedian at the Sublime Porte — set almost all of the detainees free. Khachadour Geregtsian, the mastermind behind the formation of the society, was released in 1886.

Young Armenia was an eastern Armenian group that sent couriers to western Armenia to gather information about the Armenians there. It was more of a scouting mission. Most of the future initiators of the Armenian Revolutionary Federation (ARF: Hai Heghapokhagan Tashnagtsoutioun) were part of this group. Moreover, it is interesting to note that the Ottoman government itself downplayed the issues pertaining to the formation, activities, and the subsequent dismantling of the society as an "insignificant, local foolish initiative,"[19] to avert European intervention in the internal affairs of the empire.

The formation of such societies exemplifies the process of the indoctrination of newly educated Armenian youth into an immature atmosphere of a belated "nationalism," which was the result of their exposure to the nationalist ideas of the time in Crete and the Balkans. The first full-fledged Armenian political parties materialized a decade later.

The internal constitution of 1865 had paved the way for the establishment of an educational and cultural system embodied in a growing number of schools and cultural organizations for Armenians in the eastern provinces and in Cilicia. These were augmented by an educational system created by the various missionary associations working in those areas since the 1850s. Western Armenians considered these accomplishments the epitome of Armenian enlightenment in the Armenian-inhabited provinces of the empire. Western Armenians in later years seem to have been somewhat doubtful of the revolutionary zeal manifested by their eastern Armenian counterparts.[20] Western Armenians' doubts about their eastern Armenian counterparts are now evident from archival material published during the last decade.[21]

Only in 1885 did revolutionary agitation enter the Armenian psyche in the Ottoman Empire. The first manifestation was the formation of the Armenagan Party in Van, under the leadership of an Armenian teacher, Megerditch Portukalian.[22] The Armenagan Party was nothing more than a provincial society, however, and its influence did not extend beyond Van and its environs. Portukalian was exiled to Marseilles, France, from whence he continued a periodical—albeit inconsistent—relationship with his former students.[23]

The first full-blown Armenian revolutionary and political party formed was the Social Democratic Hunchak Party (whose members are often referred to as Hunchaks). Adhering to a Marxist ideology, the party envisaged a two-step action: (1) establishing a free and independent Armenia (an immediate objective, showing the socialist/Marxist influence), and (2) striving for the creation of a democratic state structure for the fledgling Armenian republic (a more long-term objective).[24] The Hunchak Party masterminded the first and disastrous Sasun rebellion of 1894, which cost it dearly by diminishing its organizational structure. Internal disagreements between the western and eastern Armenian leaders of the party caused a rift that led to the party being divided into two distinct sections.[25] After the abortive Sasun rebellion of 1894, the Hunchaks concentrated their efforts in Cilicia and the capital, Istanbul.[26]

Hai Heghapokhakanneri Tashnagtsoutioun (Federation of Armenian Revolutionaries) was envisioned by Kristapor Mikayelian, a member of the Russian revolutionary organization Narodnaia Volia (People's Will). His intent was to bring together all Armenian revolutionary societies in western and eastern Armenia, in order to concentrate efforts and maximize results. The federation was formed in Tbilisi in the summer of 1890.[27] Two years later the unsuccessful federation gave way for the establishment of the Hai Heghapokhagan Tashnagtsoutioun (Armenian Revolutionary Federation; ARF, also known as Dashnaktsutioun or Dashnak Party).[28] The ARF also adopted socialism as its ideology but did not fully integrate it into the party program until 1907.[29] Moreover, unlike the Hunchak Party, the ARF adopted a more nationalistic tone and initiated a decentralized working environment that proved to be crucial for the success of the different bodies of the organization scattered throughout Russia, the Ottoman Empire, Europe, and the United States. Although it too was undermined by the friction between its western and eastern leaders regarding issues pertaining to ideology and tactics, the party was able to solve its internal difficulties during its general congresses.[30]

The reasoning behind the formation of the Armenian revolutionary organizations is best described by Hratch Dasnabedian, the official historian of the ARF:

> the growing appetite manifested by Russia in its wars against the Ottomans in 1828 and 1877 created hope and aspiration for Armenians in both empires. It led to massive Armenian migrations to the Russian-dominated parts of the Caucasus.... The renaissance of the Christian people of the Ottoman Empire (Greeks, Romanians, Serbians, Bulgarians) was a contagious stimulus that infected Armenians.... The impotence of the [Armenian] Patriarchate and its national bodies in asking for reforms for the Armenians in the interior...was enough for the creation of a revolutionary tendency

within the Armenians.... Moreover, the Armenian Nationalistic Movement had a peaceful reformist attitude aiming at attaining for Armenians what already was normal for the dominant Muslim population of the Ottoman Empire. These [elements] included human dignity, equality within the social, economic, and religious spheres.... If there was even some semblance of autonomy or freedom in the minds of some [Armenians], it was not yet formulated in a bold political, ideological platform.[31]

THE HAMIDIYYE REGIMENTS

Abdülhamid II's grandiose idea of creating the Hamidiyye Light Cavalry regiments in 1891 must be considered within the context of the reformist policies of his predecessors. Composed of Kurdish tribal fighters, these regiments were supposed to secure the border with Russia. Their structure was to be similar to that of the Cossack regiments employed by the Russian army.[32] Bitlis was one of the last areas of the eastern provinces not yet brought under the reformist policies of the central government. Through the advice of his brother-in-law, Muşir Zeki Paşa, the commander of the Fourth Army stationed in the eastern provinces, Abdülhamid began the formation of these regiments.[33] He believed such an action would bring the Kurdish tribes in the area under his control. But the project backfired and caused the first real Armenian rebellion in Sasun. It was the direct consequence of the coercive and intimidating actions of these tribal regiments which left Armenian villagers no other alternative but to defend themselves against excessive Kurdish extortions. The Armenian discontent was the direct result of taxes newly imposed on them by the leaders of the regiments. This amounted to an intolerable system of double taxation.[34] In some instances the Ottoman army had to interfere in order to return cattle abducted by Hamidiyye Regiments to their owners.[35]

In describing Abdülhamid II's policy in the eastern provinces of the empire, Bayram Kodaman outlines the sultan's intentions. Abdülhamid II was tired of European intrigue regarding parts of his empire. The Ottoman losses in the Balkans stiffened the sultan's stance in the east.[36]

To alleviate the condition of Armenians living at the mercy of the Hamidiyye Regiments, the Geneva *Droshak* Center of the ARF collaborated with Abdülrahman Bedirhan Bey in publishing a periodical called *Kurdistan*.[37] Abdülrahman Bedirhan Bey was the son of the legendary Kurdish chief Bedirhan, who had organized a massive revolt against the Ottoman government from 1840 to 1847.[38]

While in Geneva Abdülrahman had established close ties with the *Droshak* center. Armenian-Kurdish relations had a history before Abdülrahman Bey's arrival on the scene. In 1898 *Droshak* had published a call by an unknown Kurdish chieftain, who stressed that Kurds had been living with Armenians for almost 2,000 years and that they should not be toys in the hands of Abdülhamid II.[39] The article concluded by stating: "We have to do what Armenians are doing, because we too are being usurped and oppressed."[40] The collaboration with Abdulrahman Bey resulted in the publication of his famous article "Kürtlere Hitap" ("Koch Kurterun" in Armenian: A Call to the Kurds) in *Droshak*.[41]

Droshak's response to Abdülrahman Bey's article stressed that the issue of Armenian-Kurdish unity and collaboration deserved some thought. *Droshak* attempted to analyze Kurdish aggression against the Heyidi Kurds (1830s), Nestorians (1840s), and finally Armenians (beginning in the 1860s), which had culminated in Kurdish cruelty against Armenians in Sasun in 1894. This was especially important because of Abdülhamid II's initiative in forming the Hamidiyye bands.[42] *Droshak* also stressed that several attempts by powerful Kurdish leaders to attain independence had occurred during the nineteenth century and that Armenian peasants were always loyal to them.[43] It must be noted that Abdülrahman Bedirhan Bey later started publishing *Kürdistan* as his own gazette, with the aim of enlightening the Kurdish population of the eastern *vilayet*s.[44]

According to F. R. Maunsell, the Hamidiyye forces were becoming a real menace for the population. (Moreover, their loyalty to the central government was questionable, as in the case of the Hayderanlı tribe which counted some nine thousand tents and furnished ten Hamidiyye Cavalry Regiments.) Tribal rivalry between the Hayderanlı and Takuri (Shekak) tribes was another reason for heightened danger in the area.[45] Moreover, "[In the] Russian frontier posts, many of the officers were 'Jeunes Turcs' [Young Turks] exiled from some more favorable place, and very bitter against the way the Hamidiyye were pampered, and readily accorded ranks which took them many years of faithful service to attain."[46]

European embassies once again deplored the Kurdish actions and demanded that the government bring the brigands under control. Ottoman authorities arrested Emin Paşa, a Kurdish tribal leader who had bedeviled the Adiljevaz district in the summer of 1899. Consul Maunsell reported that he believed the Ottoman authorities were trying to impose stricter discipline on the Hamidiyye and "to check the almost unbounded license to commit crime they used to possess."[47]

Furthermore, the governor of Van was actively trying to reduce the in-fluence of Hüseyin Paşa, a Hamidiyye commander. Zeki Paşa did not back the tribal leader. The effect of the governor's actions was that the tribal leaders were more cautious for some time.[48] As the year progressed, how-ever, the Hamidiyye appeared to have a free hand from the government. Local authorities did not proceed against them without explicit orders from the palace, which was hesitant to deliver such orders due to lack of sufficient military units in the area. Therefore most of the province of Erzurum was in a "universal state of insecurity. Armenian migrant workers [en route to Russia] were in misery as they were unable to get there."[49]

To protect themselves against the Hamidiyye some Armenian villagers reached out to the Russians, asking to join the Russian Orthodox Church. Their action was also prompted by the wish to escape heavy Ottoman taxation.[50]

The latest report of 1901 from Consul Lamb in Erzurum dated Decem-ber 2, reported the formation of a new Hamidiyye Regiment composed of Kurds who are "known cut-throats."[51] It was obvious that the sultan had certain designs in mind.

In general, weaker tribes were chosen to join the Hamidiyye Regi-ments.[52] Edward Freeman's report is an example of how Kurdish tithe-farmers impoverished Armenian villages where villagers lost their land titles. The loss of Armenian land titles would become rampant in the fol-lowing years, due to the attempt to change the land tenure system and thus affect the ethnic-demographic status quo of the area.

THE MAY 1895 REFORM PROJECT

On August 1, 1894, the mountainous Armenian region of Sasun in eastern Asia Minor swarmed with regular Ottoman troops and Hamidiyye bands. The Ottoman government's official reason for the initial military concen-tration and the subsequent attack on villages and hamlets in the area was to squelch an alleged uprising.[53] Official sources also referred to frequent raids organized by bands of Armenian *fedayees* (freedom fighters) against the government in Sasun and the Muş district as a danger to peace and tranquillity in the whole region.[54]

The military offensive left more than three thousand dead and thou-sands of refugees, whose homes and villages were demolished.[55] After the massacre the Ottoman authorities began deporting a considerable part of the Armenian population to distant locations.[56] Moreover, the participation of the Hamidiyye bands gave much cause for alarm, because their recruits were largely poorer Kurdish tribal horsemen.[57]

On January 23, 1895, a commission of inquiry visited the devastated area.[58] The formation of the commission had been triggered by numerous reports about the ongoing atrocities received by the British, French, and Russian ambassadors in Constantinople and forwarded to their respective governments.[59] The findings of the European members of the commission raised serious doubts about the government's official explanation that it was responding to a "popular uprising." Instead, they viewed this as a military campaign organized by army units against a peaceful and defenseless population. Moreover, *fedayee* raids were not considered a sufficient reason to permit such a punitive action.[60] It is noteworthy that the Ottoman members of the delegation were outraged that as soon as the delegation reached the area of the insurgency the European members left them alone and started to conduct their own investigations.[61]

It was in this critical situation that the British, French, and Russian ambassadors confronted the sultan on May 11, 1895, with a translation of the "Memorandum and Project of Reforms for the Eastern Provinces of Asia Minor." The document was approved by the three Great Powers.[62] This memorandum, referred to as the "May Reform Project,"[63] contained twelve major aspects of reform and lengthy explanations regarding each.[64]

Events took a dramatic turn on September 30, 1895. The Social Democratic Hunchak Party organized a demonstration in front of the Bab-ı Ali (Sublime Porte), the seat of the government. The demonstrators demanded the implementation of the May Reform Project.[65] Viewing the demonstration as a provocation, the Ottoman government retaliated swiftly. It organized a series of massacres in Constantinople and various places in the provinces.[66]

The European powers responded with a show of force in Constantinople. Vessels of the British and French fleets engaged in a naval demonstration in October 1895 to flex their muscles. But the "entertainment" brought no tangible results concerning Armenian reforms.[67]

The new year brought renewed Armenian hopes for the revival of reforms. On January 3, 1896, under intense diplomatic pressure, the sultan approved a plan for the establishment of a Commission of Control for the Armenian Provinces.[68] Only three days later, however, British ambassador Sir Philip Currie had to inform his government that Kurdish elements were once again creating disturbances in Sasun and Talori, while government forces watched idly.[69]

On February 8, 1896, Mateos Izmirlian, patriarch of the Ottoman Armenians, presented a formal *takrir* to Rıza Paşa, the Ottoman minister
of justice, in which he painstakingly enumerated both the human and
property losses suffered by the Armenians during the 1894 massacres and
their subsequent deportations.[70]

Although European powers exerted pressure on the sultan to bring
some relief to the situation of Armenians in the interior provinces, especially in Bitlis, Abdülhamid II remained adamant. About two and a half
months after the patriarch's *takrir* was filed with the ministry of justice, on
April 24, 1896, Robert Graves (the British consul at Erzurum) reported to
Ambassador Currie in Constantinople that "a year after the massacres in
Sasun the situation in the area and effectively the whole province of Bitlis
remains very grave."[71] The European ambassadors organized a relief committee to provide much-needed aid and shelter for thousands of homeless
Armenians in Sasun.[72]

In the province of Aleppo peace was shattered when the Ottoman
army started an offensive against Zeytun.[73] The town had been under
siege by the army since December 1895.[74] On January 7, 1896, Currie had
informed the British Foreign Office that the Ottoman government had
agreed to European mediation in Zeytun and that the British and Italian
consuls at Maraş had reached the town.[75] After complicated deliberations,
the Armenians agreed to hand over their arms and accept the stationing
of Ottoman troops in the town.[76] Ambassador Currie confided to Salisbury his fear that once the Armenians had given up their weapons they
would be at the mercy of the troops and the Kurdish tribal forces aiding
the army.[77] The ambassador's premonitions were well founded. Simultaneously with events in Zeytun disturbances were spreading in other cities. In
Urfa 7,000–8,000 Armenians were massacred. Many of them were burned
alive in a church.[78]

Since the Sasun massacres, the city of Van and its environs had been in
a state of turmoil. In January 1896 the governor, Nazlm Bey, was replaced
by Ferit Saadettin Paşa, who had been instructed to deal with the Armenians of the city.[79] At the end of May the onslaught of Ottoman forces
started and was met with Armenian self-defense. The fighting continued
well into June. Hundreds of Armenians were killed, and scores of homes
were destroyed.[80]

It was under these circumstances that *amira* (Armenian notable)
Abraham Paşa (Kara-Kehia[ian]), who was believed to be close to governmental circles, visited Ambassador Currie. He confided to the British diplomat that the situation of Armenians in the interior was hopeless unless

some sort of reconciliation was reached with the sultan.[81] Interestingly, the *amira*'s visit coincided with Ambassador Currie's reception of an unsigned letter demanding the removal of Patriarch Mateos Izmirlian.[82] And Izmirlian himself did exactly that. Understanding that the whole issue of Armenian reforms was untenable, the patriarch rendered his resignation to the Ottoman government on July 21, 1896.[83] The authorities ignored the resignation for a while, although Izmirlian stayed away from his office at the patriarchate.[84] Currie remarks that Izmirlian's resignation "had to do with the Russian government," according to Russian ambassador Alexander Nelidov.[85]

Following Izmirlian's resignation a temporary committee was established to prepare for the election of a new patriarch under the presidency of *locum tenens* Archbishop Bartoghomeus (Bartholomew) Chamichian.[86] Maghakia (Malachai) Ormanian was elected patriarch on October 20, 1896.[87] He was the candidate who satisfied Abraham Paşa and other notables. In his memoirs Ormanian writes:

> If we were to look logically at Izmirlian's actions, there would seem to be no problems regarding them. However, politics is not a matter of simple logic. Here, interests, and diplomacy to achieve those interests, prevail. Izmilrlian put so much faith in international [foreign] intervention that he thought it was unnecessary to think twice about his stern position with the envoys and emissaries of the sultan. He thus closed all doors behind him. He entered the field of diplomacy yet disregarded the basic rules of that field.... He reduced Armenian issues into a matter of personal enmity between himself and the sultan. Within the inner circles of the patriarchate, he antagonized the committee members [notables], while giving credence to party representatives, who were always encouraging him to lean on foreign diplomats, especially the British ambassador [Philip Currie], to the detriment of the others [French, Russian, German, and other diplomats]. It is no wonder that sympathizers called him "the Iron Patriarch." Those people never assumed that it was better to be flexible rather than as rigid as iron.[88]

Writing about the issue of Patriarch Izmirlian's resignation, *Hnchak* stated:

> Izmirlian's predecessor, Patriarch Ashekian, who was elected in 1891, was obliged to cleanse the National Council of people with

real nationalistic feelings and to appoint others who were willing
to become instruments in the hands of the likes of Nurian and
Maksud *paşas*. However, when Izmirlian was elected in 1894 things
changed. Europe's eyes were on the Armenian Question and the
likes of Nurian and Maksud *paşas* suddenly disappeared from
the scene. This time, however, it was the likes of Abraham Kara-
Kehiaian Paşa, who entered intra-Armenian politics at a very old
age as a crony of Nurian and his faction. He was to bring shame and
dishonor upon the name of his noble family. It was telegrammed to
the *Times* [in London] that the sultan had promised 10,000 gold
coins to this traitor, if he secured Izmirlian's resignation.[89]

Currie's dispatch to Salisbury on the resignation of Patriarch Izmirlian
sheds more light on the status of the belated Armenian reforms:

March 17, Constantinople:
The secretary of the Armenian Patriarch called at this Embassy a
few days ago, and said that His Beatitude was much disheartened
by the inaction and bad faith of the Ottoman government in all
matters affecting the Armenian question. The twelve points [May
11, 1895, Armenian Reform Project] mentioned in my dispatch
No. 44 of the 17th January had been mostly rendered illusionary
by the numerous qualifications and conditions attached to them,
and the few concessions which, after being revised by the Palace,
retained any solid value, had not been executed.[90]

Currie concluded by explaining that both the patriarch and the government were apprehensive of the revolutionary committees. According
to the patriarch, the committees were to wait until Easter. If no reforms
were implemented by then, they would strike.[91]

Meanwhile British-Ottoman relations deteriorated further. Sultan
Abdülhamid II, angered over some public statements made by Queen
Victoria, sent a letter of protest to Ambassador Currie. He expressed his
regret and dissatisfaction regarding "the speech that the British queen had
delivered [in Parliament] respecting Armenian affairs." The letter ends:
"His Majesty [the sultan] thinks that it [the queen's speech] would have a
bad effect on public opinion."[92]

Nevertheless, mounting diplomatic pressure obliged the Ottoman
government to start implementing the promised reforms. But it was

obvious that the sultan was doing this under pressure.[93] During the first meeting of the Commission of Control of Armenian Reforms with the dragomans of the British, French, and Russian embassies on February 14, 1896, the commission informed the foreign dignitaries that "they were well intentioned and that the embassies should give them a free hand in their work."[94]

The commission's meeting coincided with the trial of some Armenian notables in the city of Trabzon on the Black Sea. Armenians demonstrated against the unjust rulings and the subsequent death sentences—later changed to permanent exile—rendered by the Turkish court.[95] On February 24 Ambassador Nelidov met with the sultan. According to Currie, Nelidov stated that "he is unceasingly occupied by [the] question of reforms in Anatolia and Macedonia."[96]

Outrages and attacks continued throughout eastern Asia Minor. In March 1896 U.S. missionaries in Erzurum contacted Currie regarding their security and protection from Kurdish mobs.[97] A few days later the missionaries stressed that some forty thousand Armenians in the city were in dire need of relief.[98] Meanwhile the British ambassador received some encouraging news regarding the reforms, such as the "enrollment of a new police force in Sivas."[99] A memorandum by the Commission of Control of Armenian Reforms to the government stated that some of the measures had been implemented.[100] Currie's hopes, however, were unfounded. In March 1896 a new wave of massacres swept through Harput, following some comparatively minor outrages earlier in the year.[101]

In its efforts to keep European public opinion focused on the issue of Armenian reforms the ARF's Constantinople Tsutsagan Marmin (Demonstrative Body) organized a "spectacular" operation in the capital.[102] On August 26, 1896, a group of militants took over the Ottoman Bank, the largest European financial institution in Constantinople. The Armenian agitators entered the bank with the intent of bombing it if the issue of Armenian reforms was not brought back to the forefront.[103] They entered the bank when it was full of employees and many Turkish and European customers, who were held as hostages.[104] The revolutionaries exchanged fire with the police forces surrounding the building. This resulted in scores of deaths and casualties on both sides.

Upon hearing the news of the takeover, organized mobs assaulted Armenian establishments, homes, and people on the streets throughout the Ottoman capital. The atrocities spread quickly to the suburbs and other seashore towns, where thousands of Armenians were murdered.[105]

DIRECT NEGOTIATIONS

On January 6, 1898, Ormanian informed Currie that he had delivered a new *takrir* to the sultan, consisting of sixteen points to bring some sort of relief and normalcy to Armenians in the interior. Most important of these measures were:

1. Permission to collect funds for orphans;
2. Permission of travel for traders;
3. Temporary remission of the military tax;
4. Permission for Armenians having claims against the government to return to their homes;
5. Permission for Armenians employed by the government to return to their duties;
6. Admission of Armenian students to government schools;
7. Permission for Armenians exiled to provinces to return to Constantinople;
8. Permission for patriarchal delegates to assume positions in provinces;
9. Permission to reopen parochial schools;
10. Exemption of church properties from taxes;
11. Cessation of conversions [to Islam];
12. Permission to print patriarchal press releases without censorship.[106]

Ormanian's report drew a dark picture of the situation of Ottoman Armenians. The suggestions were nothing less than a summary of the government's failure to provide even minimal civil and human rights to its Armenian citizens. Ormanian's *takrir* left no room for doubt that the Armenian community as such was facing grave danger and was on the verge of institutional destruction. In view of the pending reform program, Ormanian's report also constituted an urgent appeal to the Great Powers to follow through on their political promises to urge the Ottoman government to implement reforms. In March 1898 Ormanian called upon Currie, telling him that the sultan had issued an *irade* regarding his *takrir*. It had remained useless, however, because the document would not guarantee the implementation of the reforms formulated in his appeal.[107]

Ormanian's protest and the promulgation of the imperial *irade* provided the background for a new initiative on the part of the sultan. Once more he opened direct negotiations with the Armenian revolutionary committees.[108] Soon *Droshak* denied that a certain Bulbul (literally

"Nightingale") Efendi had approached the ARF's Paris Committee as a legitimate negotiator on behalf of the Ottoman government. Moreover, the ARF's Paris committee called the episode "a Turkish hoax."[109] Nevertheless, in a subsequent issue *Droshak* confirmed that a person named Bulbulian indeed had tried in vain to get in touch with the ARF in Paris. He was denied the opportunity.[110]

Despite the public rebuff, the Ottoman government did not give up its endeavors. In November 1898 an unidentified person wrote to the ARF Center in Geneva. The informant reported that somebody from Constantinople wanted to talk with ARF leaders and inquired whether the ARF would send someone to meet this "gentleman" in Lausanne. As it turned out, the person in question was none other than Kevork Bulbul (Bulbulian). After leaving Paris he had traveled to Lausanne. Upon his return to Paris, he had apparently gotten in touch with some Hunchaks and persuaded them that he was on official business as the envoy of the Ottoman government.[111]

Droshak published the whole affair and stated that this "gentleman" was a close friend of Enver Bey, the governor of Pera, who had masterminded the Armenian massacres in the capital after the seizure of the Ottoman Bank. *Droshak* denounced Bulbulian as a spy, probably with police credentials from Galata Seray (Constantinople police headquarters). Bulbulian's task may have been to gather information about Armenian revolutionaries and revolutionary cells in the Ottoman capital.[112]

More discreet and possibly more serious negotiations were to follow. On June 23, 1898, the British Foreign Office received a letter from "Le Parti Révolutionnaire Arménien, Comité Central" (Armenian Revolutionary Party, Central Committee). The document stated:

On November 20, 1897, a special envoy of the sultan had arrived in Paris to enter into a dialogue with Armenian revolutionary societies. Our issue is not a pardon for the revolutionaries and their safe return to the country, but rather obtaining reforms promised for the Armenians in the empire. After the talks between the envoy and the Central Committee, the envoy wanted us to continue the negotiations through the offices of the Ottoman Ambassador in Paris, Munir Bey. We reiterated our demand for the belated reforms. At the end, Munir Bey promised an amnesty for revolutionaries and to persuade the government to quicken the pace of the promised reforms. He also promised that Armenians displaced because of massacres will return to their homes and would not be subjected to hardships by the police. It was decided that Munir Bey would work toward procuring an Imperial decree from Constantinople in this regard.

We have to underline, however, that these negotiations are not final, and their future depends on how the sultan and his government react to the issue of Armenian reforms.[113]

Munir Bey was able to procure the promised decree.[114] In a note addressed to Munir Bey, the Central Committee in Paris thanked him for procuring it. The note added:

> There were a lot of promises in the document, which are not implemented yet. This means that the government is not serious regarding Armenian reforms. Prisoners are not released as was promised. Even though our attitude is sincere, your government's continuation of persecuting Armenians and other violations show that it is acting contrary to the Imperial irade. In such a situation, the final rupture of the whole negotiation process is inevitable. We ask you to transmit our note to His Majesty, the Sultan, so that he may consider the grave results of his actions.[115]

As on many similar occasions, the sultan's promises seemed to be of no tangible value. The Ottoman authorities continued their negotiations, thereby forcing the Armenian revolutionaries into passivity. At the same time, however, the ongoing campaign of repression in the eastern provinces of the empire rendered the situation of Ottoman Armenians increasingly precarious. British ambassador Sir Nicolas O'Conor described the complicated diplomatic maneuvering:

> Further papers have reached me…showing that the Armenian Committee in Paris was still, at the beginning of this month, resolved to break off all correspondence with the Ottoman Embassy, unless full effect were given to the promised amnesty [for seventeen prisoners in Constantinople and the provinces]…. The Palace seems inclined to yield. The Armenian Committee has been informed, through telegraph, that their demands are admitted in principle…. From the same quarter I hear that a telegram has been received at the Porte from the Ottoman Minister [ambassador] at Washington that the Armenian Committee of New York has decided to address a petition to the German Emperor, and to take

advantage of his visit to the Sultan to provoke some disturbance in Constantinople.[116]

A month and a half later the Hunchak center in London sent a letter to Wilhelm II, the German emperor, on the occasion of his visit to Constantinople. The letter reminded the monarch that the question of Armenian reforms was part of the Treaty of Berlin and had been endorsed by all European powers. Nevertheless, the document stressed, since the signing of the treaty in 1878 some three hundred thousand Armenians had lost their lives.[117]

The Armenian committees in Europe remained adamant in their demand to implement the belated reforms. The Ottoman government gradually tried to appear more conciliatory without changing its fundamental strategy of undermining the Armenian community. In January 1899 the Armenian Patriarchate at Constantinople reported that the government showed a slightly more moderate attitude toward Armenians. Ormanian told Currie that he had learned from palace sources that the sultan had promised to postpone the collection of the military tax for 1897 for two years.[118] Artin Paşa, however, did not share the patriarch's optimism. O'Conor (who replaced Currie as ambassador to Constantinople) had learned that:

> Artin Pasha, who is officially charged with Armenian affairs, being himself an Armenian and Under-Secretary of State for Foreign Affairs, has written to his son, Diran Bey [who was in Europe negotiating with the ARF], that Armenian grievances are left without redress, the promises of the sultan unfulfilled, and that the only answer to demands for an inquiry is to accuse Armenians of aiming at independence. He points out that such a policy is calculated to strengthen the hands of the powers that were aiming at the disruption of the Turkish Empire.
>
> This letter is interesting only as affording corroboratory evidence from a high Turkish official to several consular reports submitted to your lordship.[119]

In February 1899 Ormanian asked O'Conor whether an appeal to the Great Powers to implement reforms would be welcomed. The ambassador's answer was in the negative.[120] On leaving the embassy, however, the patriarch saw Adam Block (the embassy's chief dragoman). He told Block that "Artin Pasha had assured him that the Ottoman government would look favorably upon such a petition" and that he was acting upon this advice.[121] It is very important to note Ambassador O'Conor's report to Salisbury, concerning Artin Paşa's advice to the patriarch: "It is difficult to explain the motives that prompted Artin pasha to give this advice. But probably it was connected with some palace intrigue. Anyhow the patriarch seemed only too glad to have an excuse to escape from a position which would have compromised him with the sultan, with whom he is generally supposed to be anxious to keep on friendly terms."[122]

Meanwhile the ARF had grown increasingly disillusioned about the maneuvers of the various Ottoman envoys. *Droshak* published a summary report on these negotiations:

> We had already discussed that the government of the sultan wanted to negotiate with us [ARF]. Because lots of misguided and wrong reports were published about these negotiations in the European newspapers, we find it prudent to give our side of the story. Our readers should also be aware that the ARF ceased negotiations as of March 11 [1899].
>
> It was after the battles of August 14/26 of 1896 [the Ottoman Bank incident and its aftermath] that the sultan decided to send his envoy, Diran Bey Dadian, son of Harutiun [Artin] Paşa Dadian. Diran Bey reached Geneva on October 28 and informed the ARF that it must stop hostilities since the sultan was about to embark on a reform project in Turkey. Diran Bey emphasized that in nine months a new era would open in Turkey's history.
>
> *Droshak*'s representatives told Diran Bey that the issue was not to come to Geneva and negotiate with the ARF but to accomplish real reforms in the places where Armenian people were really hurting, that is, the homeland. Therefore stopping the hostilities was going to be achieved by the committees working inside the country, if and when they see tangible results. Three months after Diran Bey left, a new envoy, Vaghinag Ajemian, arrived in Geneva to repeat the same terms. Because nothing had changed in the status quo, he too was given the same answers. The sultan must have had long forgotten those negotiations when two events turned things upside down: the Khanasor Expedition first on July 25/August 6, 1897, and the Ottoman Bank takeover event and the explosion at its doors on August 6/18 [1896].[123] These events in themselves once again made negotiating with Armenian revolutionaries a priority for the sultan.[124]

A third envoy, Artin Paşa's nephew Drtad Bey, arrived in Geneva on October 26, 1897, to reiterate the old reforms agenda. *Droshak's* representatives were amazed that the sultan still wanted to talk after Diran Bey's "nine months" had long since expired and the situation of Armenians in the empire had worsened. *Droshak's* response was:

> Drtad Bey, who was instructed definitely to reach an agreement, implored ARF representatives to come up with a reform project, which he promised would reach the sultan through the offices of Harutiun Paşa Dadian.
>
> Our answer was that there was no need for such a reform project, since Harutiun Paşa and the sultan know it very well and it has been presented to them several times through the Patriarchate in Constantinople.
>
> Drtad Bey went to Constantinople. *Droshak* headquarters received a letter from him containing a letter from Harutiun Paşa himself about the situation. The paşa is optimistic that the reform projects he will hand to the sultan in the name of the National Committee of the patriarchate will be enforced soon.
>
> He says that as a national leader he is doing his utmost to solve the situation. Yet anything good can only come from the sultan himself.
>
> *Droshak* replied with a letter that it had informed the committees in Turkey about the reform project through its circular of January 14, 1898.
>
> The ARF also stated that in order to present a written memorandum of reforms to the government it had to confer with other Armenian parties, committees, and important national figures. Therefore the ARF asked Harutiun Paşa if he was able to communicate with the other parties and tell them that the ARF was doing this with his consent.[125]

The *paşa* replied again through Drtad Bey. He stated that the ARF might contact the other parties telling them that the *paşa* was sponsoring this initiative and that he was very serious about it. The *paşa* instructed Drtad Bey to request the ARF Geneva center to collect information from its cells in the provinces as to the extent to which the sultan's promised reforms were being implemented or not. Moreover, the *paşa* told the ARF that he would inform them on any new decrees that the sultan was to sign in terms of the promised reforms.[126] Remaining in line with its earlier strategies, Ottoman intelligence not only hoped to obtain critical evidence on Armenian political party cells throughout the empire but even to get the list of members delivered by the organization itself!

Given the sultan's record of unabatedly persecuting Armenians, the Geneva ARF Center did not accept Drtad Bey as a negotiator. Moreover, it informed Drtad Bey that it was impossible to gather all the requested information and send it to Artin Paşa. In short, the ARF saw no point in continuing the negotiations.[127]

Drtad Bey replied by saying that he understood the situation and the reason for the ARF's refusal to continue the negotiations. Returning to one main objective, he suggested that if the ARF was able to give him the written statement he would inform the party bodies about the reform project emanating from Constantinople.[128] The Ottoman agent was clearly pressed hard for information on the party's structure and influence within the empire.

The Ottoman government was determined in its objective and did not hesitate to make some substantial financial outlays. Thus Drtad Bey remained in Geneva for eight more months. He maintained constant contact with the ARF Center, passing on information forwarded by Artin Paşa from Constantinople. The data were of little practical value for the ARF, however, and often rather irrelevant. For example, he informed the ARF that twenty-five Armenian students had been accepted in the imperial universities.[129]

The ARF cells operating in Asia Minor and western Armenia shared the Geneva ARF Center's skeptical views concerning negotiations with the Ottoman government. Accordingly, they urged the Geneva center to stop any negotiations with Artin Paşa. The general feeling was that it would be better to discuss the negotiations issue at the ARF General Congress, which was to convene in April 1898.[130]

Not surprisingly, the ARF General Congress was not in favor of continuing the negotiations with Abdülhamid II through his Armenian agents. Instead the congress formulated a proposition. In order to restart the negotiations it would, in good faith, allow a three-month period for the Ottoman government to fulfill the following three demands so that Armenians could see the goodwill of the sultan:

1. A general amnesty to be implemented for all political exiles so that they could return to their homeland without fear of being prosecuted;
2. The return of all properties confiscated from Armenians during the massacres and deportations;
3. A general amnesty to be given to all Armenian political prisoners.

After the conclusion of the General Congress, when the ARF was on the verge of presenting its demands to Drtad Bey in Geneva, the situation changed dramatically. New massacres took place in the Ahlat and Pağeş regions (northwest of Lake Van). Consequently the newly elected ARF Bureau (Supreme Council) decided to add a fourth demand:

4. The strict punishment of all perpetrators of the massacres in Khlat and Pağeş in accordance with the law and the indemnification of the villages that had been pillaged.[131]

Drtad Bey received a copy of the demands signed by the ARF Western Bureau on November 2, 1898. As expected, the demands were unacceptable to the sultan. He insisted through his intermediary, Harutiun Paşa, that the ARF must withdraw its demands. In a further diplomatic twist, the Ottoman government suggested that the ARF could formulate a petition in a more acceptable manner by asking the sultan to fulfill the same "demands" out of his goodwill and righteousness.[132] Obviously the sultan never intended to accept the ARF as a legitimate partner for serious negotiations.

The Geneva ARF Center received a letter from Artin Paşa. It stated that he had been "conducting these negotiations for three years now with the consent of the sultan and in order to bring peace for, and within, the [Armenian] nation." He continued criticizing the ARF for its demands, thereby demonstrating that the Ottoman government had never regarded the negotiations as a serious diplomatic effort:

> I could have completed the process [of negotiations] by working only with the patriarchate and its bodies. However, I chose to include the Armenian parties because deep inside I believed that as an elderly and respected person the ARF would willingly speak with my representatives without any preconditions.... I presented all the demands and the pains of the Armenian nation to the proper authorities. I was able to get some small reforms in return. I thought that with time peace and prosperity would come to the Armenian nation. Therefore I urge you to listen to me carefully. I honestly believe that the salvation and the peaceful existence of the Armenian people in Turkey have been guaranteed for centuries. Moreover, the sultan has spoken about his good intentions toward the Armenians to the Patriarch and to me. We have already witnessed his work in this regard. He still sends his orders to governmental ministries and regional governors regarding the well-being of Armenians. I hope

that you will continue to have an open channel with me and I will certainly inform you of any new developments.[133]

The thinly veiled threat that any opposition to the sultan would undermine the sole basis for any Armenian existence within the Ottoman Empire was not promising. Despite the sultan's refusal to consider the ARF's demands, Drtad Bey asked for an extension of the three-month waiting period for the implementation of the demands. The deferment continued until March 1899. At that point the ARF informed Artin Paşa that it was cutting all relations with him in accordance with the decisions of its General Congress.

Still trying to buy more time, Artin Paşa wrote several times, asking the ARF to circumvent the decisions of the General Congress and to keep a channel open with him. The suggestion was aimed at creating dissent within the organization while avoiding making any substantive offer. In response the ARF ignored the *paşa*'s letters and returned them unopened on May 26, 1899. It is interesting to note that while the ARF was cutting its relations with Artin Paşa he and his representatives were being accused by the Ottoman government of being Russian spies in disguise.[134]

The ARF negotiators had been fully aware of the Ottoman government's stalling tactics. It was important for Abdülhamid II to keep Armenians engaged in negotiations, because a peace conference was soon to be held at The Hague.[135] Representatives of European powers and the Ottoman government would discuss issues pertaining to minorities in the Ottoman Empire.

The peace conference was to convene in less than two months. The sultan was unwilling to discuss his country's internal affairs there. The end of the negotiations with the ARF would be a blow for his policies. It would also mean that reforms in the Armenian *vilayet*s of the empire would definitely be brought to the peace conference. He acted quickly, infesting European newspapers with lies that the negotiations with Armenian revolutionaries were going well and that a decision would soon be reached regarding the Armenian question.

The Ottoman disinformation campaign became fully public when the Constantinople correspondent of the Correspondenz-Bureau in Vienna published a telegram on May 1, 1899: "Three members of the Geneva [Armenian] Committee have arrived at Istanbul to discuss Armenian reforms with governmental officials. Discussions have begun with Artin

Paşa [Dadian] and Enver Bey, the governor of Pera. It is rumored that the Armenian delegates have taken upon themselves to pacify the committee members."[136] The ARF was quick in refuting the sultan's telegram. It declared that the negotiations had been cut as of March 11, 1899.

On May 11 the sultan published another telegram through the same channel:

> The representatives who are going to discuss [Armenian reforms] with the Paris Committee and the two Committees of Geneva are Mehmud Paşa, minister of the interior; Artin Paşa [Dadian], advisor to the Ministry of Foreign Affairs; Ahmed Jelaleddin Paşa Tufekjibashi [manager of imperial gunpowder]; Enver Bey, governor of Pera; Drtad Bey as a referee; Kevork Bulbulian, attorney.[137] The Armenian delegates have not yet arrived. The government guarantees their freedom. Negotiations will start as soon as they arrive.[138]

Once more the ARF reacted promptly: *Droshak* immediately refuted the telegram by wiring the editors of *Frankfurter Zeitung* in Germany and *Le Temps* in France. While *Le Temps* did not publish the refutation, the *Frankfurter Zeitung* published it the next day in its May 12, 1899, issue. Moreover, in its May 16, 1899, issue the Constantinople office of the Correspondenz-Bureau partly retracted its earlier report by stating that the Armenian-Ottoman negotiations had reached an impasse and that the sultan was sending Ahmed Jelaleddin to give them a boost.[139]

Jelaleddin Bey's mission to Paris had no results, and the negotiations did not resume. Meanwhile the ARF and the Hunchak Party intensified their collaboration with the Young Turks in order to create an organizational framework that would give rise to a united front against Abdülhamid II.

THE SECOND SASUN REBELLION

The events of 1903 were a precursor to a larger campaign by Ottoman troops to bring Sasun under control. The situation was getting worse in all parts of the provinces of Bitlis and Van. Nevertheless, Armenian revolutionary bands continued their efforts to procure arms and ammunition and transfer them across the border from Russia or Persia.[140] It seems that some Kurdish tribes, especially those not affiliated with the Hamidiyye, helped Armenian revolutionaries.[141] The first tensions started in February in the plain of Muş. "The immediate cause appears to have been an affray between revolutionaries and tax-collectors, but a general belief was prevalent that the Kurds were ready for excesses, and that orders from Constantinople existed to which they could appeal in justification."[142] The Ottoman government tried to explain its measures by stating that Antranig (Toros Ozanian), leading almost a thousand revolutionaries in the mountains of Sasun, was committing outrages against Muslims. Moreover, revolutionaries had attacked tax-collecting officials, and Kurds appeared to be waiting to attack Armenians. Local Ottoman authorities had contingency plans for a massacre to proceed with their blessing. This threatening atmosphere had obliged Armenian villagers to join the revolutionaries, fearing attacks by the gendarmes, who were notorious for taking revenge on women and children.[143]

The gravity of the situation obliged Ambassador O'Conor to meet with the sultan.[144] He suggested starting negotiations with Armenian revolutionaries in order to circumvent an imminent bloodbath. Abdülhamid then "entered into a desultory history of the ingratitude and infidelity of the Armenians to the Imperial House of Osman, and cited instances of Armenians who had been employed in positions of the utmost confidence by his father and himself. Eventually he turned to the idea I [O'Conor] had thrown out, and remarked that it seemed to him deserving of consideration, and that it had already crossed his mind."[145]

After this meeting the palace ordered the patriarch to open negotiations with the revolutionaries through his representatives at Muş. Ormanian requested official company for the delegation to show official support. The patriarch also made strong representations to the sultan regarding the corruption in the provincial administration and the general ineffectiveness of the government, causing the situation to go from "worse to worst."[146] The revolutionaries rejected the patriarch's offers, stating that they would rather negotiate with European consuls as mediators.[147] Although Abdülhamid II sent the most stringent orders to avoid massacres and the local government in Bitlis formed new gendarme battalions manned exclusively with Circassians in order to check the Kurdish Hamidiyye forces, consul C. H. Heathcote Smith remarked that "it is perhaps natural that these men should avail themselves of their position as gendarmes to rob and oppress the Armenians, who dread them at least as much as the regular Kurdish *Zaptiyyes* [gendarmes]."[148]

Meanwhile Armenian revolutionaries were preparing themselves for the worst.[149] Although outnumbered, they tried to calm the population as much as possible. But their request to have European consuls as mediators suggests that they feared the worst and wanted Europe and especially Britain to be privy to the plight of their people.[150]

The government's detention and subsequent imprisonment of the bishop of Muş and the members of his council because of alleged "false declarations" coincided with the first round of fighting between Armenians and Kurdish Hamidiyye troops.[151] The governor of Bitlis brought the bishop from prison and ordered him to mediate with the revolutionaries. The bishop insisted that the governor should accompany him. Refusing to do so, the governor accused the bishop of being in league with the revolutionaries, with the intent of putting the blame for the fighting on Armenians. He also made it clear that the revolutionaries were planning to provoke foreign intervention.[152] Meanwhile the fighting had spread, amid reports of villages having been burned in Sasun. The government insisted that the Kurds were responsible for the carnage.[153]

Bewildered by the course of events, the governor ordered Father Arakel, the superior of St. Garabed Monastery, to intervene. He sent the priest to the revolutionaries with the demand that they surrender unconditionally. Without even waiting for a definite result from the priest's mission, the governor castigated him as a sympathizer of the revolutionaries and ordered his already assembled Ottoman troops to attack the Armenian stronghold. Thirty-seven villages were burned, while most of their people retreated to the mountains. Almost a thousand Armenians became refugees at this initial stage of the government's anti-Armenian campaign. The French consul witnessed similar results on the plain of Muş. The fighting continued through April and May 1904. The final tally was some four thousand Armenians killed and about three thousand refugees driven from their villages with no permission to return — not counting several thousands who sought shelter in the remaining villages of the plain of Muş and in friendly Kurdish territories.[154] Returning was futile, because most of the villages had been utterly destroyed and the rest were uninhabitable.[155] The policy of pushing Armenians out of Sasun could be deduced from O'Conor's statement to the grand vizier:

> In fact, it seemed to me...that the Government's policy was to drive the Armenians from the mountainous districts of Sassun to the Moush plains, where they would be under the eye of the authorities, but at the mercy of the Kurds. All that I heard pointed to the execution of the plan, and though, happily, the loss of life may not have been considerable, the ruin, poverty, and misery caused must

remain, and reduce these much-tried people to the verge both of
starvation and desperation.[156]

The policy of uprooting the indigenous Armenian populations from
their ancestral homeland and settling those lands with Kurds and other
immigrants from the Caucasus becomes apparent from the following diplomatic dispatch:

> Mr. Heathcote added that neither insurgents nor fugitives would
> be allowed to return to their homes without special orders from
> here, since the Vali considers Armenian inhabitants of the moun-
> tains as intruders on Kurdish property, and is evidently desirous
> that they should be constrained to settle in the plain, although
> he denies that such is his wish, but professes that the refugees are
> themselves asking to be allowed to do so.[157]

It is interesting that by the time the fighting ended the Kurdish sheikhs
had already arrived in Sasun to divide the land among themselves. According to H. S. Shipley: "The governor tried to persuade me that the Armenians of the mountainous areas were merely intruders who had settled
on Kurdish lands, either unlawfully or at best as farmers on the Metayer
[sic] system. He also asserted that the judicial examination of the refugees
showed that the majority of them desired to be established elsewhere."[158]
Moreover, the governor's leniency toward the Kurds was openly
manifested: "To the suggestion that perhaps the Kurds had committed
some excesses, he replied with an effrontery that surprised us, even in a
Turkish official, that no Kurds had taken part in the proceedings, and
that there had been no excesses whatever except those committed by the
insurgents."[159]
Upon the intervention of European consuls to bring a solution to the
refugee issue,

> the Armenian insurgents had presented five conditions to the
> French Consul, including permission for them to return to their
> homes under a guarantee of security by the Great Powers; the re-
> building of their houses and churches; the restoration to them of
> all property and live-stock stolen from them; a prohibition of no-
> mad Kurds coming into the district; and that, seeing the danger
> caused to women principally by the presence of licentious soldiers,
> no barracks should be built.[160]

When Ambassador O'Conor approached Abdülhamid II regarding the situation in Sasun, the sultan

said that the stories I had heard were lies and that the policy of the revolutionary committees was to circulate these mendacious reports throughout Europe. He did not deny that many lives had been lost on the side of the soldiers and the insurgents, and probably some innocent persons who had been forced to take up arms by the insurgents who had crossed the frontier had been killed, but he had given the most stringent orders not to allow the Kurds to approach the theatre of the disturbances, and he was confident that his orders had been obeyed.[161]

Confiscation of Armenian land was not exclusive to Sasun. In Van a Kurdish *ağa* (local notable) had settled in an Armenian village with the help of the Agricultural Bank and had started to oppress the Armenians.[162] Although some reports indicated that the return of villagers to Sasun proceeded "satisfactorily," the Hunchak Party appealed to the British government in a special letter to end the suffering and the persecution of Armenians in Sasun.[163]

Many of the revolutionaries were killed during the battles. Some were arrested, while the rest went into hiding in the mountains or on the Muş plain. In Sasun, where the fiercest of the battles had taken place, the banner of the ARF was found among the corpses, with documents and other important material that was confiscated by the government.[164]

On top of all this, new barracks were built either by confiscating existing houses or by material and relief funds earmarked for the refugees. Some reports even indicated that soldiers were destroying new homes in order to enlarge and improve their barracks. In consul William Tyrell's view:

All this raises a very grave question about relief measures. These have a tendency to pauperize the people, who look upon them as their right, and who seem to think it is the duty of foreign Governments to provide for them. And in the present state of the country, and of the attitude, both of the Armenians and the Turks, it seems as if such relief measures would be required at regularly recurring intervals — at least, there is no guarantee that all this will not happen again, when the money now spent in relief will all be wasted.[165]

TO ASSASSINATE A "TYRANT"

The highlight of the third ARF World Congress, which was convened in Sofia, Bulgaria, in 1904, was its decision to assassinate Sultan Abdülhamid II. The highly secretive project was entrusted to Kristapor Mikayelian, one of the founders of the party, who left Geneva for Bulgaria to start preparations.[166]

Interestingly enough, the newly formed Young Turk coalition had also decided to assassinate the sultan. The plan was developed by Dr. Abdüllah Cevdet, at the time an important member of the coalition. The assassination was supposed to be carried out on September 21, 1904. The conspirators, Edhem Ruhi and Arif Hikmet, went to Constantinople in disguise. A sailor who was supposed to deliver the dynamite obtained from Bulgaria to Arif left it unattended at the customs offices out of fear. The authorities found the explosives and arrested Arif through the sailor. The scheme was a complete failure.[167]

Mikayelian and Vram (Vramshabuh Kendirian) were killed in Bulgaria's Mount Vidosh area when a device exploded prematurely during an experiment.[168] The project continued, however, under the leadership of Safo (Mardiros Markarian). One of the conspirators, identified as Silvio Ricci, was actually an ARF member by the name of Kris Fenerjian.[169] The project was to be carried out on Friday, July 21, 1905, after the Friday prayers that Abdülhamid II would attend. A special carriage containing the explosive device was brought to Constantinople.[170]

Zareh Khachigian, an ARF member who had participated in the Ottoman Bank seizure, was driving the carriage, which was masterfully built in Vienna. The idea was to have it parked close to Abdülhamid's carriage and detonate it when he got in. Although the timing of the event had been calculated for months and Khachigian was able to park the carriage in the expected space, the sultan got into an unexpected conversation with the Şeyh-ül Islam (religious leader). The explosive device detonated while Abdülhamid was still away from his carriage. Zareh was killed on the spot. Safo was blamed for the failure of the operation and was ousted from the organization by the decision of the Fourth General Congress, held in Vienna in 1907. After the ARF's failed assassination attempt on the sultan, Abdüllah Cevdet gave an interview to a Swiss newspaper in which he tried to minimize the magnitude of the affair by stating that the Young Turks had tried that a year ago.[171]

Unbeknownst to the assassins, however, the plan was that if they failed a series of terrorist events would take place in Constantinople and Izmir to compensate for the failure. Thus it was decided that for eight to ten consecutive days several establishments and landmarks were to become the targets of bombings. The situation resembled a spy story. Although the event was to be similar to the 1896 occupation of the Ottoman Bank in Constantinople, it was much more elaborate. The first targets were to be the governmental palace and the building of the Public Debt Administration, then the customshouse, the Aydın and Magnisa train stations, the gas depot, and finally two bridges used by the railway.[172]

Ottoman intelligence-gathering agencies got some leads concerning the operations after arresting Kevork Hapetian, one of the ARF Izmir committee members. He seems to have been disbursing sums needed to fund the operations through his personal account at The Credit Lyonnais. The mastermind of the Izmir Operation was Hovannes Hagopian, an ARF member holding a United States passport issued under the name "John Jacobs." According to the plan, he was to occupy the French Embassy and use it as a center for negotiations as the bombing spree started.[173] Hagopian, who at the time was busy transporting arms and ammunition to the Caucasus, where they were desperately needed during the Armenian-Tatar fighting there, came to Izmir via Batum. Upon realizing that the whole affair had been undermined, he left Izmir secretly and boarded a Greek ship to Piraeus. There Hagopian became aware that the ARF's explosive devices hidden in the city for future use in the empire had been uncovered on a tip from the Ottoman government and that most active members including a local priest had been imprisoned.[174]

Moreover, the Ottoman government had bribed Greek newspapers, which were spreading rumors to the effect that Armenian, Bulgarian, and Macedonian revolutionaries were preparing to conduct terrorist acts against Greece. The sultan had even promised the Greek government immediately to sign a decree to start the building of the Larisa-Salonika railway if Hagopian and his comrades were extradited to Constantinople. The Greek government was in a dilemma. The sultan's offer was enticing. The Greeks conspired with the sultan to exile the terrorists to Egypt on a Turkish vessel, which was to take them directly to Constantinople. When the rumors subsided, however, Hagopian told Greek newspapers that Armenians would never allow themselves to work against Greece and that they were doing this to fight against the Ottomans as the Greek people had done decades earlier. Then the Greek public started pressuring the government. After two swift trials, all imprisoned Armenians were set free.[175]

THE EASTERN PROVINCES
WELCOME THE 1908 REVOLUTION

The news of the August 1908 revolution, which reintroduced constitutional government and its most appreciated prize, *hürriyet* (freedom), reverberated throughout the empire. The population of the eastern provinces, although puzzled at the speedy turn of events, accepted the change with jubilation. "At Van, Bitlis, Diarbekir, and elsewhere the Armenian and other political prisoners were released, and the Moslem and Christian elements were rejoicing on the same lines as those which have taken place at Constantinople, [and] the sea coast towns."[176] Moreover, "all the prisoners condemned in February last for their connection with the disturbances of the last two years at Erzeroum have now been released."[177]

The revolutionary zeal manifested itself in Harput (Kharpert in Armenian), Diyarbakır, Erzurum, and Bitlis: both Muslims and Christians demanded the removal of corrupt officials, who symbolized the last vestiges of the ancien régime.[178]

Armenian revolutionaries, as baffled as the population at large by this sudden onslaught of freedom, laid down their arms. "Hundreds of fugitive Armenians are returning home from Russia, and are being very well received by Kurds on the road. Others are going to Constantinople and elsewhere."[179]

In his memoirs Rupen Der Minassian indicates that the whole episode of freedom (*hürriyet*) baffled the *fedayees*. They thought it was a new trick by the government to bring them down from the mountain to arrest them en masse. Der Minassian had finally agreed to come to Muş with some one hundred and fifty *fedayees*.[180] Needless to say, the festivities at Muş put them at ease.

CONCLUSION

The single most important aspect of this discussion is that the period of Abdülhamid II's reign was indeed complex and perplexing. No major international conflagrations occurred, and the canny politics and maneuverings of the sovereign himself must be credited for this. But in the end the revolutionaries — Young Turks, Armenians, Albanians, Kurds, and Arabs — did attain their goal of reinstating the constitutional monarchy.

Although this victory was soon tested through the events of March 31, 1909, and the subsequent April events in the province of Adana, Abdülhamid II's fate was sealed. The centuries-old institution of Ottoman autocracy was seriously compromised.

Several factors were in play during this period. The Western powers had the sultan's government under tight control through the General Debt Administration Commission, which mercilessly siphoned almost 30 percent of all Ottoman revenues for payment of the interest accrued on the debts. This created a real economic challenge for Abdülhamid II at a time when he was constantly being pressed to implement needed reforms.

The whole debacle regarding the formation and activities of the Kurdish Hamidiyye Regiments in the eastern provinces can be viewed as a huge mistake on the part of Abdülhamid II. Whether he acted out of confidence that the adoption of these regiments would be a reformist move within the eastern *vilayet*s or out of military concern that these regiments would augment the meager Ottoman military presence on the border with Russia, it did nothing but alienate the Armenians in the eastern provinces. Moreover, the actions of the Hamidiyye became really advantageous for the Armenian revolutionary societies, which utilized the atrocities committed by these regiments to advance their agendas within the Armenian population. Thus it is not surprising to note that conditions really started to deteriorate in the eastern provinces only after the formation of these regiments in 1891, which paved the way for the 1894 and the 1904 uprisings in Sasun.

Finally, both the Armenian and Turkish sides maintain strongly nationalistic historiographies, which also hinders any rapprochement between them. This is especially true regarding the issue of the Armenian genocide, which is the central occupation of historians from both sides as well as many historians of different nationalities, to the detriment of the formative period of 1870–1914. New research must be conducted regarding this neglected period, which is less contentious than the conflict-laden issue of genocide. I hope that a new generation of Armenian and Turkish historians will rise to the task and ask the important and difficult questions.

NOTES

1. Although the Library of Congress transliteration system for Armenian is commonly used in rendering Armenian names, for the purpose of readability I have utilized a more simplified method of transliteration. Ottoman names have been transliterated into modern Turkish. In cases where Armenian and Turkish names of people and places have been adopted in English, those common spellings are used here.

2. A partial reference list includes the pioneering works of Louise Nalbandian and Hratch Dasnabedian on the Armenian side. On the Turkish side are Esat Urtas, Türkayya Ataöv, and Salahi R Sonyel.

3. The primary sources in this study are the Başbakanlık Osmanlı Arşivi, Istanbul (BOA); National Archives of the United Kingdom (formerly Public Record Office), Foreign Office Archives, London (FO); and Armenian Revolutionary Federation Archives, Boston (ARF). The original ARF Archives, which are housed at the Hayrenik Building in Watertown, Massachusetts, are not yet open to researchers. Only a few people (including me) have been able to do research there. Seven volumes have been printed thus far. The first four volumes were printed under the editorship of Hratch Dasnabedian, while the following volumes were printed under the editorship of Yervant Pamboukian. A word regarding the difference in editorship is in place. When Dasnabedian edited volumes 1 through 4 the archival materials were not yet classified. Hence these documents are cited by page number(s) in the volumes. From volume 5 on, Pambukian has used a reference system started in the 1980s, whereby each document had a separate archival referral number attached to it.

4. The Ottoman minorities were ruled according to a *millet* (Turkish for *community*) system, which allowed religious leaders some leverage in governing the internal affairs of their respective communities, by reporting directly to the Evkaf (Department of Religious Affairs). For more information regarding the *millet* system in the Ottoman Empire, see Kemal H. Karpat, "Millets and Nationality: The Roots of the Incongruity of Nation and State in the Post-Ottoman Era"; and Kevork Bardakjian, "The Rise of the Armenian Patriarchate of Constantinople."

5. Bardakjian, "The Rise of the Armenian Patriarchate," 98.

6. Ahmed Cevdet Paşa, *Sultan Abdülhamid'e Arzlar (Ma'ruzat)*, 129–205. This book is perhaps one of the most important primary sources regarding the Tanzimat period. It was discovered only recently within the Ottoman State Archives Directorate at Istanbul and is a must-read for any Ottomanist dealing with the Reform Period in the Ottoman Empire. Ahmed Cevdet Paşa was one of the most prominent (albeit within the shadows) leaders of this process. When Abdülhamid II asked Cevdet to write him a history of the Reform Projects for the period before his reign, Cevdet Paşa wrote what in Ottoman is known as the *Ma'ruzat*. Abdülhamid II ordered the writing of the book, which shows, if anything, that he was keen on the issue of reforms and by reading the manuscript became well aware of the projects undertaken by his predecessors. In the case of the Cilician reforms, which were initiated under the leadership of Ahmet Cevdet himself, the changes included bringing mobile *aşiret*s (tribes) of Turkmens, Circassians, and especially Kurds in the Gavur Daghı (literally, Infidel Mountain, later to be known as Jabali Bereket) and the Kurd Daghı (literally, Kurdish Mountain) into sedentary life in the cities and hamlets of the area as well as the incorporation of new towns such as Islahiye (literally, Reformed Town), Kars Pazar, Zulkadiriyye, and others.

7. Cevdet Paşa, *Sultan Abdülhamid'e Arzlar*, 139.

8. This police state can be explained within the context of the multitude of spies from all national groups of the empire, who were on the government payroll and reported to the sultan through their "intelligence" journals. I have found several such

reports from Armenian collaborators in the BOA. See, for example, BOA-Yıldız Tasnifi-Sadaret Hususi Maruzat Evrakı, 1746-521-109, Vanda icra edilen tahariyyet (Investigations completed in Van); BOA-Yıldız Perakende Evrakı-Umum Vilayetler Tahriratı (Y.PRM.UM), 2783-51-21, Sasunda tenkil edilen Ermeni Eşkiyasının saklandıkları yerlerin muhabirler vasitasiyle tesbiti (Spies' report on the hiding places of the Armenian revolutionaries who were transported to Sasun); BOA–Yıldız Tasnifi-Sadaret Hususi Maruzat Evrakı, 1730-521-93, Van civarında tahariyyet fesadcıların hakkında (Investigations in the Van area regarding revolutionary activities and agitators).

9. Contrary to established tradition, the term *sadıka* was not unique to the Armenian communities in the Ottoman Empire. The adjective was also used to denote other Christian minorities in the empire, especially the Bulgarians living under Ottoman dominion. The same can be said regarding the adjective *asiya*, which was used repeatedly to denote rebellious Balkan Christians.

10. The constitution, bearing the official Ottoman name "Ermeni Milletin Kanun-i Esasi" (Fundamental Organic Law of the Armenian *Millet*), was later duplicated for the other *millet*s within the empire. The sultan decreed the constitution and put his official seal on it in 1865. It is to be noted that the constitution did embolden the intellectuals while at the same time diminishing the power that the Armenian *amira* and *sarraf* classes, who until that point had been the real intermediaries with the palace regarding the Armenians. In fact several of the members of these groups were employed within the high echelons of the central government.

11. *Takrir* literally means a report. The Ottoman administration accepted *takrir*s from its subjects as pleas addressed to the sultan, who would consider them out of his benevolence.

12. Christopher J. Walker, *Armenia: The Survival of a Nation*, 112. Walker states that the Armenian proposals represented "some form of local self-government within the framework of the Ottoman Empire, and for a strengthening of the forces of law and order. But the leaders of Europe showed little interest in the cause of the Armenians, a people who had remained pacific, despite misgovernment. From April to June [1878] the Armenian leaders were in England, and met Lord Salisbury on 10 May; he gave them no more than platitudinous assurances. British policy had more important things to deal with than humanitarian matters."

13. Ibid., 114–15. The delegates to the Berlin Congress had signed an agreement that they were attending the congress with "clean hands." That is, their governments had not reached or signed any secret agreements with other governments attending the congress. During the congress, however, the *Globe* in London published the text of the Cyprus Convention, a secret agreement between Great Britain and the Ottoman Empire. According to this convention, the sultan agreed to lease Cyprus to Britain, which would defend the Ottoman state by force of arms. This revelation created a big commotion within the delegations to the Berlin Congress. It was only through the maneuvering genius of Bismarck that the French delegation was appeased, especially when France was awarded some leeway regarding Tunisia through a separate package.

14. Walker, *Armenia*, 115.

15. *Guberniia* is the Russian word for province. In fact Russia's policy had always been the creation of an "Armenia without Armenians." What Russia favored was transferring Cossacks and other peoples into its new periphery with the Ottoman Empire. Enticed by the Cossack regiments' action during the 1877–78 Russo-Turkish War, Abdülhamid II created the Hamidiyye Regiments as an auxiliary military force to augment the Ottoman army against new Russian incursions in the eastern periphery of the empire.

16. Hrant Pastermadjian, *Histoire de l'Arménie*, 325.

17. Hratch Dasnabedian, "Badmutyun Hay Heghapokhagan Sharzhman ou Hay Heghapokhagan Tashnagtsutyan," 35. This pioneering action of "Tebi Yergir" (going back to the interior, i.e., the Armenian provinces) was a direct result of the reformist agenda imbued in the Internal Armenian Constitution promulgated in 1865. Ironically, this also means that the Ottoman government itself, by ratifying this fundamental law, bears responsibility for the Armenian reawakening within the eastern provinces of the empire.

18. For more in-depth information regarding these organizations, see Hratch Dasnabedian, *Badmutyun Hay Heghapokhagan*, 35–61, 110.

19. Ibid., 111.

20. For example, Hrayr of Sasun, better known by his *nom de guerre* Dervish, always advocated patience and a long period of preparation for any rebellion, rather than inflicting a heavy toll on the Armenian population of the mountainous area because of amateurish acts of disobedience that were sure to catch the attention of the Ottoman authorities.

21. Yervant Pamboukian, ed., *Nyuter Ho. Hi. Ta. Badmutyan Hamar*, 355–66.

22. Portukalian was one of the first young educated Armenians to hear the call of the "country" (*yergir*, meaning the eastern provinces of the empire). He had settled in Van as early as 1878 and was later arrested and exiled as an agitator. Portukalian settled in Marseilles and started editing the journal *Armenia*. It was his students (who received the volatile essays that he penned in *Armenia*) who formed the Armenagan Party in Van in 1885.

23. The party membership later dissolved within the Hunchak Party and the ARF, while its remnants were later absorbed within the *Ramgavar Azadagan Gusagtsutyun* (Populist Freedom Party, Ramgavar), which was formed in Constantinople in 1908.

24. *Dzrakir Hnchakian Gusagtsutyan* (1897).

25. This happened in 1896. The western Armenian leaders of the party adamantly wanted a purely nationalistic party with no socialist ideology, while their eastern Armenian counterparts remained unyielding in this matter. This polarization within the party continued until 1907, when the party's General Meeting in Vienna incorporated both eastern and western Armenian demands within its general strategy. This action led many members of both convictions to leave the party for good.

26. The Zeytun rebellion of 1895 was in conjunction with the Sasun rebellion of 1894. Both acts led to further Armenian bloodshed throughout 1895 and 1896.

27. Dasnabedian, *Badmutyun Hay Heghapokhagan*, 109–22.

28. Ibid., 123–27.

29. Ibid., 128–50. The program was finally formulated and adopted during the fourth ARF General Congress held in Vienna in 1907. See note 25.

30. Ibid., 52–87.

31. Ibid., 20–22, 28–29.

32. Stephen Duguid, "The Politics of Unity: Hamidian Policy in Eastern Anatolia," 144. Duguid credits the Ottoman fear of a Russian encroachment on the eastern provinces and Armenian nationalist movements as a major motive for the creation of the Hamidiyye corps.

33. BOA-Yıldız Esas Evrakı-255-97-39, 4cu ordunun muşiri Zeki Paşa Talori ve havalesinde teftiş ederek Muşa döndüğü, Askerı hareket (Zeki Paşa, the commander of the Fourth Army, returning to Muş after inspection in Talori and its environs, military action).

34. The formation of the Hamidiyye Regiments gave the Kurdish tribes an institutional and official capacity in terms of imposing new taxes on Armenian villages. Although law-abiding citizens who were already burdened with taxation by the central government, Armenians now also had to pay Kurdish tribes for their "protection." Kurdish chieftains appointed "guards" in Armenian villages to protect them from other tribes. Armenian villagers were thus obliged to pay the guards' salaries.

35. BOA-Yıldız Esas Evrakı-263-97-47, Zeki Paşa: Kürt aşiretler, Bikranlı ve Badkanlı Ermenilerin hayvanları bölüşmek istiyor, Ordu onları alyor ve ve Ermenilere veriyor. Zeki Paşa (Zeki Paşa: The Bikranli and Badkanli Kurdish tribes want to divide cattle belonging to Armenians among themselves. The [Ottoman] army retakes the cattle, however, and gives them back to the Armenians, 1894).

36. Bayram Kodaman, *Şark meselesi ışığı altında Sultan II. Abdülhamidin Doğu Anadolu Politikası*, 7–11.

37. Garabet Moumdjian, "Armenian-Kurdish Relations in the Era of Kurdish Nationalism, 1830–1930," 309–10. In fact *Kurdistan* was first published under the editorship of Abdülrahman Bey's brother, Mithat Bey. When Abdulrahman assumed the editorship of the paper, he established close relations with the *Droshak* headquarters in Geneva. It was under these circumstances that his famous article "Kürtlere Hitap" (A Call to the Kurds) was published as a pamphlet in Kurdish. Its Armenian translation appeared in *Droshak*. Armenian revolutionary cells distributed thousands of these pamphlets within areas inhabited by Armenians and Kurds in the eastern provinces of the empire.

38. Moumdjian, "Armenian-Kurdish Relations," 281–83. See also BOA, 1716-503-98, Zeki Paşa: Anadoluda Osmanlı askeriyle Kürtlerin mezalimde bulunduğü ve Ermeniler tarafından yazılan mektupların Evrupada neşredildiği (Zeki Paşa: The publication in European newspapers of letters that Armenian [revolutionaries] had written regarding Ottoman soldiers' and Kurds' mayhem [against Armenians]).

39. It is interesting that *Droshak* did not publish the Kurdish chieftain's name, perhaps due to political reasons or because no such person existed. My impression is that this first propaganda tool was also written by Bedirkhan Bey.

40. Abdülrahman Bedirhan, "Koch Kurterun." In this issue *Droshak* gives a summary of the article, while leaving its publication to a future issue.

41. Ibid.

42. Ibid.

43. Moumdjian, "Armenian-Kurdish Relations," 277–94. During the nineteenth century Kurdish princes made several attempts to attain independence: Amir Mohammad's movement during the 1830s; Bedirhan's revolt during the 1840s;

Yezdansher's movement during the 1850s; and Sheikh Ubeydullah's movement during the 1880s. See also "Hay-Kertakan Haraberutiunner."

44. BOA-Yıldız Perakende Evrakı-Umum Vilayetler Tahriratı, 1614-42-4, [Abdulrahman] Bedirhan Paşazade Mıthatin Kürtçe olarak neşretmiş olduğu gazeta nushalarının dağıtımının engellenmesi, 1898 (The stoppage of the distribution of copies of [Abdulrahman] Bedirhan Bey's gazette, 1898).

45. BOA-Yıldız Perakende Evrakı-Umum Vilayetler Tahriratı, 1614-42-4.

46. FO 424.200, No. 88, Maunsell to O'Conor, Van, July 24, 1900; No. 31, enclosure in O'Conor to Salisbury, Constantinople, August 11, 1900, No. 279.

47. FO 424.200, No. 11, Maunsell to O'Conor, Van, January 6, 1900; No. 1 enclosure in O'Conor to Salisbury, Constantinople, January 24, 1909, No. 28.

48. FO 424.200, No. 19, Maunsell to O'Conor, Van, January 3, 1900; No. 5 enclosure in O'Conor to Salisbury, Constantinople, March. 1, 1900, No. 66.

49. FO 424.200, No. 127, Lamb to de Bunsen, [Erzurum, n.d.] enclosure in De Bunsen to Salisbury, Constantinople, October 15, 1900, No. 358. See also BOA, 270-511-115, Ermenilerin Rus Konsulun Teşvikiyle teşebbusu.

50. FO 424.200, No. 22, Lamb to O'Conor, Erzurum, February 24, 1900; No. 2, Confidential enclosure in O'Conor to Salisbury, Constantinople, March 7, 1900; No. 75, Confidential. See also BOA-Yıldız Perakende Evrakı-Arzuhal ve Jurnarlar, 2125–4748, Ermenilerin terki tabiiyetle yabancı memleketlere göşmek istedikleri, 1902 (Armenians asking to give up their [Ottoman] citizenship and settle in other countries, 1902).

51. FO 424.202, No. 97, Lamb to O'Conor, Erzurum, December 2, 1901; No. 21, enclosure in de Bunsen to Lansdowne, Constantinople, December 9, 1921, No. 439.

52. FO 424.202, No. 97.

53. BOA-Yıldız Esas Evrakı-255-97-39 (1894).

54. William Miller, *The Ottoman Empire and Its Successors*, 429. Sasun was located in the Province of Bitlis; Avedis Papazian, *Zhamanakagrutyun, Haykakan Hartsi yev Medz Yegherne*, 7. *Fedayee*, from the Arabic *fida'i*, literally means a person who is ready to be sacrificed for a cause. *Haytug*, adopted by Armenians from the Serbians, who used the appellation to refer to their freedom fighters, was used intermittently to mean *fedayee*. The adoption of this name shows the affinity that the Armenian revolutionary movement had with its counterparts in the Balkans (Serbs, Macedonians, and others).

55. Miller, *The Ottoman Empire*, 429. Miller describes the events as follows: "For three weeks in the late summer of 1894 the district of Sasun in the province of Bitlis became the scene of horrors which recalled those of Batak [where thousands of Bulgarians were massacred after an initial uprising by militants in the area]. The Kurds, aided by Turkish troops, under the command of Damad Zeki Paşa [brother-in-law to Abdülhamid II and the commander of the Fourth Ottoman Army], destroyed 24 villages, and butchered, with the most revolting cruelty, every Armenian whom they could find. Zeki was decorated for his services." See also Louise Nalbandian, *The Armenian Revolutionary Movement: The Development of Armenian Political Parties through the Nineteenth Century*, 120–22. According to Nalbandian, the "uprising" was organized by Murad (Hampartsum Boyajian), a devoted member of the Social Democratic Hunchak Party, who came to Sasun at the beginning of 1894. Mihran Damadian, another Hunchak leader at the time, was also instrumen-

tal in the organization of self-defense battles during the turmoil. See also Duguid, "The Politics of Unity," 151. Duguid plays down the role of the central authorities, however, asserting that the government stepped aside and allowed the Kurds to commit the atrocities.

56. Avedis Nakashian, *A Man Who Found a Country*, 135. Nakashian, an Armenian physician, commented on the arrival of the Armenian deportees from Sasun to Urfa: "The exiles arrived at Urfa. It was like a caravan of death. I shall never forget those tattered, pain-wracked victims, their staring eyes filled with horror, their gaunt faces. Women clinging to their starving babies, little children with bleeding feet, men, women, and children who had been slashed with swords or beaten from head to foot. Had anything in history ever compared to it? I wondered, and I doubted if it had. Tears streamed down their faces, prayers were on their lips, and when they learned that they would be safe in Urfa, they fell upon their knees and gave thanks to the God they worshiped so devoutly."

57. Nalbandian, *The Armenian Revolutionary Movement*, 161.

58. BOA-Yıldız Esas Evrakı, 1552-66-10, Sason Ermeni meselesine Tahkik Heyetinin tahkikat neticesini havi umumi raporun aslisi, 1895 (The original report containing the results of the Inspection Committee regarding the [uprising of] the Sasun Armenians, 1895). See also Miller, *The Ottoman Empire*, 429. According to Miller, the commission was appointed by the Ottoman government at the insistence of Great Britain, which demanded that British, French, and Russian delegates accompany it.

59. Nalbandian, *The Armenian Revolutionary Movement*, 122. See also Papazian, *Zhamanakagrutyun Haykakan Hartsi*, 7.

60. Miller, *The Ottoman Empire*, 429. According to Miller, "the commission officially designed as intended 'to inquire into the criminal conduct of Armenian brigands' [i.e., *fedayee* bands] conducted its proceedings with the partiality which might have been expected from this statement of its object, and proved as dilatory as most Turkish institutions."

61. BOA-Yıldız Esas Evrakı, 1552-66-10, Sason Ermeni meselesine Tahkik Heyetinin tahkikat neticesini havi umumi raporun aslisi, 1895.

62. FO 424.182.182. See also J[ohn] Kirakosyan, *Hayastane Michazkayin Divanagitudyan yev Sovetakan Artagin Kaghakakanutyan Pastatghterum*, 130–47. This book is a compilation of Russian documents relevant to the period 1828–1923.

63. Supplement to FO 424.182.182. The supplement is the main body of the reforms project, consisting of fourteen one-column pages. The original is in French.

64. Kirakosyan, *Hayastane Michazkayin*, 130. The most important of the twelve points of the May Reform Project are:

   1. Decreasing the number of provinces;
   2. Appointing suitable governors consistent with the needs of the different provinces;
   3. Granting amnesty to Armenian political prisoners;
   4. Providing the means for the return of Armenian refugees to their regions;
   5. Appointing a permanent Control Commission in Constantinople;
   6. Appointing a mobile commission to oversee implementation of reforms in the provinces;
   7. Providing reparation to Armenians in Sasun, Talori [Dalvorik] and other areas where massacres have occurred;

8. Establishing laws to reduce instances of forced conversions of religion;
9. Providing measures to sustain Armenians' rights and privileges.

65. BOA-Yıldız Esas Evrakı-Analitik Envanteri, 131-94-60, *Ermenilerin Istanbulda cikardığı karşılık ve ihtilal hareketlere dair tedbirler*, 1895 (The opposition of Armenians in Istanbul and the revolutionary movements and measures initiated by them, 1895); see also Miller, *The Ottoman Empire*, 429; and Papazian, *Zhamanakagrutyun Haykakan Hartsi*, 7.

66. Arman Kirakosyan, *Britanakan Divanagitutyune Yev Arevmtahayeri Khentire: 1830–1914*, 346. Kirakosyan's book is an important source, based primarily on British governmental documents. See also Miller, *The Ottoman Empire*, 429. In Miller's own words, "the cathedral at Urfa, the Edessa of the Crusaders, was the scene of a human holocaust, in which 3000 persons perished."

67. Archives du Ministère des Affaires Étrangères de France, Paris (AMAE), CP-T, 524, October 1895, 114–18. See also M. Şükrü Hanioğlu, *The Young Turks in Opposition*, 43.

68. FO 424.186.11.

69. FO 424.186.26.

70. Papazian, *Zhamanakagrutyun Haykakan Hartsi*, 7.

71. FO 244.182.196.

72. FO 424.186.50.

73. As noted above, Zeytun had endured several offensives since the 1850s.

74. For a complete rendering of events in Zeytun, see FO 424.186, especially documents 4, 18, 68, and 86.

75. FO 424.186.98.

76. FO 424.186.130.

77. FO 424.186.131 and 206. The latter is a telegram from Zeytun to the British ambassador in Constantinople, in which Armenians report that they have indeed handed in their arms and beg for security from the British.

78. FO 424.186.96. See also Miller, *The Ottoman Empire*, 429.

79. Y. Yesayan and L. Mkertchyan, "Inknapashpanakan Krivnere Vanum." Abdülhamid II replaced Nazim Bey with Ferit Paşa because Nazim Bey could not fully implement the sultan's policies in Van and its vicinity. Upon arriving in Van, Ferit Paşa organized the Turkish populace and arranged for all Armenian deportees to return to Van and the surrounding villages (ibid., 50).

80. BOA-Yıldız Esas Evrakı-Analitik Envanteri, 329-50-47, *Van vilayetinde bulunan Ferik Sadettin ve Van Kumandani, Ferik Şemsi paşalar tarafından telegraflara gore şehrin İngiliz konsulu bu fesadın tertipcisi olan dir*, 1896 (According to telegrams received from Col. Saadettin Paşa and the military commander of Van, Col. Şemsi Paşa, the British consul of Van, is the one who is instigating the revolutionaries, 1896). See also Yesayan and Mkertchyan, "Inknapashpanakan Krivnere Vanum," 50–54. It is interesting that the two Soviet Armenian historians try to paint a vicious picture of the British consul at Van, James Williams. According to Russian documents utilized by these authors, Williams collaborated with Ferit Paşa. He even informed the *paşa* of the route that the Armenian fighters were going to take when passing across the border into Persia. These accounts seem ridiculous when compared with the Foreign Office documents pertaining to dispatches from Williams in Van to Ambassador Currie, especially documents contained in FO 424,

vols. 186 through 190. Moreover, the writers were certainly influenced by the Soviet rhetoric of their era. They had to show that Russia was the only true friend the Armenians had at the time (1896) and that other European powers—particularly England—were sabotaging Russia's efforts to achieve the implementation of the promised Armenian reforms. See also Mikayel Varandian, *Ho.Hi.Tashnaktsutyan Patmutiun*, 1:208. Varandyan vindicates Williams and his actions by stating that he was a conscientious gentleman who was doing everything he could to save Armenian lives in Van. It seems that the Ottoman Archives are clearer in their estimate regarding the British consul in Van (see the BOA archival document cited in note 80). See also BOA-Yıldız Esas Evrakı-Analitik Envanteri, 325-50-43, Rusya ve Iran Ermeni komiteleinin Iran hududu yakınında sireyet etmesi malhuz, 1896 (The movement of Russian and Iranian Armenian revolutionaries is noticed in the border area with Iran, 1896). The Ottoman action was also determined by reports regarding the transport of arms and ammunition to Armenians in Van by Armenian revolutionary mobile groups traveling inside the Ottoman borders through Russian and Persian lands.

81. FO 424.186.144, February 29, 1896.

82. FO 424.186.154. Some prominent Constantinople Armenian notables, including Hovannes Nurian Efendi, S. Maksud(ian), and Abraham Kara-Kehia(ian), hated Patriarch Izmirlian. In fact, many notables considered him an ardent nationalist. Abraham Paşa's visit to Currie implies that the circumstances required a patriarch who could seem approachable to the sultan and his inner circle. Izmirlian was not a person to act in such a manner. Hence the notables were apprehensive of him.

83. The Armenian patriarch was the head of the Armenian *millet*. The Ottoman minorities were ruled according to a *millet* system, which allowed religious leaders some leverage in governing the internal affairs of their respective communities in the empire, reporting directly to the Ministry of the Evkaf.

84. FO 424.191.209.

85. FO 424.186.249. In 1899 the palace had already sent Mateos Efendi Izmirlian to Jerusalem (i.e., exiled him). Minister of justice Said Paşa, who was acting on the advice of Artin Paşa, took this action. See also FO 424.198.27. While in Jerusalem—as the guest of the Armenian Patriarchate there—Izmirlian was practically under house arrest. The local police constantly followed him. Every move he made was reported to Constantinople. But he was to return as patriarch after the 1908 Young Turk Revolution. Nelidov's remark to Currie that Izmirlian's resignation had to do with the Russian government remains a moot point. What did the Russian diplomat mean by stating that "the patriarch's removal was the Russian government's responsibility"? Moreover, why did Currie use such vague words in his report? One possible explanation is that Izmirlian was very close to Currie, which was not to the liking of the Russian diplomat, who worked closely with the notables to bring an end to Izmirlian's career.

86. FO 424.186.249; see also Maghakia Ormanian, *Azkabadum: Hay Ughapar Yegeghetsvo Antskere Esgispen Minchev Mer Orere, Haragits Azkayin Barakanerov Badmvadz*, 3:5062–63.

87. Ormanian, *Azkabadum*, 3:5069–71.

88. Ibid., 3:5042–44. Although Ormanian's account is an exaggeration in itself, since he had worked closely with the government on many occasions, it is very telling.

While the account paints Izmirlian as a nationalist and revolutionary, it also shows how reactionary Ormanian was. This was going to be a major problem for the Armenian revolutionary committees, who reached the point (as discussed below) of even threatening Ormanian's life if he did not change his attitude.

89. "Patriarkin Shurch — Verche Barin," page unknown. The passage from *Hnchak* clarifies why Abraham Kara-Kehia(ian) Paşa met with Ambassador Currie and under what circumstances Currie received the unsigned letter demanding Izmirlian's resignation.

90. FO 424.191.209.

91. Ibid.

92. FO 424.186.185.

93. BOA-Yıldız Perakende Evrakı-Arzuhal ve Jurnallar, 568-34-20, Ermeni Meselesi için Fransa, İngiltera ve Rusya arasında bir anlaşma olduğu ve bu husustakı mutalaat, 1896 (Concerning an agreement of France, England, and Russia vis-à-vis the Armenian question and some research material in this regard, 1896).

94. FO 424.186.226.

95. FO 424.186.228.

96. FO 424.186.230.

97. FO 424.186.288.

98. FO 424.186.317.

99. FO 424.186.308.

100. FO 424.186.318.

101. FO 424.186.111 and 324.

102. Tsutsagan Marmin was a secretive semimilitary apparatus of the ARF.

103. For a complete account of the event, see Armen Garo, *Bank Ottoman: Memoirs of Armen Karo*, 96–116. This book is a translation by Haig T. Papazian. Armen Garo, whose real name is Karekin Pastermajian, was an ARF member who participated in the takeover of the Ottoman Central Bank on August 26, 1896. After the 1908 Young Turk Revolution he was elected as a deputy from Karin (Erzurum) in the Ottoman Parliament.

104. The Ottoman government had huge debts to European countries, so the ARF chose the Ottoman Bank as a symbol representing both Ottoman and European interests in the Ottoman capital. In fact most of the officials of the bank and a good proportion of its customers were foreigners. The bank served the purpose of paying off the Ottoman debt, through the auspices of a special commission that organized the consolidation of the general debt. Moreover, according to Armen Garo, the hostages were properly fed and looked after throughout the event. They were removed to the central part of the building, where they would be out of harm's way.

105. Kirakosyan, *Britanakan*, 352–54. Kirakosyan quotes from "The Constantinople Massacre," *Contemporary Review* 70 (1896): 458, and *Spectator* 77 (September 5, 1896): 292. He also states that the sultan was informed, through his spies, that an operation by Armenian revolutionaries involving the Ottoman Bank was to take place. The sultan did nothing to stop the event from happening, however, since it was to his advantage to use the act as a valid reason for a new round of massacres. See also Miller, *The Ottoman Empire*, 430–31: "Scarcely had they [bank raiders]

been shipped on board of [the] French steamer [*sic*] the infuriated sultan took a terrible vengeance upon their innocent compatriots. For the next two days, August 27 and 28, 1896, the streets of Constantinople were the theatre of an organized massacre. The Armenian quarter was attacked by gangs of men, armed with clubs, who bludgeoned every Armenian whom they met, and forced their way into the houses of Armenians or foreigners who had Armenian servants, in pursuit of their victims. Police officers and soldiers aided, and even directed, this Turkish St. Bartholomew; and it was not until the representatives of the Powers, who had seen with their own eyes what had occurred, sent a strongly-worded note to the palace that the order was issued to stop the slaughter. Some 6000 persons perished in this horrible carnage; and in the words of a British diplomatist, it seems to have been the intention of the Turkish authorities to exterminate the Armenians.... Gladstone...made his last public utterance at Liverpool on behalf of the Armenians, and branded Abdülhamid II as 'the Great Assassin,' while the French writers pilloried him as 'the Red Sultan.' But no steps were taken to punish the author of the Armenian horrors."

106. FO 424.195.8.
107. FO 424.195.72.
108. BOA, 1628-520-122, Taşnaklarla Muhaberette bulunan kişiler (Persons who were in negotiations with the Dashnaks).
109. "Herkum Me."
110. "Azd."
111. "Yerku Khosk Banaktsutiunneru Artiv."
112. Ibid.
113. FO 424.196.82. The dispatch containing the letter is from O'Conor, the British ambassador in Paris. It is evident that the negotiations are being conducted with the ARF.
114. FO 424.196.82. The copy of the decree (dated April 15) is a supplement to FO 424.196.82. It contains all the promises made during the negotiations. For a complete account of the negotiations between Artin Paşa Dadian and the ARF, see also *Hayrenik* 7 (May 1938): 141–47; 8 (June 1938): 157–60; 10 (August 1939): 166–75; and 11 (November 1939): 148–66.
115. FO 424.197.45 (dated September 18, 1898).
116. FO 424.197.54.
117. FO 424.197.58 and enclosure 58. On Wilhelm II's visit to the Ottoman Empire, see Nazaret Naltchayan, "Kaiser Wilhelm II's Visits to the Ottoman Empire: Rationale, Reactions and the Meaning of Images."
118. FO 424.198.5.
119. FO 424.198.6. Artin Paşa's letter to Diran Bey is a supplement to the same document. O'Conor gives no indication of how he secured a copy of a personal letter that Artin Paşa had sent to his son. Moreover, the statement in the *paşa*'s letter that "such a policy is calculated to strengthen the hands of the powers that were aiming at the disruption of the Turkish Empire" can only implicate European powers and Russia in particular. Perhaps the elderly Armenian statesman had to include it, to show good faith toward the sultan, because his dispatches were censored.
120. FO 424.198.31.

121. Ibid.

122. Ibid.

123. The editor at *Droshak* is confused about the chronology of the two events. The Ottoman Bank event took place in August 1896, while the Khanasor Expedition took place in August 1897. To enumerate them in the sequence that appears in the editorial is misguiding.

124. "Turk Karavarutian Dimumnere Dashnaktsutian Het Banaktselu I." The article contains several letters exchanged between the ARF center and Diran Bey and Drtad Bey, quoted in tandem.

125. Ibid.

126. Ibid.

127. Ibid.

128. Ibid.

129. Ibid. *Droshak* states that the issue of Armenian students being accepted at the university and other such positive remarks that Drtad Bey reported were all lies.

130. Ibid.

131. "Turk Karavarutyian Dimumnere Dashnaktsutian Hed Banaktselu, II" (The Turkish Government's Appeals to Negotiate with Dashnaktsutiun, Part 2). The article contains several letters exchanged between the ARF center and Diran Bey and Drtad Bey, quoted in tandem.

132. Ibid.

133. Ibid.

134. Ibid. See also BOA-Yıldız Perakende Evrakı-Arzuhal Ve Jurnallar, 1305-40-31, Ermeni Patriği Ormanian Efendinin ve dişişleri vekilin musa'idi Artin Paşanın Devleti Aliyyeye hizmet ediyor görünerek aslında Rusyaya hizmet ettikleri ve cezalanderılmemek için yalancıktan geçinemiyorlar intibağını vermeye çalıştıkları (By showing themselves to be working for the benefit of the Ottoman Empire, the Armenian patriarch, Ormanian, and the undersecretary of Ottoman Ministry of Foreign Affairs, Artin Paşa, are in reality working for Russia but are very careful in not showing it, 1899).

135. "Turk Karavarutyian Dimumnere, II."

136. Ibid.

137. Ibid. It is clear that the negotiations were being conducted with the ARF. The mention of three separate committees (one in Paris and two in Geneva), however, was a ploy by the sultan to show that he was negotiating with all Armenian revolutionary organizations.

138. Ibid.

139. "Yerku Khosk Banaktsutiunneru Artiv."

140. BOA-Yıldız Perakende Evrakı-Arzuhal ve Jurnallar, 1556-4243-2, Ermenilerin Anadoluya girme ve silah sokma eylemleri, 1901 (Regarding Armenian bands entering Anatolia and smuggling guns into the country, 1901).

141. FO 424.206.14, Evelyn Grant Duff to Lansdowne, Tehran, January 26, 1904, No. 13, enclosure in Wratislaw to Hardinge, Tabriz, December 28, 1903, No. 27, Confidential; Hagop Manjikian, *Ho. Hee. Ta. Albom-Atlas, Tutsaznamard, 1890–1914*, 134; Rupen Der Minassian, *Hay Heghapokhagani Me Hishadagnere*, 259–62; FO 424.206.55, Tyrell to O'Conor, Van, April 11, 1904, No. 10, enclosure in O'Conor

to Lansdowne, Constantinople, May 5, 1904, No. 327. According to Tyrell: "Revolutionists are said to be continually arriving in Van, disguised as Kurds; and the Kurds are quite ready to help them to do so, allowing them to pass over the frontier, and assisting them on their way, for adequate pay."

142. FO 424.206.19, O'Conor to Lansdowne, Constantinople, February 23, 1904, No. 118.

143. Ibid.; FO 424.206.21, O'Conor to Lansdowne, Constantinople, March 1, 1904, No. 141; FO 424.206.24, Heathcote Smith to O'Conor, Bitlis, February 13, 1904, No. 5, enclosure 1 in O'Conor to Lansdowne, Constantinople, March 8, 1904, No. 155.

144. FO 424.206.31, Heathcote Smith to O'Conor, Bitlis, March 5, 1904, No. 9, enclosure in O'Conor to Lansdowne, Constantinople, March 28, 1904, No. 202. Muslims had informed consuls of a plan to attack Armenians. Some Kurdish leaders were opposed to the idea for the time being.

145. FO 424.206.25, O'Conor to Lansdowne, Constantinople, March 12, 1904, No. 166.

146. FO 424.206.26, O'Conor to Lansdowne, Constantinople, March 16, 1904, No. 176; FO 424.206.29, Shipley to O'Conor, Erzurum, March 12, 1904, No. 13, enclosure in O'Conor to Lansdowne, Constantinople, March 22, 1904, No. 195.

147. FO 424.206.33, O'Conor to Lansdowne, Constantinople, April 5, 1904, No. 63, Telegraphic; FO 424.206.499, Heathcote Smith to O'Conor, Bitlis, April 9, 1904, No.13, Confidential, enclosure 1 in O'Conor to Lansdowne, Constantinople, April 26, 1904, No. 301, Confidential. Concerning the failure of the patriarch's mission, Heathcote Smith wrote: "In the first place, the refusal of the Imperial Government to give the proceedings an official character, in accordance with the Patriarch's request that an officer should accompany his agents, will tend to throw doubt on his Beatitude's assertions that he is acting on behalf of His Majesty; and, moreover, I understand that the Patriarch himself is not regarded with any great confidence by the authority of the Armenians in these parts, and if they suspect him of being too Turkish in his sympathies, it is probable that the revolutionaries would distrust him still more."

148. FO 424.206.39, Heathcote Smith to O'Conor, Bitlis, March 19, 1904, No. 11, enclosure in O'Conor to Lansdowne, Constantinople, April 6, 1904, No. 248.

149. BOA-Yıldız Esas Evrakı, 347-50-65, Sason ve Talori taraflarında Ermenilerin fesad çıkarma niyetinde olduklarına dair mazbata, 1903 (Report regarding the intent of revolutionary activities by Armenians in Sasun and Talori, 1903).

150. FO 424.206.45, Heathcote Smith to O'Conor, Bitlis, April 2, 1904, No. 12, enclosure in O'Conor to Lansdowne, Constantinople, April 20, 1904, No. 284; FO 424.206.46, O'Conor to Lansdowne, Constantinople, April 18, 1904, No. 285, Confidential. The Porte had informed O'Conor that the number of revolutionaries was 300–400, with 100 trained peasants guarding their flank; FO 424.206.499, Heathcote Smith to O'Conor, Bitlis, April 9, 1904, No. 13, Confidential, enclosure 1 in O'Conor to Lansdowne, Constantinople, April 26, 1904, No. 301, Confidential. Heathcote Smith remarks: "Unfortunately I have no means of ascertaining the real intentions of the effective force of the revolutionaries. As to the former, it is generally believed that they have abandoned all hope of securing reforms except through European, and preferably British, intervention. If this is so, though they may have no desire to provoke hostilities, they would wish to keep

the question open as long as possible, and would be likely to regret the mere offer
of personal safety even of they could regard it as secure, unless it were the only
alternative to immediate annihilation." Der Minassian, *Hay Heghapokhagani Me
Hishadagnere*, 261–89 (a detailed account of the Sasun incidents of 1904); Manjikian, *Ho. Hee. Ta. Albom-Atlas*, 136–49.

151. FO 424.206.58, Heathcote Smith to O'Conor, Bitlis, April 23, 1904, No.18,
enclosure in O'Conor to Lansdowne, Constantinople, May 10, 1904, No. 335,
Confidential. Heathcote Smith also confirms that consular correspondence had
been tampered with. FO 424.206.59, Heathcote Smith to O'Conor, Bitlis, April
23, 1904, No. 17, enclosure in O'Conor to Lansdowne, Constantinople, May 10,
1904, No. 340. According to Heathcote Smith, "No one here has any certain
knowledge of the cause of the arrests, but some leading Armenians believe that the
Bishop was charged with sending a false report." FO 424.206.60, Heathcote Smith
to O'Conor, Bitlis, April 23, 1904, No. 19, enclosure in O'Conor to Lansdowne,
Constantinople, May 10, 1904, No. 341.

152. FO 424.206.71, Heathcote Smith to O'Conor, Bitlis, April 30, 1904, No. 20,
enclosure in O'Conor to Lansdowne, Constantinople, May 16, 1904, No. 367.

153. Ibid.

154. FO 424.206.127, Heathcote Smith to O'Conor, Muş, June 29, 1904, No. 29,
enclosure from O'Conor to Lansdowne, Therapia, July 11, 1904, No. 546
(O'Conor suspects that 4,000 deaths in Sasun are not greatly exaggerated).

155. FO 424.206.74, O'Conor to Lansdowne, Constantinople, May 24, 1904, No. 391;
FO 424.206.75, O'Conor to Lansdowne, Constantinople, May 24, 1904, No. 392,
"Memorandum by Mr. Lamb respecting affairs in Sassun," enclosure in O'Conor to
Lansdowne, Constantinople, May 24, 1904, No. 392. According to the Ottoman
government the Armenians destroyed their villages in Sasun before leaving them.
FO 424.206.81, O'Conor to Lansdowne, Constantinople, June 1, 1904, No. 420.
The information and assurances from the governor do not match the facts. The
latter admits to 2,000 refugees, but there are too many widows and orphans. FO
424.206.80, Tyrell to O'Conor, Van, May 14, 1904, No. 19, enclosure in O'Conor
to Lansdowne, Constantinople, May 30, 1904, No. 409; FO 424.206.95, Heathcote Smith to O'Conor, Muş, May 29, 1904, No. 23, enclosure 1 in O'Conor to
Lansdowne, Constantinople, June 14, 1904, No. 459 (Refugees estimated at
3,000).

156. FO 424.206.75, O'Conor to Lansdowne, Constantinople, May 24, 1904, No. 392.

157. FO 424.206.80, Tyrell to O'Conor, Van, May 14, 1904, No. 19, enclosure in
O'Conor to Lansdowne, Constantinople, May 30, 1904, No. 409.

158. FO 424.206.89, Shipley to O'Conor, Erzurum, May 31, 1904 No. 34, enclosure in
O'Conor to Lansdowne, Constantinople, June 8, 1904, No. 438.

159. Ibid.; FO 424.206.113, O'Conor to Lansdowne, Therapia, June 28, 1904, No. 513,
FO 424.206.125.

160. FO 424.206.101, O'Conor to Lansdowne, Therapia, June 22, 1904, No. 494. See
also FO 424.206.121, Heathcote Smith to O'Conor, Muş, June 22, 1904, No. 28,
enclosure in O'Conor to Lansdowne, Therapia, July 4, 1904, No. 533. Although
villagers demanded guarantees for their return to Sasun, "the Government had
ordered the Vali to offer to the refugees the choice of returning home or accepting

new land in the plain." The *vali* alleged that the palace had ordered the settlement of refugees on the plain.

161. FO 424.206.105, O'Conor to Lansdowne, Therapia, June 25, 1904, No. 496.

162. FO 424.206. 112, O'Conor to Lansdowne, Therapia, June 28, 1904, No. 510.

163. FO 424.206.108, O'Conor to Lansdowne, Therapia, June 28, 1904, No. 503 (forwards letter by local Hunchak committee); FO 424.206.114, O'Conor to Lansdowne, Therapia, July 7, 1904, No. 116, Telegraphic.

164. FO 424.206, No. 122. Tyrell to O'Conor, Van, June 10, 1904, No. 24, enclosure 1 in O'Conor to Lansdowne, Therapia, July 4, 1904, No. 534; Tyrell to O'Conor, Van, June 14, 1904, No. 26, enclosure 2 in O'Conor to Lansdowne, Therapia, July 4, 1904, No. 534.

165. FO 424.206, No. 122.

166. Hratch Dasnabedian, *H[ay] H[eghapokhagan] Tashnagtsutiune Ir Gazmutenen Minchev 1924*, 75–76. The sultan's assassination project was code-named "Nzhuiki Kordzoghutiun" (Operation: The Mare). In the fifth volume of the ARF documents series, however, a second code name, "Vishab" (Dragon), is used to denote the assassination attempt. See Yervant Pamboukian, ed., *Nyuter Ho. Hi. Ta. Badmutyan Hamar*, 103, which is a letter by Gosti Hambartsumyan, one of the members of the ARF central committee in Izmir, who was a fugitive in the city at the time. My assessment is that "Nzhuiki Kordzoghutiun" was the code name for the assassination, while "Vishab" was the code name for the events planned to take place in Izmir.

167. M. Şükrü Hanioğlu, *Preparation for a Revolution: The Young Turks, 1902–1908*, 57–58.

168. BOA-Yıldız Tasnifi-Sadaret Hususi Maruzat Evrakı-1000-499-64, Filipede Bomba Tecrubesi Yapan Ermeniler Hakkında Tahkikat İsteği (Asking for investigation regarding Armenians involved in bomb trials in Filibe).

169. Armen, "Ho. Hee. Dashnaktsutiune Balkanneru Mech: Enger Asadur Bedigiani Hushere." It was impossible for Kris Fenerjian (a Bulgarian citizen and a known ARF member) to get a visa to travel to Constantinople, so Vahan Mazmanian (another ARF member) bribed one of his employees, Silvio Ricci (a Bulgarian citizen of Italian ancestry), to get his passport. Ricci himself acquired a visa from the Ottoman consulate in Philippopolis (Filibe). It was through this altered passport that Kris Fenerjian made it to Constantinople to take part in the assassination affair; Manjikian, *Ho. Hee. Ta. Albom-Atlas*, 151.

170. BOA-Yıldız Tasnifi-Sadaret Hususi Maruzat Evrakı-1712-503-94, Ermeniler tarafından imal edilen bombaların İstanbula gönderilmesi: Muhbir: Ahmet Bey (Regarding bringing the bombs manufactured by Armenians to be used in Istanbul: Informant: Ahmet Bey). See also BOA-Yıldız Tasnifi-Sadaret Hususi Komisyonlar Maruzatı Evrakı, 1563-14-76, 1905, Sayfa 25, Yıldız hadisesiyle ilgili olarak tutuklanan Bogos Oğlu Minasianın intihar ettiği, 1905 (As an event that is tied to the Yıldız incident, Boghos Minasian commits suicide, 1905), 25.

171. Hanioğlu, *Preparation for a Revolution*, 57–58.

172. Malkhas (Ardashes Hovsepian), *Abrumner*, 380–81. Malkhas was also an ARF member from the United States. At the time he was sent from Geneva to Greece to liquidate the remnants of Hovannes Hagopian's operation. It must be noted that

he had explicit orders from the Western Bureau to do so. Upon arriving in Greece and hearing the account firsthand from Hagopian, however, he was inclined to pardon him, although the Western Bureau considered him responsible for the arrests. Hagopian was ousted from the ARF by decision of the Fourth General Congress in 1907 but later rejoined the party and held important positions during the second constitutional period in the Ottoman Empire. See also Hratch Dasnabedian, ed., *Niuter Ho. Hee. Tashnagtsutian Badmutian Hamar*, 256–57. These post-facto documents from the ARF Archives make it clear that the Izmir operation was designed to attack European interests if the assassination failed and a new wave of massacres ensued. Rosdom [Sdepan Zorian], however, is very critical of the organizers of the Izmir event. Apparently the secrecy of the operation was compromised (hence the Ottoman intelligence's knowledge of it), and Rosdom was furious about it. See also BOA-Yıldız Tasnifi-Sadaret Hususi Maruzat Evrakı-309-494-43, Atinada Va Pirede Derdest Edilen 8 Ermeniler Hakkında (Regarding the eight Armenians who were apprehended in Athens and Piraeus).

173. Pamboukian, *Nyuter Ho. Hi. Ta. Badmutyan Hamar*, 95–107. These pages contain several documents showing the desperate situation of ARF members in Izmir when the bombing plot code-named "Vosgehank" (Gold Mine: the revolutionary name given to Izmir) was uncovered by the police. This resulted in the total disintegration of the local ARF organization. Scores of its leaders were imprisoned, while the rest escaped to Egypt and the Balkans.

174. Malkhas, *Abrumner*, 382–85; FO 424.210.65, Cumberbatch to O'Conor, Smyrna, August 1, 1906, No. 55, enclosure 1 in O'Conor to Grey, Therapia, August 10, 1906, No. 547 in FO 424/210/28340. This document contains detailed reports on the findings in regard to the Smyrna bomb affair. The document states that it was an ARF operation and that prisoners were tortured to extract information. According to Cumberbatch, it was "sham justice."

175. FO 424.210.65, Nos. 386–91.

176. FO 424/216/29302, No. 81, Lowther to Grey, Therapia, August 18, 1908, No. 498.

177. FO 424/216/29295, No. 79, Lowther to Grey, Therapia, August 18, 1908, No. 491.

178. FO 424/216, No. 140, Lowther to Grey, Therapia, September 20, 1908, No. 590.

179. FO 424/216/n, No. 140, Safrastian to Shipley, Bitlis, September 1, 1908, enclosure to Lowther to Grey, Therapia, September 20, 1908, No. 590.

180. Der Minassian, *Hay Heghapokhagani*, 390–94.

13

Template for Destruction

The Congress of Berlin and the Evolution of Ottoman Counterinsurgency Practices

Edward J. Erickson

RECASTING THE STRATEGIC ENVIRONMENT

"The Berlin Peace Treaty recast the Ottoman Balkan possessions in such a way that it was not militarily feasible to defend them against either foreign aggression or internal insurrection."[1] In spite of this, Bismarck's Congress of Berlin treaty signed on July 13, 1878, had a profound effect on the military posture of the Ottoman Empire as it entered the twentieth century, particularly with regard to its military deployment and operations. After 1878 the recast situation in the Balkans forced the Ottoman Empire to dedicate more and more of its scarce military resources toward the defense of the Balkans. This outcome was largely due to the vulnerable geographic position of the Ottomans' remaining Balkan provinces imposed by the Congress of Berlin and by the increasingly strident and dangerous insurgent activities that the agreement seemed to encourage. This paper explores the relationship between the Congress of Berlin and the evolution of Ottoman counterinsurgency practices in the empire during the period 1878 to 1915.

In political terms, while reducing the "Greater Bulgaria" created by the Treaty of San Stefano, the Congress of Berlin served to create the modern country of Bulgaria, which by 1885 included the province of Eastern Rumelia as well. The strategic consequence for the Ottomans was monumentally disastrous: the new Bulgaria cut deeply into Ottoman territory in Europe, thereby partially isolating the five western Balkan provinces of Kosovo, Işkodra, Janina, Manastir (Macedonia), and Salonika. Moreover, the creation of Bulgaria nearly severed overland communications with the region, and the single-track railroad from Istanbul through Salonika to Skopje remained the only significant route available to the Ottomans.[2] This made communications with the Ottoman western provinces very vulnerable to interdiction while simultaneously making the resupply of military forces stationed there problematic. Unfortunately for the empire, in strategic terms the Berlin agreement created a theater of operations: its maintenance was critical to the national security needs of the Ottoman Empire, but it provided no strategic depth against its new Bulgarian neighbor. Unwilling to abandon the isolated provinces because of their large populations and productive economies, the Ottomans felt forced to defend them. The nearly bankrupt Ottomans did not have the financial resources to defend the entirety of the overextended empire. As a result they made a series of military policy decisions that prioritized the defense of their European provinces. This prioritization of effort in turn short-changed other theaters of operation and led to the evolution of a variety of differing counterinsurgency practices. By the time of World War I these practices had evolved into a template for destruction, which significantly affected Ottoman policy decisions regarding the Armenian insurrection in 1915.

CHANGES IN STRATEGIC POLICY
AND PRIORITIES AFTER 1878

The principal military legacy of the Congress of Berlin was the creation of a new and unfavorable strategic geography that pushed back the frontiers, resulting in the creation of a Bulgarian state that projected like a salient into the Ottoman European provinces. This was aggravated in turn by the permanent loss of the fortress zones along the Danube frontier in Europe and in the border areas around Kars and Batum in Caucasia. Combined with massive losses of men and equipment, the treaty immediately put the Ottoman Empire in a strategically defensive posture. The Ottoman strategic response was predictable and resulted in a major reorganization of armies, the construction of a new series of modern fortresses to replace the ones lost as a result of the Congress of Berlin, and a movement toward military modernization. As the new Christian kingdom of Bulgaria grew larger and more dangerous, the Ottomans, now hamstrung by inadequate finances, were forced to constrict and prioritize their military spending and outlays in line with strategic threats. This was the result of the creation of the Ottoman Public Debt Administration in 1881 by the Great

Powers, which forcibly reduced government expenditures in order to pay European creditors.[3] Thus between 1880 and 1911 the Ottomans built and gathered a disproportionate share of the empire's military strength in the Balkans at the expense of other regions.

Prior to the Russo-Turkish War of 1877–78, the Ottomans had three field armies with headquarters and operational areas in Europe; the First in Istanbul, the Second in Şumnu (essentially in what is now Bulgaria), and the Third in Manastir (in what is now Macedonia).[4] The European front absorbed about fifty-five percent of the field forces, with the remainder spread evenly in the Caucasus, Mesopotamia, and Arabia.[5] The organization of these armies was not standardized and varied greatly with local combinations of divisions and independent regiments. The Second Army was largely destroyed or captured by the Russian armies during the war, making the postwar restructuring of the Ottoman army an immediate priority. It took the Ottomans several years after the Treaty of Berlin to reorganize their seven numbered field armies, implementing the new structure in March 1881 and at the same time also standardizing their divisions along European lines.[6] In Thrace the Ottomans reconstituted the Second Army with its new headquarters in the city of Edirne.[7] In terms of force structure, the field armies were each identically organized, with two infantry divisions, an artillery division, and a cavalry division. The infantry divisions contained four infantry regiments each. For the purposes of this paper, the infantry regiment is used as the basis for analyzing force structure and deployments.

Under the 1881 reorganization, the three Ottoman field armies in Europe deployed a total of twenty-four infantry regiments, with the army's remaining thirty-two regiments assigned to the other four field armies (this meant that the Ottomans deployed forty-two percent of the force in Europe). This well-balanced deployment was made possible by the creation of a weak Bulgarian state in 1878 and by the removal of a direct Russian threat to southeastern Europe. The situation changed in 1885, however, when the Bulgarian annexation of East Rumelia placed an increasingly powerful Bulgarian adversary on the doorstep of Edirne (Adrianople) and Istanbul.

The creation of a new strategic threat in European Thrace forced the Ottomans to reconsider the army's strength and deployment. In 1888 a modernized reserve system was created, which added sixteen reserve infantry regiments to each field army in the event of war (thereby adding forty-eight infantry regiments to the wartime defense of the European provinces).[8] This alone was insufficient to guarantee the defensive integrity of the European front, however. To strengthen the European front, the peacetime manning levels of the infantry battalions assigned to the Second and Third Armies were raised to wartime authorizations of 800 men per battalion, while the First Army authorizations were raised to 500 men.[9] In the remaining armies of the empire infantry battalion peacetime manning levels were maintained at 400 men (only fifty percent of wartime authorizations). This increase in manning strengthened the Ottoman forces in Europe, but the vastly increased numbers of men brought commensurate increased costs in provisioning, equipping, and billeting.[10]

As a young and vigorous Bulgaria grew in conventional military power, it also encouraged revolutionary movements in Ottoman territory that forced the Ottomans to send even more troops to the European provinces (see the discussion below). In 1894 the Ottoman army added four active infantry divisions to its force structure; two of them went to the Third Army in Macedonia. Moreover, the Second Army in Edirne had grown to sixteen regiments by 1907, while the Third Army had grown to twenty-four regiments (making it the largest Ottoman field army). This gave the three Ottoman armies in Europe fifty-seven percent of the army's combat power but — under the army's higher manning levels on its European fronts — over seventy percent of the army's infantry rifle strength.[11]

Further reorganization and modernization occurred between 1908 and 1911, creating army corps that brought the Ottoman army in line with contemporary European practices.[12] As a part of this the Third Army headquarters moved to Caucasia while the Second Army headquarters moved to Salonika, absorbing the former Third Army area and assuming operational responsibility for the Ottoman provinces in Europe. The First Army headquarters remained in Istanbul but assumed command of the Edirne fortress. On the eve of the Balkan Wars in 1911, Ottoman forces assigned to defend Europe had grown to sixty-three percent of the force structure (89 infantry regiments of a total of 141 in the army) manned at near war establishments.[13]

Similarly, the national security and police force (originally *Zabtiye*, meaning law enforcement), which was founded in 1840, transformed in the 1870s into a national gendarmerie (*Jandarma*), which reflected the shifting strategic priorities of the empire. In 1888 European advisors reorganized the gendarmerie along military lines by including military training and ranks in the organization.[14] As it militarized and grew in size and capability the gendarmerie assumed internal responsibility for field operations against terrorists and guerrillas. At the beginning of the twentieth century the Ottoman gendarmerie was a well-led, well-trained, and competent force that was an integral component of the Ottoman internal security structure. The deployment of the gendarmerie, a force of over 26,000 men by the 1890s and modeled on the French system, reflected the national security priorities of the military: over forty percent of its strength was stationed in the European provinces.[15]

This robust growth of Ottoman military and paramilitary force structure was matched by the construction of new modern fortresses to make up for the loss of the Danube fortress quadrilateral (Silistre, Zistovi, Vidin, and Plevna) and the Caucasian fortresses (Kars, Ardahan, and Batum) in 1878. Starting in the early 1880s the Ottomans chose a number of important cities as defensive complexes and began to fortify them, similar to efforts then ongoing in Belgium, France, and Germany. This was a substantial effort that was very expensive. Ottoman engineers in Macedonia, closely advised by German officers, turned Janina and Scutari into major fortresses and established secondary fortress complexes in Salonika, Manastir, and Kosovo (as well as sixteen other fortified towns).[16] Complementing these defenses, the Ottomans heavily fortified the city of Edirne and the fortress line at Çatalca, which lay astride the key avenue of approach from Bulgaria to Istanbul. These major fortresses became the operational hubs around which the defense of Ottoman Europe was established.[17] The major fortresses consisted of concentric rings of self-sufficient forts about three kilometers outside the city that contained heavy artillery emplaced inside bomb-proof brick and earth fortifications. These forts were connected by entrenchments and later connected by telephone wires as well. By the twentieth century the ring of forts was moved out to about ten kilometers from the city centers.[18] In Caucasia the Ottomans heavily fortified the city of Erzurum as well as smaller efforts at Trabzon, Van, and Samsun. Thus in the thirty-year period after 1878 Ottoman military policy shifted toward the static defense of the empire's European and Caucasian frontiers but prioritized the construction of fortresses in the Balkan provinces.

The nearly total defeat at the hands of the Russians in 1878 also led the Ottoman sultan Abdülhamid to undertake dramatic reform efforts in rebuilding his shattered armies.[19] The best-known and most far-reaching of his reforms was to approach Germany for assistance in the retraining and reforming of the Ottoman army. Initially the sultan approached France, a traditional ally and friend. The French ignored the request, however, and in May 1880 Abdülhamid's request was accepted by the Germans instead. Led by Colonel Otto von Kaehler, the first three German officers reached Istanbul on April 29, 1882.[20] From these small beginnings the German military mission began the retraining of the Ottoman officer corps. Under

Kaehler's successor, Colmar von der Goltz, the mission had a great effect on the curriculum of the Ottoman War Academy by creating a mirror image of the German War Academy. This ensured that German theories of war, operational principles, and planning and training methods took intellectual root in the Ottoman army.[21] Moreover, almost immediately Ottoman army weapons procurement began to shift toward German manufacturing firms, such as Krupp and Mauser, in efforts to reequip Ottoman forces.[22] By 1888, for example, the army's artillery forces had acquired over a thousand quick-firing German field guns.[23] The army also procured hundreds of thousands of rifles, pistols, and other military equipment from Germany. Beyond this the German military mission had little apparent immediate impact; indeed, because of the financial costs the sultan rejected most of the German recommendations regarding the creation of a modern reserve system and modern army organization. In fact, the real impact of the German presence was strategic: it began the long process that ultimately blossomed into a friendly military relationship and alliance between the two nations.[24]

In sum these policies (force structure increases, fortification, and military reform) militated some of the negative strategic effects imposed by the Congress of Berlin. The army gradually deployed the bulk of its strength in Europe and created a new heavily armed fortress system that blocked key avenues into the empire's Balkan provinces. Over time the army was reequipped predominantly with up-to-date German weapons, and over a generation its senior officers were trained to plan and execute campaigns like their German mentors. Unfortunately for the empire, in the end none of these measures would compensate for the geographic penalty imposed by the creation of an aggressively expansionist Bulgaria, which acted as a salient cutting deeply into the transverse communications between Istanbul and the western provinces.

INSURGENCY BY COMMITTEE

The period 1878 through 1912 was one of general peace for the Ottoman Empire and for Europe as well. With the exception of the Ottoman-Greek War of 1897, the Ottoman Empire fought no conventional or major wars in this era. The Ottoman army, however, was increasingly operational in this period, as a number of insurgencies broke out in near and distant corners of the empire. This situation tended to focus the operations of the Ottoman army on counterinsurgency rather than on preparations for a large-scale conventional war. Historically, revolts had been ongoing in the

Ottoman Empire almost since its inception. A wave of separatist insurrections swept the Balkans between 1821 and 1876, culminating in the infamous "Bulgarian Atrocities." These revolts were built around nationalist
identities and were quite successful in dismembering the empire's European provinces. After 1878 a second wave of revolts swept through the
Ottoman Empire. The most notable were the Albanians, who rose up in
1880, the Armenians in 1894 and 1909, the Cretans in 1896, the Macedonians in 1896, the Kurds in 1908, and the Arabs in Yemen and the Hijaz as
well as the Libyan Sanussi in the early twentieth century. The second wave
of insurrections was driven in part by perceptions of Ottoman weakness
as well as by a European-wide surge of political agendas based on nationalist identity. Most of the insurrections were unsuccessful in achieving
independence but often led to Great Power interventions and interference
in Ottoman domestic affairs.[25] This section focuses on the evolution of
the revolutionary nationalist groups into a well-organized and effective
hierarchical dual system of revolutionary committees as well as the insurrections in Macedonia, which were pivotal to the Ottoman position in
the Balkans.

The Congress of Berlin left significant numbers of Christian ethnic minorities within the Ottoman Empire, who quickly and stridently
demanded independence or union with their respective motherlands.
Moreover, certain clauses of the treaty itself were designed to reform the
empire's treatment of its Christian minorities. In particular, article 23 obligated the sultan to reform the administration of the Balkan provinces. The
incomplete and sluggish implementation of this reform by the Ottoman
government led directly to discontent and unrest. After 1878 in Macedonia a number of insurgent groups emerged, who fought the Ottomans
(and among themselves) in attempts to gain control of the province.[26]
This situation coincided with the rise of what might be termed the modern guerrilla organization, which was a result of the introduction of Russian nihilism and Italian anarchism into radicalized revolutionary groups.
These organizations were known to the Ottomans as committees because
of their tightly constructed organizational architecture; their members
were likewise known as *komitacıs* (members of a secret political organization but also the word most commonly used in the empire to describe
the groups themselves).[27] The groups were organized hierarchically in
a military-like chain of command that extended from the top echelons
down to local village levels. In general they were initially formed outside
of the empire by exiles or revolutionaries who supported terrorist activity
inside the Ottoman provinces.

The first committees were formed by the Armenians in Geneva in 1887 (the Hunchak or Social Democratic Party) and in Tbilisi in 1890 (the Tashnagtsoutioun or Armenian Revolutionary Federation), which adopted extremely aggressive terrorist policies.[28] These two groups consolidated a preexisting network of decentralized revolutionary cells that were well armed and ideologically motivated. After 1892 the Armenian revolutionary organizations held world congresses, issued manifestos and proclamations, and secretly organized and trained military formations inside the Ottoman Empire.[29] At the same time the external committees organized internal, and ostensibly peaceful, counterpart political committees inside the Ottoman Empire itself. These committees were legal, operated openly, and were often composed of prominent locals such as teachers, priests, businessmen, and mayors. The internal committees encouraged nationalism and promoted military activity that was presented as self-defense against repression. Thus the Armenian committees evolved a dual organizational architecture consisting of both legal political organizations and secret armed military cells. This became the template used by other rebellious ethnic groups in the empire, and particularly in the Balkans, to form their own revolutionary organizations.

The Balkan committees began in the early 1890s when ethnic Bulgarian intellectuals from Macedonia formed literary societies in Bulgaria, which were in fact thinly disguised nationalist movements.[30] On October 23, 1893, men with Bulgarian sympathies formed the clandestine Internal Macedonian Revolutionary Organization (IMRO) to counterbalance the increasing influence of Serbia in the province.[31] Most of the founders were educated and had worked as teachers in Macedonia. They began by establishing a central committee and established local committees in Istib, Prilip, and Manastir in 1894. Meanwhile in Sofia the literary society transformed itself into the Young Macedonian Company, which matured into the Fraternal Union. A competing Macedonian Committee also based in Sofia soon sprang up. By 1895 it was apparent to the various groups that coordination was in order. Thus the First Macedonian Congress convened in Sofia on March 7, 1895, and the external groups in Sofia merged. Members of the IMRO also attended the congress, establishing formal contact with the external groups. Two months later the Bulgarian minister president Konstantin Stoilov met with the committee and encouraged uprisings in Ottoman Macedonia. The committees then began to organize themselves tactically into bands of armed irregulars in Bulgaria (called *cheta*s or *chete*s) for operations inside the Ottoman Empire.[32] Armed by the Bulgarian army and organized into four major *cheta*s and several smaller ones, the bands crossed into eastern Macedonia in the summer of 1895, raiding and terrorizing the Muslim population. Ottoman reprisals against villagers believed to have assisted the intruders were swift and merciless.

Encouraged by their successes the external groups convened the Second Macedonian Congress in December in Sofia and invited all the internal groups as well. Out of this congress came a refined organizational architecture with a Supreme Macedonian Committee at the top and in charge of the movement. This attempt to control the movement by the externals led to a fracturing of relations with the IMRO's central committee, which refused to recognize the Supremists (as the externals called themselves).[33]

Between 1896 and 1897 the IMRO put in place a comprehensive committee system throughout Macedonia, which secretly organized *cheta*s and trained them to use military weapons and tactics. Discipline was strict, and the various local groups were compartmentalized so that the exposure or destruction of one would not endanger the rest. In November 1897 the IRMO began a campaign of terror in Macedonia, using assassinations and bombings. These internal tactics complemented the raids into Ottoman territory conducted by the Sofia-based externals. And in 1899 at the Sixth Congress the two organizations agreed to work together.[34] Similar Serbian and Greek revolutionary groups emerged in the 1890s, although they do not seem to have been as violent as the Bulgarian movements. After 1900 the IMRO accelerated its preparations for insurrection by smuggling weapons into Macedonia, conducting military training, and inculcating nationalist propaganda in its network of revolutionary cells. Unfortunately for the Bulgarian nationalists the rift between the internal and external groups soon resurfaced, which in turn led to a badly coordinated insurrection.

The insurrection began in October 1902 in Djoumaia Bala (Cuma-i Bala), instigated by gangs crossing the border. The Ottomans quickly contained the revolt and limited it to the northeastern corner of the Salonika province. This reverse energized the IMRO to begin a comprehensive campaign of terror over the winter of 1902–3, in preparation for a major preplanned insurrection.[35] The IMRO campaign targeted the Ottoman infrastructure: railroads (including the fabled Orient Express), bridges, tunnels, gasworks, banks, and Ottoman police and army stations, using bombs and raids by armed gangs. In May the central committees began to orchestrate the actual uprising by organizing the *cheta*s into tactical groups, moving supplies and villagers into the mountains, and prepositioning medical supplies.[36] The IMRO was at its strongest in the Manastir

province and began the insurrection there on August 1, 1903, by immediately cutting the lines of communications and attacking isolated military and police outposts. This was soon followed by the seizure of narrow
passes and bridges to isolate the area.[37] Inside the main area of operations
the insurgents began to slaughter Muslim villagers. The well-prepared Ottomans ruthlessly suppressed the insurgency, however, finally crushing the
resistance in September. The fighting was so intense that it shocked the
Great Powers, which intervened to stabilize the region, but the IMRO
never recovered from this blow.[38]

While the Ottomans defeated the *komitacis* in the first decade of the
twentieth century, it was a bitter victory that resulted in a wide swath of
destruction in the European provinces. As noted below, sporadic IMRO
activities and localized revolts continued until the Balkan Wars, forcing
the Ottoman army to maintain a continuous military presence in the region that was focused largely on internal security.

Two serious outcomes affected the Ottomans as a result of these nationalist insurrections by committee. First, over a period of some twenty
years the operations of the *komitacis* in the Balkans and in eastern Anatolia
came to dominate the collective Ottoman military mind—much as the
Sepoy Mutiny of 1857 affected the British army.[39] Insurgency by committee remained a persistent concern of the Ottoman army until the final
days of the empire. The intellectual focus and interest of an entire generation of the Ottoman officer corps shifted from conventional warfare to
counterinsurgency campaigns. In the operational sense the experiences
and backgrounds of the army's professionals likewise shifted away from
large-scale conventional operations toward proficiency in small-unit operations focused on the suppression of internal insurrection.

Second, and perhaps more importantly, Ottoman understandings
of the nature of insurgency changed, as evidenced by Ottoman military
responses. In fact, the revolutionary committee architecture itself represented a fundamental shift in how insurrections were conducted within
the Ottoman Empire. Although insurrections had been nearly a constant
throughout its history, rebellion in the Ottoman Empire before the committees tended to be centered on a leader or tribe.[40] Insurrections were
often driven by heavy taxation or conscription rather than by nationalist
aspirations and were led by clearly identifiable local or regional leaders.[41]
In a sense, insurrections in the Ottoman Empire until the late nineteenth
century were characterized by an apolitical leader-centric and tribal organizational architecture. As a result, traditional Ottoman counterinsurgency strategies and tactics focused on the hunt for the leader and on
punishment for his followers by Ottoman army expeditionary columns.

The reality of the rise of the *komitacı*s forced a paradigm shift in the Ottoman intellectual approach to the question of insurrection because the committees distributed the leadership down and into the population itself. The club-like political front structure of the legal wings and the cell-like violent structure of the armed secret wings created a web of networked local leaders, who were embedded in the very fabric of the societies of particular nationalist minorities. Most *komitacı* leaders were teachers, intellectuals, merchants, and priests. In many locations they were mayors and public officials. In effect, the rise of the committees transformed the individual responsibility for rebellion of tribal leaders into collective responsibility for insurgency on the part of entire segments of the population. This paradigm shift in the nature of insurrection itself made it nearly impossible to localize and isolate those responsible for the problem, forcing the Ottomans, in turn, to evolve new counterinsurgency methods.

EARLY TWENTIETH CENTURY
COUNTERINSURGENCY PRACTICES

At the dawn of the twentieth century counterinsurgency policies based on the responsibility of civilian populations emerged as viable and acceptable practices in warfare. Three wars, in particular, set important precedents for the Western world in the way in which militaries dealt with guerrillas and irregular insurgents. These wars involved Spain in Cuba, the United States in the Philippines, and Britain in South Africa and led to the evolution of similar strategic, operational, and tactical practices by the Western powers.[42] At the strategic level, the powers sought the destruction of guerrilla and irregular military forces in order to end insurgencies and, in the case of the Boers, end a conventional war that had entered a guerrilla warfare phase. Operationally, the Great Powers employed campaign designs that focused on separating the guerrillas from their principal sources of support (the friendly civilian populations), thereby enabling the military defeat of the weakened guerrilla armies. At lower tactical levels, military commanders isolated the guerrillas by establishing fortified lines that cut their operational areas into manageable sectors and then removed the civilian populations. Simultaneously their regular and numerous forces swept the sectors clean of enemy forces by driving the guerrillas to destruction onto fixed barriers. To varying degrees these campaigns of population removal and concentration were successful, with the British in South Africa setting the standard for the complete and brutal subjugation of the Boer republics.

Political consequences and liabilities resulted from the issues of these international practices of making war and the morality of waging war so completely on innocent civilians. In all three countries investigations into the nature and conduct of operations were held, evoking a public outcry against the harsh treatment of civilians. In some cases individual military commanders were put on trial for blatantly illegal and reprehensible acts. But these wars did not result in international conventions or prohibitions against such policies and practices.

The military had few guidelines that either proscribed or prescribed direct military operations against civilians. The Western armies of the early twentieth century employed field service regulations that provided commanders with instructions regarding tactics, administration, logistics, and operations. These publications were almost exclusively technical in nature. Higher-level doctrines at the strategic and operational level were largely absent; official understandings of these subjects evolved mainly by reading classical military thinkers such as Carl von Clausewitz and Antoine-Henri Jomini. These kinds of works contained almost nothing on guerrilla warfare or insurgency, and it may be argued that counterinsurgency policies and practices in the early twentieth century were a matter of practice rather than of theory. Indeed, the major theorists of the field, such as T. E. Lawrence and Mao Zedong, were post–World War I authors. During the period examined in this paper a number of books were written about guerrilla and irregular warfare.

The best-known of these works on the subject was Col. Charles E. Callwell's *Small Wars: Their Principles and Practice*, which was first published in 1896 and which was regarded "in its day…as a minor classic of military writing."[43] Callwell's third edition appeared in 1906 and contained insights gathered directly from Britain's experiences in the Boer War.[44] Drawing on French marshal Thomas-Robert Bugeaud's Algerian campaigns of the 1840s as well as recent British experience in South Africa, Callwell articulated the conventional wisdom of his day regarding counterinsurgency. He noted that an effective campaign against well-led guerrillas was "well-neigh [*sic*] impossible."[45] Callwell maintained that success depended on good intelligence and the employment of highly mobile flying columns to give the enemy no rest. This was set in a context of denying the guerrillas the support of the population, subdividing the theater of war into sectors, constructing block house lines, and employing a "happy combination of mobile columns and of defensive posts" to drive the guerrillas to destruction.[46] Although Callwell did not mention population removal directly, he highlighted the necessity of "rendering it impossible for an enemy to exist in the country at all owing to no food or shelter being left" and advocated the destruction of property such as crops, homes, and livestock.[47] In Callwell's defense, he did note that such tactics were often counterproductive when the population remained in place.

It seems clear that about the time of the Russo-Japanese War (1904–5) the application of counterinsurgency and counterguerrilla practices among the militaries of the Great Powers was fairly uniform. These policies were punitive and involved the relocation of populations and the wholesale destruction of private property. The most successful example of the implementation of such policies was the conduct of the British in South Africa, which was singularly notable for the totality of the application of the practices of population removal and sweeping sectors clean of guerrillas. While repugnant, the British war against the Boers proved beyond the shadow of a doubt that such policies, when vigorously and thoroughly employed, might transform Callwell's "well-nigh impossible" situation into a victory.

It is equally clear that the Ottoman army and its officers intensively but informally studied these contemporary campaigns and small wars. The most notable example was Pertev Paşa, who was an Ottoman general staff officer and a protégé of General Colmar von der Goltz. Pertev and von der Goltz maintained an active correspondence concerning the lessons learned from the Boer War.[48] Von der Goltz also mentored Ahmed İzzet Paşa throughout this period, and the two maintained an active professional friendship. Ahmed İzzet later commanded the successful Ottoman counterinsurgency campaign in Yemen in 1911–12, an effort that involved twenty-nine infantry battalions. Counterinsurgency operations were actively discussed at the Ottoman War Academy in the period 1905 to 1914, although the subject itself was not a part of the regular course curriculum.[49] The wily and paranoid Abdülhamid, fearful of being overthrown by his own officer corps, forbade the inclusion of the subject of counterinsurgency as a course (as he also did for any courses involving political theory and thought).[50] Callwell's *Small Wars*, for example, was never translated into Ottoman, although it was translated into French (as *Petites Guerres* in 1899) and both the English and French editions were privately available in the empire. In spite of these prohibitions, the officers trained in the academy and war college, who were all fluent in at least one European language, read widely and maintained active understandings of contemporary military affairs.[51] It is easy to argue that the Ottoman officer corps was well grounded in its collective knowledge of what the Western world was doing in the way of small wars and counterinsurgency at the dawn of the twentieth century.

THE EVOLUTION OF OTTOMAN
COUNTERINSURGENCY PRACTICES IN EUROPE

During the period from 1878 to 1912 the primary strategic threat to the Ottoman Empire was not external attack by a neighboring country but rather insurrection by nationalist groups seeking political autonomy or independence. The most active of these groups were the Bulgarian and Armenian *komitacı*s, in Macedonia and Caucasia respectively. As noted above, the costly strategic reinforcement of the Ottoman armies in the Balkans closely paralleled both the growth of the Bulgarian state and the growth of the internal and external revolutionary *komitacı*s. The strategic "bill payers" for the increasing costs of security in Europe were the Ottoman field armies in the remaining theaters of operations (Caucasia, Mesopotamia, and the Arabian and North African provinces), which over time were denuded of men and equipment.[52] This asymmetric concentration of conventional forces in the Balkans in turn forced the Ottomans to consider alternative operational solutions to the insurgency threats elsewhere. One outcome of this situation was the parallel development of resource-driven counterinsurgency practices by the Ottoman military.[53] In Europe the powerful Ottoman Second Army and Third Army increasingly focused on counterinsurgency operations as the terrorist threats mounted. These operations, conducted in the relatively small Balkan geographic theater of operations by strong regular forces, closely mirrored the contemporary Western counterinsurgency practices of the age and were successfully executed.

As the *komitacı*s matured in strength and capability during the early 1890s, the Ottoman army had no formal doctrines about counterinsurgency warfare. Indeed, the military philosophy of the age was based on conventional Napoleonic warfare interpreted by Clausewitz and Jomini, which concentrated almost exclusively on wars between the regular forces of nation-states. The major defining small guerrilla wars of the era had yet to be fought, and the lessons learned about effective counterinsurgency practices had yet to be written down. This absence of formal and comprehensive doctrines left the door of practical application wide open for interpretation by individual officers. Ottoman foreign policy after 1878 was focused on keeping the Great Powers from intervening in domestic crises within the empire involving Christian minorities. This imperative drove the army to find quick and effective solutions when revolts broke out. Thus the question of how to suppress revolts as rapidly as possible in the Ottoman Empire was left entirely to field army commanders.[54]

In the Balkans the Third Army turned to the formation of provisional detachments (*müfrezeler*) or small, self-sufficient expeditionary forces that were tailored toward specific missions. Typically such detachments were commanded by a colonel and consisted of several thousand soldiers with artillery (a typical detachment in the suppression of the Bosnian revolt consisted of four battalions and an artillery battery).[55] In practice the detachments were positioned around the affected area of insurrection and then drove inward on a convergent point. Any rebels who might escape were hunted down by patrols commanded by Ottoman captains and lieutenants. A single detachment might deal with a small cross-border raiding party or the localized revolt of a tribe or a town. For large-scale insurrections the Ottomans employed their regular forces, broken down into a number of tactical detachments. In the case of the Bosnian revolt, which affected almost an entire province, the Ottomans initially committed thirty infantry battalions, which grew to a total of forty-four battalions over the course of the four-month counterinsurgency campaign.[56] The Ottoman forces began by wresting control of the roads and key mountain passes from the rebels then seized the major towns. Finally, the army drove the insurgents into the hills, where they were isolated and destroyed in detail. The campaigns were bitterly contested: many Ottoman battalions lost a third of their men in the Bosnian revolt. The most active counterinsurgency campaign fought by the Ottomans at the end of the nineteenth century in Europe occurred in Crete in 1896, when the Third Army put down an attempted revolt supported by Greeks from the mainland. In addition to the regular army division stationed on the island the sultan sent twelve additional infantry battalions to assist in the counterinsurgency campaign.[57]

The Macedonian insurrection of August 1903 represented a significant challenge for the Ottoman army simply because of its large scale, estimated at 25,000 men organized and armed by the IMRO *komitacıs* with perhaps 10,000 rifles.[58] The well-planned insurgency immediately cut communications and seized the key communications centers and choke points. Initially the Ottoman army, caught by surprise, sent twelve infantry battalions into the province, commanded by Ömer Rusdu Paşa. This force was clearly insufficient, so the Ottomans distributed rifles to the local Muslim inhabitants to secure the towns.[59] By the end of the month the First, Second, and Third Armies sent an additional forty battalions to reinforce the effort, and command transferred to Nasir Paşa. On August 24, 1903, Nasir Paşa reorganized his forces into "five detachments, which starting from outlying positions in the rebellious area headed toward its center…the soldiers encircled every zone controlled by the insurgents and hunted the revolutionary forces by surrounding them in an ever narrowing circle before crushing them…the soldiers systematically burned and destroyed Christian villages as for every shattered village there was a revolutionary center that was eliminated."[60] It took the Ottomans several months of using these brutal tactics to extinguish the insurrection: they burned several hundred villages, killing about five thousand civilians and forcing some thirty thousand to flee into neighboring Bulgaria.[61] About a thousand *komitacis* were killed as well as about five thousand Ottoman soldiers.[62] However many soldiers the Ottomans actually lost, the ferocity and totality of their response destroyed the cohesion and effectiveness of the Macedonian revolutionary organizations, which had difficulty recovering from this defeat.[63]

By 1907 Macedonian *komitacis* had regained enough strength to renew their terrorist campaigns, forcing the Ottomans to reinforce the army again. The sultan formed mobile detachments as well as a reinforced "special gendarmerie corps of three to four thousand men" to combat the guerrillas.[64] Characterized by a Western author as "mobile commandos" the forces totaled 12 battalions divided into 120 detachments of 30 men each.[65] The use of the term "commandos" is not reflective of the modern connotation of highly specialized individual soldiers; in the original use by the Boers it referred to a self-sufficient and highly mobile independent force. Complementing the mobile commandos, the Third Army, a force that had grown to 124 infantry battalions, employed 80 battalions in the counterinsurgency campaign, while 44 battalions sealed off the Bulgarian and Serbian borders.[66] Over the winter of 1907–8 the sultan's forces swept through Macedonia, sealing off areas of known guerrilla activity, destroying villages suspected of harboring and supporting the *komitacis*, and, finally, hunting down and annihilating the survivors by using the mobile columns. The operations quickly turned into a campaign of no quarter, in which massacre, countermassacre, and atrocity became commonplace. Nevertheless, the Ottomans ultimately again prevailed and ended the outbreaks of insurrection.

The Ottoman counterinsurgency campaigns in Macedonia against the Bulgarian *komitacis* were marked by the evolution of distinct tactics that mirrored the contemporary counterinsurgency practices of the Great Powers. Initially the army employed large numbers of regular soldiers, who were heavily reinforced by the gendarmerie. This force was used to seal the borders and isolate the tactical area of operations, often dividing it into manageable sectors. Villages thought to support the *komitacis* were raided and put to the torch when hidden arms were found, forcing the inhabitants to flee. Finally, the isolated guerrillas were then ruthlessly hunted down by independent and highly mobile Ottoman detachments. In the bitterly contested campaigns, atrocities on both sides were commonplace. The nature of the revolutionary committee structure ensured that the army viewed the entire local populations as wholly responsible for the insurrections. Taken altogether Ottoman counterinsurgency practices in the empire's European provinces can be characterized as well-organized but punitive and brutal campaigns executed by large numbers of regular forces.

THE EVOLUTION OF OTTOMAN COUNTERINSURGENCY PRACTICES IN CAUCASIA

Unfortunately for the Ottomans, instability and insurrection by committee erupted simultaneously (1890–1912) in the eastern Anatolian and Caucasian provinces. Poorly resourced to execute a coherent counterinsurgency campaign in one theater, the Ottomans found it almost impossible to conduct counterinsurgency campaigns in a second. Along the Ottoman Empire's Caucasian frontier and within its eastern Anatolian provinces, the Ottoman army evolved an alternate counterinsurgency policy characterized by vastly different force structures and tactics. This was brought about not by choice or sound national military policy but by the constraints caused by the spending priority of the European front, which absorbed both financial and human resources. This began as a result of the costs of the war and indemnities imposed by the Congress of Berlin, which caused the already shaky Ottoman finance system to collapse. The creditor nations then forced the Ottoman government to create a public debt administration in 1881 that administered tax revenues with a view toward the repayment of foreign investors.[67] This reduced government revenues to a trickle and crippled the ability of the sultan to rebuild the empire's military capacity for the next decade. Most of the available Ottoman military budget in the 1880s went toward weapons procurement and fortress construction.[68] The navy suffered terribly during this period, receiving almost no money, and the size and force structure of the army was frozen.[69] Moreover, as noted above, the internal and external Balkan threats to Ottoman national security pulled a disproportionate share of the existing force structure and resources to the European armies. Only twenty percent of the field gendarmerie was deployed in the six eastern Anatolian provinces.[70] This situation in turn created significant weakness in the empire's resource-poor eastern and outlying provinces.[71] Financial pressures increased, and in 1889 the desperate sultan ordered a study aimed at reducing the Ottoman active force from 250,000 to 130,000 men.[72] This reduction never took place because the security needs of the empire precluded its implementation, but it illustrates the severe financial strain imposed by financial weakness. Unfortunately for the government the threat of armed insurrection by the Armenian *komitacıs* grew in Caucasia, forcing the financially pressed Ottoman military to search for an adequate but "relatively inexpensive" solution, which it found in the resurrection of irregular light cavalry forces.[73]

In 1890 the sultan ordered the formation of the Hamidiye Tribal Light Cavalry, modeled on Russian Cossack regiments, as a standing force for internal security and border security.[74] Nominally organized as regiments under progovernment tribal chieftains and notables who received a stipend from the army, the units were uniformed and well armed but untrained and undisciplined. The cavalrymen in the regiments received guns and equipment but received no pay unless called into service.[75] Upon mobilization the men were paid small salaries, but the money was delivered directly to the chieftains and distributed by them. The government was always short of cash during this period and unable to pay salaries, so it attempted to accommodate the cavalrymen with tax reductions and other compensatory methods.[76] Moreover, the government was not saddled with the overhead costs of barracks, medical care, cantonments, and the training of conscripts, which led to further savings. In truth the force was expedient and inexpensive compared with the costs of maintaining an active force of similar size.[77] Most of the regiments were composed largely of Kurdish tribesmen, although Laz and Azeri regiments also existed. Within four years thirty regiments were raised, with a total strength of well over forty thousand men. Although the army established a special military school for the regimental leaders, the force remained largely unresponsive to conventional military discipline, a condition that would cause great difficulty when the regiments were committed operationally in arduous circumstances.[78]

Events coalesced in August 1894 in the Bitlis province when well-organized Armenian *komitacıs* rose in rebellion in the town of Sasun.[79] It remains difficult to pinpoint the beginning of the fighting—the Armenians blamed Ottoman persecution and massacres, while the Ottomans blamed Armenian raids on Muslim villages, which were encouraged by the Tbilisi committee as the proximate cause. In any case it fell to Fourth Army commander Zeki Paşa to suppress the insurrection. For this task his army had only the Eighth Infantry Division available in the area (which under the Ottoman manning policies was maintained at less than half strength).[80] After subtracting fixed garrisons, and even when reinforced with local gendarmerie regiments, the Fourth Army had much less than a division to deal with the insurgency. This led Zeki Paşa to mobilize his tribal cavalry regiments and send them to assist in the suppression. The undisciplined and poorly led irregulars quickly gained notoriety for excessively heavy-handed tactics that included the massacre, mutilation, rape, and pillaging of the Armenian population. It proved impossible to stop them from destroying Armenian villages thought to be supporting the *komitacıs*. About a quarter of the Armenian inhabitants of Sasun were killed, and both the rebellion and the Ottoman response spread to adjacent areas. It is clear today that much of the destruction was caused by impoverished tribesmen anxious to acquire the wealth and property of their neighbors. Armenian authors have asserted that 100,000 were killed in what became known as the Hamidian Massacres, but the French ambassador claimed a lower number (40,000). In any case eastern Anatolia became a slaughterhouse. This outcome, of course, should not have been unforeseen, given the inherent difficulty of counterinsurgency operations and the indiscipline of the tribal cavalry. Nevertheless, the willingness of the government to tolerate the atrocities of the Hamidiye cavalry damaged the reputation of the Ottoman military for the remainder of its existence.

After the suppression of the Sasun rebellion small numbers of additional regular troops were sent to the region, but never enough to maintain security. In 1896 renewed Armenian rebellions broke out in Van and Zeytun, which were again ruthlessly put down by government forces. A new commander, Saadettin Paşa, personally led several assaults and attempted to restrain the tribal cavalry; the pattern of atrocities continued.[81] As a matter of practice the irregular Hamidiye tribal cavalry in Caucasia seems to have employed more indiscriminate tactics than those employed by the regular army in Macedonia. Over the next decade a number of outbreaks of violence occurred, involving the Armenians both as victims and as perpetrators. As late as 1909 irregular tribal cavalry regiments were used in counterinsurgency operations in Caucasia.

In the early twentieth century Ottoman counterinsurgency practices in Caucasia evolved along fundamentally different lines than those evolving simultaneously in the empire's European provinces. In eastern Anatolia the nearly bankrupt Ottoman state chose a deliberately under-resourced approach caused by military policies that had prioritized its European fronts. As a result, the famously undisciplined irregular tribal cavalry regiments were the instrument of choice in the counterinsurgency campaigns waged against the Armenian *komitacı*s. These campaigns were characterized by insufficient regular troops and by the inability to coordinate operations between the army and the tribal cavalry. Success was gained in most cases by the indiscriminate destruction of Armenian villages and the wholesale slaughter of Armenians. Reciprocally, atrocities committed by the Armenian *komitacı*s and committee architecture ensured the transposition of responsibility to the general population, making things all the worse. Although they were generally successful in counterinsurgency operations, the brutal excesses of the Hamidiye cavalry enraged even the most hardened Ottoman officials. In 1911 the tribal cavalry regiments were disestablished or converted into reserve light cavalry regiments. This experiment failed miserably when the empire went to war in November 1914 and the Reserve Cavalry Corps, composed of the former Hamidiye regiments, was committed to conventional combat against the regular Russian army. Its performance was so weak and unreliable that the Ottomans immediately deactivated the entire force in December. In sum, Ottoman counterinsurgency practices in the empire's eastern Anatolian provinces can be characterized as poorly coordinated campaigns executed mostly by irregulars (rather than regulars), which were episodic, punitive, and needlessly bloody.

THE OTTOMAN ARMY
ON THE EVE OF WORLD WAR I

After 1878 Sultan Abdülhamid attempted a vast reformation of the army in an effort to create a viable military force capable of defending the empire. Hobbled by the lack of financial backing, his efforts were incompletely applied. While some components of the army flourished (notably the highly trained corps of general staff officers educated at the military and war academies), other parts atrophied. The training of the army was sadly deficient, as the money invested in fortifications and equipment took away from the training of line officers and soldiers, which was itself costly. In particular the new reserve force existed largely on paper and underwent almost no meaningful annual training, making it a useless tool. In the Balkan Wars of 1912–13 the army's shortcomings were ruthlessly exposed and reflected the financial priorities and military policies of the Hamidian government. Ottoman staff work was excellent, as was the effectiveness of the field artillery; however, mobilization and operational maneuvers and logistics were inefficient. The army's tactical performance in conventional operations, especially in leadership and battlefield coordination, was dismal: the war was a disaster.[82]

In comparison, Ottoman counterinsurgency campaigns were notably successful. This was mostly a result of the decentralization of effort, whereby Ottoman officers had to learn by themselves under very adverse conditions how to conduct counterinsurgency operations against guerrilla organizations. Most of the academically trained officers had to spend several rotations (sometimes whole careers) in Macedonia fighting on their own against ideologically motivated, well-equipped, and well-led guerrilla organizations. The main problem for them was the lack of government support as well as a lack of doctrinal tactics to combat unconventional and irregular fighters. The officers involved were quick to recognize the evolution of traditional insurgents and social bandits into *komitacı*s (ideologically motivated and highly disciplined guerrilla fighters). In a relatively short time, they understood the importance of gaining support from the population and made use of not only the potential of the Muslim population but also the different Christian groups, pitting them against each other.[83] Hence various practices and tactics were implemented independently of the government, and a more or less unofficial but widely accepted uniform counterinsurgency doctrine was in use after the 1890s. Ottoman officers also followed developments in foreign militaries by making use of their competency in foreign languages acquired at the academy and war college. For example, the British practice of constructing blockhouses in order to control and secure rugged terrain during the Boer War was immediately introduced under the same name (*blokhavz*) and widely used.[84] In effect, combat units became alternative military schools, and the officers' mess became clubs where army officers could discuss their ideas and tactics freely.

The counterinsurgency campaigns also played an important role in shaping the political consciousness of the officers, which was accelerated by interaction with the ideologies of their guerrilla enemies. The militant nationalism of the guerrillas, particularly the continuous flow of political thoughts and their types of propaganda and organization, greatly inspired the officers. In the end they applied what they had learned. Military men conducted the first political protests and formed secret organizations similar to the committees, such as the establishment of the Ottoman Union Committee (Osmanlı Ittihad Cemiyeti) in 1889 by Imperial Medical School cadets.[85] After 1904 more secret organizations were established and flourished at the field army headquarters. Unsurprisingly, the Third Army headquarters in Salonika became the epicenter of the most powerful group. In a relatively short time the Committee of Union and Progress (CUP: Ittihad ve Terakki Cemiyeti) became the most prominent and absorbed the other groups.[86] Despite much preparation and secrecy, an incompletely planned revolt unraveled in late April 1908. Abdülhamid immediately sent an investigation team with extraordinary powers. The conspirators gave the alarm and reacted with disobedience and insubordination.[87] Over the summer numerous other officers joined the rebellion, often taking up arms in the rugged Balkan mountains. The civilian population joined the cause of the officers by holding public demonstrations and sending mass petitions to the sultan. The officers were clearly making use of their accumulated experience in counterinsurgency by following the blueprints of the *komitacı*s.[88] In the end Abdülhamid gave up under intense pressure and restored the constitution that he had suspended in 1878. What came to be called the Young Turk Revolution was a remarkable victory won largely by junior officers, who were schooled in the practical art of counterinsurgency.[89] Many of the officers directly involved in these events, notably Enver Paşa, later seized control of the entire Ottoman government in 1913, while others rose to high command in the Ottoman Army. Thus on the eve of World War I these highly politicized officers, who had built their careers fighting *komitacı*s and guerrillas, were in positions of importance as the empire's decision makers at the strategic and operational level.

1915 IN EASTERN ANATOLIA — TEMPLATE FOR DESTRUCTION

The best-known Ottoman counterinsurgency campaign of the twentieth century involved the Armenians in 1915. It has come to be known by many Westerners as the "Armenian Genocide."[90] From the Ottoman perspective the insurrection of 1915 was a continuation of the work of the Armenian revolutionary committees, which was actively supported by the empire's new Russian and allied enemies. The Armenian committees were instrumental in the arming of the Armenian community in eastern Anatolia and in encouraging discontent and revolt. Importantly, what differentiates the Armenian insurrection of 1915 from previous rebellions is that it constituted an existential threat to the national security interests of the Ottoman state.[91] Thus the Ottomans, again in the position of possessing inadequate resources, desperately sought a more permanent resolution than those found in previous counterinsurgency campaigns.

In late October 1914 the Third Army staff informed the Ottoman general staff that large numbers of Armenians with weapons were concentrating for action.[92] War with the Entente broke out on November 2, 1914. Throughout the winter incidents of terrorism increased, particularly bombings and assassinations of civilians and local Ottoman officials. Ottoman intelligence tracked both the local Armenian committee leaders and the villages that hid and supported them. Minor revolts occurred in Bitlis and areas near Van in early February. In Armenian villages Ottoman officers found illustrated bulletins and posters advocating resistance and massacre of Muslims. These incidents were especially disturbing to the Ottomans because they indicated a higher degree of organization, which also included the cutting of communications lines and the interdiction of roads. Whether the Armenian committees' activities were acts of self-defense or acts of revolt remains controversial to this day.

In late February 1915 the Ottoman general staff sent warnings to its commanders, directing them to take increased security precautions. By mid-March 1915 the insurgent situation in the region had considerably worsened. The governor of Van reported numerous massacres of isolated Muslim villagers by armed groups of Armenian guerrillas, while the local Armenian community accused the governor of unprovoked massacres of Christians. Regardless of the cause, by this time the Ottomans were so concerned about the possibility of armed insurrection that they began to shift gendarmerie and army units into the area to meet the threat. In fact, armed revolts by the Armenians soon broke out in many areas of southeastern Anatolia.[93] The Russians actively supported the Armenians inside the Ottoman Empire with money, weapons, and encouragement, and the external Armenian committees formed regiments of enthusiastic volunteers who were eager to invade the Ottoman Empire.[94]

The event most associated with the beginning of the insurrection occurred when insurgents seized most of Van in a fierce attack on April 14, 1915.[95] Making things worse for the Ottomans, Armenian guerrilla bands began to interdict the vulnerable Ottoman lines of communications by cutting telegraph wires and conducting road sabotage to cut and block roads (notably along the Erzurum–Sivas corridor). The Van uprising acted as a catalyst, and uprisings broke out in many other cities in the east. The Ottomans did not have adequate forces in position to deal with the problem. In spite of months of tension the Ottoman army was largely unprepared for outbreaks of violence on the scale of the Van rebellion. As an expedient solution the Ottoman army formed paramilitary volunteer units, many of which were manned by the former members of the recently disbanded tribal cavalry regiments. The Field Gendarmerie Division and part of an expeditionary force were sent into action in mid-April at Van, along with several light cavalry regiments. Additionally, the Thirty-sixth Infantry Division was diverted briefly to the area as well. These divisions were all short of artillery, engineers, and ammunition trains. The army activated three new weak infantry divisions in April composed of older reservists. But they were unfit for combat until late summer. In fact, it was a resurrection of the perennial dilemma that had affected Ottoman military policy since 1878 — inadequate human and financial resources. The Ottomans simply did not have enough troops and equipment to deal with a widespread regional insurgency in the middle of a world war. Combat on the active fronts in Caucasia, Mesopotamia, the Sinai, and Gallipoli (on April 25) absorbed the attention of forty-three of forty-six active Ottoman infantry divisions in the spring of 1915.[96] Moreover, in the middle of a world war (unlike the period from 1878 to 1912) the Ottomans could not stand the draining pressure of an extended counterinsurgency campaign that interfered with the critical central lines of communications between Istanbul and the eastern parts of the empire.

The dynamics of operating in wartime with a resource-constrained force structure intersected with the imperative of national security and drove Ottoman decision makers, who themselves were steeped in the practical application of counterinsurgency practices, to seek a rapid and complete resolution of the Armenian insurrection before it caused the collapse of the Ottoman field armies deployed in the eastern reaches of the empire. A modern historian has characterized the Ottoman state's political response to the Armenian rebellion in this period as moving "from regional measures to general policy."[97] Likewise, the development of the Ottoman's military policy toward the Armenian rebellion can be characterized as moving from a localized response to a general counterinsurgency campaign. On April 20, 1915, the Ministry of Defense directed field commanders to use the local gendarmerie and provisional forces against the Armenians who were forming insurgent bands. Moreover, the ministry noted that it was undesirable to take regular army units and field gendarmes from the front for these tasks. In fact the experienced gendarmerie division and the regular divisions were relieved from counterinsurgency duties and were sent to the front in May. This military policy was maintained over the summer of 1915, and as late as July 28 the Ottomans were arming loyal Kurds and Cizre tribesmen to suppress the Armenians. Atrocities erupted, mirroring those that had previously occurred in the

1890s and 1909. This localized response was increasingly ineffective as the tempo of the insurgency accelerated.

Caught without the necessary military forces in position to deal effectively with an insurrection, on April 24, 1915, Enver Paşa ordered that the Armenians in the affected areas should be temporarily relocated. Several days later he ordered the arrest of all prominent Armenian leaders regardless of affiliations. On May 2 1915, Enver recommended to the Ministry of the Interior that the "Armenian rebels" be driven away from the borders and that the areas be resettled with Muslim refugees.[98] At the political level Talat Paşa, the interior minister, notified the prime minister on May 26, 1915, that "the insurgent Armenians did everything to obstruct the operations of the army against the enemy, prevented delivery of supplies and munitions to the soldiers on the battlefronts, collaborated with the enemy and that some of them joined the enemy's ranks."[99] The next day a provisional law was passed, directing the military to crush Armenian resistance and to begin rounding up Armenians in response to military necessity. On May 30, 1915, the Ottoman Ministry of the Interior issued the now infamous order to relocate the Armenian population of the six eastern provinces to locations away from the strategic lines of communications.[100] These directives did not order the extermination of the Armenians, but today they have generated a spectrum of interpretations ranging from simple relocation to ethnic cleansing and genocide. Over the coming summer the Ottomans began to concentrate all of the Armenians in the identified region for relocation. Many chose resistance, which in some cases was interpreted by the Ottomans as insurgency, making it difficult to determine the real reasons for the fighting in many locations.

Full-blown insurgencies erupted in a number of places beginning in July 1915, forcing the Ottomans to move into actual large-scale (regimental and divisional level) counterinsurgency operations using largely inexperienced regular forces and the provisionally organized irregulars. The newly formed and inexperienced divisions were ordered into action at Urfa, Tarsus, and Musa Daghı to tackle actual Armenian resistance.[101] Troops were later sent to Karahisar as well. In these actions the regulars encircled the Armenians, with some difficulty, and then moved inward, crushing resistance. In most locations, however, particularly those where the Armenians did not chose to fight, the army ordered the irregulars to gather up and remove the Armenians on foot in large convoys. By the early winter the Ottomans had forcibly relocated almost the entire Armenian population of the six eastern provinces. Thousands of insurgents were killed in this process by direct military action, and many more thousands of innocent

Armenians were massacred by irregulars or died of disease and starvation in the relocation process.

In any event, the suppression of the 1915 Armenian insurrection reflected the evolving counterinsurgency practices developed by the Ottoman army in the aftermath of the 1878 Congress of Berlin. This involved the wholesale removal of the Armenian population and the sweeping of the Armenian guerrillas from entire zones of operations by both regular and irregular forces. Moreover, the increasing reliance on undisciplined and irregular forces ensured that atrocities became commonplace. It is also likely that the intellectual transposition of responsibility for insurrection to the entire Armenian population often became an excuse for the massacre of innocent civilians. The counterinsurgency campaign against the Armenians was based on a comprehensive regional policy that relied as much on relocation as on direct military action. In application, Ottoman counterinsurgency practices against the Armenian revolt took previous practices to the next level by ending the problem with population removal. Again crippled by resources and inadequate regular force structure, the campaign itself was characterized by atrocity on a large scale. It is arguable that Ottoman counterinsurgency practices, as these evolved from 1878 to 1915, became a template for destruction.

CONCLUSION

The Congress of Berlin created the conditions and circumstances that directly led to a reappraisal of Ottoman strategic priorities as well as the rise of the *komitacı*s. This in turn led the Ottoman military to adapt itself to the changing strategic landscape by reacting to new external and internal threats. While procurement and organizational imperatives were for the most part focused on conventional and defensive acquisitions, the Ottoman operational effort in the period 1878 to 1912 focused on counterinsurgency campaigns. These campaigns involved varied applications of counterinsurgency practices that were driven by the financial constraints of the pauperized Ottoman state. Often Ottoman officers were left on their own to suppress rebellion and insurrection. The well-resourced Ottoman counterinsurgency campaigns and practices in the empire's European provinces generally conformed to the contemporary practices of the Great Powers. In contrast, the under-resourced Ottoman counterinsurgency campaigns and practices in Caucasia relied on the employment of irregular forces, whose hallmark was atrocities. It could also be said that the Ottoman military learned from its *komitacı* teachers how a secret nationalist committee might successfully overthrow the government — a lesson that metastasized in 1908 with the Young Turk Revolution.

When World War I broke out in 1914, the restive Armenians, encouraged by the Armenian revolutionary committees, rose in insurrection in eastern Anatolia. Unlike previous uprisings, the existential threat posed by the Armenians in wartime forced the Ottomans to seek a rapid and complete resolution based on population removal. Once again the resource-poor Ottomans, unable to commit adequate regular forces, suppressed the insurrection by using a combination of counterinsurgency practices. Unfortunately, within the framework of a poorly planned and executed regional relocation policy the opportunity for undisciplined irregular forces and criminals to perpetrate crimes against the Armenian population was guaranteed. The operational compromises that were made because of inadequate resources, mainly in the area of force structure and capability, became the common threads that link the evolution of Ottoman counterinsurgency practices between 1878 and 1915. In this regard, evolving Ottoman counterinsurgency practices became a template for the relocation and destruction of the Armenian population in eastern Anatolia.

NOTES

1. Mesut Uyar and Edward J. Erickson, *A Military History of the Ottomans, from Osman to Atatürk*, 213.
2. Naci Çakın and Nafiz Orhon, *Türk Silahlı Kuvvetleri Tarihi, IIIncü Cilt 5nci Kısım (1793–1908)*, map 8.
3. Niall Ferguson, *The War of the World: Twentieth Century Conflict and the Descent of the West*, 10–11.
4. The remaining armies were the Fourth in Erzurum, the Sixth in Baghdad, and the Seventh in Sana (there was no Fifth Army).
5. Twenty of thirty-six infantry regiments were stationed in Europe.
6. Çakın and Orhon, *Türk Silahlı Kuvvetleri Tarihi*, 213 and document 2 (Ottoman Armed Forces, March 1881).
7. The remaining armies were the Fourth in Erzincan, the Fifth in Damascus, the Sixth in Baghdad, and the Seventh in Sana.
8. Çakın and Orhon, *Türk Silahlı Kuvvetleri Tarihi*, 215–17 and organizational chart 5 (1891 reserve organization and mobilization areas).
9. Ibid., 215.
10. Stanford J. Shaw and Ezel Kural Shaw, *History of the Ottoman Empire and Modern Turkey*, 156. See also table 3.5, "Changes in Ottoman Departmental Budgets between 1880 and 1907," on 225, which shows that the army budget increased from 547 million kuruş in 1880 to 898 million kuruş in 1907.
11. Ibid., 234–36. In 1907 the Ottoman field armies deployed the following numbers of infantry regiments: First Army, eight; Second Army, sixteen; Third Army,

twenty-four; Fourth Army, twelve; Fifth Army, eight; Sixth Army, eight; Seventh
Army, eight. See also Merwin A. Griffith, "The Reorganization of the Ottoman
Army under Abdülhamid II, 1880–1897," 36. Griffith states that the army devoted
fifty percent of its strength to the Balkans, but this would appear to be on the
low side.

12. Edward J. Erickson, *Defeat in Detail: The Ottoman Army in the Balkans, 1912–1913*,
15–33.

13. Selahattin Karatamu, *Türk Silahlı Kuvvetleri Tarihi, IIIncü Cilt 6nci Kısım (1908–
1920)*, 147–75.

14. Çakın and Orhon, *Türk Silahlı Kuvvetleri Tarihi*, 251–53.

15. Ibid., "1888 Organized Jandarma and Zaptiye Forces," appendix chart 9 (Ek 9).

16. Karatamu, *Türk Silahlı Kuvvetleri Tarihi*, appendixed chart 3 (Ek 3). See also
Çakın and Orhon, *Türk Silahlı Kuvvetleri Tarihi*, 235, for a complete list of the
fortresses.

17. Griffith, "The Reorganization of the Ottoman Army under Abdülhamid II,"
67–70.

18. Şadi Sükan, *Türk Silahlı Kuvvetleri Tarihi, Osmanlı Devri, Balkan Harbi (1912–
1913), II Cilt, 3ncü Kısım Edirne Kalesi Etrafındaki Muharebeler*, 2–3. By 1912,
for example, the Edirne fortress contained 247 permanent artillery pieces fixed
in eighteen forts and eleven artillery battalion positions (see Erickson, *Defeat in
Detail*, 140–43, for details about the Edirne fortress).

19. See Jonathan Grant, "The Sword of the Sultan: Ottoman Arms Imports, 1854–
1914," for an excellent summation of the Ottoman budget during these years and
the decisions to purchase German weapons.

20. Uyar and Erickson, *A Military History of the Ottomans*, 205.

21. See Erickson, *Defeat in Detail*, 11–15, 21–33, 55–59, and 61–62, for varied commentary about the effect of the German military mission and Colmar von der Goltz in
particular.

22. Shaw and Shaw, *History of the Ottoman Empire and Modern Turkey*, 245.

23. Çakın and Orhon, *Türk Silahlı Kuvvetleri Tarihi*, 228.

24. See Benjamin C. Fortna, "The Reign of Abdülhamid II," 57; and M. Şükrü
Hanioğlu, "The Second Constitutional Period, 1908–1918."

25. Whether these insurrections were designed to liberate subject peoples or to provoke the Ottomans into heinous behavior remains contested today.

26. The modern connotation of a country called Macedonia with a discrete ethno-
linguistic identity had little relevance in the pre-1914 world, when the area was
the epicenter of conflicting claims advanced by armed groups of Bulgarians, Serbs,
Albanians, and Greeks.

27. Uyar and Erickson, *A Military History of the Ottomans*, 214–16.

28. Fortna, "The Reign of Abdülhamid II," 54.

29. Hratch Dasnabedian, *History of the Armenian Revolutionary Federation, Dasnaktutiun 1890/1924*, 25–33.

30. Duncan M. Perry, *The Politics of Terror: The Macedonian Liberation Movements,
1893–1903*, 36.

31. Nadine Lange-Akhund, *The Macedonian Question, 1893–1908: From Western
Sources*, 36. Duncan Perry's earlier work asserted that the founding date was No-

vember 3, 1893. This group is known as the Internal Macedonian Revolutionary Organization (IMRO) because it functioned inside the Ottoman Empire (the MRO functioned externally)

32. Perry, *The Politics of Terror*, 46–47.
33. Ibid., 54–56.
34. Lange-Akhund, *The Macedonian Question*, 48–50.
35. Ibid., 119–24.
36. Ibid., 123–24.
37. Ibid., 125–30. This is the best concise description of the 1903 revolt in the literature.
38. Austria and Russia forced the Ottomans to submit to the Mürzsteg Reform Program of October 22, 1903, which established a European-supervised gendarmerie in the affected provinces. See Lange-Akhund, *The Macedonian Question*, 141–46, for the text and commentary.
39. See Uyar and Erickson, *A Military History of the Ottomans*, 214–19, for a discussion of this topic.
40. Çakın and Orhon, *Türk Silahlı Kuvvetleri Tarihi*, 502–68.
41. Ibid. Many of the insurrections were known by the name of the leader: for example, the Ali Paşa Insurrection and the Mehmet Ali Paşa Insurrection.
42. For Spain in Cuba, see Philip S. Foner, *The Spanish-Cuban-American War and the Birth of American Imperialism, 1895–1902*; and David F. Trask, *The War with Spain in 1898*.

    For the Philippines, see Brian McAllister Linn, *The U.S. Army and Counterinsurgency in the Philippine War, 1899–1902*; and Robert D. Ramsey III, *Savage Wars of Peace: Case Studies of Pacification in the Philippines, 1900–1902*.

    For the Boer War, see Eversley Belfield, *The Boer War*; Thomas Pakenham, *The Boer War*; S. B. Spies, *Methods of Barbarism?: Roberts and Kitchener and Civilians in the Boer Republics, January 1900–May 1902*; and Keith Terrance Surridge, *Managing the South African War, 1899–1902*.
43. Douglas Porch, "Introduction to the Bison Books Edition," v.
44. C. E. Callwell, *Small Wars: Their Principles and Practice*, 140–44.
45. Ibid., 126. Callwell's chapter 11 is titled "Guerrilla Warfare in General."
46. Ibid., 135–49 (quotation on 138).
47. Ibid., 133.
48. Pertev Demirhan, *Generalfeldmarschall Colmar von der Goltz: Das Lebensbild eines grossen Soldaten*, 74–77. See also F. A. K. Yasamee, "Colmar Freiherr von der Goltz and the Boer War."
49. Yavuz Abadan, *Mustafa Kemal ve Çetecilik*, 53–56; Asim Gündüz, *Hatıralarım*, 29–32.
50. Uyar and Erickson, *A Military History of the Ottomans*, 221–22.
51. Mesut Uyar and A. Kadir Varoğlu, "In Search of Modernity and Rationality: The Evolution of Turkish Military Academy Curricula in a Historical Perspective." See also Erickson, *Defeat in Detail*, 56–57, for a discussion of the war college curriculum.
52. Justin McCarthy, Esat Arslan, Cemalettin Taşkıran, and Ömer Turan, *The Armenian Rebellion at Van*, 44.

53. See Vincent S. Wilhite, "Guerrilla War, Counterinsurgency, and State Formation in Ottoman Yemen," for detailed discussions of how resources affected the Ottoman counterinsurgency campaigns in Yemen.

54. H. Erdoğan Cengiz (ed.), *Enver Paşa'nın Anıları*, 48–51.

55. Çakın and Orhon, *Türk Silahlı Kuvvetleri Tarihi*, 582.

56. Ibid., 585.

57. Ibid., 216, 594–95.

58. Lange-Akhund, *The Macedonian Question*, 124–25.

59. It is unclear whether the Ottomans considered their Muslim citizens more reliable than Christians, but it is true that the *komitacı*s targeted Muslims in terrorist attacks. This led, over time, to more cooperative relations between the army and the local Muslim populations.

60. Lange-Akhund, *The Macedonian Question*, 128.

61. Ibid., 130.

62. Perry, *The Politics of Terror*, 140.

63. Ibid., 139.

64. Lange-Akhund, *The Macedonian Question*, 259.

65. Ibid., 260.

66. Ibid.

67. Shaw and Shaw, *History of the Ottoman Empire and Modern Turkey*, 222–24.

68. See Griffith, "The Reorganization of the Ottoman Army under Abdülhamid II," 85–87 and annex 4 ("Income vs. Military Expenditures, 1886–1895"), for detailed discussions of military expenditures.

69. Shaw and Shaw, *History of the Ottoman Empire and Modern Turkey*, 225.

70. Çakın and Orhon, *Türk Silahlı Kuvvetleri Tarihi*, "1888 Organized Jandarma and Zaptiye Forces," appendix chart 9 (Ek 9).

71. McCarthy et al., *The Armenian Rebellion at Van*, 58.

72. Griffith, "The Reorganization of the Ottoman Army under Abdülhamid II," 87.

73. Ibid., 119–22. See also Uyar and Erickson, *A Military History of the Ottomans*, 202–4. The tradition of locally organized irregular cavalry dated back to the earliest days of the Osmanli dynasty; see 53–61 for details of the Timariot Cavalry and associated frontier units.

74. Çakın and Orhon, *Türk Silahlı Kuvvetleri Tarihi*, 223.

75. Griffith, "The Reorganization of the Ottoman Army under Abdülhamid II," 122.

76. Correspondence with Dr. Mesut Uyar, Turkish Military Academy, Ankara, March 23, 2010.

77. It is important to note here that the Russians gradually decreased the size of their Cossack forces as 1914 approached and that no other Great Power chose an irregular force model for their standing armies. This speaks to the generally held idea at that time that irregular forces, and the Cossacks in particular, had limited utility on the battlefield.

78. Stanford J. Shaw, *The Ottoman Empire in World War I*, 84–86, 145.

79. Dasnabedian, *History of the Armenian Revolutionary Federation*, 51–53.

80. Çakın and Orhon, *Türk Silahlı Kuvvetleri Tarihi*, 602–3.

81. McCarthy et al., *The Armenian Rebellion at Van*, 64–68.

82. Uyar and Erickson, *A Military History of the Ottomans*, 208–11.

83. Resneli Niyazi, *Hürriyet Kahramanı Resneli Niyazi Hatıratı*, 148–52.

84. Cengiz, *Enver Paşa'nın Anıları*, 52–57; Kazım Karabekir, *Hayatım*, 379–83, 407–11, 468–75, 503–18; Rahmi Apak, *Yetmişlik Bir Subayın Anıları*, 16–23.

85. Military schools (especially the Military Academy) were the real cauldrons of dissidence and dissemination of ideologies and thoughts. See Halil Kut, *Ittihat ve Terakki'den Cumhuriyete Bitmeyen Savas*, 9–17; Karabekir, *Hayatım*, 247–349.

86. Cengiz, *Enver Paşa'nın Anıları*, 57–69, 75–76; Niyazi, *Hürriyet Kahramanı Resneli Niyazi Hatıratı*, 162–63; H. Cemal, *Arnavutluk'tan Sakarya'ya Komitacılık: Yuzbası Cemal'in Anıları*, 9–13.

87. Cengiz, *Enver Paşa'nın Anıları*, 79–90; Niyazi, *Hürriyet Kahramanı Resneli Niyazi Hatıratı*, 165–71.

88. Cengiz, *Enver Paşa'nın Anıları*, 77, 90–121; Bekir Fikri, *Balkanlarda Tedhiş ve Gerilla: Grebene*, 17–28. See also M. Şükrü Hanioğlu, *Preparation for a Revolution: The Young Turks, 1902–1908*, 217–30.

89. Cemal, *Arnavutluk'tan Sakarya'ya Komitacılık*, 21–24.

90. This paper does not address the issue of whether these events constitute a genocide or not, focusing more narrowly on the causes and effects of Ottoman counterinsurgency operations.

91. See Edward J. Erickson, "Captain Larkin and the Turks: The Strategic Impact of the Operations of HMS *Doris* in Early 1915"; and Edward J. Erickson, "The Armenians and Ottoman National Security, 1915."

92. See Edward J. Erickson, "Armenian Massacres: New Records Undercut Old Blame."

93. Erickson, "The Armenians and Ottoman National Security, 1915," 163.

94. Ibid., 150–53.

95. The most recent work on this subject is McCarthy et al., *The Armenian Rebellion at Van*, which presents a comprehensive analysis of what happened there.

96. Erickson, *Ordered to Die*, 86, 109.

97. Donald Bloxham, *The Great Game of Genocide, Imperialism, Nationalism and the Destruction of the Ottoman Armenians*, 141–51 (quotation on 145).

98. Operations Division to Ministry of the Interior, May 2, 1915, Genelkurmay Askeri Tarih ve Stratejik Etüt Başkanlığı Arşivi/Archives of the Turkish General Staff Directorate for Military History and Strategic Research, Ankara (ATASE), Archive 44, Record 207, File 2-1.

99. Talat to Prime Minister's Office, Memorandum 270, May 26, 1915, Başbakanlık Osmanlı Arşivi, Istanbul (BOA), No. 326758, quoted in Yusuf Halaçoğlu, "Realities behind the Relocation," 114.

100. Thus the Ottomans opted for the widely practiced contemporary counterinsurgency strategy of relocation (or "concentration" as it was then known) as developed by the Spanish, the Americans, and the British. It might also be mentioned that the British in Malaya and the French in Algeria in the 1950s also chose counterinsurgency strategies of population removal and relocation, moving 570,000 ethnic Chinese and over 2 million Algerians respectively.

101. See Edward J. Erickson, "Bayonets on Musa Dagh, Ottoman Counterinsurgency Operations—1915."

14

The Hamidiye Light Cavalry Regiments

Abdülhamid II and the Eastern Anatolian Tribes

Bayram Kodaman

It is well known that the Abdülhamid II period (1876–1909) has been a topic of great interest for local and foreign historians in recent years. The reason for this undoubtedly lies in the lack of scholarly research concerning the Abdülhamid II period and incomplete knowledge concerning its ins and outs. What we presently know is a product of books, articles, and newspapers that are generally written according to particular political positions and consider only certain aspects of this period. It can be said that most of these types of books and articles have been written in order either to criticize or to praise this period in a one-sided way. In this regard, scholarly research that relies on archival documents and original sources has become increasingly important. As a result of all this, the angles and ways of looking at the Abdülhamid II period have changed. The time of seeing and evaluating this period only as "despotic" and "a reaction to modernity" or only as a "reawakening of Islam" has passed.

I have found it beneficial to shed light on the Hamidiye Regiments by relying on archival documents. The regiments were established in 1891 by Abdülhamid II and gave a new face to eastern Anatolia's social, political, and economic life. This subject is not well known, or even touched on, in scholarship. In order to elucidate this topic, it is useful to give a general characterization of the period between 1876 and 1908, because it is not possible to understand the formation of the Hamidiye Regiments without discussion of other events during the Abdülhamid II period.

CHARACTERISTICS OF
THE ABDÜLHAMID II PERIOD

Centralization

Although it is indisputable that this period was despotic and centralist, despotism and centralism in the Ottoman Empire were not particular only to Abdülhamid II. If we remember the centralist and despotic policies of Mahmud II in the Ottoman Empire or those of Bismarck and the Russian tsar only shortly before this period, Abdülhamid II's relatively similar policies are not to be regarded as deviant from the norm among his contemporaries. Abdülhamid II's centralization policy is actually a logical result of the events and transformations had been occurring since the Tanzimat.[1] Much of the system that Mahmud II established was centralist and autocratic. He managed to strengthen his central control over the empire with a decree that took effect on March 1, 1840. But the establishment of local administrative councils, which Mustafa Reşit Paşa enacted in 1842, and the decree (*ferman*) on November 28, 1852, that increased the authority of the *vali*s weakened the centralist system. Due to the uprisings and disturbances that occurred in the empire between 1857 and 1861, however, the tendency for central government to increase its control in the *vilayet*s reemerged. It is possible to see traces of this tendency in the centralist spirit of the Vilayet Reform Law passed in 1864, based on the pattern of France's administrative divisions. After additional modifications of this law were passed in 1871, the Ottoman state became slightly more centralist. After this date the Abdülaziz administration developed in both an absolutist and centralist way. In short, efforts to reconcile democratization with centralization were rendered increasingly unsuccessful throughout the Tanzimat period. From 1864 onward the tendencies toward centralism gained sway over the tendencies toward democratization. At the end of Franco-Prussian War of 1870 this tendency toward centralism increased.

The experiences of the 1876 constitution (Kanun-i Esasi) and the Chamber of the Deputies (Meclis-i Mebusan), the Russo-Turkish War of 1877, and the ensuing Treaty of Berlin in 1878 brought Abdülhamid II closer to the idea of centralism. He recognized that the power that held the Ottoman Empire together was state power and that everything was connected to it. Indeed, the sultan knew that the central state could not prevent uprisings and fragmentation or keep the local forces from gaining strength once its power weakened. Therefore he was against any persistent lack of centralization.

Abdülhamid attributed both the failure of the Tanzimat supporters to implement any successful reforms and the existence of rampant military irregularity (*başıbozukluk*) in the empire to the weakness of central state power. He envisioned the establishment of a centralist state not in a constitutional and parliamentary system but only in an autocratic system and imposed his centralist vision on the authorities in Istanbul by shutting down the Chamber of the Deputies. Abdülhamid continually urged the local authorities (notables in the towns and cities) and official authorities (army commanders and *valis*) in the rural areas to adopt his vision of a centralist state. It can be said that he pursued a successful policy by establishing a well-balanced movement and by making gradual and occasionally mutual concessions. Part of this policy is seen in the Hamidiye Regiments established in eastern Anatolia.

Yet one point must be made: centralism was considered a means of achieving Islamic unity and other related reforms and was not Abdülhamid II's sole purpose.[2] Traces of this policy can be seen in the establishment of the Hamidiye Regiments.

Islamic Unity
The driving force behind the Tanzimat reforms was to create an Ottoman society in which people became Ottoman citizens, by uniting different elements in the empire around a shared nation (*vatan*), a shared dynasty, and a shared interest. Even if such aspirations were seen as logical, they did not occur naturally within the conditions of that time. Nevertheless, natural and political rights were granted to non-Muslims with good intentions and also as a result of European pressure. But tangible results were not achieved, due to European intervention and the anti-Ottoman tendencies of many non-Muslims. Finally, non-Muslims continued to stage uprisings and Muslim society became increasingly withdrawn from the government, which dampened the hopes of the administrators. A significant part of Christian society either completely split from the empire or became autonomous at the end of 1877 Russo-Turkish War and the Berlin Congress, which was enough to show that the Tanzimat proponents' "Ottomanist ideology" would not be realized.

It was not long before that the idea of Islamic unity (pan-Islamism), which originated around 1872, filled an ideological void. This idea seemed slightly more natural and practical compared to Ottomanism, because the majority of the population in the empire was Muslim and shared many traits: first and foremost, the Islamic faith and reverence for the caliphate.

By using the spiritual facilities of the caliphate together with the material facilities of the centralist system, Abdülhamid II sought to give new hopes to Muslims in a hopeless situation, to increase their belief and loyalty to the dynasty and the government, and thus to strengthen the empire both inside and outside. Therefore this policy was successful. In fact he established the view that he was the leader of the Muslims and their protector in the empire. His fame and reputation as caliph-sultan spread among the world's Muslims. By establishing the Hamidiye Regiments, the sultan easily strengthened his ties with the tribes and placed them under his command.

A Policy of Balance

The most significant method that Abdülhamid II applied in his domestic and foreign policy during his thirty-three-year reign can be summarized as a balanced policy: an attempt to maintain the authority of the palace and the Sublime Porte, and importantly his own authority, by securing a balance among competing forces in the state. His ability to remain in power for thirty-three years can be attributed to this policy. Concrete examples include opening space for pan-Islamist thought while accepting the need to implement reforms like those of the Tanzimat — even doing so successfully in the education sector — in order to balance reformist and antireformist forces (those in favor of Westernization and the conservatives against it).[3] Thus the sultan managed to appease the two sides while maintaining himself above them. Still, he wanted to balance the demands of Muslim and Christian societies through reform. All reforms during the Tanzimat period were made in response to the demands of Christians, leading to a disparity in the rights of Muslims in regions where Christians formed a large portion of the population. Therefore Abdülhamid II undertook reforms that were in favor of and even tipped the balance toward Turks and Muslims. The state maintained its authority over and provided public order for the forces in the rural areas by securing the balance between them, much in the same manner that it did in the urban areas. Abdülhamid II made efforts to bring the state above the competition between *vali*s and cities, village notables and *ağa*s in the rural areas, Christians and Muslims, and bureaucrats and the public by calculating a delicate balance.

It can be said that Abdülhamid II attempted modernization by establishing a balance between pro-Western and conservative officials. Except for some areas, however, the success rate was generally low, and the empire was also unable to save itself from collapse, because it lagged behind on the path to modernization.

Reform Policy

The state in the reign of Abdülhamid II had an undeniable need to benefit from Western civilization in order to modernize and grow. Contrary to the Tanzimat, however, it can be said to have adopted a policy in favor of putting the pro-West intelligentsia, who formed a new class, under supervision. Arbitrary revolutionary movements, which were outside the scope of supervision, were widely seen as a disaster for the empire and society, leading to a tendency toward renovations and changes that placed society under the state's control.

The intellectual class of this period undoubtedly had a big influence on the emergence of the tendency to supervise both the intelligentsia and such renovations. The emergent intellectual class of the period had two major shortcomings. First, the old Ottoman intelligentsia had been set apart as the enemy of the West in a dogmatic way, without recognizing Western civilization. The Tanzimat intelligentsia was in favor of the West and was the enemy of the traditional order, thus falling into the same dogmatism but in the opposite direction. Perhaps the paradox of the Turkish intellectual class lies in this point. In short, the proponents of the Tanzimat competed over "mastery in imitation," without taking the trouble to understand the foundation of Western civilization or analyze Ottoman social structure.[4] The second shortcoming is that members of the Tanzimat intelligentsia went to Europe to learn their own history and not to learn about Western civilization. In other words, they tried to learn Turkish, Ottoman history, and Islamic society and civilization while in Europe, even though they were commissioned to examine the foundations of Western civilization. They actually did learn a number of things. But the result was uncertain because the intelligentsia viewed Ottoman society and Turkish-Islamic civilization through European eyes and approached Turkish issues by way of solutions that Europeans had put forth. Consequently, the intelligentsia alienated Turkish society and steered it toward denial of the past and present. Thus a spiritual/intellectual, commoner/intelligentsia split emerged. The empire's intelligentsia donned the European (French-English and German) cloak and shed the Arab-Persian cloak that had long covered Turkish culture. Therefore the Turkish people, who had preserved and represented Turkish culture, were left to their own fate. Yet some of the Turkish intelligentsia worked in a positive direction.

Until 1876 a bureaucratic intelligentsia class consisting of intellectuals who possessed administrative value but no social value (as explained above) was present in the empire. Its opposite was a conservative intelligentsia class that more or less had the support of the people and (despite different tendencies) could unite based on centralist, Islamist, and pro-sultan stances.

Abdülhamid II planned to undertake reforms that would meet the demands of both intelligentsia classes by striking a delicate balance between them and would also help to strengthen centralism and Islamic unity. He even managed to establish a balance and undertake some reforms. From 1890 onward, however, the balance between the two intelligentsia classes was broken by the emergence of a third group or ideology: the Committee of Union and Progress and Turkism. In addition to these three opposing groups, non-Muslim dissenters and European interference led to an era of increasing instability and eventually brought an end to the period of Abdülhamid II.

THE GREAT POWERS AND EASTERN ANATOLIA

By the end of the 1877–78 Russo-Turkish War Russia had increased its influence in eastern Anatolia and the Balkans by breaking the established balance and became a threat to British interests. In order to balance Russian supremacy and protect its interests, Britain leased Cyprus through a secret agreement with the Sublime Porte in 1878. Britain also obtained the right to intervene in eastern Anatolia by inserting article 61, which favored the Armenians, into the Treaty of Berlin. Thus the Eastern question devolved from the Balkans to eastern Anatolia, and the "Armenian question" and the Ottoman Empire's Asian lands became the major points of debate. Britain had a large stake in this. According to article 61 of the Treaty of Berlin, "The Sublime Porte undertakes to carry out, without further delay, the ameliorations and reforms demanded by local requirements in the provinces inhabited by the Armenians, and to guarantee their security against the Circassians and the Kurds."[5] The Great Powers were to oversee the reforms that would be undertaken, and the Sublime Porte was to lose its dominion in eastern Anatolia. Britain sought to create an Armenian state that would be located on land taken from a weakening Ottoman Empire (which was then unable to stop Russia from entering its southern region), would always have the support of Europe in eastern Anatolia, and would also keep Russia from entering Iraq. Britain was already making plans to seize Egypt and influence events in the Arabian Peninsula.

In the first years Abdülhamid II showed that he trusted Britain to preserve the lands in Asia by renting out Cyprus as a military base and that he preferred Britain's policy to that of Russia. But from 1887 onward we see that he distanced himself from Britain or at least started to act more cautiously and became increasingly close to Russia. The basis for this change was Britain's occupation of Egypt and the Arabian Peninsula, its activities in regard to Iraq and Kuwait, its aid to Armenian organizations, and its protection of the Armenians. This British stance aroused the suspicions of Abdülhamid II and even frightened him, pushing him to take precautions in eastern Anatolia according to his own political understanding. In doing so he took into account the social balance (centralism, Islamism, and the Armenian threat).

The sultan started to put his policy into practice, especially from 1891 onward. After this date Britain completely changed Europe's mind regarding the Ottoman Empire and gradually turned from the policies pursued during the Tanzimat period, which tended toward protecting the integrity of the Ottoman Empire, to a policy of breaking the empire apart and destroying it. By creating the political situations in Armenia, Crete, and Macedonia, Britain constantly sought to meddle in Ottoman internal affairs and to wear the Ottoman state thin.

EASTERN ANATOLIA'S SITUATION

Even in the periods of Selim I (1465–1520) and Süleyman the Magnificent (1520–66), during which the Ottoman Empire expanded the most, the Ottomans were unable to establish full dominion over eastern Anatolia because of its geographic and social situation. Therefore no serious relationship between the central authority and eastern Anatolia could be established. The region remained autonomous until the Republican period. This made the cultural, economic, and social structures in eastern Anatolia unique. Two features of this structure stand out. First, the *ağa* order was based on wealth and particularly land ownership. Each person came under the rule of the wealthiest and most powerful in sequenced loyalty. Thus an *ağa* class emerged. Second, the sheikh order was rooted in religious customs, in the *mezheb*s (religious schools of law) and the *tarikat*s (Sufi orders). The *ağa*s brought the people in eastern Anatolia under their material influence, and the sheikhs brought them under their religious influence. These two groups were particularly influential on the tribes and the people in the rural regions.

In the *vilayet*s, *sancak*s, and *kaza*s an *eşraf* (nobility) class existed. From the Tanzimat onward, members of this group had a dominant political, administrative, and cultural status in the cities. They were able to bring the *vali*s under their influence, act as arbiters in the reforms, and participate in the local governance (in commissions and organizations) related to the reforms. They did not want the central authority to gain excessive power lest they lose such privileges.[6] The local authorities (such as *valis*, *mutasarrıf*s, *kaymakam*s, and *kadi*s) already were able to secure power easily through various means. Moreover they had been able to increase their influence by exerting pressure on the tribal chiefs and *ağa*s through official paths. Since the *eşraf*s in the cities had no trust in the reforms, they delayed their implementation and hindered them through organizations over which they had control. They also blamed the Ottoman bureaucracy for the reforms made for the Armenians.

Another characteristic of eastern Anatolia was its ethnic and religious diversity. Although Turks were the majority, minorities such as Kurds, Armenians, Circassians, Arabs, and Nestorians also lived there. While the majority of the people were Muslim and Christian, there was much religious diversity in terms of the different religious orders and schools of law. But the greatest paradox in regard to the ethnic and religious issue was that the Muslim people lived interspersed with the Christian Armenians. Although the Kurds officially recognized the central authority, they continually had the ability to move freely, outside the control of Istanbul. Therefore they often feuded among themselves and attacked villages. The Armenians did not listen to Istanbul, because their hopes of creating an independent state had been extinguished after the 1877–78 Russo-Turkish War. As noted above, the *eşraf*s also seized every manner of control over the cities.

Foreign states influenced Christian minorities via agents, consuls in eastern Anatolia, and schools with politico-religious aims that they opened. They also kept the central authority from increasing its strength by intervening in the local administrations. The British, French, and American missionary schools and colleges especially played a destructive role in eastern Anatolia. Abdülhamid II at one time closed these foreign schools (which had been opened without permission) and restricted the opening of new schools to schools that had obtained government permission in order to control them, but it cannot be said that he was fully successful.

Abdülhamid II was faced with this situation in eastern Anatolia. His vision of a centralist, Islamist, balanced reformist state was a policy experiment that was full of contrasts and clashed with international interests. This policy manifested itself in a balanced and positive way: sometimes harsh, sometimes appeasing, and sometimes moderate when forced to comply with the conditions in eastern Anatolia. But it did not lead to any transformation in the socioeconomic structure of eastern Anatolia. Yet it created a situation that favored the Muslim people politically and more or less culturally. The foundation of Abdülhamid II's policy already was to prevent the establishment of an Armenian state in eastern Anatolia and to keep the region within the borders of the empire. In short it did not pave the way for incidents in eastern Anatolia similar to events in Eastern Rumelia and Crete. When viewed from this angle, it is clear that all of the problems of eastern Anatolia were not taken into consideration. Keeping together an empire with no financial strength that was reeling back and forth was an important matter for the administrative cadres of the time.

EASTERN ANATOLIAN TRIBES
AND ABDÜLHAMID, 1878 TO 1891

The eastern Anatolian tribes, which had been relatively calm during the Tanzimat period, began to clash with one another as a result of the power vacuum created by the Russo-Turkish War of 1877–78. They also started to act insubordinately toward the local officials who represented central authority.[7] In 1878 Sheikh Ubeydullah, the chief of the tribes in the environs of Hakkari, launched an independence movement in the region between Iran and the Ottoman Empire and gained support from Britain. At first Abdülhamid II supported Ubeydullah against Iran and helped him. In 1880 the sultan tried to draw Ubeydullah to his side by dispatching his assistant Bahri Bey, the son of Bedr Khan Bey (the chief of a powerful and populous tribe that ruled over the region around Van), to Hakkari.[8] In fact he succeeded in getting Ubeydullah to focus on Iran. Ubeydullah turned against the Ottoman Empire a short time later, however, probably at the behest of Britain. Abdülhamid II, who sensed the danger, chose to ally himself with other tribal chiefs and sent some twenty-six retired officers to visit the tribal chiefs gathered in Hakkari, present them with various gifts, equip them with weapons, and train them militarily.[9] Afterward he tried to organize and arm the tribes in Şakird, Muş, Bitlis, Doğubeyazıt, Erzurum, and Hınıs, visiting their respective leaders Ahmed Ağa, Abdulkadir, İsmail Bey, Sheikh Siddik, and Seyit Ali Abdurrahman. Meanwhile Sheikh Ubeydullah had given up his ambitions and was placed under forced residency in Istanbul. He did not keep quiet, however, and was exiled to Mecca in 1883. After that Abdülhamid II continued his policy of establishing good relations with the tribal chiefs.

Britain and especially Iran did not look kindly upon Abdülhamid II's policy. Because Iran was Shiꞌi, it opposed Abdülhamid II's pan-Islamism policy and was suspicious that he would use the tribes against Iran. Britain considered the organization of the tribes to be an obstacle in implementing the reforms for the Armenians, which were to be undertaken under British supervision, and in creating a future Armenian state, to be established under British protection. Abdülhamid II believed that he could organize the tribes as long as he was friends with Russia. The Russians were already opposed to Britain's policy and against the idea of an independent Armenia, so it was not hard for Abdülhamid II to acquire their friendship.

From 1884 onward Abdülhamid II tried to form an alliance with the tribes by using a softer approach. Dinitin, the Russian consul in Erzurum, had this to say on the topic: "The Ottoman government commanded the local authorities to establish friendly relations with the tribal chiefs and to make an alliance with them through nice words and good actions."[10] The *vali*s and the military elites had a big share in implementing this policy. For instance, Ethem Paşa, who was appointed the *vali* of Hakkari in 1884, continually established good ties with the tribal chiefs, resolved the disputes between them through friendly actions, and made them friendlier to the government.[11] At the same time they would woo the tribes by distributing arms among them and make them sense the power and overlordship of the state.

Between 1885 and 1890 the Sublime Porte tried to be tolerant of the tribes in order to bring them under moderate control. It took pains to act moderately against the Armenians. In fact during these years the Armenians submitted no major complaints. They complained only of the actions of the local officials and of the tribes. Even in 1887 Said Paşa, one of the foremost Ottoman officials of the period (who had been the grand vizier on multiple occasions), wanted reforms in favor of the Armenians to be undertaken.[12] But the gradual attempt on the part of the Armenian secret terror organizations to rise up against the state in eastern Anatolia and other parts of the Empire scared Abdülhamid II. Eastern Anatolia could have been lost. Therefore he placed Armenian schools, newspapers, and other activities under close surveillance. The finding of scores of weapons in Armenian churches in searches during the 1890s pushed Abdülhamid II and the Sublime Porte toward acting more favorably toward the Muslim peoples, especially the tribes, and to forge alliances with them. Danger appeared imminent to both the empire and the tribes, so the time had come to take precautions.

THE REASONS FOR THE ESTABLISHMENT OF
THE HAMIDIYE CAVALRY REGIMENTS

The reason for the formation of the Hamidiye Regiments was not a single factor, such as the Armenian issue. The causes for the formation of the Hamidiye Regiments can be found in the policies of Abdülhamid II (as outlined in the first section of this paper). The Hamidiye Regiments were not the sole aim of Abdülhamid II's policy but were a means to an end. The following factors played a role in the formation of the regiments:

1. Establishing central authority.
2. Procuring a new sociopolitical balance in which the state could be effective in eastern Anatolia.
3. Benefiting from the tribes as a military power.
4. Hindering Armenian activism and ensuring the balance of power between the Armenians and Muslims.
5. Protecting eastern Anatolia from Russian attacks and British policy.
6. Carrying out the policy of pan-Islamism.

Central Authority

In 1877, after closing the first Chamber of Deputies, Abdülhamid II embarked upon implementing an extreme centralist system in order to liberate the empire. The sultan could not turn a blind eye to the situation of eastern Anatolia and of the tribes, which had remained outside the control of Istanbul for years. Therefore he considered it necessary to take the state's power to eastern Anatolia by linking the tribes to the center or at least bringing them closer. But in practice his agents needed to take care to avoid inciting the tribes, who lived independently and far from all types of authority and other sociopolitical forces. Also acting as the caliph, Abdülhamid II enticed the tribes, the sheikhs, and others through compromise, gifts, and betrothals and linked them to the state. Acting as a sultan, he found more concrete and convincing ways of linking them to the state. Before 1890 he distributed arms to the tribes through the *vali*s and military leaders and found various methods to fulfill his aims. Thus he attempted to confirm his status as the "patron sultan" of the tribes, which in turned engendered good relations between the tribes and the local authorities. He believed that establishing the Hamidiye Regiments would greatly improve relations between the sultan and the tribes via the local authorities. Despite the expectation of some drawbacks and negative results, he thought that with time the tribes would become accustomed to authority and submit to it. In brief, the main aim was to establish state authority in eastern Anatolia through the Hamidiye Cavalry.

A New Sociopolitical Balance

The sociopolitical and economic order in eastern Anatolia brought to light a number of traditional local forces, the most significant of which was the urban elite (*şehir eşrafı*). Members of this urban elite class did not want the central authority to strengthen, so they constantly viewed Istanbul with suspicion and blamed the Sublime Porte for the reforms. They were first to come out against Abdülhamid II's centralist policy, which they tried to stifle. The sultan perceived their objections and attempted to break their power — or balance it with another force — to bring them under his control. The nomadic and seminomadic tribes living in the rural regions provided the balancing element. The sultan tried to control the elites by organizing the tribes into military units and arming them. The tribes were Muslim, which added another security element against the Armenians.

The Tribes as a Military Power

Benefiting from the power of the tribes from a military standpoint is perhaps the most logical reason behind the establishment of the Hamidiye Regiments. Until the last period of the Ottoman Empire, an important part of not just the Christian population but the Muslim population did not perform military duties: the Ottoman government was not strong enough in some regions to implement the law that required military service. It could not recruit soldiers among the nomadic Arabs in Iraq and the Arabian Peninsula or among the tribes in Albania and eastern Anatolia.[13] The eastern Anatolian tribes were brave horseback riders, good marksmen, and heroic fighters, however, so they could serve as a natural military source for the Ottoman Empire. Even in the 1877–78 Russo-Turkish War the Ottomans benefited from the Jibranli and Hörmekli tribes.[14] The geographic conditions of eastern Anatolia hindered the mobility of the regular Ottoman army. The region's distance from the center and difficult terrain made sending reinforcements for logistical support nearly impossible. Forming military units from the tribes could remove all of these obstacles to a great extent because the tribes knew the region well and were used to all types of natural conditions. They also met their own needs. Such a military power could be of the greatest use to the Ottoman army, especially in skirmishes with bands, in narrow passes, in sudden raids, in exploring the region, and in outmaneuvering the enemy.

The idea of forming military units from tribes, who were prone toward militarism and keen on weapons and horses without being a major burden for the state, attracted Abdülhamid. He thought that these units could be established immediately and eventually would take their place in the military structure by becoming normal military units.

Hindering Armenian Activism

Seeing the Armenians' preparations for rebellion with the aid of Europe may have driven Abdülhamid to the thought of organizing the Muslim people through the Hamidiye Regiments: arming them, preparing them against the Armenians, and disrupting a potential internal uprising by establishing a balance of power. The Armenians' continual demand to disband the Hamidiye Regiments strengthened this resolve.[15] The regiments were not established as a necessary force against the Armenians, as the latter had supposed.[16] Yet sometimes the regiments got involved in incidents that the Armenians had caused; in these conditions and in light of the Armenians' general disposition, this can be seen as normal: after all, self-defense is a basic right.

Protecting Eastern Anatolia from Russia and Britain

Th possibility of benefiting from the Hamidiye Regiments in the event of a probable Russian attack was certainly an important factor behind the formation of the regiments, especially because Russia was the only power that could militarily threaten the empire in the east. The idea had already been put forth that Abdülhamid II would establish the Hamidiye Regiments, inspired by the model of the Cossack regiments in the Russian military.[17] Upon further consideration, the sultan sought to bolster the Ottoman military by delegating the tribal regiments to undertake various tasks, which bore some semblance to what the Russians did in relation to the Cossacks. But the sultan had to proceed with caution in view of his friendship agreement with the tsar (in place since 1890) and Russia's opposition to the formation of the regiments. Still, Abdülhamid II sought to gain the approval of the Russians or at least ensure their impartiality toward the idea of the regiments by calling attention to Britain's policy and the Armenian question.[18]

It can be said that Abdülhamid II viewed the Hamidiye Regiments as a means of preventing Britain from implementing its policy toward the Armenians and from provoking the Kurds against the empire. After Sheikh Ubeydullah's experiment, Abdülhamid II was quite alarmed by Britain's policy and immediately drew closer to the tribes. The Hamidiye

Regiments were a concrete part of the policy that had been applied to the tribes. In spite of Britain's aspirations the tribes remained loyal to Istanbul.

Pan-Islamism

Abdülhamid II sought to establish a direct tie between the Hamidiye Regiments and his policy of pan-Islamism in order to foster their growth. The existence of an indirect tie with the regiments was part of the policy of pan-Islamism. Abdülhamid II approached the tribes as he had done with the Muslims of the empire and foreign states: in his capacity as caliph. As the head of state, the sultan tended toward policies through which he could benefit from the tribes and subdue them to the political aims of the state, in accordance with the concept of the caliphate and sultanate. Moreover, eastern Anatolia was on the empire's eastern border, which made this all the more important. Abdülhamid II applied the same policy toward the Albanians on the western frontier, the Arab tribal chiefs in the south, and the Turkish, Kurdish, Circassian, and Karakalpak tribes in the east. By creating the Tribal Office for the Arabs, the Palace Guard Regiment for the Albanians, and the Hamidiye Regiments for the eastern Anatolian tribes, he attempted to link these regions to the center and protect the integrity of the empire.

THE ESTABLISHMENT OF THE
HAMIDIYE REGIMENTS AND THE FIRST CHARTER

The close relations that Müşir Zeki Paşa (the commander of the Fourth Army), the *vali*s, and especially Abdülhamid II had established with the tribal chiefs became increasingly strong. Müşir Zeki Paşa inspired Abdülhamid II to adopt the idea of benefiting militarily from the tribes, because the political situation in eastern Anatolia had become more precarious and the West had begun to take an interest in the region. Although Abdülhamid II had consulted other *paşa*s regarding this idea, most of them were against it. But the sultan, who ascribed the other *paşa*s' opposition to their envy of Müşir Zeki Paşa, decided to support the project because it was in line with his thinking. In his view, "in a war with Russia, tribes who are gathered as disciplined units can be of great service to us; the sense of loyalty that they will learn in organized units will also be good for them."[19] The idea of using the tribes against the outside and more particularly of making them listen to the central authority was at the forefront of the administration's plans.

I cannot say much regarding the preparations for the establishment of the Hamidiye Regiments because we currently possess no documents on the subject.[20] The earliest historical documents on this topic are dated 14–15 Nisan 1307 (April 26–27, 1891). According to these documents the foundation of the Hamidiye Regiments was initiated through the efforts of Müşir Zeki Paşa.[21] The first charter was published in 1891.[22] Article 1 of this charter, which was prepared as an Imperial Edict (Hatt-ı Hümayun), states the justification for the foundation of the Hamidiye Regiments:

> The formation of military order, whose organization is necessary to guard the state against aggressions and infractions of foreign elements, is an obligation that is extended to all of the country's general population. Since the exception of a portion of the population from this obligation has caused a deficiency in public force, it is hereby the legitimate aim of the state to increase the power of the Ottoman people by putting this legal principle [of military service] into force in the Ottoman Empire. It is hereby decreed that the formation of the Tribal Cavalry regiments, who will be called by the honorable name of the Hamidiye Soldiers [*asakir-i Hamidiye*], be undertaken. These regiments will consist of nomadic (those who dwell in tents) tribal people, who have been known for their horsemanship and who have not previously performed military service under a regular military order.[23]

This charter points to the need for the participation of the tribes in the state defense by stressing in a soft but urgent tone the duty of every individual to defend the country against the enemy. It also notes that no one from these regions had served regularly in the military. This charter, which consists of fifty-three articles and a conclusion, provides sufficient information regarding the characteristics and the establishment of the Hamidiye Cavalry Regiments.

First, the regiments consisted of no less than four but no more than six squadrons. Every regiment contained between 512 and 1,152 men (article 2). Large tribes were given the right to form one or more regiments, and small tribes were given the right to form a number of squadrons (articles 3–4). Uniting the tribes for the purpose of training and regiment formation was forbidden, however, and only tolerated in times of war under the command of the central authority or the army commanders (articles 4–5).

State-appointed enumerators undertook a population count of all males in the tribes between the ages of seventeen and forty and informed the Ministry of the Interior, the Hamidiye General Commandership, and the Center of the Imperial Army (article 6). The males that were to form the Hamidiye Cavalry Regiments were placed into three divisions: the *ibtidaiye* (ages seventeen to twenty); the *nizamiye*e (ages twenty to thirty-two); and the *redif* (ages thirty-two to forty) (article 7). By sending two sergeants from every regiment to the Center of the Imperial Army, the state subjected them to education in the Office Regiment (*mektep alayı*) and afterward promoted them to the regiments by having them perform two years of service either in Istanbul or somewhere else. A youth from each regiment was chosen and sent to Istanbul. After completing training in the Cavalry Office (*süvari mektebi*), he returned to his region and regiment as a second lieutenant (*teğmen*) (article 10). As long as the Hamidiye Regiments provided their own squadron of men, the state would give them clothes, animals, rifles, ammunition, and a banner (article 18).

Article 19 of the charter states:

Because the troops of the Hamidiye Regiments are organized from the Turkmen, Karakalpak, Kurdish, and Arab tribes, and since they dress in a way that is similar to the way in which the local tribes dress, it is necessary for three patterns to be chosen now. They should dress in a way that will distinguish them from the local people. The regiments shall have a name and number and a written trademark [*alâmet-i fârika*].

As noted above, the Hamidiye Regiments were composed of Turkish, Kurdish, and Arab tribes. It is important to stress that the view that the agenda was to arm only the Kurds does not square with the truth. Another point worth mentioning is favoritism among the tribes. The Ottomans did not take into account that such favoritism, even if it had some practical advantages, could engender long-term disadvantages.

The regiments' office cadre would be formed from the sergeants brought to Istanbul and the youths of the tribes who were taken into the Cavalry Office. If this was insufficient others were appointed from the tribal "commanders and leaders." Regular cavalry regiment officers were appointed as instructors and trainers. The war unit regiment and squadron commanders decided which members of the tribal elites would be the other military officers, such as the *kaymakam*, field major, and *kolağası* (above a captain but below a major) (articles 22–25). At the same time, those among the tribal elites who were loyal to the state and in military service would be promoted to the rank of colonel by the sultanate. But the deputy would certainly be a regular officer. With this article the state incentivized the Hamidiye Cavalry Regiments and gained further control over the tribes and regiments.

The salary that would be given to each officer of the Hamidiye Regiments and his men and methods for his appointment, wages, promotion, inspection, and discipline in war and peacetime were determined. The charter states: "Those who are not included in the Hamidiye Cavalry for any reason are held accountable to the code of laws regarding recruitment. It is not lawful for them to remain outside the public force. If necessary, extraordinary action, which may involve the use of compulsion and violence, will be taken in order to induct them into a military" (articles 26–52). Sanctions were put in place in order to make individuals in the tribes serve as soldiers. Usually they were forced to be in the regiments. From another perspective, both the authority of the center and the authority of the tribal chiefs were strengthened by the sanctions.

Through the preparation and acceptance of the charter, the formation of the regiments from the eastern Anatolian tribes continued under the supervision of Müşir Zeki Paşa. In 1891 many tribal chiefs and elites came to Istanbul, visited with Abdülhamid II, and offered their loyalty. The sultan showed them favor by giving them gifts and medals. The tribal commanders and chiefs who could not come to Istanbul went to Erzincan, the headquarters of the Fourth Army, and met with Müşir Zeki Paşa, through whom they informed the sultan of their loyalty.[24] Tribal elites increasingly made requests to visit Abdülhamid II, who was the sultan and the caliph, considering this a privilege. In the same year tribal chiefs from as far away as Hakkari, Van, and Diyarbakır sought out Müşir Zeki Paşa as an intermediary through whom they made special requests to visit the sultan.[25] In a telegram dated April 14–15, 1891, Müşir Zeki Paşa requested that the sultan issue an imperial rescript (*irade-yi seniyye*) that would order the tribal elites in Erzincan and Istanbul to return to their regions and engage in the establishment of the regiments. In the telegram he also requested that the sultan accept new visitors.[26] The following document concerns the attempts to form the Hamidiye Regiments and their results:

> In accordance with the supreme order by the imperial permission of the caliph, the number of the cavalry regiments, whose preliminary formations have been determined, and who are composed of Karakalpak clans and of Kurdish tribes living in the environs of the Van, Bitlis, and Erzurum provinces, is more than forty-five. Other than the unsettled tribes in the Diyarbakir *vilayet*, there are no

more tribes from which to form cavalry regiments in this region. The necessary inspection of the animals and of the individuals who will form the aforementioned regiments, with the specification of their remittances, is to be done by the selection of a commission. According to the statutes of imperial instruction all animals are to be branded one by one. These aforementioned measures are to be completed in three to four months.[27]

This shows that Hamidiye Regiments were formed quickly and with little trouble.

The tribes sought permission from the sultan via Müşir Zeki Paşa, as if in competition with one another, to acquire the privilege of establishing cavalry regiments. Tribes that obtained permission held a superior status in the region both de facto and de jure. By arming the tribes and recognizing their separate legal status, the government enabled the tribes to become more independent politically and socially. Over time this engendered envy among the tribes and even caused tribal clashes. The right to establish a regiment or squadron was not granted to every tribe, so the tribes who did not obtain this right secretly held a grudge against the other tribes and against Istanbul, as was the case with some tribes in the Tunceli region.[28] While the government was giving the rights to establish regiments, it left out some critical dimensions. Only tribes that were weak, loyal, and Sunni were chosen initially. But over time the government tried to broaden the scope as much as possible, to include all tribes in the Hamidiye Cavalry.

The reason for the tribes' insistence on assuming the status of Hamidiye Regiments undoubtedly has to do with the some of the provisions of the charter, particularly the provision that individual members of tribes who were not included in the regiments must serve in the regular army. For these tribes who had not served for ages or at least were not accustomed to doing military service, it seemed impossible to live under orders for years, far from their homeland. Because of the freedom of tribal life, obligatory military service ran contrary to their nature. If they were included in the Hamidiye Regiments, however, they could be spared from service in the regular military and could be counted as having done military service without moving far from their tribe and homeland. Besides this personal privilege, the question of the increased status of tribe and tribal chief, in the eyes of the caliph and on the state level, was at stake. The caliph would give the tribal chiefs belonging to the regiments hallmarks, honorific titles, and ranks and accept them at the palace. These matters were important for the morale of all of these tribes. In addition, inclusion in the regiments would bring the tribe material advantages. This came as a necessary distinction so that the tribes could protect themselves and measure up to other tribes. In brief, registration in the Hamidiye Regiments gave the tribes great privileges.

The formation of the regiments engendered a dialogue between the central authority and the tribes, and among the peoples of Eastern Anatolia, that had not existed before. This dialogue itself, leaving aside its character and results, was a major development in the relations between the government and eastern Anatolia. Taking into consideration the methods and principles of the state's military, financial, and administrative forces and the sociopolitical structure of eastern Anatolia, it appears that the government did actually choose the easiest and quickest method to achieve its goals. The government implemented the plan before getting a reaction from the tribes. The method of forming the Hamidiye Regiments did fit the tribes' psychological-social structure, especially since Abdülhamid II had no such policy of changing the social structure in eastern Anatolia. By creating a new type of balance of power, however, he tried to seize control over the state authority within the present order. In reality reinforcing the tribes by establishing the regiments and giving them special status and weapons accomplished the opposite of what Abdülhamid II understood to be centralization. But he was aware of that. Yet he joined the Hamidiye Regiments to the structure of the army and eventually hoped to take back the concessions that he had given to the tribes.[29] Therefore he saw fit to link the tribes to himself through what was at first an extremely soft and concessionary policy, without scaring them off. In this he was successful, and his esteem in the eyes of the tribes increased greatly. The Armenian incidents later kept Abdülhamid II from moving the Hamidiye Regiment policy forward and caused a number of negative results.

THE SITUATION BETWEEN 1892 AND 1895

After the first charter regarding their establishment, the formation of the Hamidiye Regiments was implemented. In a short while the number of regiments increased to thirty-six.[30] A number of military and strategic matters were taken into account in the establishment of the mounted regiments, which did not occur randomly. The process started in two regions that were chosen as the most fitting places to establish the regiments. The first was the borderland with Russia between Erzurum and Van.[31] To organize the various tribes in these border regions as soon as possible, the

Fourth Army commander, Müşir Zeki Paşa, immediately sent Mirliva Mahmud Paşa to Van, Malazgird, Hınıs, and Varto.[32] The second region encompassed the tribes who lived in northern parts of the barren land lying between Mardin and Urfa.[33]

These regions were given priority in establishing the cavalry regiments because the regiment on the Erzurum–Van line guarded against the Russian threat and the regiment on the Urfa–Mardin line guarded against the British political activities. In each of the two regions Armenian terrorist movements had become more concentrated. The central authority was hardly effective there and was trying to increase its political scope.

Regular army officers were appointed as regiment and division commanders to the cavalry units established from the tribes in these regions. The tribal chiefs were appointed as deputy commanders of regiments, lieutenant colonels, and majors, according to their capacity. Other elites of the tribe were appointed to the established regiments with the rank of lieutenant. Undoubtedly there were some exceptions to the charter, because the regular army was sometimes insufficient. Therefore the government sought to arouse the tribes' desire to form regiments, thus giving them incentive and responsibility.

The sultanate gave edicts to the established Hamidiye Cavalry Regiments. One side of these edicts was written on white glittery fabric, with a verse of the Qur'an. The other side was worked through with red satin banners and the sultan's coat of arms.[34] In these edicts the sultan explicitly specified the regiments' charter, how they were to be trained, and other matters. But not everything in the charter was successfully put into practice. After 1892, especially after the Sasun incidents on September 22, 1893, it was evident that the government was not able to keep the Hamidiye Cavalry under close supervision.[35] In spite of this, new regiments continued to be formed.

The established regiments were brought under the direct command of the Fourth Army. The organization, training, and inspection of the regiments was placed under the control of Müşir Zeki Paşa. Thus in a short time Zeki Paşa had established friendly and close relations with the tribal chiefs and tribal elites. As a result he became the tribes' protector and the only authority who could resolve issues pertaining to them. All of the tribal chiefs informed the central authority of their commitments by visiting Zeki Paşa in Erzincan. A large group that had gone to Erzincan and from there to Istanbul was accepted by the sultan even in 1893.[36] No one could do anything in relation to the tribes without the permission of Zeki Paşa. This led to many misunderstandings between the local civil

authorities and the military authorities. After gaining leverage through
Zeki Paşa, the tribes belonging to the Hamidiye Regiments no longer listened to the local government officials. The local authorities could not
even interrogate a military officer for any reason.[37] This situation caused
a divide between the *valis* and Zeki Paşa. As the son-in-law of the sultan,
Zeki Paşa was close to the palace and felt that he was above the authority
of the *valis*. It is evident that this situation had great disadvantages from
an administration standpoint.

In spite of the alliances, competition, and hidden or overt friction
caused by the Hamidiye Cavalry, regiments continued to be formed
within the framework of the state policy. According to the figures given
in the military yearbook (*salnâme-yi askeri*) of 1311 (1895), the number
of cavalry regiments had risen to fifty-six by 1895.[38] A regiment number
from one to fifty-six was assigned to each regiment. Only regiments fifty-
one, fifty-two, fifty-three, fifty-four, and fifty-five were placed under the
command of the Fifth Imperial Army in Syria because of their proximity. The other fifty-one regiments were placed under the direct command
of the Fourth Imperial Army, with headquarters in Erzincan. The *kaymakam* (lieutenant-colonel) commanded the colonels and twenty of the
Hamidiye Regiments in the Fourth Army. None of these regiments completed the six-year transition stipulated by the first charter. Therefore they
were unable to become trained and organized units. For these reasons they
would be contacted when their turn came.

THE SECOND CHARTER

Based on the experience gained from the four-year implementation of
the first charter regarding the Hamidiye Regiments and other social and
political experiences during this time, the sultan saw fit to prepare and
put into force a second charter. He aimed to add what the first charter
was lacking and to discipline the regiments further. He thought that a
number of conflicts that the Hamidiye Regiments had created in social,
political, and administrative areas could be smoothed out and that further
drawbacks could be prevented. With the intensification of the Armenian
incidents, however, the Armenians and their European supporters blamed
the adverse political environment on the implementation of the Hamidiye
Regiments and other such policies. They viewed the tribes who belonged
to the regiments as the ones who created the disturbances and the incidents. Therefore the Ottoman government sought to rein in the regiments
and tribes, without giving in to such accusations.

The second charter was put into force on May 13, 1896 (30 Zilkade 1313).[39] It consists of 121 articles with 12 sections and an addendum. In addition it contains a short section called a "special article" in the brief introduction and conclusion:

A. Introduction
1. Formation (Articles 1–7)
2. Individuals (Articles 8–14)
3. Accumulation (Articles 15–21)
4. Missions, uniforms, and weapons (Articles 22–25)
5. Commanders and officers (Articles 26–34)
6. Advancement of ranks (Articles 35–42)
7. Matters of discipline and punishment (Articles 43–54)
8. Merit (Articles 55–62)
9. Administration (Articles 63–64)
10. Exemption and recompense (Articles 65–72)
11. Inspection (Articles 73–79)
12. Artillery (Articles 80–81)
13. Duties of the regiments and commanders in building up the military and recruiting soldiery (Articles 82–88)

B. Addendum
1. Rotation (Articles 95–99)
2. Staff committees (Articles 100–111)
3. Temporary administration during exceptional intervals (Articles 112–14)
4. Education during exceptional intervals (Articles 115–21)
5. Special article

In general the first and second charters are not very different. The fundamental articles and the political and military thoughts are preserved with exactness, except for the differences explained below.

The second charter stipulates that the regiments are to be called either the "Hamidiye Light Cavalry Regiments" or the "Hamidiye Cavalry Regiments," that four regiments constitute a brigade, and that a division will be established from the regiments by decision of the High Officials of General War when necessary. It has no changes in the other matters. The second charter places greater emphasis on having the cavalry and foot soldiers trained by the regiments (including the *redif*, *nizamiye*, and *ibtidaiye*) in a timely manner. It also stipulates more strongly that no one belonging to the *ibtidaiye-nizamiye* divisions can leave the country without obtaining permission from the regiments' tribal chiefs. The divisions can also be transferred by land to other regions "by decree of the sultan." The charter repeats that the regiments will be formed from the Turkmen, Kurdish, Karakalpak, and Arab tribes and that the elites can be officers of varying ranks, except lieutenant and colonel. But in some cases squadrons led by tribal chiefs and commanders of regiments can be appointed. In practice they were often consulted on this decision.

The second charter gives increased emphasis to discipline and punishment. The stipulation regarding any movement that is contrary to the charter is made clear. According to article 54, fights between tribes, particularly during peacetime, will be strongly punished:

> Old rivalries between two tribes during peacetime will be prejudicial to order in the country. Commanders and officers of regiments who perpetrate mass killing against each other and who do not obey orders to disperse are subject to execution, hard labor, temporary exile, and imprisonment according to the introductory principles that will come into effect after cross-examination. Those understood to be in violation of these principles are sentenced to service in the *nizamiye* line for an extended period in the cavalry regiments in the distant regions.

This article indicates that infighting between tribes existed to a certain extent, that it agitated the government and the regional peoples, and that the government sought to put an end to these types of incidents through strong measures. Thus it is clear that Hamidiye Regiment policy caused a degree of friction between the tribes and that the regiments had not yet been put under full control.

An important place is reserved in the second charter for a subject that is not found in the first. This difference is the inclusion of several rights and privileges afforded to the tribes belonging to the regiments under the subheading "exemption and recompense." This section is important, so some excerpts are cited here:

> With the stipulation of exemption from paying the supreme treasury the previously collected tithe [*âşâr*] and animal taxes [*ağnam*], the commanders, officers, and individuals in the light cavalry regiments who are from among the tribes and clans are to be exempted only from taxes [article 65].
> The aforementioned exemption includes the personal and dividends taxes of the individuals who are commanders, officers, and

of the three ranks in these regiments and their private property and annexations to dwellings, because these are basic necessities. This exemption is to be used only for themselves and their families. This exemption does not apply to real estate, roofed property, and distant relatives [article 66].

The individuals and officers in these three ranks also are given assistance with the costs of transportation provisions. However, transportation of the regiments is specifically assigned to the tribes [article 67].

With the tax exemptions granted to the tribes, the Ottoman state managed to attract more men to the Hamidiye Regiments and to expedite recruitment. The position of the government in this regard was perceived as normal, because the tribes had never paid full taxes. But it managed to win the tribes over to the state by legally recognizing certain exemptions. For ages the only relations between the state and the tribes had been through tax collection, so the tribes saw the state as a tax-collecting institution. Through its new approach the state wanted to show that it was a protector at the same time. The lifting of the *âşâr* tax was not particularly important for the tribes, because the nomadic and seminomadic groups did not subsist much from farming. Thus only the *ağnam* (animal) tax remained incumbent upon the tribes. They could easily hide their sheep and goats in the mountains and then show the officials from the tax-collecting office fewer animals than they actually owned to get away with paying a lower tax.[40]

Besides these exemptions, the state stipulated a number of rights regarding compensations. Families who lost a son or husband in war were put on the salaries of veterans, those who lost a horse in war were given another horse or other compensation, and certified officers were granted the right of retirement. Regiments who participated in pursuing bandits were treated as if they had participated in a war. The tribes belonging to the regiments were prohibited from banditry under this article: the state sought to instill them with a sense of responsibility by charging them with the duty of pursuing and crushing bandit movements. In brief, the state wanted to use the tribes to ensure security, especially since its own forces were inadequate.

The conclusion of the charter clearly explains the status of the personnel of the regiments and their training, whether within a six-year period or afterward. According to this part of the charter, each year a squadron would be trained under the supervision of regular officers, sergeants, and corporals. All squadrons would repeat such training four times per year. In the last two years all squadrons would undergo training exercises at the same time. The authorities would conduct this training only during an appropriate season to avoid harming agricultural production. They also kept military training under armed supervision. This would be a type of "civil defense" training that would ensure the continuation of the tribes' normal life. Military training sessions primarily focused on bringing order and organization to the cavalry. These consisted of mounting and dismounting horses, military lessons, and patrolling and reconnaissance tasks.

One of the most salient points of the charter was the provision that the tribes could have their children educated in the military schools, to create a continual resupply of regiment and squadron personnel. The policy of establishing the Hamidiye Regiments was only to fulfill temporary military purposes. But it was part of a long-term policy through which the state sought to carry out its agenda of changing the tribes' cultural, social, political, and economic lifestyle by educating future tribal chiefs and elites in state schools and transforming the tribes into elements that directly benefited the state. The provision of state education was limited only to the children of tribal elites, however, leaving the subject open to varying interpretations. Yet, considering the scope of the empire and that the movement toward state education had only recently begun, the approach taken in eastern Anatolia was an important start. It can also be said that the state placed great importance on bringing eastern Anatolia within the scope of its state schooling project.[41] Some parts of the charter can elucidate this matter:

> Each year from each light cavalry regiment, a child from among the children of the commanders and the officers, who can read and write and who is between the ages of sixteen and eighteen, is accepted to the military school [Mekteb-i Harbiye] and is sent to Istanbul. These children, who are summoned from the province of Trablusgarb, spend some three years in cavalry classes [article 115].[42] At the end of these three years they are appointed as second lieutenant and deputy to their individual cavalry units. Since the officers who have an education in this manner and who enter the regiment with a certificate deserve the rights of certified officers, they maintain the right of priority, as do other certified officers, to rank promotion [article 117]. It is natural that this rule be revoked during an intermittent period. If the children of the officers in the light cavalry regiments so desire, they are required to undergo the

preparation of state cavalry officers by completing their education in the military school in an orderly manner [article 118].

There are so many sons of tribal chiefs in the schools that in order to facilitate their completion of education after entering the military school [Mekteb-i Harbiye] it may be necessary to place them in the advanced [*rüşdiye*] schools near the regiment boards in Erzurum, Baghdad, Diyarbakır, and Van during the evenings. The children that will be sent to advanced military schools in these four places, the preparatory [*idadi*] schools in Baghdad and Erzurum and the *rüşdiye* schools in Diyarbakir and Van, will be quartered ten each in the dormitories. Payment will be made to the Ministry of the Military Offices [*mekâtib-i askeriye nezareti*] [article 119]. Children will be accepted to the advanced military school [*rüşdiye*] only for a particular time [article 120]. If the officers make a petition to the esteemed military school [Mekteb-i Harbiye] to serve in the regular cavalry, since they have the authorization to go to the light cavalry regiment, they are sent to one of the organized armies together with other school colleagues [article 121].

By opening the doors of all the military schools to the tribes by these pronouncements the state provided that the children of the tribal leaders could become military officers either in their own regiments or in the ranks of the Ottoman army. The Hamidiye Regiments became more effective with certified and educated officers. It appears that the state found accepting children to the schools to be the most practical way of integrating the tribes. If we consider the role that the officers who graduated from the military school played in World War I and the National Front (*kuvay-i milli*), the policies implemented during this period can be seen from a positive angle. Besides the aforementioned military (*harbiye*), preparatory (*idadi*), and advanced (*rüşdiye*) schools many children of the tribes were educated through the Tribal Office (*aşiret mektebi*) opened by Abdülhamid II and were then sent back to their tribes.[43] Many tribal chiefs and elites, by requests to the sultan, allowed their children to go those schools, which shows that the education policy was adopted by the tribes.[44]

The "special clause" added at the end of the charter stipulated that the tribal regiment officers could not be appointed to the civil service but could be deployed to the civil service as members of the local council, because members in this council were not legally prohibited from military service. This stipulation allowed tribal elites to have a voice in the local administrations through membership in the council. Thus balance was established in the administrative councils, traditionally controlled only by the urban elite (*şehir eşraf ve âyânı*). The urban elite opposed the Hamidiye Regiments, so they were not enthralled with the appointment of those belonging to regiments to membership on the council.

As in the first charter, the second charter's most glaring flaw is that it did not clearly specify what the legal and administrative rights of the Hamidiye Regiments and of the tribes belonging to the regiments would be in relation to the individuals and establishments who represented the central government in civil administration as *vali*s, *mutasarrıf*s, and *kaymakam*s. Because of this lack of clarity many significant matters arose that weakened the state authority administratively. The Hamidiye Regiments were technically under the authority of the Fourth and Fifth Armies. But because of the distance and the difficulty of transportation between the army commanders — especially Müşir Zeki Paşa in Erzincan — and the tribes, it was not possible to check on the regiments or obtain exact information. Nevertheless, due to the locations of the *vali*s and the authority that they held, they could more easily and effectively check on the tribes and take swift precautions if necessary. Because this matter was not carefully taken into consideration, de facto and de jure friction arose both between the military and civil authorities and between the civil authorities and the tribes. In practice the policy of the Hamidiye Regiments resulted in a number of drawbacks.

REQUESTS FROM THE TRIBES
TO ESTABLISH THE REGIMENTS

As noted, it was the sultan who requested the participation of the tribes in the regiments. He did not force them to participate. To the contrary, he received many applications for participation in the regiments and recognized some tribes to the chagrin of others. In such conditions, the tribal elites sent petitions as soon as possible to the sultan and to Zeki Paşa, requesting permission to establish a regiment and assuring them of their commitment and loyalty to the state. The second charter contained many stipulations that would favor the tribes who belonged to the regiments, so the number of requests to form a regiment increased.

Some of the tribes in southern Anatolia either petitioned the state not to give permission to establish the regiments (or at least delay this) or sought to obtain permission. For instance, a petition dated 11 Teşrin-i Sani 1312 (November 23, 1896) from a tribe in the environs of the Mardin *sancak* known as the Havass-ı Hümayun is quite interesting:

As your humble servants, the villages in which we live and which are part of the Mardin *sancak* and known by the name of the Havass-ı Hümayun are among the villages of the Kiki Haçan, Kiki Çakan, Milli, and Dokuri tribes, who are found in the depths of the Mardin desert, and who are part the Hamidiye cavalry. We are mixed within these tribes and our character and life is like theirs. A while before the establishment of the Hamidiye cavalry, our population was counted but not registered. However, since we were subservient to the government and listened to the words of the [government] organization that came from Mardin, it was our population that was accepted to be registered before the other aforementioned tribes. Before, you honored them by accepting them to the Hamidiye units. Our tribe was deprived of such honor. However, our tribe, known by other tribes by the name of the Havass-ı Hümayun, has been subservient and loyal for a long time. Therefore we request that we be a part of the Hamidiye cavalry and always, before everyone else, are ready to sacrifice our soul and possessions for our sultan and the state. In the event that honor and acceptance is given to us to be a Hamidiye regiment in a like manner, it is clear that our agriculture in the fields and orchards will increase, since the desired public order and security will be provided. After all, our praise and loyalty to our Dignified Majestic Emir of the Believers [the sultan] will be the reason for justification, before all else, in the field of truth... [sixteen stamps of the village heads and elites, 11 Teşrin-i Sani 1312, Havass-ı Hümayun tribal chief].[45]

In the same way some of the other tribes in eastern Anatolia submitted various applications to enter the regiments as well. The following text is a summary of a petition that the chief of the Sinan tribe and accompanying tribal elites in the Bitlis region sent to the sultan through the "Honorable Aide-de-Camp of the Sultan," Field Marshal Şakir Paşa.[46]

May the life and grandeur of the sultan be prolonged. Our tribe, which is from the Sinan tribe, servants [of the sultan] who came from the deserts of Diyarbakır with the Hussan Haydaran [tribe] and other tribes of Kurdistan in the heavenly age of Sultan Selim and who are both settled and unsettled in the Çukur *kaza* and its environs in the Bitlis *vilayet* and some of whom are included in the registers, consists of more than 7,000 men known for their bravery in cavalry and marksmanship.[47] All members of our tribe are ready to lay down their lives for the sake of the most imperial of the kings [the sultan]. We have previously undertaken the formation of servants [of the sultan] into cavalry and foot soldier [brigades] to form the honorable Hamidiye Regiments. Yet since our regiment was too large after having been formed, we created two registers of cavalry. Many of our horses were branded. Now the complete delay of our regiments, during which time an additional 1,000 horses of ours were branded on the official order of the commandership, is the cause of the general despair and forlornness of your servants. Even if a small part of our tribe is registered (since other tribes who have been accepted to the regiments are registered in part also), it is our strong hope that we, your servants, will be seen as worthy of your royal mercy in view of this matter, especially since other tribes who have been accepted to the regiments and who form a much smaller part than our tribe have been included in the registry. The cavalry regiment units that have been accepted and registered from the Cibranlı, Hasnanlı, Haydaranlı, and other tribes number one more than has been accepted from our tribe. Therefore our tribe needs, by imperial decree, its remaining entire part to be accepted and formed, in his kingly shadow [his majesty], into the regiments. It is our plea that an imperial decision be made and a decree announced, to the commandership of the regiments under the Fourth Army and to the Bitlis *vilayet*, that our regiments be formed and registered, that his kingly justice and mercy will not reject our request for loyal service, and that he will not settle for the deprivations and desperations of the people, their clans, and their peers, who are available to form a regiment and who are much too numerous and crowded, and that he will also not settle for their woes, with all of their families, until their last fainthearted breaths. The love of mercy is of his Excellency our Lord, the Commander of the Faithful. [Signed by tribal chief Ramazan and chief Abdülmecid].[48]

This document, upon close inspection, points out a number of concrete facts about the tribes and the Hamidiye Regiments. A large part of the tribes had already made requests to form Hamidiye Regiments. The prevalence of such requests cannot be attributed to the rights and privileges granted to the tribes by the state charter alone. As noted, the foundation of such privileges consisted of exempting the tribes from the payment of some taxes. The tribes, from whom the state had not been able to collect full taxes for hundreds of years, could pay only a partial tax or simply not pay at all. They were outside the control of the state and not under its authority. Their seminomadic and nomadic lifestyle facilitated their independent movement. In this situation the basis for the tribes' requests to enter the regiments was not only the privileges recognized by the state but also other factors. First, through the Hamidiye Cavalry the tribes wanted to ensure their own security with the help of the state and to make their political and social situations official and strengthen them. Second, they sought to be on the same level with other tribes in the Hamidiye Cavalry and to increase their own rank and status in the state.

As the elites of the Sinan tribe indicate in their document, coming under the order of another tribal chief through participation in the regiment weakened their own tribe's force. This situation was disadvantageous for the chief who was unaffiliated with the regime. It was thought that forming another regiment would be the best way to prevent this from happening, thereby ensuring their authority, strength, and a balance of power with other tribes. Hence it was not hard to understand why the Sinan tribal chiefs Ramazan and Abdülmecid, who could supply more than 7,000 men of military age to create six or seven regiments, made a request to form a regiment.

The rights granted by the state to establish regiments clearly specify how, when, and to which tribes authority would be given. Therefore the right of establishing regiments was continually granted in a random way, which benefited the tribal chiefs, who had relations with the palace, Sublime Porte, and Müşir Zeki Paşa. This engendered sadness and envy in other tribes. The greatest example of this is the situation of the Havass-ı Hümayun and Sinan tribes detailed above. This random policy of the state caused competition and rivalry among tribes.[49] But the state sought to quell the rivalry through the Hamidiye Regiments. This infighting could be prevented little by little if it was limited in scope. The Fourth Army commander, Müşir Zeki Paşa, had particular authority to make the tribes listen to his words.

THE HAMIDIYE REGIMENTS AFTER 1895

In the wake of the escalation of the Armenian incidents, the Great Powers sought to reinforce the implementation of reforms in eastern Anatolia by giving the Sublime Porte a warning. Moreover, a number of requests indicate that the boundaries of the tribes' winter and summer quarters were fixed and that their movements were checked. Abdülhamid II, relying on his friendship agreement with Russia, did not accept these requests verbatim but prepared a different reform bill. He sent Müşir Zeki Paşa, under the title inspector-general of Anatolia, to eastern Anatolia in 1895 to have him conduct necessary investigations and take precautions. But before the incidents subsided they escalated once again. In 1896 the reaction and intervention of Europe turned violent. The situation in eastern Anatolia became quite dangerous. Furthermore, Abdülhamid II sought to bring the Hamidiye Regiments to order by dispatching Saadettin Paşa to Van, on the one hand,[50] and to take the "necessary precautions of ensuring the order and discipline of the Hamidiye Regiments" by sending an encoded telegraph to Şakir Paşa in 1897 (1313), on the other.[51] On his orders Şakir Paşa and Zeki Paşa prepared a mutual report in three months and sent it to the Sublime Porte in December 1897 (Kânunevvel 1313). The report, which reflected the views of the official authority concerning the Hamidiye Regiments, became a matter of prominence (therefore its most relevant parts are cited below).

Yet the most authoritative of the officials in relation to eastern Anatolia, Müşir Zeki Paşa, both as general inspector and aide-de-camp and as the commander of the Fourth Army, accepted that full order and discipline were not established among the Hamidiye Regiments. As a result he acted reasonably and realistically in searching for the reasons for the lack of discipline in the regiments and for a solution. Thus he became the primary informant on the current situation in the Sublime Porte and the palace. Şakir Paşa and Zeki Paşa explained the reasons for the lack of discipline among the tribes belonging to the regiments as follows:

1. Lack of proper instruction as to the laws and charters.
2. The fact that the Hamidiye Regiments were not directly under the Imperial Army.
3. Inability to establish order and loyalty, of any military essence, because the staff officers in charge of army property were deprived of the means to strengthen their authority.
4. "The nobility of the country, who are shareholders in the affairs of the government either as members [of the government] or as distinguished and influential elites, have not been spared from the arbitrary power of the tribal chiefs on account of the formations [of regiments]. Therefore they relied on misinformation from some of the *vali*s and the *mutasarrıf*s and sought, in meddling in the formations, to secure interests that they had lost. Incidents and complaints against those belonging to the regiments, even if they were against individuals not belonging to the regiments, were framed in a way that cast the blame

on the regiments, associates, and others and implicated the perpetrators' connection to the Hamidiye officers. Thus the regiments and officers were forced into a state of insecurity by the government without cause. The main cause for these incidents was the delay in direct communication between the tribes and the center of the caliphate and the consequent inability to establish order and discipline."

5. A lack of ability on the part of the squadron and regiment commanders who were appointed from the army to the Hamidiye Regiments. None of them were able to carry out affairs in a way that ensured discipline and order because they felt compelled to maintain a false friendship with and curry the favor of "tribal chiefs in order to procure the commutation of rations and salaries gathered from the tribes' *âşâr* and *ağnam* taxes."

6. The fact that the habits and actions of the tribes, to which they had grown accustomed from old, could not be corrected in the desired way, especially since tribal elites had direct communication with the army commanders and would bypass the regiment commanders.[52]

Şakir Paşa and Zeki Paşa sent a report of their general observations to the Sublime Porte, attaching a detailed bill of thirty articles related to the reinstituting of the Hamidiye Regiments. In this bill they tried to remove the defects of the previous charters, generally those concerning the Hamidiye Regiments. They also introduced further precautions that they considered necessary for thorough inspections.[53]

The bill consisted of five sections, the first of which touched on matters related to increased military organization. According to the second section of the bill:

It is necessary that the de jure formation of the fifty-seven Hamidiye Light Cavalry Regiments consist of several army corps. Since it is administered directly by the Imperial Army in the committee of independent regiments, it is not possible to complete the order and discipline of the troops in this situation because the Imperial Army has been in grave trouble. Therefore it is stipulated that the fifty-seven regiments be temporarily divided into seven groups, since they are quite strong, thereby attaining a level determined by law. Of these seven the commander of the Urfa brigade is already present. Three brigades are given over to the brigadier general of the regular cavalry of the Imperial Army. It is necessary that three qualified lieutenants from the commanders of different classes of

the Imperial Army be appointed to lead the remaining three brigades. They are to live in the center of Malazgird. It is also necessary
at least to appoint an individual to the Hamidiye General Commandership as a major general. The appointment of general staff
to accompany the general commander according to the necessary
registration is also needed.[54]

According to this article Şakir Paşa and Zeki Paşa would divide the
regiments into seven brigades. They included in the bill a list that shows
the centers of the brigades, which tribes the brigades would consist of, the
tribes' names, and how many of each would constitute a regiment. The brigades were to be formed along the Russian and Iranian borders. It should
not be too hard to understand the military and strategic implications of
this. The number of regiments belonging to the brigades ranges between
five and nine. Table 14.1 shows that large tribes formed four or five regiments. The tribes that had more regiments became dominant in their respective regions and managed to shift the social balance in their favor. The
Husnanlı tribe in Viranşehir (in the Milli and Malazgird environs), with
five regiments, and the Haydaranlı tribe, with eight regiments, came to be
the most powerful tribes. Some tribal chiefs were revered by and active in
the palace and the Sublime Porte because of their power and influence in
the region. Table 14.1 shows the tribes' names, how many regiments they
formed, and the regiments to which they belonged.[55]

The Fortieth Regiment established by the Karapapak tribe in Sivas was
not under any brigade, so it was militarily trained under the supervision
of the Sivas commandership and with the help of the cavalry squadron
there.[56] Other matters in the first section of the charter include the question of a greater sense of military spirit and loyalty among the tribes, their
mastery of horsemanship, the appointment of officers, increased effectiveness of the squadron and regiment commanders, and prohibition of direct
communication between the tribes and the army commanders.

The part in the second section with the subheading "Reinforcement
of the Regiments" contains three articles that touch on matters related
to the duties and participation of the tribal individuals in the regiments
and squadrons.[57] The third section touches on obedience to the chain of
command during peacetime, the punishment of insubordinates, military
service in the regular cavalry regiments, and promotion to the rank of
officer. In addition it lays out the punishment to be exacted according to
law upon regiments involved in pillage and plunder operations among

TABLE 14.1. Tribes in Regiments of the First to Seventh Brigades

TRIBE	REGIMENT NUMBER	TRIBE	REGIMENT NUMBER
First Brigade (Center: Karakulliya Regiments)		**Fourth Brigade (Center: Erciş)**	
		(?)	13, 14, 15
Zilan	3, 4, 5	Hayderanlı	16, 21, 22, 23, 24, 26
Karapapak	6, 9		
Adamanlı	10, 11	**Fifth Brigade (Center: Başkale)**	
Haydaranlı	12, 37	Mukri (?)	17
Celâli	38	Milan	18
Şazili	57	Şimsikie	19
		Şukufti	20, 26
Second Brigade (Center: Homs)		Takuri	39
Cemadanlı	8, 31		
Ciranlı	32, 33, 34	**Sixth Brigade (Center: Mardin)**	
Zırikanlı	35	Milli	41, 42, 43, 44
Cibranlı	36	Karakeçi	45, 46
		Tay	47
Third Brigade (Center: Malazgird)		Miran	48, 49
Sıpkanlı tribe	1, 2	Artuşu	50
Karapapak tribe	7		
		Seventh Brigade (Center: Urfa)	
Hüsnanlı tribe	26, 27, 28, 29, 30	Kays	51, 52
		Berâzî	53, 54, 55

Source: BBA, *Yıldız Esas Evrakı*, section 14, document no. 2287, envelope 126, carton 11.

themselves or against other peoples. Brigade and regiment commanders are put in charge of these matters.

The fourth section explains "Administration and Reforms" as well as how and from whom taxes are taken. Article 18 states:

Reforms are to be made to the Hamidiye Light Cavalry Regiments. The law code, which has been presented by sultanic decree, exempts commanders and officers in the Hamidiye from the *âşâr* and *ağnam* [taxes] but not from [military] service. However, they will be exempted from some responsibilities toward the state and obligated for others. The *âşâr* and *ağnam* taxes collected from the tribes will provide the salaries of the commanders and the officers who form the aforementioned regiments and who recruit the squadrons in the brigades. Furthermore, the sultan specifically decrees to the invited Hamidiye squadrons that not one *akçe* [Ottoman coin] be left out in the collection of the *âşâr* and *ağnam* imposts, the former collected after the month of Eylül [September] and the latter collected in the spring. Collection is to be commissioned by the subdivisions [*liva*] and *kazas*. Under the commission of the subdivision, officers and individuals are to be accompanied by collectors. Collections are to be done in such a way so that not a single grain is left out. No one other than the tribes affiliated with the regiments has the right to benefit from these exemptions. The Hamidiye Regiment commanders are to assist the collectors in gathering the taxes on real estate, dividends, and properties belonging to the tribes. The aforementioned commanders are held accountable for inaction in this regard.[58]

The fifth section, which deals with "Just Procedures," covers some of the most interesting issues. Since the foundation of the regiments a number of legal issues had arisen between civil and judicial authorities, which caused the Hamidiye tribes to come out against both types of authority. The Hamidiye Regiments, through their irresponsible actions, rendered the local authorities virtually ineffective. While the regiments found it acceptable to be under the authority of the Imperial Army and the sultan, they found the decisions of the court and the orders of the *vali*s, *mutasarrıf*s, and *kaymakam*s unacceptable. This situation led to a number of controversies between the civil and military authorities and made the local authorities turn against the regiments. To mitigate these circumstances Şakir Paşa and Zeki Paşa established the following legal stipulations, which addressed the legal responsibilities of the Hamidiye Regiments in relation to military, civil, and judicial authorities:

1. "The commanders and officers of the Hamidiye are subject to the courts of the regular army in cases of felonious activity between themselves and the people and are subject to the legal articles on war rulings found in the military laws in the military law code" (article 24).
2. "Individuals of the Hamidiye who are suspected of crime who are issued a legal writ by the regular military courts are, like the *redif*s, arrested by officers of justice [*zabıta-ı adliye*] and are held in civil government jails" (article 26).

3. "Legal writs issued against commanders and officers of the Hamidiye are submitted to the military authorities. The military authorities are obligated to notify the court of the [suspect's] imprisonment, arrest, and status at the military office" (article 27).

4. "At the end of the trial the judgment of those charged with a crime, if approved by the appeals court, is put into effect. In accordance with military law, the convicted Hamidiye commanders and officers are handed over to the civil government after being stripped of their rank" (article 29).

5. "Although Hamidiye commanders are permitted to use a lawyer while in court at the time of trial, they must be present [in court] and cannot decline to be present, according to the rules of justice" (article 30).

Thus the regiments' accountability to the civil and military governments was made clear. The bill concludes by specifying that officials found to be in opposition to the Hamidiye Regiments would be punished. On the one hand, the bill gave the regiments new status and disciplined them. On the other hand, it took precautions against propaganda against the regiments.

The diagnosis of the lack of discipline and order in the Hamidiye Regiments and the social structure of eastern Anatolia that Şakir Paşa and Zeki Paşa undertook undoubtedly appears logical and correct. In addition, they managed to devise measures that were appropriate for local conditions and that brought the Hamidiye Cavalry to a state of greater discipline. They sent continual reports to the Sublime Porte about eastern Anatolia and the regiments, enabling the government and the sultan to keep a close eye on the positions and political actions of the regiments and the tribes in the region. Therefore it can be said that the policy in relation to eastern Anatolia was not random, although it was somewhat flexible, befitting the conditions there. This policy was necessitated by the social and political structure of the eastern region. It helped secure the loyalty and order of the Hamidiye Regiments. The state managed to show its authority in eastern Anatolia and over the tribes through the Hamidiye Regiments.

THE HAMIDIYE REGIMENTS
DURING THE FINAL YEARS OF ABDÜLHAMID II

In spite of its well-intentioned efforts in regard to the Hamidiye Regiments from its establishment until 1897 and the law codes, charters, and various bills, the state was still unable to achieve its desired result.[59] Although the state still made attempts to bring the Hamidiye Regiments to order after 1897, the nature of the regiments did not change much in practice. Thus these attempts were not completely successful. Even provincial yearbooks, provincial histories, and memoirs spoke of friction between the tribes and the nobility and elites, of tribal rivalry, and of the incidents that the tribes caused between 1897 and 1908.[60] The internal and external political events of the empire and the characteristics of the region played a significant role in the unraveling of the situation in this way. Therefore the Sublime Porte and the palace were forced to follow a flexible policy because of these incidents. While the charters that resulted from this flexible and concessionary policy were complete on paper, they could not be duly implemented. Hence the tribes belonging to the regiments remained more or less free in their movement.

In spite of all this, progress was made in the relations between the regiments and the tribes belonging to the regiments. Furthermore, the central authority managed to ensure obedience on many issues. An important development should be noted, however. Various political and social circumstances beginning in 1895 did not permit the implementation of the charters, so the Sublime Porte and the state became the target of increased criticism because of the emerging disturbances. This situation undermined the state authority and the Sublime Porte and may also have weakened the tribes' faith in the central authority in a number of instances. The European emphasis on eastern Anatolia reforms certainly left the Sublime Porte in a state of hesitation. Administrators, not necessarily of their own will, moved toward implementing reforms that the Muslim people in eastern Anatolia would not like. This conflicting situation could eventually have alienated many of the tribes from the central authority. Even under the influence of local and foreign propaganda, the tribal regiments that were formed could have developed a bad attitude toward the state. Abdülhamid II, who experienced such dangerous situations, stopped pursuing the old policy of bringing the tribes closer to the state and pushed for a second plan. In an environment of increased internal opposition and foreign pressure, in which Macedonia was becoming a greater problem, he believed that he could save eastern Anatolia by stressing a personal policy in relation to the Hamidiye Regiments.

The basis of Abdülhamid II's policy toward the tribes and the regiments was the establishment of a direct connection between the Sublime Porte and the tribes, without an intermediary. In putting this policy into force, he showed his trust in his title and position as caliph. Although the tribes had physically lived somewhat independently and separately from Istanbul for hundreds of years, he maintained their commitment to the office of the caliph in spirit. The tribes' positive view of Abdülhamid II's Islamist policy facilitated the sultan's political aims. This gave rise to a personal relationship involving the tribal chiefs, sheikhs (spiritual leaders), and Abdülhamid II, which strengthened the sense of guardianship, respect, and loyalty that was fundamental in relations between the caliph and believers. Furthermore, no power existed that could set up an obstacle in these relations.

With this policy Abdülhamid II sought to persuade the tribes to accept him as the protector of the Muslim people, in a manner that was independent from the Sublime Porte. Both the tribes and the urban elite and nobility class cast doubt on the Sublime Porte, viewing it as too much in agreement with Europe. They generally concluded that it sought to implement the reforms in favor of the Armenians in eastern Anatolia. Abdülhamid II benefited from this psychology of the tribes and the Muslim people and easily cast further doubt and suspicion on the bureaucrats in the Sublime Porte, Europe, the Armenians, and even the internal opposition, thus assuming greater supremacy, esteem, and authority.

Abdülhamid II did not just pay lip service to establishing relations with the tribal chiefs and sheikhs but formed a solid alliance by providing the tribes with a number of concrete benefits. For instance he made the tribes feel that he was protecting them by giving them weapons and ammunition. He also appointed members of the tribe to various ranks such as full colonel and *paşa*, thus solidifying his role as the protector. By bringing the children of the tribal chiefs to Istanbul, educating them, protecting them, and appointing them to civil service positions, his well-timed policy ensured their commitment and loyalty. Abdülhamid II offered the following response to critics of his policies:

> By giving various ranks, the tribal *ağa*s that we have made officers are satisfied with their situation and will learn a little discipline.... Still I know that I am criticized because I had the children of the tribal leaders brought to Istanbul and gave them civil service positions. For many long years we used the Christian Armenians in the civil service. Why wasn't I criticized then? In addition, I do not protect the children of Bedr Khan and do not host them at Istanbul. It seems that they are criticizing and blaming me because the country's security is being threatened. What a shame!

This is not interpreted in the way that was desired. In any case, I believe that I am on the correct path in my policy toward the tribes.[61]

This passage makes it clear that Abdülhamid II was sure of the correctness of his personal policy that he was implementing. Because of his belief, he continued the policy of controlling the tribes by forming personal relationships in his capacity as caliph until 1908. Therefore it can be said that the tribes and the tribal regiments became further committed to Abdülhamid II and more distanced from the state and the government. With time this commitment and loyalty to the sultan helped accustom the tribes to listening to the commands of the government and to committing themselves to the state to a certain extent. If Abdülhamid had not mediated with his personal policy, the Sublime Porte might have had greater control over the tribes, albeit in a limited way. The existence of discord and friction between the tribes and the local authorities, who were an extension of the Sublime Porte, supports this claim. Abdülhamid II's mediation helped decrease this friction to an extent. But in spite of the flexible and concessionary policy that the sultan pursued in regard to the tribes, the tribal regiments and affiliates could not be brought to order. The matters addressed in the charters were not implemented, because of these incidents and developments. Therefore Abdülhamid II chose at least to form a stronger bond with the tribes. Various internal and external factors inhibited the strengthening of an orderly military power and the full development and establishment of the Hamidiye Regiments. Both these impediments and the continuance of the tribes' old traditions caused the stipulations of the charters to remain only on paper. The policy of drawing the tribes to the side of the state forces through the Hamidiye Regiments and ensuring their support for the state was more important than bringing them under complete control. This aim was achieved and eventually kept the Armenians from forming an independent Armenian state in eastern Anatolia. Hence the Hamidiye Regiments spared eastern Anatolia the fate of becoming a second Eastern Rumelia or Macedonia. The tribes and the Muslim peoples gained confidence and security in defending themselves and eastern Anatolia by keeping close watch and acquiring weapons.

In conclusion it can be said that in spite of all efforts the Hamidiye Regiments could not become an organized military force.[62] The tribal chiefs and *ağa*s continually dominated the regiments, so they did not easily bend to the strict demands of military order. Thus they could not learn the principles and rules of modern warfare. Although this caused a number of complaints, Abdülhamid II continued to protect and develop Hamidiye Regiments, which had always borne his imprint.[63]

THE HAMIDIYE CAVALRY
AFTER THE SECOND CONSTITUTION

The governments established after the declaration of the Second Constitution revamped the Hamidiye Cavalry instead of dismantling it. They formed two commissions, the first headed by Maj. Hacı Hamdi Bey of Trabzon for the tribes near the Russian border and the second headed by Fahrettin Altay for the tribes in the southeast.[64] These commissions inspected the registration of the tribes, removing the names of those who were deceased and adding those who were of age. In addition, they inspected the horses of the regiments and gave new ranks to the tribal elites. Thus the new formations were completed by 1910.

Meanwhile the name of the regiments was changed to Tribal Regiments by Mahmud Şevket Paşa. Fahrettin Altay says that some wanted to change the name to Oğuz Regiments for a while, but this idea was eventually abandoned.[65] Over the next few years the government attempted to keep the ties between the tribes and Istanbul close by giving the Tribal Regiments new banners and ordinances. The Karakeçili tribe (located around Urfa) and the Milli tribe (at Viranşehir), who were divided into three regiments, participated in the Balkan Wars.

After the Second Constitution the state wanted Tribal Regiments to serve as assistance units that would undertake guerrilla warfare according to modern military techniques. To that end a number of new charters and instruction codes were drawn up.[66] These took into consideration the war techniques of newly developed cavalry units.

The new charter, drawn up in 1910 (1328 [Hicri]/1326 [Maliyya]), lists sixty-four regiments in the Tribal Regiments.[67] The first article stipulates that the formation and coordination should be undertaken and that the old charter should be abrogated. Table 4.2 shows the organization of the personnel of the Tribal Regiments according to the new charter.

The period for a salaried soldier in the regiments was twenty-seven years, from the age of eighteen to the age of forty-five. Those aged eighteen to twenty-one were in the *ibtidaiye*, those aged twenty-one to twenty-three were in the *nizamiye*, and those aged thirty-five to forty were in the *redifiye*. The *ibtidaiye* and *redifiye* divisions were supplied the following pieces of equipment in accordance with the charter: rifle, sword, lance, sheath, boots, laundry, raincoat, fur cap, provender bag, dressing

TABLE 14.2. Personnel of the Tribal Cavalry Divisions (1910)

REGIMENT PERSONNEL

1 Regiment Commander	A major or lieutenant colonel of the regular army
1st and 2nd Tribal Chief	From a tribe with a major. If the regiment consists of two or three squadrons the second major will be the chief. Chiefs who have attained the ranks of lieutenant colonel and captain (*kolağası*) will keep their rankings
1 Regiment Clerk	From the regular army
1 Second Clerk	From the tribe. If the tribe has no eligible person then an assistant from the regular army will be assigned
1 Imam	From the tribe
1 Lieutenant Doctor	—
1 Lieutenant Veterinarian	One major is appointed for each three regiments
1 Lieutenant Apothecary	—
1 Gunsmith	One gunsmith is appointed to two or three regiments depending on the region

SQUADRON PERSONNEL

1 Lieutenant	From the regular army; serves as squadron commander
1 1st Lieutenant	From the regular army; serves as team leader
1 2nd Lieutenant	From the tribe; serves as team leader

PERMANENT PERSONNEL

2 Regiment Scribes	From the tribe; if not available, then from the regular army
1 Gunsmith Assistant	—
20 Storage Keepers	From the tribe

Source: *Aşiret Hafif Süvari Alayları Nizamnamesi.*

for wounds, saddle set, spade, canteen, rope, reserve rations, reserve fund, reserve goods, and horseshoes. The men were to have all of these supplies with them. Some would have equipment that would be of benefit in destruction and fortification.

The new charter had seventy-one articles and is significantly different from the old one. It was put into force on August 19, 1910 (12 Şaban

TABLE 14.3. Personnel of the Tribal Cavalry Divisions (1912)

Division Commander	Brigadier General
General Staff	Major or lieutenant
Additional Officer	Lieutenant or first lieutenant
Recruitment Officer	Regiment commander or regimental secretary
Civil Officer	—
Subordinate Officer	—
Concierge (*odacı*)	—

Source: *Aşiret Süvari Alayları Nizamnamesi.*

1328 [Hicri]/6 Ağustos/Ab 1326 [Maliyya]) and was rewritten in 1912 to contain 120 articles, under which the Tribal Regiments were reformed.[68] According to these amendments the Tribal Regiments were united and became the Tribal Cavalry Divisions. The personnel of the divisions are shown in table 14.3.

Although there is no significant difference in the regiment and squadron personnel from the earlier charter, an increasing number of regular officers were appointed to the personnel and fewer tribal elites were appointed. Beyond this a seven-person Tribal Cavalry Inspectorate was created, which was headed by the major-general.

The duties of the Tribal Cavalry Regiments and the methods for their training are laid out in the 1911 instruction code.[69] The code applied tactical and strategic instructions from some of the foreign armies to the Tribal Regiments to increase their effectiveness. Accordingly the duties of the regiments supported by the army consisted of dispersing enemy cavalry units, weakening their power, misleading them, diverting them, crushing them, and undertaking other guerrilla warfare tactics.

We cannot know for sure what results these more militarily profound charters had in practice after the Second Constitution. But the tribal regiments had some military duties both in World War I and in the national War of Independence and contributed to the defense of eastern Anatolia.

CONCLUSION

No serious research has yet been undertaken on the Hamidiye Light Cavalry Regiments established in 1891. The topic has often been misunderstood or at least seen only as a military issue. But it is not possible to isolate the Hamidiye Regiments (with their different aspects) from other issues in recent Turkish history. First, the history of the Hamidiye Regiments sheds light on Abdülhamid II's policies, because the incidents were a part or extension of these policies. Second, the role that the regiments played in social and political life was particularly important. Most importantly, the Hamidiye Regiments were closely connected to Abdülhamid II's policies of centralism, his policies of balance between social and political forces, his Islamic thought, his reform efforts, and his military views. The archival documents used here were somewhat limited. But when the cataloging of the Yıldız Archives is completed a greater number of documents will be available to shed light on the issue. This paper is a start in developing analyses in that direction by revealing the basic outline of the Hamidiye Regiments.

NOTES

This chapter was translated from Turkish by Brad Dennis.

1. Stephen Duguid, "The Politics of Unity: Hamidian Policy in Eastern Anatolia."
2. Ibid., 139–41.
3. Ibid., 141.
4. Said Halim Paşa, *Buhranlarımız*, 107.
5. The Treaty of Berlin, 1878, Article LXI.
6. Başbakanlık Archives, Istanbul (BBA), Yıldız Esas Evrakı, Section 31, no. 76/35, envelope 76, carton 81.
7. M. Şerif Fırat, *Doğu İlleri ve Varto Tarihi*, 93.
8. Halfin, *19. Yüzyılda Kürdistan Üzerinde Mücadele*, 107.
9. Ibid., 115.
10. Ibid., 122.
11. The *padişah* would appoint the *vali*s himself. The *vilayet*s were tied to the Dahiliye Nezâriti. The authority of the *vali*s was limited, and they corresponded directly with the palace. See Enver Ziya Karal, *Osmanlı Tarihi*, 327.
12. Osman Nuri, *Abdülhamid-i Sâni ve Devr-i Saltanatı: Hayât-i Husûsiye ve Siyâsiyesi*, 821–22.
13. Paul Rohrbach, *Hatt-ı Saltanat*, 9.
14. Fırat, *Doğu İlleri ve Varto Tarihi*, 93.
15. Nuri, *Abdülhamid-i Sâni ve Devr-i Saltanatı*, 840.
16. General V. F. Mayewski, *Van ve Bitlis Vilayetleri Askeri Istatistiki*, 125.
17. Rohrbach, *Hatt-ı Saltanat*, 9.
18. Ali Vehbi Bey, *Pensées et souvenirs de l'ex-Sultan Abdulhamid*, 16–17.
19. Ibid., 16.
20. During research in the Başbakanlık Archives, I found no such documents.
21. BBA, Yıldız Documents, section 13, document no. 76/1, envelope 76, carton 81 (14 Nisan 1307). These two documents are in the form of notes written to Abdülhamid II by Yaver-i Ekrem Şakir Paşa.
22. BBA, Yıldız Documents, section 37, document no. 47/27, envelope 47, carton 113

(*Tensikat-ı Askeriye Cümlesinden olarak Hamidiye Süvari Alayları'na dair Kânun-nâmedir, Dersaadet 1308*).

23. Ibid.

24. BBA, Yıldız Esas Evrakı, Section 31, document no. 76/1, envelope 76, carton 81.

25. Ibid. The private room of the palace (*mabeyin*) accepts the visits of two persons from every regiment, but only with the tribal chiefs.

26. Ibid. A telegraph line between eastern Anatolia and Istanbul was completed at that time.

27. Ibid., telegram dated 14 Nisan 1307 (April 26, 1891).

28. Fırat, *Doğu İlleri ve Varto Tarihi*, 93.

29. Vehbi, *Pensées et souvenirs de l'ex-Sultan Abdulhamid*, 16.

30. Fırat, *Doğu İlleri ve Varto Tarihi*, 95.

31. Fahrettin Altay, *10 Yıl Savaş (1912–1922) ve Sonrası*, 54.

32. Fırat, *Doğu İlleri ve Varto Tarihi*, 95.

33. Altay, *10 Yıl Savaş (1912–1922) ve Sonrası*, 55.

34. Ibid.

35. Violent incidents between Muslims and Armenians had occurred since the Armenians revolted in the Sasun *kaza* of Bitlis in October 1893. Müşir Zeki Paşa went to Sasun and crushed the incident. This show of force by the state increased the esteem of the central authority in the eyes of the tribes. The Fourth Army commander enhanced his authority over the tribes.

36. Fırat, *Doğu İlleri ve Varto Tarihi*, 96.

37. Mayewski, *Van ve Bitlis Vilayetleri*, 196.

38. *Salnâme-i Askeri*, 514–78. The military yearbooks include only the numbers of regiments and the names and ranks of their commanders. They contain no information regarding the tribes to which they belonged or the regions in which they were located.

39. BBA, Yıldız Documents, section 37, document no. 47/28, envelope 47, carton 113, 30 Zilkade 1313. In a letter written by inspector-general Şakir Paşa on 3 Zilkade 1313 (April 16, 1896), it appears that the second charter was put into force before it was printed. I cite the date of the printed charter. For the letter of Şakir Paşa, see BBA, Yıldız Esas Evrakı, section 31, document no. 76/19, envelope 76, carton 81.

40. Mayewski, *Van ve Bitlis Vilayetleri*, 198.

41. For the education movement during the Abdülhamid II period, see Bayram Kodaman, "II. Abdülhamid Devrinde İlk ve Orta Öğretim."

42. It is understood here that the children from the Trablusgarb province were schooled in the Mekteb-i Harbiye.

43. Bayram Kodaman, "II Abdülhamid ve Aşiret Mektebi."

44. Ibid.

45. BBA, Yıldız Esas Evrakı, Kısım A, document no. 21/IV, envelope 21, carton 131.

46. Ahmed Şakir Paşa was born in Istanbul on May 26, 1838 (2 Rebiülevvel 1254), the son of Çapanzade Ömer Hulûsi. In February–March 1857 (Recep 1273) he finished studies in the Harbiye military school. In 1878 he was appointed as the ambassador at St. Petersburg, where he served for ten years. On August 4, 1889 (7 Zilhicce 1306), he was appointed as the deputy *vali* in Crete. On July 4, 1890 (16 Zilkade 1307), he assumed the title "Honorable Aide-de-Camp of the Sultan." On August

25, 1895 (4 Rebiülevvel 1313), he was appointed to the General Inspectorate of Anatolia and remained in that position until his death. He died on October 20, 1899 (8 Teşrinevvel 1315). His grave is in Sinop. See Zeki Pakalın, *Sicill-i Osmanî Zeyli*, 4119–20.

47. It is noteworthy that these tribes left the Diyarbakır environs and were withdrawn to more northern sections. The aforementioned Sultan Selim was probably Selim the Grim (Selim Yavuz). Were these tribes in the hands of the state or did they migrate by themselves? Were they situated in the more northern part of the regions for state purposes or for their own reasons? These matters are important from the standpoint of eastern Anatolian history. These tribes were quite numerous and lived in a wide range of regions.

48. BBA, Yıldız Esas Evrakı, section A, document no. 21/V, envelope 21, carton 131.

49. Fırat, *Doğu İlleri ve Varto Tarihi*, 97–98. This type of infighting frequently occurred between the Cibran and Hörmekli tribes in the environs of Tunceli. Many tribes competed and became enemies of one another.

50. Nuri, *Abdülhamid-i Sâni ve Devr-i Saltanatı*, 831.

51. BBA, Yıldız Esas Evrakı, section 14, document no. 2287, envelope 126, carton 11.

52. BBA, Yıldız Esas Evrakı, section 31, document no. 76/35, envelope 76, carton 81.

53. Ibid.

54. Ibid.

55. BBA, Yıldız Esas Evrakı, section 14, document no. 2287, envelope 126, carton 11.

56. Ibid.

57. See articles 11, 12, and 13 of the bill.

58. Ibid., article 18.

59. No original documents that elucidate the situation of the Hamidiye Cavalry between 1897 and 1908 are available. In spite of research in the Başbakanlık Archives on this topic, I did not come across any documents on this period. After the cataloging of the Yıldız Archives has been completed, I believe that many documents on the Hamidiye Cavalry will be found and that these documents will provide further information.

60. Şevket Beysanoğlu, *Kısaltmış Diyarbakir Tarihi ve Abideleri*, 95–97; Fırat, *Doğu İlleri ve Varto Tarihi*, 97–98.

61. Vehbi, *Pensées et souvenirs de l'ex-Sultan Abdulhamid*, 17.

62. Karal, *Osmanlı Tarihi*, 364.

63. Said Paşa, *Said Paşa'nın Hatıratı*, 2:272.

64. Altay, *10 Yil Savaş (1912–1922) ve Sonrası*, 55.

65. Ibid. On the name "Oğuz Regiments," the military minister Mahmud Şevket Paşa said: "[I]t is nice but after saying it time and again the regiments seem stale. It is best to call them tribal regiments." Ibid., 57.

66. These instruction codes and charters are found in the Milli Kütüphane.

67. *Aşiret Hafif Süvari Alayları Nizamnamesi.*

68. *Aşiret Süvari Alayları Nizamnamesi.*

69. *Instruction Guidelines on the Proceedings (CERAD) of the Tribal Light Cavalry Regiments.*

PART IV

Ethno-religious Cleansing and Population Transfers in the Balkans and the Caucasus

15

Ignoring the People

The Effects of the Congress of Berlin

Justin McCarthy

The Congress of Berlin was the type of Great Power deliberation frequently seen in the heyday of European imperialism: statesmen, often without any real knowledge of the regions whose fates they were deciding, drew boundaries on maps, ignoring both demographic realities and the wishes of the people involved. Thus were the idiosyncratic boundaries of Sub-Saharan Africa and the dangerous borders of the modern Middle East created. Ethnic and religious realities of regions were seldom considered and, if considered at all, were always secondary to European politics.

HUMAN RIGHTS AND THE CONGRESS OF BERLIN

The concept of human rights was surely known to the representatives of the powers who met in Berlin. As has always been known (then and now), the purpose of the congress was to restrain Russia. Russia's plans for the Balkans and eastern Anatolia were to be curtailed as far as possible without war. It is no exaggeration to state that the effects of the congress's decisions on the peoples of the Ottoman Empire were never a consideration of the delegates. Their concern was the balance of power, not human rights. Nevertheless, their decisions had a great and largely destructive effect on the peoples of the Ottoman Empire.

POPULATION OF THE BALKANS

Had the powers wished to consider the people of Ottoman Europe, they might have created a far different map than the one they imposed on the Balkans.

MAP 15.1. The Ottoman Empire in 1876

MAP 15.2. Southeastern Europe: Boundaries according to the Treaty of Berlin, 1878

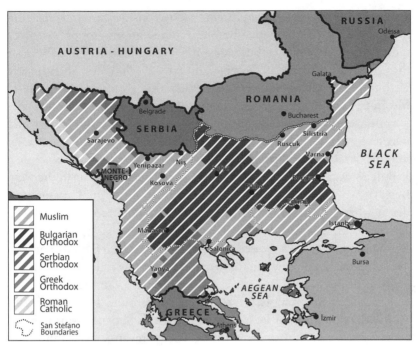

MAP 15.3. Majority Population by Religious Group, 1876

The population of Ottoman Europe before the 1877–78 War was by no means overwhelmingly Christian (map 15.3). Excluding Istanbul and its hinterlands, it included 4.2 million Muslims and 6.8 million non-Muslims.[1] It is impossible to assess the ethnic breakdown of the non-Muslims accurately, because many of the Ottoman population records listed only "Muslim" and "Non-Muslim" categories. The population of each ethnic group was diffuse, seldom centered in one region. The Bulgarian population, for example, was proportionally greater in part of the Edirne Province, south of Bulgaria proper, than it was in the area of the Bulgarian Principality created in 1878. Nor did the different religious communities live in compact groups within the provinces: Bosnia Province was 50 percent Muslim, 36 percent Orthodox (Serbian), and 13 percent Catholic (Croatian),[2] and the communities were scattered throughout the province. Serbs in Bosnia were a greater percentage of the population in the subprovinces (*sancak*s) in the west, on the Austrian border, than they were in the provinces adjoining Serbia. And the religious groups in many regions were commingled down to the village level.

It is possible, although impressionistic, to consider how Ottoman Europe could have been divided by ethnic and religious groups.[3] Map 15.3 indicates the majority populations in the Ottoman Balkans. Because the Ottomans only registered population by religion, not language, the sections of the map look more unified than they were in reality. Bosnia's Muslims were mainly Slavic-speaking. Muslims in western Ottoman Europe were mainly Albanian-speaking, while Muslims in eastern and northeastern Ottoman Europe were mainly Turkish-speaking, with a significant number of Bulgarian-speaking Muslims (Pomaks). Those shown as Bulgarian on the map were mainly Macedonian-speaking in the west, Bulgarian-speaking in the center and east. It should be noted, however, that neither the Russians at San Stefano nor the powers at Berlin showed any recognition that Macedonians existed.[4]

Had countries been created along ethnic lines, the religious "borders" indicated on the map would have had to be redrawn, because drawing maps according to majorities would have left sizable minorities in each region: Dobruja, for example, was 56 percent Muslim and 44 percent Christian. The population of Bosnia was evenly split between Muslims and Christians, although the Christians were by no means allied.[5] Bulgarians were one-third of the population in the area in northeastern Bulgaria that is marked as Muslim. Only massive population exchanges would have created truly compact nation-states. This would have resulted in hardships, but nothing compared to the hardships and forced population movements that had taken place in the recent war and the even worse mortality and migration that was to come. Short of retaining the unity of Ottoman Europe in some form, the creation of states such as those on the map would have been the only reasonably just way to forge a new southeastern Europe.

The powers at the Congress of Berlin never considered the possibility of creating states based on actual population numbers. They gave little indication of being in any way interested in the ethnic makeup or the desires of the people that they were moving on their diplomatic chess board. The only delegate who brought up the injustice of awarding Muslim populations to the new Christian states was the Ottoman delegate, Alexander Karatheodori, who protested the granting of Muslim lands to Montenegro.[6] His objections were futile; the lands were given to Montenegro anyway. The delegates felt that the Montenegrins should be given the land equivalent to the Muslim territory they had conquered in the recent war ("un accroissement de territoire équivalent à celui que le sort des armes avait fait tomber entre les mains des Monténégrins leur devait être accordé").[7] The Muslim inhabitants, as shown below, were soon either killed or evicted.

THE NEW MAP OF THE BALKANS

The boundaries created by the Congress (see map 15.2) seem almost designed to be as unfair as possible: Serbia was granted Muslim land in Niş but not the region of Bosnia that had a Serbian majority. Romania's prize, Dobruja, had a Turkish majority before the war. All but small sections of the region granted to Montenegro had a Muslim majority. It was the Bulgarian Kingdom, however, that was given the most unreasonable boundaries: a large area with a prewar Turkish majority in the northeast became part of Bulgaria but not the region in the west, where a majority were Bulgarian Orthodox. Turkish towns such as Varna became part of Bulgaria; Ohrid, the chief see of the Bulgarian Church, did not. Eastern Rumelia, the portion of Bulgaria that was autonomous but at least theoretically retained by the Ottomans, was overwhelmingly Bulgarian in population, unlike Bulgaria proper.

Bulgarian ethnic considerations had been much better served by the Treaty of San Stefano (see map 15.3). It put the Bulgarians in the new Bulgaria. Of course, San Stefano Bulgaria still held a sizable Muslim minority, but no one, either at San Stefano or at Berlin, cared about the wishes of those Muslims.

MINORITIES AND THE NEW STATES

The rights of minorities were not completely omitted from the Treaty of Berlin, if only theoretically. The treaty was forthright in guaranteeing the rights of minorities in the new or enlarged Balkan states. For example, the treaty made the following demands on Bulgaria:

> The following points shall form the basis of the public law of Bulgaria:
>
> The difference of religious creeds and confessions shall not be alleged against any person as a ground for exclusion or incapacity in matters relating to the enjoyment of civil and political rights, admission to public employments, functions, and honours, or the exercise of the various professions and industries in any locality whatsoever.
>
> The freedom and outward exercise of all forms of worship are assured to all persons belonging to Bulgaria, as well as to foreigners, and no hindrance shall be offered either to the hierarchical organization of the different communions, or to their relations with their spiritual chiefs.[8]

Using the same formulation in each case, the treaty guaranteed the civil and religious rights of minorities in Montenegro, Serbia, and Romania. The provisions envisaged systems of government that would have been exemplars of intercommunal justice, for their time. If applied in the United States at the time, the provisions would have canceled the disabilities of Native Americans and African Americans. If they were applied in Great Britain, the Irish would have seen their political and agrarian rights actualized. If the provisions were applied in the colonies of the European empires, the colonies would have ceased to exist. Of course, the Europeans gave no thought to their own practices or to the philosophical ramifications of human rights legislation; nor could they have considered that their pious guarantees for the Balkans were anything but declarations of unenforceable good intentions, at best.

Like later international treaties, the Treaty of Berlin had no system of enforcement. Protection of minority interests was left completely to the governments of the new states. Those governments were often the ones organizing attacks on minorities, particularly Muslim minorities. The Europeans knew this. European diplomats in the Balkans had written voluminous testimony on abuses against Muslims.[9] Given that the delegates at the Berlin Congress knew well what was still happening to the Muslims of the conquered regions, it is impossible to believe that their pious sentiments on human rights were anything but hypocrisy.

The new countries set about almost immediately to erase the official presence of minorities, a practice that was to be accelerated after the Balkan Wars. Greeks and Macedonians officially ceased to exist in Bulgaria, subsumed in government documents and practice into the Bulgarian nationality and the Bulgarian Church. In the 1887 Bulgarian census, for example, 98 percent of the Christian population was listed as Bulgarian Orthodox. This was perhaps literally true, as all traces of the Greek Orthodox Church had been erased in favor of the Bulgarian Exarchate Orthodox Church. Serbia and Romania followed the same practice.

The results of the congress's lack of consideration for the people of the Balkans can best be seen in a brief description of the populations of the region.

Romania

The congress awarded the region of Dobruja (Mouths of the Danube) to Romania (see map 15.4). Once again the powers did not consider the prewar population in their award. Russia demanded Bessarabia, the region east of the River Pruth that had been part of Romania.[10] The region had

MAP 15.4. Ottoman Dobruja, 1876

an ethnic Romanian majority, but no one but the Romanians felt that this was a factor to be considered. In exchange, Romania was given Dobruja, a region with a Muslim Turkish/Tatar majority — Romanian land was taken, and Turkish land given in compensation. Few provisions show such a complete disregard for the people affected by the powers' play with maps.

Much of the Turkish population had fled Dobruja at the beginning of the war. They were simply not allowed to return. The Muslim population of Dobruja declined from 184,000 (56 percent of the total) in 1870 to 32,000 in 1879. The Christian population, presumably swelled by Romanians from Bessarabia, increased from 142,000 to 177,000.

Serbia and Montenegro

At the congress it was stated that all the inhabitants of Montenegro would have complete religious freedom. The delegates recognized that disturbances were occurring in the Montenegrin conquest region, but the congress decided that troubles in the Montenegrin conquest should be

MAP 15.5. Bosnia, Serbia, Montenegro, and the Ottoman Empire: 1876 and 1878 Borders

resolved by the Ottoman Empire and Montenegro and were not part of its business.[11] The Turks, of course, had no way to stop the Montenegrins from killing or evicting the Muslims. Soon after the congress, virtually no Muslims remained in the area occupied by Montenegro.

The Niş region (see map 15.5) was awarded to Serbia. Its original Muslim population of 131,000 declined to 12,000.[12] Many of these were soon replaced by Serbs migrating from territories retained by the Ottomans. Serbia did not admit the existence of Slavic-speaking Muslims, who, if they were recognized at all, were listed officially as "Turks."

Greece

The congress left the question of Greek territorial gains for later deliberation. In 1881 Greece was given Thessaly (see map 15.6), which had a Muslim population of approximately 40,000, one-fifth of the total population. Little is known of the reasons for Muslim emigration, but the first accurate Greek census of Thessaly, in 1911, listed only 3,000 Muslims.[13]

Bosnia-Hercegovina

The greatest mortality for both Muslim and Christian populations in Bosnia-Hercegovina had come in the 1875 Serb rebellion in Bosnia and the subsequent Ottoman-Serbian War of 1876. Due to Austrian occupation, the province was spared the effects of the 1877–78 War. Nevertheless,

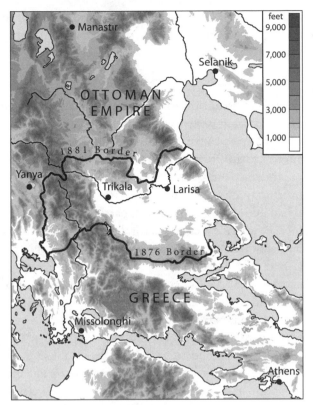

MAP 15.6. Greece and the Ottoman Empire: 1876 and 1881
Borders

the 1875–76 troubles and large Muslim emigration from Bosnia caused a
significant diminution of population. The Serb population decreased by
7 percent and the Muslim population by 35 percent.[14] Although Muslim
mortality in 1875–76 was high, many—perhaps most—of the lost Muslims were emigrants who had no wish to live under Austrian rule. (The
Austrians in fact treated the Muslim population better than did any of
the other Balkan states.)

At the congress the Austrians stated that 200,000 people had fled their
homes in Bosnia-Hercegovina in the 1875–76 disturbances and that the
Ottomans would never be able to pacify the province. Russia agreed. This
ignored the fact that the Ottomans had in reality pacified the province
in 1876.[15]

The *sancak* of Yenipazar, originally tied to the Ottoman Bosnian province, had been largely given to Montenegro in the Treaty of San Stefano.[16]
The Berlin Congress placed it within the Ottoman Empire, although

under Austrian occupation. This was in no way due to the Muslim majority in the *sancak* (63 percent), which was never mentioned at the congress. The cause was Austrian fear of an enlarged and empowered Montenegro.[17]

Bulgaria

The Muslim population of Bulgaria (the new Bulgarian state and Eastern Rumelia) declined precipitously during and immediately after the 1877–78 War, from 1,480,000 to 676,000, a 54 percent loss. Of these, 515,000 became refugees in the Ottoman Empire; 289,000 were dead. (It should be noted that these are almost entirely civilian deaths not military deaths, as are the other mortality and migration statistics presented here.) Many of the dead had been killed by Russians, particularly by Cossacks acting alongside local Bulgarians. Perhaps naturally, the Russians had no wish to bring wartime actions to the table at the congress. The other powers also had no wish to do so.[18]

The Turks were not the only refugees. A large number of Bulgarians migrated into Eastern Rumelia and Bulgaria. The 1905 Bulgarian Census listed 37,000 immigrants from Edirne Province, 38,000 from Manastır Province and Selanik Province, and 13,000 from "other parts of the Ottoman Empire" (assumed to be mainly from Yanya Province and Kosova Province). Earlier Bulgarian statistics did not include Eastern Rumelia, although the statistics indicate that many Bulgarians went there.[19] The majority of the migrants had died before 1905; demographic projections of the number of migrants show them to have been approximately 187,000.

The Jews

Because of the prewar practice of publishing population numbers only as "Muslim" and "non-Muslim" in most Ottoman provinces it is usually impossible to enumerate the migration and mortality of Jews during and after the 1877–78 War. Where statistics on Jews are available, such as in Bosnia, it appears that they suffered as badly as Muslims. Jewish organizations complained bitterly over the placement of Jews under the notoriously anti-Semitic regimes in Serbia and Romania.[20]

AFTER THE CONGRESS: EXCLUDING THE REFUGEES

Each of the Balkan countries excluded the Muslim and Jewish refugees who had left during the war.[21] Indeed, the treaty made no specific mention of refugees. In most cases those who had left were theoretically allowed to return for two or three years after 1878 depending on the country. In reality, the borders were closed to them. The recent history of persecution and death would have made swift repatriation a dubious consideration for the refugees in any case. Not even the Muslims who had remained in the new states, such as those who had taken refuge in northeast Bulgaria, were allowed to return to their homes (see the discussion below).[22]

The Treaty of San Stefano had envisaged the creation of commissions that would assess property ownership "under the superintendence of Russian commissioners." Unclaimed property was lost after two years: "At the expiration of the two years mentioned above all properties which shall not have been claimed shall be sold by public auction, and the proceeds thereof shall be devoted to the support of the widows and orphans, Mussulman as well as Christian, victims of the recent events."[23]

The Treaty of Berlin mentioned only those who had left the occupied regions. The formula for each state was the same, as in the example of Bulgaria: "Mussulman proprietors or others who may take up their abode outside the Principality may continue to hold there their real property, by farming it out, or having it administered by third parties."[24]

Whatever the treaties stated, the reality was the loss of Muslim property that had been taken by Christians during the war. Muslim refugees had no diplomatic or legal mechanism to claim their property. The refugees in the Ottoman Empire or still within the new states, such as the refugees from Dobruja and central Bulgaria who had fled to the Şumla-Varna region, lost everything. The refugees who had remained within the borders of the new states could theoretically go back to their old villages to claim their land. Those foolish enough to attempt this were met by angry mobs and were often killed. Survivors fled a second time.[25]

As an example of the impossibility of refugees returning to their homes, British diplomatic observers recorded the situation in Bulgaria and Eastern Rumelia. Russian soldiers cooperated with Bulgarians to exclude Turks, destroying the old homes of Turkish refugees, and the Turks were not allowed to build new homes. Refugees had been promised food and housing by the Russian occupiers; none was provided, and they starved. It was often impossible for refugees to return, as Bulgarian bands roamed the roads, robbing and killing the refugees. Refugees soon learned that their homes and farms had been lost forever.

The refugees who had gone to what remained of the Ottoman Empire in Europe had no way ever to claim their property, despite treaty assurances that they could sell or rent it out. No Bulgarian, Romanian, Montenegrin, or Serbian would act as an agent for Turkish refugees.

Land would first have had to be seized from the Christian peasants who had occupied it. Attempting this would likely have been a death sentence. Police force would have been needed, but the Bulgarian, Eastern Rumelian, Serbian, Montenegrin, and Romanian governments did not offer their services.

The Ottoman government protested these treaty violations to the powers, with no result.

The problem was the lack of any enforcement method in the Treaty of Berlin. Assuming, against all evidence, that the powers had any real concern for Muslim refugee landowners, what could be done unless they were willing to enforce the treaty? Seizures of land had taken place in villages all across the Balkans. None of the new Balkan governments could have carried out the treaty directive. Attempting to return land seized from Muslims by Christian peasants would have sparked revolts, perhaps even toppled states. And enforcing the payment of rent to Turks who had been forced into exile was a laughable concept. An external force was needed for enforcement, and none was ever even considered at the Congress of Berlin.

It can surely be argued that politics and the fear of a European war stood in the way of the creation of a mechanism to protect human rights. Russia might have refused to accept the concept of Great Power intervention in matters of refugees' return to their land, although this seems to be too small a matter to lead to war.[26] More likely, given the lack of any mention of the refugee problem at the congress, the powers simply did not wish to be involved.

EASTERN ANATOLIA

Compared to what was done in Ottoman Europe, the alterations made to the Treaty of San Stefano in the Ottoman east (see map 15.7) were slight. In essence the Treaty of Berlin afforded the Ottomans a slightly improved defensive position in the northeast. They still lost Batum and Kars, the linchpins of the defense of Anatolia. Given the lack of accurate statistics, no one knows exactly the total wartime mortality during and immediately after the war. It seems, however, that it was proportionately less than the losses in the Balkans.

As it did in the Balkans, the congress ultimately paid little attention to demographic realities in the Ottoman east. Its consideration of the Russian conquests there, however, was one of the very few times that the nature of the population was considered at all. Lord Salisbury resisted the grant of Kars and Ardahan to the Russians on the ground that to do so

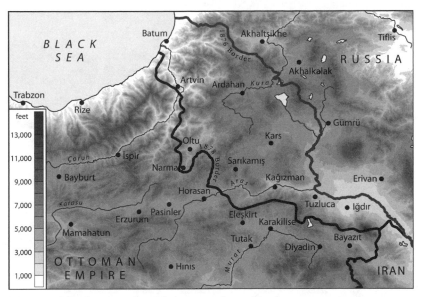

MAP 15.7. Northeastern Anatolia: 1876 and 1878 Borders

would lessen Ottoman power in Asia and would make future peace in the region difficult. Disraeli asked that "[e]thnographic considerations" be taken into account.[27] They were not so considered, and Kars and Ardahan were granted to the Russians.

Statistics on the populations of the region taken by Russia before the war, and indeed until the 1897 Russian census, are virtually nonexistent; wartime deaths are unknown. Both Armenians and Turks migrated across the new border. The Treaty of San Stefano had guaranteed free passage from the newly Russian lands for Turks;[28] it offered similar unhindered passage for Armenians who wished to follow departing Russian troops.[29] Perhaps 100,000 Armenians went to Russian Transcaucasia (see map 15.8), including the newly conquered Kars, Ardahan, and Batum regions. A minimum of 110,000 Muslim Turks, Kurds, and Laz crossed into the Ottoman Empire during and immediately after the war. These are extremely tentative statistics.[30]

ARTICLE 61

The main problem in the east was article 61 of the Treaty of Berlin, which was similar to a section of the Treaty of San Stefano.

> The Sublime Porte undertakes to carry out, without further delay, the improvements and reforms demanded by local requirements

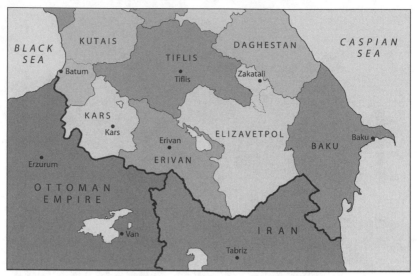

MAP 15.8. Russian Transcaucasian Provinces after 1878

in the provinces inhabited by Armenians, and to guarantee their security against the Circassians and the Kurds.

It will periodically make known the steps taken to this effect to the Powers, who will superintend their application.[31]

Armenian groups, armed with impassioned pleas from the Armenian patriarch of Constantinople, had demanded that they be given independence or autonomy in eastern Anatolia. Judging by the lack of consideration given the question at the congress, the powers actually cared little about the Armenians. They could have used the fact that the Armenians were a distinct minority in the areas they claimed (even then well known) as an excuse not to take action, but instead they simply ignored any real ramifications of the Armenian question. They had to say something for the Armenians, however. The Armenian cause had a sizable following in European countries, especially among religious groups, who used the Armenians as a weapon in their holy battles with the Muslim Turks. Thus article 61 came about. It really said little beyond platitudes, but it was to prove a diplomatic difficulty in the years to come.

Article 61 gave the powers carte blanche to interfere in eastern Anatolia whenever they wished. Because the article lacked all specifics, it was always easy to say that the Ottomans had not carried out their promises well enough. And the term "superintend" could take on ominous meaning for the Ottomans. Even the phrase "in the provinces inhabited by Armenians" was a problem. Armenians inhabited nearly every province in the Ottoman Empire. The Armenian population was, in fact, most dense in İzmit near Istanbul. Armenians, though, were not a majority in any Ottoman province. So where did the powers actually have the right to "superintend"?

From 1878 onward, the powers cited article 61 in complaints about the state of Armenians in the Ottoman Empire. This was to a certain extent salutary: the Ottomans did what they could to increase their policing power in the east. They attempted to enlist Armenians in the police force and in the provincial bureaucracies, although this proved to be a failure when Armenian groups began to assassinate Armenians who cooperated with the government. Ultimately, however, the effect was far from beneficial: the powers forced the Ottomans to relinquish control of their far eastern provinces, creating "inspectorates" headed by Europeans in Erzurum and Van Provinces. Only the advent of World War I kept the inspectorates from wresting political control from the Ottoman government and the creation of what were in effect autonomous countries that favored minority populations.[32]

Russia obviously intended to use article 61 as a wedge for constant interference and — the European political situation permitting — as a *casus belli* for future wars. After all, Russia had begun the 1877–78 War on the pretext of aiding Ottoman Christians.

The Ottomans could only lose from article 61. No matter what reforms they managed, it could be said that they were not doing enough. In any case, the Ottomans could do very little in eastern Anatolia. Any reforms would take a long time. The problem, as the Russians knew well and the other powers should have realized, was financial.

The Ottomans were anxious that reforms be put in place in eastern Anatolia. Even if one believes (I think unjustly) that the Ottoman government had no interest in the well-being of Armenians, the Ottomans had definite interest in reforming the east. Both Muslims and Christians suffered from the depredations of Kurdish tribes. Troubles in the east meant a constant drain on the exchequer and kept taxes from being collected. But the Ottomans could not pay what was needed for true reform. Reform, especially the pacification of Kurdish tribes, depended on military force, and soldiers had to be paid.

Although the situation gradually improved, for some time after the 1877–78 War the Ottoman government could only afford to put garrisons

in major cities. Tribes who preyed on Muslim and Armenian agricultural-
ists were mobile. By the time soldiers reached affected areas the raiders
were gone. Interdicting gun shipments of Armenian rebels would have
meant a great increase in border guards. Many more men were needed.
And the soldiers who did exist were often not in a position for action
against tribes and rebels. In 1904 soldiers in Van rioted. They had not been
paid in eight months, but their primary complaint was that they did not
have enough to eat.

The congress did not advance the cause of reform in the Ottoman east.
Quite the contrary: the Treaty of Berlin made it more difficult for the Ottomans to pay for reform. It took no notice of one of the most damaging
elements of the Treaty of San Stefano, leaving in place the war reparations forced on the Ottomans. Added to the Ottoman government's other
debts, the effect of the reparations was to make it impossible to carry out
the reforms called for in the Berlin Treaty. The amount of the reparations
was staggering: 310 billion rubles, slightly reduced in the Constantinople
Convention of 1882 to 802,500,000 French francs.[33] The same convention,
recognizing that the Ottomans could never pay such a sum, set an "annuity" of 350,000 lira (8,050,000 francs) to be paid to Russia. Even though
this meant that the total would not be paid for 100 years,[34] it was still impossible for the Ottomans to pay the annuity. It must be remembered that
by 1879 the Ottoman Empire was essentially bankrupt. In today's dollars
350,000 lira a year would be more than $100 billion.[35]

The reparations were obviously unpayable, as the Russians knew. In
addition to gaining purely economic advantages, the Russian intention in
imposing the indemnity was twofold — to hamper the economic and military development of the Ottoman Empire by starving the government of
funds and to force the empire to accede to Russian wishes in exchange for
leniency in collection. The best example of this was Russian opposition to
the construction of railways to the Ottoman east. In addition to their commercial benefits, railways were needed to bring soldiers to the east quickly.
The Russians opposed this for obvious military reasons, but rapid movement of soldiers was needed to bring military might against Kurdish tribes
and Armenian rebels. The Ottomans did not have nearly enough soldiers
to garrison all the potential trouble spots of the empire. They needed to
be able to bring soldiers in quickly. By threatening to demand arrears in
payment of the war indemnity, the Russians kept the railroad from being
built.[36] The fact that improving Ottoman policing power in the east would
have improved life for both Christians and Muslims was ignored.

CONCLUSION

Historians have usually considered the Congress of Berlin only from the standpoint of European diplomacy and the European balance of power. Indeed, anyone reading the standard work on the Congress, W. N. Medlicott's *The Congress of Berlin and After*, would find virtually no consideration of the effects of the Treaty of Berlin on the peoples of the conquered territories.

The Russians had initiated the 1877–78 War with two objectives in mind — to maximize Russian power in the Balkans and Anatolia and to bring independence to the Slavic Christians, especially the Bulgarians, whom they saw as their protégés. Their success in maximizing their power was somewhat limited by the Congress of Berlin but was still great. The Russians managed to keep both Bessarabia and the most formidable Ottoman defense region of northeastern Anatolia — essentially the same victories they had written into the Treaty of San Stefano. The congress limited the success of the Russians' second aim by reducing the size of Bulgaria and leaving land to the Ottomans. In the Balkan Wars, however, Christian states were ultimately to conquer all the Ottoman European land envisaged for new Christian states in the Treaty of San Stefano. The forced migration of the Muslims of the Balkans, ignored by the Congress of Berlin, was to culminate in the Balkan Wars, until the Muslim population of the regions taken by Romania, Serbia, Montenegro, and Greece was only half of what it had been in 1876. The Christians of the Balkans were to become official members of the dominant religion in each state, no matter what their personal choice was. The Treaty of Berlin was unjust in itself, but its later ramifications were worse. By ignoring the people, the Congress of Berlin had set the pattern that was to lead to later disaster.

NOTES

1. There is not enough space to describe all the calculations of the populations given here. They are taken from my book *Death and Exile: The Ethnic Cleansing of Ottoman Muslims, 1821–1922*; "The Population of Ottoman Europe before and after the Fall of the Empire"; "Muslims in Ottoman Europe: Population from 1800 to 1912"; and "The Demography of the 1877–78 Russo-Turkish War."

2. These and other calculations include some rounding error (carried out to more decimal places, the percentages would have equaled 100).

3. This analysis is based on Ottoman population records, considered in the sources listed above in note 1. There was no lack of population estimates from each of

the ethnic groups, which showed completely different population distribution. The best compilation of estimates of the Muslim population is in Alexandre Popovic, *L'Islam Balkanique: les musulmans du sud-est européen dans la période post-ottomane*. Popovic offers clear-headed analysis of the figures. Standard contemporary statistical compilations, such as *Bevölkerung der Erde*, were only as good as their sources, which were usually deficient and often outright fabrications. The best published collections of Ottoman population summaries are Kemal H. Karpat, *Ottoman Population, 1830–1914; Demographics and Social Characteristics*; and Cem Behar, *Osmanlı İmparatorluğu'nun ve Türkiye'nin Nüfusu*. Two books by Hans-Jürgen Kornrumpf, *Die Territorialverwaltung im östlichen Teil der europäischen Türkei vom Erlass der Vilayetsordnung (1864) bis zum Berliner Kongress (1878) nach amtlichen osmanischen Veröffentlichungen* and *Die Territorialverwaltung im östlichen Teil der europäischen Türkei vom Berliner Kongress (1878) bis zu den Balkankriegen (1912/13) nach amtlichen osmanischen Veröffentlichungen*, contain both Ottoman and European statistics but are particularly valuable for their information on geography and boundaries. On population statistics for Bulgaria, see Ömer Turan, *The Turkish Minority in Bulgaria (1878–1908)*, 79–98.

4. The question of a separate Macedonian existence at the time (an intractable subject) is not considered here.

5. See the section "Minorities and the New States" below.

6. Congress of Berlin: protocols 10 and 12. The powers did give some small consideration to Christian religious and ethnic differences. For example, as one of its reasons for diminishing the size of Bulgaria, Britain voiced concern that Greeks would be put under Slavic rule if Bulgaria extended to the Aegean and Lake Ohrid, an area where there were actually very few Greek Orthodox (Treaty of Berlin: protocol 2). The protocols of the Congress were published in *Les Protocoles du Congrès de Berlin*.

7. Congress of Berlin: protocol 8, annex 1.

8. Treaty of Berlin: article 5. The treaties of Berlin and San Stefano were published in Thomas Erskine Holland, *The European Concert in the Eastern Question*.

9. National Archives of the United Kingdom (formerly Public Record Office), Foreign Office Archives, London (FO), FO 195/1136, 1137, 1184, 1185, 1189, 1252, 1253, 1254, and 424/59. Bilal Şimşir published a voluminous collection of these documents in *Rumeli'den Türk Göçleri*. The British printed a large number of Muslim complaints, along with those of their own consuls, in Great Britain, Foreign Office, *Turkey, No. 45 (1878), Further Correspondence Respecting the Affairs of Turkey*.

10. The territory had been taken from Russia in the Paris Treaty of 1856.

11. Congress of Berlin: protocol 10.

12. McCarthy, "Muslims in Ottoman Europe," 36–38, and *Death and Exile*, 104.

13. The estimate of 40,000 is extremely conservative. Some contemporaries gave numbers well above 50,000 Muslims. See Popovic, *L'Islam Balkanique*, 119–21. A Greek census in 1881 gave a total population of 254,744 but provided no figures by religion or ethnicity.

14. The Catholic population actually increased by 7 percent, while the Jewish population, always tied to the fate of the Muslims, decreased by 25 percent. The population of Bosnia is considered in Justin McCarthy, "Ottoman Bosnia, 1800 to 1878."

15. Congress of Berlin: protocol 8.

16. Preliminary Treaty of San Stefano: article 1.
17. W. N. Medlicott, *The Congress of Berlin and After: A Diplomatic History of the Near Eastern Settlement*, 95–96 (the original edition was published in 1938).
18. The evidence was extensive. See McCarthy, *Death and Exile*, 59–108.
19. The 1881 Bulgarian Census, which did not include Eastern Rumelia and gave only partial migration statistics, listed 32,000 "born in Thrace and Macedonia." The number of Bulgarian refugees has been calculated by comparison to standard demographic tables.
20. See Max J. Kohler and Simon Wolf, *Jewish Disabilities in the Balkan States: American Contributions toward Their Removal, with Particular Reference to the Congress of Berlin*; and Zvi Keren, "The Fate of the Jewish Communities of Kazanlık and Eski-Zağra in the 1877–78 War."
21. See McCarthy *Death and Exile*, 86–88.
22. For a description of this in Macedonia, see Marija Pandevska, "The Refugee Crisis in Macedonia during the Great Eastern Crisis (1875–1881)."
23. Preliminary Treaty of San Stefano: article 11.
24. Treaty of Berlin: article 12.
25. See the many examples of the treatment of these refugees in McCarthy, *Death and Exile*, 81–94, and the sources in note 9.
26. Count Nikolai Ignatiev felt that the Russians were not willing to go to war over the results of the Berlin Congress. Medlicott, *The Congress of Berlin and After*, 12.
27. Congress of Berlin: protocol 14.
28. Treaty of Berlin: article 21,
29. Treaty of Berlin: article 27. Migrants were assured the right to sell their property, but the degree to which this actually took place is not known. Many of the migrants were wartime refugees, so it is doubtful that much property was sold.
30. For a description of the difficulties in arriving at these figures, see McCarthy, "The Demography of the 1877–78 Russo-Turkish War," 56–62.
31. Treaty of San Stefano: article 16.
32. The Ottomans took advantage of the war to repudiate the inspectorates. On the inspectorates, see Justin McCarthy, Esat Arslan, Cemalettin Taşkıran, and Ömer Turan, *The Armenian Rebellion at Van*, 144–48, 166–69. See also Joseph Heller, *British Policy towards the Ottoman Empire*, 107–11; FO 371/2137, Beaumont to Grey, Constantinople, December 4, 1914, "Annual Report, 1913"; W. J. Van der Dussen, "The Question of Armenian Reforms in 1913–1914"; "Communiqué of the Ministry of the Interior, April, 1330," April 28, 1914, Başbakanlık Osmanlı Arşivi (BOA), DH.KMS., D:2-2/5 F:20-1; "Dahiliye Nezaretinin 15 Nisan 1330 tarihli atama yazısı," cited in Zekariya Türkmen, "Birinci Dünya Savaşı Öncesinde İttihat ve Terakki Hükümetinin Doğu Anadolu Islahat Projesi ve Uygulamaları," 258.
33. The initial reparations in the Treaty of San Stefano were much larger. The treaty listed the following reparations: War Expenses, 900,000,000 rubles; Damage to the South Coast of Russia, 400,000,000; Damage to the Caucasus Region, 100,000,000; Claims of Russian Subjects and Establishments in Turkey, 10,000,000; Total, 1,410,000,000 rubles. This total included 1,100,000,000 rubles considered to be payment for regions taken by Russia, leaving 300,000,000 in reparations and 10,000,000 for the claims of Russian subjects.

34. The Russians kindly decided not to charge interest.
35. It is nearly impossible to make accurate comparisons without recourse to statistics like producer price parity, which cannot be properly calculated for the nineteenth-century Ottoman Empire. One Ottoman lira (*mecidiye*) officially converted to $4.29 in 1880. Based on the change in the American Consumer Price Index, the dollar equivalent of 350,000 lira would be worth $41 billion; based on the change in the American Gross Domestic Product per capita, it would be $427 billion. These figures do not give a satisfactory estimate of the actual buying power of 350,000 lira in 1880, but they are sufficient to show the value of that sum. Contemporary exchange rates have been drawn from Hermann Schmidt, *Tate's Modern Cambist*, 918–19.

     No attempt has been made here to put the reparations into economic perspective, because the finances of the Ottoman Empire were in such a precarious state that any addition to expenditures could lead to disaster. For comparison of the cost of the reparations relative to Ottoman wages, see Süleyman Özmucur and Şevket Pamuk, "Real Wages and Standards of Living in the Ottoman Empire, 1489–1914." For the place of the reparations in the Ottoman budget, see Stanford J. Shaw, "The Nineteenth-Century Ottoman Tax Reforms and Revenue System."
36. Michael R. Milgrim, "An Overlooked Problem in Turkish-Russian Relations: The 1878 War Indemnity," 533–35.

16

The Treaty of Berlin
and the Tragedy of the Settlers
from the Three Cities

Mustafa Tanrıverdi

INTRODUCTION

Population movements are the most important social consequence of the Treaty of Berlin (1878). Because the treaty recognized the emergence of new states and thus established new national borders, the mass population movements ran rampant in the Balkans and the Caucasus and approximately 5 million Turkish Muslims started flocking into the Ottoman Anatolia.

The Ottoman Empire, which was not ready to contain such large-scale settler movements into its interior, encountered many socioeconomic, political, and administrative difficulties. The Ottoman state established commissions and appointed civil servants to solve these problems and to provide settlers with whatever they needed. Yet this was not an easy task. One of the most important reasons why the empire failed to contain the settler influx was the sheer number of settlers. Another important context was the Turko-Russian War of 1877–78, which came pretty much out of nowhere and resulted in extensive losses of territory. Thus the Ottomans simply did not expect such severe consequences of the war.

The settlers who flocked into the Ottoman interior included people from Kars, Ardahan, and Batum (Elviye-i Selâse).[1] According to article 58 of the Treaty of Berlin, the Ottoman Empire left the Three Cities to the control of Russia, which created monumental changes in social, commercial, military, and administrative structures of Elviye-i Selâse. Accordingly, the Turkish-Muslim population of the region who started suffering from these transformations decided to leave their homes for Anatolia.

Between 1877 and 1918 more than 100,000 Turkish Muslims left the Three Cities, and the frontiers between Russia and the Ottoman Empire became suitable grounds for resettlement by non-Muslims. In accordance with the Russian policy of cleansing the region of the Turkish-Muslim elements, new ethnic groups were encouraged to settle there. At the same time, Russia resettled large numbers of Armenian communities around Kars and Ardahan, deeming the Armenians more welcoming of Russian policies.

Such population movements and corresponding resettlements left a deep imprint on Anatolia; thus studies on such demographic changes are important vehicles to understand modern Turkey. Hence many studies have focused on the population movements from Crimea, the Caucasus, and the Balkans. Yet such extensive population movements require more micro-scale studies, which do not exist (as for the population influx from Kars, Ardahan, and Batum into Anatolia). While it is by no means complete, this paper focuses upon the reasons and consequences of population movements from the three *sancak*s into the Ottoman interior and portrays the painful lives of the settlers by using the archival holdings of the Başbakanlık Osmanlı Arşivi (BOA), Genelkurmay Askeri Tarih ve Stratejik Etüt Başkanlığı Arşivi (ATASE), and several secondary sources.

THE ROAD TO THE TREATY OF BERLIN

As a result of political developments in the Balkans, Russia declared war in the Ottoman Empire on April 24, 1877.[2] Once the war started, Russia struck an alliance with Romania (which was an Ottoman vassal state), ordering its troops to cross over the Danube. Serbia and Karabagh sided with Russia as well. In the Caucasus Russian forces first invaded Kağızman, Ardahan, and Beyazıt and then besieged Kars. While the efforts of Ahmet Muhtar Paşa hindered the Russian invasion of Kars at first, Russian forces took control of the city in December 1877.[3] Having failed to stop the Russian advances into the interior, the Ottoman Empire signed an armistice with Russia on January 31, 1878.

After the armistice, Russia chose San Stefano (Yeşilköy) as the diplomatic setting to hold the discussions on a peace treaty. By doing so Russia intended to show its might both to the Slavs in the Balkans and to European powers.[4] Russia imposed its own terms without any consultation with the European powers, and the Ottoman side signed the Treaty of

San Stefano. Article 29 of this treaty stipulated that the agreement in San Stefano was a "preliminary treaty" ("Mukaddemat-ı Sulhiye"). When Britain and Austria argued that this peace treaty could only be finalized in a congress attended by the signatories of the Treaty of Paris in 1856, preparations for a permanent resettlement started.[5]

On June, 13, 1878, a congress for a final peace treaty between the Russians and Ottomans met at the Palace of Radziwil. After a month of discussion it produced the terms of the Treaty of Berlin: a list of further political and military concessions on the part of the Ottoman Empire.[6] This treaty was an important watershed in Ottoman history. In addition to significant losses of territories in Europe and Asia as well as other military and political defeats, the empire lost its most populated areas, inhabited by up to 5 million people, mostly non-Muslims. In the aftermath of the treaty the control of the Ottomans was reduced to Anatolia and today's Middle East. Accordingly the ratio of Muslims in the Ottoman population significantly increased.[7]

The terms of the Treaty of Berlin also transformed the dynamics of Elviye-i Selâse. According to the Treaty of San Stefano, Elviye-i Selâse as well as Eleşkirt and Beyazıt were given to Russia as part of the war reparations, accounting for 1,110 million rubles of the 1,410 million total monetary claims of the Russians.[8] The issue of Kars, Ardahan, and Batum was discussed in the fourteenth protocol of the Congress of Berlin on July 2, 1878. In compliance with the wishes of the British minister of foreign affairs, Lord Salisbury, the congress first discussed the matters relating to Kars and Ardahan. Salisbury argued that leaving Kars and Ardahan to Russian control would destroy Ottoman credibility and influence across Anatolia and would make it difficult to maintain security around Kars and Ardahan. Yet he did not push his agenda further, once the meetings between British and Russian representatives made it clear that Russia had no intention whatsoever of leaving the region.[9] As Russia secured its hold over Kars and Ardahan, the next issue to be discussed was the future of Batum.

Batum was an integral part of the negotiations in the congress. While the discussions focused on the possibility of turning Batum into a free port, Russia obviously argued against such proposals. A free port zone in Batum would help the European commercial stakes in the region. Accordingly Lord Salisbury defended the notion of either returning Batum to Ottoman control or creating a free port zone. Trying to contain the Russian influence around the region, Salisbury presented his plan on the Ottoman Straits to Prime Minister Disraeli on July 2. It included an acknowledgment of the Russian control over Batum but expected Russians to accept the British proposal on the Straits, which included the British naval access to the Black Sea through the Straits. These British ambitions changed the mind of Russian prime minister Aleksandr Gorchakov on Batum. Russia accepted the British proposal that projected the creation of a free commercial port in Batum.[10]

These decisions made in the protocols can be seen in articles 58 and 59 of the Treaty of Berlin. Kars, Ardahan, and Batum would be under the control of Russia (article 58), and Batum would be a free commercial port (article 59).[11]

THE BEGINNING OF MIGRATIONS AND ELVIYE-I SELÂSE UNDER RUSSIAN CONTROL

The reassertion of Russian rule over Elviye-i Selâse by the Treaty of Berlin played a large role in the Turkish-Muslim population's decision to migrate. Within a few years thousands of people from the region migrated into the interior of Anatolia. Obviously, these migrations created serious troubles. Even the decision to migrate itself was a manifestation of a larger tragedy.

Migrations from Kars, Ardahan, and Batum into the Ottoman interior had started in the first years of the nineteenth century. Certain events caused these migrations to take place, such as the first Russian invasion of Kars in 1807, the Turko-Russian War of 1828–29, and the Crimean War of 1853–56, which also took place in the Caucasus. Such wars brought about tragedies across the region; thousands of people were massacred in this fighting. In 1855 the people of Kars were presented with a *gazilik* (honorary title for the victorious) medal and granted a three-year tax exemption for their bravery and extensive losses in wartime.

But the Turko-Russian War of 1877–78 was the worst tragedy of the century. It not only brought about destruction but also caused migrations, exile, and captivity. The telegram dated September 5, 1878, from Kars to Mabeyn-i Hümâyûn Baş Kitabet-i Celilesi (Grand Office of the Chief of Staff of the Ottoman Palace) explicitly depicts the tragedies of the war. Sent approximately ten months after the invasion of Kars by the Russian forces, this telegram provides an insider's view into the daily tragedies and shows how the Russian forces destroyed the city in such a short time. Motivated by religious and statist concerns, the people of Kars continued to supply the Ottoman army, but forty-four days of Russian attacks resulted in the destruction of most buildings in the city. All the properties of Turkish-Muslim people were burned to ground. Most of the Turkish

Muslims in the city were killed, and more than half of the people in Kars suffered terribly on the fronts of the war or during the invasion of the city. As a result of Russian looting that lasted three days and nights, even the wealthiest people in the city got significantly poorer and needed help. Once the Russian forces torched the city, more than five hundred shops and all the merchandise in them were seriously damaged or destroyed. As a result of this destruction and massacre, the people of Kars left the city for Erzurum and resettled there temporarily. Those who could not or chose not to migrate continued to suffer for the next forty years.[12] This period of Russian invasion is still remembered in the region as the "forty-year-long dark days."

In his article "Kars'tan Hicret Ederken" (While Migrating from Kars), Tahsin Nihad describes the painful journey like this:

> Women, children, and the old took to the roads. Right before they climbed the hill, they threw sorrowful looks at their hearths once again. This unlucky group of people was in tears. The fog that brought together their tears this morning was about to lift, and there were no young girls any longer who were washing rugs on the river that passed through their dear homeland. Allah's name was not echoed any longer from the white minarets that pierced through the lifting fog. To them, their homes, with no smoke coming out of their chimneys at this point, seemed to constitute a small black hill of stone and dirt. The enemy soldiers who were marching down the hill across from them were moving forward swiftly in order to perch on this hill like a eagle.[13]

The Turkish-Muslim people of Elviye-i Selâse obviously were not in favor of leaving their homeland that they had inhabited for centuries. Thus the local population reacted to the Russian assertion of control over the region by sending telegrams to the Ottoman authorities. They made it clear that the Ottoman administration knew their resentment about the decision to leave them under Russian control.

The telegram dated April, 13, 1878, from the Batum Headquarters to the Central Command describes the views of the locals of Batum on the consequences of the war. According to this document, the majority of the population in Batum rejected Russian control and suggested some alternative solutions, having heard that Batum was left to Russia as part of the war reparations. The locals suggested collecting the necessary amount of money among themselves. If this was not possible, they suggested taking a loan from a European bank, which they could pay back according to a proper timetable.[14] The people of Ardahan showed similar reactions, pointing to their discontent with the loss of Ottoman control. If Ardahan was given as part of the war reparations, they demanded facilitation of the process of migration into the Ottoman Empire.[15]

It is clear from the telegrams sent from Kars, Ardahan, and Batum to the central Ottoman authorities that the Turkish-Muslim population of the region was not willing to migrate. The invasion of their homeland and the assertion of Russian control over it caused deep resentments among these locals. The people of Elviye-i Selâse made it clear that they were ready to make any sacrifice to avoid Russian control. All of these efforts and suggestions proved useless, however, because the Ottoman state was not in proper economic shape to pay the war reparations. Thus Elviye-i Selâse had to be left to Russian rule.

Accordingly, the Turkish-Muslim populations of nearly all villages and towns of Elviye-i Selâse waited for the right time to start their migration into the Ottoman interior. The *tezkire* (memorandum) prepared by Sadrazam Kamil Paşa on December, 26, 1886, speaks to this point. According to this document, the people of Çıldır, Ardahan, Kars, Batum, and Oltu and the surrounding villages wanted to migrate. Four villages of Batum as well as the people of Kağızman, Camuşlu, and Livana (Artvin) even prepared petitions indicating their intention to leave their homelands. The locals in Batum flocked to the docks for this purpose as well, leaving their household items and animals behind in their houses. Having considered the possible detriments to its tax collection, Russia did not allow the people of Batum to get on board the ships in the winter of 1886. Thus hundreds of families were left in despair in the Caucasus. The chargé d'affaires in the Caucasus asked the Ottoman state for possible options for transporting these families into the interior. All of the official documents of the families who were about to migrate were sent to the Office of the Ottoman Ministry of Foreign Affairs. The official replies to such local inquiries indicate that the Ottoman central authorities found it suitable to settle these settlers in the Ottoman interior and mentioned that the Russians were aware of this process of resettlement. They also asked that the process of resettlement should start by determining how many settlers were to be relocated in a particular Ottoman province and then distribute the settlers in their respective ports of departure accordingly.[16]

Therefore the Turkish-Muslim people of the region started their difficult journeys because they were not presented with any other option. The young and old, men and women, took the roads to Anatolia in order to

TABLE 16.1. The *Sancak* of Kars in 1288 (1871)

		MALE POPULATION		
KAZA	VILLAGES	MUSLIM	CHRISTIAN	TOTAL
Kars	110	11,110	519	11,629
Şuregel	84	2,320	1,015	3,335
Zaruşad	74	3,325	—	3,325
Kağızman	58	2,825	950	3,775
Total	326	19,580	2,484	22,064

Source: *Salnâme-i Vilâyet-i Erzurum*, 143.

find peace and happiness. They could not find anyone to sell their properties to, so they burned down their houses with their own hands.

In order to increase the pace of migrations, the Russian government
provided the proper legal context and further incentives. On February, 8,
1879, the Treaty of Istanbul was signed between Russia and the Ottoman
Empire. Article 7 of this treaty says that the Turkish-Muslim people of
Elviye-i Selâse were free to sell their properties and migrate in the following three-year period, effective immediately after the date of the treaty.
After the end of this three-year period those who had sold their properties
but failed to cross the border would become Russian subjects.[17] This article
clearly suggests that the Turkish Muslims were encouraged to migrate. Accordingly, the ratio of Turkish Muslims to the Christian population in the
region changed in favor of the latter in the following years, and new ethnic
groups were introduced to the demographic equation.

The changing demographic patterns can be seen through a comparative analysis of censuses taken before and after the Russian control in the
region. The following tables include the demographic statistics for certain years from Kars, Ardahan, and Batum. Table 16.1 shows statistics for
the *sancak* of Kars for the year 1288 (1871), taken from the yearbook of
Erzurum.

Table 16.2 (from the same yearbook) shows the demographic statistics
on the *sancak* of Çıldır, including the *kaza* of Ardahan.[18]

Table 16.3 shows the population of the *sancak* of Batum in 1870, 1872,
1873, and 1874, according to the yearbook of the *vilayet* of Trabzon.

Table 16.3 clearly shows that the Turkish-Muslim sector of the population was in the majority and Armenians constituted one of the largest
Christian groups in the region (the exact number of Armenians cannot

TABLE 16.2. The *Sancak* of Çıldır in 1288 (1871)

| KAZA AND NAHIYE | VILLAGES | MALE POPULATION | | |
		MUSLIM	CHRISTIAN	TOTAL
Kaza of Oltu	70	5,711	296	6,007
Kaza of Namervan (Narman)	48	3,137	339	3,476
Nahiye of Tavusker	28	3,041	—	3,041
Kaza of Ardahan	110	6,786	—	6,786
Nahiye of Göle	76	2,942	19	2,961
Nahiye of Poshov	49	3,337	—	3,337
Nahiye of Çıldır	31	1,995	—	1,995
Kaza of Ardanuç	51	5,213	549	5,762
Nahiye of Şavşad	53	5,801	647	6,448
Nahiye of Penek	68	5,226	25	5,251
Total	584	43,189	1,875	45,064

Source: *Salnâme-i Vilâyet-i Erzurum*, 144.

be derived from the table). Other non-Muslim groups also lived there, but the Armenians were the only one with a settled community. The Russian invasion brought about changes in administrative structures, and the *kaza*s of Oltu and Ardahan were integrated into the *sancak* of Kars. Thus a significant transformation of the demographic pattern of the region occurred after the arrival of the Russians. According to the Russian census taken twenty years after the invasion (1897), the *sancak* of Kars had 162,723 males and 129,755 females, totaling 292,478.[19] Similar changes occurred in the following years. In İbrahim Hilmi Bey's "Kafkasya Hakkında Erkâm," published in the *Ati* newspaper (1918), the population of Batum was 183,100, while the *sancak* of Kars had 396,200 people.[20] This change was not caused by a natural growth of population over twenty years but by Russian attempts to plant colonies in the region. The 1897 tsarist census divided the population of Kars into two groups, "colonized" and "indigenous" (table 16.4).

The year 1878 was clearly the turning point for the increase in colonized groups. Such an increase in the number of ethnic groups on a borderland cannot be explained by the growth of cross-border commerce. It was caused by the policies during the reign of Russian tsar Alexander

Table 16.3. The *Sancak* of Lazistan (Batum) in 1870, 1872, 1873, and 1874

KAZA AND NAHIYE	VILLAGES	DISTRICTS	MALE POPULATION					
			CATHOLIC	ARMENIAN	RUM	CIRCASSIAN	MUSLIM	TOTAL
Nefs-i Batum (Central Batum)	—	1	4	17	41	429	113	604
Kaza of Batum	18	—	—	—	—	1,008	2,800	3,808
Kaza of Çürüksü	17	—	—	—	—	—	3,686	3,686
Kaza of Acara-ı Sufla	34	—	—	—	—	—	5,150	5,150
Nahiye of Acara-ı Ulya	22	—	—	—	—	—	5,810	5,810
Nahiye of Maçahel	26	—	—	—	—	—	3,955	3,955
Kaza of Hopa	23	—	—	—	—	—	4,496	4,496
Nahiye of Arhavi	34	—	—	—	—	6	6,637	6,643
Nahiye of Gönye	21	—	—	—	—	472	4,178	4,650
Kaza of Atina	25	—	—	—	—	87	7,980	8,067
Nahiye of Hemşin	33	—	—	104	—	—	6,493	6,597
Kaza of Livana	58	5	1,229	312	—	—	14,431	15,972
Kaza of Habekelaskur	11	—	—	—	—	—	2,243	2,243
Total	322	6	1,233	433	41	2,002	67,972	71,681

Source: Kudret Emiroğlu, ed., *Trabzon Vilayet Salnamesi*, 2:185 (1870), 4:201 (1872), 5:177 (1873), 6:183 (1874) (data for all four years).

TABLE 16.4. Inhabitants of Kars in 1897

GROUPS		POPULATION	
Colonized Group	Russian	10,695	
	Polish	12	
	Greek	23,525	
	Estonian and Mordvin	280	
	Ossetian	2,330	
Indigenous Group	Kurd	26,434	
	Armenian	37,094	
	Ashur (Chaldean)	321	
	Iranian	81	
	Turk	41,823	
	Turkman	8,893	Turkish Language Group
	Karapapak	24,134	
	Noghai	2,556	

Source: Ortaylı, "Çarlık Rusyası Yönetiminde Kars," 181.

III, who implemented similar Slavicization and colonization policies elsewhere in Russia.[21] Furthermore, the number of people who spoke Turkish in Kars also decreased greatly right after 1878.

Russian subjects were divided along confessional lines in the region. Similarly, Muslims were divided into the two categories of Sunni and Shiʿi Islam. Table 16.5 shows the major religious groups in Kars.

The total non-Muslim population in Kars was 100,898, while the Muslim population was 123,418 (table 16.5). In order to police the Muslim population more efficiently, the Russian authorities appointed hierarchical religious heads for each Muslim group.

One of the most important reasons for the demographic changes such as the increase in the number of colonized groups and decrease in the number of Turkish Muslims was the large-scale population movements in and out of Elviye-i Selâse. As a result of the migrations from 1878 to 1918, thousands of Turkish Muslims left the Three Cities. Those who stayed in the region came face to face with harsh political realities of the Russian rule.

TABLE 16.5. Religious Groups in Kars

RELIGIOUS GROUP	MALE	FEMALE	TOTAL
Orthodox	18,142	17,188	35,330
Sektan[a]	6,488	6,276	12,764
Armenian-Gregorian	26,016	24,964	50,980
Armenian-Catholic	500	459	959
Protestant	469	392	861
Jewish	—	4	4
Muslim (Shiʻi)	7,715	7,289	15,004
Muslim (Sunni)	54,789	50,529	105,318
Yazidi	1,648	1,448	3,096

Source: Ortaylı, "Çarlık Rusyası Yönetiminde Kars," 182.
[a] The people of this group were reactionary in belief and tradition. They first opposed the church reform during the time of Tsar Alexei Mikhailovich and patriarch Nikon and then migrated to Caucasia and later to Kars. Among the people of the region they are also known as *malakan*.

First, the Russian government initiated many administrative changes in the region. Two military *oblasts* (*vilayets*) were created in the region by integrating Ardahan, Posof, Göle, Çıldır, and Oltu with Kars and Ardanuç and Artvin with Batum. These two military administrative units were then put under the control of the governor of Tbilisi. The *oblasts* of Kars and Batum were governed by military governors with the rank of general, while other *sancaks/okrugs* were under the charge of *mutasarrıfs* with the rank of colonel. By establishing *başmuhtarlıks* (small administrative units), Russians transformed the administrative structure into the order of *vilayet, sancak, kaza, nahiye,* and *başmuhtarlık*.[22]

The railroads from Kars and Batum were connected to Tbilisi, the center of the southern Caucasus. By functionalizing the trade route of Batum, Tbilisi, and Tabriz to replace the Trabzon, Erzurum, and Tebriz route, Russia turned Batum into the commercial center of the Caucasus and Iran.[23] Batum became the third port on the Black Sea (after Odessa and Istanbul), serving the hinterland of the Caucasus and Central Asia. Even though the diplomatic terms defined Batum as a free commercial port, Russia made it a military port.[24]

In addition to these administrative and commercial transformations, Russia also developed a particular policy for education in the region.

According to the census of 1876/77, the three *rüşdiye* (middle schools) in Kars, Kağızman, and Çıldır were the highest institutions of education in the *sancak*. The Russian administration did not open middle schools or high schools in Kars until 1898. Furthermore, the budget set aside for educational purposes in Kars and in Daghestan was the lowest in the Caucasus. These policies cannot be explained by the difficulties that the geography of the region presented to the implementation of state policies and realization of investments. Rather, they were rooted in the deliberate Russian strategy to raise ignorant but loyal individuals in the region.[25] The tsarist educational policies in the region started changing in 1905, with the Russian defeat at the hands of the Japanese. Until that time the people of the area were only able to get Qur'ans and Mawlid (a work by Süleyman Çelebi, depicting the birth of Muhammad) books from Anatolia, but after 1905 the locals started having access to the newspapers from Azerbaijan and the Crimea.[26] In 1910 the region had 12 state schools and 143 Muslim schools. While the underdevelopment of secular educational institutions was part of the Russian state policy, it was also as the result of Turkish-Muslim opposition to Russian rule, manifested in the rejection of Russian institutions.[27]

The major reason why Russia implemented such heavy-handed policy changes in the administrative, economic, and educational structure of the region was to strengthen its control. In a way the strategic value of the region forced Russia to aspire to these changes. Once Russia had added Kars, Ardahan, and Batum to its territories, they were aware that these were important gains in the Caucasus. In order to build a strong defense line against the Ottoman Empire, Russia attempted to establish a solid military administration in the southern Caucasus.[28]

Elviye-i Selâse was the source of important Russian aspirations in the political and commercial arena. Accordingly, Russia had established relations with the region in earlier times. Before 1877, for instance, a Russian civil servant in Kars was responsible to the consulate in Erzurum. Kars was an integral part of the Caucasian trade and a center of commerce. For this reason, the Ottoman government had established a commercial court with six members and one head. Despite the difficulties in transportation, the postal system and the telegraph facilities were still functional under the Ottomans.[29]

Kars had a symbolic importance for the British as well. The Russian conquest of the city caused extensive coverage in English newspapers and thus awareness among the English public, increasing the British concern over the Russian advances. For instance, the *Times*, one of the newspapers closest to the government, suggested that Britain would mediate between the Ottomans and Russians "for the sake of humanity" and "for her own interests." The *Standard* and *Morning Post* argued that the British stakes in the East were at risk and that the recent developments forced Britain to make a decision in its policy orientation. The *Morning Post* further argued that Britain needed to set aside its neutrality. The Ottoman control across Anatolia, the newspaper maintained, was critical for the security of Britain.[30]

Aware of the strategic value of the region, Russia made use of the existing Armenian population to extend its control over the trade routes in and out of Kars. Beginning in the seventeenth century, the Armenian merchants came to control the trade between the Ottoman Empire and Iran, Russia, and the European countries.[31] The final Russian objective in the region was to integrate the Ottoman Armenians formally with Russia. Accordingly, the Russian policy increasingly came to favor the Armenians of Kars and Ardahan.[32]

THE MIGRATION ROUTES OF THE SETTLERS

The people from Elviye-i Selâse who settled in Anatolia used both land and sea routes. The settlers from Kars and Ardahan usually chose the land route, while the ones from Batum preferred the sea route. The geographical position of each city to some degree determined the nature of the route.

The settlers who arrived in the port of Batum waited for days and nights for the ferries that were to take them to Anatolia. The ferry of İdare-i Mahsusa, which served the Batum area only once a week, could not meet the increasing demand, and the number of settlers waiting in the port to be transported continued to grow. Some of the settlers changed their minds because of these delays and returned to their homeland. The ones who waited for their turn crowded the port area for days and nights. At the same time, new arrivals of settlers worsened the situation. Among them were the settlers from the *sancak* of Çıldır who went to Batum to migrate to the interior.[33]

Some of the settlers took alternative routes, reaching the ports of Trabzon, Samsun, and Sinop; from there they were transported to their respective port cities or to the cities in Anatolia. By orders from the Commission of Settlers, the settlers who arrived in Istanbul were sometimes dispatched to their respective areas of resettlement without even being allowed to land on the shores of Istanbul.[34]

Those who arrived in the port of Samsun first resettled in the city temporarily. Then some of them were sent to Istanbul and some to other provinces. Those sent to Istanbul were resettled in their permanent areas of settlement.[35] On the shores of the Black Sea, the port of Sinop was less frequented by the settlers than the ports of Trabzon and Samsun. Yet from the report sent to the Commission of Settlers on January, 20, 1888, it is clear that a Russian ship carrying 1,500 settlers anchored in the port of Sinop.[36]

Settlers who opted for the land routes from Elviye-i Selâse were sent to the interior from Kars to Erzurum. Erzurum functioned as the central gathering point for these settlers, who were later distributed to their respective areas of permanent resettlement.[37] But this process of redistribution was not necessarily quick and thus unproblematic. The document sent to the Bab-ı Ali on May, 15, 1880, shows that the settlers sent from the environs of Kars, Çıldır, and Ardahan to the *vilayet* of Erzurum were in misery because of delays in the process of permanent resettlement.[38]

The central function of Erzurum as a center of redistribution on the land routes was the main reason for the concentration of settlers in the city. The authorities of the *vilayet*, for instance, demanded the resettlement of the accumulated settlers around the Dersim area, which had fertile lands. Excluding the settlers who had come from the Kars area and settled earlier, more than 15,000 settler families were in Erzurum by May 5, 1879. Because of the increase in the number of settlers and potential movements from Elviye-i Selâse, a commission was set up in the city to provide for the settlers' needs. This commission was active in organizing the relocation of the settlers from Elviye-i Selâse. In the Istanbul decree May 5, 1879, the governors of Erzurum and Sivas were asked to determine appropriate empty plots of land for resettlement around these cities. By March of 1880 eight thousand families from Erzurum had been resettled on these lands. Similar migratory patterns continued on the same routes in the following years, and this number increased to thirty thousand settler families.[39]

The increase in the number of settlers also caused a number of problems on the land routes. A report sent to the Ministry of War mentions that Armenian *chete*s attacked the settlers who left Kars and Sarıkamış for the interior. The *chete*s, centered in Karaurgan, stole ninety cows, six horses, and two hundred kilos of cereal as well as food and money from a settler community of over a hundred families. They also gathered the female settlers in a barn and stole their valuables.[40] On the same route, the settlers on the way to the Erzurum and Beyazıt area were attacked by Russian soldiers, leaving many dead and wounded.[41]

THE SETTLERS BECOMING OTTOMAN CITIZENS

The developments in the nineteenth century led the Ottomans to restructure their legal system in accordance with European notions of citizenship. In 1869 Tabiiyet-i Osmaniye Kanunnamesi was accepted. This law, inspired by the 1851 French law, provided the first legal context for citizenship irrespective of religious principles. It considered everyone who lived in the land of the sultan to be an Ottoman national.[42] Due to important demographic fluctuations, the issues of citizenship gained further importance.

The Ottoman government divided those who migrated into its territories into two groups: *muhacir* (settler) and *mülteci* (refugee). These legal definitions and contexts were finalized in the 1911 İskân-ı Muhâcirîn Nizamnamesi. Accordingly, those who migrated into the empire with the approval of their state were called *muhacir*s, while those who sought refugee in the Ottoman realm and thus asked for Ottoman nationality were called *mülteci*s.[43] The Ottoman state provided housing and provisions to the *muhacir*s. In this legal context, the migrants from the Three Cities were legally *muhacir*s.

Once the migrants from Elviye-i Selâse entered the Ottoman territory, they had to accept Ottoman nationality. The migrations were from Russian territories, so a Russian passport was needed for the process. The Ottoman officials considered those who came with their passports to be *muhacir*s and treated them accordingly.[44] The *muhacir*s were also required to present the document of denaturalization that they had obtained from the Russian authorities to the Ottoman officials. Then the *muhacir*s started the process of Ottoman naturalization by sending their petitions to the ministry or to the relevant local authorities.[45]

While the Ottoman state accepted the *muhacir*s as citizens, they also needed to pass an identification check. This process was under the control of the Ministry of the Interior and its corresponding local Directorate of Common Safety. The *muhacir*s were asked to present documents indicating that they came from Elviye-i Selâse.[46] If they did not have passports, problems occurred.[47]

At the same time, a fine was applicable to those who failed to finish this process of naturalization. For instance, the report sent to the *vilayet* of Sivas on July 17, 1889, shows that some *muhacir*s from Kars and Ardahan failed to complete the process. The daily difficulties that the *muhacir*s faced led the authorities to forgo the fine for such delays, however, and instead encourage the *muhacir*s to complete the process.[48]

While the Ottoman authorities deemed the process of naturalization quite important, *muhacir*s tended to delay or totally avoid it. Some *muhacir*s in Anatolia who did not finish the procedures and were caught by the authorities came up with excuses not to complete the process. For example, some argued that they were just guests in the region or were visiting their relatives and about to return home once their visit was done. The purpose behind such delays and avoidances by the *muhacir*s was to circumvent taxation and conscription.

RELOCATION OF THE SETTLERS

The resettlement process of *muhacir*s was carried out by the *muhacir* commissions. Issues of migration and migrants were handled by the institution of Şehremaneti until 1859.[49] After this date, though, a new institution was necessary for such issues because the developments in the Balkans and Caucasus significantly increased the number of migrations and thus necessitated a new institutional framework for large-scale demographic movements. In 1860 Istanbul alone received approximately ten thousand *muhacir*s. Sadrazam Ali Paşa realized the extent of the problem; after discussions in the Meclis-i Vâlâ-yi Ahkâm-i Adliye (Supreme Council of Justice), the Ottoman state decided to establish a new commission of *muhacir*s.[50]

After the Russo-Turkish War of 1877–78, the Commission of Settlers became a larger institution: the Commission of the Resettlement of *Muhacir*s. Later Directorates of the Resettlement of *Muhacir*s were created in each *vilayet*, under the control of the Directorate of General Resettlement in Istanbul.[51]

The *muhacir*s who reached Ottoman soil were first sent to their temporary areas of resettlement by the Commission of Settlers and then to their permanent region of resettlement. The *muhacir*s resettled primarily on empty state lands and *vakf* properties.[52]

While the *muhacir*s from Elviye-i Selâse were resettled in almost all Anatolian cities, they concentrated in certain regions. The *muhacir*s from Kars and Ardahan were primarily resettled in and around Sivas, Erzurum, Amasya, and Tokat,[53] while the ones from Batum were sent for resettlement to cities like Bursa and Istanbul.

During the process of resettlement, the settlers' labor skills determined whether they were to be sent to a rural or an urban area. The Ottoman government resettled civil servants, scholars, and those with skills suitable to urban contexts in cities.[54] For instance, Mehmed Tahir Efendi was *shaykh* of the lodge of Ebü'l-Hasan El-Harakani, an Islamic mystic in tenth-century Kars. After the Russian invasion, Mehmed Tahir Efendi migrated from Sivas to Kars. The authorities resettled him in the Alibaba neighborhood of central Sivas, where a Nakşibendi lodge existed.[55] *Muhacir* Cemal from Kars, in contrast, was resettled in Bandirma, a seaside town, because his occupation was boat-building.[56]

Despite these examples, the *muhacir*s from Elviye-i Selâse were usually resettled in areas with suitable agricultural lands, because they were mostly farmers. In a sense these resettlements of *muhacir* farmers contributed to the development and diversification of Anatolian agriculture. For example, the introduction of the metal plow to the *vilayet* of Sivas, which can be considered an agricultural breakthrough, was because of the *muhacir*s from Kars.[57]

The *muhacir*s were usually distributed to existing villages. In some cases, though, a village was created from scratch just for the *muhacir*s. For instance, two new villages named Seyfiye and Kolcular were established around the Beyazıt fields of Bursa when forty *muhacir* families were resettled in the area. As an another example from Bursa, a neighborhood named İclaliye was established around the Yıldırım district, with the approval of the Ministry of the Interior, after the resettlement of thirty-five households of *muhacir*s from Batum and Ardahan.[58] Around the Eylice area of Bursa, a new village named Burhaniye was established after the resettlement of 139 *muhacir*s from Ardahan.[59] Another neighborhood named Abadan was created in Sivas for 100 households of *muhacir*s from Kars.[60] The *sancak* of Beyazıt received 268 households, totaling 1,739 individuals. While 1,193 of them were resettled in existing villages, new villages were established for 546 of them. These villages were named Şahverdi Harabesi, Kilise Harabesi, Gürgürek Harabesi, and Muradyüzü Harabesi.[61]

It is interesting to see that most of the newly established villages were named after the Ottoman sultans. This act of naming suggests the *muhacir*s' gratitude to the Ottoman state, which embraced them in a time of hardships. These feelings of gratitude also partially emerged as a result of the Ottoman policies such as granting lands to the *muhacir*s and giving them daily provisions, thus saving them from hunger and further misery. Examples of naming new villages and neighborhoods after an Ottoman sultan can be found almost everywhere across Anatolia. The village established by the *muhacir*s from Ardahan in the Ilgın *kaza* of Konya was named Mecidiye;[62] the neighborhood established in the Çorum *kaza* of Yozgat for the *muhacir*s from Kars was called Hamidiye; the neighborhood established in Çorum for thirty settler families from Kars was named Selimiye;[63] the village established in the Çanak district of the *kaza* of Etrenos for the resettlement of twelve *muhacir* families (forty-six individuals) from Batum was called Osmaniye;[64] and the village established in the *kaza* of Aksaray in Niğde for the seventeen households of resettled *muhacir*s from Kars was named Reşadiye (in reference to the ruler of the period, Sultan Mehmed Reşat).[65]

In some instances the *muhacir*s were sent somewhere else after their resettlement. For example, four hundred *muhacir* families migrated from the *sancak* of Çıldır to the *sancak* of Muş and were later constantly ordered to resettle. In a petition sent to the governor's office of the *vilayet* of Bitlis, Mehmed İshak, speaking on behalf of the *muhacir*s, said that they did not understand why they were constantly resettled in different places and that these multiple resettlements created terrible conditions.[66]

A map of the routes of migrations from Elviye-i Selâse makes it clear that the migrations stretched over wide spaces. In accordance with the Ottoman policies of resettlement that preferred the distribution of *muhacir* groups in smaller numbers to different territories, the *muhacir*s from Elviye-i Selâse were resettled in places like Erzurum, Istanbul, Tokat, Bursa, Aydın, and Aleppo.[67]

PROBLEMS AFTER THE RESETTLEMENT

Hunger and Misery

Having left their properties behind and taken to the difficult path of migration, the *muhacir*s came face to face with issues of hunger and misery when they reached the areas of resettlement. This had many causes: the long process of resettlement, lack of lands to till and harvest, and at times the Ottomans' failure to distribute aid among the *muhacir* groups. The continuing decline in the Ottoman economic and administrative structures worsened the problems, which were already difficult to handle.

Most of the *muhacir*s were children, which increased the death rates, mostly due to hunger. Among the 335 individuals in 71 *muhacir* families sent from Batum to Şile, 155 were under the age of eighteen. Only 53 were over the age of fifty.[68] Two reasons explain these age gaps. First, people above the age of fifty often did not venture on such a long journey full of hardships. Second, these older people did not want to leave their homelands despite terrible conditions.

Migration was a process of terrible human suffering. Even though the settlers spent long years in their new homelands, they still could not adjust to a new life. For instance, Mehmed Şerif and his family from Kars were sent to Niksar of Sivas for resettlement. Yet they were not fully resettled even after five years had passed. He traveled to Istanbul to complain to the authorities about the misery of his family. The Commission of Settlers' reply shows that a plot of land was allocated to him but that the Official of Lands in the region disputed the allocation. Thus Mehmed Şerif remained without land for years. He and his family were willing to resettle in Niksar and thus were sent there with the promise that the final process of resettlement would take place in Niksar.[69] A document dated September 4, 1880, sent to the Commission of Settlers deals with a similar situation for the *muhacirs* from Batum who were sent to Gemlik. They were in misery and hunger for a long time, because the process of resettlement was not finalized. The *muhacirs* wrote a petition, asking for help and a solution to their dilemma.[70]

The problems of hunger that the *muhacirs* often faced were closely related to the areas of resettlement and to the dynamics of the period. Resettlement of *muhacirs* in cities, towns, or villages presented different problems in each context. The cities posed the severest threat. For instance, those who were sent to Istanbul experienced horrible conditions. The capital had received settlers from the Balkans, Crimea, and Caucasus, and the corresponding rise of the city's total population worsened the problems of public hygiene, food supply, and housing. Those who were sent to Istanbul and were waiting for the final decision of resettlement were provided accommodation in public buildings, empty houses, military barracks, and inns. When these spaces could not meet the demand, available rooms in the existing residential areas were rented out to provide accommodation, or the *muhacirs* were distributed as guests to the people of Istanbul. Even so, sometimes the only solution was to ask the *muhacirs* to live in tents. The *muhacirs* from Elviye-i Selâse who were sent to Istanbul found misery in the capital instead of peace and harmony.[71]

The settlers from Elviye-i Selâse who were sent to much more distant provinces of Anatolia were faced with even more difficult days. The return to the Three Cities was not possible because of the distance, and the journey took a very long time, with similar themes of hunger and misery. The petition sent to the *vilayet* of Syria by 120 *muhacirs* from Kars who were resettled in Damascus highlights these themes. They asked for help and the allocation of plots of land and noted that they would face the severe threat of hunger if lands were not distributed among them sooner than later.[72]

The *muhacirs* who were resettled in villages also faced such problems, because their land did not produce a harvest in certain years. For instance, the *muhacirs* from Batum who were resettled in the Sultaniye village of the *kaza* of Gemlik in Bursa failed to harvest any cereal from their land that year. They wanted to go back to Batum because they did not even have enough to eat. The Kaymakamate of Gemlik, aware of their situation, sent provisions to the *muhacir*s, which only lasted for a few days. Alternative measures were sought: the *muhacir*s were relocated to the empty plots of land close to the *kaza* of Kul.

The governor's office in Bursa explained the reason for such problems as a result of the large number of *muhacir*s. The research conducted by the Office of the Governor shows that while 8,656 households and 34,269 individual *muhacir*s had been resettled by December 24, 1881, 1,929 households and 8,546 individuals were not yet resettled but were given temporary accommodation in *kaza*s and villages. Of these 8,546 settlers, 450 widows, orphans, and needy people were given housing in available rooms of *medrese*s, lodges, *imaret*s (charitable institutions, mostly soup kitchens), and empty buildings; but 8,096 had to wait a little longer for the final resettlement.[73]

The hunger and misery among the *muhacir*s led the Ottoman state to take measures to alleviate some of their problems. For instance, the Regulations of the Resettlement of the *Muhacir*s (İskân-ı Muhâcîrin Talimatnamesi) projected a daily provision of food and money for settlers who were sent to Istanbul and other parts of the country until they were fully resettled. Yet after 1880 there were some cuts to these projected provisions for the settlers because of the economic consequences of the Turko-Russian War of 1877–78.[74]

While the Ottoman state initiated the processes necessary to meet the demands of the *muhacir*s,[75] certain problems prevented the state from providing for all of the *muhacir*s. Some of them had not yet been resettled and were thus technically still in migration, so they did not benefit from any Ottoman provisions.[76] Furthermore, when the *muhacir*s were given some wheat to sow their land, they consumed the seed wheat because they simply did not have anything else to eat.[77]

Another problem that worsened the misery was the difficulty that the *muhacir*s had in selling their properties and land in their former homelands. The Ottoman state appointed officials to help them facilitate this process. For instance, the Karapapaks from the *sancak* of Çıldır declared that they wanted to migrate, but the authorities warned them to wait until the Ottoman officials came to expedite the process.[78]

The Issues of Orientation and Settler Relations with the Locals

It was not easy for the *muhacir*s to abandon their old habits and become oriented to a new life. Most of them simply did not share the local culture of their respective areas of resettlement. They were resettled in places far from their other family members, so they felt lonely and culturally isolated. In addition, the local reaction to the newcomers was rarely positive, which contributed to their isolation.

Some of the *muhacir*s had been nomads in Elviye-i Selâse, and it was difficult for them to adapt to the requirements of a new sedentary life. For instance, a group of settlers from Kars first migrated to Erzurum and then proceeded to Sivas. They chose their own land of resettlement and set up their tents. Once the local authorities recognized them, they were shown a permanent area for resettlement and were banned from traveling from place to place and resettling wherever they wished without the permission of the authorities. They were also told that legal procedures would begin if they did not carry the necessary documentation proving their legal status as *muhacir*s.[79]

Some of the *muhacir*s also had a difficult time adjusting to the different climatic conditions. For instance, thirty households from Batum were resettled in Selimiye village of the *kaza* of Gemlik. The village was located at a high altitude and created problems for these *muhacir*s, particularly during the winter months. Accordingly, Emin Beyefendi, who was one of the notables of the village, offered to allocate land for the *muhacir*s on his farm and to build a mosque and school. He sent an official application to the Şura-yı Devlet (Council of State) for the recognition of this new village, named Hayriye. Emin Beyefendi provided the necessary funds for the construction of the mosque and school.[80] In this respect it is clear that buildings with social purposes such as mosques and schools were important parts of the process of resettlement in new villages.

Climatic difficulties were not only problematic for the *muhacir*s from Batum. The *muhacir*s from Kars who were resettled in the Alayurt region of Sivas experienced similar problems. These settlers who bought land and houses in Alayurt rejected the Ottoman demands to pay the *ağnam-ı resmiye* (sheep-goat tax) and *öşür* (tithe) of the last four years, arguing that the air and water of the region were not suitable for them. Their representative, Yusuf, presented a petition to the authorities and contacted the Commission of Settlers. The commission made a decision that was quite important for all *muhacir*s: the Ottoman state was not to demand any taxes, *ağnam-ı resmiye*, or other monetary claim for the next two years for the *muhacir*s coming from Rumelia, Anatolia, and Batum into the Ottoman interior. This decision encompassed not only the *muhacir*s who were resettled or were about to be resettled but also those who were yet to reach Ottoman soil.[81] With this decision the Ottoman state showed that it had taken the necessary care in resolving the orientation problems of the *muhacir*s.

One of the most common reasons for orientation problems was the difficulties that the *muhacir*s experienced with the local populations. The natives of the resettlement areas did not want any *muhacir*s in their region and even threatened the settlers to make them leave. This obviously added extra troubles for the *muhacir*s. One interesting case from Bursa sheds light on the complexity of the problems. A group of 450 *muhacir*s from Batum resettled in the Karaıslah region of the *nahiye* of Cebeli Atik in the *vilayet* of Bursa received threats from the local population to leave the region, even though the *muhacir*s had started constructing the mosque, the school, and their houses. As a result of increasing pressures, Batumlu Mehmed reported the issue to the authorities of the *vilayet*, arguing that their relocation would create terrible conditions for the whole *muhacir* community.[82] By a decision of the Commission of Military Inspection, led by the secondary judge İsmail Hakkı Paşa, the *muhacir*s were asked to stay in the region. In the end the *muhacir*s completed the construction of the mosque, school, and residences in the village of Karaıslah and resettled in the area.[83]

Most of the problems between the *muhacir*s and the local populations arose because the settlers wanted to have a plot of land for their own food supply. Yet most of the arable lands were under the ownership of the local people. The *muhacir*s thus wanted to make use of these lands. Hence the distribution of these lands was crucial for the survival of the settlers.

A petition sent to the Meclis-i Mebusan by Başrahip Agop and his friends, who lived in the *kaza* of Kangal in Sivas, reports the problem of land between the *muhacir*s and the local population: "The *muhacir*s from Kars who migrated to Sivas in 1878 and 1879 were resettled in the 8,000-acre land of Başrahip Agop and his friends; yet the *muhacir*s took possession of some of this land after a while." Agop and his friends demanded the return of the lands.[84]

Out of the fear of hunger and misery, the *muhacir*s ended up resettling in the lands of locals who did not want to share their land. Such cases even led to some skirmishes between the two groups. For instance, the inhabitants of the village of Hüseyingazi Tekkesi of Çorum attacked the lands of the *muhacir*s and destroyed the produce in the fields. This created dire times for the settlers, facing hunger and disease. Many *muhacir*s asked the local administration to intervene, but their situation did not improve for years to come. The letter sent by the *muhacir*s of Kars in Hüseyingazi Tekkesi to the Ottoman government on June 24, 1919, shows that their problem was still unsolved at that date. As an interesting twist, the *muhacir*s' rhetoric of criticism increasingly sharpened and targeted the Istanbul administration under Abdülhamid II, gaining an important political element. The settlers argued that it was the oppressive rule of Abdülhamid II that caused them to suffer this much pain and prevented them from gaining the attention of the higher Ottoman administration in regard to their problems. With the Young Turk Revolution of 1908, the *muhacirs* were also caught in the general atmosphere of hope and a possible change in the imperial system. They hoped that revolution, which was inspired by the notions of justice and liberty, would solve their problem, end the persecution in the village of Hüseyingazi Tekkesi, and return their lands that the locals had come to control.[85] Yet not much changed, and the problems of the *muhacirs* remained. For approximately twenty years they continued their lives with the dominant patterns of hunger and misery. In a petition sent to the Sadaret (Office of the Grant Vizier) in 1919, they said that if they were not accepted as Ottoman citizens and could not reach a level of comfort they wanted to go back to Kars under Russian occupation. They asked for help to this effect.[86]

In some instances the local authorities demanded that the lands given to the *muhacirs* be given back. These cases obviously worsened the problems of orientation for the *muhacirs*. For example, when the *muhacirs* in the town of Aziziye in Sivas learned that the local authorities were about to sell the pasture that they had been using for ten years, they contacted the Bab-ı Ali and the Ministry of the Interior to prevent the sale, arguing that this would create terrible conditions for the *muhacir* community.[87] The problem remained unsolved and resurfaced after only two years. For the *muhacirs*, the distribution of lands and pastures was critical, because they lived by farming and animal husbandry. When they were resettled on fertile lands and pastures, some people wanted to usurp their fields even through scams.

In order to usurp the lands and pastures of the *muhacirs* from Kars in Aziziye in Sivas, some of the merchants from Kayseri and Sivas argued that their lands and pastures were under the control of the military and thus were open to bids from any buyers in an auction. Obviously their intention was to buy the land and pastures for themselves. When they failed to do so, they went to court and demanded half of the properties. The *muhacirs* reported the situation to the Bab-ı Ali by sending a petition and arguing that even taking away half of their land would cause their destruction, asking the sultan to help solve the problem.[88]

Some of these disputes over lands and pastures between the locals and the *muhacirs* in fact had political and social aspects. The *muhacirs* were of Turkish-Muslim origin, while the local inhabitants where they were resettled were non-Muslims. This tended to transform the nature of such disputes, even leading to ethnic conflicts. For instance, a similar dispute over land took place between the Karapapak tribe, which migrated from Kars and resettled in the *kaza* of Resülayn in the *sancak* of Zor, and the local population of Mardin. A letter sent to Sadaret on April 18, 1889, reported that the Karapapak *muhacir*s had attacked the local population in Mardin, who complained about the aggressive attitudes of the settlers. Most of the complaints came from Christian quarters, so the dispute threatened to turn into a conflict between the Muslims and Christians. It was rumored that two mounted *muhacir* horsemen would come and create mayhem in Mardin. The spread of such rumors created a very tense atmosphere in the city.[89]

Constant complaints by the Christians attempted to define the Karapapak *muhacir*s as disreputable people, which the Ottoman state soon noticed. The state asked the Mutasarrıfiya of Mardin to investigate the situation.[90] A document sent to the *vilayet* of Diyarbakır also includes a reply to the Christians' complaints about the Karapapaks. According to this document, the authorities asked the Christians to cease groundless complaints about the Karapapaks. Because the *muhacir*s suffered from hunger and misery, a decree was sent to the general of the Gendarmerie and the *vilayet* of Mousul that the *muhacir*s should be conscripted and employed in this way.[91]

As these examples show, the Ottoman state took the necessary measures when conditions such as the conflicts between *muhacir*s and locals called for a response. By establishing commissions and bringing charges against the guilty, the state wanted to show its care and attention to local conflicts. The commissioners were given per diem provisions for their duties, which clearly indicates that the commissions were official bodies for such particular cases.[92] Most of the complaints were presented by the Christians, making it clear that conflicts between communities had a political twist. One of the most important causes for this was the Christian population's reactions to demographic changes.

Settler Demands to Go Back to Their Homeland
Because of orientation problems, many *muhacir*s intended to go back to their former homelands. A report from the *vilayet* of Erzurum on July 23, 1901, stated that the *muhacir*s from the *sancak* of Kars who had traveled to Sivas but failed to find a proper place for resettlement had decided to go back to Kars and were returned to the *sancak* of Beyazıt by the soldiers on the border. These *muhacir*s were eventually sent to Amasya for resettle-

ment. They wandered around Amasya for a while and spent some time in the center of the area but still wanted to go back to the *sancak* of Beyazıt. A report sent from the *vilayet* of Sivas indicates that the clear reason why these *muhacir*s could not be resettled and always wanted to go back was their intention to live with their relatives in Beyazıt.[93]

While the *muhacir*s insisted on going back to Beyazıt, the Ottoman state sent committees of advice to convince them that it would be more advantageous for them to stay on Ottoman soil. First the *muhacir*s were convinced to resettle in Koçkiri, but this did not last long either. In order to keep them in place, the local administration offered daily provisions, showed them possible places for resettlement, and even started constructing houses for them.[94]

Most of the returns of the *muhacir*s were from the regions around Sivas and Erzurum. The *muhacir*s of Kars and Ardahan who migrated to Sivas wanted to go back because their petitions to the local administration proved useless and they continued to live in graveyards or in the middle of the street. In fact, as a result of the investigations that took place after the complaints by the *muhacir*s, it became clear that there were *miri* (public), empty, and *vakf* lands available for the construction of 10,000 houses. Yet these lands were under the control of *bey*s and *ağa*s in the region, who constantly incited the local population against the *muhacir*s so that they could protect their lands. In order to put an end to bad treatment of the *muhacir*s and resettle them as quickly as possible, Mustafa Paşa was appointed as the official of resettlement for the *vilayet*s of Sivas, Malatya, Elazığ, and Ankara. These measures did not solve the problems fully, however, and some of the *muhacir*s of Kars in Sivas returned to Kars in 1882.[95]

Such returns of *muhacir*s were not welcome in Russian quarters. Russia made its position clear: anyone who returned would be exiled to Siberia. As a legal framework, article 325 of the Russian Penal Code stated that "fugitives from the army or anyone who has left Russia without the permission of the government deprive themselves of their civil rights. Once they come back home, they are exiled to Siberia as a punishment." This legal threat was enough to prevent the return of most settlers from the Ottoman interior back to the Three Cities.[96]

One of the most important reasons why the Russian authorities tried to prevent the return of the *muhacir*s to their former homelands was their policy of demographic engineering in Elviye-i Selâse. While Russia encouraged the decrease of the number of Turkish-Muslim people in the Caucasus, it also encouraged the migration of Christians into the region.

The replacement of Muslim nomads in the region by sedentary Armenians partly explains the Russian policies, which targeted an agricultural
economy and growth in the Caucasus. From a political standpoint the
settlement of Armenians in the region rendered the population politically
desirable and also created a buffer between the Ottomans and Russia. In
order to change the demographical patterns in the region, Russia did not
officially announce the benefits of Christian migration into the area but
circulated a rumor among the Christian groups that whoever migrated
into the Caucasus would greatly benefit.[97]

CONCLUSION

The transfer of Kars, Ardahan, and Batum from Ottoman control to Russia according to article 58 of the Treaty of Berlin caused deep social and
administrative transformations in the region. The Turkish-Muslim population of the region protested against the Russian yoke and reported their
reactions to the Ottoman authorities by sending telegraphs to Istanbul.
They argued that the Ottomans had multiple options for meeting Russia's
monetary demands. The people could gather the necessary amount among
themselves, the Ottoman government could increase taxes, or the government could receive loans from European banks. The people said that they
were ready to pay their share if given time.

Such proposals from the population of Elviye-i Selâse should be placed
within the socioeconomic, political, and administrative context of post-
Ottoman years in the region. The Russian policies during the Turko-
Russian War of 1877–78 and its aftermath pushed the Turkish Muslims
in the region to seek such alternatives. Yet the Ottomans' inability to push
harder for such changes forced the Turkish-Muslim locals to migrate.

Russia encouraged these migrations as well. In 1879 Russia made the
Ottomans accept the terms of the Treaty of Istanbul. The seventh article
of the treaty allowed migration of local populations to take place in the
next three years.

The migrations from Elviye-i Selâse into Anatolia not only highlighted
the themes of death, tragedy, and nostalgia for what was left behind but
also transformed the socioeconomic and demographic fabric of Anatolia.
In the end these migratory movements were not individual acts but collective movements with larger sociopolitical outcomes. The Ottoman
policies of resettlement simply were not capable of containing such large
population movements into Anatolia, although most of the time they
were well planned. Administrative, political, and economic dilemmas

partially explain this problem. These migratory patterns caused serious harm to the socioeconomic integrity of the Ottoman state as well. Yet the biggest tragedies were those of the settlers.

When the Turkish-Muslim peoples of the region left their homeland for Anatolia, Russia resettled what it saw as "loyal" groups in the region and increased the ratio of Christians in the local population. From 1878 to 1918 Elviye-i Selâse stayed under Russian control. Those Turkish Muslims who could not migrate and thus lived under Russian rule were forced to abstain from their sociocultural traditions. This is why the Russian control is still remembered in the region as the "forty-year-long dark days."

NOTES

This chapter was translated from Turkish into English by Ramazan Hakkı Öztan.

1. The term "Elviye-i Selâse" designates the three *sancak*s (Kars, Ardahan, and Batum) that the Ottomans lost to Russia. This term gained currency in the literature after the Berlin Treaty of 1878.

2. Enver Ziya Karal, *Osmanlı Tarihi*, 57.

3. Even though the Ottoman army successfully defended its western flank around Plevna and its eastern flank around Kars, thus preventing a swift Russian victory, the events that took place during the defense of Plevna demoralized the Ottoman government. It asked for an armistice, which was signed on January 31, 1878. Fahir Armaoğlu, *19. Yüzyıl Siyasi Tarihi (1789–1914)*, 489–519; Hans Kohn, *Panislavizm ve Rus Milliyetçiliği*, 32; Justin McCarthy, *Osmanlı'ya Veda İmparatorluk Çökerken Osmanlı Halkları*, 89; Karal, *Osmanlı Tarihi*, 58.

4. Karal, *Osmanlı Tarihi*, 64.

5. Nihat Erim, *Devletlerarası Hukuku ve Siyasi Tarih Metinleri, Cilt I (Osmanlı İmparatorluğu Antlaşmaları)*, 400; Armaoğlu, *19. Yüzyıl Siyasi Tarihi*, 523.

6. For the full text of the treaty, see *Muahedat Mecmuası*, 110–41.

7. Kemal H. Karpat, *Osmanlı Nüfusu (1830–1914): Demografik ve Sosyal Özellikleri*, 67.

8. The instructions given to the Ottoman representatives by Istanbul included the return of the Eleşkirt Valley and Beyazıt to Ottoman control; the maintenance of Ottoman control in Batum; and finally the cancellation of the Russian monetary demands. The Ottomans could not realize their goals, except for Eleşkirt and Beyazıt. Ali Fuat Türkgeldi, *Mesâil-i Mühimme-i Siyasiyye*, 63–64.

9. *Muahedat Mecmuası*, 379.

10. "Disraeli achieved his success on Batum as a result of his meeting with Gorchakov on July 7. In his letter to the Queen that talks about this meeting, Disraeli said that the issue of Batum was fast approaching a 'pleasing' solution and secured the tsar's promise that Batum would be a free and commercial port." Mithat Aydın, "İngiliz-Rus Rekabeti ve Osmanlı Devleti'nin Asya Toprakları Sorunu (1877–1878)," 276; *Muahedat Mecmuası*, 381; *Vakit* 976 (10 Temmuz [July 10] 1878); *Vakit* 978 (12 Temmuz [July 12] 1878); Armaoğlu, *19. Yüzyıl Siyasi Tarihi*, 522; M. Fahrettin Kırzıoğlu, *Kars Tarihi*, 553.

11. *Muahedat Mecmuası*, 138–39.

12. Başbakanlık Osmanlı Arşivi (BOA), Y. PRK. AZJ, 2/20, telegram dated September 5, 1878, sent from Kars to the Mabeyn-i Hümâyun Baş Kitabeti Celilesi.

13. Nihad quoted in Süleyman Erkan, *Kırım ve Kafkasya Göçleri (1878–1908)*, 82.

14. Genelkurmay Askeri Tarih ve Stratejik Etüt Başkanlığı Arşivi (ATASE), ORH (Genel Kurmay Başkanlığı Askeri Tarih Stratejik Etüt Dairesi Başkanlığı Arşivi Osmanlı-Rus Harbi Kataloğu), Kutu: 71, Gömlek: 85, Belge: 85-1, telegram sent from the Batum Headquarters to the Central Command.

15. ATASE, ORH, K. 90, G. 63, B.63-1, telegram sent by Koca Mehmed, the viceholder of the Ardahan Office, to the Mabeyn-i Hümâyun Baş Kitabeti Celilesi.

16. BOA, DH. MKT, 1387/69.

17. Erim, *Devletlerarası Hukuku ve Siyasi Tarih Metinleri*, 426.

18. Ardahan was a *kaza* of the *sancak* of Çıldır, which was part of the *vilayet* of Erzurum. Selçuk Günay, "Resmi Devlet Sâlnâmelerine Göre (H.1263–1334) Osmanlı İmparatorluğu'nun Seneler İtibariyle Mülkî Taksimatı," 103; *Salnâme-i Vilâyet-i Erzurum*, 144.

19. İlber Ortaylı, "Çarlık Rusyası Yönetiminde Kars," 181.

20. *Ati* 66 (7 Mart 1334/March 7, 1918).

21. Ortaylı, "Çarlık Rusyası Yönetiminde Kars," 181.

22. Selçuk Ural, "Yakınçağ'da Kars."

23. *Tanin* 3357 (16 Nisan 1334/April 16, 1918). "Batum is the door to the Caucasus and Central Asia and is the third most important port in Black Sea after Odessa and Istanbul. Each year imports through Batum amounted to approximately 50 to 60 million *pud* (one *pud* equals about 13 *okka* [one *okka* equals 1,283 grams]). These imports included primarily products of grain like kerosene [*gaz yağı*], manganese, wool, cotton, and corn. Mostly in Batum, Russian capital built many factories producing matches, sugar, pasta, and soap as well as many mills and gas tanks" ("Kars, Ardahan, Batum," *Ati* 72 [13 Mart 1334/March 13, 1918]); Charles Issawi, "The Tabriz-Trabzon Trade, 1830–1900: Rise and Decline of a Route," 24.

24. *Ati* 72 (13 Mart 1334/March 13, 1918); W. E. D. Allen and Paul Muratoff, *1828–1921 Türk-Kafkas Sınırındaki Harplerin Tarihi*, 206.

25. Ortaylı, "Çarlık Rusyası Yönetiminde Kars," 190.

26. Kırzıoğlu, *Kars Tarihi*, 553.

27. Ortaylı, "Çarlık Rusyası Yönetiminde Kars," 185. The opposition to the Russians was led by the imam of Evliya Mosque, Molla Muhyiddin Efendi, and Yusuf Zülali Efendi. While Molla Muhyiddin Efendi turned the mosque and his house into a school, Yusuf Zülali Efendi wrote many articles to rekindle the nationalist sentiments among the public. Kırzıoğlu, *Kars Tarihi*, 553.

28. Yuluğ Tekin Kurat, "1878–1919 Arasında Türk-Rus İlişkileri," 138.

29. Ortaylı, "Çarlık Rusyası Yönetiminde Kars," 178.

30. Aydın, "İngiliz-Rus Rekabeti," 276.

31. M. Sadık Bilge, *Osmanlı Devleti ve Kafkasya Osmanlı Varlığı Döneminde Kafkasya'nın Siyasi-Askeri ve İdari Taksimatı (1454–1829)*, 168–69.

32. Günay Çağlar, "Türkiye-Sovyet Rusya Arasında Türkiye'nin Bugünkü Kuzey-Doğu Sınırının Belirlenmesi Süreci ve Kars Antlaşması," 276.

33. Nedim İpek, *İmparatorluktan Ulus Devlete Göçler*, 58; BOA, A.MKT. MHM, 342-13.

34. BOA, Y.A.RES, 657/2431.

35. BOA, ZB (Zabtiye Nezareti), 12/114-3.

36. BOA, DH. MKT, 1555/114.

37. ATASE, ORH, K. 25, G. 44, B.44-1.

38. BOA, Y.PRK. BŞK, 3/5.

39. İpek, *İmparatorluktan*, 54; Kemal Çilingiroğlu and İbrahim Tuğcu, *Kars*, 22.

40. *Ermeniler Tarafından Yapılan Katliam Belgeleri (1914–1919)*, 208.

41. Erol Kaya, "1877–1878 Harplerinde Ağrı Bölgesinde Göç Hareketleri," 207.

42. Ilhan Unat, *Türk Vatandaşlık Hukuku (Metinler-Mahkeme Kararları)*, 8; Işıl Özkan and Uğur Tütüncübaşı, "Türk ve Alman Hukukunda Çifte Vatandaşlığa İlişkin Gelişmeler," 617.

43. İpek, *İmparatorluktan*, 18.

44. BOA, DH. MKT, 255/69.

45. BOA, DH. MKT, 911/60.

46. BOA, DH. EUM. ECB, 4/47.

47. BOA, DH. MKT, 491/40. "The application for the birth certificate of İbrahim oğlu Mustafa from the Kars *muhacir*s had been made; and after the review of his case, his identity has been verified, and the decision made that there is no obstacle for him to become an Ottoman subject."

48. BOA, DH. MKT, 1639/43.

49. "Şehremaneti" was the first term used to describe the local administrative structure in the empire that fulfilled the duties of today's modern municipality, such as policing duties and issues of public health.

50. Ahmet Cevat Eren, *Türkiye'de Göç ve Göçmen Meseleleri Tanzimat Devri, İlk Kurulan Göçmen Komisyonu, Çıkarılan Tüzükler*, 54.

51. Ibid.

52. Mehmet Esat Sarıcaoğlu, "İskan-ı Muhacirin İane Pulları: Osmanlı Devleti'nin Göçmen Harcamalarında Uyguladığı Bir Finansman Yöntemi," 605.

53. BOA, Y. Mtv, 110/132; *BOA*, DH. MKT, 398/28.

54. Eren, *Türkiye'de Göç ve Göçmen Meseleleri*, 82.

55. BOA, DH. MKT, 2015/98, report sent to the Ministry of Finance, dated October 28, 1892.

56. BOA, DH. EUM. ECB, 4/47.

57. Donald Quataert, *Anadolu'da Osmanlı Reformu ve Tarım 1876–1908*, 36.

58. BOA, DH. MKT, 739/60, *tezkire* dated July 28, 1903.

59. BOA, DH. MKT, 631/25.

60. BOA, İ. ŞD, 106/6353.

61. BOA, Y. A. Hus, 314/85, report sent to the *mutasarrıfıya* of the *sancak* of Beyazıt, dated December 3, 1894.

62. BOA, DH. MKT 1907/113, writ sent to the *vilayet* of Konya, Divân-ı Hümâyun, and the Commission of Settlers, dated January 5, 1892.

63. BOA, İ. DH. 984/77697-1, *BOA*, İ. DH, 984/77697-2, report sent to the *mutasarrıfıya* of the *sancak* of Yozgat, dated March 28, 1884.

64. BOA, DH. MKT, 354/11.

65. BOA, İ. DH, 1491/1330.S/36.

66. BOA, DH. MKT 1566/104, writ sent to the *vilayet* of Bitlis, dated January 17, 1889.

67. BOA, DH. MKT, 2663/17.

68. BOA, Y. PRK. KOM, 3/36-2, register charting the *muhacir* group that migrated from Batum to Şile in terms of household, age, sex, and name, dated January 8, 1887.

69. BOA, DH. MKT, 1498/110, memorandum sent to the *vilayet* of Sivas, dated January 8, 1882.

70. BOA, DH. MKT, 1333/66.

71. İpek, *İmparatorluktan*, 18; BOA, DH. MKT, 1466/26.

72. BOA, DH. MKT, 516/15.

73. BOA, Y. PRK. KOM, 3/36-2.

74. Erkan, *Kırım ve Kafkasya Göçleri*, 172.

75. BOA, A. MKT. MHM 514/22. ("As long as they stayed in Koçgiri, they were given provisions, shown their areas of resettlement, and even permitted to build their own houses").

76. BOA, DH. MKT 1333/95-1/1.

77. Hilmi Uran, *Meşrutiyet, Tek Parti, Çok Parti Hatıralarım (1908–1950)*, 67.

78. BOA, DH. MKT, 1324/93.

79. BOA, DH. MKT, 1348/16.

80. BOA, DH. MKT, 187/2.

81. BOA, DH. MKT, 1383/25.

82. BOA, DH. MKT, 274/39-1.

83. BOA, DH. MKT, 274/39-2

84. BOA, DH. MKT, 2790/96-3.

85. BOA, DH. MKT, 2879/88, petition sent to the *vilayet* of Ankara, dated June 24, 1919.

86. BOA, DH. MKT, 2879/88.

87. BOA, DH. MKT, 1863/78.

88. BOA, DH. MKT, 91/43.

89. BOA, DH. MKT, 1617/38.

90. BOA, DH. MKT, 1624/124.

91. BOA, DH. MKT, 1624/124, memorandum given to the *vilayet* of Diyarbakır, May 25, 1889.

92. BOA, DH. MKT, 511/60-2.

93. BOA, A.MKT. MHM, 514/22.

94. Ibid.

95. İpek, *İmparatorluktan*, 55.

96. BOA, MB.HPS.M, 9/39.

97. For instance, according to the announcement made for the Christians in the Ünye region, the families who migrated to Russia in 1879–80 were given farmlands and 15 rubles as well as immunity from being conscripted into the army. In addition they were promised not to be taxed in the next seven or ten years, sometimes even twenty when their lands failed to yield a harvest. Justin McCarthy, *Ölüm ve Sürgün*, 135–36.

17

Two Different Images

Bulgarian and English Sources on the Batak Massacre

Tetsuya Sahara

Batak is a small town on the northern edge of the Rhodope range. It is well known among Bulgarians as one of the most sacred places in their memory of national independence, representing the suffering as well as glory. Among outsiders, however, the story of Batak is rather complicated. Bulgaria became an autonomous principality through the Berlin Congress in 1878, which was an aftermath of the Russo-Turkish War of 1877–78. The war broke out in the midst of the diplomatic turmoil caused by the international criticism of the Ottoman misrule. The Ottoman government was widely denounced for having failed to provide protection to its Christian subjects and accordingly caused the humanitarian catastrophe known as the "Bulgarian Atrocities," in which Batak played a crucial role. As this context shows, the role of Batak in Bulgarian national independence is somewhat remote and indirect. For all this distance, or rather because of it, the memory of Batak still constitutes an essential part of the Bulgarian national self-image and a source of dispute over its modern history.

The purpose of this paper is not to assess the historical facts concerning the Batak incident but to elucidate the biased approach of the international community by contrasting the images of the incident in international media coverage and in Bulgarian historiography.

THE BATAK MASSACRE DESCRIBED BY BULGARIAN SOURCES: PRIMARY SOURCES AND THEIR CHARACTERISTICS

Despite its huge political repercussions, the direct witnesses of the incident are rather scant. Only three primary sources written in Bulgarian exist: the memoirs of Zahari Stoyanov and Angel Goranov and the fieldwork of Hristo Popkonstantinov.[1] Of the three, Stoyanov's memoir is by far the best known and has played a major role in formulating the popular image of the incident that has been continuously reprinted. As the material for historical study, however, it is less reliable than the other two sources. Although Stoyanov was a member of the Bulgarian Revolutionary Committee that played the major roles in staging the uprising, he did not have direct access to what happened in Batak in April 1876. His writings were drawn from the reports of various witnesses who watched the event directly or indirectly. Moreover, his work is saturated with revolutionary romanticism: the event is simplified into a moral story where justice (revolutionary Bulgarians) fought against evil (Muslim oppressors and counterrevolutionaries).

In contrast, the memoir of Angel Goranov provides us with a much more detailed and complicated picture. He was the son of Peter Goranov (1829–1925), the leader of the Batak uprising. Although Goranov was a student in high school at the time of the massacre, he was appointed a secretary of the military council of Batak. As this career suggests, his information basically represents the same view of the revolutionaries as in Stoyanov's memoir and must have come from virtually the same sources. As a direct participant of the event, however, Goranov writes with far greater reliability as a primary source. Moreover, his personal background must have given him a moral obligation to explain the story from a more balanced viewpoint. Goranov's mother, Marga, was the daughter of Angel Kavlakov, one of the influential elders of Batak. Kavlakov was a moderate and called for restraint from the radical revolutionaries before the outbreak of hostilities. When the battle turned out unfavorably for the Batachanins, he tried to negotiate with the Muslim assailants and eventually took the lead in disarming the villagers. Owing to this behavior, Stoyanov strongly denounced Kavlakov as a counterrevolutionary and characterized him as a typical "Chorbadzhiya."[2] In contrast, Goranov gave a more plausible explanation of the circumstances in which Kavlakov had to make the difficult decision. As a whole, Goranov's work is more objective.

The writings of Hristo Popkonstantinov rely on a completely different kind of source. He was an ethnographer who did interviews with Muslims who directly participated in the massacre. Although they are composed of fragmentary evidence, they are valuable, especially as auxiliary information to verify the accuracy of the two other sources.

BATAK AND ITS VICINITY BEFORE THE INCIDENT

These Bulgarian sources give us pictures of the bloodbath that took place during April 1876. Batak was a small mountain village. According to a modern Bulgarian historian, the village had no more than a hundred houses in 1819. Then it grew rapidly and was several times larger by the eve of the incident. It is certain that the majority of the population were immigrants who had arrived there during the first three quarters of the nineteenth century.[3] According to Goranov, the villagers principally lived by forestry and carpentry, but stock-breeding seemed to be equally important.[4]

From a religious point of view, the village was completely Christian. It had no Muslims except for a few guards sent by the local authority. In contrast, the region surrounding the village was predominantly Muslim. It had several settlements with a Christian population, but all of them were either small hamlets or mixed villages that also had Muslim peasants. Most of the neighboring villages were dominated by Muslims. Due to the rapid growth during the nineteenth century, Batak turned out to be the largest Christian village in the northern Rhodope and was often viewed as the Christian outpost in the midst of a Muslim world.[5]

From an ethnic point of view, the Muslims were often referred to by others as Pomaks and even called themselves by that name, while the Christians mainly identified themselves as ethnic Bulgarians. Although it is not easy to give a brief explanation of Pomaks, they are Muslims whose mother tongue is a Bulgarian dialect. Therefore, despite the difference in religion, the population shared the same linguistic tradition. Most of the people spoke the same dialect of the Bulgarian language.[6] Some authors even claim that the Pomaks came from the same ancestral roots as the Christian Bulgarians, though this is still disputed. But some contemporaries did believe in this theory, as Angel Goranov put it: "At first, the settlers lived on good terms with Muslims despite the difference of faith. They generally retained and respected old family ties. Familial ties were kept among Pelyuvats, Kavlakovs, Balinovats, Vranchovats, Karkalyacho-vats, Peychinovats, Garkovats, Tsuryuvats, Kanyuvats, etc., and the same family names even existed among the Chepino Pomaks. When someone came to Batak, he visited the house whose host bore the name of his family. Elderly people remember the time when they exchanged various gifts with their distant relatives."[7]

The same author, however, testifies that the peaceful coexistence
had already ended by the middle of the nineteenth century and that the
Batachanins felt surrounded on all sides by infidels who were "fanatical
and hostile" to them. According to Goranov, this was partly caused by a
religious purification process within the Muslim communities. He tried to
explain it as follows: "Various imams constantly threatened the Muslims
with punishment for their deviation in the legends, traditions, customs,
and songs. As a result, they gradually forgot the past, got used to the present situation, lived within the narrow limits of the new fanatical faith, and
began to show a cold attitude then open hostility to the Batachanins."[8] But
there seem to have been other reasons for the growing tension between
the two communities, and Goranov admitted that the Batachanins played
their parts in this development:

> These relations became even more acute when the strife began over
> forests, pastures, and grasslands located around the lake and very
> often ended in bloody events. The incessant activities of Batak lum-
> berjacks destroyed forests around the village, transforming the hills
> into lofty meadows, and enlarged the boundaries of the village to-
> ward the mountains of Dorkovats, Kostandovats, Rakitovats, and
> Yenimahale. Eventually hidden attacks, lootings, mutual violations
> of possessions, and even secret murders began. As a result, mutual
> enmity and hatred grew seriously.[9]

This passage reveals the two important elements of the background of
the bloodbath in 1876. First, the antagonisms of the neighboring Muslims
had their roots in the flourishing economic activities of the Batachanins.
The Muslims felt enmity as the Batachanins were expanding their share of
economic activities at the cost of their own territory. This took the form of
the dispute over the public land and developed into an open clash between
the two communities. The accuracy of Goranov's observation can be at-
tested by the following information as well. In 1873 the elementary school
in Batak was burned down. According to a Bulgarian newspaper, the incident had the following background: "The fire was set by *Turks* of the
nearby village Enimahala. It seems to have been done out of the hostilities
whose origin lies in a land dispute. The two villages have since long been
engaged in a struggle over the ownership of pastures between them."[10]

Equally important is the nature of this struggle. Although Goranov
does not disclose it openly, the passage above suggests that the conflict
was conducted in a reciprocal manner. The Christians were not one-sided

victims, as the following information from Goranov indicates: "Although they were confronted with the constant instigation of imams and softas [students of Islamic schools] to kill Christians, it was the Pomaks that had to send out scouts during Ramadan or Bayrams for fear that the Batachanins would behead them. The fear for Batak was not confined to the neighbors but well known to the people living in remote places."[11]

Goranov testifies that the antagonisms had already taken a decisive form by the middle of the century. A bloody incident occurred at Batak during the Crimean War. A reserve unit from Macedonia wanted to spend the night in Batak, but the village head refused. The Muslims tried to kill him, but the armed villagers allowed him to flee into the forest.[12] The situation became even more tense after the war. The Batachanins began to feel threatened by Muslim herdsmen, who often intruded into their meadows with arms in hand. The villagers could not even appear in their gardens.[13] But their plight did not last long. The Bulgarians could not rely on the help of the Muslim authorities in Dospat who were in charge of the region, so the Batachanins organized a military band led by a fighter known as Todor the Hayduk. According to Goranov, his band succeeded in "cleansing the Dospat forests of Turkish brigands" within a few years. They even "attacked the military institutions and threw all the Pomaks into disarray."[14]

To sum up, the Bulgarian sources testify to the existence of deeply rooted hostilities between the Batachanins and their Muslim neighbors. The enmity had a long history, at least more than twenty years, and grew over time. It must have originated in economic factors, in which the struggle over the pasture played the most decisive role. The Muslims felt that the Batachanins had violated their possessions, while the Batachanins were indignant at the intrusion of the Muslim herdsmen into their meadows. The conflict involved several bloody incidents in which both sides committed atrocities. The constantly conflicting relations between the two communities must have affected the behavior of the people during April in 1876.

PREPARATION FOR THE INSURRECTION

Owing to their precarious relations with the neighboring Muslim villages, the villagers of Batak were by and large inclined to radical options. So the village naturally became a center for sympathizers of the radical nationalists who were preaching armed struggle for national independence. A secret committee was established and became one of the most important radical centers on the eve of the April Uprising. Zahari Stoyanov testifies that Batak was among the three most important centers of the uprising, together with Koprivshtica and Panagyurishte, in the fourth "revolutionary region."[15]

The main organizer of the Batak uprising was Peter Goranov. He was an influential person among the Christians in the region and was once elected a judge of the local court. At the same time, he kept secret contact with the radical nationalists whose center was in Romania. When the revolutionary committee decided to stage an uprising, Peter Goranov took charge of the military preparations at Batak.[16]

Under Goranov's direction the villagers began to purchase arms and munitions. In theory the preparation must have been done in secret, but Angel Goranov testifies to a completely different scene. Many villagers, regardless of age and gender, participated in the military preparation and soon transformed the village into "a military camp." They abandoned daily activities and concentrated on target practice and stockpiling of provisions. Villagers gathered in large groups in the market, taverns, and squares, where they displayed their rifles, pistols, gunpowder, and knives. The outskirts of the village became a testing ground for the newly purchased weapons. Agents were dispatched to various places to purchase weapons and gunpowder.[17] The preparation was not hidden from the eyes of the Muslim neighbors. The villagers even went to the Pomak villages to buy rifles and pistols, selling their cows and bulls in exchange.[18] As a result, by the time the uprising started the rebels had about 2,000 well-trained fighters, 500 flintlock rifles, 380 pistols, 6 revolvers, 8 repeaters, 150 yatagans (swords), and several cannons.[19]

THE BEGINNING OF THE UPRISING

The uprising broke out on the night of April 21. The two main Bulgarian sources, Stoyanov and Goranov, convey almost the same story about what led the rebels to rise up. A few villagers who had visited the nearby city of Pazardzhik (Pazarcık) brought news of an unusual situation. The government officials came out of their office in apparent disarray. Alarmed by their attitude, the people began to shout: *giaur geliyor* (infidels are coming). The merchants quickly closed the shops and returned home. In a short while the market became completely deserted. Upon hearing this news the rebels of Batak took it for granted that the general uprising had taken place. Then Peter Goranov convened a meeting at the school during the night and decided to take action.[20] The next day the rebels organized an official ceremony. A ritual service was performed by the village priests, who prayed for the victory of the Christian fighters. It was attended by many villagers and gave the impression that the entire village agreed on the uprising. As Stoyanov put it: "In addition to the warriors, the service was attended by many women and children, both young and old. They were all overjoyed."[21]

Stoyanov describes the first actions: "The members went out of the school and sounded the wooden bell of the church. The villagers were all awakened, and armed men took up their positions half an hour away from the village. It was midnight of April 22."[22] So it seems that the rebels refrained from committing provocations. But the story described by Angel Goranov is entirely different. He testifies that the rebels first attempted to kill Muslim agents in the village. The attack was abortive because of the betrayal of the innkeeper, who had let them slip out the back door.[23] Goranov also gives us more detailed information concerning the rebel actions. After the proclamation of the uprising the first orders to the council were to send several people to the most important strategic locations in the neighboring mountains as standing guards. They were instructed to disarm all the Muslims, report to headquarters everything that took place, and select couriers and snipers who would be stationed on the remote peaks as scouts to check the nearby Pomak villages and the government forces in the Pazardzhik plain.[24]

At the time of the uprising the Batachanins had about 1,100 soldiers, divided into two battalions. Each of them was subdivided into platoons and companies. In addition they had 30–50 cavalrymen.[25] With this force, the rebels began to attack Muslim travelers who were traveling along the road near the village. They ambushed and killed many Muslim civilians in the dark bushes of the mountains. The mountain sentinels of Batak found horsemen with military supplies riding on the forest trails and killed two of them. Another platoon kidnapped a Muslim student. He was unarmed and begged for his life in exchange for conversion, but the rebels instantly executed him. The other platoon ambushed a convoy of Macedonian Pomaks, killed three of them, and let the rest flee. The survivors managed to escape to a Muslim village and informed the authorities in Pazardzhik of the Batak uprising. Upon hearing the news the government immediately mobilized the reserves and distributed rifles and ammunition to the Muslim population.[26]

These provocations and indiscriminate killings threw the Muslim neighbors into a panic. Ahmed Ağa of Barutin, the police chief of Dospat region, dispatched two policemen to assess the situation on April 24. They came to one of the village outposts and asked permission to enter the village. Both of them were unarmed. The outpost commander met them and told them that "the Bulgarians of Batak took up arms to liberate themselves from the tyranny of the Sultan and that *they were ready to fight to the last drop of their blood*" (emphasis added). The two policemen were subsequently released. But on their way back they were shot dead by the commander.[27] This was apparently an open challenge to the Ottoman state.

The event profoundly shocked the Pomaks in the neighborhood of Batak. Angel Goranov explains their anxiety: "As it was not likely that military forces from Pazardzhik would come to protect their villages, the Muslim notables of Rakitovo, Dorkovo, Kostandovo, and Korovo held a meeting and unanimously decided to go to Batak and beg the commander not to consider them opponents."[28]

On April 25 the Pomaks led two hundred armed men and arrived at the outskirts of Batak.[29] They sent a Bulgarian messenger to propose a peace talk. The rebels accepted the offer and agreed on the exchange of delegates. At the negotiating table the Bulgarian side explained the reason for their action and tried to justify the violence. According to Goranov, they said: "The Bulgarians of Batak have rebelled against the tyrannical government of the sultan, not against the peaceful Turkish population, which they would let live in brotherly love. Nevertheless, as they have declared freedom, they have decided to defend it and to stand up for the other Bulgarians as well."[30] Stoyanov describes the same declaration: "The Bulgarian people can no longer endure the hated slavery. They do not want to remain submissive *reaya*s, as their ancestors were. For this purpose, they took up arms today, rejecting the mercy of the Sultan and claiming their human rights. They seek much-needed freedom. They don't have anything against the civilian population and want to live with their Turkish neighbors in fraternity."[31] Although we can notice a slight difference in the terminology, both versions coincide on the point that the rebels promised not to attack Muslim civilians so long as they kept neutrality. The authors presumably intended this as a sign of goodwill from the Bulgarians to their Muslim neighbors that was later betrayed by the massacre. But this was not the case. The exemption of civilian targets contradicted the earlier conduct of the rebels, who had killed Muslims without discrimination. The real intention of this proposal can be found in the following context.

After declaring their cause, the rebels ordered the Muslims to help the Bulgarians in their villages move to Batak with their property. They even threatened an open assault if the Muslims failed to fulfill this order within twenty-four hours, saying that "their villages would be end up in dust and ashes."[32] According to the original decisions of the committee, Batak was to serve as a center for several villages; but owing to the premature outbreak of the uprising no other villages could join. So the villagers of Batak had to fight alone, except for small groups coming from the nearby villages. The rebels wanted to consolidate their position by adding reinforcements. Therefore they offered generous conditions. The Muslim delegates accepted the conditions. They even promised to follow every order given by the rebel leaders. After the negotiations both sides retreated. The rebels took the result as a diplomatic victory and returned home, chanting and shouting triumphantly.[33]

The next day, however, several Muslims and the heads of the Bulgarian quarters met again at the outskirts of the village. The Bulgarians openly declared that they declined the offer to move to Batak because they did not want to do so. They also asserted that they did not see any inconvenience in living together with the Pomaks and that they wanted to stay and meet their final fate at their homes during this disturbance.[34] So the Batachanins had to fight alone.

THE OUTBREAK OF HOSTILITIES

The situation remained calm until April 30, when the sentry noticed a number of armed *başıbozuk*s (irregulars) coming along the mountain path from the direction of Dospat. The next morning they arrived at Peter's Hill, a fifteen-minute walk from the village. The irregulars were Pomak peasants coming from the villages south of Batak led by the police chief, Ahmed Ağa Barutinli. A Batak villager who was captured in the woods brought the police chief's message, demanding that the Batak leaders immediately submit to him, hand over all the weapons, and release the two Muslim captives within two hours. Otherwise he would attack the village and take the weapons by force.[35] Upon hearing this Peter Goranov immediately convened a meeting and dispatched three delegates to the camp of Ahmed Ağa. They were instructed to deliver the following message: "The villagers of Batak are no longer *reaya*s. They have already done away with the humiliating regulations saying that a bowed head would not be cut off by a sword. They have formally declared independence with arms in hand. *They are ready to shed their last drop of blood for the sake of independence*" (emphasis added). They also said that if Ahmed Ağa used force they would respond in kind.[36] In this way the rebels refused to surrender and declared that they would fight to the last ditch.

Then both sides began to assemble in war formations. The outbreak of hostilities was inevitable. As Stoyanov put it: "Two hostile nations, one eager for freedom, the other for loot and robbery, now standing opposite each other, railing from a distance, preparing their rifles, gnashing teeth, got ready to clash with one another as if two wild beasts met for the first time."[37]

Stoyanov and Goranov agree that the Muslims were superior in numbers and that the village was surrounded by the Muslims from the north and south. It was apparent that the Bulgarians were in quite a vulnerable position. But the two authors give us different stories about the first battle. Stoyanov asserts that the Bulgarians were victorious in the initial battles and that they managed to defend their position, inflicting huge casualties on the Muslim side. The first open fire took place when the Muslim force approaching from the north tried to take a Bulgarian position. According to Stoyanov:

> A contingent of *başıbozuk*s came to a location known as the Middle Graveyard.... The first gunshot came from this position, and the Turkish standard-bearer fell to the ground. Someone took his place, but he followed the same fate. The Turks fired more than a hundred guns in reprisal, and the rebels returned fire in exchange. A fierce battle was carried out. The battle lasted four hours, from 8 o'clock to 12 in the Turkish reckoning. Another battle was carried out in the lower part of the village. There were constant reinforcements on the Turkish side from the direction of Dospat. For all their numerical superiority, however, the Turks could not take the Bulgarian position. They were even forced to retreat toward the outskirts of the village. They left seven corpses and innumerable wounded on the battlefield. On the Bulgarian side, only a few got injured.[38]

Goranov gives us a more nuanced story:

> Those who came from the north made a quick attack on the village, burning the houses located there and approaching the barns. Peter Goranov came against them with forty soldiers and opened first fire at a place called the Graveyard.... A continuous battle began. At the first exchange of fire, the *başıbozuk*s lost several soldiers and were forced to withdraw from their position.... After this battle, the enemy attacked the position in Galagonkata.... The *başıbozuk*s

put pressure on the Bulgarian positions with a great force. Both sides formed a dark cloud of smoke that made it impossible to see anything for a while. The enemy made use of it for their advance. Then the Red Crescent was about to wave over the rebels' position. Hence the *başıbozuk*s shot at Goranov's company. The bullets came from two sides and flew over their heads. Several people were killed or injured, and the rest fled. The last effort that Goranov made with his servant Kolyu Cholaka was to fire the cannon against Galag-onkata, but there was no ammunition to load; he was forced to descend the hill and followed his comrades into the village.[39]

Thus the two sources contrast sharply on the result of the first battle. While Stoyanov is adamant about the success of the Bulgarians, Goranov frankly admits defeat. Which one is more reliable? A clue can be found in the information gathered by Popkonstantinov from the Pomak partici-pants in the battle: "The Pomaks began to attack the village and opened fire. The rebels replied in the same way. The battle lasted for about three hours. During the battle, the Pomaks were continuously pressing on and entered the village. Some were killed and wounded on both sides."[40] This version therefore coincides with the one given by Goranov.

Stoyanov's story has another weakness. He admits that the massacre started on May 1, the very next day after the first battle. If the Bulgarians were victorious in the first battle, why did they give up so soon? Stoyanov tries to explain this contradiction by the betrayal of some Bulgarian leaders. According to him, the betrayal started even before the first exchange of fire. The Bulgarians had their headquarters on the hill dominating the main battlefield and stationed the main fighting unit of 400 soldiers there. Shortly before the first battle, Peter Goranov led a reconnaissance com-pany to take a hill commanding the Muslim position. So he was absent from the main position. At this very moment several "very influential persons in the village" or "Chorbadzijas" allegedly came to the position and persuaded the people to give up arms. As a result of this "internal betrayal," many soldiers returned to the village, abandoning the position to the enemy.[41] Owing to this strategic mistake, Stoyanov suggests, the Bulgarians could not make use of the initial military success.

In contrast, Angel Goranov describes the same process as follows. When Peter Goranov led a reconnaissance and reached high ground to monitor the enemy, 200–300 Pomaks descended from their position in the direction of the rebels. He gave the order to yell at the attackers to halt their advance, but the enemies suddenly turned to the west, hastily rushed to Holy Trinity hill, and seized it. "Pressed by the threat, many rebels abandoned their positions and retreated into the village."[42] Therefore it seems more plausible that the reason for the loss of the main position lay in a strategic mistake of Peter Goranov when he demoralized the fighters by leaving the commanding position.

THE ESCAPE OF PETER GORANOV

Whether or not the Bulgarians were successful in the first battle, as night fell the skirmishes ended. During the night the Muslims encircled the village and put it under siege. Stoyanov describes the scene: "Dogs barked and howled in an unusual way with their heads up. Their voice was accompanied by wild cries of the *başıbozuk*s, who yelled at their yet-to-be-captured victims like wild beasts. These voices were coming from the mouths of no less than three thousand Pomaks."[43] At this very moment one of the most mysterious events concerning the Batak incident occurred. Stoyanov gave it only a short comment: "Several people, including Goranov, escaped from the village during the night through a valley."[44] He does not give a detailed explanation of the important question of why the main commander escaped from the battlefield, leaving his fellow villagers at the mercy of their enemies.[45]

Angel Goranov, in contrast, tries to explain the urgent circumstances in which his father had to make a difficult decision. According to him, the situation of Batak after the first battle was very terrible. After dark the Turks had conquered all the heights around the village. They shot at the village, killing and injuring many villagers even on the streets. They also threw fireballs made of oiled cloth, and some houses and barns were burned. Frightened by the scene, "the population, regardless of gender or age, gathered in the church, the school, and the house of Trendafil Kerelov. They considered these places safer, more appropriate for self-defense, and less likely to be burned."[46] In light of this description, it is clear that the defense line of the rebels had been totally broken. Therefore, according to Goranov, his father claimed that the only possible salvation was to escape from the village and hide in the mountains. He allegedly said: "There is no doubt that the village will be set on fire and burned. The *başıbozuk*s are so many. As no defense has been prepared in the village, there is no hope to avoid the destructive fires that have already started." Those who had gathered in the school and church accepted the proposal. But the villagers led by Trendafilov did not agree to leave the village, because they thought it better to defend themselves inside the village. As a result, only some of the villagers who supported Goranov decided to leave the village. His followers then set out for the positions manned by the Pomaks, but many of them were prevented from escaping because of the heavy barrage coming from the enemy side. Only two hundred armed soldiers succeeded in breaking through the enemy's line and arriving at the safe place.[47]

If we believe Goranov's story, it poses a serious question: why did the rebel leader who had just sworn to fight to the last ditch several hours before decide so easily to end the uprising and abandon the village? The rebels had committed various provocations that they must have known would cause reprisals from the Muslim side. The leader's claim that the village was defenseless surely contradicted all his earlier courageous remarks and instigation. The decision might have come from his realist calculation of the military situation resulting from the loss of strategic positions in the first battle. Even so, a question arises: did he miscalculate the scale of the Muslim reaction? In any case, the chief commander abandoned his followers and left them in a fatal situation. Therefore, as Goranov writes, it was natural that many people began to accuse him, saying that the principal agitator of the uprising was the first to abandon the village. He was even shot at by a villager when he was passing by a bridge on his escape route.[48]

THE MASSACRE

The flight of Peter Goranov and his followers made the village even more vulnerable to the enemies' attack, as it was obvious that it had lost the most reliable soldiers. The resistance was reduced to sporadic shootings from several houses and buildings. Now the Muslim offenders could freely enter the village and began to loot and plunder those vacant houses whose inhabitants had taken shelter in more reliable places. Everywhere the village was covered with flame. The fire spread by itself.[49]

The first massacre took place in the lower quarter that was cut off from the rest of the village. The people who remained there took shelter in a house. According to Angel Goranov, 200–300 people were there, but the defense was maintained only by a few.[50] Stoyanov asserts that the Bulgarians effectively defended themselves even in this plight. "The enemy lost 46 men, while our damage was only two killed and three wounded."[51] But his assertion apparently contradicts the actual situation. Therefore he again claims betrayal by "Chorbadzhiyas" who invited the enemy in.[52] The scarcity of information makes it impossible to verify his claim. In any case, one thing is certain: the Bulgarian resistance could not last long.

For all their numerical and strategic superiority, the Muslims had their own problems. According to the Bulgarian sources, the Muslims convened a meeting during the slaughter in the lower quarter. The heads of bands and prominent leaders from different villages gathered around Ahmed Ağa. At the meeting the Muslim commanders expressed discontent and grievances. The complaints focused on the loss of soldiers and concern about the food supply. It is alleged that the casualty list amounted to 96 names.[53] This episode suggests many things. First, the position of Ahmed Ağa as the chief commander was not strong enough to impose his will on the Muslim fighters. The Muslim force was composed of various small units, usually organized by a village, and each of them had its own leader and commander. Ahmed Ağa acted as the coordinator of those units. Therefore he had to consult with the other leaders and persuade them by noting the opportunity for plunder. Second, the Muslim side had suffered relatively heavy losses in the battle and accordingly must have harbored a sense of vengeance. The strong feeling of revenge for the lost soldiers may account for the extent of the atrocities that followed. Third, the Muslims were running short of food as early as the third day of the siege, which shows that they did not expect a long battle and that their military preparations were made on the spot. They must have taken it for granted that the Bulgarians would surrender when they demonstrated their numerical supremacy. The stout resistance and the fierce battle surprised them and thus added fuel to their hostilities. The scarcity of provisions must have made the booty even more necessary.

After the meeting Ahmed Ağa sent a messenger to the Bulgarian side and proposed a ceasefire on the condition of their disarmament. The Bulgarians accepted the offer, and their representative, Angel Kavlakov, came to the Muslim camp for negotiation. Ahmed Ağa accepted him with courtesy and assured him that no harm would be done if the Bulgarians handed over the weapons. Kavlakov delivered the message to the Bulgarian leaders, who finally agreed to give up fighting. When the disarmament was completed, however, the plundering and massacre started.[54]

The looters entered the village and broke into the empty houses in search of booty and sport. At the sight of this some Bulgarians fled into the mountains, but the majority had to take shelter in the church and the school. The church was relatively well defended, so the Muslims first broke into the school. The people inside showed signs of resistance but in vain. Some of them were instantly executed. The rest were burned alive as the plunderers set fire to the building.[55]

The largest number of villagers took shelter in the church. The courtyard and the interior were filled with people. They tried to organize a desperate resistance and held on for some time, but to no avail. The Muslim fighters finally broke into the buildings. Indiscriminate mass killing followed, and a huge number of people including women and children were slain. The killing and plundering lasted for several days. The village was turned into a pile of rubble.[56]

THE PICTURE OF THE BATAK MASSACRE
PROVIDED BY THE BULGARIAN SOURCES

To sum up, the Bulgarian sources describe the course of events that led the massacre in Batak as follows. The more or less peaceful relations of the village with the surrounding Pomak communities had broken in the middle of the nineteenth century. The relationship became especially tense after the conflict over the expanding meadows of Batak. Long before the uprising, the villagers of Batak felt insecurity and hostility to their Muslim neighbors. The villagers agreed to stage an uprising, even knowing that it would lead to an open confrontation with the Pomak fighters. They embarked on massive preparations for the uprising and accumulated a significant amount of weapons and munitions. When a rumor of the outbreak of the "April Uprising" reached the village, the villagers decided to join it and started military activities on their own. The activities were not confined to defensive measures but included apparently provocative ones. They randomly attacked and killed Muslim travelers who happened to come close. They executed two unarmed policemen dispatched by Ahmed Ağa. They intimidated their Muslim neighbors and threatened to destroy their villages if they were not obeyed.

Even when the main units of Muslim irregulars arrived in the village, the Bulgarians refused to surrender and declared that they would fight to the last ditch, expressing their will for independence and making it clear that there was no room for compromise. The battle broke out after opening fire from the Bulgarian side. A significant number of Muslim soldiers were killed during the battle. Sources disagree on whether the Bulgarians were successful in the first battle or not, but they admit that the rebel leader, Peter Goranov, along with many young soldiers, abandoned the village in the night. It is indisputable that their evacuation made the village more defenseless and more vulnerable to the Muslim attacks. Indeed, the defense broke down the next day, and the villagers had to take shelter. Sporadic massacres and lootings had taken place as early as the second day. The rest of the villagers were at the brink of total catastrophe. At this very moment Ahmed Ağa proposed a ceasefire. But immediately after the Bulgarians handed over their weapons the wholesale massacre began. In light of this story, we can conclude that the people of Batak were attacked because they had started an uprising that aroused serious anxiety on the part of their Muslim neighbors. In other words, they gave the pretext for their attack. This by no means justifies the subsequent massacre, of course, which constituted a crime against humanity.

THE BATAK MASSACRE
DESCRIBED BY THE ENGLISH MEDIA

The news of the April Uprising and its aftermath was slow in reaching the outside world. Even in the Western circles in Istanbul people received very little detailed information on what had happened in the northern Rhodope for a while. Only ambiguous rumors about the massacre of the Christian population came to the ears of those who had personal ties with the region. Edwin Pears, a British barrister who had settled in Istanbul a few years earlier and worked as an amateur correspondent for the London-based *Daily News*, describes the circumstances: "In the spring of 1876 rumours began to come into Constantinople of a dark and ugly business in Bulgaria."[57] One of the centers of such rumors was an American missionary school known as Robert College. The school had many Bulgarian students and was in a position to get fragments of information through them or their relatives. One of the teachers, Albert Long, was especially interested in the situation because he formerly had been a missionary stationed in Bulgaria for seven years. Long received a number of letters from Bulgaria telling a dreadful story. According to Pears, the contents could be summed up as follows: "Orders had gone out from the Turkish authorities to the Moslem villagers to kill their Christian neighbours."[58]

Albert Long was much shocked by those rumors and began to write up a long report based on them.[59] He and his boss, George Washburn (the president of Robert College), petitioned Sir Henry Elliot, the British ambassador in Istanbul, to use his influence on behalf of the Bulgarians. The ambassador did not consider their report of sufficient importance or authenticity to communicate to his government and returned the documents. Long and Washburn then gave copies of their report to their friend Edwin Pears as well as a correspondent of the *Times*. While the *Times* did not take the report seriously, the *Daily News* published the letter of Pears under the title "Moslem Atrocities in Bulgaria" on June 23, 1876.[60]

The article created a sensation among the British public. Pears listed the names of thirty-seven villages that had allegedly been destroyed and asserted that the innocent Christian inhabitants had been indiscriminately tortured or killed by the Muslims.[61] Two members of Parliament asked the government about the validity of the information on June 26. The prime minister, Benjamin Disraeli, denied its authenticity and testified that "the information which we have at various times received does not justify the statements made in the journal."[62] Indeed the British ambassador had already reported to his government that the statements about the atrocities had been taken chiefly from information furnished by the American missionaries.[63]

When Pears learned that his article had been accused of inaccuracy, he sent his second letter to the editorial page of the *Daily News* on June 30. It was published on July 8. The article confirmed the first letter and increased the number of destroyed villages to sixty.[64] Therefore one of the two members of Parliament renewed his inquiries. Disraeli repeated the same answer but admitted that they had not yet had time to receive any reply to the inquiries made.[65]

The validity of the letters of Pears turned out to be a sensitive agenda for the British Parliament. Despite the wide repercussions, Pears's source of information was narrow and ambiguous. As to the source of information for his first letter, Pears recollects: "I collected a number of *rumors* and made much use of the information with which *Dr. Long furnished me*" (emphasis added). Even when the accuracy of his report was criticized by Disraeli, he did not make an effort to cross-examine his earlier informants. As he put it, "Thereupon I saw various friends, and especially Dr. Long and Dr. Washburn, who furnished me with translations of a mass of correspondence, from which I wrote a second and longer letter to the *Daily News*."[66] It is obvious that his letters were nothing but a patchwork of the hearsay diffused among the Western circles in Istanbul.

The shortcomings of Pears's account on the event do not stop there. He was apparently obsessed by a stereotype of Muslim misrule and could not distinguish groundless rumors from solid facts. Thus he wrote in his book published in 1913: "Now, orders for a Turkish massacre meant a free licence to soldiers, mostly barbarians from Anatolia, and to a small number of Circassian refugees who had recently been dumped down into the country by the Turks, to violate women, kill men, women and children, and take possession of or destroy their property. The orders were issued in April 1876, by the Ministers of Abdul Aziz."[67] In his memoir published in 1916 he reiterates the same account that he had given forty years before. "It should be understood that at this time there was no revolt in Bulgaria, though there had been considerable expression of discontent. The idea of the Turks was to crush out the spirit of the Bulgarian people, and thus prevent revolt."[68] His obstinacy is astonishing: the first English translation of Zahari Stoyanov's memoir had appeared three years earlier.[69]

In spite of all these shortcomings, Pears's amateurish account mixed with the stereotyped image of Muslim misrule had set the tone for the ensuing media coverage, as shown by the following episode. A London journal criticized the accuracy of Pears's account by claiming that the names of the destroyed villages did not figure in any known map. Pears had no possibility of refuting this criticism, so he asked the newspaper to dispatch "a competent correspondent" who would report on the subject on his behalf. The editors of the *Daily News* hastened to send Januarius MacGahan, an Irish-American journalist, to Bulgaria. Pears recalled the selection as "a happy one." When he arrived in Istanbul, MacGahan immediately made contact with Pears and got a detailed briefing. In this way Pears could imbue MacGahan with a preconceived idea and entrust him to accomplish the work that he himself could not.[70]

MacGahan, for his part, had been attracted to the rumors.[71] He first tried to interest the *Herald* but failed. Then he applied to the *Times* of London, again to no avail. As his biographer put it, "According to the history of the newspaper covering the years 1841–84, the *Times* declined Mac-Gahan's services because 'of his reputation for sensational proclivities.'"[72]

In the meantime two different authorities began to gather information on the situation in Bulgaria. After the second discussion in Parliament, the British government decided to send its own agent to Bulgaria. Walter Baring, a secretary of the embassy in Istanbul, was chosen for the task and started on July 19. Simultaneously an American diplomat was charged with the same duty by his government. Some contemporaries asserted that this U.S. fact-finding mission was an impartial humanitarian effort, as the U.S. government did not have any particular political interest in the region. But such an assessment is misleading. The person who assumed the task was Eugene Schuyler, who had formerly worked at the U.S. embassy in St. Petersburg and had just been appointed consul-general and secretary of the legation in Istanbul. He was a self-acknowledged "Slavophile" and doggedly believed in the Russian-made image of Muslim misrule, according to which the Christians had no rights. Moved by his personal conviction, Schuyler asked permission to make an investigatory trip to Bulgaria immediately after his arrival at Istanbul in early July. His request was instantly accepted by a U.S. official who was watching the political crisis in the British Parliament with concern.[73] In his letter of July 21 Schuyler explained the aim of his trip: "No doubt you have heard something already of the frightful atrocities perpetrated in Bulgaria by the bashi-bozouks and

Circassians…. I hope to bring back irrefragably proved facts which will show to the civilised world what sort of a Government is this of England's protégé in the East."[74] It is obvious, therefore, that he had predetermined not to assess the situation from an impartial point of view but to find evidence of Muslim atrocities.

Schuyler started his journey on July 23. He was accompanied by Mac-Gahan, although the reason for this is not altogether clear. The following remarks by Pears may provide grounds for speculation. "The selection of Mr. MacGahan was a happy one. He was a friend of Mr. Schuyler's. Both of them had been in Central Asia and knew something of Russia."[75] They could have gone with Baring, who set out four days earlier, but instead they preferred to make the journey with Prince Tseretelev of the Russian embassy. Schuyler employed a guide who spoke the local languages, a Bulgarian from Robert College.[76]

When he reached central Bulgaria, Schuyler paid utmost attention to avoiding contact with Muslim informants on the assumption that they would control his investigation. This might be seen as a sign of prudence. But his behavior seems a little extreme. "I avoided staying in Turkish houses, as I would thus have been prevented from having free access to the Bulgarians."[77] Such an attitude inevitably made him rely overwhelmingly on the Christian sources, especially in the investigation at Batak.

Batak was one of the most important destinations of their trip and one of the first places they visited. The reason is simple: Pears had mentioned the destruction of this village in his letters. Batak had already become a symbol of Muslim atrocities. Schuyler and MacGahan traveled almost directly to Batak and reached Peshtera, the last Christian village on the road to Batak, as early as August 1. When they arrived, the Muslim county head visited them and offered a guide to Batak. They declined the offer and insisted on staying at a Christian house that night. The Christian villagers welcomed them with extraordinary fervor. MacGahan describes the scene. "The poor people were only too glad to receive our party…for they looked to us for encouragement and protection against their Mussulman rulers. As soon as the Mudir [*sic: müdir*] went away, what appeared to be the whole population of the town seemed to flock into the court-yard of our house."[78] The reason for this unusual reception immediately became clear: "The people who had these stories to tell us we soon found were not the people of the place, but of Batak…. They were mostly women who had lost their husbands, and in many cases their children, whose houses had been burnt…. They all told their stories with sobs and tears, beating their heads and wringing their hands in despair."[79]

The unexpected encounter with the victims of the Batak massacre was rather convenient for Schuyler and MacGahan. They listened to the stories with utmost interest until late in the night and again the next day. They were "besieged all the morning by the same people who had blockaded us the night before." It was true that "their stories were so much alike," but the two investigators were much impressed by the very monotony and soon sympathized with the stories. They even promised "to do something for them" when they returned to Istanbul. Some of the people insisted on accompanying the party to Batak and explaining the site in their own words.[80]

It took four hours to reach Batak along a narrow mountain path. A much easier road existed, but the guide led them the harder way for some unknown reason.[81] The longer trip inevitably shortened the time that the travelers could spend in their investigation, because Batak had no facility to accommodate them. Even if staying had been possible, they would not have done so, as Schuyler confessed in his letter of August 3: "I was glad to escape from the fearful sight and equally terrible stench."[82] It is certain that Schuyler and MacGahan visited Batak for a relatively short time, presumably several hours at most. This prevented them from engaging in the most elementary forensic investigation and made it inevitable that they would rely heavily on the testimony of the survivors. That may partly explain why they made serious mistakes even in such an elementary point as counting the number of houses. As noted above, modern Bulgarian historians estimate the number of houses up to five hundred and the population at four thousand. Schuyler and MacGahan, however, believed the number of houses to be nine hundred and estimated the original population at nine thousand by counting ten to each house.[83] This error led them to assume that the number of victims was much larger than it actually was. They employed a primitive method of calculation: they estimated the scale of casualty by subtracting the number of survivors from the original population.

During their stay in Batak Schuyler and MacGahan observed several sites of murders, including the school and the church. Then they hurriedly returned to Pazardzhik the same day. At Batak they saw only the ruins and the scattered skeletons with rotten flesh, but the terrible sight of the huge number of corpses left to the mercy of wild dogs was enough to arouse strong indignation. As MacGahan put it, "Of all the cruel, brutal, ferocious things the Turks ever did, the massacre of Batak is among the worst! Of all the mad, foolish things they ever did, leaving these bodies to lie here rotting for three mouths un-buried is probably the maddest and most foolish!"[84] Their outrage was so great that they took the scene as evidence of an alleged attack on the innocent population. Schuyler put it in his official report: "The sight of Batak is enough to verify all that has been said about the acts of the Turks in repressing the Bulgarian insurrection."[85]

It is true that the pile of corpses including women's clothes and small skulls was evidence that indiscriminate mass killing had been committed. But the dead bodies could not provide the detailed context of the massacre. Nevertheless, Schuyler could eloquently explain the process in his letter on August 3: "Here fully six thousand people were massacred in cold blood by Ahmed-Aga, after they had given up their arms and had made no resistance."[86] The tone became even harsher in his report prepared a week later: "This village surrendered without firing a shot, after a promise of safety, to the Bashi-Bazouks [*sic*], under the command of Ahmed Aga of Burutina [*sic*]."[87] Schuyler mentioned nothing about the situation before Ahmed Ağa proposed the (false) ceasefire, let alone the initial provocations of the Bulgarian side. Perhaps he could not get the information from his informants. But he also had no interest in the topic. His aim was to ascertain "the manner in which the troops did their work" from the testimony "gathered on the spot from persons who escaped from the massacre," not to assess the situation as a whole. Otherwise he could not have said: "I am unable to find that the Bulgarians committed any outrages or atrocities, or any acts which deserve the name."[88]

The same mindset was shared by MacGahan. As for the insurrection, he claims: "There was a weak attempt at an insurrection in three or four villages, but none whatever in Batak, and it does not appear that a single Turk was killed here" or that "[t]he inhabitants offered any resistance whatever when Achmet-Agha [*sic*], who commanded the massacre, came with the Basha-Bazouks and demanded the surrender of their arms."[89] His explanation, however, naturally poses a question: why did the villagers possess so many weapons that had to be surrendered? MacGahan's answer: "It must not be supposed that these were arms that the inhabitants had specially prepared for an insurrection. They were simply the arms that everybody, Christians and Turks alike, carried and wore openly as is the custom here."[90] This opportunistic explanation apparently contradicts the principle of Muslim society that the arming of non-Muslims was strongly restricted. The practice was well known among the contemporary Europeans; MacGahan himself asserted: "There is no security for life or property in Bulgaria. The Turkish population is armed; the Christians have been disarmed, and the former do as they please. There is nothing, absolutely nothing to restrain them, but their own consciences, and what a restraining power that is can be inferred from the horrors of Batak. The

Bulgarians are unresistingly robbed and plundered daily by their Mussul-man neighbors."[91]

As we have seen in the Bulgarian sources, both insurrectionists and the Pomak perpetrators agree that the villagers of Batak had been armed and committed various act of provocation, including random killing. There-fore if Schuyler and MacGahan had visited one of the Pomak villages on their way to and from Batak they could have gotten a more plausible ex-planation of the Bulgarian armament. But even at the start of their mission they were obsessed with sympathy for the victims: "why sympathise with the strong against the weak, when the weak are so evidently in the right!"[92] Their insistence on the innocence of the Bulgarians was therefore not the result of "careful investigation" but the typical outcome of the victim-ori-ented analysis arising out of the conviction that the perpetrators are liars.[93]

In the case of MacGahan, moreover, this conviction was strengthened by his biased image of Muslim society. He was apparently obsessed with the stereotype of fanatic and barbaric "Turks." His level of knowledge on Islam is clear from his assertion on the motive for indiscriminate killing: "When a Mohammedan has killed a certain number of infidels he is sure of Paradise, no matter what his sins may be. Mahomet probably intended that only armed men should count, but the ordinary Mussulman takes the precept in its broader acceptation, and counts women and children as well."[94] In the same way he insists on the innate greediness of the "Turks" as the main reason for the massacre: "The village of Batak was compara-tively rich and prosperous; it had excited the envy and jealousy of its Turk-ish neighbours, and the opportunities of plunder to the Turks…was more than they could resist."[95]

MacGahan's letter dated August 2 appeared in the *Daily News* about a week later. Schuyler sent a preliminary draft to his chief, which was pub-lished on August 22. The tales of MacGahan shocked the public with their graphic description of the grotesque scene of massacre, while Schuyler's report gave it a tone of credibility, having been written as an official docu-ment by the consul-general and secretary of legation of the United States. Despite being the outcome of the same investigation, the two reports interactively created a "profound sensation" in Great Britain and other European countries.

At that very moment William Gladstone, who had long been con-ceiving a plan to make use of the news as the device to attack his rival Disraeli, launched a political campaign by publishing a pamphlet under the title *Bulgarian Horrors and the Question of the East*. Making use of the sensationalism of the reports by MacGahan and Schuyler, he succeeded in triggering an outburst of indignation in England against the Muslim perpetrators of the horrors. As Pears put it, "Public meetings were held in nearly every important town in the British Islands. Members of all political parties, of all the churches, all the living historians including Freeman, Carlyle, and Froude, joined their voices in the denunciation of the most wanton and brutal attack which had been made on a race within living memory."[96] The agitation spread throughout Europe, especially in Russia.

In his pamphlet Gladstone presented a story of the "Bulgarian Atrocities" almost identical to the accounts of Pears, MacGahan, and Schuyler. According to Gladstone, the Ottoman rule in Bulgaria was nothing but brutality and slavery. Bulgarians had every reason to stage an uprising to make known their grievance to the outside world. The "Turks," however, made use of this modest protest to eliminate their source of concern, taking it as the pretext for punishment. This view was no accident: Gladstone conceived the image based almost exclusively on the information provided by the three authors.

Gladstone explains how he got acquainted with the event: "By a slow and difficult process…through the aid partly of newspaper correspondence, and partly of the authorised agent of a foreign State, but not through our own Parliament, or Administration, or establishments abroad…we now know in detail that there have been perpetrated, under the immediate authority of a Government, crimes and outrages, so vast in scale as to exceed all modern example."[97] Out of all the "newspaper correspondence," he admires the coverage of the *Daily News* as "the most weighty" and "splendid."[98] Gladstone then expresses his gratitude to Schuyler for having made "the responsibility of silence…too great to be borne" through his report.[99] It is true that Gladstone used Baring's report as well, but only as additional reinforcement. He also disparages it as "too late…to hope to convince Europe."[100]

Gladstone not only obtained his image of the "Turkish atrocities in Bulgaria" from the reports of Pears, MacGahan, and Schuyler but also had a political plan and the strategy to materialize it. In his discourse Gladstone constantly takes a tone of humanitarian concern. He presents himself as a man who makes much of human rights and asserts that "of all the objects of policy, in my conviction, humanity…is the first and highest."[101] He emphasizes that his actions are just and impartial because they arise from pure humanitarian concern.

From this platform Gladstone further claims that those who are imbued with the same humanitarian mission must be equally just and impartial and accordingly trustworthy. It is noteworthy that Gladstone and the three authors of the "Bulgarian Horrors" mutually applauded each other as impartial humanitarians. Pears admired Gladstone's action as "a generous demonstration of human sympathy with a suffering people and of indignation against its oppressors."[102] Gladstone, in turn, applauded Pears as "the gentleman who has fought this battle with such courage, intelligence, and conscientious care."[103] This echoes his contention about the validity and trustworthiness of Schuyler's report on the basis that the United States "enters into this matter simply on the ground of its broad human character and moment."[104]

The same logic was applied to repudiate the facts that did not coincide with Gladstone's contention. The most important was information that the Bulgarians had committed acts of violence that provoked reprisals. Gladstone adopted the following logic of denial. "It may be thought that a defence for the Turks is to be found in the allegations of cruel acts done by the revolted Bulgarians. On this plea, I take leave to assert that there is no such defence; nor the shadow of it." First, "[o]utrages by oppressed inferiors do not excuse like outrages by the race which has held them down... by superior force." Second, "assertions from Turkish agents of outrages by Bulgarians are of no more weight, than their denials of outrages by Turks, which are shown by impartial reports to be valueless." Third, "the assertions by Christian Commissioners of the Porte that the insurgents committed deeds of atrocity, are of no higher value, until we know that they were men of integrity and of courage, who would both wish and dare to speak the truth."[105] To sum up, Gladstone took the same stance as the three authors discussed above: the perpetrators were liars because they were Muslims.

The allegedly impartial, conscientious, humanitarian, and therefore "trustworthy" information of the three authors was imbued with the stereotyped image of Turkish misrule. The same was true of Gladstone, who displays his understanding of history:

> Let me endeavour very briefly to sketch what the Turkish race was and what it is.... They were from the black day when they first entered Europe, the one great anti-human specimen of humanity. Wherever they went, a broad line of blood marked the track behind them; and, as far as their dominion reached, civilisation disappeared from view. They represented everywhere government by force, as opposed to government by law. For the guide of this life they had a relentless fatalism: for its reward hereafter, a sensual paradise.[106]

In the light of this assessment, we can safely conclude that Gladstone as well as the three authors instantly saw the event as a one-sided massacre of innocent Christians owing to their stereotyped prejudice against Islam and Muslim society. Convinced by this belief, they did not hesitate to adopt the victim-oriented method of gathering and analyzing the information. According to them, the Bulgarians were telling the truth because they were Christians, who were the inherent victims under Muslim rule. In contrast, the testimony of the "Turks" (and those Christians who sided with them) was unreliable because they were Muslims, who were always the perpetrators. The method was further justified and fortified by their belief that the Muslims or "Turks" were savage barbarians, alien to European "civilization." Those who believe in such a simple picture of good and evil often feel it necessary to do something for the sake of the victims. In other words, they are apt to take on the responsibility to do something good.

As noted, the "do-goodism" of MacGahan and Schuyler had already been displayed during their investigation, when they promised the Bulgarians to do "something" for their sake. A question arises: what was concretely in their mind as a possible measure? For them the Ottoman government was absolutely unreliable; they believed in the story that the massacre was organized and ordered by the authorities. Moreover, even if the authorities had intended to take action, they asserted, they could have done nothing effective to mitigate the plight of the victims because the country was in "a state of complete anarchy." MacGahan claims: "The Turkish authorities fail in the two great functions of government — the administration of justice and the maintenance of order."[107] The logical outcome of this assessment was "a foreign intervention." Schuyler hastily drew up a plan for the appointment of a commission for the protection of the people. The commission would see to the hanging of those who commanded the irregulars, the disarming of the Muslim population, the rebuilding of the burned villages, and the indemnification of the people for their losses at the expense of the Ottoman government.[108]

Not surprisingly, Gladstone shared the same opinion and agreed with MacGahan and Schuyler on the necessity of effective punishment for the perpetrators. But those who must be penalized were not confined to the ones who directly committed or abetted the atrocities but included the Ottoman government as a whole.[109] Therefore "the question is not only whether unexampled wrongs shall receive effectual and righteous condemnation, but whether the only effective security shall be taken against its repetition."[110] In Schuyler's view, the measures should be taken under

the aegis of an international commission. But Gladstone declined this option and proposed unilateral action by the British government. Instead of
the plan of concerted intervention by the European powers, he proposed
that the British government should declare distinctly that "for purposes
of humanity alone" it had "a fleet in Turkish waters" and that the fleet
would be "so distributed as to enable its force to be most promptly and
efficiently applied on Turkish soil for the defence of innocent lives, and to
prevent the repetition of those recent scenes."[111] But this was no more than
an initial step in his self-styled humanitarian mission; the final aim of the
plan was to rid Bulgaria of all Ottoman institutions. Gladstone claimed:
"Let the Turks now carry away their abuses in the only possible manner,
namely by carrying off themselves. Their Zaptiehs and their Mudirs, their
Bimbashis and their Yuzbachis, their Kaimakams and their Pashas shall
clear out from the province they have desolated and profaned."[112]

At this point Gladstone disclosed his real intention: Bulgaria should
become a protectorate of the British government. His insistence on humanitarian concerns was, after all, a camouflage of this expansionist plan.
Indeed the elimination of the Ottoman rule and the replacement of it with
a British protectorate were justified as "the only reparation we can make…
to the civilization which has been affronted and shamed…to the moral
sense of mankind at large."[113] Gladstone did not even hesitate to claim that
the concern about humanitarian catastrophe should take precedence over
existing jurisprudence: "Now there are states of affairs, in which human
sympathy refuses to be confined by the rules…of international law."[114] In
this claim we may even see one of the forerunners of the "humanitarian
intervention" of the late twentieth century.

CONCLUSION

The Batak incident was reported by contemporary authors both in Bulgaria and in the English-speaking world. The two sources generally agree
that a huge number of villagers were slaughtered by the Muslim irregulars
after disarming themselves. The stories of the mass killing portrayed by
the two sources are also identical. The killing was indiscriminate: a number of women and children, along with their husbands and fathers, were
shot, stabbed, mutilated, suffocated, and burned. It is indisputable that a
wholesale massacre took place.

Another common feature of the two sources is that they relied on
the same information provided by the local people who witnessed the
bloodbath at first hand. Although they shared the same kind of witnesses,
however, their explanation for the event had marked differences and dis-

crepancies. The Bulgarian sources admit, and even eloquently claim, that the villagers of Batak staged an uprising that eventually led to an open confrontation with the irregulars recruited among their Muslim neighbors. They had been relatively well prepared for the uprising and started it of their own will. After inciting the insurrection, they carried out a variety of military activities, including the indiscriminate murder of Muslim travelers. They threatened to destroy the villages of the Muslim neighbors who came to negotiate a peace deal. Even when the main body of Muslim irregulars appeared at the outskirts of the village, the Bulgarians refused to surrender and declared that they would fight to the last ditch. They opened fire first. During the battle a significant number of Muslim soldiers were killed. After the first battle and after entangling the village in a critical situation, the rebel leader along with many young soldiers fled Batak, leaving it fatally defenseless. As a result the defense was demolished. The villagers had to take shelter in several buildings. At this very moment Ahmed Ağa proposed a false armistice, and the massacre began.

The British sources, in contrast, seldom mention the military preparation on the Bulgarian side and claim that the village was virtually unarmed. They say nothing of the military activities and even claim that the Bulgarians did not resist at all: they offered no provocation and killed no Muslim soldiers. Instead they assert that the Bulgarians were massacred only because they were Christians.

The discrepancies do not reduce the credibility of the two kinds of sources on the fact of massacre. Indiscriminate massacre indeed took place: many people were annihilated. The Bulgarian sources testify that the mass killing occurred after provocations by the Bulgarians, so it can be considered an act of excessive reprisal. The action of the perpetrators, of course, cannot be justified by saying so; it constitutes a crime against humanity. But it cannot be denied that the Bulgarians gave the pretext for the Muslim violence. The British sources, in contrast, claim that the Bulgarians were killed without reason, with no pretext. The mass killing was therefore unilateral human slaughter by the Muslim aggressors. The discrepancies are not small. It seems certain that the difference in the context must have produced a different moral judgment than the one that appeared in British society, even allowing for the moral inclination of Christian Europe during the nineteenth century.

What produced these marked discrepancies? Two different answers are possible. British investigators might have been misled by unanimous manipulation of information put forward by the victims. The first mediators who conveyed the stories of massacre to the outside world must have been struck by the letters written by the Bulgarian intellectuals, who had every reason to sympathize with the sufferings of those who belonged to the same nation. The investigators who went to the site three months later believed the stories of unilateral aggression told by the survivors of the bloodbath. They probably curtailed the whole story in order to concentrate on the explanation of the depth of the victims' anguish. They paid most of their attention to attracting the sympathy of outsiders and did not disclose the tales that they deemed irrelevant.

Another hypothesis is that the mediators were too obsessed with their own paradigm to examine the data seriously and impartially. As noted, Edwin Pears, Januarius MacGahan, Eugene Schuyler, and William Gladstone all displayed a very biased image of Islam and the Ottoman society. They were imbued with the stereotype of Muslim misrule and therefore instantly accepted the news of mass murder as another proof of this theory. All of them believed in more or less the same ready-made explanation for the origin and background of the massacre: innate greed mixed with fanaticism brought about the Muslim atrocities. Because they had already prepared the answer, they left no room for another explanation from the onset. They had no intention of examining the validity of the news, which would challenge their premise that all the victims were innocent because they were Christians.

The two reasons are not mutually exclusive but rather interrelated. In other words, the discrepancies between the British and Bulgarian sources may well be a result of the interaction between the endeavors of the victims to attract outside compassion and the foreign sympathizers who had their own agenda. The outsiders were both eager to write and willing to be attuned to the simple picture of good and evil in which the Turkish government instructed the savage Muslims to annihilate innocent Bulgarians.

NOTES

1. Zahari Stoyanov, *Zapiski po balgarskite vastanie* (originally written and published in 1884); Angel Goranov (Boycho), *Vastanieto i klaneto v Batak: Istoricheski ocherk*; Hristo Popkonstantinov, "Chepino: Edno balgarsko kraishte v severozapadnite razkloneniya na Rodopskite planini."

2. "Chorbadzhiya" is a technical term widely used in Bulgarian historiography. Originally it was the popular title given to the Christian notables. After independence it acquired additional connotations. Chorbadzhiyas became negative figures who betrayed the national cause and sided with the Ottoman oppressor out of their own greed and selfishness.

3. Yanko Yanev asserts that it must have had more than five hundred houses with a population of approximately four thousand in 1876: Yanev, "Batak prez Vazrazhdaneto," 54.

4. Goranov, *Vastanieto i klaneto*, 4.

5. Yanev, "Batak prez Vazrazhdaneto," 58.

6. According to Yanev, the overwhelming majority of the Muslim population in the vicinity of Batak were Pomaks. He even asserts that contemporary Turkish villages like Nova Mahala, Fotinovo, Borino, and Gyovren must have been Pomak until the nineteenth century: Yanev, "Batak prez Vazrazhdaneto," 55. Although Yanev's narrative tone is apparently affected by his nationalist beliefs, we must note that contemporary Bulgarian historiography admits that the perpetrators of the massacre were Pomaks, not ethnic Turks.

7. Goranov, *Vastanieto i klaneto*, 8.

8. Ibid.

9. Ibid.

10. *Iztochno Vreme*, June 17, 1874 (emphasis added). The denomination "Turks" is different from the modern notion of a ethnic group. The "Turks" were apparently Pomaks. This type of confusion occurs very often in the nineteenth-century Bulgarian sources. In fact, many contemporaries (both "Bulgarians" and "Pomaks") paid little attention to the difference. "Turks" and "Pomaks" were almost synonymous in this region.

11. Ibid., 4.

12. Ibid., 5.

13. Ibid., 9.

14. Ibid.

15. Stoyanov, *Zapiski po balgarskite vastanie*, 905.

16. Goranov, *Vastanieto i klaneto*, 16, 21–22.

17. Ibid., 20.

18. Ibid., 23.

19. Ibid., 27.

20. Stoyanov, *Zapiski po balgarskite vastanie*, 907–9; Goranov, *Vastanieto i klaneto*, 33.

21. Stoyanov, *Zapiski po balgarskite vastanie*, 909.

22. Ibid., 909.

23. Goranov, *Vastanieto i klaneto*, 34–35.

24. Ibid., 36.

25. Ibid., 38.

26. Ibid., 40–41.

27. Ibid., 42–43.

28. Ibid., 44.

29. According to Stoyanov, the event took place on April 24. As noted above, the narratives of Stoyanov and Goranov are identical in principle but contain many differences in detail, especially in the case of the first military actions of the Batachanins. Stoyanov did not mention the provocation and indiscriminate killing by the Bulgarians, which makes his explanation of the event strange. According to him, the Muslims noticed the military preparations of Batak and appeared on the outskirts of the village with 200 armed men. The villagers of Batak opposed them with 350 fighters, including 40 cavalrymen. When the fighters appeared at the scene, the Muslim side dispatched a Bulgarian to propose a peace negotiation. Thus Stoyanov tries to suggest that the Muslims first showed an militant attitude but abandoned the option of war when they learned of the military supremacy of the Batachanins.

But the unusual activities of the Bulgarians had since long been noticed by the Muslims. So it is unnatural that the Muslims would have been suddenly alarmed by the signs of uprising consisting of nothing but the stationing of scouts at several positions, if we believe Stoyanov's story. It is more plausible that the Muslims found it necessary to negotiate with Bulgarians because they had been threatened by the wanton killings described by Goranov.

30. Goranov, *Vastanieto i klaneto*, 45.

31. Stoyanov, *Zapiski po balgarskite vastanie*, 910.

32. Goranov, *Vastanieto i klaneto*, 46.

33. Stoyanov, *Zapiski po balgarskite vastanie*, 911.

34. Goranov, *Vastanieto i klaneto*, 47.

35. Ibid., 51. According to Stoyanov, the police chief said: "Otherwise, he will let the brute force of his '*başıbozuk*' formation unleash on them." Stoyanov, *Zapiski po balgarskite vastanie*, 912.

36. Stoyanov, *Zapiski po balgarskite vastanie*, 912. According to Goranov, the phrase was as follows: "The Batachanins in no way surrender [their] arms, with which they have declared freedom and independence. If Ahmed Ağa wants to take it by force, they are ready to fight." Goranov, *Vastanieto i klaneto*, 51.

37. Stoyanov, *Zapiski po balgarskite vastanie*, 913.

38. Ibid., 915.

39. Goranov, *Vastanieto i klaneto*, 58.

40. Popkonstantinov, "Chepino," 240.

41. Stoyanov, *Zapiski po balgarskite vastanie*, 913–14.

42. Goranov, *Vastanieto i klaneto*, 54–55.

43. Stoyanov, *Zapiski po balgarskite vastanie*, 916.

44. Ibid., 918.

45. Stoyanov tries to persuade readers that Peter Goranov's action was an abortive night raid. But even if that is the case, the question of why his units did not return after the operation still remains. Ibid., 918.

46. Goranov, *Vastanieto i klaneto*, 59.

47. Ibid., 60.

48. Ibid.

49. Ibid., 64.

50. Ibid., 64–65.

51. Stoyanov, *Zapiski po balgarskite vastanie*, 920.

52. Ibid., 923. Goranov gives us a different story. "The next morning [May 2], the Turks of Yeni Mahale, who were the main force in the attack on the Bogdanov house, sent a messenger with an offer to surrender.... After this messenger, several Muslims of Yeni Mahale who were close friends to the villagers yelled at [the people] behind the neighboring buildings and tried to persuade [them] to surrender weapons to them and to come out to extinguish the fire. The inmates at Bogdanov's house were lured by the friendly assurances and decided to surrender." But when the inmates handed over the weapons, the Muslims gathered around the house and began massacring them; Goranov, *Vastanieto i klaneto*, 65–66.

53. Ibid., 73–74.

54. Ibid., 75–81; Popkonstantinov, "Chepino," 240.

55. Goranov, *Vastanieto i klaneto*, 86–89.

56. Ibid., 94–97.
57. Edwin Pears, *Forty Years in Constantinople: The Recollections of Sir Edwin Pears, 1873–1915*, 14.
58. Ibid., 15.
59. American Protestant missionaries made the official report on the event as late as September 1876. According to Ömer Turan, "the reason why the Missionaries have not spoken before is that they have heard plenty of stories but, not being able to obtain satisfactory evidence of their (truth), they have refrained from writing in reference to them." Turan, *The Turkish Minority in Bulgaria 1878–1908*, 50. In the light of this information, Long's action was personal, and he did not fully ascertain the reliability of the information on which his report was based.
60. Edwin Pears, *Turkey and Its People*, 210.
61. Ibid., 17.
62. Disraeli quoted in William Gladstone, *Bulgarian Horrors and the Question of the East*, 22.
63. Eugene Schuyler, *Selected Essays with a Memoir by Evelyn Schuyler Schaeffer*, 62.
64. Pears, *Forty Years in Constantinople*, 17.
65. Gladstone, *Bulgarian Horrors*, 23.
66. Pears, *Forty Years in Constantinople*, 17.
67. Pears, *Turkey and Its People*, 209.
68. Pears, *Forty Years in Constantinople*, 17.
69. Zachary Stoyanoff, *Pages from the Autobiography of a Bulgarian Insurgent*.
70. Pears, *Turkey and Its People*, 212.
71. Januarius MacGahan was a famous pro-Russian propagandist and one of the earliest examples of "yellow journalism" in the nineteenth century. He had been a correspondent in Russia and became a favorite in the tsar's court. He married a lady from an old Russian family in 1872; Richard Millman, "The Bulgarian Massacre Reconsidered," 228.
72. Dale Walker, *Januarius MacGahan: The Life and Campaigns of an American War Correspondent*, 170.
73. Schuyler, *Selected Essays*, 62.
74. Ibid., 63–64.
75. Pears, *Forty Years in Constantinople*, 18.
76. Schuyler, *Selected Essays*, 63–64.
77. Ibid., 65.
78. Januarius MacGahan, *The Turkish Atrocities in Bulgaria: Letters of the Special Commissioner of the Daily News, J. A. Macgahan*, 18.
79. Ibid.
80. Ibid., 18–19.
81. Ibid., 20–21.
82. Schuyler, *Selected Essays*, 71.
83. MacGahan, *The Turkish Atrocities*, 24.
84. Ibid., 30.
85. Schuyler, *Selected Essays*, 93.
86. Ibid., 71.
87. Ibid., 93.
88. Ibid., 94.

89. MacGahan, *The Turkish Atrocities*, 25.

90. Ibid., 25.

91. Ibid., 69.

92. Ibid., 14.

93. Richard Millman even characterizes the fact-finding mission of the two as follows: "Schuyler and MacGahan, hating the Ottomans, found ample evidence in their tour for such feeling, and in their reports justified their prejudices and contempt by describing the enormity of what they had heard and observed." Millman, "The Bulgarian Massacre Reconsidered," 229.

94. MacGahan, *The Turkish Atrocities*, 27.

95. Ibid., 32. Interestingly enough, the theory was echoed by Edwin Pears, who not only agreed with MacGahan's opinion on the Batak case but even generalized this greed as the basic motive of the Muslim atrocities against the Christian population in the Ottoman Empire. "In all the Moslem atrocities, Chiot, Bulgarian and Armenian, the principal incentive has been the larger prosperity of the Christian population; for, in spite of centuries of oppression and plunder, Christian industry and Christian morality everywhere makes for national wealth and intelligence." Pears, *Turkey and Its People*, 214. Was it mere accident that the two main architects of the media coverage of the "Bulgarian Horrors" shared the same conviction that the Christians were oppressed because they were more industrious and therefore more prosperous?

96. Pears, *Turkey and Its People*, 216.

97. Gladstone, *Bulgarian Horrors*, 11.

98. Ibid., 21.

99. Ibid., 33.

100. Ibid.

101. Ibid., 51.

102. Pears, *Turkey and Its People*, 216.

103. Gladstone, *Bulgarian Horrors*, 11.

104. Ibid., 34.

105. William Gladstone, *Lessons in Massacre*, 24–25.

106. Gladstone, *Bulgarian Horrors*, 12–13.

107. MacGahan, *The Turkish Atrocities*, 74.

108. Ibid., 75.

109. MacGahan claims that "these men carried out the wishes and intensions [sic] of the Government, if not the positive orders." Ibid., 13. Although this conclusion was sheer speculation based on the information that some of the *başıbozuk* commanders were promoted after the event, Gladstone adopted the same conclusion and asserted that "the authors of the crimes are the agents, the trusted, and in some instances, the since-promoted servants, of the Turkish Government." Gladstone, *Bulgarian Horrors*, 12.

110. Gladstone, *Bulgarian Horrors*, 10.

111. Ibid., 43.

112. Ibid., 61–62.

113. Ibid., 62.

114. Ibid., 47.

18

The Rhodope Resistance and Commission of 1878

Ömer Turan

EVENTS THAT LED TO THE RHODOPE RESISTANCE

The Ottoman-Russian War of 1877–78 was planned and conducted as "the war of races and extermination."[1] This was the definition of Prince Vladimir Tcherkasski, the pan-Slavist president of the Bulgarian Commission, which was established to arrange the administration of Bulgaria after the war. The Turkish and Muslim presence in the Balkans was going to be wiped out. Ultimately a new Bulgaria where the Bulgarians were the majority was going to be created. Not only Turks and Muslims but all non-Bulgarian communities (Jews, Protestants, Catholics, Greeks, and others) were unwanted and attacked. The Turks and Muslims were the biggest group, so they were the main target. Briefly, the total Muslim population of today's Bulgaria was about 1.6 million before the war and was reduced to about 800,000 in the early 1880s, which means that half of them were killed or forced to migrate; many of them also died on the road because of disease, cold, and hunger.[2]

The Russians employed special Cossack cavalries (who preceded the main Russian army) in the destruction of the Muslim communities.[3] Armed Bulgarian bandits were the other group designated to eliminate the Muslim Turks. The destruction of Balvan, a Turkish village with 200 houses three hours away from Tirnovo on the road to Selvi, is a good example of their method. Many places had similar experiences. On July 7 two squadrons of Cossacks came to Balvan. They first surrounded the village and collected the arms. They paid for the bread and hay they collected. On the following day two other squadrons of Cossacks arrived and again surrounded the village. They were accompanied by a number of armed Bulgarians from neighboring villages. They drove off all the cattle of the village and stripped the people and their houses. "They then set the village on fire in many places at once, and fell upon the inhabitants as they attempted to escape, cutting down men, women, and children, and driving them back into the flames. The Cossacks, who formed an outer cordon around the village, looked on quietly whilst these deeds were being perpetrated."[4]

The news of the massacres and cruelties caused a panic among the Turks and migration toward the south. Not only the Turks of the Dobruja area but also the Turks of northern Bulgarian places such as Ruse, Plevna, Nikopol, and Tirnovo joined them. Their destination was either Varna or Shumen. Varna was chosen because of its port as a way to reach Istanbul. British consul R. Reade described the wave of migration from Varna on July 14: "On my way back to Varna I could see nothing but Muslim men, women and children flying in a state of terror in the direction of Varna."[5] Shumen was also considered a safe place because it was the headquarters of a huge Ottoman army. Horsemen with lances attacked the refugees while they were hiding. Even nine-month-old infants were cut down. Consul Reade visited a group of eighteen wounded women and children in a dervish lodge in Shumen. Eight of them were nine years old or younger and were wounded by lances on their thighs, heads, legs, and other places. Nine of them were women and girls aged twelve to forty, wounded on their breasts or backs. The shoulder and back of the only fifty-five-year-old woman were wounded, and her right hand had been cut off.[6] The European journalists in Shumen made a common declaration on July 20, reporting the inhuman war crimes they had witnessed against the Turks, how they were massacred in their villages or while they were escaping, and how women and children had not been spared.[7]

After a short fight in July, the Russian forces easily captured the Shipka (Şipka) Pass in the Balkan Mountains. It was the only natural barrier on their way to Istanbul. As a result, the Ottoman armies in the area were cut into three separate groups: one in Shumen, one in Silistra (Silistre), and one in the southern Balkans. After crossing the Shipka Pass, the Russian forces under the command of Gen. Joseph Gurko conducted terrible massacres in the area, at Kyzanlik, Stara-Zagora, and Nova-Zagora. On the order of British ambassador Sir Henry Layard, Consul Blunt and his assistant Calvert went to the area and investigated the cruelties in the district of Kyzanlik. In his detailed and extended report, dated December 30, 1877, Consul Blunt described how the Cossacks and Bulgarians, provoked and protected by the Russians, had massacred civil Turks with no regard for their age or sex. As usual, the Russian soldiers first disarmed the Turks and distributed the arms they collected to the Bulgarians. Pretending to search for arms, the Russian soldiers went into the houses, searched every hole and box, and took whatever they liked. After the main bulk of the Russian army left, the Turks were left to the mercy of the Cossacks and Bulgarians and faced all kind of massacres. The Turks lost all their horses, sheep, and cattle. Their houses and mosques were burned. The Bulgarians also spread rumors among the Turkish villagers that Edirne had fallen, the Ottoman sultan had fled to Damascus, and so forth.[8]

Although Süleyman Paşa's army failed in its attempts to recapture the Shipka Pass in August and September 1877, it remained in the southern skirts of the Balkans and saved (at least for the time being) the Muslim population of that area from further Russian and Bulgarian cruelties. The end of the heroic defense by Osman Paşa's army in Plevna on December 10 was the end of the war in practical terms. The Ottomans were the losers. In the January 1878 the Russians captured Sofia, Samokov, Kyzanlik, Philippopolis (Filibe), and Edirne. The atrocities and destruction were indescribable. Not only Russian and Bulgarian swords but also cold and hunger killed the refugee groups.

On the demand of the Ottoman government, the Edirne Armistice was signed on January 31, 1878, and the Treaty of San Stefano on March 3, 1878. A Bulgarian Principality was established from the Black Sea to Lake Ohrid, from the Danube River to the Aegean Sea. After having dreamed of it for ages, the Russians were able to reach the Mediterranean Sea through Bulgaria. Only one natural obstacle stood in their way: the Rhodope Mountains and its Muslim Turkish and Pomak inhabitants.[9]

THE CAUSE AND NATURE
OF THE RHODOPE RESISTANCE

Muslim Turks and Pomaks of the Rhodopes were aware of a possible result of the Russian-Bulgarian occupation of the area. They heard the stories of the victims of the occupied areas from the Muslims who reached the Rhodope Mountains. Although the Treaty of San Stefano had been signed, the Russian and Bulgarian cruelties continued in the southern Balkans. The Muslim Turks and Pomaks of the Rhodopes therefore felt obliged to protect their lives, properties, and honor and did not allow the Russian troops and their Bulgarian helpers to penetrate into their territory. They were not prepared for such a defense. Even though they did not receive any help, weapons, or ammunition, they used their geographic advantage and resisted. They were sometimes called insurgents, sometimes guerrillas, sometimes mountaineers, sometimes *başıbozuk*s (Muslim irregulars), and sometimes a national army.[10]

In his report to Sir Henry Layard on March 10, 1878, Consul Calvert described how all Muslim houses (even their doors) and mosques were plundered and destroyed in the area of Philippopolis. Assuring them protection, the Grand Duke Nicholas asked the Turkish fugitives who were hiding in the Rhodope Mountains to return to the plain. Their living conditions were so atrocious that thousands decided to accept this invitation. Unfortunately, the families were fired upon by the Bulgarians while en route, and their remaining possessions were plundered. The young women were violated by the Bulgarians and the Russian soldiers. Many of the sick, children, women, and men were left to die in the snow. Because of these cruel proceedings the mortality among the refugees increased terribly.[11]

Consul Calvert reported from Edirne on April 16 that a group of armed Bulgarians of Mustafa-Paşa and Çirmen (Tchirmen) had attempted to reach Sel-bukrum, a Turkish village on the edges of Rhodope Mountains, on April 14. Their purpose was to plunder the rich farmstead of İzzet Ağa. The Muslim inhabitants of Sel-bukrum and neighboring villages opposed them, and combat began. A detachment of 200 Cossacks joined forces with the Bulgarians. The Muslims managed to be victorious. Eight Cossacks were lost, and one officer went missing. The Russian troops returned to Mustafa-Paşa. It was thought that the Russians would require 5,000 or 6,000 men to ensure Russian authority in that area. The number of guerrillas in that part of the Rhodopes was about 3,000 or 4,000, with headquarters at Bahadir-Yatadjak. The Turkish mountaineers were defensive. Their objective was to resist Russian penetration into the highlands.[12]

On April 25 two Istanbul-based newspapers, the *Levant Herald* and *Turquie*, also reported news about the rise of the Muslim population in the Rhodope Mountains. The *Herald* said that on April 12 a huge group of Bulgarians of Mustafa-Paşa and Hasskeui (Hasköy) had assailed twelve Muslim villages in the district of Harmen, killed twenty-three people, and set fire to the houses. In the Hasskeui district forty villages were burned, and fifty-six people were killed. The Muslim population of Çirmen and Hasskeui wrote to the Ottoman government, describing the atrocities. The Muslim population of Demotica telegraphed the Ottoman government on April 17, complaining of Bulgarian cruelties and asking for help.[13] *Turquie* reported similar news.[14]

A British adventurer Sinclair, who called himself Hidayet Paşa, led the resistance until October 1878. He told the European commissioners at Kara-Tarla that large masses of the refugee groups had changed their direction to the Rhodope Mountains because the Russian army that held the control of the area of Shipka Pass completely in January did not allow the refugees to return to their homes. When a Russian column advanced to Gümülcine (Gumuldjina), the armistice was signed; refugees were encouraged to return to their homes. Some of the refugees believed the promises and returned, but they were punished and oppressed. Then the resistance began, under the leadership of a certain Omer, Kara Yusuf, and their friends. The Bulgarians attacked them but denied doing so. Eleven Russian battalions, supported by Bulgarian legions, attacked the resistance groups in April. The fighting continued for nine days. Although the Russians drove the volunteers as far back as Kara-Tarla, they could not go further and could not suppress the resistance. The Russians occupied Couchalar, and Kara-Tarla became the headquarters of the movement. The lines were established on the occasion of the armistice and were maintained.[15]

Consul Calvert at Philippopolis reported to Layard on April 23 that twelve Turkish villages in the district of Hasskeui had been destroyed by the Russian troops two or three days earlier. The male inhabitants took up arms and fled to the mountains. Women and children of these villages suffered at the hands of the Russian troops and Bulgarian auxiliaries. Serious fighting occurred in the villages, involving the Russians, Bulgarians, and *başıbozuk*s. A Russian surgeon told the French consul that a regular battle had taken place; the Russians lost 600 men, the Turks 2,000 or 3,000. The Russian general Stabilin, however, minimized the number of destroyed villages, the amount of fighting, and the number of Muslim irregulars. Although other accounts estimated 25,000 or 30,000, he claimed that they had not numbered even 2,000.[16]

According to Tevfik Bıyıklıoğlu, the men of twenty-one Turkish villages of Hasskeui that had been destroyed by the Russian troops armed themselves and fled to the mountains. The men from the destroyed villages, deserters from Süleyman Paşa's army, and inhabitants of the area did not allow the Russian troops to penetrate into the Rhodopes. The uprising first occurred at Sultan Yeri and Ahi-Chelebi. The first engagement took place at Sel-bukrum above Çirmen on April 14, 1878. The power of the resistance in those days was 25,000–30,000 mountaineers. The movement soon spread south to the neighborhood of Gumuldjina; the Pomaks of Sitchandjik Mountain also joined them. Fighting between the Pomaks and the Russians occurred in the northern districts of the Rhodopes, between Philippopolis and Tatar-Pazarcık (Tatarpazarcık), and continued in the following months.[17]

In his report of April 20 from Edirne, Consul Calvert stated that fighting was taking place between the Russians and the Pomak population of the Kritchma (Kriçma/Kričma) valley, between Philippopolis and Tatar-Pazarcık. It was not clear which side won these battles, but hostilities occurred farther south as well. The Russians captured three or four Pomak villages and destroyed them. The Russian troops were also fighting against the Turkish mountaineers above Hasskeui. The first engagement took place in the neighborhood of Sel-bukrum on April 14, between a detachment of Cossacks and guerrillas who possessed four Krupp guns that had been abandoned during Süleyman Paşa's retreat. The Russians concentrated in that direction with about 12,000 troops: 8,000 from Philippopolis and 4,000 from Edirne. They were supported by some mountain-guns. Around Çirmen fighting was continuing. By April 17 the Russian losses amounted to 58 men and 2 officers. The Russians were also obliged to send 500 infantrymen from Edirne, 4,000 from Mustafa-Paşa, and two battalions from Demotica to the guerrillas at Demirler-Djemaati, two hours' away from Ortaköy. The chief stronghold of the movement seemed to be the inaccessible mountain district of Sultan Yeri (Sultanyeri), west of Demotica. Fighting was continuing there. A Russian force of 12,000 men from Demotica was operating in the area. On April 18 an engagement took place. The Russians were reported to have lost 500 soldiers and 8 officers. Neither side had a clear victory at any of the sites. A large force was sent to Sultan Yeri to occupy it. They had more than enough to handle. Two thousand infantry and three *sotnia*s (units with 170 men) of Cossacks had been sent toward the south in great haste the day before. The movement extended southward around Gumuldjina. The Pomaks of Sitchandjik Mountain also took up arms.[18]

The resisting mountaineers organized a delegation and presented a report on their situation to the British Embassy in Istanbul in the name of 250,000 Pomaks. The representatives of the resisting Muslim population of southern Philippopolis and Edirne described their cause, requesting support from the British government for their resistance against the Russian attacks and cruelties. On May 16, 1878, in the name of a temporary government, they applied to the Great Powers of the Paris Treaty of 1856 and explained their position. They said that the European powers should examine the reasons that led them to resist. They had to defend their lives, property, and honor. Their resistance was not against a legitimate government. The Treaty of San Stefano was not applicable unless it was accepted by the Great Powers. They demanded a new agreement to protect their region from further outrages. The area that they were protecting was fully Turkish and Muslim and also sheltered 100,000 Muslim refugees. Russians and Bulgarians occupied their territories after the Treaty of San Stefano. Although the Ottoman Empire had given that area to the Bulgarian

Principality, they did not consider that government legitimate without approval of the European powers. The Russians and Bulgarians perpetuated all kinds of horrors and ineffable cruelties in every place they occupied. In order to stop that, the Muslim resisters had resorted to arms. All the areas under the Russian occupation were in a state of anarchy, but they had established order in their region. They asked the European powers to send observers to see the differences between the two areas. They did not want the Europeans to give any land southwest of Maritza (Maritsa) to Bulgaria. Four million Muslims living in the area they protected preferred death to Bulgarian rule, which was known for its horrors and cruelties.[19]

The members of this resistance did not have enough means to defend themselves. They were made up of the inhabitants of the area, refugees, and some soldiers left from the armies of Süleyman Paşa and Osman Paşa. They had acquired some weapons from these armies. One of their sources of weapons and ammunition was the Russian troops. On May 10 they were reported to have 35,000 soldiers in their national army but only 15,000 rifles and very little ammunition.[20] According to another report, the number of insurgents was 25,000, not counting small groups; only one-fifth of the insurgents were armed; if they had enough arms, their number could have reached 60,000.[21] The members of the resistance applied to Queen Victoria through the British consul at Thessalonika, asking for British protection and for two battalions of soldiers. They also applied to the Ottoman government but got nothing. None of the Great Powers supported them or gave weapons or ammunition. According to the letter from a person in direct communication with the leaders of the resistance to Ambassador Layard on July 1, 1878, the native people of the area were fighting bravely for their honor, without any weapons and ammunition. The area sheltered 100,000 refugees. They had no food, only hunger; no doctors or medicines, only disease.[22]

At the request of the Russians, the Ottoman government sent two high-ranking officers, Vasa Efendi and Sami Paşa, to the Rhodope Mountains to negotiate with the rebels and convince them to give up arms. They left Istanbul on May 2. That evening they met the general commander of Edirne, General Delliusgausen. The day after they reached Philippopolis, on May 4, they met the general commander of the Russian forces there, General Stobissine. Showing them the places of resistance on the map from Hasskeui to Stanimaka, he explained the Russian position and informed the Ottoman officers that they had sent additional forces to Stanimaka, Deirmendere, Pechtera, Markova, Eliatcha, Mandera, Sarnitch Cassaba, Sitova, Lelkova, and Djourien. In the following days the mediators went to the Rhodopes, made observations, and asked the resistance leaders to give up their weapons, but the rebels refused. They told the mediators that when they had handed in their arms to the Russians in the past the Bulgarians, who had taken over these weapons, had attacked them in spite of the Russian promise to protect their lives, properties, and honor. The mediators witnessed the destruction. They added the names of fifty-five villages destroyed by the Bulgarians: Tartar-keuy, Babalar, Borevadjikli, Mussatli, Guidirlar, Foundoukli, Karamaular, Yeni-Mahalle, Mursallar, Guerine, Kouchavlar, Boyardji-keuy, Penderdjik, Caracaya, Vara Deir-men, Yeni-Bazar (Yenipazar), Kukviran, Moila Musallar, and Cara Tarla in the District of Hasskeui; Milkova, Timroueh, Chirocalaka, Bey-keuy, Tourou-Imatli, and Tchanakgillar in the District of Stanimaka; and Sa-tioglar, Keremeler, Kodja-oglar, Duidichli, Reis-keuy, Servichli, Kireb-chilar, Yatahlar, Sahfabi, Sari-Ibli, Souitchoh, Moustchali, Tekke-keuy, Kodja-beyler, Kalaidjilar, Behirli, Karadja-at, Sari-demirdje, Otli-feha, Ineh-bighdji, Kordjouli, Mahmoudlar, Baldjilar, Tcheltikdji, Senilemichli, Seymen, Abrachlar, Sakali, Omaroba, and Turhmenler in the District of Caradja Dagh.[23] General Stabilin was not satisfied with this attempt, however. He thought that the officers were too young and inexperienced to convince the rebels and asked Istanbul to send a superior officer to complete that mission.[24]

The resistance was still continuing in the following weeks and months. Many thousands of Muslim refugees were in extreme distress in the area, so around the third week of June Consul Calvert (who was the president of the International Relief Society at the time) decided to send someone to the Rhodope Mountains to report on the situation of the refugees. The society and Ambassador Layard gave some money to Dr. Cullen, a well-known and reliable person, to traverse the district as far as possible in ten days and collect information. After leaving Istanbul, he visited Lagos, Xanthi, Gumuldjina, Kilkona, Farfarlar, Djuma, Kirligali, Arda Valley, Assaralti, Kiujeri, Daridere, and Schahimlar and returned to Xanthi. He also visited sixty small villages. He estimated that the number of Muslim refugees was about 150,000 and that 70 percent of them were widows and orphans. Their numbers were increasing daily as a result of the Russian and Bulgarian attacks and burning of the villages. Thousands of women and children, unable to get any help, had died a lingering death from starvation. As many as 250 women and children were found in one place, without a single man among them. In several villages women and teenage girls were found naked, huddled together.[25]

After giving detailed information about the distribution of the refugees, their number at each location, and their situation, Cullen also presented a list of villages burned and plundered by the Russians and Bulgarians in the *kaza* of Hasskeui since signing the Treaty of San Stefano. He also gave the numbers of inhabitants and the names of the villages: Idemush, Yuresgulek, Rochaslee, Tatakui, Horoslar, Clescher, Allan Mahalah, Shiperlee, Kumurgee, Kisserkul, Karakjacia, Cumbular, Karamanlar, Foundoujak, Dourakui, Sheremetter, Gabrova, Mollah Moussabah, Rushhalliler, Karatlar, Kiretchtarler, and Koken-karrieh. In another list Cullen provided the names of the villages burned and plundered by the Bulgarians and Russian troops in the Philippopolis District, on May 28 and 29, 1878: Softischa, Bugutova, Dranova, Cunkurkui, Borova, Belitza, Yerkenprese, Orstritza, Hardeovo, Lakovitza, Lebourmahale, and Yundus-mahale. He added that in all of these villages many women and girls had been violated and many were abducted.[26]

Calvert's report on June 28 stated that he had received no important news from the resistance for more than three weeks. The parties kept their positions. The Russians claimed that they had driven back the mountaineers close to Drama but were obliged to return to occupy their positions, which they considered more advantageous. During their advance Russians or Bulgarian auxiliaries burned a number of Turkish places in the district of Ruptchus, including Softeshti, Dranova, and Gunduz-Mahalessi. In contrast, the advancing Russians found Bulgarian and Christian villages untouched.[27]

The resistance developed spontaneously. It was an independent act of the local people against the Russian cruelties. Consul Calvert in his report dated July 4 described the movement as defensive. They took up arms only when they were attacked.[28] Their official letters were signed by a group of people instead of a single leader. For instance, their request letter sent to Ambassador Layard had the seals of ten names. Their other letters to the Ottoman government and to newspapers bore the seals of either 25–30 public representatives or 100 village councils. But they did have some leaders. Ahmet Ağa Tamraslijata, for instance, stood at the head of the temporary government.[29] Yusuf Cavus controlled the movement in the eastern Balkans, from Emine Burnu to Shipka. Hidayet Paşa (Sinclair) met the European Commission on Kara-Tarla as the commander of the national army. Kara Yusuf and Hacı İsmail were among the other leaders of the movement. The Ottoman commissioners who visited the Rhodopes in early May to convince them to end the resistance stated that the leaders of the movement were Ali Paşa and Kerim Paşa, Hacı Emin, Hüseyin Çavuş, Molla Murad, and Şaban Ağa in the Stanimaka, Tchitak, and Hasskeui regions.[30]

During the Berlin Conference, the Russian representative, Count Peter Shuvalov, promised the villagers permission and protection to go back to their villages on behalf of the Russian emperor if they gave up their arms and ceased hostilities. Lord Salisbury, the British minister of foreign affairs, telegraphed this news to the British Embassy in Istanbul on July 2.[31] Sir Henry Layard in Istanbul passed this information to the Ottoman government. The Ottoman grand vizier was glad to see that the British government was paying attention to the refugees. He said that he would communicate this news to the leaders in the Rhodopes and send a commissioner to convince them to stop the hostilities. His only objection was that the reports called them insurgents, since they were only defending their lives and properties and the honor of their wives.[32]

We have no information as to whether Istanbul sent that commissioner or not. But in those days Russians and Bulgarians were still burning and plundering Turkish villages, violating the women, and murdering the old men and children. Rear-Admiral Sir J. Commerell gave this information from Gelibolu on July 8 and emphasized that the source was not Turkish.[33] The Muslim inhabitants of the settlements in Rhodope area, as in the other occupied areas of Rumelia, kept sending letters to the British Embassy in Istanbul, complaining of the Russian, Cossack, and Bulgarian cruelties and destruction.[34]

But the Russian ambassador, Prince Alexei Labanov, clearly stated to his colleagues at the meeting of the ambassadors in Istanbul on July 15 (on the authority of Prince Alexander Dondukov Korsakov, the imperial commissioner) that the Muslim refugees could not be allowed to return to their villages. He claimed that the Russian administration had no means of protecting them from the Bulgarians.[35] Prince Dondukov Korsakov said similar things to the European commissioners when they visited him at his office in Philippopolis on July 21. It was clear that the Russians were not willing to allow the repatriation of the Muslim refugees and that the words of Count Shuvalov were just a political maneuver during the conference in Berlin.

THE WORK OF THE INTERNATIONAL COMMISSION
SENT TO THE RHODOPE MOUNTAINS

The Congress of Berlin met to redraw the map of the postwar situation in the Balkans, the Caucasus, and the Middle East on June 13, 1878. In its session of July 11 the Berlin Congress decided to establish a European Commission consisting of representatives from the participatory powers and send it to the Rhodope Mountains to examine the situation of the refugees.[36] The ambassadors of the European powers met on July 15 and 17 at the British embassy in Istanbul and selected the members of the commission: Austrian military attaché Col. R. Raab; British consul-general J. Henry Fawcett; French consul C. Challet; a second secretary to the Russian Embassy named Basilii; second dragoman of the Italian Embassy D. Graziani; and a German vice-consul named Müller. Naşit Paşa, ex-governor of the *vilayet* of Syria, and Rıza Bey were the delegates of the Ottoman government in the commission.[37]

The ambassadors also gave joint instructions for the commissioners:

> These gentlemen are commissioned to proceed to the district of the Rhodope, and to the neighbouring country, in order to inquiry into the condition of the emigrant population in those localities, and into their sufferings. They will estimate, as far as possible, the number of these refugees, will endeavor to ascertain the places from whence they come, their race, their religion, the motives which have compelled them to leave their country, and which still prevent their return. They will ascertain what measures can be taken for the immediate relief of their sufferings, and for continuing such relief until these refugees can be repatriated and restored to their homes with every security for their existence.
>
> They will consult, if necessary, with the Russian authorities in order to concert the measures to be taken for effecting the repatriation of the refugees, and for obtaining the means of affording immediate relief, if that is practicable. In case the Commissioners should consider that measures suggested to them by information acquired on the spot are capable of immediate application, they shall refer to their respective Ambassadors upon the subject. The Russian and Turkish military authorities will assist the Commissioners in the accomplishment of the mission which is entrusted to them. The commissioners will proceed in the first instance to Philippopolis, will there place themselves in communication with the Russian authorities, and from thence will organize their exploration as they think best.[38]

After a short preparation, the commissioners left Istanbul. Their mission lasted for about a month. They visited Philippopolis, Lagos, Xanthi, Gumuldjina, Kirkova, Mastanly, Kerdjalli, Kara-Tarla, Couchalar, Ortaköy, Plavon, Temiler, Ketenli, and Ilya, made observations, met with the representatives of the fugitives and leaders of the revolt, asked them questions, and got their answers. They assembled three more times after returning to Istanbul in mid-August. The commissioners had a total of twenty-nine meetings, the last one being on August 25, 1878. From the beginning of the process to the end, the Russians tried to limit the commission's work. Even at the meeting of the ambassadors on July 15 Prince Labanov did not want the commission to go beyond the Russian lines or the refugees to return to their homes, which were under Russian occupation.[39]

The commission had its first meeting on July 21, 1878, at the Philippopolis railway station. Colonel Raab was chosen unanimously as their president and authorized to speak on behalf of the commission. Consul Challet served as the secretary. They communicated with Prince Dondukov Korsakov, the imperial Russian commissioner in Bulgaria, to ask him for safe-conduct and an escort in localities under his jurisdiction. On the same day, the commission visited him. The meeting with the prince reflected the position of the Russian administration in regard to the cruelties toward the Turks in Bulgaria and situation of the refugees. Claiming that the hatred was so strong among the two populations that it was unable to maintain order, the Russian administration was preventing the refugees from returning to their homes. By listing the difficulties and not promising protection, it was proving its unwillingness to accept the refugees back. The Russian administration was also trying to belittle the revolt in the Rhodope Mountains by denying the engagements between the Russian forces and the insurgents. Just after the interview with Prince Dondukov Korsakov, the commissioners decided to go to the district of Gumuldjina first. It was not advisable to take the shortest route from Philippopolis, however, because of the lack of security and road conditions. Therefore they decided to go back to Edirne by rail on the same day. From Edirne they were going to Dedeağaç by train. Afterward a war ship provided by the British government was going to take them either to Lagos or to Cavala, whichever they chose.[40]

The commission held its third meeting on July 24 at the Austro-Hungarian Lloyd's Agency at Lagos. Prince Dondukov Korsakov employed an aide named Yusefovich as his intermediary with the civil and military authorities under his orders, to provide free passage in all the areas under Russian control and to accommodate them in any way necessary in order for them to accomplish their mission. The commissioners decided to continue their journey and met several refugee groups on the way. They interviewed refugees and took some notes about their situations. Upon

MAP 18.1. The Rhodopes

entering Xanthi, they saw a considerable number of refugees and unanimously decided to stop there to speak with the authorities, notables, and
refugees. A common form of interview was accepted to elicit "the date of
the arrival of the emigrants, the place whence they come, what they are
doing, what they receive, what are their prospects, what they can do, the
reasons for their departure, and of their stay being prolonged, and, finally,
the measures taken with respect to them, both past and present, so as to
instruct the Commission as to the decisions to be at once taken, and those
which it may be requisite to take in the future."[41]

Before beginning to interview the refugees in Xanthi, the commission
met the *kaymakam*, the members of the *meclis* formed in the town to help
the refugees, and some town notables, half Muslim and half Christian.
From the information that the commission gathered from the interviews
it appeared that the first emigrants had arrived there ten days before the
Russians occupied Philippopolis. The *kaza* had about 60,000 refugees.
Although the inhabitants helped the refugees with all they had available,
it was not enough; the refugees had to be sent away as soon as possible.
About 50,000 of them were sent to the coast of Anatolia and other places

on ships sent by the Ottoman government. About 10,000 refugees still remained in the *kaza* and its villages. The refugees could not bring anything with them. Even one of the richest people of Philippopolis, for instance, needed to be helped. Almost all of them were Muslims, along with a few Gypsies. The refugees were receiving aid from the government and a society. Half an *oke* (*okka*) of flour (641 grams) or 300 *drachm*s of bread was given to each person. A register listed the names of the refugees in the *kaza* and their age, sex, and place of origin. Their health was not perfect but satisfactory; according to two doctors, the refugees were suffering from intermittent typhoid fever. Only 7 to 10 percent of them were able-bodied; the rest were old men, women, and children, including a lot of orphans. Some were the children of people who had been massacred, and the others did not know whether their parents were alive or not.[42]

The commissioners met the refugees on their second day in Xanthi, on July 25. They listened to the refugees all day. The lists of refugees who had been distributed to the villages and received relief estimated their number at about 7,500. Representatives of refugees from different places met with the commission. After hearing the spokesperson of each group, the commissioners freely asked questions of any member of the groups they chose. Delegates of refugees from Tatar-Pazarcık; Pazarcık; Philippopolis; Stara-Zagora, Çirmen, and environs; Loftcha, Isladie, and Statizza; Plevna and its environs; and Orkhanie, Selvi, and Sofia presented their stories and were interrogated by the commissioners. Many heart-breaking events were described. During the interrogation, some of the women who had been raped demanded poison rather than bread.[43]

Russian commissioner Basilii objected first to the spokesman of a group then to the method of collecting information. Claiming that the commission had exceeded its limits several times, he said that he would leave the commission and go back to Istanbul if the commission did not confine itself to receiving general statements, without entering into details. At the end of the session all the members of the commission signed the procès-verbal. For the first time Basilii included a reservation: "Protesting against the proceedings of the Commission."[44] He retained this reservation in the procès-verbal for each of the following sessions. The Russian commissioner's objection was the topic of the next session, held on the following day, July 26, at Xanthi. Supporting Basilii, Müller proposed not to go into details of the motives. After discussions, the suggestion was voted down.[45] The British, French, Austrian, and Italian commissioners sent telegrams to the Austrian and British ambassadors in Istanbul, stating that their Russian colleague was attempting to stop the work of the commission and threatening to withdraw from it. They were directed to continue their work as long as they were the majority.[46]

The commission reached Gumuldjina on Saturday, July 27, and stayed there until the end of the month. Seven sessions were held there. Graziani presented the notes he had taken en route about the refugee groups they had met. The commission interviewed the authorities of the town and was informed that the *kaza* had from 60,000 to 70,000 refugees. The delegates of refugees from Tatar-Pazarcık; Philippopolis; Stara-Zagora; Hasskeui; Kyzanlik and Nova-Zagora; Demotica, Tcherpan, and Carlova; and Loftcha, Tirnovo, Plevna, Selvi, and Gabrova made presentations and explained their conditions (including how they had been treated by the Russians and Bulgarians, how they had left their countries, and how they would like to go back). The delegation from Demotica also gave information about the resistance in the Rhodope Mountains, as stated in the procès-verbal of the session:

> These emigrants bear witness that there are insurgents in the Rhodopes; one of them has two sons among them, and they themselves have fought on several occasions. Forty-five or fifty days ago two fights took place at Tcheutekly and at Acha Mahale, after which there was an exchange of two prisoners. Three days before these two fights one Petco, accompanied by sixty Bulgarians and twenty Russian soldiers, arrived at the out-posts. They entered a village named Tesmolu, pillaged it, killed a woman, and went away. The object of the insurgents is to prevent the Russians from extending their lines. For their part they will never make an attack upon them. There are huts in which women are living; the Russians come there in search of them, and dress them like Europeans. But since sentinels have been placed, they have been unable to get at them.

The commission then listened to widows and orphans. The widows from Plevna, Sofia, Ihlima, Philippopolis, and Kyzanlik told their heartbreaking stories, including how they had escaped, how their husband and relatives had been killed, how they had been abused by the Russian soldiers, how they were surviving, and what they expected.[47]

In the evening of July 29, during the eleventh session, the commissioners learned that Basilii had resigned from the commission due to health problems and been replaced by a dragoman of the Russian Embassy in Istanbul named Leschine. In the following sessions the delegates of the refugees in the villages of Gumuldjina and refugee groups from the *kaza*s of Isladie, Loftha, Kyzanlik, Plevna, Selvi, Philoppopolis, and Widdin were heard. After describing the terrible horrors they faced, and the massacres they had witnessed, all of them said that they had experienced very good relations with the Bulgarians until the Russians came. One of them also said that the Russians gave the arms collected from the Turks to the Bulgarians, placed the Bulgarians before the troops, and forced them to fire on the Turks. None of the refugees were willing to return home. They would prefer to be thrown into the sea by the Seven Powers. On the morning of July 31 the commission received a huge number of petitions about stolen property and movable effects of the refugees.[48]

During the first week of August the commission went to Kirkova, Mastanly, Kerdjalli, and Kara-Tarla, the heart of the Rhodope Mountains and the resistance. They met refugee groups and authorities and made observations. On August 6 at Kara-Tarla the commission met with Sinclair (Hidayet Paşa), commander-in-chief of the national forces of the Rhodopes. In this interesting meeting, according to the procès-verbal of the twenty-first session, Sinclair explained the beginning and causes of the resistance, the fighting in April, and establishment of lines between the Russians and national forces (as described above). He spoke about the visit of Sami Paşa and Vasa Efendi. He described the battles that had taken place in May and in the following months and stated:

> On the 27th May the right wing was attacked, and the Bulgarian villages claimed the protection of the National troops against the Russians. Engagements took place constantly during eight or ten days, until the treachery of the Kaimakam of Ahi-Chelebi, which threw the population into a panic, and induced them to take flight. In these combats the Commander saw with his own eyes the Russians firing on inoffensive people. He learned, through his officers, that an old man was crucified on trees: he did not see this. Since then they daily receive summons from the Russian army, and fighting continues at the outposts.[49]

According to the procès-verbal of the twenty-first session, Sinclair described the number and situation of the refugees under his jurisdiction and gave his opinion about their future. They were estimated at more than 100,000, from Demotica to Nevrecope. The majority of men had perished in the battles, so they were mostly women and children. The necessities of the refugees and the outposts were provided through the help of the native population. He suggested that the Turks who had been born in the mountains not be removed and be kept with their families and employed in the construction of roads. Yet the Turks from the plain of Pomak could be moved with less difficulty. Bringing the Turks and Bulgarians together was not favorable. He pointed out to the commission that the Bulgarian villages in the lines under his command were intact, while the enemy was still destroying the Turkish villages. Sinclair did not allow any brigandage and punished perpetrators very severely. He was displeased that the peasants working in the fields were still being fired upon. Sinclair counted twelve burned villages in the Bogot direction and concluded that some of the emigrants could be colonized in the Rhodopes by starting small industries such as wool or tobacco as well as building roads.[50]

After listening to Sinclair, the commission continued to interview the representatives of the surrounding villages, hearing the groups of women first. Women from Kararits-Igriler said that they had been violated by the Russian soldiers, who did not even spare an eight-year-old girl. Commenting that the statement about the little girl needed verification, Russian commissioner Leschine opposed going into personal details and accusations against the Russian army. Accompanied by some Russian officers and soldiers, the commission made an excursion into the neighborhood of Kara-Tarla on August 7. In eleven hours they visited nine villages. The excursion gave them a chance to observe the degree of Russian cruelties directly. Most of the villages were burned completely. In the evening of the same day the commissioners held their twenty-second session, at Kara-Tarla. They presented the notes of the excursion and approved their contents.[51]

When the commissioners went to Couchalar on August 8, they saw that 210 of 230 village houses had been burned by the Russians. The villagers of Couchalar and Karadjalar reported that when they went to work in their fields, without arms or any other weapons, Bulgarians or Russians fired at them and seized their animals. The Russian commissioner opposed these statements. Backed by the German commissioner, he claimed that these people were not refugees but inhabitants of the area. The other commissioners, however, did not accept this. They said that these people were refugees because they belonged to burned villages and were living in the mountains. In the following days the commission went to Ortaköy, Platon, and Ilya; listened to Bulgarian and Muslim villagers; and returned to Istanbul.[52]

The commission met three more times in Istanbul to finalize its report. The draft report written by the secretary of the commission was presented in its first meeting on August 17. After listening to the draft,

Russian commissioner Leschine stated that he had to resign from the commission because of the views expressed in the report. He said that the commission had exceeded its limits; the conduct of the Russian troops in the territory that they occupied during and after the war was not its subject. Müller supported this view. After some discussions, the draft was read again; all the other commissioners agreed to accept its contents, with some modifications.[53]

The modified report was discussed again on August 22. Leschine (who had resigned) and Raab (who was ill) were not present. Müller was dissatisfied with the modifications. He was of the opinion that the object of the commission was philanthropic. Without touching on the conduct of the Russian troops, the report had to deal with the means to assist the refugees in the Rhodopes. The commissioners said that the conduct of the Russian army was the reason why the refugees had fled from their homes. Therefore it had to be mentioned. They accepted some modifications, however, to please Müller. In their third meeting on August 25 the commissioners (without Leschine and Raab) discussed the final report. They still could not satisfy Müller. Italian commissioner Graziani then proposed that the commissioners who had no problem with the text of the collective report should present it to their ambassadors separately, with an identical letter. The representatives of England, Turkey, and France accepted it, and the work of the commission was terminated.[54]

What were the contents of the final report? The introduction presented the establishment of the commission, its form, and its duties. It stressed that in describing the events the commissioners were careful not to use aggressive language about the Russian army. They were obliged to report what they had observed, however, and what they had been told. The introduction then listed their working principles and the places visited.[55]

After this introduction the report gave the numbers of the refugees in the places visited: 7,000 refugees in the district of Xanthi, 62,000 in Gumuldjina, 10,000 in Kerdjalli, about the same number in Mastanly, and 150,000 in the area between Demotica and Nevrecope, which was defended by the Muslims. It was impossible to give an exact number of the refugees, but all of them were Muslims who had escaped from the Russian-occupied territories in Bulgaria and Rumelia.[56]

The report then described why and how the Muslim refugees living in the places that the commission visited had left their original places. In order to give an idea of the degree of Russian and Bulgarian cruelties, it reported the events in Harmanli. More than two thousand children had been thrown into the Maritza and Ourloudere rivers by their mothers while they were escaping from the Russian troops. The mothers had to choose whether to let the Russians kill their children or throw them into the river, and they preferred the latter.[57]

The report mentioned how the Bulgarians were used by the Russians against the Muslims. In spite of all the cruelty they had endured, the Muslims were not full of inveterate hatred against the Bulgarians. They did not touch the rich Bulgarian villages in their territories. For instance, the district of Gumuldjina had 60,000 Muslim refugees living under the most terrible stress, but the Bulgarians were able to live among them. Also, some Bulgarians had helped their Muslim neighbors and saved their lives.[58]

The commissioners found that the Muslim refugees did not exaggerate in describing their situations and complaining to the commission. The commissioners had randomly chosen and visited twenty villages among the eighty villages destroyed and burned since June 1 and verified the claims. "Devastation stretched along a line of more than 150 kilometers, marked out by the advanced posts of the Russian army."[59]

The report also mentioned the issue of repatriation of the refugees. The Russians had promised a safe return to their homes but did not keep their promise. The refugees who trusted the Russian promises and returned to their places were attacked and killed either on the road or at their destinations. The commissioners were convinced that the Russians had never really been willing to allow their return. Therefore the commissioners made some suggestions about how the return of the refugees could be achieved and how they could survive upon their return.[60]

When Commissioner Fawcett presented the final report of the commission to Ambassador Layard on August 28, he also presented the letter that each commissioner was submitting. He said that when it had been read for the first time at the meeting of August 17 the Russian commissioner's reaction had not been negative. Fawcett blamed "higher political influences," stating: "I have not the slightest doubt that this draft Report would have been approved, if we could have discussed at Adrianople. Unfortunately, at Constantinople higher influences produced at the very first sitting an obstinate and systematic opposition on the part of the German Delegate, and at the second the absence of Colonel Raab, the Austrian Delegate, on the ground of indisposition." The rest of the commissioners suggested the establishment of an International Commission to deal with safe repatriation.[61] Ambassador Layard wrote to London on August 28, criticizing the attitude of the German and Austrian commissioners. He expressed his view that the ambassadors had ordered the commissioners not to sign the final report.[62]

The report had no consequences whatsoever. In his letter dated September 1 Layard informed his government that Count Ferenc Zichy, the Austrian ambassador in Istanbul, was hoping for a meeting of the ambassadors to review the report of the commission and make suggestions to their governments for the relief and repatriation of the Muslim refugees. But the Russian ambassador refused to attend any meeting on that subject. He insisted that according to protocol 18 of the Berlin Conference there was nothing for the ambassadors to do after the establishment of the commission.[63]

In the following days nothing changed. In his letter to London dated September 27 Layard wrote that he had made some attempts to take some further steps but could not achieve anything. The Russian ambassador refused to meet to discuss the matter. The ambassadors of the signatory powers were not doing anything in terms of the implications of the report or the helpless refugees. Layard noted that

> the reports of the commission have consequently been allowed to remain a dead letter, and the object which the Congress of Berlin had in view of finding means to alleviate the sufferings of the Mussulman fugitives in the Rhodope districts, and of restoring them to their home, has been frustrated, and the result of the arduous labours of the Commission has only been to raise a controversy as to the authors of the unparalleled cruelties and outrages committed upon the Mahommedan population of Bulgaria and Roumeli.... They have been left without help; they are still wandering homeless and almost naked; and a very large proportion of them must perish of cold and hunger as soon as the cold weather, which is now rapidly approaching, sets in.

The sources of the private charities had been exhausted, and the Rhodope Muslim population could not help the refugees anymore.[64]

CONCLUSION:
THE RHODOPES AFTER THE TREATY OF BERLIN

The Rhodope resistance was one of the consequences of the Russian cruelties conducted during the Ottoman-Russian War of 1877–78. Russian soldiers, Cossack cavalries connected with the Russian army, and coerced Bulgarian volunteers destroyed the Turkish Muslim cities and villages. They demolished and burned their mosques and houses; injured and killed Muslim civilians, without sparing children, the elderly, and women; and even raped Muslim women and young girls. Their aim was to eradicate the Turkish Muslim presence from Bulgaria by killing them or forcing them to leave the country. Despite the signing of Treaty of San Stefano, the Russian and Bulgarian cruelties toward the Muslim civilians of Bulgaria continued.

The Rhodopes were not occupied by the Russians during the war. But the Muslim population of the Rhodopes knew Russia's intentions and attitude toward Muslims from the more than one hundred thousand refugees who had reached the Rhodopes. The Treaty of San Stefano gave the Rhodopes to Bulgaria, which opened an access to the Mediterranean for Bulgaria and therefore for Russia. The Russian attempt to occupy the Rhodopes caused the resistance of the Muslims there. They were not prepared for resistance: they had no weapons, ammunition, support, or assistance, yet they managed to resist the aggressors in order to save their lives, honor, and property. The combat lasted for months. The Russians faced a hard struggle.

The situation of the refugees and the resistance in the Rhodopes got the attention of the Berlin Conference. An international commission was established and sent to the Rhodopes to examine the situation of the refugees and their reasons for being there. The commissioners were the representatives of the powers who had signed the Treaty of Berlin. In July and August 1878 the commission went to the Rhodopes, interrogated the refugees, listened to resistance leaders, and collected firsthand information about the miserable situation of the Muslim refugees and the Russian atrocities inflicted on them.

The Berlin Conference remapped the Balkans, however, even before the commission was sent to the Rhodopes. By giving the southern side of the Arda River back to the Ottoman Empire, Bulgarians — and therefore Russians — were prevented from gaining access to the Mediterranean Sea. The rest of the Rhodopes were given to the autonomous Eastern Rumelian Province. When the commission completed its investigation in the Rhodopes and returned to Istanbul to write its final report at the end of August, the Berlin Conference was not functioning anymore. The commissioners could not agree unanimously on the content of the final report. The English, French, Italian, and Turkish commissioners together wrote a report and presented it to their ambassadors individually.

Although the southern Rhodopes were given back to the Ottomans by the Berlin Treaty, the northern Rhodopes were still left for the Bulgarians. Therefore Muslim refugees and inhabitants of the Rhodopes kept their position, did not recognize the Eastern Rumelian government, and did not give up their arms. In early August, according to a dispatch from Istanbul to Reuter's, the Russians ordered the Rhodope Muslim insurgents to evacuate the territory within ten days or be attacked. Two leaders of the resistance went to Istanbul to consult with Ambassador Layard. Evacuation of the Rhodopes was not expected.[65] The fighting continued in August and September 1878.

The European Commission established by the Berlin Conference, its work, and its report did not bring any help to the refugees and to the population of the Rhodope area. Dr. Cullen, a medical man who worked for the Red Cross during the war, reported on November 6, 1878, that none of the 150,000 refugees of the area had returned to their homes since the commissioners had visited the Rhodopes. In the district of Daridere thousands of refugees were crowded together in the last stage of misery and want. Many of them would perish in the winter of 1878–79.[66] Yet the survivors managed on their own in their de facto autonomous status for years. After the Balkan Wars and World War I they even established their own governments, although they did not last long.

NOTES

1. Bilal Şimşir, "The Turkish Muslim Population of the Civilian Administrative Organization of Bulgaria and the Provinces of Danube and Adrianople during the Russo-Turkish War in 1877–1878," 87 (from D. G. Anuchin, "V. A. Cherkasskii i grazhdanskoe upravlenie v Bolgarii 1877–1878," *Russkaia Starina* 84 [St. Petersburg, 1895]: 31).
2. On the treatment and suffering of the Turks and Muslims of the Balkans during and after the Ottoman-Russian War of 1877–78, see Ömer Turan, *The Turkish Minority in Bulgaria (1878–1908)*; Bilal N. Şimşir, ed., *Turkish Migrations from the Balkans (Documents)*; Zeynep Kerman, trans., *Rusların Asya'da ve Rumeli'de Yaptıkları Mezalim*; Nedim İpek, *Rumeli'den Anadolu'ya Türk Göçleri, 1877–1890*; and Hüseyin Raci Efendi, *Zağra Müftüsünün Hatıraları*. For the suffering of the Jews during the war, see Zvi Keren, "The Fate of the Jewish Communities of Kazanlık and Eski-Zağra in the 1877/78 War."
3. For the Cossacks, see Philip Longworth, *The Cossacks*.
4. National Archives of the United Kingdom (formerly Public Record Office), Parliamentary Papers (PP), 1877, 92: 490.
5. PP, 1878, 81:105–6.
6. PP, 1877, 92:513–14.
7. For the names of the journalists, see Kerman, *Rusların Asya'da ve Rumeli'de Yaptıkları Mezalim*, 24–25; for the names of their journals, see Şimşir, *Turkish Migrations from the Balkans (Documents)*, 1:151.
8. National Archives of the United Kingdom (formerly Public Record Office), Con-

fidential Prints (CP), 1878, FO 881/3651, Report by Consul Blunt on the Effect of the Russian Invasion of Roumelia, dated December 30, 1877.

9. For Pomak identity and history and Bulgarization and Christianization campaigns in the nineteenth century and twentieth century, see Ömer Turan, "Pomaks, Their Past & Present"; Hüseyin Memişoğlu, *Pomak Türklerinin Tarihi Geçmişinden Sayfalar.*

10. There are not many sources on the resistance in the Rhodope Mountains. For the Turkish classic about that Muslim resistance and the other Muslim resistances in the Rhodopes in the following years, see Tevfik Bıyıklıoğlu, *Trakya'da Milli Mücadele*; and Ömer Turan, "Rodoplarda 1878 Türk-Pomak Direnişi ve Rodop Komisyonu Raporu."

11. PP, 1878, 81:794.

12. PP, 1878, 81:810.

13. "The Musulman Rising in Thrace," *Levant Herald*, April 25, 1878.

14. *Turquie*, April 25, 1878.

15. PP, 1878, 82:580–81.

16. PP, 1878, 81:828.

17. Bıyıklıoğlu, *Trakya'da Milli Mücadele*, 1:19.

18. PP, 1878, 81:830–31.

19. Bıyıklıoğlu, *Trakya'da Milli Mücadele*, 1:22–23.

20. National Archives of the United Kingdom (formerly Public Record Office), Foreign Office Archives, London (FO), FO 358/4, 258 (Confidential/3624).

21. FO 78, No.358/5, 708–9 (Confidential/3634).

22. PP, 1878, 81:879–80.

23. PP, 1878, 81:865–70. I listed the names of the villages as they were written in the document in French.

24. PP, 1878, 81:828.

25. PP, 1878, 81:887–88.

26. PP, 1878, 81:889.

27. PP, 1878, 81:882.

28. PP, 1878, 81:884.

29. Bıyıklıoğlu, *Trakya'da Milli Mücadele*, 1:21. On Ahmet Ağa Tamraslijata, see Bernard Lory, "Ahmed aga Tamraslijata: The Last Derebey of the Rhodopes."

30. PP, 1878, 81:866.

31. PP, 1878, 81:897.

32. PP, 1878, 81:939.

33. PP, 1878, 81:879.

34. PP, 1878, 81:897–939.

35. PP, 1878, 81:944.

36. For the text of the resolution, see PP, 1878, 81:879. This commission was named differently in the documents. Sometimes it was called the European Commission, sometimes the International Commission, and sometimes the Rhodope Commission.

37. PP, 1878, 81:944–45.

38. PP, 1878, 81:945–46, 82:510–11.

39. PP, 1878, 82:510.

40. PP, 1878, 82:514–16.
41. PP, 1878, 82:516–21.
42. PP, 1878, 82:520–22.
43. PP, 1878, 82:522–31.
44. Ibid.
45. PP, 1878, 82:531–36.
46. PP, 1878, 81:952–56.
47. PP, 1878, 82:537–55.
48. PP, 1878, 82:555–58.
49. PP, 1878, 82:558–81.
50. PP, 1878, 82:581.
51. PP, 1878, 82:582–86.
52. PP, 1878, 82:591–97.
53. PP, 1878, 82:598–99.
54. PP, 1878, 82:599–605.
55. PP, 1878, 82:611–12.
56. PP, 1878, 82:613.
57. Ibid.
58. PP, 1878, 82:614.
59. Ibid.
60. PP, 1878, 82:615–16.
61. PP, 1878, 82:617–18.
62. PP, 1878, 82:618–19.
63. PP, 1878, 82:588–91.
64. PP, 1878, 82:619.
65. "The Insurgents in Roumelia," *New York Times*, August 6, 1878.
66. PP, 1878–79, 71:144.

Conclusion

On the Road Back from Berlin

Frederick F. Anscombe

Convention dictates that surveys of late Ottoman history conform to a model of distinct periods separated by narrative-changing events: the rise and fall of the Nizam-i Cedid (1792–1806); irreversible modernization under Sultan Mahmud II starting with abolition of the janissaries (1826); wider-ranging reformism in the Tanzimat period bookended by the Hatt-i Şerif of 1839 and the proclamation of the constitution in 1876; the reaction resulting from the accession of Sultan Abdülhamid II and military defeat by Russia (1876–78); and the Young Turk Revolution (1908).[1] This conventional presentation merits fresh consideration, because it tends to highlight change at the cost of underplaying significant continuities from one "era" to the next, except perhaps to aver an Ottoman desire to change in emulation of Christian Europe throughout most of the period. Some "turning points," notably the one in 1839, did bring meaningful change to the basic patterns and trajectory of Ottoman political life, but others mattered less than is usually portrayed. If the 1876–78 period may serve as an example, it is obvious that the Treaty of Berlin confirmed great territorial losses for the empire and thus harmed future Ottoman geographic cohesion; particularly in political affairs, however, the war's end in many respects brought continuity or, if a turning point it must be, then reversion back to patterns seen earlier in the nineteenth century.

Such an assertion does not deny new "facts on the ground" created by the war and its settlement, including not only the loss of territory and Christian populations but also the social upheaval caused by the large numbers of Muslims who died or became refugees. The argument presented here focuses rather on the Ottoman practice of politics pre- and post-Berlin and considers four issues related to the "reaction" commonly thought to have characterized Abdülhamid's reign after 1878: the

Islamization of imperial politics; the shift, seen at least in the sultan's palace, from liberalizing Westernization to "Oriental" despotism; the transfer of authority from the open, public bureaucracy, headed by the Sublime Porte, to the closed, private recesses of Yıldız Palace; and the rise to preeminence of ethnicity as the marker of identity among the Ottoman population. This last issue concerns the spread of mass political agendas of ethnic-national separatism, which reflects the perceived importance of ethnic conflict in triggering the war with Russia, the validation of nationalism at Berlin, and Abdülhamid's determination to suppress nationalist movements. The durability of these four issues derives primarily from understandable, well-entrenched conceptions of the period commonly termed "the reform era" (1826–78) that emphasize parallels between the Ottoman experience and those of Christian European states such as Britain and France rather than stress the correspondence of innovation to the Ottoman perception of imperial needs.[2] When the period of armed conflict in 1875–78 and the Treaty of Berlin are situated in their Ottoman environment, it becomes clearer that they did not affect political practice as much as believed, because they only confirmed rather than altered the fundamental goal of reform in the empire: strengthening the state's ability to defend itself against Christian European powers.

THE OTTOMAN REFORM ERA

Perceptions of 1878 as a fundamental turning point in Ottoman history derive from a Eurocentric reading of the half-century from Mahmud II's dissolution of the janissary corps to the proclamation of the constitution (1826–76). Christian Europe was the enemy against whom reform was targeted; according to the dominant view, however, the state in the latter part of Mahmud's reign committed itself irrevocably to modernizing reforms that were to remake the empire along Western lines, a process that really took shape with the Tanzimat inaugurated by the proclamation of the Hatt-i Şerif of Gülhane in 1839. The Tanzimat period saw the expansion of reform from the focus on professionalization of the imperial military, financial, and administrative services of Mahmud's time to a much broader program of remaking state and society. Carter Findley, in a concise summary of the Tanzimat, picked out the leading themes of transformations seen in the period: legislation, education and elite formation, expansion of government, intercommunal relations, and the political process itself.[3] Most accounts apparently accept that the model followed by the key reformers (Sultan Mahmud II himself and the *paşa*s of the Tanzimat: Mustafa Reşid, Fuad, Ali, and Midhat) was fundamentally Western. It offered a regimen of Europeanization based upon secularization, liberalization (with equality of Muslim and non-Muslim providing the touchstone), democratization (culminating in the constitution), and rationalization (a nicely adaptable term that suggests standardization but also depersonalization, such as the rule of a law in whose eyes all citizens are equal and advancement based upon talent rather than connections). As one standard text puts it, "westernization, secularism, and centralization remained enshrined in the pantheon of Ottoman elitist values throughout most of the century [of reforms]."[4]

Symbolic of the close association of reform with Western states is the stress laid upon exposure to European practice experienced by Mustafa Reşid (formerly a diplomat in Paris and London) and Fuad and Ali (products of the new Ottoman Foreign Office). Consonant with this notion is the belief that the reformers worked closely with the ambassadors of European countries such as France and particularly Britain, who advised on the design and implementation of measures.[5] The emphasis in such accounts has shifted somewhat in recent years, with less admiration addressed to the Western model-setters and more given to the Ottoman originators of ideas echoing developments in Christian Europe, but the belief survives that the urban and educated parts of Ottoman society desired to be, and succeeded in becoming, "modern Europeans." To quote from a well-regarded history of the Middle East: "Behind these guiding ideas [of reform] there lay another one, that of Europe as the exemplar of modern civilization and of the Ottoman Empire as its partner."[6]

While it would be a serious mistake to dismiss everything in the pattern described as wrong, portrayals of the Mahmud II/Tanzimat reform period commonly focus attention upon the same select trees at the expense of overlooking the forest. The jump from noting the appearance of European-style clothes (army uniforms and bureaucrats' frock coats), architecture (Dolmabahçe palace), or arts (Giuseppe Donizetti) in Istanbul to asserting an Ottoman desire for Westernization covers a greater distance than many assume — no one should confuse Sultan Abdülhamid's well-known weakness for mystery stories with a longing to remake the empire in Christian Europe's image. The popularity of Eastern motifs in Western societies (Wolfgang Amadeus Mozart in *alla turca* mode, the Royal Pavilion in Brighton, zouave uniforms in European and American armies, and fezzes worn by lounging Englishmen "in mufti" and Masonic Shriners) likewise connoted awareness but hardly a desire to become "Oriental," any more than the rise (halted abruptly after 1990) of Russian studies in North Atlantic Treaty Organization member countries during the Cold War betrayed an identification with Sovietization or vaudeville's and

Hollywood's peculiar penchant for blackface minstrelsy in the first half of the twentieth century marked a longing to become African American. All sectors of Ottoman society, most emphatically including the political elite, were aware of Europe and its power. The Ottoman ruling class could ill afford to be deaf to ambassadors' advice, any more than it could ignore their warnings and threats, but this does not mean that such counsel was as welcome as the ambassadors (and subsequent historians) believed it to be. In order to appreciate this fact, it is necessary to remember the fundamental purpose of Ottoman reform efforts: strengthening the empire's capacity to defend itself against the existential threat posed by a historically hostile and increasingly powerful Christian Europe.

Mahmud's destruction of the janissary corps was triggered but not caused by the failure to crush the Greek revolt that erupted in 1821; it was rather the culmination of growing desperation resulting from a string of military defeats suffered at Christian European hands. The empire lost its 1768–74, 1787–92, and 1806–12 wars with Russia, its 1787–91 struggle with Habsburg Austria, and in practice its 1798–1801 conflict with France; despite suffering terrible human and economic damage, the empire limited territorial losses thanks to other pressures upon the victors (especially Austria, which returned Belgrade in the Peace of Sistova) and alliance with more effective powers (Egypt was "regained" in 1801 largely through British efforts). Ottoman arms could not protect even the Holy Cities in the Hijaz, which fell into Wahhabi hands until Mehmed Ali staged a reconquest in 1813. In comparison to this record of futility, the failure to crush Christian rebels in Belgrade and the Morea immediately was lamentable but not critical (and in both cases the revolts eventually succeeded only due to Russian and, in the Morea, also British and French intervention). Mahmud II's reforms, much like Selim III's Nizam-i Cedid of 1792–1806, aimed only to correct this glaring military inferiority. The Tanzimat merely took a more holistic approach to achieving a very similar ultimate goal: preserving the state's independence and territorial integrity in the face of threats from Europe. Insofar as they have any validity, the panoply of themes that provide structure to many accounts of the reform era (secularization, liberalization, Westernization) could only be secondary to the main purpose. This clarity of design should become evident through closer attention to what the Hatt-i Şerif of Gülhane actually declared, rather than the meaning read into it by contemporary Western and subsequent commentators.

In his Gülhane decree Sultan Abdülmecid addressed the main unresolved problems that he inherited from Mahmud II, all concerned with the effort at self-strengthening undertaken by the imperiled state. The Tanzimat literally were measures to reform, reshape, and bring order to three areas critical to self-defense where Mahmud had bungled as imperial commander: protection of life, liberty, and property (an issue to which we will return); the orderly assessment and collection of taxes; and the sustainable recruitment and retention of men for the military. The last of these carried the most obvious weight in imperial defense. Mahmud had created the modern conscript army, but its terms of service were extremely harsh and the burden of manning it fell overwhelmingly on the Turkish-speaking population of Anatolia and the Balkans. It should have been no surprise that such an army failed to perform well against equally trained but better-officered forces fielded by Russia and the province of Egypt. The Tanzimat succeeded in improving army morale and performance by lightening the terms of service and spreading them more evenly across the Muslim population of the empire.[7]

An even more pressing need addressed by the Tanzimat, however, was the problem of paying for the modern military, which consumed far more than half the state budget at the end of Mahmud's reign.[8] Mahmud had failed to correct any of the weaknesses in a revenue system that depended upon tax-farming, but after 1839 the state introduced serious measures designed to streamline both the assessment and collection of taxes. Steps introduced included census and cadastral surveys, appointment of salaried provincial tax collectors to bypass tax-farmers, and the consolidation of the wide array of noncanonic traditional levies into a single personal tax assessed according to each person's measurable wealth.[9] Although these reforms were difficult and time-consuming to implement and succeeded only partially in eliminating the inefficiencies and inequities that had beset the state's revenue system, the increasing rationalization of tax-collecting and troop-raising systems made possible the creation of a truly modern military in the latter half of the nineteenth century. These measures, generated in response to the recognized needs of the state rather than any concern with secularization, liberalization (other than promoting the rule of law), Muslim-Christian equality, or Westernization, constituted the Tanzimat-i Hayriyye (beneficent measures to bring order) introduced into central and provincial administration that gave the era its name and defining character.[10]

With recognition of the fundamental purpose of reform, it becomes easier to see that the Treaty of Berlin, marking yet another devastating defeat at the hands of Russia and the subsequent seizure of territory by all major powers but Germany and minor states such as Serbia and Greece, did not automatically trigger a radical reorientation of Ottoman politics. It is the faulty picture of the Ottoman Empire following a European path that explains the impression that 1878 marked a turning point away from the Western course of modernization. Westernization did not end, because it had never really started. Abdülhamid II, the supposedly terrible, reactionary sultan, similarly did not undo decades of secularization by adopting an Islamist orientation, because the state to be saved by rapid reform had remained fundamentally Muslim throughout the preceding decades. Reform programs had always been devised under pressure and were indeed "top-down." Abdülhamid's despotism simply transferred back to the palace the autocracy that Mahmud II had developed to its highest form and the *paşa*s of the Tanzimat also employed. Finally, the real threat to continuation of the empire did not lie in ethnic nationalism within its borders but, as before, in the designs of European states that felt much freer to attack a non-Christian empire than any other "real" member of the Concert of Europe.[11]

WESTERNIZATION

In light of European powers' attitudes toward the Ottoman Empire, it would be helpful to preface further discussion of the nature of the Ottoman state by considering the problem of what the "Westernization" often mentioned in accounts might have meant. It is important in this regard to give definition to the Eastern question. The question was less "how to save the empire" than "how to manage its dissolution without causing a general European crisis." The relationship between Christian Europe and the empire remained fundamentally oppositional: all major states, including Italy, made war on the empire or took territory except Germany — and Bismarck hardly showed much interest in Istanbul's wishes while orchestrating the carve-up at Berlin. What attraction could "Westernization" hold for the empire?

If Westernization carried an essentially political meaning, involving bureaucratic development and rationalization of state affairs, then it happened in Christian Europe only a few decades before it reached Istanbul. While Eastern question–flavored perceptions of the Ottoman state as "ramshackle" persist, such a dismissal overlooks the fact that every state and empire in Europe at the end of the eighteenth century was similarly ramshackle by modern standards. In political and state development as in military affairs (and the two were very closely related), the French Revolution and the Napoleonic period broke the old model and set precedents that the rest of Europe would chase for the remainder of the nineteenth century. Each European regime saw the vital necessity of increasing state power in line with its neighbors, but each also devised its own processes and structures to make more efficient use of resources. The Ottoman state did the same after 1839; as this process occurred in rapid succession in Christian Europe and then the Ottoman Empire, it seems sensible to see modernization in both east and west as a drive for efficiency rather than a process of becoming "Western."

If Westernization is understood in the more likely sense of a broader cultural outlook, then it is an even less comfortable description of the Ottoman reform era, in regard to no less important a concept than secularization. Just as the Ottoman Empire remained a Muslim state until its collapse, the European powers remained self-consciously Christian well into the twentieth century and pressed consistently for the betterment of specifically Christian communities in the empire. Secularism, understood as the divorce of religion from public affairs, was no more the goal of European states than it was of the Ottoman Empire, and the concept did not influence their advice to the government in Istanbul any more than it shaped their own domestic agendas. They pushed for de-Islamization of Ottoman law and administration, of course, but they also demanded that the Ottoman state formally recognize and protect the autonomy of non-Muslim religious communities, resulting in institutionalization of the *millet* system.[12] The clear linkage drawn today between modernization and secularization did not exist in any meaningful way in the Tanzimat era; modernization in both Christian Europe and the Ottoman Empire aimed not at erasure of religion but rather at the strengthening of the state along the lines of the military and revenue promises made in the Gülhane decree. It should perhaps be considered tangential to this process of modernization, therefore, that European powers pushed the interests of Ottoman Christians and the empire defended the effective supremacy of Muslims.

In both cases, the European and the Ottoman, histories of the nineteenth century that have downplayed the allegiance to religious identity shown by states have consistently overlooked the continued strength of religion exhibited by the wider populations in all states from Britain to Russia to the Ottoman Empire.[13] The eclipse of religious themes in historiography can be explained in part by present-day attitudes to faith and in part by the rise of nationalism, the new tool most heavily used by regimes to make the growing burdensomeness and intrusiveness of the state tolerable for their populations as they sought to strengthen their domestic authority and military power. In most cases, nationalism was a largely state-fostered ideology, but at its strongest it did not clash with the population's religious beliefs.[14] The deep roots of Russian identity in Orthodoxy are well known, of course, but Britain in the nineteenth century still identified closely with the Church of England. Real Catholic emancipation was granted only in 1829, and Benjamin Disraeli (who could enter Parliament, let alone become prime minister, only because of his baptism into the Anglican church at age twelve) was vilified on religious grounds, being accused of supporting the Ottoman Empire in the 1870s because he was really a Jew.[15] The citizenry of France, the other leading liberal power, was hardly consistently better disposed toward Jews, as the Dreyfus Affair of 1894 showed, and North Africans who did not distance themselves from Islam had little hope of recognition as "évolués."[16] Among Germans the power of religion was strong enough to trigger (Protestant) Bismarck's *Kulturkampf* against the autonomy of Catholic institutions and clergy in regions recently incorporated into the new German Empire in the 1870s — a struggle that Bismarck did not clearly win.

The *Kulturkampf* shows best where the growth of the (nation-)state could clash with religious bodies: a key point of the struggle was control over institutions devoted to training and caring for the population, especially those involved in education, which the state needed to use in building national identity. In most cases, however, the modernizing state attempted simply to co-opt the religious authorities (as German states had already done with the Protestant churches but could not easily do with the Catholic hierarchy headquartered abroad) rather than choosing the far riskier approach of challenging them directly. From the nineteenth to the twentieth centuries all European governments (with the partial exception of France after 1905, where the excesses of the Dreyfus Affair created an anticlerical backlash) deepened the relationship between church and state by embedding religious institutions in the "Establishment." This relationship became sufficiently unequal to be termed "secularism" only with the tremendous boost to state power triggered by the cataclysmic decades after 1914 — a period of such shocking brutality that belief in an all-powerful and all-caring God could not survive unscathed — and the concomitant rise of militantly materialist ideologies such as communism.

Christianity remained a fundamental element of European culture, identity, and politics, so the portrayal of Ottoman reform as a broad process of Westernization appears even less appropriate than in the circumscribed area of state development. The problem of intent in reform also raises anew the question of how much reconsideration of legitimacy measures, or "what the state stood for," after 1878 was likely or needed, especially in possible rethinking of the state's ideological basis.

ISLAMIZATION

Much of the negative image of changes ensuing from the Peace Treaty of Berlin is difficult to separate from the persona of Sultan Abdülhamid II, who presided over the empire for three decades after the peace and whose reputation has long been distinctly sour. In recent years historians have treated Abdülhamid in more balanced fashion, although such revision frequently involves less a reconsideration of his reputation as a reactionary (the Red Sultan who instigated massacres of Christian Armenians and the reclusive autocrat) than a recognition that he did surprisingly well in furthering reform, given the adverse circumstances in which the empire found itself after 1878.[17] There is nothing to be gained from attempting here a more actively sympathetic portrayal of Abdülhamid, who certainly was neither liberal democrat nor man of the people. The focus remains on the basic continuity with the more-admired Tanzimat period, which has been subjected to less revisionism than Abdülhamid's reign but which provides the contrasting example against which his less pleasant characteristics are implicitly measured. Most such comparison in which he fares poorly bears some relationship to his championing of Islam.

Where continuities have now been recognized from the Tanzimat into Abdülhamid's time, they derive from the last two promises of the Gülhane edict, those concerning most clearly the mechanics of the state's efforts to rebuild its strength against external threats and internal challenges. Certainly under Abdülhamid many of the Tanzimat themes highlighted by Findley (such as education and elite formation and the growth of government) continued unabated or even accelerated. The apparent discontinuities from one period to the next derive from failing to recognize the importance of, and the real audience for, the decree's less mechanistic but more moral or ideological first promise: security of life, property, and honor. Accounts of the reform era almost invariably portray this promise as a bid for support from liberal Western states such as Britain in the empire's struggle to contain its rebellious governor of Egypt, Mehmed Ali Paşa. From this idea springs the assumption that the edict declared the legal equality of all Ottoman subjects, thus couching the bid for European support in a liberalizing, secularizing act designed to appeal to the empire's Christians. If the Tanzimat began with the leveling of a religiously justified hierarchy, then Abdülhamid's reassertion of Islam as a guiding political principle marked a definite end to that period. The problem with this view is that the Gülhane promise actually targeted the Muslim population of the empire more than the Great Powers or the non-Muslims in the population.

Mahmud II was a disastrous sultan, and his shortcomings as a military and fiscal reformer have already been noted briefly; most severe, however, was the damage he did to popular support for the dynasty and to the willingness of its subjects to make sacrifices in its defense. Although he is known to have viewed Christians with deep suspicion, especially the "Greek" Orthodox whose patriarch of Constantinople was killed in 1821 following the outbreaks of revolts in the Morea and the Danubian Principalities, it was Ottoman Muslims who suffered most from unexpected and arbitrary despoliation and death at the hands of the sultan's men. This despotic mode of rule first triggered Mehmed Ali's revolt and then left the throne vulnerable to the Egyptian governor, because the Muslim population that provided the dynasty with its core support would not rush to defend it against a seemingly more upright, more effective Muslim leader. Transitory European Christian support by itself would not secure the state, and whatever military and financial improvements were promised in the Gülhane decree would remain only theoretical reforms, if the population that supplied troops for the army and most of the regime's income remained disaffected.[18]

Gülhane's first purpose was to heal the rift between the state and the Muslim population upon which it depended, and both the men of the Tanzimat and Sultan Abdülhamid II knew this; at no time after 1839 would Ottoman statesmen carelessly cast the Muslim identity of the state into doubt. Statements to the effect that European models shaped reforms and that modernizing moves established equality between Muslims and non-Muslims, thereby furthering secularization, are still routine but miss the point of efforts to change.[19] Nowhere is the ideology of the state more readily revealed than in the area of law, which was of fundamental importance to any self-consciously Islamic regime. Findley rightly stressed legal reform as the first theme of the Tanzimat, but the standard narrative of the period too readily encourages the assumption that man-made legislation must have meant breaking free from the state's roots in supposedly hidebound religious law. This was not the case. Throughout Ottoman history "man-made" legislation (*kanun*: regulation by sultanic decree) inevitably formed a significant part of the empire's legal structure, made necessary by the significant non-Muslim population that could not follow much of the law of a religion to which it did not adhere. But there is also no doubt that such legislation was legitimated by the notion that it did not contravene Sharia. Tanzimat-era legal reform conformed fully to that deeply entrenched model, at least until the declaration of equality before the law of all Ottoman subjects in 1856 (see the discussion of the Reform Decree below), and after 1856 the state still adhered to that established practice as far as circumstances permitted.

This continuity of consciously Islamic legal practice can be seen in the new penal law code issued by the state in 1840, for example, which modern accounts frequently describe as based upon French law, as confirming the equality before the law of Muslims and non-Muslims and by implication as superseding all extant Ottoman penal law and its application.[20] The code, however, was much more limited in scope than is usually acknowledged, being designed primarily to enact formally some of the main promises of the Gülhane decree and to regulate the power of the social and especially political elite by confirming that the life, property, and honor of all subjects, no matter how low, were protected against all others, no matter how lofty, except where a penalty was justified by court procedure. To prevent the perversion of justice, bribery and other forms of "corruption" were made punishable crimes. And, of course, everyone must pay taxes. The code clearly recognized hierarchy and made no effort to erase inequality from society. Nothing in these confirmations and additions to the established practice of either *kanun* or *siyaset* (the sultan's regulation of his servants appointed to positions of power) clearly contravened Sharia, moreover, a fact stressed in the code itself.[21] This pattern continued in Tanzimat-era legislation concerning areas in which there was already an established Ottoman Sharia-*kanun* code of practice, culminating in the Mecelle, the civil code explicitly based upon Hanafi interpretation.[22]

In issuing the Mecelle, the state did act with some audacity in defining punishments for crimes, mandating the application of the less severe punishments deemed legitimate by Hanafi opinion, but it was only in 1917 that Istanbul sharply limited the applicability of Sharia per se. The Ottoman state thus maintained Islamic law as much as possible under conditions that required unprecedented strengthening of the state and extension of its reach in society, coupled with the need to defend against European efforts to promote the interests of non-Muslims. This was no drive to secularize. Even the limited innovation involved in mandating which Hanafi interpretations to use resulted from the state's newfound need to control more closely the application of law, as well as the actions of all state officials traditionally regulated by *siyaset*, in order to prevent the renewal of the turmoil seen in the provinces during the pre-Tanzimat period. Integral to this need for control was the wish to minimize opportunities for incidents involving non-Muslims that could create openings for Christian European states to interfere. Illustrative of the power of European pressure, and of the reasons why the state saw a clear interest in exercising such control over legal affairs traditionally recognized as wholly Islamic, was the convoluted matter of policing conversion between Islam and Christianity.

In the early Tanzimat period there was an apparent rise of forced conversion to Islam, especially targeting Christians, carried out ad hoc at the local level in the provinces. If true, this probably resulted from a wave of religious angst among Ottoman Muslims who had grown sensitive to threats to the Islamic state through the experience of futile wars against foreign powers and Christian rebels as well as perceived injustices wrought by the state itself. This concern for religion was primarily directed against European protégés among Ottoman non-Muslims. Forced conversions and other signs of inequality for Christians upset the European powers, and they pressed Istanbul vigorously to protect Christians from such efforts and to stop all punishment of Muslims who (re)converted to Christianity. The Ottoman regime had to bow to foreign demands, repeatedly reminding Muslims that "there is no compulsion in religion" and in many cases requiring that cases of apostasy be decided in Istanbul. The masterful stroke in Istanbul's handling of competing external and internal pressures came in the transfer of accused apostates to the capital: their guards apparently allowed the prisoners ample opportunity to escape custody before reaching Istanbul, where a trial would arouse both domestic and foreign passions.[23] This neat solution to a delicate problem, preserving the correct position of the Islamic state in the eyes of the majority of the population and yet deflecting the anger of Christian powers abroad, would not have been possible without Istanbul's assertion of tighter control over legal procedure and punishment, the focus of "secularizing" law reform in the Tanzimat period.

Arrogation to the capital of control over the handling of issues that could provoke intense foreign interest also marks the Reform Decree/ Islahat Fermanı of 1856, the first real tampering with the Islamic principles underpinning law, state, and society. Even this measure, however, must be seen not as an effort to secularize and Westernize but rather the opposite, as a gamble thought worth taking in order to preserve the Islamic Ottoman state's independence against Christian Europe.[24] Sultan Abdülmecid issued the decree as a clear quid pro quo for the promises made immediately thereafter by the European powers in the Peace of Paris. Most importantly for Istanbul, the empire was admitted to the Concert of Europe and to legal equality with Christian states in (European) international law. Furthermore, it gained a guarantee of territorial integrity, strengthened subsequently in a separate agreement among Britain, France, and Austria that any infraction would be a *casus belli*. The Treaty of Paris also lessened the practical Russian threat by mandating the demilitarization of the Black Sea. Preservation of independence and territorial integrity had been the fundamental goal of all major reform efforts since the Nizam-i Cedid, so Istanbul was willing to pay a significant price for these assurances. The Reform Decree provided what the Ottomans' Christian allies in the Crimean War demanded: legal equality with Muslims for non-Muslims and the formal recognition of *millet* privileges. Other measures, such as the assertion of the sultan's right to decide on the building of new places of worship for non-Muslims, were not new, not only because they echoed the principle already seen in measures such as the guidance of handling conversion disputes but also because the sultan had always had such rights in managing non-Muslim communal affairs.[25]

In applying the promised equalization of Muslims and non-Muslims, however, the Tanzimat reformers attempted to heed the wishes of the Muslim population and keep intact the Islamic identity of the state as much as possible without endangering the gains won from Christian Europe. Under continuing foreign pressure, for example, the government introduced another penal code in 1858 and a commercial code in 1861 that drew upon French law, but only after the failure of an attempt to create an easily comprehensible guide to Hanafi *fiqh* (jurisprudence) that would make Ottoman law less mysterious to litigants, not only foreign and domestic non-Muslims but also Muslims who could understand Turkish but not Arabic. This effort to make Hanafi law open and predictable for all led eventually to the codification of the Mecelle.[26] The military, a main target of the Tanzimat, remained thoroughly Muslim despite the provision to conscript non-Muslims contained in the Reform Decree. This preservation of the state's defense forces as a fundamentally Muslim institution was only right in the eyes of stalwarts of the reform movement.[27]

Further indications of the continuing strength of Islamic identity in both state and society appear in two features always profiled highly in the discussions of the last decade of the Tanzimat period: the activities of the Young Ottoman opposition group and the introduction of the constitution in 1876. Historical accounts of the Young Ottomans acknowledge readily that their protests were couched in Islamic terms, but the stress usually falls upon the "liberal" ideas that the group generally espoused, including notably constitutionalism.[28] While this also is not factually

wrong, such a rendering glosses over a basic motive driving the Young Ottomans and also touching a significant part of the population, which gave
the group more impact than small dissident factions expatriated to distant
countries normally enjoyed. The Young Ottomans criticized the oligarchy
of Tanzimat reformers not for their despotic rule per se, but because they
excused autocracy on the grounds of strengthening the state against Christian threats but then repeatedly failed to stand up for Muslim interests
against European pressure in Syria, in Crete, and in the western Balkans.[29]
Constitutionalism offered the means to force the oligarchs to consider the
views of the wider Muslim population before deciding the regime's stance
on sensitive issues regarding Europe and Ottoman Christian affairs.

It was initially such Muslim popular pressure that led to the issue of
the constitution in 1876, and this document that retrospectively strikes
so many as evidence of Western influence confirms at its start that the
Ottoman Empire was an Islamic state. Facing a crisis that could well result in another catastrophic war with Russia and possibly other European
powers, the insecure and isolated regime hoped to use the constitution to
rally the active support of the population that most mattered to survival
of the state. Whether or not to give a voice to non-Muslims in the parliament was a matter of intense debate in the clique led by Midhat Paşa that
pushed the several sultans of 1876 to issue the constitution. The issue was
decided only by Midhat's belief that barring non-Muslims would rob the
constitution of any symbolic force in massaging tense relations with the
Christian powers.[30] Midhat, who harbored no delusions that even European champions of liberalism were trustworthy friends of the Ottoman
Empire, had eminently practical reasons for choosing the form of constitutionalism that he did.[31]

Although Abdülhamid II prorogued parliament when it became clear
that the war with Russia had been lost, it was only natural that he continued to act as described in the constitution, as "Supreme Caliph, [who] is
the Protector of the Muslim religion."[32] The effective loss of much of the
Balkan Christian population sealed by the Treaty of Berlin and, just as
importantly, the deflation of whatever dreams remained that any European power was disposed to aid the empire in accordance with the Paris
agreements removed much of the incentive to maintain only relatively
discretely the Muslim nature of the state that had existed since 1856. With
a heavy preponderance of Muslims in the population under his authority, any policy that failed to use this potential means of maintaining active loyalty would have been foolhardy. Whoever wished to engineer
the continued strengthening of the state, after all, had to find renewed

ideological justification following the Tanzimat program's evident failure to enable the empire to defend its territory and independence against foreign threats. The resurrection of openness in the Muslim direction of politics succeeded because it was not a radical change that could encourage popular confusion and disorientation but rather a recommitment to a long-standing ideal.

Confirming this recognition of such fundamental continuity between the Tanzimat and Hamidian worldviews are the various hints that many of the features noted as evidence of secularization and Westernization in the Tanzimat could still be found in the later "reactionary" Islamizing period. Abdülhamid suspended the constitution, but he did not annul it, any more than he annulled the bulk of the Tanzimat's modernizing achievements noted by Findley. Also much in line with the predicament of Tanzimat statesmen, Abdülhamid's regime could hardly afford to distance itself from the major Christian states but rather showed renewed commitment to attempting to play the European powers against each other, regardless of the heightened feeling that none of them could be trusted.[33] According to one analysis submitted to Abdülhamid in the early 1880s, for example, London had designs upon the entire stretch of land from Basra to Egypt, as its occupation of the latter territory proved. Britain's aggressiveness derived from its concerns about the security of India, the territory that made Britain anything more than a third-rate power, according to the analysis. Yet Istanbul had to court rather than confront London: it was the only power capable of keeping Russian designs in check. It also would be best positioned to prevent further seizures of land by the French, who had recently taken Tunisia.[34] Such an attitude speaks of a realism that ought to be detectable in earlier reformers still commonly portrayed as enamored of the West.

SULTANISM AND NATIONALISM

In addition to the more open avowal of the Islamic nature of the state, two features of post-Berlin politics in the Ottoman empire deserve review here: the transfer of power from the bureaucracy to the palace and the growth of nationalism among the Ottoman population. Of these two issues, the first is easier to address briefly.

To say that power rested with the bureaucracy during the Tanzimat seems misleading, at the least, because it conflates the undoubted growth of the bureaucracy with the leading role in determining reform played by the Sublime Porte/Grand Vizierate. The Ottoman Empire had a long tradition, dating back at least to the mid-seventeenth century, of powerful grand viziers wielding the day-to-day power in imperial affairs, and the Tanzimat marked another period of such vizierial vigor. Also strongly reminiscent of earlier periods was the vital importance of personal connections (*intisab*) in gaining promotion in the administrative ranks (the bureaucracy). The three leading "Men of the Tanzimat," Mustafa Reşid, Fuad, and Ali Paşas, all gained access to power as clients of elder statesmen and, once in power, built their own political households in the upper echelons of the bureaucracy. The "bureaucracy" itself held no independent power: it was the tool used to implement decisions made by its autocratic head — as many surveys of the Tanzimat note, reform was "from the top down." This description fits not only the imperial picture of state-over-society but also the nature of the state itself. The fact that the decisive voice in ordering the policies to be executed by the bureaucracy shifted from the Porte to the palace, from one seat of illiberalism to another, changed more in appearance than in practice. That the sultan implemented his Islamic initiatives in part through nonofficial channels did mark an innovative practice, but the burden of administration remained firmly in the hands of the bureaucracy, which indeed grew in size under Abdülhamid.

Of all the persistent notions about the Ottoman reform era and especially about the decades after the Treaty of Berlin, perhaps none is as entrenched as the idea that nationalism became an intractable and indeed mortal threat to the survival of the empire. A similar assumption used to reign over the field of Habsburg history but now has been seriously challenged, and a similar skepticism seems fully merited in considering the history of the late Ottoman Empire, a country always administered within a religious rather than ethnic frame of reference.[35] It was World War I, a catastrophic conflict that traumatized the "winners" and destroyed all the major states in the losing alliance (as well as one of the winners' original comrades in arms), that broke the Ottoman Empire. Even by a time as late as the end of the empire, nationalism was far from a strong, unifying force in newly post-Ottoman territories. Insofar as nationalism presented a challenge to the prewar imperial regime, it resulted from a major factor distinguishing the Ottoman situation from the Austro-Hungarian one: the presence of numerous neighboring states eager to foment unrest in hopes of causing the fracturing, if not total collapse, of the empire.[36] The Treaty of Berlin, in lowering the landmass-to-frontier ratio, presented the Ottoman Empire with a worsened tactical situation in which revanchist nation-state neighbors played an important role, but within the empire's borders home-grown nationalism was a manageable part of the Ottoman self-defense problem.

While nationalism is a subject that has fascinated scholars for decades, much that has been written about it misses basic facts that merit constant remembrance. National identity (in most cases ethnic in nature, featuring people who feel linked to one another by bonds of language, culture, and historical experience), the basis of nationalism (the belief that the members of the nation also should have a common future that they themselves control, preferably in an independent state run by and for them), is episodic and situational.[37] Even in the most totalitarian state, there is never simply one identity felt, and nationality rises to prominence only in response to circumstance; even in the most nationally minded societies, other identities (of kinship, locale, occupation, or religion) come to the fore in "non-national" situations. Nationalism is also almost inevitably oppositional: group solidarity means nothing in practice without the existence of another, rival group, the classic foreign or internal enemy. Both conditions predispose nationalism to be dependent upon the modern state, because the state as it developed from the late eighteenth century ever more clearly had the power and interest to foster such identities and also to implement intrusive policies based upon ethnicity. Ethnic groups rarely oppress each other spontaneously or without direction, in part because ethnic groups (in the modern sense used in reference to nation-states) almost never have clear natural or innate definitions but rather depend upon states to impose the necessary mental boundaries of "us" and "them" for the imagined community. In the Ottoman case, the state had no obvious interest in promoting ethnic national identity. In most circumstances it devised policies of universal applicability or, where that was not possible, based not on ethnicity but rather on religion. As most students of nationalism acknowledge, moreover, the spread of the idea depends upon the growth of literacy; throughout the nineteenth century the great bulk of the population, Muslim and non-Muslim alike, remained illiterate, especially the majority of the population that lived outside urban areas. Even among the urban literati, those who embraced nationalism most wholeheartedly tended to be the young and especially the "romantics" (poets, schoolteachers, and the underemployed "intelligentsia") rather than the more practically minded commercial mainstream.[38] Antagonistic to Ottoman rule and weakly rooted in the would-be national milieu, nationalists tended to be expatriates (many having converted to their new faith while studying abroad) living in European capitals such as Vienna and Paris or, following the retreat of Ottoman control, in territories such as Serbia and Wallachia. In confirming opportunities for nationalists to reside in security close to Ottoman borders, and by granting independence to openly revanchist host regimes in formerly Ottoman territories, the

Treaty of Berlin ensured nationalism among expatriates as a permanent feature of the Ottoman "near abroad"; but the direct threat to Ottoman rule posed by the fieriest revolutionaries was practically nil.

There was no successful nationalist rebellion in Ottoman history. This assertion certainly does not deny that serious grievances triggered significant unrest in specific locales and times, but most such grievances that sparked the best-known revolts resulted from factors other than nationalism, including the collapse of legal protections for life and property (Belgrade in 1804, Wallachia and Morea in 1821, and eastern Anatolia in the 1890s) and extreme poverty (Hercegovina in 1875). Muslim-Christian antagonism that could reach intense levels also played a large part in some conflicts (such as Belgrade and eastern Anatolia), and the revolts also should be seen properly as uprisings by Christians in a particular region rather than as ethno-national liberation struggles made inevitable by the multiethnic nature of the Ottoman state. It was Christian sympathy that garnered European support for uprisings, from the Russian attack in support of the "Greeks" in 1828–29 to the notably devout William Gladstone's drumbeat of anti-"Turkish" (meaning Muslim) propaganda over the "Bulgarian Horrors" that roused feverish anti-Ottoman sentiment in Britain in 1876–78. Where the state administered mixed populations with reasonable competence, local conditions might suffer spikes in tension that intrigued nationalist agitators, but most resident Christians saw greater hope for the future in avoiding acts of rebellion that brought a very real risk of death or absolute ruin. Bulgaria in 1875–76 offers an example of this, with expatriate agents provocateurs hoping to take advantage of Ottoman preoccupation with the peasant revolt in Hercegovina to stage a liberation uprising but only succeeding in lengthening their record of futility in igniting the flames of widespread nationalist revolution.[39]

Most nationalist agitators presumably realized that their schemes — quixotic plots that were little more than blood-spattered grand gestures (attacks on offices of the Ottoman Bank became a favored tactic) — posed no more threat to the state than other acts of murder, theft, arson, and vandalism did. If they hoped that such deeds would galvanize the slumbering nation into action, they consistently suffered disappointment; the only plausible purpose behind such schemes was to provoke an overreaction that would bring European intervention. It was this prospect that most concerned the Ottoman state, in part because it was only too conscious of its own precarious policing power.[40] The initiative might lie with nationalist groups, but the key to the success or failure of each plot rested primarily in Ottoman hands, because the reaction of the state was crucial. In the case of the attack on the Ottoman Bank in Istanbul organized by the expatriate Armenian Dashnak group in 1896, for example, the state reacted too slowly to halt massacres of innocent Armenians in the capital, which prompted strong European protests about the need for reform in Armenian affairs and the increased alienation of Britain from the Ottoman Empire. In 1903, by contrast, the army and police in Salonika quickly rounded up the Internal Macedonian Revolutionary Organization (IMRO) cell that blew up the Ottoman Bank and several other targets there. The episode spread few shock waves in the city, the rest of Macedonia, or the capitals of Christian Europe.[41]

In all parts of the empire, of course, Ottoman control eventually came to an inglorious and frequently bloody end, usually through direct Christian European pressure rather than domestic unrest, and all imperial lands were transformed into autonomous or independent countries. In both southeastern Europe and western Asia, post-Ottoman regimes had to place high priority on creating the nation. Their projection of the desired nation's unity and struggle for freedom back into the Ottoman period still shapes assumptions that nationalism among subject peoples was a critical threat to Ottoman survival. Nationalism also offers an easy answer to the question of why Christians did not fully embrace the concept of Ottomanism, or reintegration into the empire as equal citizens, which would have necessitated renunciation of privileges protected by both the capitulatory and *millet* systems. The enduring Islamic nature of the state provides a more plausible partial explanation, but the simple willingness to remain loyal to the state as long as it was not overbearing and acted in accord with its obligations to uphold law and order should also be recognized.[42] This made Christian as well as many Muslim populations more likely to support decentralization than independence.

Macedonia after 1878 illustrates well both the limited appeal of nationalism and the continuing threat to the empire posed by the Christian powers of Europe. Each of the newfound states on its borders adopted a program of irredentism against Ottoman lands (first and best exemplified by Greece's "Megali Idea," which viewed all Ottoman Orthodox Christians as "Greeks" awaiting redemption) as an important part of creating the nation, giving a purpose to the massive expansion of bureaucratic and military institutions that were designed to consolidate the state's hold over newly won territory and population.[43] All Macedonian territory was claimed by one or more of its neighbors: Greece, Bulgaria, Serbia, and Montenegro. One feature making Macedonia an unusual arena for anti-Ottoman irredentism, however, was the acknowledged role of the views of those targeted for redemption. Under the terms of the creation of the Bulgarian Exarchate (1870), Orthodox parishes could decide which church authority to follow, the Slavic Bulgarian or the established Greek patriarchate. This caused the neighboring states to devote major efforts to teaching Orthodox Macedonians that they were Greek/Bulgarian/Serbian. Suitable instruction was provided through educational and cultural missions and through paramilitary (and also regular military) violence targeting villagers who did not answer quickly and satisfactorily the question "What are you?" Such thuggery spurred the growth of the IMRO, whose slogan "Macedonia for the Macedonians" reflected the resentment felt toward alien irredentist powers. Irritation even prompted a plan for creation of a Slav Macedonian loyalist-Ottoman autocephalous Orthodox church that would keep Bulgarian interventionism at bay.[44] Elements within the IMRO fit the decentralist model better than the separatist one and at least discussed cooperation with the Committee of Union and Progress. Irredentism in Macedonia also eventually spurred the Ottoman army there to enter politics, bringing about the Young Turk Revolution in 1908: echoing the Young Ottoman movement of the 1860s, Muslim dissatisfaction with Abdülhamid II's inability to repel foreign interference in Macedonia by either the Great Powers or the neighboring states prompted the call to replace autocratic rule with constitutionalism. As Ali and Fuad knew better than the Young Ottomans, so Abdülhamid was also most conscious of the futility of confrontation, with even victorious military responses to neighbors' irredentism (Montenegro in 1853, Serbia in 1875, Greece in 1897) being negated by Great Power intervention.

Macedonia's example illustrates the continuity between the pre-Berlin period and the Hamidian era. Sectors of the population, both Muslim and non-Muslim, were aware of ethnic identity to varying degrees, but in most cases this consciousness did not evolve into an active sense of nationalism, the belief that ethnicity required an independent state of and for the nation's people. The Ottoman state generally avoided policies that would heighten consciousness of ethnicity as a politically consequential issue. The practical implications for Christians of the continuing Muslim identity of the state naturally kept religious identity more salient than later nationalist renderings of history acknowledge.[45] "Nationalism" threatened to become a critical issue for the empire only insofar as it was instigated by irredentist and Great Power states manipulating non-national populations.

In at least one case, however, state action did promote national sensibilities as a direct consequence of decisions made at Berlin. The promises of territory to Greece and Montenegro contained in the treaty spurred unprecedented efforts by Muslim and Christian Albanians to unite to prevent the loss of lands considered "Albanian." This was initially not an anti-Ottoman movement, but when Istanbul tried to enforce the transfers mandated in the treaty, conflict between central authority and provincial populations resulted. The self-defense movement took further a sense of ethnic identification as politically important that had become very apparent during the reign of Mahmud II, although the earlier example of consciously Albanian resistance to Istanbul's dictates was overwhelmingly a Muslim movement.[46] Much as in 1878, however, the earlier movement grew out of a sense that Istanbul's policies were threatening specifically the well-being and honor of Albanian Muslims. Muslims still provided the backbone of the Albanian movement that emerged in 1878, preventing its transformation into a lastingly anti-Ottoman resistance league, but the greater role taken by Christians did aid the development of Albanian national identity. Albania thus proved very difficult to control for the energetic centralizers dominant in Istanbul after 1909. The CUP-dominated state undid whatever gains Abdülhamid had made. Having recognized the threat of ethnic division within Muslim ranks, he had devoted attention to reconfirming ties of loyalty to the state based upon religion among Albanians and other groups in sensitive frontier areas, including Kurds and Arabs, whose notions of ethnic solidarity could develop along paths similar to that of the Albanians if territorial security conditions worsened.[47]

CONCLUSION

When considering the slow breakup of the Ottoman Empire and the place within that process occupied by the Treaty of Berlin, it is important to view the extent of the damage done in 1878 from a longer-term perspective. Berlin ratified the loss of significant territory and population, and the permanent displacement of yet more people, but the treaty did not fundamentally alter either the predicament or the nature of the Ottoman state. The territorial losses merely took their place in a series of such events dating back to 1699, and it can be argued that the losses accepted at Karlowitz in that year (notably Hungary and the Morea), at Küçük Kaynarca in 1774 (which freed Russian access to the Black Sea and saw the Crimea withdrawn from the Ottoman sphere), and at Edirne in 1829 (which ratified the unprecedented creation of autonomous or independent states to reward Christian subjects who had revolted) were more shocking or meaningful for the future direction of imperial politics and policy. It is true that the Treaty of Berlin confirmed to the empire that the promises of territorial integrity made at Paris in 1856 were null and void; but disappointing as this may have been, it can hardly have been previously inconceivable, given one guarantor's demonstrated willingness to land troops in Ottoman territory (the French response to the confessional fighting in Lebanon and Damascus in 1860) and Russia's ability to renounce without penalty the demilitarization of the Black Sea in 1871.

As in the issue of Parisian promises, most of the patterns highlighted in standard accounts of the post-Berlin Hamidian period also bear strong links to past practices. Abdülhamid did not innovate sharply in adopting a more openly Islamic approach to domestic and international politics, because the Ottoman state had always been of and for Muslims first. Since the reign of Mahmud II, moreover, it had tended strongly toward autocracy, and the oligarchic state of the Tanzimat adapted itself relatively easily to Abdülhamid's idea of monarchy. This pattern of illiberal rule was only to be expected in a state facing intractable security problems, and great room for misunderstanding nineteenth-century Ottoman history lies in confusing the willingness to invent, beg, steal, or borrow whatever could strengthen the state's ability to defend itself with the wish to become "Western." Until the final collapse of the empire following defeat in war against Russia, Britain, and France, the only threat that really mattered to its survival was from the Christian powers of Europe. All that any such state needed to trigger offensive action, military or political, was a pretext; as strenuously as Ottoman authorities tried to police potential pretexts, they could not forestall them all. The Treaty of Berlin may have hastened the opening of some opportunities for the Christian powers (for example, by the call for reforms in Armenian provinces), but it did not create or even significantly alter the fundamental vulnerability that bedeviled the Ottoman regime in the twilight of empire.

NOTES

1. Recent examples include Carter Findley, *Turkey, Islam, Nationalism, and Modernity: A History, 1789–2007*; and Erik Zürcher, *Turkey: A Modern History*.
2. The drawing of parallels is understandable because it challenges the often-smug assumption of Christian European moral, technical, and intellectual superiority over caricatured "Turks" that is still strong, although not as pervasive as it long was. For examples from a field directly relevant to this volume (Eastern question historiography), see M. S. Anderson, *The Eastern Question, 1774–1923: A Study in International Relations*; and David Fromkin, *A Peace to End All Peace: Creating the Modern Middle East, 1914–1922*.

3. Carter Findley, "The Tanzimat," 16.

4. Donald Quataert, "The Age of Reforms, 1812–1914," 766. The qualification that these were elite values is important, but most accounts make little attempt to gauge nonelite perspectives, suggesting either that the nonelite thought roughly the same way or that only the elite view mattered.

5. This overall pattern appeared in standard-setting works of the 1960s: Bernard Lewis, *The Emergence of Modern Turkey*; and Roderic Davison, *Reform in the Ottoman Empire, 1856–1876*. It has survived in relatively sound health since the 1960s: Stanford J. Shaw and Ezer Kural Shaw, *History of the Ottoman Empire and Modern Turkey*; Zürcher, *Turkey*; Justin McCarthy, *The Ottoman Turks: An Introductory History to 1923*; Caroline Finkel, *Osman's Dream: The Story of the Ottoman Empire, 1300–1923*; and M. Şükrü Hanioğlu, *A Brief History of the Late Ottoman Empire*.

6. Albert Hourani, *A History of the Arab Peoples*, 272. For a discussion of the inadequacy of "Westernization" as a term to describe the reform era, however, see İlber Ortaylı, *İmparatorluğun En Uzun Yüzyılı*, 14–22. On the shift in emphasis from Eurocentrism toward indigenous roots of change, see Donald Quataert, "Ottoman History Writing and Changing Attitudes towards the Notion of 'Decline.'"

7. On the evolution of terms of military service, see Erik Zürcher, "The Ottoman Conscription System in Theory and Practice, 1844–1918."

8. Yavuz Cezar, *Osmanlı Maliyesinde Bunalım ve Değişim Dönemi (XVIII. yy dan Tanzimat'a Mali Tarih)*, 279–80.

9. For a summary of these reforms, see Findley, "The Tanzimat," 25–26.

10. It was such administrative, financial, and military rationalization that constituted "instituting the beneficent reorganizations" in outlying provinces such as Albania and Bosnia that had not been touched in the first wave of reforms. See, for example, Başbakanlık Osmanlı Arşivi, Istanbul (BOA), Cevdet Dahiliye 4347, February 20, 1845.

11. Certainly there were wars between Christian states of Europe in the nineteenth century after 1815, but the Congress of Vienna system worked reasonably well until the late 1840s; thereafter the most significant intra-European conflicts (Austrian struggles in Italy and Prussian wars with Denmark, Austria, and France) were launched and completed in such short order that the Concert of Europe had little opportunity to intervene. The pattern survives the test provided by the main apparent exception, the Crimean War, which was triggered by Russian underestimation of Anglo-French willingness to fight for the Muslim empire that Russia again attempted to bully — and miscalculation of Austrian readiness to maintain at least friendly neutrality.

12. Benjamin Braude and Bernard Lewis, eds., *Christians and Jews in the Ottoman Empire*.

13. Although often treated in modern historiography as a vaguely comic notion, the Holy Alliance organized by Russia in 1815 reflected a serious idea of the time: that the immense destruction wrought by the revolutionary and Napoleonic period should never afflict Christendom again. All states in Europe but the Ottoman Empire (for obvious reasons) and the Papal State (which neither Orthodox Russia nor Protestant Prussia strongly wished to include) were invited to join, and almost

all did. It foreshadowed in some respects the European Union. The alliance failed largely because one major state, Britain, refused to join. Paul W. Schroeder, *The Transformation of European Politics, 1763–1848*, 558–59.

14. The tight relationship between religious and national identity in Britain, for example, has been well covered by several authors, including Linda Colley (*Britons: Forging the Nation, 1707–1837*) and John Wolffe (*God and Greater Britain: Religion and National Life in Britain and Ireland, 1843–1945*).

15. Anthony Wohl, "'Dizzi-Ben-Dizzi': Disraeli as Alien."

16. The Dreyfus Affair began in 1894 with the baseless accusation of treason against a Jewish French army officer, Alfred Dreyfus, who was to spend years under brutal conditions in the penal colony of Devil's Island; the Catholic likely betrayer of military secrets never faced serious investigation. Natives of French North Africa, particularly Algeria, which was not a colony but legally incorporated into France after 1848, were treated as subjects, not citizens, until they were deemed to have "evolved."

17. See, for example, François Georgeon, "Abdülhamid II (1876–1909)"; and Benjamin C. Fortna, "The Reign of Abdülhamid II," 38–40. The most significant work in changing thought about Abdülhamid's period was Selim Deringil's *The Well-Protected Domains: Ideology and the Legitimation of Power in the Ottoman Empire, 1876–1909*.

18. For more on the problems of Mahmud's reign and the transition to the Tanzimat, see Frederick Anscombe, "Islam and the Age of Ottoman Reform."

19. Zürcher, *Turkey*, 52–54, Hanioğlu, *A Brief History of the Late Ottoman Empire*, 73.

20. Lewis, *The Emergence of Modern Turkey*, 109; Davison, *Reform in the Ottoman Empire*, 44; Finkel, *Osman's Dream*, 452; Hugh Poulton, *Top Hat, Grey Wolf and Crescent: Turkish Nationalism and the Turkish Republic*, 51.

21. For a partial text of the code, see Reşat Kaynar, *Mustafa Reşit Paşa ve Tanzimat*, 302–12. Hanioğlu, *A Brief History of the Late Ottoman Empire*, 74, is one of the few accounts that seriously notes the tie to Sharia.

22. Rudolph Peters, *Crime and Punishment in Islamic Law: Theory and Practice from the Sixteenth to the Twenty-first Century*, 127–33.

23. Selim Deringil, "'There Is No Compulsion in Religion': On Conversion and Apostasy in the Late Ottoman Empire, 1839–1856."

24. As Deringil suggests, moreover, it is also possible to read the 1856 decree not just as "freedom of religion" but, for Muslims, as "freedom to protect the religion." Ibid., 556.

25. For the texts of these agreements and the decree, see J. C. Hurewitz, *Diplomacy in the Near and Middle East, a Documentary Record: 1535–1914*, 149–56.

26. Ahmed Cevdet Paşa, *Tezâkir 1–12*, 64–66.

27. Christoph Neumann, "Whom Did Ahmed Cevdet Represent?"

28. Zürcher, *Turkey*, 71–74, Hanioğlu, *A Brief History of the Late Ottoman Empire*, 104.

29. For insight on Young Ottoman criticism, see Nazan Çiçek, "The Eastern Critics of the 'Eastern Question': The Young Ottomans, 1866–1871."

30. Engin Akarlı, "The Problems of External Pressures, Power Struggles, and Budget-

ary Deficits in Ottoman Politics under Abdülhamid II (1876–1909): Origins and Solutions," 99–100.

31. When governor of Baghdad, for example, Midhat placed no faith in British assurances that they had no intention of seizing eastern Arabia. Frederick Anscombe, *The Ottoman Gulf: The Creation of Kuwait, Saudi Arabia, and Qatar*, 20–29.

32. Cited in Jacob Landau, *The Politics of Pan-Islam: Ideology and Organization*, 11.

33. F. A. K. Yasamee, "Abdülhamid II and the Ottoman Defence Problem."

34. Başbakanlık Osmanlı Arşivi, Istanbul (BOA), Yıldız Mehmed Kamil Paşa 86-37/3623, undated. The analysis bears no signature but presumably was composed by Kamil Paşa (see Feroze Yasamee's discussion of Kamil in chapter 2 of this volume).

35. On Austria-Hungary, see Alan Sked, *The Decline and Fall of the Habsburg Empire*; see also his essay "Historians, the Nationality Question and the Downfall of the Habsburg Empire," on the historiography of the "nationalities problem." Since Sked's book was published, studies that confirm the weakness of the idea that nationalism doomed the empire have multiplied. For a recent example, see Pieter Judson, *Guardians of the Nation: Activists on the Language Frontiers of Imperial Austria*. For recent works in Ottoman history that still assert the importance of nationalism, see Karen Barkey, *Empire of Difference: The Ottomans in Comparative Perspective*; and Hanioğlu, *A Brief History of the Late Ottoman Empire*.

36. The exception to this stark difference in the case of Austria-Hungary was Serbia, which was seen after 1903 as an active source of disruption for the Austro-Hungarian Orthodox Slav population — and the deep antipathy aroused by this lone case of a nation-state that fomented unrest triggered World War I.

37. Rogers Brubaker, Margit Feischmidt, Jon Fox, and Liana Grancea, *Nationalist Politics and Everyday Ethnicity in a Transylvanian Town*, highlights this fact. The study consistently downplays factors that help to create "national" situations, however; by ignoring or sometimes serving as apologists for the majority community, the authors effectively imply that nationalism is practically sui generis within a minority group, which undercuts their work in identifying its situational nature.

38. Michael Palairet, *The Balkan Economies c. 1800–1914: Evolution without Development*, 162–63, citing the case of Bulgaria.

39. British reports reveal how unplanned, unimportant, and non-nationalist the "April Uprising" was (the provocateurs apparently did not appeal to national sensibilities but rather spread the rumor that Russian troops were invading the empire and the Turks were coming to massacre Christians, sparking scattered killing of Muslims and widespread flight into the mountains). Richard Millman, "The Bulgarian Massacres Reconsidered." See also chapter 17 by Tetsuya Sahara in this volume, which describes a revolt that was more tragicomic than serious as a threat to Ottoman rule. The lack of Bulgarian interest in rising up for national liberation is reflected in the title of the bitter poem "Ne sme narod" (We Are Not a Nation/People) by Petko Slaveikov (1875).

40. The empire was the only major European state that had to use its regular military for police duties as well as for international warfare in the late nineteenth century.

41. Mark Mazower, *Salonica, City of Ghosts: Christians, Muslims and Jews, 1430–1950*, 264–68.

42. For examples from an Arab province, see Butrus Abu-Manneh, "The Christians between Ottomanism and Syrian Nationalism: The Ideas of Butrus al-Bustani"; and Stefan Wild, "Ottomanism versus Arabism: The Case of Farid Kassab (1884–1970)."

43. Victor Roudometof, "The Social Origins of Balkan Politics: Nationalism, Underdevelopment, and the Nation-State in Greece, Serbia, and Bulgaria, 1880–1920."

44. Alexander Maxwell, "Krsté Misirkov's 1903 Call for Macedonian Autocephaly: Religious Nationalism as Instrumental Political Tactic." On the general lack of practical popular support for any of the revolutionary groups, either external or internal, see Hugh Poulton, *Who Are the Macedonians?* 48–64.

45. This is nicely illustrated by the response of puzzled villagers in Macedonia who were asked by an activist from Greece if they were Greek or Bulgarian: "Asking each other what my words meant, crossing themselves, they would answer me naïvely: 'Well, we're Christians — what do you mean, *Romaioi* or *Voulgaroi?*'" Mark Mazower, *The Balkans: From the End of Byzantium to the Present Day*, 50.

46. Anscombe, "Islam and the Age of Ottoman Reform." There was significant Catholic Malësorë participation in a Muslim-led revolt originating in Shkodër in 1835, but that uprising had a less explicitly Albanian nature than the widespread movement of 1831. Istanbul's policies in Bosnia also pushed development of a protonational Bosnian identity in the 1820s and 1830s; but with those lands lost to Austro-Hungarian occupation after 1878, Bosnian nationalism could not become a serious problem for the Ottoman Empire.

47. An obvious example of such efforts was the Tribal School established in Yıldız palace. See Eugene Rogan, "Aşiret Mektebi: Abdülhamid II's School for Tribes."

Glossary

ağnam-ı resmiye: sheep tax or animal tax.

alaylı: officer who has risen from the ranks.

Bab-ı Ali: Sublime Porte (literally "high gate"), a term applied to the Ottoman government.

başıbozuk: irregular, rebel.

berat: document recognizing someone as the subject of a foreign power, entitled to *aman* (legal protection).

çiftlik: privately owned farm.

çorbacı: Christian local notable in the Balkans.

Crimean War of 1856: conflict involving the irredentist Russian Empire and an alliance of France, the British Empire, the Kingdom of Sardinia, the Duchy of Nassau, and the Ottoman State, which tried to stop Russian expansion over the Ottoman territories.

Dashnak: Armenian Revolutionary Federation (ARF), founded in 1890.

dhimmi: protected and tributary Christian or Jewish inhabitant of a Muslim state.

Elviye-i Selâse: the three cities of Ardahan, Batum, and Kars.

eşraf: local community leader.

eyalet: Ottoman province.

*fedayee*s: Armenian irregular volunteers committed to sacrificing their lives for the nationalist cause.

Hamidiye Regiments: informal Kurdish cavalry established during the reign of Abdül-hamid II.

Hunchak: Hunchakian Revolutionary Party, founded in Geneva, Switzerland, in 1887.

irade: degree of the sultan.

İttihad-ı Avrupa: Concert of Europe.

kaymakam: governor of a *sancak*.

kaza: judicial and/or administrative district (subunit of a *sancak*).

kmet: tenant farmer.

komitacılık (çetecilik): rebel, member of a secret revolutionary organization.

Meclis-i Mebusan: Chamber of Deputies (lower house of Parliament).

mektebli: officer who has graduated from military academy.

miri: state-owned real estate.

muhacir: settler.

mülteci: refugee.

mutasarrıf: governor of a subprovince.

mutasarrıflık: subprovince.

müvazene-yi Avrupa: equilibrium of Europe.

nahiye: Ottoman administrative unit, subdivision of a *kaza* administered by a *müdür* (director).

öşür (ushr): tithe.

Ottomanism: equality of all male subjects before the law.

paşa: general term for a territorial governor.

paşalik: territory governed by a *paşa*.

Pomak: Bulgarian-speaking Muslim.

Rumeli: European province of the Ottoman Empire.

sancak: military administrative unit (original meaning); administrative unit ruled by a *mutasarrıf* (after the Tanzimat in 1839).

takrir: report or plea addressed to the sultan, who considers it out of his benevolence.

Tanzimat: general term applied to the Ottoman administrative and governmental reforms of the period from 1839 to the 1870s.

Torbes: Macedonian-speaking Muslims.

vakf (*vakıf*, pl. *evkaf*): endowment or properties of a religious foundation, usually land.

vali: governor of *vilayet*.

vilayet: Ottoman province, replacing the *eyalet* in 1864.

Vilayet-i Sitte: Six Provinces (Erzurum, Van, Bitlis, Diyarbakır, Mamuretülaziz [Elazığ], and Sivas); sometimes called "Western Armenia," although Armenians represented only about 25 percent of the total population.

Vlach: descendant of the romanized pre-Slav Balkan population.

Chronology of Ottoman History (1828–1909)

1826 Destruction of the Janissaries
1832 Battle of Konya
1833 Treaty of Hünkar-İskelesi with Russia
1838 Anglo-Ottoman Convention
1839 Tanzimat begins with the Hatt-ı Şerif (Imperial Rescript) of Gülhane
1839–61 Abdülmecit I
1853–56 Crimean War
1856 Hatt-ı Şerif
1856 Treaty of Paris
1861–76 Abdülaziz I
1875 Bulgarian insurgency in Batak
1875 Serbia and Montenegro declare war against the Ottoman state
1875 (April) Slavic-Orthodox rebellion in Hercegovina
1875 (October) Ottoman bankruptcy
1876 Abdication of Abdülaziz I
1876 First Ottoman Constitution
1876 Murad V (deposed in August)
1876 (December) Istanbul Conference
1876–1909 Abdülhamid II
1877 (March) London Conference
1877 (April) Russia declares war against the Ottoman state
1878 (March) Treaty of San Stefano
1878 (June) Cyprus Convention with Britain
1878 (June–July) Congress of Berlin and Treaty of Berlin
1881 Formation of Public Debt Administration
1885 Occupation of Eastern Rumelia by Bulgaria
1887 Establishment of Hunchak (Bell) Revolutionary Party in Switzerland
1890 Armenian Rebellion in Erzurum
1890 Establishment of Armenian Revolutionary Federation Party (Dashnak) in Tbilisi
1890 Kumkapı incident organized by Hunchak Party
1894 Armenian Rebellion in Sasun and Zeytun
1895 Bab-ı Ali demonstrations in Istanbul
1895 Memorandum and Project of Reforms for the Eastern Provinces
1896 Armenian nationalist (Dashnak) attack at the Ottoman Bank in Istanbul
1896 Armenian Rebellion in Van
1896–97 Insurrection in Crete; war with Greece
1908 Young Turk Revolution and restoration of the Constitution
1909–18 Mehmet V
1911 Ottoman war with Italy over Libya

1912–13 Balkan Wars
1914 World War I begins
1918–22 Mehmet VI
1920 French and British mandate over Syria, Lebanon, Iraq, and Palestine
1923 Proclamation of the Republic of Turkey

Bibliography

Archives and Unpublished Sources

Archives du Ministère des Affaires Étrangères de France/Archives of the Ministry of
Foreign Affairs of France, Paris and Nantes (AMAE).

Archivio Storico del Ministero degli Affari Esteri/Historical Archive of the Ministry of
Foreign Affairs, Rome (ASMAE).

Arhiv Bosne i Hercegovine/Archive of Bosnia-Herzegovina, Sarajevo (ABH).

Arhiv Srbije (Turski statisticki pregled, Statisticko odeljenje Ministarstva finansija
Srbije)/Archives of Serbia (Turkish Statistical Review, Statistical Department of
the Serbian Ministry of Finance), Belgrade.

Arkhiv Vneshnei Politiki Rossiiskoi Imperii/Archive of the Foreign Policy of the Russian Empire, Moscow (AVPRI).

Arkivi Qendror Shtetëror/Albanian Central State Archives, Tirana (AQSH).

Armenian Revolutionary Federation Archives, Boston, Mass. (ARF).

Başbakanlık Arşivi/Prime Ministerial Archives, Istanbul (BBA).

Başbakanlık Osmanlı Arşivi/Office of the Prime Minister Ottoman Archives, Istanbul
(BOA).

Genelkurmay Askeri Tarih ve Stratejik Etüt Başkanlığı Arşivi/Archives of the Turkish
General Staff Directorate for Military History and Strategic Research, Ankara
(ATASE).

Haus-, Hof- und Staatsarchiv/Austrian State Archive, Vienna (HHStA).

Milli Kütüphane/National Library of Turkey, Ankara.

National Archives of the United Kingdom (formerly Public Record Office), Foreign
Office Archives, London (FO).

National Archives of the United Kingdom (formerly Public Record Office), Parliamentary Papers and Confidential Prints, London (PP and CP).

U.S. National Archives, College Park, Md. (NA).

Published Sources

Collections of Documents

Başbakanlık Devlet Arşivleri Genel Müdürlüğü. *Bosna-Hersek İle İlgili Arşiv Belgeleri.*
Ankara: Başbakanlık Basımevi, 1992.

Bericht über die Verwaltung Bosnien und der Hercegovina. Vienna: K. und K. Gemeinsame Finanzministerium, 1906.

Dasnabedian, Hratch. ed. *Niuter Ho. Hee. Tashnagtsutian Badmutian Hamar.* Vol. 2.
N.p., n.d.

Die Ergebnisse der Volkszählung in Bosnien und der Hercegovina vom 10. Oktober 1910.
Sarajevo: Landesregierung für Bosnien und Hercegovina, 1910.

Ermeniler Tarafından Yapılan Katliam Belgeleri (1914–1919). Ankara: Başbakanlık Devlet Arşivleri Genel Müdürlüğü Yayını, 2001.

Great Britain, Foreign Office. *Turkey, Correspondence respecting Affairs in Turkey, No. 1.* London: Harrison and Sons, 1876.

———. *Turkey, Correspondence respecting Affairs in Turkey, No. 2.* London: Harrison and Sons, 1876.

———. *Turkey, Correspondence respecting Affairs in Turkey, No. 3.* London: Harrison and Sons, 1876.

———. *Turkey, Correspondence respecting Affairs in Turkey, No. 24, No. 26, No. 33, No. 36, No. 38, No. 39.* London: Harrison and Sons, 1878.

———. *Turkey, No. 15.* In *Accounts and Papers of the House of Commons,* 3, 146. London: Harrison and Sons, 1877.

———. *Turkey, No. 27, Further Correspondence respecting the Preliminary Treaty of Peace between Russia and Turkey, Signed at San Stefano, 3 March 1878.* London: Foreign Office, 1878.

———. *Turkey, No. 45 (1878), Further Correspondence Respecting the Affairs of Turkey.* London: Harrison and Sons, 1878.

Hansard's Parliamentary Debates. Vol. 1 (1877). N.p., n.d.

Hansard's Parliamentary Debates. Vol. 232 (February 8, 1877–March 15, 1877). N.p., n.d.

Kirakosyan, J[ohn]. *Hayastane Michazkayin Divanagitudyan yev Sovetakan Artagin Kaghakakanutyan Pastatghterum.* Yerevan: Hayastan Publishing, 1972.

Ortschafts- und Bevölkerungs-Statistik von Bosnien-Herzegowina nach dem Volkszählung- sergebnis vom 1. Mai 1885. Sarajevo: Amtliche Ausgabe, 1886. Appendix.

Osmanlı Belgelerinde Bosna-Hersek: Bosna i Herzegovina u Osmanskim Dokumentima. Istanbul: Başbakanlık Devlet Arşivleri Genel Müdürlüğü, 2009.

Pamboukian, Yervant, ed. *Nyuter Ho. Hi. Ta. Badmutyan Hamar.* Vol. 5. Armenian Revolutionary Federation Archives. Beirut: ARF Publications, 2007.

Sammlung der für Bosnien und die Hercegovina erlassenen Gesetze, Verordnungen, und Normalweisungen 1878–1880. Vol. 1. Vienna: Kaiserlich-königliche Hof- und Staats- druckerie, 1880–81.

Stenographische Sitzungs-Protokolle der Delegation des Reichsrathes. Vienna: Kaiserlich- königliche Hof- und Staatsdruckerei, 1893 and 1896.

OTHER SOURCES

Abadan, Yavuz. *Mustafa Kemal ve Çeteçilik.* Istanbul: Varlık Yayınevi, 1972.

Abu-Manneh, Butrus. "The Christians between Ottomanism and Syrian Nationalism: The Ideas of Butrus al-Bustani." *International Journal of Middle East Studies* 11 (1980): 287–304.

———. "Sultan Abdülhamid II and Shaikh Abdulhuda Al-Sayyadi." *Middle Eastern Studies* 15 (1979): 131–53.

Adanır, Fikret. *Die Makedonische Frage: Ihre Entstehung und Entwicklung bis 1908.* Wiesbaden: Steiner Verlag, 1979.

Adanır, Fikret, and Hilmar Kaiser. "Migration, Deportation, and Nation-Building: The Case of the Ottoman Empire." In *Migrations et migrants dans une perspective historique: Permanence et innovations,* edited by René Leboutte, 273–92. Florence: European University Institute, 2000.

Adjarian, Herachyah. *Classification des dialectes arméniens.* Paris: H. Champion, 1909.

Ağanoğlu, H. Yıldırım. *Osmanlı'dan Cumhuriyet'e Balkanlar'ın Makûs Talihi.* Istanbul: Kum Saati, 2001.

Akarlı, Engin. "The Problems of External Pressures, Power Struggles, and Budgetary Deficits in Ottoman Politics under Abdülhamid II (1876–1909): Origins and Solutions." Ph.D. diss., Princeton University, 1976.

Akgün, Ahmet. "Bulgaristan'da Asimilasyon ve 'Zavallı Pomaklar' Adlı Bir Risale." *Balıkesir Üniversitesi Sosyal Bilimler Enstitüsü Dergisi* 8(13) (May 2001). http://sbe .balikesir.edu.tr/dergi/edergi/c8s13/makale/c8s13m1.pdf.

Ali, Rabia, and Lawrence Lifshultz, eds. *Why Bosnia?: Writings on the Balkan War.* Stony Creek, Conn.: Pamphleteers Press, 1993.

Aličić, Ahmed S. *Pokret za autonomiju Bosne od 1831. do 1832. godine.* Sarajevo: Orijentalni institut u Sarajevu, 1996.

Allen, W. E. D., and Paul Muratoff. *1828–1921 Türk-Kafkas Sınırındaki Harplerin Tarihi.* Ankara: Genelkurmay Basımevi, 1966.

Altay, Fahrettin. *10 Yıl Savaş (1912–1922) ve Sonrası.* Istanbul: n.p., 1970.

Anderson, Benedict. *Imagined Communities: Reflections on the Origin and Spread of Nationalism.* New York: Verso, 1991.

Anderson, Margaret Lavinia. "'Down in Turkey, Far Away': Human Rights, the Armenian Massacres, and Orientalism in Wilhelmine Germany." *Journal of Modern History* 79 (March 2007): 80–111.

Anderson, M. S. *The Eastern Question, 1774–1923: A Study in International Relations.* London: Macmillan, 1966.

Andric, Ivo. *The Bosnian Chronicle.* New York: Praeger, 1993.

———. *The Bridge over the Drina.* Translated by Lovett F. Edwards. Chicago: University of Chicago Press, 1977.

———. *The Development of Spiritual Life in Bosnia under the Influence of Turkish Rule.* Edited and translated by Zelimir B. Jurici and John F. Loud. Durham: Duke University Press, 1990.

Anghie, Antony. *Imperialism, Sovereignty and the Making of International Law.* Cambridge: Cambridge University Press, 2004.

Anscombe, Frederick. "Islam and the Age of Ottoman Reform." *Past and Present* 208 (2010): 159–89.

———. *The Ottoman Gulf: The Creation of Kuwait, Saudi Arabia, and Qatar.* New York: Columbia University Press, 1997.

Apak, Rahmi. *Yetmişlik Bir Subayın Anıları.* Ankara: Türk Tarih Kurumu Basımevi, 1988.

Apostolski, Mihailo, et al., eds. *Kresnenskoto Vostanie, 1878–1879.* Skopje: Makedonska akademija na naukite i umetnostite, 1982.

Armaoğlu, Fahir. *19. Yüzyıl Siyasi Tarihi (1789–1914).* Istanbul: Alkım Yayınevi, 2006.

Armen. "Ho. Hi. Dashnaktsutiune Balkanneru Mech: Enger Asadur Bedigiani Hushere." *Hayrenik* 12, no. 107 (October 1933).

Arslanoğlu, Cem-Ender. *Kars Millî-İslâm Şûrâsı ve Cenubigarbî Kafkas Hükûmeti Muvakkata-i Milliyyesi.* Ankara: Azerbaycan Kültür Derneği Yayınları, 1986.

Artinian, Vartan. *The Armenian Constitutional System in the Ottoman Empire: A Study of Its Historical Development.* Istanbul: n.p., 1988.

Aşiret Hafif Süvari Alayları Nizamnamesi. Istanbul: n.p., 12 Şaban 1328 [1910].

Aşiret Süvari Alayları Nizamnamesi. Istanbul: n.p., 6 Mart 1328 [1910].

Aydın, Mahir. *Şarkî Rumeli Vilayeti.* Ankara: Türk Tarih Kurumu Basımevi, 1992.

Aydın, Mithat. "İngiliz-Rus Rekabeti ve Osmanlı Devleti'nin Asya Toprakları Sorunu (1877–1878)." *A. Ü. Türkiyat Araştırmaları Enstitüsü Dergisi* 38 (2008): 253–88.

"Azd." *Droshak* 3–83 (March 1898): 31.

Babuna, Aydın. "The Bosnian Muslims and Albanians: Islam and Nationalism." *Nationalities Papers* 2 (2004): 287–321.

———. *Die nationale Entwicklung der bosnischen Muslime, mit besonderer Berücksichtigung der österreichisch-ungarischen Periode.* Frankfurt: Peter Lang, 1996.

———. "The Emergence of the First Muslim Party in Bosnia-Hercegovina." *East European Quarterly* 2 (1996): 131–51.

———. "Nationalism and the Bosnian Muslims." *East European Quarterly* 2 (1999): 195–218.

Babuş, Fikret. *Osmanlı'dan Günümüze Etnik-Sosyal Politikalar Çerçevesinde Göç ve İskan Siyaseti ve Uygulamaları,* Istanbul: Ozan Yayıncılık, 2006.

Baker, Valentine. *War in Bulgaria: A Narrative of Personal Experiences.* London: Sampson Low, 1879.

Baleva, Martina, and Ulf Brunnbauer. *Batak kato Mjasto na Pametta: Izložba/Batak — ein bulgarischer Erinnerungsort: Ausstellung.* Sofia: n.p., [2007].

Balfour, Michael. *The Kaiser and His Times.* London: Cresset Press, 1964.

Balibar, Etienne. "Is There a 'Neo-Racism'?" In *Race, Nation, Class: Ambiguous Identities,* edited by Etienne Balibar and Immanuel Wallerstein, 23–24. London: Verso, 1991.

Banac, Ivo. *The National Question in Yugoslavia: Origins, History, Politics.* Ithaca: Cornell University Press, 1984.

Bardakjian, Kevork. "The Rise of the Armenian Patriarchate of Constantinople." In *Christians and Jews in the Ottoman Empire,* edited by Benjamin Braude and Bernard Lewis, 89–100. Vol. 1. New York: Holmes and Meier Publications, 1982.

Barkey, Karen. *Empire of Difference: The Ottomans in Comparative Perspective.* Cambridge: Cambridge University Press, 2008.

Bartl, Peter. *Albanian: Vom Mittelalter bis zur Gegenwart.* Regensburg: Pustet, 1995.

———. *Die albanischen Muslime zur Zeit der nationalen Unabhängigkeitsbewegung (1878–1912).* Ph.D. diss., Wiesbaden, 1968.

Bartov, Omer. *Mirrors of Destruction.* Oxford: Oxford University Press, 2000.

Bass, Gary J. *Freedom's Battle: The Origins of Humanitarian Intervention.* New York: Vintage Books, 2008.

Bataković, Dušan T. *The Kosovo Chronicles.* Belgrade: n.p., 1992.

Bauman, Zygmunt. *Modernity and the Holocaust.* Ithaca: Cornell University Press, 1989.

Baykal, Bekir Sitki. "Pitanje Bosne i Hercegovine i osmanska država 1878. godine." In *Naučni skup: Otpor austrougarskojokupaciji 1878. godine u Bosni i Hercegovini,* edited by Milorad Ekmečić, 95–108. Sarajevo: ANU Bosne i Hercegovine, 1979.

Bayur, Hikmet. "Yeni Bulunmuş Bazı Belgelerin Işığında Kamil Paşa'nın Siyasal Durumu." *Belleten* 35, no. 137 (1971): 76.

Bayur, Hilmi Kamil. *Sadrazam Kamil Paşa: Siyasi Hayatı.* Ankara: Sanat Basımevi, 1954.

Bedirkhan, Abdulrahman. "Koch Kurterun." *Droshak* 4, no. 115 (June 1901): 65–67.

Behar, Cem. *Osmanlı İmparatorluğu'nun ve Türkiye'nin Nüfusu* Ankara: T. C. Başbakanlık Devlet İstatitik Enstitüsü, 1996.

Belfield, Eversley. *The Boer War*. London: Archon Books, 1975.

Bencze, Lászió. *The Occupation of Bosnia and Herzegovina in 1878*. New York: Columbia University Press, 2005.

Benjamin, Walter. *Illuminations*. Translated by Harry Zohn. New York: Schocken Books, 1968.

Berić, Dušan. "Bosna i Hercegovina od kraja XVIII veka do 1914: U najnovijoj jugoslovenskoj istoriografiji." *Zbornik Matice srpske za istoriju* 37 (1988): 183–200.

———. "Pogled na literaturu o otporu austrougarskoj okupaciji 1878. u Bosni i Hercegovini." In *Naučni skup: Otpor austrougarskoj okupaciji 1878. godine u Bosni i Hercegovini*, 365–85. Sarajevo: Akademija nauka i umjetnosti Bosne i Hercegovine, 1979.

Bey, Ali Vehbi. *Pensées et souvenirs de l'ex-Sultan Abdulhamid*. Paris: n.p., n.d.

Beydilli, Kemal. "1828–1829 Osmanlı-Rus Savaşında Doğu Anadolu'dan Rusya'ya Göçürülen Ermeniler." *Türk Tarihi Belgeleri Dergisi* 8, no. 17 (1988): 410.

Beysanoğlu, Şevket. *Kısaltmış Diyarbakir Tarihi ve Abideleri*. Istanbul: Diyarbakır: Diyarbakır Tanıtma Derneği, 1963.

Bilge, M. Sadık. *Osmanlı Devleti ve Kafkasya Osmanlı Varlığı Döneminde Kafkasya'nın Siyasi-Askeri ve İdari Taksimatı (1454–1829)*. Istanbul: Eren Yayıncılık, 2005.

Bıyıklıoğlu, Tevfik. *Trakya'da Milli Mücadele*. 3d ed. 2 vols. Ankara: Turkish Historical Society, 1992.

Bloxham, Donald. *The Great Game of Genocide, Imperialism, Nationalism and the Destruction of the Ottoman Armenians*. Oxford: Oxford University Press, 2005.

Blumi, Isa. "Capitulations in the Late Ottoman Empire: The Shifting Parameters of Russian and Austrian Interests in Ottoman Albania, 1878–1912." *Oriente Moderno* 83, no. 3 (2003): 635–47.

———. "The Dynamics of Identity: The Albanian in the Ottoman Empire." In *ACTA Viennensia Ottomanica Akten der 13 CIEPO-Symposiums*, ed. Gisela Prochazka-Eisl, 21–34. Vienna: University of Vienna, 1999.

———. *Reinstating the Ottomans: Alternative Balkan Modernities, 1800–1912*. New York: Palgrave, 2011.

———. *Rethinking the Late Ottoman Empire: A Comparative Social and Political History of Albania and Yemen, 1878–1918*. Istanbul: ISIS Press, 2003.

———. "Thwarting the Ottoman Empire: Smuggling through the Empire's New Frontiers in Ottoman Yemen and Albania, 1878–1910." *International Journal of Turkish Studies* 9, nos. 1–2 (Summer 2003), 255–74.

Boeckh, Kathrin. *Von den Balkankriegen zum Ersten Weltkrieg: Kleinstaatenpolitik und ethnische Selbstbestimmung auf dem Balkan*. Munich: R. Oldenbourg, 1996.

Bogičević, Vojislav. "Emigracije Muslimana Bosne i Hercegovine u Tursku u doba austro-ugarske vladavine 1878–1918 god." *Historijski zbornik* 3 (1950): 175–88.

Boissevain, Jeremy. *Friends of Friends: Networks, Manipulators and Coalitions*. Oxford: Basil Blackwell, 1971.

Boswell, Charles. *Armenia and the Campaign of 1877*. New York: Cassell, Petter and Galpin, 1878.

Bourne, Kenneth. *The Foreign Policy of Victorian England, 1830–1902*. Oxford: Clarendon Press, 1970.

Božić, Ivan, Sima Ćirković, Milorad Ekmećić, and Vladimir Dedijer. *Istorija Jugoslavije*. Belgrade: Prosveta, 1972.

Branch, Taylor. *The Clinton Tapes*. New York: Simon and Schuster, 2009.

Brass, Paul. "Elite Competition and Nation Formation." In *Nationalism*, edited by John Hutchinson and Anthony Smith, 83–89. Oxford: Oxford University Press, 1994.

———. "Ethnic Groups and Nationalities: The Formation, Persistence and Transformation of Ethnic Identities." In *Ethnic Diversity and Conflict in Eastern Europe*, edited by Peter Sugar, 1–68. Santa Barbara: ABC-Clio, 1980.

———. *Ethnicity and Nationalism: Theory and Comparison*. New Delhi: Sage Publications, 1991.

———. *Language, Religion and Politics in North India*. New York: Cambridge University Press, 1974.

Braude, Benjamin, and Bernard Lewis, eds. *Christians and Jews in the Ottoman Empire*. Vol. 1. New York: Holmes and Meier, 1982.

Bridge, F. R. and Roger Bullen. *The Great Powers and the European States System, 1815–1914*. London: Longman Group Limited, 1980.

Browning, Christopher R. *The Path to Genocide: Essays on Launching the Final Solution*. Cambridge: Cambridge University Press, 1992.

Brubaker, Rogers, Margit Feischmidt, Jon Fox, and Liana Grancea. *Nationalist Politics and Everyday Ethnicity in a Transylvanian Town*. Princeton: Princeton University Press, 2006.

Brunn, Gerhard, Miroslav Hroch, and Andreas Kappeler. Introduction to *The Formation of National Elites*, edited by Andreas Kappeler, 1–10. New York: New York University Press, 1992.

Brunnbauer, Ulf. "Ethnische Landschaften: Batak als Ort des Erinnerns und Vergessens" (also in Bulgarian). In *Batak kato Mjasto na Pametta*, 98–105. Sofia: Iztok-Zapad, 2007.

Bullough, Oliver. *Let Our Fame Be Great: Journeys among the Defiant Peoples of the Caucasus*. New York: Basic Books, 2010.

Burdett, Anita L. P., ed. *Historical Boundaries between Bosnia, Croatia, Serbia, Documents and Maps, 1815–1945*. London: Archive Editions, 1995.

Bury, J. T., ed. *The New Cambridge Modern History: The Zenith of European Power, 1830–70*. Vol. 10. Cambridge: Cambridge at the University Press, 1960.

Buzan, Barry, Ole Waever, and Jaap de Wilde. *Security: A New Framework for Analysis*. Boulder: Lynne Rienner, 1998.

Çağlar, Günay. "Türkiye-Sovyet Rusya Arasında Türkiye'nin Bugünkü Kuzey-Doğu Sınırının Belirlenmesi Süreci ve Kars Antlaşması." *A. Ü. Türkiyat Araştırmaları Enstitüsü Dergisi* 17 (2001): 275–304.

Çakın, Naci, and Nafiz Orhon. *Türk Silahlı Kuvvetleri Tarihi, IIIncü Cilt 5nci Kısım (1793–1908)*. Ankara: Genelkurmay Basımevi, 1978.

Callwell, C. E. *Small Wars*. N.p., 1896.

———. *Small Wars: Their Principles and Practice* (1896). Lincoln: University of Nebraska Press, 1996.

Canis, Konrad. *Bismarck's Aussenpolitik 1870–1890: Aufstieg und Gefährdung*. Paderborn: Friedrich Schöningh, 2004.

Cecil, Lady Gwendolen. *Life of Robert, Marquis of Salisbury.* 2 vols. London: Hodder and Stoughton, 1921.

Celil, Celilê. *XIX. Yüzyıl Osmanlı İmparatorluğu'nda Kürtler.* Translated by Mehmet Demir. Ankara: Öz-Ge Yayınları, 1992.

———— (Dzhalile Dzhalil). *Intifadat al-Akrad 'Am 1880.* Translated by Siyamand Sirti. Beirut: Dar al-Kitab Press, 1979.

Cemal, H. *Arnavutluk'tan Sakarya'ya Komitacılık: Yuzbası Cemal'in Anıları.* Edited by Kudret Emiroğlu. Ankara: Kebikeç Yayınları, 1996.

Ćemerlić, Hamdija, ed. *Naučni skup: 100 godina ustanka u Hercegovini 1882. godine.* Sarajevo: ANU Bosne i Hercegovine, 1983.

Cengiz, H. Erdoğan, ed. *Enver Paşa'nın Anıları.* Istanbul: İletişim Yayınları, 1991.

Çetin, Atilla. "Rumeli Vilayetlerinin Durumu Hakkında Safvet Paşa'nın II: Abdülhamid'e Sunduğu 1880 Tarihli İki Önemli Arizası." *Tarih Enstitüsü Dergisi* 15 (1997): 565–71.

————. *Tunuslu Hayreddin Paşa.* Istanbul: Kültür ve Turizm Bakanlığı, 1988.

Cezar, Yavuz. *Osmanlı Maliyesinde Bunalım ve Değişim Dönemi (XVIII. yy dan Tanzimat'a Mali Tarih).* N.p.: Alan Yayıncılık, 1986.

Chapman, Maybelle Kennedy. *Great Britain and the Baghdad Railway, 1888–1914.* Northampton, Mass.: Smith College Press, 1948.

Cheragh, Maulavi Ali. *The Proposed Political, Legal, and Social Reforms in the Ottoman Empire and Other Mohammadan States.* Bombay: Education Society's Press, 1883.

Chevalier, Michel. *Les montagnards chrétiens du Hakkâri et du Kurdistan septentrional.* Paris: University of Paris-Sorbonne, Department of Geography, 1985.

Çiçek, Nazan. "The Eastern Critics of the 'Eastern Question': The Young Ottomans, 1866–1871." Ph.D. diss., University of London, 2005.

Çilingiroğlu, Kemal, and İbrahim Tuğcu. *Kars.* Istanbul: Yeni Sabah Matbaası, 1943.

Colley, Linda. *Britons: Forging the Nation, 1707–1837.* New Haven: Yale University Press, 1992.

Cooper, Henry R., Jr. "The Image of Bosnia in the Fiction of Ivo Andric." *Serbian Studies* 3, nos. 1–2 (Fall/Spring 1984–85): 83–105.

Čubrilović, Vaso. *Bosanski ustanak 1875–1878.* Belgrade: Srpska kraljevska akademija, 1930.

————. "Istočna kriza 1875–1878: i njen značaj za međunarodne odnose koncem XIX I početkom XX veka." In *Međunarodni naučni skup povodom: 100-godišnjice ustanka u Bosni i Hercegovini,* 1:15–30. 3 vols. Sarajevo: Akademija nauka i umjetnosti Bosne i Hercegovine, 1977.

Cunningham, Allan. *Eastern Questions in the Nineteenth Century: Collected Essays.* 2 vols. London: Frank Cass, 1993.

Cutler, Allan Harris, and Helen Elmquist Cutler. *The Jew as Ally of the Muslim: Medieval Roots of Anti-Semitism.* Notre Dame: University of Notre Dame Press, 1986.

Dabağyan, Levon P. *Sultan Abdülhamit II ve Ermeniler.* Istanbul: Kum Saati Yayınları, 2001.

Dakin, Douglas. *The Greek Struggle in Macedonia, 1897–1912.* Thessaloniki: Institute for Balkan Studies, 1966.

Dasnabedian, Hratch. *Badmutyun Hay Heghapokhagan Sharzhman ou Hay*

Heghapokhagan Tashnagtsutyan. Edited by Yervant Pambukian. Beirut: Hamazkayin Vahe Setian Printing House, 2010.

———. *H[ay] H[eghapokhagan] Tashnagtsutiune Ir Gazmutenen Minchev 1924.* Beirut:
Hamazkayin Vahe Setian Printing House, 1984.

———. *History of the Armenian Revolutionary Federation, Dasnaktutiun 1890/1924.*
Milan: OEMME Edizioni, 1990.

Davison, Roderic. "The Ottoman Empire and the Congress of Berlin." In *Der Berliner
Kongress von 1878: Die Politik der Grossmächte und die Probleme der Modernisierung
in Südosteuropa in der Zweiten Hälfte des 19. Jahrhunderts,* edited by Ralph Melville
and Hans Jürgen Schroeder, 205–23. Wiesbaden: Steiner Verlag, 1982.

———. *Reform in the Ottoman Empire, 1856–1876.* Princeton: Princeton University
Press, 1963.

Dawidowicz, Lucy. *The War against the Jews.* New York: Holt, Rinehart and Winston,
1975.

Dawn, C. Ernest. *From Ottomanism to Arabism: Essays on the Origins of Arab Nationalism.* Urbana-Champaign: University of Illinois Press, 1973.

Demirağ, Yelda. "Ayastefanos'tan Berlin Kongresine Giden Süreç: Batı'nın Osmanlı'ya
Yönelik Politikası." In *Prof. Dr. Fahir Armaoğlu'na Armağan,* edited by Ersin
Embel, 123–53. Ankara: Türk Tarih Kurumu Yayınları, 2008.

Demirhan, Pertev. *Generalfeldmarschall Colmar von der Goltz: Das Lebensbild eines
grossen Soldaten.* Göttingen: Verlags-Anstalt, 1960.

Deringil, Selim. "Legitimacy Structures in the Ottoman State: the Reign of Abdülhamid II (1876–1909)." *International Journal of Middle East Studies* 23 (1991): 345–59.

———. "'There Is No Compulsion in Religion': On Conversion and Apostasy in the
Late Ottoman Empire, 1839–1856." *Comparative Studies in Society and History* 42
(2000): 561–68.

———. *The Well-Protected Domains: Ideology and the Legitimation of Power in the
Ottoman Empire, 1876–1909.* London: I. B. Tauris, 1998.

Der Minassian, Rupen. *Hay Heghapokhagani Me Hishadagnere.* Vol. 4. Beirut: Hamaz-
kaine V Setian Press, 1975.

Devereux, Robert. *The First Ottoman Constitutional Period: A Study in the Mithat Constitution and Parliament.* Baltimore: Johns Hopkins Press, 1963.

Die grosse Politik der Europäischen Kabinette. 39 vols. Berlin: Deutsche Verlagsgesell-
schaft für Politik und Geschichte, 1922–27.

Dincer, Celal. "Osmanlı Vezirlerinden Hasan Fehmi Paşa'nın Anadolu Bayındırlık
İşlerine dair Hazırladığı Layiha." *Belgeler* 5–8(9–12) (1968–71): 157–62.

Djordjević, Dimitrie. *Izlazak Srbije na jadransko more i konferencija ambasadora u Londonu 1912.* Belgrade: [Slobodan Jović], 1956.

Donia, Robert J. *Islam pod dvoglavim orlom: Muslimani Bosne i Hercegovine 1878–1914.*
Sarajevo: Zoro Zagreb, Institut za istoriju Sarajevo, 2000.

———. *Islam under the Double Eagle: The Muslims of Bosnia-Herzegovina, 1878–1914.*
New York: East European Monographs, 1981.

———. *Sarajevo: biografija grada.* Sarajevo: Institut za istoriju Sarajevo, 2006.

Donia, Robert, and John V. A. Fine. *Bosnia and Herzegovina: A Tradition Betrayed.*
New York: Columbia Press, 1994.

Doyle, Jonathan Klier. *Imperial Russia's Jewish Question, 1855–81*. Cambridge: Cambridge University Press, 1995.

Doyle, M. W. *Empires*. Ithaca: Cornell University Press, 1986.

Doynov, Dojno. *Kresnensko-Razloškoto Våstanie*. Sofia: n.p., 1979.

Duce, Alessandro. *L'Albania nei rapporti italo-austriaci, 1897–1913*. Milano: Giuffre, 1983.

Duguid, Stephen R. "Centralization and Localism: Aspects of Ottoman Policy in Eastern Anatolia, 1878–1908." Master's thesis, Simon Fraser University, 1979.

———. "The Politics of Unity: Hamidian Policy in Eastern Anatolia." *Middle Eastern Studies* 9, no. 2 (April 1973): 139–55.

Džaja, Srećko. *Konfessionalität und Nationalität Bosniens und der Herzegowina: Voremanzipatorische Phase 1463–1804*. Munich: R. Oldenbourg Verlag, 1984.

Dzrakir Hnchakian Gusagtsutyan. 2d ed., abridged. London: n.p., 1897.

Efendi, Hüseyin Raci. *Zağra Müftüsünün Hatıraları*. Translated by M. Ertugrul Duzdag. Ankara: Iz Yayincilik, 2009.

Ekmečić, Milorad. "Istorijski značaj ustanka u Bosni i Hercegovini 1875–1878." In *Međunarodni naučni skup povodom: 100-godišnjice ustanka u Bosni i Hercegovini*, vol. 1, 49–89. Sarajevo: ANU Bosne i Hercegovine, 1977.

———. "Karakteristike Berlinskog kongresa 1878. godine." *Prilozi* 17, no. 18 (1981): 73–99.

———, ed. *Međunarodni naučni skup: Problemi istorije Bosne i Hercegovine 1850–1875*. Sarajevo: ANU Bosne i Hercegovine, 1987.

———, ed. *Naučni skup: Otpor austrougarskoj okupaciji 1878. godine u Bosni i Hercegovini*. Sarajevo: ANU Bosne i Hercegovine, 1979.

———. "Rezultati jugoslovenske istoriografije o istočnom pitanju 1875–1878." In *Jugoslovenski istorijski časopis* 1–2 (1977): 55–74.

———. *Ustanak u Bosni 1875–1878*. 2d ed. Sarajevo: Veselin Masleša, 1960.

Emiroğlu, Kudret, ed. *Trabzon Vilayet Salnamesi*. Vols. 2 (1870), 4 (1872), 5 (1873), and 6 (1874). Ankara: Trabzon İli ve İlçeleri Eğitim, Kültür ve Sosyal Yardımlaşma Vakfı, 1993.

Ensor, R. C. K. *England, 1870–1914*. Oxford: Oxford at the Clarendon Press, 1968.

Erdost, Muzaffer İlhan. *Şemdinli Röportajı*. Ankara: Onur Yayınları, 1993.

Eren, Ahmet Cevat. *Türkiye'de Göç ve Göçmen Meseleleri Tanzimat Devri, İlk Kurulan Göçmen Komisyonu, Çıkarılan Tüzükler*. Istanbul: Nurgök Matbaası, 1966.

Erickson, Edward J. "Armenian Massacres: New Records Undercut Old Blame." *Middle East Quarterly* 13, no. 3 (Summer 2006): 67–75.

———. "The Armenians and Ottoman National Security, 1915." *War in History* (Sage Publications, UK) 15, no. 2 (April 2008): 141–67.

———. "Bayonets on Musa Dagh, Ottoman Counterinsurgency Operations—1915." *Journal of Strategic Studies* 28, no. 3 (June 2005): 529–48.

———. "Captain Larkin and the Turks: The Strategic Impact of the Operations of HMS *Doris* in Early 1915." *Middle Eastern Studies* 46, no. 1 (January 2010): 151–62.

———. *Defeat in Detail: The Ottoman Army in the Balkans, 1912–13*. Westport, Conn.: Praeger, 2003.

———. *Ordered to Die: A History of the Ottoman Army in the First World War*. Westport, Conn.: Greenwood Press, 2001.

Erim, Nihat. *Devletlerarası Hukuk ve Siyasi Tarih Metinleri, Cilt I (Osmanlı İmparatorluğu Antlaşmaları)*. Ankara: Türk Tarih Kurumu Yayınları, 1953.

Erkan, Süleyman. *Kırım ve Kafkasya Göçleri (1878–1908)*. Trabzon: Kafkasya ve Orta Asya Ülkeleri Uygulama ve Araştırma Merkezi Yayını, 1996.

Ermeniler Tarafından Yapılan Katliam Belgeleri (1914–1919). Ankara: Başbakanlık Devlet Arşivleri Genel Müdürlüğü Yayını, 2001.

Ermeni Milletin Esasi Kanunı. N.p., n.d.

Feis, Herbert. *Europe: The World's Banker, 1870–1914*. New Haven: Yale University Press, 1930.

Ferguson, Niall. *Empire: The Rise and Demise of the British World Order and the Lessons for World Power*. 2d ed. New York: Basic Books, 2004.

———. *The War of the World: Twentieth-Century Conflict and the Descent of the West*. London: Penguin Books, 2006.

Fikri, Bekir. *Balkanlarda Tedhiş ve Gerilla: Grebene*. Istanbul: Belge Yayınları, 1978.

Filandra, Šaćir. *Bošnjačka politika u XX. Stoljecu*. Sarajevo: Sejtarija, 1998.

Filipović, Muhamed, ed. *Socijalistička Republika Bosna i Hercegovina, Separat iz drugog izdanja Enciklopedije Jugoslavije*. Zagreb: Jugoslavenski leksikografski zavod, 1983.

Filipović, Nedim, ed. *Savjetovanje o istoriografiji Bosne i Hercegovine (1945–1982)*. Sarajevo: ANU Bosne i Hercegovine, 1983.

Findley, Carter. "The Tanzimat." In *The Cambridge History of Turkey*, vol. 4: *Turkey in the Modern World*, edited by Reşat Kasaba, 11–37. Cambridge: Cambridge University Press, 2008.

———. *Turkey, Islam, Nationalism, and Modernity: A History, 1789–2007*. New Haven: Yale University Press, 2010.

Fine, John V. A., Jr. *The Late Medieval Balkans: A Critical Survey from the Late 12th Century to the Ottoman Conquests*. Ann Arbor: University of Michigan Press, 1987.

Fink, Carole. *Defending the Rights of Others: The Great Powers, the Jews, and International Minority Protection, 1878–1938*. New York: Cambridge University Press, 2004.

Finkel, Caroline. *Osman's Dream: The Story of the Ottoman Empire, 1300–1923*. London: John Murray, 2005.

Fırat, M. Şerif. *Doğu İlleri ve Varto Tarihi*. N.p., 1961.

Foner, Philip S. *The Spanish-Cuban-American War and the Birth of American Imperialism, 1895–1902*, vol. 1: *1895–1898*. New York: Monthly Review Press, 1972.

Fortna, Benjamin C. "The Reign of Abdülhamid II." In *The Cambridge History of Turkey*, vol. 4: *Turkey in the Modern World*, edited by Reşat Kasaba, 38–61. Cambridge: Cambridge University Press, 2008.

Friedman, Francine. *The Bosnian Muslims: Denial of a Nation*. Boulder: Westview Press, 1996.

Fromkin, David. *A Peace to End All Peace: Creating the Modern Middle East, 1914–1922*. London: Penguin, 1991.

Fukuyama, Francis. "The End of History?" *National Interest* 16 (Summer 1989): 3–18.

Fuller, William C., Jr. *Civil-Military Conflict in Imperial Russia, 1880–1914*. Princeton: Princeton University Press, 1985.

———. *Strategy and Power in Russia, 1600–1914*. New York: Free Press, 1992.

Garo, Armen. *Bank Ottoman: Memoirs of Armen Karo*. Translated by Haig T. Papazian. Detroit: n.p., 1990.

Gavranović, Berislav. *Bosna i Hercegovina u doba austrougarske okupacije 1878. godine*. Sarajevo: ANU Bosne i Hercegovine, 1973.

Geiss, Immanuel, ed. *Der Berliner Kongress 1878: Protokolle und Materialen*. Boppart am Rhein: Harald Boldt Verlag, 1978.

Gellner, Ernest. *Nationalismus und Moderne*. Berlin: Rotbuch Verlag, 1991.

Georgeon, François. "Abdülhamid II (1876–1909)." In *Pax Ottomana: Studies in Memoriam Prof. Dr. Nejat Göyünç*. edited by Kemal Çiçek, 409–24. Ankara: Yeni Türkiye Yayınları, 2001.

Georgiev, Velichko, and Stajko Trifonov. *Pokrăstvaneto na Bălgarite Mohamedani 1912–1913: Dokumenti*. Sofia: Akad. Izdat. Marin Drinov, 1995.

Germanov, Stojan. *Makedoniya: Istoriya i Političeskata Sădba*. Vol. 1. Sofia: n.p., 1994.

Gibb, H. A. R. "Lutfi Pasa on the Ottoman Caliphate." *Oriens* 15 (1962): 287–95.

———. "Some Considerations on the Sunni Theory of the Caliphate." In *Studies on the Civilization of Islam*, edited by Stanford J. Shaw and William R. Polk, 141–50. Boston: Beacon Press, 1962.

Gilligan, Emma. *Terror in Chechnya: Russia and the Tragedy of Civilians in War*. Princeton: Princeton University Press, 2009.

Giulkhandanian, Abraham. "Heghapokhakan Sharzhman Skizbe Taroni Mej." *Hairenik Monthly* 17, no. 9 (October 1939): 96–97.

Gladstone, William. *Bulgarian Horrors and the Question of the East*. London: John Murray, 1876.

———. *Lessons in Massacre*. London: J. Murray, 1877.

Gong, Gerrit W. *The Standard of "Civilization" in International Society*. Oxford: Oxford University Press, 1984.

Goranov, Angel (Boycho). *Vastanieto i klaneto v Batak: Istoricheski ocherk*. Plovdiv: D. V. Manchov, 1892.

Gourvish, T. R., and Alan O'Day, eds. *Later Victorian Britain, 1867–1900*. London: Macmillan, 1988.

Grant, Jonathan. "The Sword of the Sultan: Ottoman Arms Imports, 1854–1914." *Journal of Military History* 66, no. 1 (January 2002): 9–36.

Gregorian, Vartan. "The Impact of Russia on the Armenians and Armenia." In *Russia and Asia: Essays on the Influence of Russia on the Asian Peoples*, edited by Wayne S. Vucinich, 166–218. Stanford: Hoover Institution Press, 1972.

Griffith, Merwin A. "The Reorganization of the Ottoman Army under Abdülhamid II, 1880–1897." Ph.D. diss., University of California, Los Angeles, 1966.

Grmek, Mirko, Marc Gjidaram, and Niven Simac. *Le nettoyage ethnique: Documents historiques sur une ideologie serbe*. Paris: Fayard. 1993.

Günay, Nejla. *Maraş'ta Ermeniler ve Zeytun İsyanları*. Istanbul: IQ Kültür Sanat Yayıncılık, 2007.

Günay, Selçuk. "Resmi Devlet Sâlnâmelerine Göre (H. 1263–1334) Osmanlı İmparatorluğu'nun Seneler İtibariyle Mülkî Taksimatı." M.A. thesis, Erzurum, 1980.

Gündüz, Asim. *Hatıralarım*. Istanbul: Kervan Yayınları, 1973.

Gutman, Roy. *A Witness to Genocide*. New York: Macmillan, n.d.

Güven, Melek Sarı. "Kevork Pamukciyan'ın Tarih Perspektifinden Olaylara Bakışı."
    M.A. thesis, Ankara University, 2006.

Guzina, Ružica. *Opština u Srbiji 1839–1918*. Belgrade: n.p., 1976.

Habiçoğlu, Bedri. *Kafkasya'dan Anadolu'ya Göçler ve İskanları*. Istanbul: Nart
    Yayıncılık, 1993.

Hacikyan, Agop Jack, Gabriel Basmajian, and Edward S. Franchuk. *The Heritage of
    Armenian Literature: From the Eighteenth Century until Modern Times*. Detroit:
    Wayne State University Press, 2000.

Hacısalihoğlu, Mehmet. *Die Jungtürken und die Mazedonische Frage, 1890–1918*.
    Munich: Oldenburg Verlag, 2003.

———. *Doğu Rumeli'de Kayıp Köyler: İslimye Sancağı'nda 1878'den Günümüze Göçler,
    İsim Değişiklikleri ve Harabeler*. Istanbul: Bağlam, 2008.

Hadžibegović, Iljas. *Bosanskohercegovački gradovi na razmeđu 19. i 20. Stoljeca*. Sarajevo:
    Oslobođenje public, 1991.

———. *Postanak radničke klase u Bosni i Hercegovini i njen razvoj do 1914. Godine*. Sara-
    jevo: Svjetlost, 1980.

———. "Radnički socijalistički pokret u Bosni i Hercegovini do kraja prvog svjetskog
    rata i stvaranje zajedničke države 1918. godine." *Prilozi* 17, no. 18 (1981): 121–53.

Hadzijahić, Muhamed. "Uz prilog Prof. Vojislava Bogičevića." *Historijski zbornik* 3
    (1950): 189–92.

Halaçoğlu, Yusuf. "Realities behind the Relocation." In *The Armenians in the Late
    Ottoman Period*, edited by Türkkaya Ataöv, 100–142. Ankara: Turkish Historical
    Society, 2001.

Halfin. *19. Yüzyılda Kürdistan Üzerinde Mücadeleler*. Ankara: Komâl Yayınları, 1976.

Hanioğlu, M. Şükrü. *A Brief History of the Late Ottoman Empire*. Princeton: Princeton
    University Press, 2008.

———. *Preparation for a Revolution: The Young Turks, 1902–1908*. Oxford: Oxford Uni-
    versity Press, 2001.

———. "The Second Constitutional Period, 1908–1918." In *The Cambridge History of
    Turkey*, vol. 4: *Turkey in the Modern World*, edited by Reşat Kasaba, 62–111. Cam-
    bridge: Cambridge University Press, 2008.

———. *The Young Turks in Opposition*. New York/Oxford: Oxford University Press,
    1995.

Harris, David. *A Diplomatic History of the Balkan Crisis of 1875–1878: The First Year*.
    London: Archon Books, 1969.

Hauptmann, Ferdinand. *Borba Muslimana Bosne i Hercegovine za vjersku i vakufsko-
    mearifsku autonomiju: Građa*. Sarajevo: Arhiv Bosne i Hercegovine, 1967.

———. "Die Mohammedaner in Bosnien und Hercegovina." In *Die Konfessionen (Die
    Habsburgermonarchie 1848–1918)*, edited by Adam Wandruska and Peter Urban-
    itsch, 670–701. Vienna: Verlag der österreichischen Akademie der Wissenschaften,
    1985.

———. *Die österreichisch-ungarische Herrschaft in Bosnien und der Herzegovina 1878–
    1918: Wirtschaftspolitik und Wirtschaftsentwicklung*. Graz: Institut für Geschichte
    der Universität Graz, Abt. Südosteuropäische Geschichte, 1983.

———. "Privreda i društvo Bosne i Hercegovine u doba austro-ugarske vladavine

(1878–1918)." In *Prilozi za istoriju Bosne i Hercegovine 2*, edited by Enver Redžić, 99–211. Sarajevo: Akademija nauka i umjetnosti Bosne i Hercegovine, 1987.

Hayes, Carlton J. H. *A Generation of Materialism, 1871–1900*. New York: Harper, 1941.

Hayes, Paul. "British Foreign Policy, 1867–1900: Continuity and Conflict." In *Later Victorian Britain*, edited by T. R. Gourvish and Alan O'Day, 151–74. New York: St. Martin's Press, 1988.

"Hay-Kertakan Haraberutiunner." *Droshak* 4, no. 115 (June 1901): 67–68; *Droshak* 5, no. 116 (July 1901): 81–82.

Hecter, Michael. *Containing Nationalism*. New York: Oxford University Press, 2001.

Hegel, G. W. F. *The Phenomenology of Spirit*. Translated by A. V. Miller. Oxford: Clarendon Press, 1977.

Heller, Joseph. *British Policy towards the Ottoman Empire*. London: Cass, 1983.

Hentsch, Thierry. *Imagining the Middle East*. Montreal: Black Rose Books, 1992.

"Herkum Me." *Droshak* 2, no. 82 (February 1898): 23–24.

Hinsly, F. H., ed. *The New Cambridge Modern History*, vol. 11: *Material Progress and World-Wide Problems, 1870–1898*. Cambridge: Cambridge at the University Press, 1962.

Hinton, Alexander Labon, ed. *Annihilating Difference: The Anthropology of Genocide*. Berkeley: University of California Press, 2002.

History of the Turko-Russian War. London: Adam and Co., 1880.

Hofmann, Tessa, and Gerayer Koutcharian. "The History of Armenian-Kurdish Relations in the Ottoman Empire." *Armenian Review* 4 (1986): 1–45.

Holborn, Hajo, ed. *Aufzeichnungen und Erinnerungen aus dem Leben des Botschafters Joseph Maria von Radowitz*. 2 vols. Berlin/Leipzig: Deutsche Verlags-Anstalt, 1925.

Holland, Thomas Erskine. *The European Concert in the Eastern Question*. Oxford: Clarendon Press, 1885.

Hourani, Albert. *A History of the Arab Peoples*. Cambridge, Mass.: Belknap Press of Harvard University Press, 1991.

Hovannisian, Richard G. "The Armenian Question in the Ottoman Empire, 1876 to 1914." In *The Armenian People from Ancient to Modern Times*, edited by Richard Hovannisian, 2:203–38. 2 vols. New York: Macmillan, 1997–2004.

———. *Armenia: On the Road to Independence, 1918*. Berkeley: University of California Press, 1967.

Hristov, Petko. "Granicite na Šopluka i/ili Šopi bez granica." In *Hidden Minorities in the Balkans*, 67–83. Belgrade: n.p., 2004.

Hubka, Gustav. *Die österreichisch-ungarische Offiziersmission in Makedonien, 1903–1909*. Vienna: Tempsky, 1910.

Huntington, Samuel. "The Clash of Civilizations." *Foreign Affairs* 72, no. 3 (1993): 22–50.

Hurewitz, J. C. *Diplomacy in the Near and Middle East, a Documentary Record: 1535–1914*. Vol. 1. Princeton: D. van Nostrand, 1956.

Ikenberry, G. John, and Charles A. Kupchan. "Socialization and Hegemonic Power." *International Organization* 44 (1990): 283–315.

Imamović, Mustafa. "Bosna između Osmanske i Habsburške carevine u Istočnoj krizi 1875–1878 godine." In *Međunarodni naučni skup povodom: 100-godišnjice ustanka*

u Bosni i Hercegovini, drugim balkanskim zemljama i istočnoj krizi 1875–1878.
godine, edited by Rade Petrović, 341–50. 3 vols. Sarajevo: ANU Bosne i Herce-
govine, 1977.
———. *Historija Bošnjaka*. Sarajevo: Bošnjačka zajednica kulture Preporod, 1998.
———. *Historija države i prava Bosne i Hercegovine*. Sarajevo: Magistrat, 2003.
———. "O historiji bošnjačkog pokušaja." In *Muslimani i bošnjastvo*, edited by Atıf
Purivatra, Mustafa Imamović, and Rusmir Mahmutćehayić, 33–69. Sarajevo: Musli-
manska bibliotheka, 1991.
———. *Pravni položaj i unutrašnji politički razvitak Bosne i Hercegovine od 1878 do 1914.*
Sarajevo: Svjetlost, 1976.
İnal, İbnülemin Mahmud Kemal. *Osmanlı Devrinde Son Sadrazamlar*. Istanbul: Milli
Eğitim Basımevi, 1969.
İnalcık, Halil. "Islamic Caliphate, Turkey and Muslims in India." In *Shari'ah, Ummah
and Khilafah*, edited by Yusuf Abbas Hashmi, 14–34. Karachi: University of Kara-
chi, 1987.
*Instruction Guidelines on the Proceedings (CERAD) of the Tribal Light Cavalry Regi-
ments*. Istanbul: n.p., 1327 [1909].
İpek, Nedim. *İmparatorluktan Ulus Devlete Göçler*. Trabzon: Serander Yayınları, 2006.
———. *Rumeli'den Anadolu'ya Türk Göçleri, 1877–1890*. Ankara: Türk Tarihi Kurumu,
1994.
Ippen, Theodore. "Das religiöse Protectorat Österreich-Ungarns in der Türkei." *Die
Kultur* 3 (1902): 298–310.
Issawi, Charles. "The Tabriz-Trabzon Trade, 1830–1900: Rise and Decline of a Route."
International Journal of Middle East Studies 1, no. 1 (1970): 18–27.
Jagodić, Miloš. *Naseljavanje Kneževine Srbije 1860–1861*. Belgrade: n.p., 2004.
Jakšić, Grgur. *Bosna i Hercegovina na Berlinskom kongresu*. Belgrade: SAN, 1955.
Jelavich, Barbara. *History of the Balkans, Eighteenth and Nineteenth Centuries*. 2 vols.
Cambridge: Cambridge University Press, 1995.
———. *The Ottoman Empire, the Great Powers, and the Straits Question, 1870–1887.*
Bloomington/London: Indiana University Press, 1973.
———. *Russia's Balkan Entanglements, 1806–1914*. Cambridge: Cambridge University
Press, 1991.
Jelavich, Charles, and Barbara Jelavich. *The Establishment of the Balkan National States,
1804–1920*. Seattle/London: University of Washington Press, 1977.
Jokanović, Vlado. "Elementi koji su kroz istoriju djelovali pozitivno i negativno na
stvaranja bošnjaštva kao nacionalnog pokreta." *Pregled* 2 (1968): 241–63.
Jovanović, Jagoš. *Stvaranje črnogorske drzave i razvoj črnogorske nacionalnosti: Istorija
Črne Goreod pochetka VIII vijeka do 1918 godine*. Cetinje: Narodna knjiga, 1948.
Jovanović, Slobodan. *Vlada Milana Obrenovića II*. Belgrade: n.p., 1991.
Judson, Pieter. *Guardians of the Nation: Activists on the Language Frontiers of Imperial
Austria*. Cambridge, Mass.: Harvard University Press, 2006.
Juzbašić, Dževad. *Jezičko pitanje u austrougarskoj politici u Bosni i Hercegovini pred prvi
svjetski rat*. Sarajevo: Svjetlost, 1973.
Jwaideh, Wadie. *The Kurdish National Movement: Its Origins and Development*. Syra-
cuse: Syracuse University Press, 2006.
Kapidžić, Hamdija. "Agrarno pitanje u Bosni i Hercegovini za vrijeme austrougarske

uprave (1878–1918)." *Godišnjak Društva istoričara Bosne i Hercegovine* 19 (1973): 71–96.

———. *Der Aufstand in der Hercegovine im jahre 1882: Auszüge.* Graz: Selbstverlag, 1972.

———. "Prilog istoriji hercegovačkog ustanka 1882." *Godišnjak istorijskog društva Bosne i Hercegovine* 2 (1950): 207–16.

Karabegović, Ibrahim, ed. *Bosna i Hercegovina od najstarijih vremena do kraja Drugog svjetskog rata.* 2d ed. Sarajevo: Preporod, 1998.

Karabekir, Kazım. *Hayatım.* Edited by Faruk Özerengin. Istanbul: Emre Yayınları, 1995.

Karal, Enver Ziya. *Osmanlı Tarihi* (1962). Vol. 8. Ankara: Türk Tarih Kurumu Yayınları, 2007.

Karatamu, Selahattin. *Türk Silahlı Kuvvetleri Tarihi, IIIncü Cilt 6nci Kısım (1908–1920).* Ankara: Genelkurmay Basımevi, 1971.

Karpat, Kemal H. "The Migration of the Bosnian Muslims to the Ottoman State, 1878–1914: An Account Based on Turkish Sources." In *Ottoman Bosnia: A History in Peril,* edited by Markus Koller and Kemal Karpat, 121–40. Madison: University of Wisconsin Press, 2004.

———. "*Millets* and Nationality: The Roots of the Incongruity of Nation and State in the Post-Ottoman Era." In *Christians and Jews in the Ottoman Empire,* edited by Benjamin Braude and Bernard Lewis, 1:141–70. 2 vols. New York: Holmes and Meier Publications, 1982. Republished in *Studies on Ottoman Social and Political History: Selected Articles and Essays,* edited by Kemal Karpat, 611–46. Leiden/Boston: E. J. Brill, 2002.

———. *Osmanlı Nüfusu (1830–1914): Demografik ve Sosyal Özellikleri.* Istanbul: Tarih Vakfı Yurt Yayınları, 2003.

———. "The Ottoman Attitude towards the Resistance of Bosnia and Hercegovina to the Austrian Occupation in 1878." In *Naučni skup: Otpor austrougarskoj okupaciji 1878. godine u Bosni i Hercegovini,* edited by Milorad Ekmečić, 147–72. Sarajevo: ANU Bosne i Hercegovine, 1979.

———. *Ottoman Population, 1830–1914: Demographics and Social Characteristics.* Madison: University of Wisconsin Press, 1985.

———. "The Social and Political Foundations of Nationalism in South East Europe after 1878: An Interpretation." In *Der Berliner Kongress von 1878: Die Politik der Grossmächte und die Probleme der Modernisierung in Südosteuropa in der Zweiten Hälfte des 19. Jahrhunderts,* edited by Ralph Melville and Hans Jürgen Schroeder, 385–410. Wiesbaden: Steiner Verlag, 1982. Republished in Kemal H. Karpat, *Studies on Social and Political History,* 352–84. Leiden: Brill, 2002.

———, ed. *Studies on Social and Political History.* Leiden: Brill, 2002.

———. *The Turks of Bulgaria: The History, Culture and Political Fate of a Minority.* Istanbul: Isis, 1990.

———. "1878 Avusturya İşgaline Karşı Bosna-Hersek Direnişiyle İlgili Osmanlı Politikası." In *Balkanlar'da Osmanlı Mirası ve Ulusçuluk,* edited by Kemal Karpat, 151–96. Ankara: İmge Yayınları, 2004.

"Kars Oblast." In *Brockhaus and Efron Encyclopedic Dictionary.* St. Petersburg: n.p., 1890–1907.

Kaya, Erol. "1877–1878 Harplerinde Ağrı Bölgesinde Göç Hareketleri." *Erzincan Eğitim Fakültesi Dergisi* 10, no. 1 (2008): 203–10.

Kaynar, Reşat. *Mustafa Reşit Paşa ve Tanzimat*. Ankara: Türk Tarih Kurumu, 1954.

Kemura, İbrahim. "Proglas muslimanske akademske omladine u Beću od 1907 godine." In *Prilozi (Institut za istoriju)* 13 (1977): 334–45.

Kennedy, Paul. *The Rise and Fall of the Great Powers: Economic Change and Military Conflict from 1500 to 2000*. New York: Random House, 1987.

Kent, Marian, ed. *The Great Powers and the End of the Ottoman Empire*. London: George Allen and Unwin, 1984.

Keren, Zvi. "The Fate of the Jewish Communities of Kazanlık and Eski-Zağra in the 1877/78 War." In *The Ottoman-Russian War of 1877–78*, edited by Ömer Turan, 113–30. Ankara: Middle East Technical University Department of History and TDV Yayın Matbaacılık METU, 2007.

Kerman, Zeynep, trans. *Rusların Asya'da ve Rumeli'de Yaptıkları Mezalim*. Istanbul: Turk Dunyasi Arastirmalari Vakfi, 1987.

Khan, Mujeeb R. "Bosnia-Herzegovina and the Crisis of the Post-Cold War International System." *East European Politics and Societies* 9, no. 3 (Fall 1995): 459–98.

———. "External Threats and the Promotion of a Trans-national Islamic Conciousness: The Case of the Late Ottoman Empire and Contemporary Turkey." *Islamic World Report* 1, no. 3 (1996): 115–28.

———. "From Hegel to Genocide in Bosnia: Some Moral and Philosophical Concerns." *Journal of Muslim Minority Affairs* 15, nos. 1–2 (January and July 1994): 1–30.

———. "The 'Other' in the Balkans: Historical Construction of 'Serbs' and 'Turks.'" *Journal of Muslim Minority Affairs* 16, no. 4 (January 1996): 49–63.

Khrimian, Megerditch. *Haykoyzh*. Istanbul: Asadurian Press, 1908.

Kiniapina, N. S. "Osnovnye Etapi Politiki Rossii v Vostochnom Krizise 1875–1878 gg." In *Rossiia i Vostochnii Krizis 70-kh Godov XIX v*, edited by I. A. Fedesov et al., 6–22. Moscow: Izdatel'stvo Moskovskogo Universiteta, 1981.

Kirakossian, Arman J. *British Diplomacy and the Armenian Question: From the 1830s to 1914*. Princeton: Gomidas Insitute Books, 2003.

Kirakosyan, Arman. *Britanakan Divanagitutyune Yev Arevmtahayeri Khentire: 1830–1914*. Yerevan: Gitutyun Publishing, 1999.

Kırzıoğlu, M. Fahrettin. *Kars Tarihi*. Istanbul: Işıl Matbaası, 1953.

Klicin, Dimitrije. "Otpor Muslimana protiv okupacije." *Gajret: Kalendar za god 1939* (1938): 227–46.

Kodajova, Daniela. "R. W. Seton-Watson's Views of the Habsburg Monarchy, the Ottoman Empire and Russia." In *Great Britain and Central Europe, 1867–1914*, edited by Robert Evans et al., 123–34. Bratislava: VEDA, 2002.

Kodaman, Bayram. "Hamidiye Hafif Süvari Alayları (II. Abdülhamid ve Doğu Aşiretleri)." *Tarih Dergisi* 32 (1979): 427–80.

———. *Şark Meselesi Işığı Altında Sultan II. Abdulhamidin Doğu Anadolu Politikası*. Istanbul: Orkun Yayınevi, 1983.

———. "II. Abdülhamid Devrinde İlk ve Orta Öğretim." Associate professorship thesis, Ankara University, 1976.

———. "II Abdülhamid ve Aşiret Mektebi." *Türk Kültürü Araştırmaları Dergisi* 15, nos. 1–2 (1976): 263.

Kohl, Horst, ed. *Anhang zu den Gedanken und Erinnerungen von Otto Fürst von Bismarck*. 2 vols. Stuttgart/Berlin: Cotta, 1901.

Kohler, Max J., and Simon Wolf. *Jewish Disabilities in the Balkan States: American Contributions toward Their Removal, with Particular Reference to the Congress of Berlin.* Publications of the American Jewish Historical Society 24. New York: Lord Baltimore Press, 1916.

Kohn, Hans. *Panislavizm ve Rus Milliyetçiliği.* Trans. Agah Oktay Güner. Istanbul: Kervan Yayınları, 1983.

Kojeve, Alexandre. *Introduction to the Reading of Hegel.* Assembled by Raymond Queneau. Edited by Allan Bloom. Translated by James H. Nichols, Jr. New York: Basic Books, 1969.

Kornrumpf, Hans-Jürgen. *Die Territorialverwaltung im östlichen Teil der europäischen Türkei vom Berliner Kongress (1878) bis zu den Balkankriegen (1912/13) nach amtlichen osmanischen Veröffentlichungen.* Munich: J. Trojenik, 1983.

———. *Die Territorialverwaltung im östlichen Teil der europäischen Türkei vom Erlass der Vilayetsordnung (1864) bis zum Berliner Kongress (1878) nach amtlichen osmanischen Veröffentlichungen.* Freiburg: Schwarz, 1976.

"Kotch Kurterun." *Droshak* 6, no. 86 (June 1898): 51–52.

Kraljačić, Tomislav. *Kalajev režim u Bosni i Hercegovini (1882–1903).* Sarajevo: Veselin Masleša, 1987.

Krikorian, Mesrob K. *Armenians in the Service of the Ottoman Empire, 1860–1908.* London: Routledge, 1977.

Kruševać, Todor. *Sarajevo pod austro-ugarskom upravom 1878–1918.* Sarajevo: Narodna štamparija, 1960.

Küçük, Cevdet. *Osmanlı Diplomasisinde Ermeni Meselesinin Ortaya Çıkışı, 1878–1897.* Istanbul: Istanbul Universitesi, 1984.

Kuneralp, Sinan, ed. *The Queen's Ambassador to the Sultan: Memoirs of Sir Henry A. Layard's Constantinople Embassy, 1877–1880.* Istanbul: ISIS, 2009.

Kuneralp, Sinan, and Gül Tokay, eds. *Ottoman Diplomatic Documents on the Origins of World War One: The Macedonian Issue, 1879–1912.* Istanbul: Isis, 2011.

Kuran, Ercümend. "Küçük Said Paşa (1840–1914) as a Turkish Modernist." *International Journal of Middle East Studies* 1, no. 1 (1970): 124–32.

Kurat, Akdes Nimet. *Türkiye ve Rusya: XVII. Yüzyıl Sonundan Kurtuluş Savaşına Kadar Türk-Rus İlişkileri 1798–1919.* Ankara: Ankara Üniversitesi, 1970.

Kurat, Yuluğ Tekin. "1878–1919 Arasında Türk-Rus İlişkileri." In *Ankara Üniversitesi Dil ve Tarih-Coğrafya Fakültesi Tarih Bölümü Tarih Araştırmaları Dergisi* 16, no. 27 (Ankara, 1992): 133–43.

Kut, Halil. *Ittihat ve Terakki'den Cumhuriyete Bitmeyen Savas.* Istanbul: 7 Gün Yayınları, 1971.

Ladas, Stephen. *The Exchange of Minorities: Bulgaria, Greece, and Turkey.* New York: Macmillan, 1932.

Landau, Jacob. *The Politics of Pan-Islam: Ideology and Organization.* Oxford: Oxford University Press, 1994.

Lange-Akhund, Nadine. *The Macedonian Question, 1893–1908: From Western Sources.* New York: Columbia University Press, 1998.

Langer, William L. *The Diplomacy of Imperialism, 1890–1902.* 2d ed. New York: Alfred A. Knopf, 1956.

"Law on Agrarian Relationships." In *Agrarno pitanje u novooslobodjenim krajevima*

Srbije posle srpsko-turskih ratova 1878–1907, ed. Slobodanka Stojičić, 131–37. Leskovac: n.p., 1987.

The Layard Papers: A Memoir of His Embassy to Turkey. Vols. 5–8, sections 12–13. N.p., n.d.

Lazarev, Ivan Davidovich. *Prichiny Bedstvii Armian v Turtsii: Otvetstvennost' za Razorenie Sasuna*. Tiflis: Tip. I. A. Martirosiantsa, 1895.

Lee, Dwight E. *Great Britain and the Cyprus Convention Policy of 1878*. Cambridge, Mass.: Harvard University Press, 1934.

Les Protocoles du Congrès de Berlin. St. Petersburg: Trenké and Fusnot, 1879.

Lewis, Bernard. *The Emergence of Modern Turkey*. Oxford: Oxford University Press, 1961.

———. "Watan." *Journal of Contemporary History* 26 (1991): 526–33.

Lewy, Guenter. *The Armenian Massacres in Ottoman Turkey: A Disputed Genocide*. Salt Lake City: University of Utah Press, 2005.

Libaridian, Gerard J. *Modern Armenia: People, Nation, State*. New Brunswick, N.J./London: Transaction Publishers, 2004.

———. "Revolution and Liberation in the 1892 and 1907 Programs of the Dashnaktsutiun." In *Transcaucasia, Nationalism and Social Change: Essays in the History of Armenia, Azerbaijan, and Georgia*, edited Ronald Grigor Suny, 187–98. Ann Arbor: University of Michigan, 1983.

Lieven, C. B. *Empire: The Russian Empire and Its Rivals*. New Haven: Yale University Press, 2001.

Lilić, Borislava. *Istorija Pirota i okoline (1878–1918)*. Vol. 2. Belgrade: n.p., 1990.

Lindow, Erich. *Freiherr Marschall von Bieberstein als Botschafter in Konstantinopel, 1897–1912*. Danzig: A. W. Kafemann, 1934.

Linn, Brian McAllister. *The U.S. Army and Counterinsurgency in the Philippine War, 1899–1902*. Chapel Hill: University of North Carolina Press, 1989.

Longworth, Philip. *The Cossacks*. New York: Holt, Rinehart and Winston, 1970.

Lory, Bernard. "Ahmed aga Tamraslijata: The Last Derebey of the Rhodopes." In *The Turks of Bulgaria: The History, Culture and Political Fate of a Minority*, edited by Kemal H. Karpat, 179–202. Istanbul: ISIS Press, 1990.

MacGahan, Januarius. *The Turkish Atrocities in Bulgaria: Letters of the Special Commissioner of the Daily News, J. A. Macgahan*. London: Bradbury, Agnew and Co., 1876.

Maclean, Arthur John. *Grammar of the Dialects of Vernacular Syriac*. Cambridge: Cambridge University Press, 1895.

Madsen, Wayne. "Did NSA Help Target Dudayev?" *Covert Action Quarterly* 61 (1997): 47–49.

Madžar, Božo. "Izvještaji austriskog generalnog konzula Vasića…od septembra 1875. do juna 1876. godine." *Glasnik arhiva i Društva arhivskih radnika Bosne i Hercegovine* 14/15 (1975): 238–98.

Magas, Branka. *The Destruction of Yugoslavia: Tracking the Breakup, 1980–92*. London: Verso, 1993.

Maier, Charles. *The Unmasterable Past: History, Holocaust, and German National Identity*. Cambridge, Mass.: Harvard University Press, 1988.

Makdermot, Mersiya. *Za Svoboda i Săvăršensto: Bografiya na Yane Sandanski*. Sofia: n.p., 1987.

Maksić, Jelena, and Anica Lolić. *Bibliografija jugoslovenske literature o velikoj istočnoj krizi 1875–1878*. Vol. 1. Belgrade: Istorijski institut, 1979.

Malcolm, Noel. *Bosnia: A Short History*. New York: Macmillan, 1994.

———. *Kosovo: A Short History*. New York: Harper Perennial, 1999.

Malkhas (Ardashes Hovsepian). *Abrumner*. Tehran: Farabi Publishing, 1982.

Mandić, Mihodil. *Povijest okupacije Bosne i Herzegovina 1878*. Zagreb: Matica Hrvatska, 1910.

Manjikian, Hagop. *Ho. Hee. Ta. Albom-Atlas, Tutsaznamard, 1890–1914*. Los Angeles: Modern Type Printing and Lithography, 1992.

Mann, Michael. *The Dark Side of Democracy*. New York: Cambridge University Press, 2005.

Mardin, Şerif. "Modernization of Social Communication." In *Propaganda and Communication in World History*, edited by Harold D. Laswell et al., 381–443. Honolulu: University Press of Hawaii, 1979.

———. *Religion and Social Change in Modern Turkey: The Case of Bediüzzaman Said Nursi*. Albany: State University of New York Press, 1989.

Marriott, J. A. R. *The Eastern Question: An Historical Study in European Diplomacy*. Oxford: Clarendon Press, 1918.

Marx, Karl. *The Economic and Philosophic Manuscripts of 1844*. Edited by Dirk J. Struik. New York: International Publishers, 1964.

———. "On the Jewish Question." In *Selected Writings*, edited by David McLellan, 39–62. Oxford: Oxford University Press, 1977

Maxwell, Alexander. "Krsté Misirkov's 1903 Call for Macedonian Autocephaly: Religious Nationalism as Instrumental Political Tactic." *Studia Theologica* 5 (2007): 165–67.

Mayewski, General V. F. *Van ve Bitlis Vilayetleri Askeri Istatistiki*. Translated by Mehmet Sadık. Istanbul: Matbaa-i Askeriye, 1912.

Mazower, Mark. *The Balkans: From the End of Byzantium to the Present Day*. London: Phoenix Press, 2002.

———. *Dark Continent: Europe's Twentieth Century*. New York: Vintage Books, 2000.

———. *Salonica, City of Ghosts: Christians, Muslims and Jews, 1430–1950*. London: Harper Perennial, 2004.

———. "Violence and the State in the 20th Century." *American Historical Review*. http://www.historycooperative.org/journals/ahr/107.4/ah0402001158.html.

McCarthy, Justin. *Death and Exile: The Ethnic Cleansing of Ottoman Muslims, 1821–1922*. Princeton, N.J.: Darwin Press, 1995.

———. "The Demography of the 1877–78 Russo-Turkish War." In *The Ottoman-Russian War of 1877–78*, edited by Ömer Turan, 51–78. Ankara: Middle East Technical University Department of History and TDV Yayın Matbaacılık METU, 2007.

———. *Muslims and Minorities: The Population of Anatolia and the End of the Empire*. New York: New York University Press, 1983.

———. "Muslims in Ottoman Europe: Population from 1800 to 1912." *Nationalities Papers* 28, no. 1 (2000): 29–43.

———. *Ölüm ve Sürgün*. Istanbul: Inkılap Yayınevi, 1998.

———. *Osmanlı'ya Veda İmparatorluk Çökerken Osmanlı Halkları*. Istanbul: Etkileşim Yayınları, 2006.

———. "Ottoman Bosnia, 1800 to 1878." In *The Muslims of Bosnia-Herzegovina*, ed. Mark Pinson, 54–83. Cambridge, Mass.: Harvard University Press, 1994.

———. *The Ottoman Turks: An Introductory History to 1923*. London: Longman, 1997.

———. "The Population of Ottoman Europe before and after the Fall of the Empire." In *Proceedings of the Third Conference on the Social and Economic History of Turkey*, ed. Heath W. Lowry and Ralph Haddox, 275–98. Istanbul: Isis, 1990.

———. *Turks in America: The Creation of an Enduring Prejudice*. Salt Lake City: University of Utah Press, 2010.

McCarthy, Justin, Esat Arslan, Cemalettin Taşkıran, and Ömer Turan. *The Armenian Rebellion at Van*. Salt Lake City: University of Utah Press, 2006.

McMeekin, Sean. *The Berlin-Baghdad Express: The Ottoman Empire and Germany's Bid for World Power, 1898–1918*. London: Penguin/Allen Lane, 2010.

McMurray, Jonathan S. *Distant Ties: Germany, the Ottoman Empire, and the Construction of the Baghdad Railway*. Westport, Conn.: Praeger, 2001.

Medlicott, W. N. *Bismarck, Gladstone and the Concert of Europe*. London: University of London, Athlone Press/New York: Greenwood Press, 1956.

———. *The Congress of Berlin and After: A Diplomatic History of the Near Eastern Settlement, 1878–1880*. London: Methuen and Co., 1938. 2d ed. London: Frank Cass, 1963.

Međunarodni naučni skup povodom: 100-godišnjice ustanka u Bosni i Hercegovini, drugim balkanskim zemljama i istočnoj krizi 1875–1878. godine. Ed. Rade Petrović. 3 vols. Sarajevo: ANU Bosne i Hercegovine, 1977.

Melson, Robert. *Revolution and Genocide: On the Origins of the Armenian Genocide and the Holocaust*. Chicago: University of Chicago Press, 1989.

Melville, Ralph, and Hans Jürgen Schroeder, eds. *Der Berliner Kongress von 1878: Die Politik der Grossmächte und die Probleme der Modernisierung in Südosteuropa in der Zweiten Hälfte des 19. Jahrhundert*. Wiesbaden: Steiner Verlag, 1982.

Memisoğlu, Hüseyin. *Pomak Türklerinin Tarihi Geçmişinden Sayfalar*. Ankara: 1991.

"Mi." *Musavat*, November 13, 1906.

Mihailovich, Vasa D. "The Tradition of Kosovo in Serbian Literature." In *Kosovo: Legacy of a Medieval Battle*, edited by Wayne S. Vucinich and Thomas A. Emmert, 142–50. Minneapolis: University of Minnesota Press, 1991.

Mikić, Đorđe. "O kolonizaciji stranih seljaka u Bosni i Hercegovini u vrijeme austrougarske uprave." In *Migracije i Bosna i Hecegovina*, edited by Nusret Šehić et al., 181–93. Sarajevo: Institut za istoriju u Sarajevu, Institut za proučavanje nacionalnih odnosa Sarajevo, 1990.

Milgrim, Michael R. "An Overlooked Problem in Turkish-Russian Relations: The 1878 War Indemnity." *International Journal of Middle East Studies* 9, no. 4 (1978): 519–37.

Milićević, Milan Dj. *Kraljevina Srbija—Novi krajevi*. Belgrade: n.p., 1884.

Miller, William. *The Ottoman Empire and Its Successors*. Cambridge: Cambridge University Press, 1966.

Millman, Richard. *Britain and the Eastern Question, 1875–1878*. Oxford: Clarendon Press, 1979.

———. "The Bulgarian Massacres Reconsidered." *Slavonic and East European Review* 58, no. 2 (April 1980): 218–31.

Minoski, Mihajlo. *Politikata na Avstro-Ungarija sprema Makedonija i Makedonskoto prošanje (1878–1903)*. Skopje: Kultura, 1982.

Moumdjian, Garabet. "Armenian-Kurdish Relations in the Era of Kurdish Nationalism, 1830–1930." *Bazmavep* 1–4 (1999): 268–347.

Muahedat Mecmuası. Vol. 5. Ankara: Türk Tarih Kurumu Yayınları, 2008.

Mzali, M. S., and J. Pignon. "Documents sur Khereddine." *Revue Tunisienne* 18, 19–20 (1934), 21, 22, 23–24 (1935), 26 (1936), 30, 31–32 (1937), 33 (1938), 41, 42 (1940).

Nakashian, Avedis. *A Man Who Found a Country.* New York: Crowell, 1940.

Nalbandian, Louise. *The Armenian Revolutionary Movement: The Development of Armenian Political Parties through the Nineteenth Century.* Berkeley: University of California Press, 1963.

Naltchayan, Nazaret. "Kaiser Wilhelm II's Visits to the Ottoman Empire: Rationale, Reactions and the Meaning of Images." *Armenian Review* 42 (1989): 47–78.

Narochnickij, A. L. "Balkanskij krizis 1875–78 gg. i velikie deržavi." In *Medunarodni naučni skup povodom: 100-godišnjice ustanka u Bosni i Hercegovini, drugim balkanskim zemljama i istočnoj krizi 1875–1878. godine,* edited by Rade Petrović, 31–48. Vol. 1. Sarajevo: ANU Bosne i Hercegovine, 1977.

Nersisian, Mgrtich Gegamovich. *Hay Zhogovurti Azatagrakan Paykare Turkakan Brnapetutian Tem 1850–1890.* Yerevan: Gitutiun, 2002.

Neumann, Christoph. "Whom Did Ahmed Cevdet Represent?" In *Late Ottoman Society: The Intellectual Legacy,* edited by Elisabeth Özdalga, 117–34. London: Routledge Curzon, 2005.

Neumann, Iver B., and Jennifer M. Welsh. "The Other in European Self-Definition: An Addendum to the Literature on International Society." *Review of International Studies* 17 (1991): 327–46.

Nikić, Andrija. "Bibliografija Hercegovačkog ustanka (1875–1878)." In *Medunarodni naučni skup povodom 100-godišnjice ustanka u Bosni i Hercegovini, drugim balkanskim zemljama i istočnoj krizi 1875–1878. godine,* 2:333–43. Sarajevo: Akademija nauka i umjetnosti Bosne i Hercegovine, 1977.

Nikolić-Stojančević, Vidosava. *Leskovac i oslobodjeni predeli Srbije 1877–78.* Leskovac: n.p., 1975.

Nirenberg, David. *Communities of Violence: Persecution of Minorities in the Middle Ages.* Princeton, N.J.: Princeton University Press, 1998.

Niyazi, Resneli. *Hürriyet Kahramanı Resneli Niyazi Hatıratı.* Edited by Nurer Uğurlu. Istanbul: Örgün Yayınevi, 2003.

Njegos, P.P. *The Mountain Wreath.* Translated and edited by Vasa D. Mihailovich. Irvine, Calif.: Charles Schlacks, Jr., 1986.

Norman, C. B. *Armenia and the Campaign of 1877.* London/Paris/New York: Cassell, Petter and Galpin [1878].

Novotny, Andre. *Österreich, die Türkei und das Balkanproblem im Jahre des Berliner Kongresses (Quellen und Studien zur Geschichte des Berliner Kongresses 1878).* Graz/Cologne: B. Filser, 1957.

Nuri, Osman. *Abdülhamid-i Sâni ve Devr-i Saltanatı: Hayât-i Husûsiye ve Siyâsiyesi.* Istanbul: Kitaphane-yi İslam ve Askeri, 1327 [1911].

Nye, Joseph S. "The Soft Power." *Foreign Policy* 80 (1990): 153–70.

Okey, Robin. "British Impressions of the Serbo-Croat Speaking Lands of the Habsburg Monarchy — Reports to the Foreign Office 1867–1908." In *Great Britain and Central Europe 1867–1914,* edited by Robert Evans et al., 61–76. Bratislava: VEDA, 2002.

———. *Taming Balkan Nationalism: The Habsburg "Civilizing Mission" in Bosnia, 1878–1914*. New York: Oxford University Press, 2007.

Ormanian, Maghakia. *Azkabadum: Hay Ughapar Yegeghetsvo Antskere Esgispen Minchev Mer Orere, Haragits Azkayin Barakanerov Badmvadz*. Antilias: Cilician Catholicosate Publishing House, 2001.

Ortaylı, İlber. *İmparatorluğun En Uzun Yüzyılı*. Istanbul: Hil Yayın, 1987.

———. *Osmanlı'da Milletler ve Diplomasi Seçme Eserleri III*. Istanbul: Türkiye İş Bankası Kültür Yayınları, 2009.

Özkan, Işıl, and Uğur Tütüncübaşı. "Türk ve Alman Hukukunda Çifte Vatandaşlığa İlişkin Gelişmeler." *Ankara Üniversitesi Hukuk Fakültesi Dergisi* 57, no. 3 (2008): 599–634.

Özmucur, Süleyman, and Şevket Pamuk. "Real Wages and Standards of Living in the Ottoman Empire, 1489–1914." *Journal of Economic History* 62, no. 2 (June 2002): 293–321.

Pakalın, Mehmed Zeki. *Son Sadrazamlar ve Başvekiller*. Vol. 4. Istanbul: Ahmet Sait Matbaası, 1944.

Pakalın, Zeki. *Sicill-i Osmani Zeyli*. Vol. 19. N.p.: Türk Tarih Kurumu Kütüphanesi'ndeki El Yazması, n.d.

Pakenham, Thomas. *The Boer War*. New York: Random House, 1979.

Palairet, Michael. *The Balkan Economies c. 1800–1914: Evolution without Development*. Cambridge: Cambridge University Press, 1997.

Pamuk, Sevket. *The Ottoman Empire and European Capitalism, 1820–1913: Trade, Investment and Production*. Cambridge: Cambridge University Press, 1987.

Pandevska, Marija. "The Refugee Crisis in Macedonia during the Great Eastern Crisis (1875–1881)." In *The Ottoman-Russian War of 1877–78*, edited by Ömer Turan, 98–112. Ankara: Middle East Technical University Department of History and TDV Yayın Matbaacılık METU, 2007.

Pandevski, Manol. "Kresnenskoto vostanie vo Makedonija od 1878–1879 godina: Predpostavki, nadvoreshno vlijanie, tek, karakter." In *Kresnenskoto vostanie vo Makedonija 1878–1879: Materiali od nauchniot sobir odrzhan po povod 100-godishninata od vostanieto* (Berovo, October 1–4 1978. godina). Skopje: Makedonska akademija na naukite i umetnostite, 1982.

Papazian, Avedis. *Zhamanakagrutyun, Haykakan Hartsi yev Medz Yegherne*. Yerevan: National Academy of Sciences, 2000.

Pappé, Ilan. *The Ethnic Cleansing of Palestine*. Oxford: Oneworld, 2006.

Paşa, Ahmed Cevdet. *Sultan Abdülhamid'e Arzlar (Ma'ruzat)*. Transcribed/translated by Yusuf Halacoğlu. N.p.: Babıali Kültür Yayıncılığı, 2010.

———. *Tezâkir 1–12*. Edited by Cavid Baysun. Ankara: Türk Tarih Kurumu, 1991.

Paşa, Ibrahim Ethem. *Plevne Hatıraları (Sebat ve Gayret, Kıyametten Bir Alamet)*. Edited by Seyfullah Esin. Istanbul: Tercüman, 1979.

Paşa, Kamil. *Hatırat-ı Sadr-ı Esbak Kamil Paşa*. Vol. 1. Istanbul: Matbaa-ı Ebuzziya, 1329.

Paşa, Mahmud Celaleddin. *Mirat-i Hakikat*, 3 vols. Istanbul: Matbaa-ı Osmaniye, 1326–7.

Paşa, Rıza. *Hülasa-ı Hatırat*. Istanbul: Matbaa-i Askeriyye, 1325/1909.

Paşa, Said. *Said Paşa'nın Hatıratı*. 2 vols. Istanbul: Sabah Matbaası, 1912.

Paşa, Said Halim. *Buhranlarımız*. Istanbul: Tercüman, 1970.

Pastermadjian, Hrant. *Histoire de l'Arménie*. Paris: n.p., 1964.

"Patriarkin Shurch — Verche Barin." *Hnchak* 9, no. 7 (April 2, 1896).

Pears, Edwin. *Forty Years in Constantinople: The Recollections of Sir Edwin Pears, 1873–1915*. London: Herbert Jenkins, 1916.

———. *Turkey and Its People*. London: Methuen/New York: George H. Doran, 1912.

Perry, Duncan M. *The Politics of Terror: The Macedonian Liberation Movements, 1893–1903*. Durham, N.C.: Duke University Press, 1988.

Peters, Rudolph. *Crime and Punishment in Islamic Law: Theory and Practice from the Sixteenth to the Twenty-first Century*. Cambridge: Cambridge University Press, 2005.

Petrović, Rade, ed. *Medunarodni naučni skup povodom: 100-godišnjice ustanka u Bosni I Hercegovini, drugim balkanskim zemljama i istočnoj krizi 1875–1878. godine*. 3 vols. Sarajevo: ANU Bosne i Hercegovine, 1977.

———. "Pokret otpora protiv austrougarske okupacije 1878. godine u Bosni i Hercegovini." In *Naučni skup: Otpor austrougarskoj okupaciji 1878. godine u Bosni i Hercegovini*, edited by Milorad Ekmečić, 15–69. Sarajevo: ANU Bosne i Hercegovine, 1979.

Pflanze, Otto. *Bismarck and the Development of Germany*. 3 vols. Princeton: Princeton University Press, 1990.

Pinson, Mark. "The Muslims of Bosnia-Herzegovina under Austro-Hungarian Rule, 1878–1918." In *The Muslims of Bosnia-Herzegovina: Their Historic Development from the Middle Ages to the Dissolution of Yugoslavia*, edited by Mark Pinson, 84–128. Cambridge, Mass.: Harvard University Press, 1993.

Pirenne, Henri. *Muhammad and Charlemagne*. Translated by Bernard Miall. New York: Barnes and Noble, 1955.

Popkonstantinov, Hristo. "Chepino: Edno balgarsko kraishte v severozapadnite razkloneniya na Rodopskite planini." *Sbornik za narodni umotvoreniya i knizhnina* 15 (1898): 222–65.

Popović, Alexandre. *L'Islam Balkanique: Les musulmans du sud-est européen dans la période post-ottomane*. Berlin: Osteuropa-Institut an der Freien Universität Berlin, 1986.

Popović, Vasilj. *Agrarno pitanje i turski neredi za vreme reformnog režima Abdul Medžida (1839–1861)*. Belgrade: SAN, 1949.

Porch, Douglas. "Introduction to the Bison Books Edition." In *Small Wars, Their Principles and Practice* by Colonel C. E. Callwell, v–xviii. Lincoln: University of Nebraska Press, 1996.

Poulton, Hugh. *Top Hat, Grey Wolf and Crescent: Turkish Nationalism and the Turkish Republic*. London: C. Hurst and Co., 1997.

———. *Who Are the Macedonians?* 2d ed. Bloomington: Indiana University Press, 2000.

Powell, James M., ed. *Muslims under Latin Rule, 1100–1300*. Princeton: Princeton University Press, 1990.

"Pravila." In *Zbornik zakona i uredaba izdanih u Knjažestvu Srbiji*, 33:239–41. Belgrade: n.p., 1878.

Prelacy of the Armenian Apostolic Church of America, ed. *Hayrig: A Celebration of His Life and Vision on the Eightieth Anniversary of His Death (1907–1987)*. New York: Prelacy of the Armenian Apostolic Church of America, 1987.

"Privremeni zakon o uredjenju oslobodjenih predela." In *Zbornik zakona i uredaba izdanih u Knjažestvu Srbiji*, 32:251–70. Belgrade: n.p., 1878.

Prunier, Gerard. *The Rwandan Crisis: History of a Genocide*. New York: Columbia University Press, 1995.

Purivatra, Atif, et al., eds. *ABC Muslimana*. Sarajevo: Bosna, 1990.

Quataert, Donald. "The Age of Reforms, 1812–1914." In *An Economic and Social History of the Ottoman Empire*, vol. 2: *1600–1914*, edited by Suraiya Faroqhi et al., 759–944. Cambridge: Cambridge University Press, 1997.

———. *Anadolu'da Osmanlı Reformu ve Tarım 1876–1908*. Istanbul: Türkiye İş Bankası Kültür Yayınları, 2008.

———. *The Ottoman Empire, 1700–1922*. 2d ed. Cambridge: Cambridge University Press, 2005.

———. "Ottoman History Writing and Changing Attitudes towards the Notion of 'Decline.'" *History Compass* 1 (August 2003): 1–9.

Radušić, Edin. "Bosna i Hercegovina u britanskoj politici od 1857. do 1878. godine." Ph.D. diss., Faculty of Philosophy, Sarajevo, 2008.

———. "Uloga Velike Britanije u promjeni državno-pravnog statusa Bosne i Hercegovine 1878. godine." *Radovi Filozofskog fakulteta u Sarajevu (Historija, Historija umjetnosti, Arheologija)*, 14, no. 1 (2010): 263–80.

Raffi [Hakob Melik Hakobian]. *The Fool: Events from the Last Russo-Turkish War (1877–78)*. Translated by Donald Abcarian. Princeton: Gomidas Institute, 2000.

Ramet, Pedro. "Die Muslime Bosniens als Nation." In *Die Muslime in der Sowjetunion und in Jugoslawien*, edited by Andreas Kappeler, Gerhard Simon, and Georg Brunner, 107–17. Cologne: Markus Verlag, 1989.

Ramsey, Robert D., III. *Savage Wars of Peace: Case Studies of Pacification in the Philippines, 1900–1902*. Fort Leavenworth, Kans.: CSI Press, 2007.

Rassam, Hormuzd. *Asshur and the Land of Nimrod*. Cincinnati: Curts and Jennings, 1897.

"Referati sa Međunarodnog naučnog skupa: Historiografija o Bosni i Hercegovini 1980–1988" (1999). *Prilozi/Contributions*, 29 (2000): 89–139.

Reid, James J. *Crisis of the Ottoman Empire: Prelude to Collapse*. Stuttgart: F. Steiner, 2000.

Ristić, Jovan. *Foreign Relations of Serbia, 1848–1872*. N.p., n.d.

———. *Serbian Diplomacy: The Serbian Wars of Liberation and Independence, 1875–1878*. N.p., n.d.

Rizvić, Muhsin. *Bosansko-muslimanska književnost u doba preporoda 1887–1918*. Sarajevo: El kalem, 1990.

Roberts, Elizabeth. *Realm of the Black Mountain: A History of Montenegro*. Ithaca: Cornell University Press, 2007.

Robinson, Ronald Edward, John Gallagher, and Alice Deny. *Africa and the Victorians: The Climax of Imperialism in the Dark Continent*. 2d ed. London: Macmillan, 1981.

Rogan, Eugene. "Aşiret Mektebi: Abdülhamid II's School for Tribes." *International Journal of Middle East Studies* 28 (1996): 83–107.

Rohrbach, Paul. *Die Bagdadbahn*. Berlin: Wiegandt, 1911.

———. *Hatt-ı Saltanat (Bağdad Demiryolu)*. Istanbul: İfham Matbaası, 1313 [1915].

Rolo, P. J. V. "Derby." In *British Foreign Secretaries and Foreign Policy*, edited by Keith M. Wilson, 106–7. N.p., n.d.

Roudometof, Victor. *Nationalism, Globalization, and Orthodoxy: The Social Origins of Ethnic Conflict in the Balkans*. Westport, Conn.: Greenwood Press, 2001.

———. "The Social Origins of Balkan Politics: Nationalism, Underdevelopment, and the Nation-State in Greece, Serbia, and Bulgaria, 1880–1920." *Mediterranean Quarterly* 11 (2000): 144–63.

Rudolph, Suzanne Hoeber, and Lloyd Rudolph. "Modern Hate." *New Republic*, March 22, 1993, 24–29.

Ruthner, Clemens. "Habsburg's Little Orient: A Post/Colonial Reading of Austrian and German Cultural Narratives on Bosnia-Herzegovina, 1878–1918." *Kakanien Revisited* (June 22, 2008): 1–16. http://www.kakanien.ac.at/beitr/fallstudie/CRuthner5.pdf.

Salnâme-i Askeri. Istanbul: n.p., 1311 [1895].

Salnâme-i Vilâyet-i Erzurum. Erzurum: Erzurum Vilayeti Matbaası, 1871.

Salt, Jeremy. *Imperialism, Evangelism and the Ottoman Armenians, 1878–1896*. London: Frank Cass, 1993.

Šamić, Midhat. *Francuski putnici u BiH u XIX stoljeću (1836–78) i njihovi utisci o njoj*. Sarajevo: Veselin Masleša, 1981.

Sarıcaoğlu, Mehmet Esat. "İskan-ı Muhacirin İane Pulları: Osmanlı Devleti'nin Göçmen Harcamalarında Uyguladığı Bir Finansman Yöntemi." In *Osmanlılar*, 603–11. Vol. 4. Ankara: Yeni Türkiye Yayınları, 1999.

Sarkisyanz, Manuel. *A Modern History of Transcaucasian Armenia: Social, Cultural, and Political*. Leiden, Netherlands: E. J. Brill, 1975.

Sartre, Jean-Paul. *Anti-Semite and Jew*. Translated by George J. Becker. New York: Grove Press, 1962.

Sarukhan, Arakel Zatiki. *Haykakan Khndire yev Azgayin Sahmanadrutiune Tiurkahayum*. Tiflis: Elektrasharzh Tparan Epokha, 1912.

Sasuni, Garo. *Kürt Ulusal Hareketleri ve Ermeni-Kürt İlişkileri (15.yy'dan Günümüze)*. Translated by Bedros Zarataryan and Memo Yetkin. Istanbul: Med Yayınevi, 1992.

Sazonov, S. D. *Fateful Years, 1909–1916: The Reminiscences of Serge Sazonov, Russia's Minister for Foreign Affairs — 1914*. London: J. Cape, 1928.

Scherer, Friedrich. *Adler und Halbmond: Bismarck und der Orient 1878–1890*. Paderborn: Friedrich Schöningh, 2001.

Schmidt, Hermann. *Tate's Modern Cambist*. London: Effingham Wilson, 1880.

Schmitt, Carl. *The Concept of the Political*. Translated by George Schwabb. New Brunswick: Rutgers University Press, 1975.

Schopoff, Atanas. *Les réformes et la protection des Chrétiens en Turquie, 1673–1904*. Paris: Plon-Nourrit et Cie, 1904.

Schroeder, Paul W. "Did the Vienna Settlement Rest on a Balance of Power?" *American Historical Review* 97, no. 3 (June 1992).

———. "The Nineteenth Century Balance of Power: Balance of Power or Political Equilibrium?" *Review of International Studies*, 15 (April 1989): 135–53.

———. "The 19th-Century International System: Changes in the Structure." *World Politics* 39, no. 1 (October 1986): 1–26.

———. *The Transformation of European Politics, 1763–1848*. Oxford: Oxford University Press, 1994.

Schuyler, Eugene. *Selected Essays with a Memoir by Evelyn Schuyler Schaeffer*. New York: Charles Scribner's Sons, 1901.

Scott-Baumann, Michael, ed. *Years of Expansion: Britain, 1815–1914*. London: Hodder and Stoughton, 1999.

Šehić, Nusret. *Autonomni pokret Muslimana za vrijeme austrougarske uprave u Bosni i Hercegovini*. Sarajevo: Svjetlost, 1980.

———. "Ustanak u Bosni i Hercegovini 1875–78. u jugoslovenskoj istoriografiji u posljednjih deset godina (1965–1975)." In *Medunarodni naučni skup povodom: 100-godišnjice ustanaka u Bosni i Hercegovini*, ed. Rade Petrović et al., 2:7–19. 3 vols. Sarajevo: Akademija nauka i umjetnosti Bosne i Hercegovine, 1977.

Serbian Literary Quarterly, Kosovo 1389–1989. 3 vols. Belgrade: Association of Serbian Writers with Serbian Pen Center, 1990.

Seton-Watson, R. W. *Britain in Europe, 1789–1914: A Survey of Foreign Policy*. Cambridge: Cambridge at the University Press, 1937.

———. *Disraeli, Gladstone and the Eastern Question*. London: n.p., 1935.

———. *The Role of Bosnia in International Politics (1875–1914)*. Raleigh Lecture on History, British Academy, 17. London: Humfrey Milford Amen House, 1931.

Sevgen, Nazmi. *Doğu ve Güneydoğu Anadolüda Türk Beylikleri: Osmanlı Belgeleri ile Kürt-Türkleri Tarihi*. Ankara: Türk Kültürünü Araştırma Enstitüsü, 1982.

Shaw, Stanford J. *The Jews of the Ottoman Empire and the Turkish Republic*. New York: New York University Press, 1991.

———. "The Nineteenth-Century Ottoman Tax Reforms and Revenue System." *International Journal of Middle Eastern Studies* 6 (1975): 421–59.

———. "The Ottoman Census System and Population, 1831–1914." *International Journal of Middle East Studies* 9 (1978): 323–38.

———. *The Ottoman Empire in World War I*, vol. 1: *Prelude to War*. Ankara: Turkish Historical Society, 2006.

Shaw, Stanford J., and Ezel Kural Shaw. *History of the Ottoman Empire and Modern Turkey*, vol. 2: *Reform, Revolution and Republic: The Rise of Modern Turkey*. New ed. Cambridge: Cambridge University Press, 1977.

Shields, Sarah. *Mosul before Iraq: Like Bees Making Five-Sided Cells*. Albany: State University of New York Press, 2000.

Silyanov, Hristo. *Osvoboditelnite Borbi na Makedoniya* (1933). Vol. 1. Sofia: Izd-vo Nauka i izkustvo, 1983.

Simpson, A. W. Brian. *Human Rights and the End of Empire: Britain and the Genesis of the European Convention*. New York: Cambridge University Press, 2005.

Şimşir, Bilal N., ed. *British Documents on Ottoman Armenians*. Vol. 1. Ankara: Türk Tarih Kurumu Basımevi, 1989.

———. *British Documents on Ottoman Armenians*. Vol. 2. Ankara: Türk Tarihi Kurumu Basımevi, 1983.

———. *Contribution à l'histoire des populations turques en Bulgarie, 1876–1880*. Ankara: TTK, 1966.

———. *Rumeli'den Türk Göçleri*. 2 vols. Ankara: Türk Tarih Kurumu, 1968, 1970.

———. *Rumeli'den Türk Göçleri, 1877–85*. Ankara: TTK, 1989.

————, ed. *Turkish Migrations from the Balkans (Documents)*. 3 vols. Ankara: Turkish Historical Society, 1989.

————. "The Turkish Muslim Population of the Civilian Administrative Organization of Bulgaria and the Provinces of Danube and Adrianople during the Russo-Turkish War in 1877–1878." In *The Ottoman-Russian War of 1877–78*, ed. Ömer Turan, 79–97. Ankara: Middle East Technical University Department of History and TDV Yayın Matbaacılık METU, 2007.

————. *The Turks of Bulgaria (1878–1985)*. London: K. Rustem and Brothers, 1988.

Sked, Alan. *The Decline and Fall of the Habsburg Empire*. London: Longman, 1989.

————. "Historians, the Nationality Question and the Downfall of the Habsburg Empire." *Transactions of the Royal Historical Society*, 5th series, 31 (1981): 175–93.

Skendi, Stavro. *The Albanian National Awakening, 1878–1912*. Princeton: Princeton University Press, 1967.

Slaveikov, Petko. "Ne sme narod" (1875). In *Nationalism, Globalization, and Orthodoxy: The Social Origins of Ethnic Conflict in the Balkans* by Victor Roudometof, 136. Westport, Conn.: Greenwood Press, 2001.

Snyder, Timothy. *Bloodlands: Europe between Hitler and Stalin*. New York: Basic Books, 2010.

Somakian, Manoug Joseph. *Empires in Conflict: Armenia and the Great Powers, 1895–1920*. London: I. B. Tauris, 1995.

Sonyel, Salahi R. *The Ottoman Armenians: Victims of Great Power Diplomacy*. London: K. Rustem and Brother, 1987.

Sowards, Steven. *Austria's Policy of Macedonian Reform*. Boulder: University of Colorado Press, 1989.

Spasić, Milovan. "Podaci o agrarnim odnosima hrišćana u oslobodjenim krajevima, okruga Topličkog i Vranjskog za vreme turske vladavine." In *Vranje kroz vekove*, 255–69. Vranje: n.p., 1993.

Speer, Robert Elliott. *Hakim Sahib, the Foreign Doctor: A Biography of Joseph Plumb Cochran, M.D., of Persia*. New York: Fleming H. Revell Company, 1911.

Spies, S. B. *Methods of Barbarism?: Roberts and Kitchener and Civilians in the Boer Republics, January 1900–May 1902*. Capetown: Human and Rousseau, 1977.

Staub, Ervin. *The Roots of Evil: The Origins of Genocide and Other Group Violence*. Cambridge: Cambridge University Press, 1989.

Stavrianos, L. S. *The Balkans since 1453*. London: Hurst and Co., 2000.

Stenografske beleške o sednicama Narodne skupštine za 1879–1880. Belgrade: n.p., 1880.

Stojančević, Vladimir. "Jedan dokument o agrarno-pravnim odnosima posle srpsko-turskog rata 1877–78." In *Arhivski almanah*, 1–2, 279–82. Belgrade: n.p., 1968.

————. "Jugoistočna Srbija u vreme oslobodjenja 1877–1878." *Leskovački zbornik* 15 (1975): 71.

————. "Kodžabaša trnske kaze Arandjel Stanojević i srpsko-bugarski spor oko Trna i Znepolja 1878–1879." *Istorijski časopis* (Belgrade) 25 (1978–79): 195–96, 199–200, 209–16.

Stojanović, Mihailo D. *The Great Powers and the Balkans, 1875–1878*. 2d ed. Cambridge: Cambridge at the University Press, 1968.

Stojičić, Slobodanka. *Agrarno pitanje u novooslobodjenim krajevima Srbije posle srpsko-turskih ratova 1878–1907*. Leskovac: n.p., 1987.

————. *Novi krajevi Srbije 1878–1883*. Leskovac: Narodni muzej, 1975.

Stojković, Momir, ed. *Balkanski ugovorni odnosi 1876–1996: Dvostrani i višestrani međunarodni ugovori i drugi diplomatski akti o državnim granicama, političkoj i vojnoj saradnji, verskim i etničkim manjinama*. Vols. 1–2 (1876–1918). Belgrade: Službeni list SFRJ, 1998.

Stoyanoff, Zachary. *Pages from the Autobiography of a Bulgarian Insurgent*. Translated by M. W. Pottee. London: Edward Arnold, 1913.

Stoyanov, Valeri. *Turskoto Naselenie v Bălgariya Meždu Polyusite na Etničeskata Politika*. Sofia: Lik, 1998.

Stoyanov, Zahari. *Zapiski po Balgarskite Vastanie*. Sofia: Balgarski pisatel, 1977.

Sućeska, Avdo. "Neke specifičnosti istorije Bosne pod Turcima." In *Istorijske pretpostavke Republike Bosne i Hercegovine, Prilozi 4*, edited by Enver Redžić, 43–57. Sarajevo: Institut za istoriju radničkog pokreta, 1968.

Sućeska, Avdo, et al. *Istina o Bosni i Hercegovini, Činjenice iz istorije Bosne i Hercegovine*. Sarajevo: Altermedia, NUBBiH, 1991.

Sugar, Peter. *Industrialization of Bosnia-Herzegovina, 1878–1918*. Seattle: University of Washington Press, 1963.

Sükan, Şadi. *Türk Silahlı Kuvvetleri Tarihi, Osmanlı Devri, Balkan Harbi (1912–1913), II Cilt, 3ncü Kısım Edirne Kalesi Etrafındakı Muharebeler*. Ankara: Genelkurmay Basımevi, 1993.

Suljević, Kasım. *Nacionalnost Muslimana: Između teorije i politike*. Rijeka: Otokar keršovani, 1981.

Sumner, B. H. *Russia and the Balkans, 1870–1880*. Oxford: Clarendon Press, 1937.

Suny, Ronald Grigor. *Looking toward Ararat: Armenia in Modern History*. Bloomington: Indiana University Press, 1993.

Surridge, Keith Terrance. *Managing the South African War, 1899–1902*. Woodbridge, Suffolk: Boydell Press, 1998.

Sutter, Berthold. "Machttcilung als Bürgschaft des Friedens: Eine Denkschrift des Botschafter Heinrich von Calice 1896 zur Abgrenzung des Interessensphären zwischen Russland und Österreich am Balkan." *Mitteilungen des österreichischen Staatsarchivs* (1984): 290–324.

Swartz, Marvin. *The Politics of British Foreign Policy in the Era of Disraeli and Gladstone*. Oxford: Macmillan and St. Antony's College, 1985.

Taffs, Winifried. *Ambassador to Bismarck: Lord Odo Russell, First Baron Ampthill*. London: Frederick Muller, 1938.

Taylor, Alan J. P. *The Struggle for Mastery in Europe: 1848–1918*. Oxford: Oxford University Press, 1957.

Tejlor, A. Dž. P. *Borba za prevlast u Evropi 1848–1918*. Sarajevo: Veselin Masleša, 1968.

Tepić, Ibrahim. *Bosna i Hercegovina u ruskim izvorima (1856–1878)*. Sarajevo: Veselin Masleša, 1988.

Thackston, Wheeler M. *Kurmanji Kurdish: A Reference Grammar*. Cambridge, Mass.: Harvard University Press, 2006.

————. *Sorani Kurdish: A Reference Grammar with Selected Readings*. Cambridge, Mass.: Harvard University Press, 2006.

Todorova, Maria. "Identity (Trans)formation among Bulgarian Muslims." In *The Myth of "Ethnic Conflict": Politics, Economics, and "Cultural" Violence*, ed. Crawford

Beverly and Ronnie D. Lipschutz, 471–510. Berkeley: University of California Press, 1998 (http://www.escholarship.org/uc/item/8k7168bs).

Tokay, Gül. "Ayastefanos'tan Berlin Antlaşmasına Doğu Sorunu." In *Çağdaş Türk Diplomasisi 200 Yıllık Süreç*, edited by Ismail Soysal, 189–202. Ankara: TTK, 1999.

———. "The Macedonian Question and the Origins of the Young Turk Revolution, 1903–1908." Ph.D. diss., University of London, 1994.

———. "Macedonian Reforms and Muslim Opposition during the Hamidian Era: 1878–1908." *Islam and Christian-Muslim Relations* 14, no. 1 (2003): 51–65.

———. "Makedonya Reformları ve Güvenlik Güçleri." In *Türkiye'de Ordu, Devlet ve Güvenlik Siyaseti*, edited by İsmet Akça and Evren Balta, 125–46. Istanbul: Bilgi Universitesi, 2010.

———. *Makedonya Sorunu: Jön Türk İhtilalinin Kökenleri, 1903–1908*. Istanbul: Afa, 1995.

———. "Ottoman-Bulgarian Relations, 1878–1908." *Balkanistica* 14/1 (2000): 117–35.

———. "Ottoman Diplomacy at the Congress of Berlin, June–July 1878." In *The Russo-Ottoman War of 1877–1878*, edited by Ömer Turan, 242–59. Ankara: TDV Yayın Matbaacılık, 2007.

Tomashevich, George Vid. "The Battle of Kosovo and the Serbian Church." In *Kosovo: Legacy of a Medieval Battle*, edited by Wayne S. Vucinich and Thomas Emmert, 203, 213–14. Minneapolis: University of Minnesota Press, 1989.

Trask, David F. *The War with Spain in 1898*. New York: Macmillan, 1981.

Trifonov, Stajko. *Istorija na Bulgarija*. Sofia: n.p., 2000.

Turan, Ömer, ed. *The Ottoman-Russian War of 1877–78*. Ankara: Middle East Technical University Department of History and TDV Yayın Matbaacılık METU, 2007.

———. "Pomaks, Their Past & Present." *Journal of Muslim Minority Affairs* 19, no. 1 (January 1999): 79–93.

———. "Rodoplarda 1878 Türk-Pomak Direnişi ve Rodop Komisyonu Raporu." *Türk Kültürü Araştırmaları* 34, nos. 1–2 (Ankara, 1998): 129–56.

———. *The Turkish Minority in Bulgaria (1878–1908)*. Ankara: Türk Tarih Kurumu, 1998.

Turgay, A. Üner. "Circassian Immigration into the Ottoman Empire, 1856–1878." In *Islamic Studies Presented to Charles J. Adams*, edited by Charles J. Adams, Wael B. Hallaq, and Donald Presgrave Little, 193–217. Leiden/New York: E. J. Brill, 1991.

Türkgeldi, Ali Fuat. *Mesâil-i Mühimme-i Siyâsiyye*. Edited by Bekir Sıtkı Baykal. 3 vols. Ankara: Türk Tarih Kurumu, 1987.

"Turk Karavarutian Dimumnere Dashnaktsutian Het Banaktselu, I." *Droshak* 4, no. 95 (April 1899): 59–61.

"Turk Karavarutian Dimumnere Dashnaktsutian Hed Banaktselu, II. *Droshak* 5, no. 96 (April 1899): 76–77.

Türkmen, Zekeriya. "Birinci Dünya Savaşı Öncesinde İttihat ve Terakki Hükümetinin Doğu Anadolu Islahat Projesi ve Uygulamaları." In *Yedinci Askerî Tarih Semineri Bildirileri*, 239–68. Vol. 2. Ankara: Genelkurmay Basımevi, 2001.

Turović, Dobrosav Ž. *Gornja Jablanica: Kroz istoriju*. Belgrade: n.p., 2002.

Uçarol, Rifat. *Siyasi Tarih (1789–1999)*. Istanbul: Filiz Kitabevi, 2000.

———. *1878 Kıbrıs Sorunu ve Osmanlı-İngiliz Anlaşması (Ada'nın İngiltere'ye Devri)*. Istanbul: Edebiyat Fakültesi, 1978.

Unat, Ilhan. *Türk Vatandaşlık Hukuku (Metinler-Mahkeme Kararları)*. Ankara: Ankara Üniversitesi Siyasal Bilgiler Fakültesi Yayınları, 1966.

United Nations. *International Convention on the Prevention and Punishment of the Crime of Genocide*. New York, December 9, 1948.

Ural, Selçuk. "Yakınçağ'da Kars." In *Kars "Beyaz Uykusuz Uzakta,"* edited by Filiz Özdem, 109–10. Istanbul: Yapı Kredi Yayınları, 2006.

Uran, Hilmi. *Meşrutiyet, Tek Parti, Çok Parti Hatıralarım (1908–1950)*. Istanbul: Türkiye İş Bankası Kültür Yayınları, 2008.

Uras, Esat. *The Armenians in History and the Armenian Question*. Translated by Süheyla Artemel. Ankara: Documentary Publications, 1988.

Uyar, Mesut, and Edward J. Erickson. *A Military History of the Ottomans, from Osman to Atatürk*. Santa Barbara, Calif.: Praeger, 2009.

Uyar, Mesut, and A. Kadir Varoğlu. "In Search of Modernity and Rationality: The Evolution of Turkish Military Academy Curricula in a Historical Perspective." *Armed Forces & Society* 35, no. 1 (October 2009): 185–89.

Uzuncarsılı, İsmail H. "II. Abdülhamid'in İngiliz Siyasetine dair Muhtıraları." *İstanbul Edebiyat Fakültesi Tarih Dergisi* 7 (1954): 51–56.

Van Bruinessen, Martin. *Agha, Sheikh, and State: The Social and Political Structures of Kurdistan*. London/Atlantic Heights, N.J.: Zed Books, 1992.

Van der Dussen, W. J. "The Question of Armenian Reforms in 1913–1914." *Armenian Review* 39, no. 1 (Spring 1986): 11–28.

Varandian, Mikayel. *Haykakan Sharzhman Nakhapatmutiune*. 2 vols. Geneva: Hradarakutiun HHD, 1912.

———. *Ho.Hi.Tashnaktsutyan Patmutiun*. Vol. 1, Paris: 1932. Vol. 2, Cairo: Husaper Press, 1950.

Vezenkov, Alexander. "Die neue Debatte über das Massaker von Batak: Historiographische Aspekte." In *Batak kato Mjasto na Pametta*, 117–24. Sofia: Iztok-Zapad, 2007.

Vlora, Ekrem Bey. *Lebenserinnerungen*. Vol. 1. Munich: Oldenbourg, 1968.

Vrankić, Petar. *Religion und Politik in Bosnien und der Herzegowina (1878–1918)*. Paderborn: Ferdinand Schöningh, 1995.

Waever, Ole. "Securitization and Desecuritization." In *On Security,* edited by Ronnie D. Lipschutz, 46–86. New York: Columbia University Press, 1995.

Walker, Christopher J. *Armenia: The Survival of a Nation*. New York: St. Martin's Press, 1990.

Walker, Dale. *Januarius MacGahan: The Life and Campaigns of an American War Correspondent*. Lincoln: Authors Guild Backprint.com, 1988.

Wallach, Jehuda L. "Bismarck and the 'Eastern Question': A Re-Assessment." In *Germany and the Middle East, 1835–1939*, edited by Jehuda L. Wallach, 23–29. Tel Aviv: Institut für Deutsche Geschichte, 1975.

Wank, Solomon "The Disintegration of the Habsburg and Ottoman Empires: A Comparative Analysis." In *The End of Empire?: The Transformation of the USSR in Comparative Perspective*, edited by Karen Dawisha and Bruce Parrott, 94–120. Armonk, N.Y.: M. E. Sharpe, 1997.

Weber, Eugen. *Peasants into Frenchmen: The Modernization of Rural France, 1870–1914*. Stanford: Stanford University Press, 1976.

Weeks, Richard G. "Peter Shuvalov and the Congress of Berlin: A Reinterpretation." *Journal of Modern History* 51 (1979): 1055–70.

Wendt, Alexander. *Social Theory of International Politics.* Cambridge: Cambridge University Press, 1999.

Wild, Stefan. "Ottomanism versus Arabism: The Case of Farid Kassab (1884–1970)." *Die Welt des Islams* 28 (1988): 607–27.

Wilhelm II. "Tischrede in Damaskus (8. November 1898)." In *Reden des Kaisers: Ansprachen, Predigten, und Trinksprüche,* edited by Ernst Johann, 81f. Munich: Deutscher Taschenbuch-Verlag, 1966.

Wilhite, Vincent S. "Guerrilla War, Counterinsurgency, and State Formation in Ottoman Yemen." Ph.D. diss., Ohio State University, 2003.

Wilson, Reverend Samuel G. *Persian Life and Customs.* New York: Fleming H. Revell Company, 1895.

Wohl, Anthony. "'Dizzi-Ben-Dizzi': Disraeli as Alien." *Journal of British Studies* 34 (1995): 375–411.

Wolffe, John. *God and Greater Britain: Religion and National Life in Britain and Ireland, 1843–1945.* London: Routledge, 1994.

Woodward, Llewellyn. *The Oxford History of England: The Age of Reform, 1815–1870.* 2d ed. Oxford: Oxford at the Clarendon Press, 1988.

Wooley, John. "The Armenian Catholic Church: A Study in History and Ecclesiology." *Heythrop Journal* 45, no. 4 (2004): 416–20.

Yanev, Yanko. "Batak prez Vazrazhdaneto." In *Istoriya na Batak,* edited by Yanko Yanev. N.p., 1995.

Yasamee, F. A. K. "Abdülhamid II and the Ottoman Defence Problem." *Diplomacy and Statecraft* 4 (1993): 26–34.

———. "Colmar Freiherr von der Goltz and the Boer War." In *The International Impact of the Russo-Japanese War,* edited by Keith Wilson, 193–210. London: Acumen, 2001.

———. *Ottoman Diplomacy: Abdülhamid II and the Great Powers, 1878–1888.* Istanbul: Isis Press, 1996.

Yavuz, M. Hakan. *Islamic Political Identity in Turkey.* New York: Oxford University Press, 2003.

———. "Nationalism and Islam: Yusuf Akçura, 'Üç Tarz-i Siyaset.'" *Oxford Journal of Islamic Studies* 4 (1993): 175–207.

———. "The Patterns of Political Islamic Identity: Dynamics of National and Transnational Loyalties and Identities." *Central Asian Survey* 14 (1995): 341–72.

Yavuz, M. Hakan, and Mujeeb R. Khan. "Turkish Foreign Policy and the Arab-Israeli Conflict: Dynamics of Duality." *Arab Studies Quarterly* 14, no. 4 (Fall 1992): 69–94.

"Yerku Khosk Banaktsutiunneru Artiv." *Droshak* 6, no. 97 (June 1898): 90–92.

Yesayan, Y., and L. Mkertchyan. "Inknapashpanakan Krivnere Vanum." *Banber Yerevani Hamalsarani* 1 (1975): 48–59.

Yılmazçelik, İbrahim. *XIX. Yüzyılın İkinci Yarısında Dersim Sancağı: İdari, İktisadi ve Sosyal Hayat.* Elazığ: Çağ Ofset Matbaacılık, 1999.

Young, Pamela. "Knowledge, Nation, and the Curriculum: Ottoman Armenian Education (1853–1915)." Ph.D. diss., University of Michigan, 2001.

"The Yugoslav Peoples in the XIX Century and the Beginning of the XX Century (to

1914), Bosnia and Herzegovina." In *The Historiography of Yugoslavia 1965–1975*. Belgrade: Association of Yugoslav Historical Societies, 1975.

"Zakon o podeli prisajedinjenog zemljišta na okruge i srezove." In *Zbornik zakona i uredaba izdanih u Knjažestvu Srbiji*, 34:32–34, 196–209. Belgrade: n.p., 1879.

"Zakon o privremenom upravnom podeljenju i snabdenju sa vlastim oslobodjenih predela." In *Zbornik zakona i uredaba izdanih u Knjažestvu Srbiji*, 32:308–15. Belgrade: n.p., 1878.

"Zakon o sudjenju i o zakonima, po kojima će se suditi u prisajedinjenim predelima." In *Zbornik zakona i uredaba izdanih u Knjažestvu Srbiji*, 34:71–77. Belgrade: n.p., 1879.

Zbornik zakona i uredaba izdanih u Knjažestvu Srbiji. Vol. 34. Belgrade: n.p., 1879. Reprinted in 2 vols. Belgrade: n.p., 1968.

Zerdeci, Hümeyra. *Osmanlı Ulema Biyografilerinin Arşiv Kaynakları*. Ankara: Türkiye Diyanet Vakfı Yayınları, 2008.

Zürcher, Erik. "The Ottoman Conscription System in Theory and Practice, 1844–1918." *International Review of Social History* 43 (1998): 437–49.

———. *Turkey: A Modern History*. London: I. B. Tauris, 1993, 1997, 2004.

Contributors

Frederick F. Anscombe,
Birkbeck College,
University of London (UK)

Aydın Babuna,
Boğaziçi University (Turkey)

Isa Blumi,
Georgia State University

Brad Dennis,
University of Utah

Edward J. Erickson,
Marine Corps University

Mehmet Hacısalihoğlu,
Yıldız Teknik University (Turkey)

Mujeeb R. Khan,
University of California, Berkeley

Bayram Kodaman,
Süleyman Demirel University (Turkey)

Justin McCarthy,
University of Louisville

Sean McMeekin,
Yale University and
Bilkent University (Turkey)

Garabet K. Moumdjian,
University of California,
Los Angeles

Edin Radušić,
University of Sarajevo
(Bosnia and Hercegovina)

Tetsuya Sahara,
Meiji University (Japan)

Peter Sluglett,
University of Utah

Miroslav Svirčević,
Institute for Balkan Studies,
Belgrade (Serbia)

Mustafa Tanrıverdi,
Kafkas University (Turkey)

Gül Tokay,
Istanbul (Turkey)

Ömer Turan,
Middle East Technical University,
Ankara (Turkey)

Feroze A. K. Yasamee,
University of Manchester (UK)

M. Hakan Yavuz,
University of Utah

Index

Abdülhamid II, 23; assassination attempt against, 332; balanced foreign policy of, 27, 32, 385, 393; called "red Sultan," 47, 345n105, 543; centralization policy of, 383–84, 389, 392–93; concern about alliance with Britain of, 75; consultations concerning foreign policy by, 61; continuity of reforms with Tanzimat period of, 543–49; creation of Hamidiyye Regiments by, 47, 310, 394; cultivation of relations with Germany by, 76, 355–56; friendship agreement with Russia of, 388, 394; initiation of "police state" by, 304; lost faith in Britain after Conference of Berlin, 26; massacre of Armenians in Constantinople by, 317, 345n105; meetings with British ambassador about Armenian fighting of, 228, 331; overthrow of, 92, 334; pan-Islamism of, 32–35, 38, 206, 384–85, 395; personal relationship with Kurdish tribal chiefs of, 38, 39, 418–21; played one European state against another, 32; policy in eastern Anatolia of, 47–49, 297–98, 310, 328, 389–90, 391–93, 395; problems faced by, 19–20; protest of Queen Victoria's statement on Armenia, 316; reform policy of, 386–87; resumed title "caliph," 35, 119; restored constitution, 372; suspended constitution, 549; two main problems of, 19–20
Abdülmecid, 538, 546
Abraham Paşa, 314–15
Aghvanian, Grigoris Vartabed, 281
Ahmed Muhtir Paşa, Manastir Vali, 232
Akarlı, Engin, 19-20
Albanian Committee, 129–30
Albanian League, 127, 128

Albanians: bribed to move to Ottoman territory, 244; chose to either leave or stay in new Serbian state, 158–60; importance to Montenegro of lowland, 243; left out of Treaty of Berlin, 261; Ottoman state and, 128; reaction to Treaties of San Stefano and Berlin of, 127–30; resistance to homogenization projects of Serbia and Montenegro of, 240, 242; Treaty of Berlin spurred both Muslims and Christians to develop national identity, 554–55
Ali Paşa, Mehmet, 128, 231, 276
Anatolia, eastern: Abdülhamid II's policy in, 389–90; awarding of Kars and Ardahan to, 440–41; British-Russian power struggle and, 287; Circassians in, 275–77; counterinsurgency campaign in, 372–76; Dersim region of, 283–85; economic transformation of after war, 45, 296; effect of Russo-Turkish War on, 275; ethnic and religious diversity in, 274–78, 389; foreign influence in, 389; Hamidiye Regiments in, 369–70; lack of full Ottoman control in, 275; languages of, 274; local-level conflicts of interest in, 278–81; missionaries in, 277–78; Muslim refugees from not allowed to return or claim property, 439–44; post-San Stefano migrations across new border of, 441; power struggle among Christians in, 279; social structure of, 388–89; state-level conflicts of interest in, 281–86; urban elite against strengthened central authority of, 393; violence in, 280–81, 285–86. See also Armenians; Kurds
Anatolian Railway Company, 90, 92
Andrássy, Gyula, 177, 183
Andrássy Note, 171–72